THE BEGINNINGS

OF THE ENGLISH NEWSPAPER

1620–1660

This book will appeal to political, social, and literary historians, and to readers interested in the history of journalism and mass communications. The author, once a cub reporter on a Chicago tabloid, is Associate Professor of English Literature, University of Rochester, and author of *The Levellers — A History of the Writings of Three Seventeenth-Century Social Democrats: John Lilburne, Richard Overton, William Walwyn* (Harvard University Press, 1955).

THE BEGINNINGS
OF THE ENGLISH NEWSPAPER

1620–1660

Joseph Frank

✻

HARVARD
UNIVERSITY PRESS

Cambridge, Massachusetts

1961

Distributed in Great Britain
by Oxford University Press, London

Publication of this book has been aided
by a grant from the Ford Foundation

Library of Congress Catalog Card Number 61–13735
Printed in the United States of America

PREFACE

A WORK of art needs no preamble; most works of scholarship do. This book, which attempts to describe in detail the first forty years of the English newspaper, requires a preface because the subject is complex, the ingredients many. The next few pages therefore attempt to explain why and how the book came to be written.

The "why" involves a mixture of luck and inclination. In a sense I stumbled onto and into the early newspaper, for while working on the Levellers I found I had to consult some of the London weeklies of the 1650's — and there was no short cut by way of a good book on the beginnings of English journalism. As to inclination, I was briefly a cub reporter. But I also feel that there is a need for a comprehensive account of the early newspaper. Such an account can fill a gap which extends across the fields of literature and history, and thus provide easier access to understanding the cultural and political patterns of both the seventeenth and twentieth centuries.

This gap was, if not filled in, at least surveyed before I came to it. Samuel Rawson Gardiner, for his monumental work on the period of the English Civil War, examined many newspapers. So did his successors and disciples, Sir Charles Firth and Godfrey Davies. But all of them used the early newspaper mainly to corroborate the details of history. The one book devoted to the subject appeared in 1908: J. B. Williams, *A History of English Journalism to the Foundation of the*

Gazette. It is only mediocre. Williams was such an ardent Royalist that, like Mr. Dick in *David Copperfield*, he was preoccupied with King Charles's head. Also, he often read only the first and last few numbers of a newspaper, skipping the bulky middle of many series. Even so, his work supplies a superficial narrative of English journalism's first forty-five years, as well as several biographical tidbits. Other historians of the English newspaper have acknowledged that it had a beginning, and usually they give the pre-Restoration weeklies a chapter. Invariably, however, such chapters are thin and brief, and for fifty years they have been heavily indebted to Williams.

More valuable than these quick surveys are certain studies which examine the pioneer press from a specialized angle. Leslie Hotson, for *The Commonwealth and Restoration Stage*, sifted the subliterature of the times, as did J. Milton French for *The Life Records of John Milton*; and Hyder Rollins in his anthology of English ballads from 1640 to 1660, *Cavalier and Puritan*, utilized many newspapers for his introduction and notes. Stanley Morison has told the story of the physical development of London journals, *The English Newspaper, 1622–1932*, and devoted a functional chapter to the first four decades. Fredrick Siebert, *Freedom of the Press in England, 1476–1776*, provides a summary of the generally hostile official context in which early journalism grew up, while Matthias Shaaber's *Some Forerunners of the Newspaper in England, 1476–1622*, does an excellent job of surveying the ancestry of the press.

The bibliographical spadework has been invaluable. Folke Dahl's painstaking *Bibliography of English Corantos and Periodical Newsbooks, 1620–1642*, has served as the spinal column for my first chapter. Volume II of the *Catalogue of the Pamphlets, Books, Newspapers, and Manuscripts Relating to the Civil War, the Commonwealth, and Restoration, Collected by George Thomason, 1640–1661*, contains an easy-to-use list of Interregnum weeklies that is at least 99 per cent accurate and amazingly complete. With a few exceptions it can stand as the primary bibliography for most of this study. The catalogues of several libraries with collections of early newspapers have also been helpful, as has *A Census of British Newspapers and Periodicals, 1620–1800*, compiled by R. S. Crane and F. B. Kaye. Finally, Katherine Kirtley Weed's and Richmond Pugh Bond's *Studies of British Newspapers and Periodicals from Their Beginning to 1800* has provided a check-list of secondary works written before 1941. In short, my problem was not to find the newspapers but to read them.

Of the approximately 8,000 separate issues of several hundred newspapers published in English or England before the Restoration I have read slightly more than 7,500. Most of those I missed were scattered numbers of long-run weeklies; a few I have not bothered with because they were described elsewhere; and some were not available. But the task of reading this mass of poor printing was made easier because I was not trying to rewrite the history of the mid-seventeenth century. As a result I was able to scan rather than devour many straight news stories, though on occasion I found myself emotionally involved in such events as a local by-election or a London murder. I have assumed, however, that the reader has some acquaintance with Interregnum history. As the newspapers show, it was an exciting period.

Certain mechanical items require mention. First, quotations: I have tried to keep their flavor by retaining seventeenth-century spelling and capitalization, though I have made some changes in punctuation for the sake of clarity and have corrected such obvious errors as transposed or upside-down letters. I have also consistently changed "then" to "than" when it is used in a comparative sense; and I have usually not preserved italics, since early typesetters often used them when they were short of normal type or when the case which held them was easier to reach. Second, notes: I have employed short titles, a necessity in a one-volume work on the seventeenth century. Also, as soon as the newspapers begin to be paged consecutively throughout a series, my notes include the page reference, except in those instances where the pagination is so confused as to be meaningless and in about a dozen places where I neglected to ascertain the page. Third, semantics: on the basis that a small dose of retroactivity can be harmless and functional I have used "newspaper" to describe these pioneer weeklies, though the word did not become common until the eighteenth century. In addition, I have included among early newspapers many publications which appeared only once but which were intended to be periodical. Fourth, dates: throughout I have used the modern method in which the year begins on January 1.

Completely unmechanical are my acknowledgments. Without help I could not have solved my own logistic problems or found the time to write this book. I therefore owe much to many institutions and individuals.

I would like to begin with thanks to the Henry E. Huntington Library and Art Gallery. As a Huntington Fellow for 1955–56 I was able to work in the most pleasant and stimulating surroundings. The late Godfrey Davies was always available to answer questions and chat about the seventeenth century. John Pomfret, the Director, was cordial and helpful, and the entire staff did everything to make my thirteen months there happy and productive. I would also like to thank the University of Rochester. By means of a generous grant-in-aid I was able to purchase some 3,000 separate newspapers on microfilm and thus work with them on my home grounds. The University also gave me a year's leave of absence and then a sabbatical to pursue my studies. The Library, under the directorship of John Russell, supplemented this help by providing every facility and service I could ask for, usually without my having to ask. Next my thanks to the John Simon Guggenheim Memorial Foundation for granting me a fellowship for 1958–59. Both the money and the free time enabled me to stay close to my typewriter for those long and uninterrupted periods which are so essential.

In the course of my research I had to visit several libraries, all of which were cooperative. My thanks, therefore, to the libraries at Harvard and Yale, the New York Public, the Newberry, and the Library of the School of Journalism at Syracuse University. And my special thanks to Richard Dillon and the staff of the Sutro Branch of the California State Library for the two uninhibited weeks during which I roamed through the collection of seventeenth-century newspapers. The following libraries, which I was unable to visit, were helpful in filling requests for microfilm: the British Museum, the Library of Congress, the Bibliothéque National, the Bodleian, the Guildhall Library of London, and the libraries of the University of Minnesota and the University of Texas. In particular I would like to express my gratitude to Mr. B. E. Freeman of the John R. Freeman Company in London. Because of the vicissitudes attendant on working with the British Museum by mail, Mr. Freeman personally supervised the microfilming of some 30,000 pages in the Thomason Collection.

Among the individuals who assisted me are Professor Willson Coates, who was always willing to serve as a sounding-board and check point for various views of mine; C. V. Wedgwood, who was generous with her enthusiasm and knowledge; Professor Ruth Adams, who helped me to unmix many metaphors; Henrietta Wolff and Ruth Sykes, who had to hurdle scotch tape and scrawled notations to type the manuscript; and Betsy Pitha, who did a yeoman job on the index. And finally my wife: Margery not only weeded my prose but kept my ivy tower cozy and buttressed. The rest is on my shoulders.

J. F.

Rochester, New York
June 1960

CONTENTS

Illustrations

Following page 194

The first English newspaper, published by Pieter van den Keere in Amsterdam, December 2, 1620

The Continuation of our former Newes, Number 26, April 8–17, 1623

Mercurius Britanicus, Number 92, July 28–August 4, 1645

Mercurius Pragmaticus, Number 17, January 4–11, 1648

The Moderate, Number 16, October 24–31, 1648

A Perfect Diurnall, Number 288, January 29–February 5, 1649

Mercurius Democritus, Number 61, June 22–29, 1653

Mercurius Politicus, Number 316, June 26–July 3, 1656

Mercurius Civicus, Number 3, May 18–25, 1643

THE BEGINNINGS

OF THE ENGLISH NEWSPAPER

1620–1660

CHAPTER I

THE UN-ENGLISH
ENGLISH NEWSPAPER

1620–1642

THE newspaper now in your living room may be the massive Sunday edition of *The New York Times* or a thin neighborhood weekly consisting of advertisements and local items. Yet they have in common three attributes which differentiate them from other forms of publication and which can be applied retroactively to determine when the newspaper had its beginnings. The first is that a newspaper is printed, not written by hand. As a result it has always been potentially available to a large audience. Second, a newspaper is published at regular and frequent intervals — and during the seventeenth century the normal interval was a week. Weekly publication, in turn, distinguishes the early newspaper from the nonrecurrent pamphlet of news and from the precursors of the modern magazine which were issued monthly or semi-annually. Third, a newspaper concentrates on current events, though in the seventeenth century there were many borderline journals whose concern with news was dubious. Finally, in this book a newspaper is considered English if it was printed either in English or in England. Thus some of the earliest newspapers which were published in Amsterdam, as well as two French language papers printed in London, qualify as "English newspapers."

Though the newspaper necessarily came after the invention of printing, the remote ancestors of Hearst and Beaverbrook can be traced back 3,700 years, to the Fifth Dynasty kings of ancient Egypt who had annals transcribed on their tombs.[1] More recently Julius Caesar instituted a gazette of official news that was regularly posted in a public spot and then copied by scribes who, in all likelihood, sold these copies.[2] By the middle of the sixteenth century the newsletter — that is, the handwritten letter of news, commissioned by a person or group to whom the political and economic events of the day were matters of urgent importance — was quite common; and at least as early as 1568 a regular newsletter was sent out from London.[3] The Fugger Letters, which extend from that year to 1605, contain much that is exciting and penetrating, while the letters of John Chamberlain provide an incisive if somewhat oblique commentary on the English scene for the first quarter of the seventeenth century.[4] Indeed, the uncensored handwritten newsletter is a rich vein for the historian well into the eighteenth century.

The immediate predecessors of the early newspaper were a mixed breed, including not only newsletters but ballads, proclamations, political tracts, and any other form of communication that at once gratified and whetted the public appetite for news.[5] Of these the type closest to its successor was the single pamphlet describing some topical event, often with lurid or partisan details. Such "relations," which go back almost as far as Gutenberg, became more frequent and influential during the later sixteenth and earlier seventeenth centuries,[6] until both in England and on the continent they began to be superseded by more regular, if often less lively, periodicals of news.

What was probably the first of these periodicals was certainly more regular than lively. In 1594 a semiannual publication written in Latin, published in Cologne, and entitled *Mercurius Gallobelgicus* began its forty-year career of publicizing and summarizing the diplomatic and military vicissitudes of the dying Holy Roman Empire.[7] Even if it was not the earliest printed periodical of news, it was the first to circulate in England, where it achieved enough notoriety to call forth a derogatory epigram from John Donne. The earliest journal of news to appear with approximately weekly regularity was published in Augsburg in 1609, though Amsterdam in 1607 may have been briefly able to boast some kind of weekly paper.[8] By 1620, under the stimulus of the spreading Thirty Years' War, Amsterdam had become the center of European journalism.[9]

In retrospect the earliest printed weeklies were the highly predictable offspring of a century of evolution. The postmasters of Europe's leading cities had long functioned as the men who collected the news in their areas and then forwarded it to such central transmission points as Venice, Rome, Vienna, Nuremberg, and Antwerp. In short, the postmasters were a rudimentary press service. Their dispatches when assembled in professional newsletters almost always consisted of a series of short paragraphs, each with a rubric specifying the place of origin and date. When the news began to be printed, both this method of collecting it and this manner of presenting it were retained. In addition, it became almost as easy for a publisher to synchronize his printed compilations with the weekly posts which now connected most of the major continental cities as it had been for him to synchronize them with the semiannual trade fairs, as he had done in the case of *Mercurius Gallo-belgicus*.[10] The next step was also logical: the translation of these new weeklies into different languages in order to stimulate and to satisfy a potentially larger demand for news. Since this step merely involved problems of literal translation, first from Latin, then from Italian, German, and Dutch, it required no change in the newspaper's content or format, no major enlargement of the one-man staff who normally assembled and edited the postmasters' reports.

In 1620 the first newspaper in French was published in Amsterdam.[11] At the end of that year a successful Dutch map-engraver, Pieter van den Keere, brought out a single sheet of small folio size, consisting of two columns of news on each side, in English.[12] Van den Keere had lived and worked in England, he remained in contact with English printers and booksellers, and in Amsterdam he was involved in the printing and selling of news.[13] Since he was also ambitious, the appearance at his shop on December 2, 1620, of the first newspaper in English is not surprising. Between that date and September 18, 1621, van den Keere issued fifteen numbers of a paper that, starting with the second, was usually given the title *Corrant out of Italy, Germany, &c.*[14] Obviously this coranto, the term normally applied to these single-sheet compilations of news, was not a weekly, the time between numbers ranging from four to forty-six days. But it did approach twice-monthly frequency and it was continuous. In fact, the *Corrant*'s coverage of the Thirty Years' War during this period left no large gaps, and it was this war that was the major stimulus to the growth of the newspaper in western Europe.

In November 1619 Frederick, the Elector Palatine, had complicated what might have remained a local struggle for power by accepting the crown of Bohemia. Not only was he the son-in-law of James I but the dynastic storms which immediately began swirling around his weak head more and more acquired the appearance of a war between Catholicism and Protestantism. Consequently the English public took a prompt and partisan interest in what was happening in central Europe.[15] It was to this interest, concentrated in London, that van den Keere addressed himself, not to the much smaller English audience in the Netherlands. That he did not miscalculate is indicated by the fact that in April 1621 another Amsterdam publisher started exporting corantos in English to London.[16]

These Dutch-English corantos, and the newspapers printed in London which quickly superseded them, raise the question of where the old newspapers are. Folke Dahl estimates that between 1620 and 1642 at least 1,000 separate issues of different papers were published in English.[17] Of this number, individual copies of only about one-third have survived. Then, if one provisionally accepts Dahl's figure of 400 copies for the normal press run of these early newspapers and includes the few duplicates that are still in existence, he arrives at a survival rate of roughly .013 per cent.[18] Yet this extremely low percentage of immortality should not be unexpected. Three centuries ago, as now, old newspapers had little individual value, and from the beginning they served to line pots or to wrap fish.[19]

Certainly these Amsterdam-published English newspapers would not have been treasured because of their literary sparkle. Since they consisted largely of verbatim translations of Dutch periodicals, they were not tailored for a specifically English audience. The news was arranged in a haphazard fashion, presumably as it came into the publisher's office. The publisher or his editor, if he bothered with one, made no attempt to integrate the various items, to provide continuity, or to avoid repetition. On the other hand, each number did manage to transmit, if only in their externals, the major political and military events that had occurred on the continent since the previous issue. Stylistically these corantos tended to be plodding and impersonal, and they lacked both highlights and human interest. The passive voice and impersonal "it," not to mention the editorial "we," are thus by no means modern innovations. For instance, here, from the first English newspaper, is the preliminary report on one of the major early battles of the Thirty Years' War:

Out of Ceulen [Cologne], the 24 of November [1620].

Letters out of Neurenburghe . . . make mention, that they had advise from the Borders of Bohemia, that there had beene a very great Battel by Prage, between the King and the Duke of Beyeren [Bavaria], & many 1000. slaine on both sides, but that the Duke of Beyeren should have any folks

with in Prage is yet uncertaine. . . . The cause that here comes no certainty
thereof is this, That all passages are so beset, and so dangerous to travaile,
that it is to [be] wondered at, & not enough to be written of, what roveing,
spoyling and killing is done dayly uppon all wayes.

Because they avoided the personal and the poignant these single-
sheet corantos were able to print a large quantity of semiofficial news.
Occasionally stories that had made their slow and hazardous way
from Turkey or the East Indies were included, though most of the
news came from and was centered on central and western Europe.
At least on the surface this news was generally accurate and rumors
were usually labeled as rumors. Despite the handicaps of bad roads,
mutual suspicion, and official secrecy, all made worse by war, the
postmasters continued to do an efficient job of forwarding the news.

When this news arrived in Amsterdam, the publisher's chief task
was to assemble enough items to fill two pages, while his major
problem was that he sometimes had to tone down a story so it would
be inoffensive. Though he allowed himself to slant the news toward
the cause of the Protestants (the Imperialist forces fighting against
Frederick were often referred to as "the enemy," and on occasion
Catholic victories were minimized), he gave the news both good and
bad, and he usually kept his vocabulary neutral. Further, these Amsterdam publishers saw to it that their newspapers were almost completely nonpolitical. They made no attempt to suggest the causes or
real issues of the Thirty Years' War and they printed no news involving Dutch politics. Then, too, these pioneer papers reveal no
concern for either people or The People. Despite many passing
accounts of villages destroyed and cities besieged, the news concentrated on the overt maneuverings of a few princes and military
leaders. Only between the lines can one sense the crescendo of terror
and devastation of a war that was rapidly becoming total. Indeed,
when an item like the following did intrude, it is noteworthy both
for its rarity and for its hint of unpublicized horrors:

The children heere [Hungary] are much troubled with sores and botches,
whereof many dye, and yet in this fearfull time, wee see not many ancient
people weepe, but rather pray unto God to take their children out of the
world before them, that they may not see the great misery . . . which is
like to fall upon us.[20]

But the most conspicuous feature of these first newspapers in
English was their total avoidance of any news having to do with
England. They contained a few references to British soldiers serving
in continental armies, and they might mention the fact that an English

ambassador had arrived at a foreign court. The rest, as far as English news is concerned, was silence. Thus van den Keere's fifth number was shorter than the Dutch coranto from which it was translated because he deleted thirty-four innocuous lines concerning James's foreign policy.[21] These first English newspapers were, then, English only in language and point of sale, not in source or content.

The Dutch publishers who between December 1620 and September 1621 put out the first twenty-seven numbers of newspapers in English were being cautious for economic rather than ideological reasons. James I was upholding a strong tradition when he viewed any public discussion of state affairs with an extremely jaundiced eye. Since Henry VII censorship had been a well-exercised part of the crown's prerogative. A Star Chamber decree of 1586 set up a comprehensive system of limiting the number of printers in England and of censoring their products, and this decree was given additional teeth in 1637.[22] Meanwhile James had become even more sensitive to criticism than Elizabeth had been. In January 1621, through the English ambassador to the Netherlands, he induced the States General to ban the export of corantos to England.[23] That this ban was not enforced helps to explain why, six months later, James reissued a domestic proclamation against the "great liberty of discourse concerning matters of state." [24]

Though the imported newspaper was by no means the chief offender in any such liberty of discourse, the king's concern was increased because by this time the news was also being printed in London. Sometime before August 1621 a bookseller named Thomas Archer began issuing corantos. None of these first English-published newspapers has survived, but contemporary letters indicate that they resembled their Amsterdam counterparts and that they came out at approximately weekly intervals.[25] By mid-summer Archer was in jail, charged with having published an unlicensed news-sheet on the war in the Palatinate.[26]

The next attempt at starting a newspaper in England was more successful. In September 1621, just after Archer's presses were dismantled, a certain N.B. "got license to print them [corantos] and sell them, honestly translated out of the Dutch." [27] During September and October he published seven corantos, each an acknowledged translation of an Amsterdam journal.[28] N.B. was probably Nathanial Butter, a man who had been involved in book-publishing since 1604, though Nicholas Bourne, another person who figures large in the early newspaper, is an alternate candidate.[29] Yet the name of Butter had been connected with some fifty relations of news in the early 1600's, and now it promptly called forth a series of predictable puns from various satirists. If Butter was N.B., he and Archer share the honor of being England's first newspapermen.

At first it was a shaky honor. After these seven tentative corantos there was a gap of two or three months. Then the pioneer English newspaper took a step away from its Dutch forebears. Early in 1622, in combination with certain other booksellers and printers, N.B. modified the format in which the approximately weekly news again began to be printed. From a single sheet of small folio size they shifted to a quarto pamphlet usually consisting of from eight to twenty-four pages. Thereafter, until the founding of the *Gazette* in 1665, all English newspapers were published in this semipamphlet form, and people viewed them as "books" of news; hence their title pages and their being "authored" rather than "edited."

Though the public may have viewed them as books, people were still greedy for current news of the Thirty Years' War. Butter and his colleagues took advantage of this. Between May and October 1622 they issued their unnumbered and variously titled newsbooks at the rate of about two a week. Together these approximately forty newspapers constituted an adequate narrative of what was happening on the continent. Indeed, besides much repetition in successive issues, they constituted more than one narrative, since during the middle of 1622 there were at least two competing series.[30] Yet in style and content these competing papers were not only very like one another but, except for the change in format, very like the Dutch corantos from which they continued to derive the bulk of their news. Perhaps for the London market a little more of a Protestant bias was allowed to show, but under the sharp scrutiny of the censor English news remained taboo.[31] One newsbook of these months had no indication of who printed it, probably because it included this passage reflecting on the timidity of English journalism: "I understand by many messengers that your corantos in England are so translated, and obsequious to the Dutch Coppies, that they never mention any exployt of the English, nor vouchsafe to attribute the glory of any enterprise unto them. . . ."[32] Not quite, for on occasion there were brief references to English volunteers involved in Europe's battles, and in one instance a correspondent referred, in passing, to James's peace-loving foreign policy.[33] But the last newspaper in this group conveniently summed up the case for caution by remarking that it would "meddle with nothing but justifiable actions" and tell "nothing but shall be befitting" to its audience; and the editor then shied away from a story concerning England to talk about events in Spain and Italy.[34]

In two ways, however, these earliest newsbooks were closer to the modern newspaper than were the corantos. First, their title pages anticipated today's headlines both by synopsizing, even if at excessive length, the leading stories in that issue and by tending to emphasize the more sensational items. Second, the hand of an editor, though it was a very faint hand, can begin to be seen. Thus in one instance the English editor accused his foreign rivals (and sources) of "shamelesse exaggeration"; in another he announced that he thought it a good idea "to muster the Newes, which belongs to the same place, as it were into one Armie" so that the reader would "receive the occurrences all together"; in a third he complained about the large number and contradictory qualities of reports from abroad.[35]

This shadowy editorial hand was probably that of the publisher, the man who took care of the business end of the paper and at whose shop it was sold. But since he relied for his news on Dutch, and to a lesser extent, on German corantos, he also needed the services of a translator — and in one number Butter referred to the "transcriber" of the news, while Bourne and Archer mentioned having the Dutch journals translated.[36] The publisher-editor supplemented these translations with letters which he contracted for, including newsletters, or which increasingly came to his hand from Englishmen abroad.[37] It was his job, too, to arrange the news, a process which took little time and energy since in most cases items were set up in type in the order and form in which they arrived. He was also responsible for occasional asides, for a rare bit of rewriting, and for seeing to it that no imprudent stories were included. But with the formation of the first newspaper syndicate, in October 1622, this shadowy editorial hand briefly acquired some substance.

Starting in mid-October the newsbooks began to be numbered consecutively and to be issued at approximately weekly intervals. Thus the fiftieth and final paper of this first of thirteen numbered series came out in October 1623; while a second and slightly less regular series consisting of forty-seven numbers lasted fifteen months, until December 1624. Thereafter, with some increase in the irregularity of appearance (a fixed day of the week did not become an avowed objective until 1641) and with a marked decrease in the number of copies which have survived, these thirteen successive series make up almost the entire output of the English newspaper until 1642. This relative regularity and continuity resulted from the amalgamation of the five men who had published newsbooks during the early months of 1622 into what can only be called a news syndicate, in this case a monopoly licensed by the crown.[38]

For two years, until Archer withdrew from the partnership to try his luck with a rival series, this syndicate, probably headed by Butter, had no direct competition.[39] What small profits could be made from journalism were concentrated in the hands of a few men; and they seem to have been interested in profits, for they were careful not to jeopardize their government-granted monopoly. One of the rare items with an English date line was a report from Plymouth of a Dutch-Spanish naval battle, and one issue risked a list of the chief English officers who were with Sir Horace Vere when he surrendered Mannheim.[40] But except for an occasional oblique reference, news of England remained conspicuous by its absence. These first fifty numbered newspapers also retained the economical habit of adjusting their day of appearance to the accumulation of enough news to fill twenty-four pages: twice two numbers appeared on the same day, while in one case consecutive issues were separated by seventeen days. Indeed, the only significant distinction between this first series of numbered newsbooks and its immediate predecessors was the larger role taken by the editor.

Almost certainly this grandfather of English editors was Thomas Gainsford, a man who had been a captain in the Irish wars, who had traveled far and written much, and who for several years had been acquainted with Butter.[41] Strangely enough, he showed flashes of temperament and personality which, despite the absence of a battered fedora and a drooping cigarette, still conform to Hollywood's picture of the typical newspaperman. For instance, he viewed his competitors as inferior:

We should also present you with the French news, but that for some, who neither know what hath past before, nor how businesses depend one upon another, have patcht up a Pamphlet with broken relations, contradicted newes of Sea-fights, and most non-sence Translations of matters of State; we cannot but informe you how you have been wronged, and we prevented, by those who would have thrust out any falsitie if they were but perswaded that the novelty will sell it.[42]

Or he could indirectly brag about the difficulties of his own job:

Whereas hitherto I have published for the Readers satisfaction divers letters both written and printed in the Dutch Tongue, and so by way of connexion proposed the affayres of Europe, especially Germany; and that therefore I finde some that would as it were pull me back by the sleeve for running too fast away with the newes, as if the Dutch-men were partiall on their owne side: I have now lighted upon other Letters . . . some in Latin, some in Spanish, and most in Italian, from which I have extracted the whole occurrences of the last Moneth . . . only by way of Caution let me intreat you neither to expect an order from Prioritie of date, nor any such exactness as men are tyed to in a continued Story. For in plaine tearmes, for anything I see they that writ these letters had them by snatches. . . .[43]

Sometimes he was apologetic, in one case admitting to an unintentional but clumsy bit of plagiarism; sometimes cynical, as when he referred to some "broken stuffe" which he was using "to fill up a blancke Page."[44]

Besides these affinities with his stereotyped descendants, Gainsford displayed signs of professional competence. He did more than the early publishers with arranging and selecting the news from abroad, and this series of newspapers was therefore more coherent than its predecessors. Amsterdam was still the main source of news, but the editor was freer in using other sources.[45] He also tried to explain the seasonal quality of military news and to let his readers know about the sporadic and uncertain nature of cross-Channel posts.[46] Finally, he could be especially careful to distinguish between rumor and certainty.[47] Even so, this first series of numbered newsbooks remained choppy, superficial, and except for an occasional informative gloss and revealing aside, generally impersonal.

The second series of numbered newsbooks underwent little change, though there was a decline in the frequency with which they were issued. This decline can be partly explained by trouble in the syndicate. Archer quit to found a rival newspaper, and by September 1624 only Butter and Bourne remained in the partnership.[48] But the first thirty numbers in this second series have a special interest in that, better than any other pre-Civil War newspaper, they reflect the personality of an editor. After Number 30 (July 3, 1623) a gap of two months occurred, during which time Gainsford died of the plague.[49] Shortly after his death Butter and Bourne standardized the opening words of their title to "The continuation of the [or our] weekly [or weekely] newes"; they also standardized the contents of their newsbooks so that editorial asides and transitions disappeared.

Before they did this, Gainsford's asides offered an additional explanation of why the newspaper was temporarily declining in output, for they reveal that the public was angry at the news. In reply to a variety of complaints the editor several times announced that he was trying to do an honest job, that he was being as reliable and objective as his foreign sources permitted, and that he was not personally to blame for the defeats of the Protestant forces.[50] Occasionally he even allowed himself an anguished outburst, such as this chronic editorial lament:

Gentle Readers, for I am sure that you would faine be known by that Character, how comes it then to passe that nothing can please you? For either custome is so predominant with you, or corruption of nature caries such a mastring hand, that you must be finding fault, though you have no cause. If we afford you plaine stuffe, you complaine of the phrase, and per-adventure cry out, it is Nonsense; if we adde some exoneration, then you are curious to examine the method and coherence, and are forward in saying the sentences are not well adapted; if the newes be forcible against the Em-perour, you breake forth, it is impossible, and all is invention; if it tend to the dejection of the Country, you seeme to commiserate and wonder at the misfortune; if we talke of novelty indeed, you make a doubt of the verity; if wee onely tell you what we know, you throw away the booke, and breake out, there is nothing in it, or else it is but a repetition of the former weekes newes: In a word, what ever we endeavor is wrested by the scrue of passion, and whether good or bad, is fashioned to strange formes by the violence of humor and over-swaying of opinion.[51]

A few months later he again reprimanded the public: since they de-manded news, all the poor editor could do was to give it to them to the best of his ability — a reprimand that could be shortened to "leave me alone." [52]

This was one of Gainsford's final complaints. A little later he departed from journalism and the world. The remainder of this second series then showed a slight increase in the amount of oblique English news, a slight decrease in coherence.[53] Also, an advertisement made its first ap-pearance in a newsbook. It lacked the polish and urgency of Madison Avenue, but it did manage to suggest that the publisher was working on a map that the reader ought to buy:

In the last printed news of September 11 [1624], I told you there could be no perfect description of the siege of Breda . . . since this, is come over a perfect description of the same, the substance whereof is . . . set downe in this Relation. I doe propose likewise to cut the Map, wherein you may with the eye behold the siege, in a manner as lively as if you were an eye-witnesse: you may not expect this Map this six dayes.[54]

The newsbooks in the third numbered series, consisting of fifty num-bers and covering the thirteen months from December 1624 to January 1626, were like the immediately post-Gainsford numbers: full of the external maneuvers of the Thirty Years' War and containing nothing that could be labeled home news. One minor change was that the im-print on the title page no longer gave the names of individuals but stated that the issue was "printed for Mercurius Britannicus," a device that Butter and Bourne employed for two and a half years. In part this name was a sort of early trade-mark, in part an attempt to borrow some of the luster of *Mercurius Gallobelgicus.*[55] Of the presumably fifty issues of the fourth series, extending to January 1627, only three complete numbers have survived. Except that they ran to sixteen instead of twenty-four pages, they indicate little shift in content or method. The survival rate was equally low for the fifth series, which came to an end early in 1628. Sixteen pages was now the accepted length, caution continued to be the rule, and all these newsbooks had an increasingly difficult time trying to disguise the fact of Catholic victories on the continent.

By the end of this fifth numbered series Butter and Bourne had been publishing newspapers in England for six years, more than long enough to provoke a response from their literary contemporaries, the most prominent of whom was Ben Jonson. In 1626 his play *The Staple of News* was presented on the public stage, then at court.[56] A reading of it may explain why it was not a hit at either place, but its liveliest scenes vigorously portrayed the new phenomenon of organized "news-mongering." With more zest than accuracy Jonson satirized an office that was the headquarters both for the Butter-Bourne enterprise and for one or more of the professional writers of newsletters — hence the mixture of foreign and domestic news which was there retailed. Jonson managed to suggest the bustle and excitement of an embryonic Fleet Street and to imply that the gullible, in all levels of society, were hungry for news. But the news-mongers were dishonest and venal. (It is very possible that Nathaniel, the clerk of the office, was modeled on Butter, while Cymbal, the "Master of the Staple," recollected Captain Gainsford.) The news they dispensed was a commodity, a staple, which they produced to gratify the whims of the public. In the process they enjoyed themselves, but they were confidence men rather than news men.

This attitude toward the pioneer journalists was echoed in other literary and subliterary works of the time. (Appendix A is a sampling of some of the more significant attacks between 1625 and 1632.) In all these works two complaints counterpointed each other: that the public was stupid and presumptuous in its desire for news, and that the men who gratified this desire were swindlers and liars. Thus, in addition to the unfriendly eye of the government, the vicissitudes of the posts, the bad news from overseas, and the complaints of the public, the early publishers and editors had a group of vociferous critics to contend with.

Yet the vigor and frequency of these attacks suggest that the circulation of the pioneer newspaper was not negligible in terms of that era, though no figures remain to support this. Moreover, Butter's and Bourne's extreme care not to offend the ever-present censor indicates that they wished to avoid the suppression of a money-making enterprise.[57] During the 1620's they sold their newsbooks for two pence a copy, then in the early 1630's, in the face of a declining market, they probably raised the price to three pence.[58] In all likelihood the average cost of printing one of these early newspapers came to about a half-penny a copy,[59] while the costs of gathering the news were kept at a minimum by the publishers' heavy reliance on foreign newspapers and on newsletters. If they ever paid for the private letters which they included, such payments must have been small — and presumably then as now getting into print was enough payment for most nonprofessional correspondents. Printing costs were kept down by the use of cheap type and paper and simple typography. Since the newsbooks were sold at the shop of the printer and the bookstall of the publisher, distribution costs were almost nonexistent. Finally, various contemporary allusions to such men as Captain Gainsford strongly hint that they usually led a hand-to-mouth existence. Taking all these necessarily speculative factors into consideration, as well as the fact that 250 copies seems to have been the common unit for setting printing rates,[60] it is likely that the average newspaper of the 1620's had a circulation of about 500, though when business was bad this might have slipped to 250. At the same time, there is ample evidence that each copy had several readers, including those friends and relatives in the country to whom Londoners regularly mailed the news.

Probably Butter and Bourne hit the low point of their circulation during their sixth and the first part of their seventh series. Since they now tried to maintain their profits, or cut their losses, by more closely gearing supply to demand, they issued many fewer numbers when the news consisted almost entirely of Catholic victories or of quickly exploded rumors of Protestant successes. Consequently in the eighteen months from March 1628 to August 1629 Butter and Bourne published only forty-one numbers, and by April 1631 they had added only twenty-five more. At the low point for the early newspaper, but ironically just as Gustavus Adolphus was beginning his victorious march into the Empire, the publishers inserted this plaintive and prophetic notice:

. . . This yeare 1630, is like to produce more action in Christendome than was this hundred yeares; and more newes is like to come to our hands. If wee may receive better encouragement than we have done, for we have lost by our publication both our labour and a great deale of money this tenne moneths, which was the cause we published scarce one a moneth . . . we presume we shall now fit their humour with action enough every weeke if their purses be as ready to pay as wee shall bee ready to publish. . . .[61]

Despite these alleged financial losses, Butter and Bourne wished to stay in business. One of the most lurid fiascos in the history of British foreign policy was the unsuccessful attempt in 1628 to relieve the Huguenot forces in La Rochelle which were defying the French government. In almost the only newspaper to contain any mention of this disaster were two stories: one, a delayed item from an English ship off the French coast, told how hungry the inhabitants were at the time of the town's surrender; the other, from Plymouth, reported the safe arrival of the English fleet. That is all.[62]

But caution combined with Protestant victories began to pay off. In the six-month period from May to November 1631 Butter and Bourne published their sixteen-page paper with almost weekly regularity, and in the ensuing ten-and-a-half months they issued an additional fifty numbers. All of them showed little change from their immediate predecessors, until in 1631 the guiding hand of an editor again became evident. Sometime during that year William Watts, a learned and well-traveled clergyman, took over the editorship.[63] Under him the paper's Protestant bias, now stimulated by the campaigns of Gustavus Adolphus, was more marked, occasionally blatant.[64] Also Watts, through his continental and courtly connections, had easier access to eye-witness accounts, and some of these first-hand stories are still gripping and graphic.[65]

In October 1632, however, the government descended on Butter and Bourne. Charles, like James, did not approve of public discussion of news, including foreign news; and his disapproval was no doubt intensified by the flattering references to Gustavus Adolphus, a decisive and successful Protestant monarch, that then poured from the presses of London. Butter and Bourne had both been recurrently investigated by various government agencies; now, at the instigation of the Spanish ambassador, the King's Council officially banned all newsbooks.[66] Though the publishers were not thrown in jail (they had not violated the original patent authorizing them to print translations of the foreign corantos), their newspaper was effectively silenced. This happened at a bad time. Presumably the circulation of their newsbooks was rising, stimulated by the Protestant victories of late 1631 and early 1632, and Butter and Bourne were now putting out *The continuation* with weekly frequency. That this profitable situation would have continued is indicated by three prompt developments: a rise in the number of news ballads sold on the streets of London, a resumption of the importation of Dutch newsbooks, and the publishers' urgent petition to be allowed to stay in business.[67] Butter and Bourne even went so far as to bribe a secretary of state, but the answer to their plea remained no.[68] For six years newspapers were banned in Britain.

During at least the first of these six years part of the slack was taken up by an Amsterdam publisher, Jan van Hilten, who exported, or smuggled, corantos printed in English to London.[69] The rest of the gap Butter and Bourne attempted to fill by continuing to publish an approximately semiannual digest of the news, under the editorship of Watts, which they had begun in January 1632. Its thirteen numbers, each well over a hundred pages, supplied an adequate, if verbose and unselective, summary of continental news until the early months of 1639.[70] But these compilations, like *Mercurius Gallobelgicus*, belong to the history of the magazine, not of the newspaper.

The newspaper again got under way late in 1638 when Butter and Bourne, probably after having more successfully practiced a bit of bribery, and after having promised to pay £10 yearly toward the repair of St. Paul's, were relicensed to issue their newsbooks.[71] Now, however, they had to operate under the greater limitation of the Star Chamber decree of 1637. The publishers were protected by their new patent against both foreign and domestic competition. At the same time they faced the actuality, not just the threat, of pre-publication censorship because the new decree set up specific censors for each type of publication, including newspapers, and strengthened the penalties for any violations.[72] Butter and Bourne, despite their legal monopoly, did not have smooth sailing.

The final rough voyage of the newspaper devoted only to foreign news can be briefly summarized. In the first place, the censors were unpredictable and perverse. By the beginning of 1641 Butter felt impelled to complain to his readers:

Wee had thought to have given over printing our Forraigne avisoes, for that the Licenser (out of partiall affection) would not oftentimes let passe apparent truth, and in other things (oftentimes) so crosse and alter, which made us almost weary of Printing, but he being vanished (and that Office fallen upon another, more understanding in these forraine affaires . . .), We are again (by the favour of his Majestie and the State) resolved to goe on in Printing, if we shall finde the World to give a better acceptation of them (than of late) by their Weekly buying them.[73]

And he concluded his complaint with the promise, never fulfilled, to publish on a fixed day of the week. In the second place, developments at home were beginning to quench the English thirst for foreign news. To counteract the resulting decline in sales Butter and Bourne devised two expedients: they reduced the size of their paper to four pages, thus cutting costs; and they frequently issued several numbers on the same day, thus forcing conscientious consumers to buy as many as four to keep up with the current news.[74] These small newsbooks of 1639 and early 1640 showed other signs of economy. No longer were they graced with any sort of title page, plain or elaborate; they displayed almost no trace of editorial supervision, and they relied even more heavily than before on literal translations from foreign corantos. Understandably, business remained poor. Bourne withdrew from the partnership some-time before April 1640, and in that month Butter tried to lift sales by going back to the earlier newsbook format: sixteen pages, a title page that included a summary of the news, and approximately weekly pub-lication. Even so, he was not confident, and in announcing this change Butter served notice that, if a rise in circulation were not forthcoming, "we shall be forced to put a period to the Presse, and leave every man to the pleasing of his own fansie by a more uncertaine restrained way of private letters, or verball news, which cannot but suffer much altera-tion according to the affection of the Relater." [75]

Though he postponed carrying out this threat, Butter's days as a suc-cessful news publisher were coming to an end, as his newspapers of 1641 and 1642 testify. To their inherited faults they added the liabilities of poorer translation, sloppier typography and proofreading, and ex-tremely sporadic publication. By mid-1642, despite the fact that he was still assuring his readers that he intended "to continue the printing of the Forrein Occurrents now every week, or at least every fortnight," he was whistling in the dark.[76] In one of his final numbers appeared a notice that a certain item was designed "to take all suspition from the Crown of England." [77] To the wary reader such a disclaimer was merely one of many indications that the day of the newspaper of domestic news had arrived. It had. Thereafter Butter intermittently tried to re-vive his un-English newsbooks and to become involved in the publica-tion of national news. But a weekly of 1643 was essentially right when it reported that "the greasie ghost of Nathanial Butter . . . walks about in print no more." [78] It was more than two decades later, however, when Butter finally did give up the ghost; he died in 1664 a poor and ap-parently neglected old man.[79]

Butter's troubles and his descent into poverty suggest some of the hazards and frustrations of early journalism. But except indirectly and largely in terms of what they avoided, the pioneer newspapers con-tribute little solid information concerning their own vicissitudes and growth. At the same time they do, of course, reveal a great deal about their immediate historical context, about the world, exclusive of Eng-land, in which they developed. Thus the first three-quarters of the Thirty Years' War are fully if thinly depicted in their pages, and some of the supplemental details, especially those few classifiable as human-interest items, can add warmth, if not much light, to today's knowledge of the earlier seventeenth century.

For instance, one of the clichés among students of the past is that human nature does not change very much, and there is ample evidence for this in the pre-1642 English newspaper. One example is a report from the Palatinate in 1622 which mentioned that the local inhabitants were learning to make "good English beere." [80] Similarly, between the newsbooks' generally impersonal lines, glimpses of the unchanging horrors of war sometimes emerge: a burned farmhouse, a weeping peasant, children dead of starvation, the stench of dead bodies.[81] Perhaps man's inhumanity to man is constant: to the accounts of raping, looting, murdering can be added stories of anti-Semitism that might have come out of Germany three hundred years later.[82] Finally, it is debatable whether or not the following item, dealing with the aftermath of an international conference in 1631, shows that the agenda of diplomatic meetings have changed much since then: "Many women and yong Gentlewomen, who never before had any children, have been brought to bed since the late Dyet and Assembly at Regensburgh, which is very notable." [83]

Presumably, too, the newspaper reader of 330 years ago was not very different from his descendant today. The ballads hawked on the streets of London featured accounts of crime, violence, and magic, usually with lurid woodcuts; and these ballads, rather than the newsbooks of the period, were the true forerunners of modern yellow journalism. Yet the newspapers did, on occasion, compete with them by means of juicy crime stories or detailed descriptions of an execution.[84] Much more common, however, were anticipations of Sunday-supplement miracles and pseudo-scientific tales. These took the form of accounts of apparitions, visions, and monstrous births. Apparitions ran the gamut from diabolic to godly, visions ranged from the piously vague to the astrologically elaborate, and the monstrous births came to some sort of climax in the report from Switzerland of a cow giving birth to a boy and a girl.[85]

In addition to such generalized human-interest stories, a few more personal items got into print. Momentarily, for instance, Gustavus Adolphus seems real and alive in an anecdote about his having a friendly chat with an enemy soldier.[86] For another moment the heavy curtain of war parts slightly to show a group of German boys being scolded for pretending they were Swedish soldiers.[87] And a short and impersonal account of some English sailors stranded in Greenland for nine months provides a glimpse of stoical courage and hardihood.[88] Infrequent stories allow one briefly to enter a strange or remote scene. Such is the account from Cairo of the Jewish colony burning Nile reeds to mitigate the plague; or the story from Goa, via Vienna, that Prester John (probably the name for the king of Abyssinia) had been converted to Catholicism; or the roundabout report from Batavia that Dutch women were in such short supply that thirty European men had married natives.[89] Such, too, are a few stories whose interest lies not in what they say but where they are from: a report of fighting in Brazil, periodic references to turmoil within the farflung Turkish empire, and an account from Virginia in 1622 of the massacre of 300 white people by the Indians — the first extended item about North America to appear in an English newspaper.[90] Yet within twenty years remote stories of this sort had largely become passé. By 1642 London had replaced Amsterdam as the staple of news, and the newspaper devoted to English affairs was ready to make its entrance into the arena of journalism.

CHAPTER II

THE FIRST ENGLISH
NEWSPAPERS

November 1641 to January 1643

THE direct ancestors of the newspaper devoted to English news
were the Dutch corantos and then the newsbooks dealing with
foreign events, but a collateral ancestor turns out to be eminently native.
Early in 1621, the year in which the first English-printed corantos appeared, Parliament reconvened after a seven-year hiatus. James not only
had increasing trouble with this Parliament, but his privy council was
kept busy trying to curtail the widespread attacks in pamphlet and pulpit on his apparent ally the king of Spain. Because of the public's growing concern over a foreign policy that seemed anti-Protestant, interest
in both the dramatic events of the Thirty Years' War overseas and the
verbal battles at Westminster rose to an unprecedented high.[1] Thus at
about the same time that Thomas Archer was jailed for printing foreign
news, the professional writer of domestic news was getting his start:
not the man who penned newsletters for a single patron or a small
group, but the scrivener who, at approximately weekly intervals and
for a fee, sent out large numbers of handwritten reports.[2]

These reports were descended from private newsletters and from the custom of distributing copies of certain speeches made in Parliament, a custom that went back to the middle of Elizabeth's reign. At first these copies were the highly polished products of the speaker's leisure. But as an embryonic party grew up in opposition to the crown, it became politically expedient to violate Parliament's own rules of secrecy by attempting to inform people outside of Westminster about what was going on inside.[3] Consequently what started out as a careful and almost private copy of a speech became, in the early seventeenth century, a hasty and often inaccurate transcript done by commercial scriveners, who then sold as many as seventy-five handwritten duplicates.[4]

The next step was to increase the circulation of these speeches, most of them hostile to royal policy, by printing them.[5] What their initial circulation was in 1621 is not known, but one such speech in 1640, when tensions and public interest were high, was reported to have sold 4,500 copies.[6] The men who by hook or crook got hold of these speeches and printed and peddled them were the same men who had recently begun to send out semipublic newsletters. Thus in a sense the professional domestic journalist preceded domestic journalism by two decades. In 1628–29 at least two such journalists were producing competing series of nonprivate handwritten newsletters; and because of the fireworks occasioned by the Petition of Right, both series concentrated almost exclusively on events within Westminster.[7]

During the eleven years between 1629 and 1640, when Charles ruled England without Parliament, the printed Parliamentary speech of course disappeared, as did, in all likelihood, the relatively widely circulated newsletter. Then the situation changed — for England and for the newspaper. In 1637, if the legend is true, an obscure woman in an Edinburgh church threw a stool at a bishop but missed his head. Even so, this event signaled the beginning of Charles's violent troubles, first with the Scots, then with the English, then with his own head. Consequently, while Nathanial Butter was struggling to issue his sporadic newsbooks, the din of events at home increasingly drowned out the cries for foreign news. Just as twenty years earlier public interest in the Thirty Years' War had made the publication of foreign news possible and profitable, now the publication of national news could be financially worthwhile, if it became possible. It did.

With the convening of the Long Parliament in November 1640, Westminster again took a dominant position in the public limelight. From Parliament, as well as from pamphlet and pulpit, various factions began to appeal to the people for support.[8] Moreover, by late 1640 the government's hawklike censorship of the press had started to weaken. Though ecclesiastical commissions and Parliamentary committees continued to indulge in occasional licensing and frequent official growls, their attempts at effective control grew more feeble. In particular, as the king's position came under heavier attack, the crown's most active agents of enforcement, the members of the Stationers' Company, gradually shifted their allegiance to Parliament.[9] Between July 1641, when the Star Chamber and Court of High Commission were abolished, and March 1642, when Parliament itself got a temporary grip on the reins of censorship, there was a period during which the press, though still harassed, was comparatively free. Newsstands did not immediately appear on the streets of London, but in November 1641 the first newspaper dealing with events in England could be bought in the vicinity of Old Bailey.

A few days before it appeared, two relevant books came out: one, a compendium of many newsletters reporting on the first year of the Long Parliament; the other, its companion volume, a collection of Parliamentary speeches which had previously been separately printed.[10] Almost certainly the same man who assembled these two books edited the first English weekly of home news: *The Heads of Severall Proceedings In This Present Parliament*, November 22–29, 1641. In a dull and impersonal style and with some inaccuracies it summarized the news from Ireland, told briefly of Charles's reception on his return to London, and devoted most of its space to a bare narrative of events in Parliament. Of the climactic debate on the Grand Remonstrance, when tempers were frayed and swords rattled, it reported in a decidedly un-Hearstian manner only that "the house was twice divided upon the question for the passing of the said Remonstrance without any alteration, and for the publishing thereof, and the greater part carried it, in both there being great opposition and debate about it."

For two weeks John Thomas, the publisher of this paper, had no direct competition. Yet the excitement of the times stimulated a demand for cheap and up-to-date news that not even the superficiality of this first truly English newspaper could dampen. By mid-December a second weekly was on the market: *The Diurnall, or The Heads of all the Proceedings in Parliament*. It showed some improvement in that it subdivided the week's news into separate days and gave a more inviting synopsis on the outside page. Further, by confining itself to goings on within Parliament, it provided a more accurate if equally undramatic summary. Except for the undercurrent of anti-Catholicism that was the inevitable accompaniment of any discussion of the rebellion in Ireland, *The Diurnall*, like *The Heads of Severall Proceedings*, stayed carefully neutral between king and Parliament. So, too, did a third weekly, which came on the scene late in December.[11]

This quick proliferation of newspapers of English news raises almost insoluble bibliographical problems, for the earliest publishers were concerned with making money, not with making journalistic history — much less with making it clear. During the first four months of the domestic newspaper, publishers formed and dissolved partnerships almost weekly; titles changed, and changed hands; plagiarism was rampant. Take, for instance, the seventh week in this chaotic history, that of January 3 to 10, 1642. John Thomas, now joined by Nathanial Butter in a partnership that lasted two weeks, published *Diurnall Occurrences: Or The Heads of several Proceedings.* This was the fourth number of a paper bearing approximately the same title, or if a different system of reckoning is used, the seventh number of a paper in which Thomas had a hand. During the same week a man named Hammond published the third issue of *Diurnal . . . Touching the daily proceedings in Parliament,* a paper which the week before had competed with a rival of the same title. Also available on January 10 was *The Diurnall Occurrences in Parliament,* the second in a series of four issues bearing that name and printed by William Cooke. It had to compete not only with the similarly titled paper put out by Thomas and Butter but with the second number of a short-lived and plagiarized paper called *The Diurnall Occurrances in Parliament.* To complete the picture for that week, Butter put out his own paper of domestic news, *The Passages in Parliament,* which survived only one issue.[12] (Appendix B, a chronological listing of the newspapers published in England from November 1641 to May 1642, attempts to unravel this bibliographical snarl.)

Such, in general, was the situation until the end of March. At least eight different newspapers, most of them running to only two or three consecutive issues, rose and fell during the first three months of 1642, and in the process remained comparatively unmolested by king or Parliament.[13] Star Chamber had been abolished, Parliament was busy with more important matters, and the Stationers' Company was immersed in its own problems. On March 28, however, the House of Commons, after several preliminary rumbles, resolved that all unlicensed newspapers should be suppressed — and none dealing with domestic news had yet been licensed.[14] Five printers were ordered brought to the House as delinquents, and eight newspapers promptly ceased publication.[15] But not for long. Within two months weeklies of home news could again be bought in London, and by the actual start of the Civil War in August more than a dozen additional short-lived newspapers had reared their heads.

All these newspapers of late 1641 and early 1642 were similar. They were printed on cheap paper with mediocre type.[16] Eight pages was the standard length with, in most cases, the first page devoted to the title and to a synopsis of the news. Monday was the customary day of publication, for the mails to the north left London Tuesday morning.[17] Consequently any Londoner who wanted an easy way to inform his rural compatriots of the current news could send them a weekly news-book. The price in London was only a penny, though the postage was higher.[18] (What the purchasing power of a penny was in 1642 is hard to ascertain, harder to translate into present-day terms, but probably it would buy about a quarter of a pound of beef or mutton.) [19]

The business and personnel arrangements of these newspapers were even simpler than those of the weeklies of foreign news: the domestic newspaper did not need the services of a translator. The editor collected and wrote the news. The publisher, almost always a bookseller, was the entrepreneur and, sometimes, the printer. It was at his shop that the paper could be bought, the women who hawked the news on the streets of London being a later development. In some cases, especially during these early months, the publisher was his own editor, his own staff, and in a few instances he might be the staff for more than one newspaper.[20]

He or his editor collected the news in one of two ways: either it was given to him by a member of Parliament or he picked it up in tavern or market place or the precincts of Westminster. This accounts for the varying degrees of accuracy both between rival series and within the same series. William Cooke's *Diurnall Occurrences in Parliament*, December 27, 1641–January 2, 1642, was, for instance, more reliable than its three competitors for that week; and *A True Diurnal of the Passages in Parliament*, in its account of the news from January 17 to 24 and in its use of "we," strongly suggests that it was a first-hand summary. This reliance on a common source, whether at first or second hand, does much to explain the large amount of duplication in the content of these newspapers. Plagiarism and pirating played their part, but, to cite only one example, four of the six newsbooks for the week of January 10 to 17 were obviously dependent on the same source for the news of Parliament which filled their pages.[21]

Because the news from Westminster reached the editor or publisher by way of members of Parliament or their cronies, the newspapers had a pro-Parliamentary orientation. At first this bias was latent, not overt, as can be seen in the essentially similar accounts of the king's theatrical and inept attempt in January 1642 to arrest the leaders of the opposition. One such account was neutral:

His majesty placing himself in the Speakers Chayr, Told them [the House of Commons] he came to demand those men of them which he had sent for the day before; but none of them being there, he told them he expected they should send them to him so soon as they returned thither; and so left the House and went back to White-Hall guarded as before; and so soone as the king was gone, the House all adjourned till the next day one of the clock, to consult of the Kings demands.[22]

A second account was still drab (note that it ignored the pregnant fact that the king was guarded), and only slightly less subdued in its anti-king implications:

About two of the clock his Majesty came into the House of Commons, and the Speaker rising out of his place, he sate therein, and demanding of his Prisoners Mr. Pym &c. who were not there to be found, hee made a short Speech, commanding the House to send them to him, so soone as they came, otherwise he would take them where he found them, and wished them to proceed in their affayres, without any feare of his concordancy with them to all their just requests, or words to that effect. So demanding his prisoners againe, he left the House, never going to the Lords house at all, but returning to the Court.

His Majesty being gone, the House of Commons after some small time of the scanning thereof, presently adjourned in discontent till the next morning.[23]

But subsequent stories of early 1642 gave clearer signs of the pro-Parliament coloration in the bloodstream of these first newspapers. Such phrases as "breach of privilege" were inevitably used in follow-up accounts of the king's attempt to arrest Pym and his fellow leaders. Anti-Catholicism was increasingly evident. Thus the weeklies soon drew a tight connection between the court, especially the queen, and the "rebels" in Ireland, whose "atrocities" got regular coverage.[24] The newspapers, too, recurrently featured reports of Catholic plots, such as the story of the French cook who planned to poison certain members of Parliament, and then, a little later, rumors of impending Catholic intervention in the affairs of England by Danes or French or other presumed dupes of the Pope.[25] The pro-Parliament crowds who flocked and rioted around Westminster were given brief but sympathetic notice, and throughout the first three months of 1642 petitions which praised Parliament were invariably mentioned, sometimes featured.[26] Yet in general the bias of these weeklies was still subdued and indirect, and no early editor took an open stand against the king or in favor of Parliament.

Not only were these pioneer domestic papers ostensibly neutral and actually cautious, but they were extremely impersonal. Asides, comments, explanations, transitions, all were absent, and the style approached that official language used in Parliament's own Journals.

Again, this should occasion no surprise. Even though it was still technically illegal for M.P.'s to divulge their actions to outsiders, they remained the papers' major, almost exclusive, source of news. Further,
the publishers wanted to avoid antagonizing any group either in or on
the threshold of power, a course that was hard to follow when king
and Parliament were openly battling for sovereignty. Then, too, publishers and editors were inexperienced, with the result that they played
safe by adhering closely to semiofficial news and an official style.

This impersonality makes the veil between the journalists of three
centuries ago and today particularly difficult to penetrate. Of the first
and most important of these early newspapermen, however, something
is known. Samuel Pecke started his career working for a bookseller.
He then became a copyist or scrivener, turning next to the compilation
of nonprivate newsletters. But, according to one contemporary, the
fifteen shillings a week Pecke earned was not enough for a gay bachelor
to live on, so he shifted to printed journalism.[27] In the words of another
contemporary, Pecke "was once a Stationer, till he crept into a hole in
Westminster Hall where indeed he began his trade of inditing or fram-
ing, and so rose at last to the style of the Diurnall-writer." [28] This same
pamphleteer also furnished an unflattering picture of Pecke: he looked
like a "bald headed buzzard . . . a tall thin-faced fellow, with a Hawks
nose, a meagre countenance and long runnagate legs, constant in nothing but wenching, lying, and drinking." [29] In spite of these avocations,
Pecke almost certainly was the editor of the first domestic English newspaper. Probably he next edited a weekly which from January through
March 1642 appeared under the title of *A Perfect Diurnall of the Passages
in Parliament*, besides having a hand in other papers. By 1643 he had
gained a certain amount of public notice, even a modicum of respectability: in that year he was jailed, he became the acknowledged editor of
the then most successful newspaper, and he joined the Stationers' Company.[30] The lanky Samuel Pecke had arrived for a long stay in journalism.

Yet any such lengthy career was made extremely difficult by the
ambivalence toward publicity of those in power. On the one side was
their desire for public support and acclaim, on the other their tendency
to view themselves as an initiated elite who alone could cope with the
arcana of state. This ambivalence was as characteristic of the Long Parliament as it is of the modern Pentagon. John Pym, for instance, could
work in a glare of publicity or almost entirely hidden from public
view. Similarly, the House of Lords during the early months of 1642
could track down certain "seditious" printers and in March join with
the Commons in adopting a resolution to suppress newsbooks; then in
May it could shut an official eye while weekly newspapers quietly crept

back onto the London scene.[31] And creep back they did, at first tenta-
tively, then with a rush, increasing from two separate numbers in May
to twenty-six in August, and staying at about that figure until the end
of 1642.

During the second half of that year the newspapers remained essentially what they had been during its first three months. Yet a few tendencies which soon became conspicuous were now more visible. The
most important was the growth of partisanship, the move away from
cautious neutrality, though throughout the Interregnum expediency
and partisanship were often indistinguishable. Regardless, the threat of
civil war, then war itself, not only heated blood but caused partisanship,
real or apparent, to be the safer course. In London this meant that anti-
Royalism made a journalist less liable to suppression by Parliament and
more popular with the urban public. At the same time, anti-Royalism
was a tricky proposition. At this point in the history of England, if one
was playing things safe, anti-Royalism could involve no direct attack
on the king or on the institution of kingship. Nor could it involve a
serious affront to any one of the three amorphous groups within Parliament: those who pushed for a vigorous prosecution of the war, those
who sought a quick accommodation with the king, and those who,
occupying a center position, shifted back and forth between them.[32]

Even before the brief clamp-down on the newspapers in March,
partisanship had safely exhibited itself in the form of anti-Catholicism,
a tenet to which almost everyone, Royalist or Parliamentarian, Anglican
or Presbyterian, at least paid lip service. From the start newspapers
could, without real danger, derogate the queen, for she was both a foreigner and a Catholic, and it was public knowledge even before she fled
England that she was dickering with other countries to gain their support for the crown. Moreover, articulate indignation against Irish rebels
and "Jesuiticall" agents did not force one into a domestic political
category. Consequently anti-Catholicism, usually with a chauvinistic
accompaniment, remained one of the safe themes of the English newspaper during the entire Civil War period. (There is a close parallel between the English weeklies' treatment of Catholicism in the 1640's and
1650's and the American press's treatment of Communism three hundred years later. In both cases the enemy was viewed as foreign, subversive, ungodly, and in both cases attacking that enemy did not necessarily place one in any firm niche in national politics.) In addition, the
newspapers of later 1642 became more explicit in their pro-Parliament
orientation. Derogatory adjectives to describe the king's adherents increased in frequency and intensity. The "malicious and disaffected
party," the "bloody minded Cavaliers," "the malignant party," all be-

came accepted synonyms by late summer 1642. Also, the number of stories about Royalist atrocities rose steadily.[33] Finally, adjectives, sentences, even occasional paragraphs, generally favorable to Parliament were progressively more in evidence. By the end of the year such a comment as the following, though not yet a commonplace, was no longer a rarity:

It being notoriously evident to the whole world how that the Parliament have and do labour for a peace, there being little need to urge them in that particular if it might be obtained upon honourable tearmes; but to have a peace without bringing Traytors and delinquents to punishment (the onely causers of this warr), without secureing of our Religion, Lawes, and Liberties, no warr can be so cruell as such a peace, as by the effects would soun appeare, which I pray God preserve this Kingdome from.[34]

This quotation can, without being overworked, also point out the caution inherent in these early newspapers even when they sounded their most militant. "Traytors and delinquents" referred to the king's "evil counsellors," itself a phrase in common use from 1642 to 1648, for it was easy to employ in attacking the Royalists without directly reflecting on the king. Further, the writer of the above passage, by linking the need for a vigorous prosecution of the war with the hope for an early and essentially nonrevolutionary peace, avoided directly antagonizing any of the major groupings within Parliament. Though an item like this could not have been pleasing to the peace party, it named no names and took no explicit positive stand. In fact, one of the extremely rare passages in a newspaper of 1642 that did exude some revolutionary heat is in such marked contrast to the normal journalistic prudence of that day that it is momentarily startling. Here is how an anonymous editor concluded a lurid story of Royalist atrocities at Brainford:

It was very credibly reported that his Majesty riding by some of the dead corps laughed and seemed to rejoyce at their fall, and some other matters which I forbeare to speake of, with hopes that it was otherwise.[35]

But the qualifying clause with which this sentence ends was the rule, what preceded it the exception.

In July *A Diurnall and Particular of the Last Weekes daily Occurrents from his Majesty*, a more significant exception, appeared in London. It contained stories about the king's popularity, the excellence of Charles's army, and the "mirth, good Victuals and drink" which were allegedly a feature of the Cavalier headquarters in York. In short, it effectively mocked the followers of Parliament and bolstered the supporters of the king. Yet since this first in a long line of pro-Royalist papers was surreptitiously printed by someone who did not expect to stay in business long, it could afford to buck the official pressures of its time and place; and though it survived only one number, within six months it had a durable successor.[36]

In addition to signs of increasing partisanship, there were many indications during the later months of 1642 of greater editorial competence. This incipient professionalism resulted from the accumulation of experience by a few editors and publishers. Each of the early newspapers continued to be produced by one or two men, and these men, in turn, benefited from a reduced mortality rate among competing weeklies. From June through September, seventeen separate papers lasted only one number; in October and November only four died aborning; in December none.[37] Another by-product of this relative stability was the regularization of certain titles. "A Perfect Diurnall" carried over a respectable and salable name from the period before the brief suppression of the newspapers; consequently between June and December, ten separate series adopted it in one form or another. (Appendix C attempts to clear a path through this bibliographical labyrinth.) The use of "Speciall Passages" and "A Continuation" in a variety of titles was a further indication of stability, and also of intense competition. Yet this competition itself was becoming stabilized. Usually only about half-a-dozen publishers were now stealing titles from each other, their less zealous colleagues having withdrawn from journalism.[38]

In this struggle for survival both methods which biologists attribute to the evolutionary process were employed: that of nature red in tooth in claw, and that of co-operation. In the first category were stealing of titles, counterfeiting of title pages, plagiarism of stories.[39] In the second was the fluid dissolving and re-forming of partnerships, a device which harked back to the time when Butter and his fellows, instead of battling each other, amalgamated. As a result the mortality rate was higher among newspapers than it was among publishers. For instance, a printer named Robert Wood published one number of *A Perfect Diurnall* on his own; he then combined briefly with two other printers to put out weeklies with that same title, before joining a third man to bring out a longer-lived series of *A Perfect Diurnall*. A publisher could thus be down without being out, and the casualty rate among editors was no higher. Pecke, for one, seems to have had his right hand in one series of *A Perfect Diurnall*, his left hand in another; while other competing papers of later 1642 show enough similarity to indicate that they were authored by the same man. The resultant accumulation of experience by publishers and editors was thus sufficiently concentrated to begin to show.

On a mechanical level it began to show in the continuous pagination from number to number within a series,[40] as well as in better-printed first pages on which the title became more prominent and the date and publisher's name more clearly set forth. The most striking of the improved title pages was that of Francis Coles's *A Perfect Diurnall,* which after mid-September featured a woodcut of the House of Commons in session surrounding the title and filling most of the upper half of the outside page. This conspicuous design was probably not employed for aesthetic reasons but to distinguish this Pecke-edited paper from rivals and attempted counterfeits, and possibly to indicate the publisher's political sympathies.

Coles was connected with two other innovations. For three months he and Francis Leach published a paper which appeared approximately twice a week.[41] Coles also attempted a sixteen-page paper covering two weeks which simplified the news by subdividing it daily into Parliamentary items and "Other certain Newes for the Day." It lasted one number.[42] Another publisher (not Butter) took a chance on swimming against the current by putting out a paper devoted solely to foreign affairs — it too lasted one issue.[43] A third, with equal success, filled his paper with non-London reports.[44] And two or three publishers employed the device of affixing the name of the Clerk of the House of Commons either on the title page or at the end of the paper, probably to suggest the authenticity of the contents.[45]

Yet almost all newspapers had certain sales-building techniques in common. Monday remained their normal day of publication so that Londoners could read them before sending them to the country by the Tuesday post. In the words of one editor, this could "save much labour in writing of Letters." [46] Also, at one time or another almost every weekly of late 1642 printed a sensational rumor, the most melodramatic being the story that the king was about to desert his forces and ally himself with Parliament.[47] Though such reports were usually labeled as rumors, some of them may have been intended to exert the appeal of today's extra. Moreover, by the end of 1642 almost every editor felt confident enough to indulge in bits and pieces of purple prose, the following being a sample of an early attempt at livelier reporting:

It is most certain that the same night the false alarm was here at London, the cry of Arm Arm being heard through all the streets, untill an infinite number of people gathered together with lanthorns had given light to their understandings to see their errour, [that] the rest was most complete by the like arrangement of the Cavaliers, for they were also at the same time in an uproare at Kingston, for they presently left the town and got away in the night as fast as they could, crying Arm Arm, the Round-heads are comming.[48]

Finally, by the close of the year several journalists were willing to try their hands on intriguing human-interest stories, such as the account of a girl who disguised herself as a soldier so she could stay near her lover, or the item about Parliamentary troops reluctantly drinking water in a town which the Royalists had recently evacuated, but not before they had "let out all the Beere." [49] One writer picked up the story that Parliament was planning to prohibit the wearing of party colors; and some editors probably collected fees from a few military leaders and local magnates, in return for which they praised the exploits of these men.[50]

The various journalistic developments of late 1642 came to a head in two of the better newspapers, one of them the Coles-Pecke *A Perfect Diurnall*. From September on, this paper regularly filled its eight pages with what can be called Westminster officialese. Its contents, that is, consisted of reports of the doings of Parliament written in a style that was unadorned and legalistic. The military news and items from Scotland and Ireland which constituted the paper's not strictly Parliamentary material were related in a similar style, as if, as was usually the case, they were derived from official reports. In one way this was a virtue, for it meant that Pecke was relying very heavily on his Parliamentary source or sources, and that, as a result, his newspaper was comparatively reliable. Probably people then purchased it for much the same reason that they today buy *The New York Times*, since it contained more straight news than its competitors.[51] Yet unlike the *Times*, Pecke's *Diurnall* was not only dull and unvaried, but indiscriminate in that its editor made little effort to distinguish between the significant and the trivial or to dig beneath the surface.

The second of these two newspapers was less typical but more interesting. From September 1642 to January 1643 *England's Memorable Accidents*, published by Stephen Bowtell, illustrated the direction in which the newspaper was moving rather than the point at which it had arrived, primarily because it was more anti-Royalist than its fellows. Cavalier atrocities were played up, and the king's army was exaggeratedly treated at one time as a massive threat, at another as a disorganized rabble.[52] God was on the side of Parliament, as he was in all London weeklies, but the editor of *England's Memorable Accidents* gave a stronger impression of being in close touch with the deity.[53] Finally, this paper devoted more space than its competitors to praising the citizens of London who were gallantly supporting the cause of God and England, gallantly fighting the Catholic anti-Christ and the anti-English foreigner.[54] In short, *England's Memorable Accidents* was partisan in the same manner and along the same lines as other London weeklies —

but more so. It was also a bit off the beaten path in that it allotted more room to news from non-Parliamentary sources, especially military items. Then, too, the editor had a greater knowledge than most contemporary journalists of military problems, as well as greater interest in the actual progress of the war. Consequently *England's Memorable Accidents* was less homogeneous in style and content than other weeklies of late 1642. But again this is relative: if from the historical spectrum of journalism one had to choose a color for Bowtell's paper, it too would be gray.

Even so, by January 1643 the early English newspaper, though its garb was still not colorful, was no longer in swaddling clothes. A few publishers and editors had gained experience in the dissemination of news and the exploitation of partisanship. But more important was the fact that a London public now existed that was sufficiently large and hungry for news to guarantee the continuance of the domestic newspaper. The major stumbling block to the gratification of this public was that a political faction might become strong enough to set up an effective censorship. At the moment the swaying fortunes of war made such an event unlikely.

CHAPTER III

CHILDHOOD

January to September 1643

FORTUNATELY for the history of journalism no really effective censorship was reimposed until the end of the 1640's. In June 1643 Parliament passed an ordinance to regulate the press, but this law did little to muzzle existing newspapers or to prevent the rise of new ones. Such legislative laxity was not the product of any liberal principle held by the leaders of Parliament; rather it was the result of what was happening on the scattered battlefields of the Civil War and, to a lesser extent, on the streets of London. In October 1642 the first major battle of the war, Edgehill, had proved indecisive, and in November the Royalist army had briefly threatened London. By early 1643 the sentiment for peace was rising in the city, while within Parliament the line between peace party and war party was becoming sharper, the power of the middle group shrinking. In the streets around Westminster crowds sometime shouted for peace, while from many Puritan pulpits the clergy called for blood.[1] Such an atmosphere produced neither the stability nor the compromise then necessary for a truly crippling censorship.

In times of tumult, when traditional restraints are breaking down, the more strident the voice, the larger the hearing. In the 1640's strident voices were, for the first time in the history of England, sustainedly calling for massive public action. Among these voices of early 1643 that of the fledgling newspaper was, if not yet a shout, no longer a whisper. Six weeklies entered the year with a momentum of experience and a probably growing circulation. Francis Coles was the publisher or co-publisher of two: the Pecke-edited *A Perfect Diurnall*, and *A Continuation of Certain Speciall and Remarkable Passages*. Walter Cook and Robert Wood published two competing papers, their titles identical with those put out by Coles. *Speciall Passages*, probably published by Humphrey Blunden, had outlasted its rivals with the same title, and *England's Memorable Accidents* survived until mid-January. Three new newspapers now also added to the din: *Mercurius Aulicus*, *Certaine Informations*, and *The Kingdomes Weekly Intelligencer*. Particularly with the first of these, a new chapter in the history of early English journalism began.

On January 1, 1643, a newspaper appeared at Oxford, now the headquarters for the king, its first number called the *Oxford Diurnall*. In the following week this became *Mercurius Aulicus* — the Court Mercury — a title which the paper kept until its demise in September 1645. From the start this was a distinctive weekly: it was not published in London, it was pro-Royalist, and January 1 was a Sunday. Yet these differences were interlocking, for the fact of being published in Oxford meant that *Mercurius Aulicus* had to be anti-Parliament, and Sunday publication represented a deliberate mocking of Puritan sabbatarianism. This contrariness and mockery remained characteristic of *Aulicus* throughout its relatively long career. From first to last it was devoted to attacking the supporters of Parliament, including journalists, but it usually did so with enough cleverness to be effective. Despite the fact that it was heavily outnumbered by pro-Parliament weeklies, and though the cause which it supported became increasingly lost, journalistically it managed to hold its own.

But when *Aulicus* first appeared, the barricade it manned seemed lined with plush. The Royalists were convinced that their armies were superior to the Parliamentary forces, their own apparent unity an optimistic contrast to the divisions among their opponents. Thus the opening sentence of the first number conveyed the conviction that truth, Royalist truth, would triumph:

The World hath long enough been abused with falsehoods: And there's a weekly cheat put out to nourish the abuse amongst the people, and make them pay for their seducement. And that the world may see that the Court is neither so barren of intelligence as it is conceived, nor the affaires thereof in so unprosperous a condition as these pamphlets make them, it is thought fit to let them truly understand the state of things, that so they may no longer pretend ignorance, or bee deceived with untruths.

And the editor proceeded, in an equally easy style, to dispense a concoction of facts and propaganda intended to puff up the Royalists and shrivel the adherents of Parliament. Consequently *Aulicus* was important to the development of English journalism because it immediately became the exemplar of clever partisanship, and because it soon provoked equally clever counterattacks.

The paper's editorial office was probably located in Oriel College, in the same building where the executive committee of the king's privy council met, and it was printed by Henry Hall, who in 1644 was appointed Printer to the University.[2] John Birkenhead was the regular editor, though other Royalists briefly took over the job. Born the son of a saddler in 1616, Birkenhead was an Oxford graduate who became a protégé of Archbishop Laud. In 1640 he was made a fellow of an Oxford college and, three years later, a newspaperman.[3] Aubrey in his *Brief Lives* described him as "exceedingly bold, confident, not very grateful to his benefactors; would lye damnably. He was of midling stature, great goggli eies, not of a sweet aspect." [4] Whether or not Birkenhead's goggly eyes made him a better journalist is debatable; but the smallness and strategic importance of Oxford, the location of *Aulicus*'s office, and Birkenhead's own associations with leading Royalist policy-makers, all helped to give his paper an air of authority.

From the beginning *Aulicus* followed a pattern of dividing each day's news into three parts: the news itself, Birkenhead's comments on it, and his refutation of parallel items in the Parliamentary press. This triple treatment caused his paper normally to consist of twelve pages, not of the eight common to its antagonists. Because Birkenhead was smart and contentious, and because the news, from his point of view, gradually worsened, his refutation of London editors occupied progressively more space. Birkenhead's favorite tactic was sowing seeds of dissension among opponents of the king. In his second number he tried to set Parliament against London, in his third he featured a quarrel between certain Parliamentary generals, and in his fourth he claimed that the recent election of the Lord Mayor was illegal and hence he should not be obeyed. In subsequent issues Birkenhead attempted to divide the war party from the rest of the House of Commons, the Commons from the Lords, both from the business interests of London, London from the rest of England, and England from Scotland — all before he had been in operation three months.

A second area in which Birkenhead quickly showed expertness was the loaded horror story. Like the London editors he emphasized atrocities committed by the other side's armies. But unlike them he could count on traditional reverence for the crown and on national habits of snobbishness to underline the bloody and low attributes of the "rebels." Within a month he included accounts of a wicked plot to kidnap the queen and of a nefarious scheme to murder Charles. Within two months he made it clear that the leaders of the anti-Royalists were men of low pedigree and less intelligence, easily misled by bloody warmongers and blasphemous sectaries.[5]

Birkenhead also rapidly became proficient in the partisan selection of news. Though military actions were limited in winter, the editor regularly played up any minor skirmish won by the Royalists. Nor did he fail to try his hand at human-interest stories, especially those involving the royal family, which might enlist sympathy for the king's cause.[6]

What, then, was the reaction to *Aulicus* in the London papers during the first three months of 1643? Generally little or none. *England's Memorable Accidents* died in the middle of January, its editor still convinced that God was on the side of Parliament and that despotism was evil.[7] Blunden's *Speciall Passages*, though it became more anti-Royalist, ignored *Aulicus*. At the same time, it is the best example of the way in which certain papers, either inadvertently or because they were honest, gave intermittent support to Birkenhead's allegations of serious splits within the House of Commons. In particular, one January issue of *Speciall Passages* criticized Parliament's direction of military affairs and implied that it might be wise to replace the Earl of Essex.[8] Since Essex was supported by Pym and the moderate wing of the war party, any attack on him involved taking a stand on the side of the more extreme militants in Parliament or, if one reads between the lines, possibly on the side of the peace party.[9] In any case, these splits, of which the Earl was the cynosure and of which Birkenhead was fully aware, were sometimes reflected in the Parliamentary press of the first half of 1643. Such asides as that in *Speciall Passages*, as well as a few of its news stories, hinted that all was not harmonious among the leaders of the Parliamentary coalition, but such hints did not yet mean that any editor was taking a specific stand, much less agreeing with *Aulicus*.

The remaining four papers which had survived from 1642 — the *Perfect Diurnalls* published by Coles and by Cook and Wood, and the competing issues of *A Continuation of certain Speciall and Remarkable Passages* put out by Coles and Leach and by Cook and Wood — continued to concentrate on straight news, with the same careful pro-

Parliament bias they had previously shown. Even so, Coles, Leach, and Pecke spent from January to April 1643 in the Fleet, where they had been sent by the House of Lords, presumably for devoting too much space to a peace petition from the London apprentices.[10] Despite this, the two papers with which Coles and Pecke had been connected kept coming out. In both, as in Cook's and Wood's weeklies, there was almost no hint, except for an infrequent denial, of any split within the Parliamentary coalition.[11] Pecke's temporary successor and his colleagues may have become slightly more proficient in their few attempts at graphic reporting, slightly more consistent in their labeling rumors as rumors. Otherwise these four newspapers showed little change — sufficient proof of their impersonality, since approximately 50 per cent of their regular staffs were in prison.

Of the two long-run newspapers which, in addition to *Aulicus*, got their start early in 1643, *Certaine Informations* was by and large indistinguishable from the publications of Coles and Leach and of Cook and Wood.[12] *The Kingdomes Weekly Intelligencer*, the other and more important newcomer, began its journalistic life on January 3, 1643 — a life which lasted, without change of title, until late 1649, and then, with a different title, for another six years. Almost certainly edited by Richard Collings,[13] this paper also ignored *Aulicus* as it fell into the over-all pattern of other London journals. But *The Kingdomes Weekly Intelligencer* was not quite the same as its fellows. In the first place, Collings was more outspoken than other editors in his generalized praise of Parliament, more insistent in stressing the theme of the king's evil advisors and in identifying Royalist with Papist.[14] In the second place, though Collings' style was also saturated with official language, *The Kingdomes Weekly Intelligencer* occasionally betrayed signs of a sense of humor, as in the probably manufactured anecdote of a Royalist dying of a swelling in the head, thus dying a Round-head.[15] In the third place, Collings or his publisher instituted certain typographical improvements that made the paper more readable. Of these the most significant was an ancestor of the headline closer to its descendant than the title-page summaries employed by other newspapers. In his first few numbers Collings at the top of his outside page printed the place from which that week's most important news had come. With Number 5 this became almost a headline, not in terms of largeness of type but in the attempt to point up the leading item or items briefly and with punch. "Queen's Landed" is one early sample, "Cessation interrupted" another.[16] Later these embryonic headlines sometimes became quite fancy, this one from early May being a good sample:

Redding yeelded is.
Hereford taken is.
Hopton beaten is.
Malignants grieve I wis.[17]

During its first few months *The Kingdomes Weekly Intelligencer* showed precocity in one other respect: what can be called competitive specialization. Apparently Collings felt that the public was receiving adequate news of Parliament from other papers, so he cut down his coverage of Westminster and gave the saved space to a fuller treatment of military affairs. He seems to have been a soldier, and in April he somewhat pretentiously announced that he was returning to the wars, for he doubted that the Parliamentary army could dispense with him.[18] Apparently it could; after a gap of only one week, *The Kingdomes Weekly Intelligencer*, still edited by the same man, was back in business. Even so, Collings showed a close familiarity with military tactics, and he had a regular correspondent in Wales to keep him abreast of military developments there.[19]

Thus by the spring of 1643 Birkenhead's competitors, though they were not in his class as shrewd propagandists, were presenting the news in a relatively full and straightforward manner, even with a few embellishments. Their style tended to be colorless, their approach superficial, and their attempts at anti-Royalist propaganda clumsy. And none of them had yet taken direct notice of *Aulicus*. When they did, it was because certain Royalists had begun to get sporadic numbers of Birkenhead's paper reprinted in London, thereby supplementing the smuggled copies.[20] In April, therefore, the London weeklies began to attack *Aulicus* directly, and in the following months these attacks increased in number and fervor.[21]

Birkenhead in the meanwhile did his best to provoke them. As it daily grew more evident that the king was not going to win an easy victory, if he won at all, Birkenhead's divide-and-conquer items became more urgent. Like both his associates and his opponents, he was aware that the Parliamentary coalition would disintegrate as the forces opposing it weakened, and he worked hard to hasten the disintegration. In so doing he exerted his greatest centrifugal pressure by his attacks on Essex and, through Essex, on Pym's leadership of Parliament. In April, for instance, Birkenhead claimed that both civilians and soldiers had lost confidence in the general. At the same time he went out of his way to characterize Pym and Lord Say as the leaders of the war party — fine leaders, he implied, who could not even pick a good field commander.[22] Birkenhead also alleged that the general's victory at Reading was Pyrrhic: that Essex had to dig five large but secret pits in which "to cast the greatest part of those poore wretches . . . for feare the true number of the slaine might disconsolate their party." [23]

Yet Essex and Pym were intermittently opposed on their home grounds by an extremist group, of whose members Henry Marten was the most flamboyant. Birkenhead did not neglect the attempt to link Pym with these proto-republicans, here as elsewhere using the device of guilt by association. Marten, a member of Commons, wished to depose the king and abolish the House of Lords; and Pym, the real leader of Parliament, was accordingly responsible for the subversion of England's most sacred institutions.[24] Thus when Pym threatened the House of Lords with absorption by the Lower House, Birkenhead utilized this threat to tighten the putative liaison between Pym and Marten.[25] More direct, but following the same track, were his assaults on a colonel in the Parliamentary armies named Cromwell, a bloody and greedy boor who delighted in defacing churches.[26] What kind of a war was this anyway? — and Birkenhead repeatedly called attention to the fact that the Presbyterians, then Parliament's most important backers in numbers, wealth, and pulpit publicity, were growing increasingly discontented with the march of events.[27] If the Royalists could be tarred with the brush of Catholicism, certainly the "rebels" could be blackwashed as atheists and radicals. In this process Birkenhead, though he was no Senator McCarthy, was more adept than his competitors in the use of innuendo and smear.

The story of these competitors from April through June, as in the earlier months of 1643, is at once simple and confusing: simple in that the London newspapers were essentially similar, confusing in that the minor differences between them were not insignificant. Generally they remained unchanged in style and content. Their crowded and official-sounding pages were still filled with relatively full accounts of the surface of events at Westminster and on the battlefields, with an occasional foreign item, such as the death of the king of France, meriting a paragraph. But in two respects all of them showed a slight shift away from their practices of the first quarter of the year: an increasingly overt display of anti-Royalism, including allotting more space to dissensions at Oxford, and a greater emphasis on military news.

One by-product of these basic similarities was a diversification of day of publication. *The Kingdomes Weekly Intelligencer* had from the start regularly been published on Tuesday, as had, since late 1642, *Speciall Passages*. By February 1643 the competing runs of *A Continuation of Certain Speciall and Remarkable Passages* had settled on Thursday, though other long-run papers stuck with Monday. Presumably there were now enough readers in London for some publishers to ignore the lure of the Tuesday post to the country.[28]

This choice of differing days of publication suggests that the competition among the small circle of London publishers continued intense. The rival *Continuations* not only came out on the same day but employed similar formats. On Monday the competing *Perfect Diurnalls* tried to attract the same general group of readers, the series with which Coles was connected still displaying its woodcut of the House of Commons. Further, the day of the counterfeit had not yet passed. Twice *The Kingdomes Weekly Intelligencer* came out in two numbers, one of them forged;[29] and several times Coles's woodcut appeared on the title page of Cook's and Wood's *Perfect Diurnall*. Finally, within this limited group of publishers competition was keen enough for their products to have a resilient quality, and a paper could quickly bounce back from temporary extinction. *Certaine Informations* skipped six weeks in May and June, then came back to sporadic life. Though Coles and Pecke were just getting out of jail, their *Continuation* missed only two numbers during the second quarter of 1643, while that published by Cook and Wood missed three and expired in mid-May. Both *Perfect Diurnalls* were completely regular, but *Speciall Passages* skipped two weeks, as did *The Kingdomes Weekly Intelligencer*. Connected with some of these gaps and intermittent revivals were minor moves by printers and publishers in the game of journalistic musical chairs.[30] As a final sign of this competition, it is probable that the spring of 1643 saw the onset of the primitive newsboy: the men and, more often, the women who hawked their wares on the streets of London, dodging hostile officials and, whenever possible, collecting more than the penny which was the newsbook's standard price.[31]

Today the competition in the automobile industry has led to an essential similarity of product; but it has also led to an accentuation of minor differences in competing models: an extra taillight here, a fancier fender there. So too with the early newspapers. Take, for instance, *The Kingdomes Weekly Intelligencer*, among the best of the London weeklies. One of its assets was the attempt to present the news clearly in terms of format. At first Collings had numbered each item consecutively, a device he dropped in May and partially replaced with a pointing hand to indicate important news. In June, for no apparent reason, he eliminated his headlines, though typographically his paper remained slightly superior. He also, more than his fellow editors, tried to give the impression that his reports were first-hand. Thus after his brief army stint he announced that he had come back to London "to informe my selfe the best I can, and to communicate the truest Intelligence I can get." [32] Such statements were common, but in Collings' case they combined with his evident knowledge of soldiering and his familiarity with recent history to suggest that his voice was authoritative.[33]

The two *Perfect Diurnalls* remained almost indistinguishable, and both came to an end in mid-June. Pecke's release from jail in April had little effect on the one for which he worked, though his hand is probably evident in a few personal and professional touches, such as in the cautious proviso that "as matters in some parts goe well for the Parliament, so in other parts they goe but indifferent, such is the chance of warre like to a pair of dice: hee that wins at this cast may happen to lose at the next." [34] Possibly Pecke's careful touch can also be seen in his praise of London's patriotism and Pym's leadership, though both these categories of obvious flattery were exploited by other editors. Like them, too, Pecke tended to exaggerate Parliamentary military victories and minimize defeats. None of these men did this sufficiently blatantly to prevent a judicious reader from getting the gist of the news, but in Pecke's hands this slanting was milder and less frequent. Finally, both his and his rival's *A Perfect Diurnall*, if viewed en masse for these three months, gave a slightly fuller coverage of the news than did other London papers, with Pecke's series showing some superiority.[35]

The competing series of *A Continuation* were as similar as the *Perfect Diurnalls*, which they closely resembled. If Pecke edited one *Continuation*, he is not much in evidence — except perhaps when the editor of Coles's paper claimed that he was an eye-witness to a Parliamentary conference between Lords and Commons on how to deal with a Royalist plot in London, and that he took notes.[36] Though the editor employed by Cook and Wood displayed as much caution and initiative as Pecke, this did not prevent his *Continuation* from dying in May.[37]

Of the other established newspapers, *Certaine Informations*, after its six-week hiatus, came back on the journalistic scene unchanged: crowded, superficial, dull, pious, and showing few signs of editorial guidance. *Speciall Passages*, which disappeared in July 1643, was not much different, though a little more coherent and vigorous. One of its asides, however, was reminiscent of Captain Gainsford, for it reminded the public that the job of an editor was not easy:

> In some weeks some of these many Relations may in some particulars faile; especially being (as usually they are) the soonest and earliest of any report that comes; the consideration whereof may (happily) render the Reader more judicious, lesse censorious.[38]

And another story suggests another vicissitude: by hinting that Essex was moving too slowly, the editor conveyed the impression that his own militant inclinations were being repressed by his businesslike caution.[39] Yet such repression was then the rule for everyone engaged in periodical publication. (A man writing a pamphlet could be much less inhibited.) Perhaps the clearest proof of this self-conscious caution was the fact that no newspaper of 1643 raised its voice against threats by Parliament to suppress "malignant" books and to regulate the London press. The news of such threats was given, but no editor indicated that he opposed censorship or had an inkling of how it might affect him. Then in mid-June Parliament's bark briefly changed to a bite.

Just before this, two new periodicals made themselves theoretically available to censorial reaction. One of them was not strictly a newspaper, though it at first appeared with approximately weekly regularity and dealt with current events. But *Mercurius Rusticus* was too highly specialized to be a paper of news, for it covered only atrocities committed by the Parliamentary armies. Each number was thus a blood-curdling collection of "barbarous out-rages." Published at Oxford, it did with a bludgeon what Birkenhead was doing with a rapier.[40]

The second new periodical of May 1643 also purported to specialize, but in this case it was very much a newspaper. *Mercurius Civicus* included the phrase "Londons Intelligencer" in its subtitle to show that here was a weekly particularly concerned with news of the metropolis. This specialization turned out to be sporadic and fuzzy, but even so there are many indications that the editor sometimes viewed himself as addressing a local rather than a national audience. In this sense, his was the first big-city newspaper. It was also the first illustrated newspaper.[41] Starting with the third number (May 18–25) the title page was usually graced with one or two woodcuts. These woodcuts, almost always the head of a prominent person, were crude, and the paper's publishers later reduced costs by using the same cut to represent different people. None the less, *Mercurius Civicus* was undeniably illustrated, an asset that made it comparatively conspicuous and probably more salable. It also differed from its fellows of May and June in its more frequent animadversions on *Aulicus*, and its occasional remarks against the London press.[42] Mainly, however, *Mercurius Civicus* covered the news in the standard manner. In fact, its intermittent use of rhymed headlines and of a hand to indicate important items are strong evidence that Richard Collings was now working for two newspapers, *The Kingdomes Weekly Intelligencer*, which appeared on Tuesday, and *Mercurius Civicus*, which came out on Thursday.[43]

These two new newspapers of May 1643, *Mercurius Rusticus* and *Mercurius Civicus*, further aggravated the chronic problem of censorship. The former added to Parliament's irritation with the Royalist press; the latter marked another inroad into the traditional province of the Stationers' Company. In the flood of unauthorized books, pamphlets, and newspapers, many of them pouring from secret presses, the historical privileges and vested financial interests of the registered stationers were being swept away.[44] In the immediate preliminaries to and opening scenes of the Civil War this group, the traditional arm of enforcement for governmental censorship, could do almost nothing. One of its agents, Joseph Hunscott, appears recurrently in the official records ferreting out seditious printers, but even his zeal accomplished little.[45] In April, therefore, the Stationers addressed a *Humble Remonstrance* to Parliament asking that they be given power to seek out and prosecute violators of their patents and that the number of presses in London be curtailed.[46]

To this request Parliament gave a sympathetic ear. It had already taken action against certain weeklies for being too accurate in their news (the arrest of Pecke and Coles, for instance) or for being too full in their coverage of Parliamentary debates (one number of Cook's and Wood's *A Perfect Diurnall* having been officially condemned for this reason). Both Houses were also concerned over the surreptitious printing of Royalist propaganda in London. Consequently in June, having passed a preliminary ordinance in March and under continued pressure from its generally loyal supporters in the Stationers' Company, the House of Commons set up a new law to control the press. In part the law was an attempt to strengthen the position of the established printers and booksellers by ordering that all printed matter be entered in the Stationers' Register and by giving the company renewed power to protect the copyrights of its members. This it was to do by having the right to refuse to enter a transgressing publication and to prosecute, with the aid of the government, any unlawful printers and publishers. But in the main the law was Parliament's attempt to establish itself as the heir, in terms of control of the press, of Star Chamber and High Commission. The ordinance of June 1643 also set up a Parliamentary Committee of Examinations to look into various potentially subversive books and pamphlets before they appeared; and to make this prepublication censorship effective the committee appointed certain specialized censors, one of whose province was the newsbook.[47]

On paper this law looked worse than it turned out to be. Temporarily, however, it did bring some order into the confused ranks of the early newspaper. Though it did nothing to curtail the Royalist press at Oxford, and though most of the surreptitious London presses remained sufficiently well hidden to go on printing "scandalous" pam-

phlets, the law eliminated most counterfeit newspapers, cut down on
the appropriation of competing titles, and simplified the ensuing history
of English journalism. Moreover, because many members of Parliament
continued to oscillate between their habitual respect for secrecy and
their new desire for large-scale public support, and because the dis-
agreements between incipient political parties in the House of Commons generated mounting tension, the impact of the new act was
promptly cushioned.

The most important immediate effect on journalism of this ordinance
was the stabilization of titles, since almost all the men who printed
and published newspapers quickly registered their titles with the Stationers' Company. Of these newspapers the one with the most prestige
and circulation was the Coles-Pecke *A Perfect Diurnall*. On July 3 the
first number in a new series came out, a series that lasted until October
1649. It was now published by Coles and Laurence Blaikelock and
could be purchased at either of their shops. Since Cook's and Wood's
Diurnall was no longer in business, the new publishing team dropped
the title-page woodcut of the Commons in session; otherwise the paper
showed no major change.

Pecke's opening statement in this new series could have applied to
its predecessor, but it was especially pertinent to the more than three
hundred numbers which were to constitute the now established and
only remaining *Perfect Diurnall*:

> . . . You may henceforth expect from this relator to be informed onely
> of such things as are of credit, and of some part of the proceedings of one
> or both houses of Parliament fit to be divulged, or such other news as shall
> be certified by Letters from the Army, and other parts, from persons of
> speciall trust. . . .

A reputation for truthfulness and a concern to avoid antagonizing those
in power continued to be the route to success among all editors and
publishers who did not conspicuously ally themselves with a partisan
group; and Pecke, having sampled jail, never again fell off the political
tightrope. Hence *A Perfect Diurnall* remained a competent record of
public events. Cromwell's early military exploits, for instance, were
given comparatively full coverage, and the battle of Newbury received two detailed pages.[48] Pecke's treatment of military news, in
fact, supported his contention that he did his best not to transmit unconfirmed reports. In addition, his handling of events at Westminster,
though invariably cautious and usually superficial, was accurate. In one
of the early numbers of this new series he even pointed out an error
he had made the previous week.[49] Then, too, Pecke's bias was obvious

enough to be easily discounted. Thus his report of a "new disease" at Oxford that was claiming one hundred victims a week was almost certainly taken with several grains of salt, for such stories represented Pecke as a propagandist, a role which he played clumsily but not very often.[50] In general, therefore, *A Perfect Diurnall* was the newspaper of the 1640's whose coverage of important news was fullest and most accurate. Apparently this paid: twice in the summer of 1643 Pecke mentioned the public demand for his paper.[51]

This demand was not a response to Pecke's style, which remained adequate but dull, though it began to show an acquired skill in the art of paragraphing. This skill may have been the result of his close adherence, in this new series of *A Perfect Diurnall*, to a rigidly chronological arrangement of the news. Such an arrangement, which almost every newspaper of the time followed, had the advantage of a certain amount of clarity, as well as that of making the editor's job easier. But it had the frequent disadvantage of promoting blindness, for often the last page was filled with smaller and then even smaller type. The middle pages of the paper, which usually included the news of the first five days of the week, were set up early. Then, if much material came in on the sixth or seventh day, it was squeezed onto the last page — and sometimes the squeezing was so rigorous that one needs a magnifying glass to read the final paragraph. Also, if the paper had proto-headlines or a title-page summary, then the top of the front page was not set up until the last minute so that it could include mention of any important late items.

Of the other established London papers, *The Kingdomes Weekly Intelligencer* stayed on its previous course until it temporarily expired in mid-August when Collings again left for the wars, this time to do three months of military service.[52] Consequently *Mercurius Civicus*, after a gap of three weeks, acquired a new editor. He retained the external trademarks of title-page woodcuts and semi-headlines, some of them in rhyme, and the internal trademark of more frequent stories in praise of the citizens of London. In one respect, however, *Mercurius Civicus* changed: it began to lean toward the Presbyterian point of view. The split between Presbyterian and Independent was still mainly in the future, and no paper that directed its appeal to the London middle-class could then be anti-Presbyterian. But *Civicus* went out of its way to praise a book by William Prynne, the darling of the city's Presbyterians, and it displayed a great deal of enthusiasm for the Solemn League and Covenant which was forging an irksome bond between Parliament and Scotland.[53]

Because both Collings and his temporary successor were inclined toward what would become the Presbyterian party, their anti-Royalism in mid-1643 was momentarily more evident than that of their London colleagues. The knot between foreign Catholicism and the cause of Charles was tied more tightly in the pages of *Mercurius Civicus*, and Royalist atrocities received a bigger play. Just before his departure Collings made an indignant joke about Rupert's "burning love to England," and he seemed more concerned than, say, Pecke about the damage done by Royalist propaganda.[54] Yet this anti-Royalism differed in degree, not kind, from that in other London papers, and *Mercurius Civicus* was essentially a crowded and not very discriminating compilation of news.

Two such compilations existing from an earlier day went out of business in mid-1643, their demise hastened by the June ordinance and the competition of more salable weeklies. *Speciall Passages* appeared once in July, then disappeared.[55] *A Continuation of certain Speciall and Remarkable Passages* managed four numbers during July and August and three during September and October before it too departed from the journalistic scene. Its editor claimed that only "the importancy of some friends" kept him in business that long;[56] but apparently he did not have enough friends to justify Leach and Coles in continuing the paper.

These departures were balanced by the arrival of two new papers, both of which, under various titles, occupy bulky niches in the early history of the newspaper. Indeed, *The Parliament Scout* is among the more interesting documents in the subliterature of the Interregnum. An offshoot of the turmoil of civil war was the two-sided phenomenon that pamphlets and newspapers were being addressed to a public that was relatively unacquainted with the written word, and that men hitherto excluded from the domain of literature were now doing much of the writing.[57] One such man, John Dillingham, in the late 1630's was a tailor in White Friars. In 1639 he began to supplement his income by writing newsletters for his patron, Lord Montague.[58] Despite this apprenticeship in journalism, Dillingham was still naïve and loquacious when he became the editor of a printed weekly. As a result his newspaper was characterized by an amateurishness, a lack of professional inhibition, that makes it especially revealing. The opening statement of the first number of *The Parliament Scout* (June 20–27, 1643)[59] can illustrate this, for it epitomizes Dillingham's long-winded style, his homespun appeal, and his apparently artless approach to the world:

And considering withall the condition the Kingdome now stands in, when the Times is the only study, and that then I finde a necessity that a right Intelligence be kept and imparted throughout the Kingdome of the proceedings of the Parliament and their Armies, to the end the well-affected party, who are willing to sacrifice life and fortune for their Religion and Liberty, and the good of the King and Kingdome, may from time to time be informed and receive encouragement; and that the Malignants themselves, seeing the Candid proceedings of the Parliament, may . . . be convinced and converted. . . . It is held requisite that some weekly account be given of the daily Occurrences Collected from such sure hands that the Printer need not be ashamed to produce his Author . . . which worke for the present I am . . . much solicited into, and shall doe my best, though it will be with such weaknesse that I shall rather doe it to chaulke out the way for some more able, and to invite them to so necessary a service for the good of the Kingdome, than do it as it ought to be.

Subsequent numbers of *The Parliament Scout* were in keeping with this preamble. Dillingham employed the standardized anti-Royalist arguments, but he did so at greater length and with more hyperbole than most of his fellows. For instance, ". . . the people of England, had they been unanimous for their own good, might have been the ballancing power of Christendome, and the glory of the world, are now become slaves and villaines to French, Irish, Papists, and others. . . ." [60] Like Collings, Dillingham devoted much space to military news, and on occasion he showed a personal familiarity with camp and battlefield that suggests he was once a soldier.[61] Further, he had one or two "Scouts" with the army who regularly sent him accurate though verbose reports.[62]

Politically Dillingham was a little left of center. He consistently supported Essex and Pym's leadership of Parliament. At one point he asked for a fair draft to increase the strength of the Parliamentary armies, at another he was comparatively mild in his animadversions on certain sectaries, and at a third he was the one journalist of the day to forego scorn in his account of the riotous presentation of a peace petition by a crowd of London women.[63] Intermittently, too, his paper contained brief hints of the editor's democratic origins and orientation: for instance, an aside to the effect that in one battle the Royalist soldiers fought as if they were to be made barons or knights, the Parliamentary soldiers as if they were guarding the liberties of posterity.[64]

These leftist tendencies, combined with Dillingham's naïve optimism, probably meant that *The Parliament Scout* was initially intended to appeal to two partially new groups: the less sophisticated Londoner and the countryman. The first group can only be inferred but the second was announced, for Dillingham early stated that he stood "engaged to country friends. . . For their satisfaction only he reports." [65] Since the paper came out at the end of the week, the editor may have felt that his version of the news, even if it was a few days late, would have adequate rural appeal.

The second new paper of the summer and fall of 1643, *The Weekly Account*, began its lengthy career on a Wednesday early in September.[66] Though at first it bore a loose resemblance to *A Perfect Diurnall*, it lacked Pecke's accuracy and professional touches. Also, it was sufficiently perturbed by *Aulicus* to start life with a detailed refutation of Birkenhead.[67] Later Daniel Border, the editor, would play a larger part in journalism; now he was merely the writer of a conventional newspaper.

The arrival on the scene of *The Parliament Scout* and then of *The Weekly Account* was not ignored by Birkenhead, who promptly included them in his castigations of the lying London press.[68] And *Aulicus* was becoming less subtle. The tide of battle in the late summer of 1643 was turning against the king, and by September the alliance between Parliament and Scotland had become inevitable. Birkenhead's attempts to conquer by dividing therefore became more extended and more blatant. Not only did he continue to probe for weak spots in the net which held together Parliament, London, and the army, but he added regular attacks on the Solemn League and Covenant. Further, he now delighted in calling attention to the unrepresentative nature of Parliament, using such phrases as "the House of *three* Lords" and constantly implying that the Commons had a proportionately low head-count.[69] Two of his more adept thrusts from this period were a sentimental account of the reunion of Charles and Henrietta Maria, and the reprinting of a possibly faked letter from a London soldier's wife begging her husband to come home from the wars.[70]

The increasing obviousness of Birkenhead's tactics almost certainly did not prevent their being effective, particularly since, in the field of propaganda, he still had little competition from London editors. In fact, intermingled with his ubiquitous insults against them were occasional touches of condescending tolerance. But in September the situation changed. At the end of his thirty-fifth number he took brief notice of a new London weekly: "All other Newes (I mean Lyes) you must expect from a fine new thing borne this week called Mercurius Britannicus. For Mercuries (like Committees) will beget one another." With the onset of *Mercurius Britanicus* Birkenhead had a rough antagonist to contend with — and Parliament had its own propaganda journal.

CHAPTER IV

EARLY ADOLESCENCE I

September 1643 to July 1644

NEWSPAPERS have always had a close connection with politics, often with dirty politics. When newspapers were young and politicians neophytes in the art of bidding for large-scale public support, the connection between them was at first tenuous and clumsy. Quickly, however, many modern techniques of political journalism put in their appearance: the planted item, the inadequately denied rumor, the inside story. In embryo all these devices had been used by the London press to support Parliament, and in a more fully developed way by Birkenhead in behalf of Royalism. Now the chief job of the editor of Parliament's new propaganda journal, *Mercurius Britanicus*, would be to refute Birkenhead. But since the men who hired him increasingly disagreed on who their enemies were, and consequently on how Birkenhead should be refuted, he found himself more and more involved in the intricacies of party politics.

This involvement was prefigured even in the birth of *Mercurius Britanicus*, late in August 1643. First, the paper's title was not intended to recall the newsbooks of the 1620's but to suggest that here was a paper for the entire nation. (*Aulicus*, however, promptly pointed out that the title's second word was misspelled, with the result that *Britanicus* never did pick up its missing "n.") Second, though this new weekly went through the normal process of being licensed and entered in the Stationers' Register, it seems to have been issued with the special blessings of General Essex.[1] Third, it began life with a staff of more than one man; in fact, according to a hostile contemporary, it was launched by four or five "conspirators in wit." [2] Finally, as in the case of *Aulicus*, *Britanicus's* editors had the co-operation of people in the know.

At the start the chief editor was Captain Thomas Audley, a "short, swarthy, Chess-nutt colour'd" man.[3] Obviously no Adonis (good looks seem to have been incompatible with early journalism), Audley was shrewd. An unfriendly newspaper claimed that his military experience had been acquired mainly in London pubs and that he was not the sort to risk life or limb in battle.[4] In addition, despite the fact that he was soon in trouble for taking a wrong tack in *Britanicus*, he promptly became a deputy licenser of the press.[5] But Audley was not so shrewd as his assistant, Marchamont Nedham. Indeed, Nedham was the most professional of all Interregnum journalists: the most professional both in his competence and in his willingness to sell himself to the highest bidder. Consequently his journalistic career winds like a bright if changing colored thread through the history of the early English newspaper, nor did it end with the Restoration.

Nedham was born in Oxfordshire in 1620 of genteel and well-educated parents. In 1637 he was graduated from Oxford. Then, after a brief stint of teaching school, he became a successful law clerk, also finding time to study medicine.[6] His first newspaper job, at the age of twenty-three, was as Audley's right-hand man, and he apparently got it by his reputation for a sharp tongue and a facile pen.[7] Presumably Audley was in charge of collecting the news, Nedham of writing it up, though their other "conspirators in wit" almost certainly helped in both functions.[8]

From the start *Britanicus* was closer to *Aulicus* than to the London journals. Essentially it was *Aulicus* squared, for its main purpose was to counter *Aulicus*, to negate the negative. Within a few months Audley and Nedham were devoting three-quarters of their space to answering and smearing Birkenhead and his employers, only one-quarter to summarizing the news. Yet, if Anthony à Wood's later testimony is correct, *Britanicus* quickly became the best-selling of the Parliamentary weeklies.[9]

One reason for this popularity was the unexpected style of *Britanicus*, since its language was often rough, caustic, and outspoken. The first number indulged in harshly loaded case histories of some Lords who had deserted to Oxford, the third featured a bitter assault on the queen, and the tenth included an indictment of the king for being pro-Catholic. Such attacks were headier items than the more oblique and toned-down criticism in other London papers. Mainly, however, Audley and Nedham aimed their fire at *Aulicus*, now an especially inviting target since its London circulation alone was allegedly up to five hundred.[10] In so doing they shot at Birkenhead directly by name-calling and obliquely by refuting his stories. When *Aulicus* directed attention to the small number of M.P.'s, *Britanicus* reacted by claiming that there were eighteen in the House of Lords, 160 in the House of Commons, and that it was the Oxford Parliament that was a mockery of representative government.[11] When *Aulicus* assailed the Solemn League and Covenant, in the ensuing week *Britanicus* defended it.[12] Even when *Aulicus* printed a poignant letter from the wife of a soldier in the Parliamentary army, *Britanicus* had an equalizing if profane letter from a Cavalier.[13] Thus the first year of journalistic warfare between *Britanicus* and *Aulicus* resembles a tennis match between two capable players: what one hits, the other returns — and today's spectator gradually develops a stiff neck.

During the first few months of that year *Britanicus* had no trouble with the men, probably including Pym, who originally promoted a paper to counter *Aulicus*. But in the spring of 1644 some of the cracks appearing within the Parliamentary coalition began to be reflected in its pages. Until then, by concentrating on attacking Birkenhead and smearing the Royalist cause in general or in personal terms, Audley and Nedham had been able to postpone taking sides publicly between Presbyterian and Independent, between Parliament and army. After Pym's death at the end of 1643 this became more difficult, which may help to account for the highly eulogistic "Elegie on Master Pym" that appeared in the sixteenth number of *Britanicus*.[14] So eulogistic is this poem, in fact, that its concluding lines become humorous in their praise of the political rather than personal attachment which Pym evoked among his followers:

> Teares are too narrow drops for him,
> And private sighes too strait for Pym;
> None can completely Pym lament,
> But something like a Parliament,
> The publike sorrow of a State
> Is but a griefe commensurate,
> We must enacted passions have,
> And laws for weeping at his grave.[15]

To *Aulicus* Pym's death was a happy event: "loaded with various diseases," he made "a most loathsome and foule carkasse." [16] Thus Birkenhead continued to rate and berate the anti-Royalists. During the final months of 1643 his emphasis was still on conquering by dividing. But now to his collection of soft spots within the Parliamentary coalition he added the Assembly of Divines, vulnerable because of its display of discord between Presbyterian and Independent. Further, he gave more space to that wild growth of heresies which, he alleged, was the inevitable result of tampering with established religion.[17] Particularly effective at this time, too, was his toying with the stock argument that Parliament was not fighting against the king but against his evil advisors. Birkenhead modified this only slightly to make it come out that the Roundheads planned "to kill the King in his owne defence." [18]

Aulicus usually did not lower itself to attack individual London papers, except *Britanicus*, but it regularly heaped scorn on them collectively by correcting their news, pointing out their sins of omission, and ridiculing their subservience. In this squabbling, Birkenhead's major weapon remained the counterstory, and sometimes, especially in the increasing rivalry between *Aulicus* and *Britanicus*, the counter-counter-story. A graphic example is his reply to an accumulation of stories about Royalist blasphemies: the account of a Parliamentary soldier committing buggery — and on a Sunday, too! To this Audley and Nedham predictably responded, first by denying the incident, then by rewriting it with the human culprit now a Cavalier.[19]

The fact that *Britanicus* was bearing the brunt of answering *Aulicus* meant that most weeklies of late 1643 kept to the tracks they had already set for themselves. *The Kingdomes Weekly Intelligencer* had suspended publication in mid-August when Collings went off to the wars. When he returned in November, it was to resume where he left off.[20] Again his paper was devoted to a relatively straightforward presentation of the news, including an emphasis on non-Westminster events. Despite a normal quota of anti-Royalist reports and sentiments, Collings usually paid Birkenhead in kind by ignoring him. He also managed to steer clear of involvement in intra-Parliament disputes, though once in December he briefly displayed his inclinations toward the Presbyterian party.[21]

During these three months *A Perfect Diurnall* remained the most reliable vendor of straight news; consequently it too paid little attention to *Aulicus*. Nor was Pecke's recurrent indignation at events in Ireland inconsistent with the aims of his paper, though his correspondents there viewed Irish Catholics as a subhuman species. Such, however, was the accepted view and any marked deviation would have stigmatized an editor as a knave or a fool. Pecke was neither. Also in tune with his time and place were his now more open attacks against Charles.[22] In fact, one of the clues to Pecke's longevity as a newspaperman was his ability to respond to shifts in public or official opinion.

One superficial aspect of Pecke's responsiveness or time-serving was his skill in anticipating certain types of news, a skill of which he was quite proud. For instance, he discussed a problem in Anglo-Dutch relations; then the following week, when news of the imminent arrival of Dutch ambassadors in London was permitted, he reminded his readers of that earlier discussion.[23] A second and more important aspect of his ability to serve the times was his deftness in avoiding offense even in the most delicate situations. Here, for example, is his account of how Essex seemed in the process of being eased out of his command:

> The Commons also had consultation touching some alterations and amendments for the better explanation and enlargement of Sir William Wallers Commission, and upon the result of all they appointed a Committee to treat with the Earl of Essex for his approbation and concurrence therein.[24]

Finally, on a more profound level, Pecke's occasional theological asides suggest that he preferred to travel along the middle road of Puritanism, between sectarian enthusiasm and Presbyterian orthodoxy. In so doing he had plenty of company, and he could be safe and conventional in attacking the "Superstitious ceremonies" of the Laudian church or in approving, on religious ground, the stripping of Henry VII's chapel.[25] Further, he did not yet have to commit himself on the theological issues already pocking the face of English Puritanism.

Like *A Perfect Diurnall*, the other established London papers generally displayed during the last quarter of 1643 only the gradual development of their earlier tendencies, not any reversals of form. *Mercurius Civicus* moved, if almost imperceptibly, toward partisan Presbyterianism,[26] at the same time becoming more of a London newspaper. The editor now frequently claimed that "the affairs of London are the maine things," and, what is more important, he followed this up by giving more space than his rivals to metropolitan news.[27]

Dillingham's *Parliament Scout* also kept to its own path, though the fact that it stumbled rather than strode made that path somewhat irregular. For instance, in one number Dillingham prefaced a paragraph of foreign news by saying that it involved "far off" places and that, anyway, continental battles were not important;[28] yet he quite frequently devoted half a page to European events. One week he seemed inclined toward religious toleration, another week he derogated it.[29] But for all its confusion and verbosity, *The Parliament Scout* retained its tinge of pink. On one occasion Dillingham urged the destruction of the Royalist armies, not the besieging of their towns; on another he expressed compassion for the lot of the common soldier.[30] But being an editor, especially a relatively outspoken one, was, as Gainsford had long ago discovered, a weary process. "Our Scout is much discouraged," Dillingham lamented early in December,

and hath thoughts of adventuring abroad no more; the reason he gives is, he cannot be allowed to tell the truth but he undergoes the censure of [being] a Malignant; if he doth not vapour and say such a one was routed, defeated, when they scarce saw one the other, then they say he is partiall: but being importuned by some speciall private friends, he resolves to go abroad a while longer.[31]

And Dillingham stuck to his resolution.

The Weekly Account continued to come out on Wednesday and to model itself on *A Perfect Diurnall*. Not so well written and organized as Pecke's paper, and exhibiting its piety more conspicuously, Border's crowded weekly steered a middle course. At one point, perhaps inadvertently, certainly ambiguously, Border summed up the policy of the cautious Interregnum editor: "I shall endeavour to lead your expectations to their owne ends, and that by so eaven and so faire a way that . . . you shall not stick on an uncertaintie, neither stumble at untruth." [32] Border was later to change his tune; now, however, *The Weekly Account* was largely unaltered from its first numbers of July 1643.

Certaine Informations, which had appeared irregularly during the summer, resumed regular publication in October.[33] Bishop and White, who were publishing *Britanicus* on Tuesday and *The Kingdomes Weekly Intelligencer* on Thursday, thus filled out their string with this Monday newspaper. *Certaine Informations*, though it gave most of its space to military news, showed the new influence of Audley and Nedham in the stridency of its anti-Royalism. In fact, its generally conventional pages were now adulterated by an increasingly shrill strain of religiosity and by a particularly horrified reaction to Cavalier blasphemies and atrocities.[34] Despite the fact that it was intended to compete with *A Perfect Diurnall*, it lacked Pecke's sureness of touch; it also lacked Nedham's cleverness. In the forest of early English journalism *Certaine Informations* was a stunted tree.

One of the characteristics of this forest was that as old trees fell, new ones took their place; and until October 1649, when the Commonwealth effectively cracked down on the press, the new growth was relatively lush. During the final months of 1643 four nonephemeral new weeklies sprang up. The shortest-lived was *Remarkable Passages*, which lasted only from early November to late December. In retrospect, probably its most interesting feature was its changes in title: its first two numbers, with fine inconsistency, were subtitled "*Impartially* relating the Proceedings of the Protestant and *Papisticall* armies . . ." (my italics); Number 3 then announced in its full title that the news was now being presented in "a better Coppy than formerly." The publisher also experimented with various forms of title-page summary and with numbering each item, while the editor showed a few signs of personality in his use of the first person and his search for nonofficial adjectives. Otherwise, *Remarkable Passages* was typical of the papers of its short day.

A second new weekly, *The Kingdomes Weekly Post*, started in November 1643, died in January 1644, came back in 1645, again died, and in 1648 revived for the last time. Edited by Border, the editor of *The Weekly Account*, it was also a standard production: much military news, much piety, much hostility to Royalist and Catholic, and little liveliness of style or evidence of editorial selectivity. But Border, more than his fellows, often wrote as if he were on the defensive, and even the first number of his new paper began with a semi-apology:

> The English newes is now a days cut into so many fashions that it must be a rare wit whose invention can exceed in some things not old . . . yet this honest Post ventures in his travelling weeds to present his newes to the City, as well as to the rest of the Kingdome, without any gilded glosings, invented fixions, or flattering Commentaries. . . .

And the fifth number of *The Kingdomes Weekly Post* (November 28–December 6, 1643) included an attack on Pecke that reads in part like an attempt by Border to bolster himself.[35]

A third new newspaper of late 1643, *The True Informer*, began its approximately three years of life in September. Edited probably by Henry Walley, the licenser of the weekly press, it came out on Saturday, now the only day of the week not already occupied.[36] In general it was the paper closest to *A Perfect Diurnall*. Its editor was cautious, restrained, and able to compress the news without undue garbling. He could also speak about his job with a certain amount of tact and confidence:

> Truth is the daughter of Time. Relations of Battels, fights, skirmishes, and other passages and proceedings of concernment are not alwaies to be taken or credited at the first hand, for that many times they are uncertaine, and the truth doth not so conspicuously appeare till a second or third relation. And hence it is that victories sometimes fall much short of the generall

expectation; and battles oftentimes prove but skirmishes, and great over-throwes related to be given to the enemy prove oftentimes equall and bal-lancing losse on both sides.[37]

As can be seen in this passage, *The True Informer*'s prose, as well as its attitude toward news, was functional. So, too, was its employment of quasi-headlines and brief title-page summaries, though its attempts to break down the news by place were sometimes inept.

In December both *A Perfect Diurnall* and *The True Informer* took time to give a brief boost to *The Scotish Dove*.[38] Whether or not this fourth of the new newspapers of late 1643 deserved it is debatable. George Smith, its editor, was a pious and garrulous man, probably from the north of England.[39] Part idealist, part hypocrite, he wrote a news-paper that was at once zealous and oily. The first number bragged about the difficulty of getting news from the north and also set the tone for the verbose anti-Royalism of succeeding issues.[40] In the third number (October 27–November 3, 1643) Smith announced that his chief concern would be with news of Scots, especially of their army in England, but he subsequently showed himself very lax in such spe-cialization. (On the other hand, the *Dove* may have had some connec-tion with one or more of the Scottish commissioners in London. The paper began when the alliance between Scotland and Parliament was being cemented; it came to an end, three years later, when the Scottish army was withdrawing across the border.)

As an editor Smith was generally amateurish. He manifested little feeling for selectivity or order in presenting the news, and at irregular intervals he poured out tangles of purple prose. Moreover, like Border, he seems to have felt on the defensive. Usually he responded by lashing back at *Aulicus*, but he also spattered some of the London weeklies with his contumely.[41] Yet it is this lack of professionalism, plus these touches of paranoia, that make *The Scotish Dove* at once repellent and inviting. This ambivalence is particularly characteristic of the paper's opening paragraphs, before Smith settled down to giving the news, mostly military, which normally filled three-quarters of his space. He began his fourth number, for instance, with this crudely punctuated announcement:

It is a wonder to see the stupidity of the common multitude of English people: And the Malignitie of some desperate Spirits, willfully ignorant, and inexorable in malice: partly by corrupt nature, and partly by Jesuiticall seducements, the working of Antichrist, by the mystery of iniquity; to the amasement of the world, and miserable destruction of these three Kingdoms: and this is part of our Doves errand at this time, to inform the judgements of the ignorant.

He then went on to underline the fact that he thought his readers stupid and that it was his role to see that "the judgments of men might be rectified, and established, in causes and things." [42] This sense of mission, of using his newspaper to reform rather than to inform, was oddly enough combined with Smith's ostensible view that it was too bad that people were so interested in newsbooks that they would "scarcely bestow money to buy a bigger or better booke, nor time to reade it." [43] Consequently *The Scotish Dove* was a mixture of anomalies. On its title page it bore a woodcut of a dove from whose beak floated the motto "holy innocency is blessed," and under this picture was the injunction "Be Wise as Serpents, Innocent as Doves." Smith was neither.

Besides *The Scotish Dove*, Smith probably edited one ephemeral paper of late 1643, *New Christian Uses*, an unctiously pious and vague commentary on the events of early October that failed to have a second number.[44] In all likelihood he also edited *The Compleate Intelligencer*, four or five numbers of which appeared during November.[45] It featured the innovation of devoting about a fourth of its eight or sixteen pages to "resolving" the news, to, that is, asking and answering certain questions relevant to the week's events. Thus the editor was able to take a verbose position in favor of aid from the Scots, of the prosecution of Laud, of unity between Presbyterian and Independent. Such "resolutions" did not involve any real risks, but in style and intention they were the precursors of the full-fledged editorial.[46]

During two of the weeks that *The Compleate Intelligencer* was indulging in anti-Royalist editorializing, the cause of the king was being supported by a surreptitious London journal dedicated to attacking *Britanicus*, a worthier target than Smith.[47] And during one of these two weeks a nonsurreptitious London paper entitled *Informator Rusticus* made a bid for rural as well as urban circulation.[48] But the strangest of the fly-by-night publications of the end of 1643 was *The Welch Mercury*, which, surprisingly, lasted three numbers.[49] It was certainly the first and perhaps the only attempt in the history of journalism to write a newspaper entirely in dialect. Though the editor managed to make some of his reports lively and anecdotal, the English language is such that it becomes almost impossible to read when, for instance, "g" is humorously changed into "c."

But during the first week of 1644 any Londoner who wanted to read his newspaper in English had a dozen to choose from. On Monday he could select *A Perfect Diurnall*, *Certaine Informations*, or *Aulicus* — which despite its Sunday dateline probably came out in London on Monday. Tuesday he had *The Kingdomes Weekly Intelligencer*; Wednesday, *The Weekly Account* or the newly revived *A Continuation*

of certain Speciall and Remarkable Passages; and Thursday a choice between *Britanicus* and *Civicus*. Friday brought forth three papers: *The
Parliament Scout*, *The Scotish Dove*, and a new weekly, *Occurrences
of Certain Speciall and Remarkable Passages*. On Saturday the reader
either acquired *The True Informer* or went newspaperless. On Sunday
he rested. Probably no one, with the exception of George Thomason,
who tried to collect every newspaper and pamphlet, purchased a paper
daily. Yet the fact that a single publisher might have a hand in two or
three newspapers indicates that a sizable number of readers purchased
more than one a week.[50] Further, there is ample evidence that many
Londoners retained the habit of sending papers to their country cousins
and friends, and that each copy, both in the city and in the hinterlands,
had several readers.

The circulation of any one paper, however, remains something of a
mystery. First, historians disagree about the population of London in
the mid-seventeenth century. In the absence of a census, the consensus
is that the city and its immediate environs held about 500,000 people.[51]
Assuming that approximately half the adult males could read, there
would then be a potential metropolitan audience for the newspaper of
roughly 60,000, or one-eighth of the total population.[52] Second, no
newspaper of the Interregnum provides any circulation figures. Even
so, one can approach a solution to the problem by means of some
seventeenth-century clues and twentieth-century guesswork. Apparently 200 copies was the minimum circulation of any Civil War newspaper,[53] and at this level no publisher could break even, much less show
a profit. Probably 3,000 copies was the maximum. This upper limit
can be set by computing the production of two hand-presses, each
operating for twelve hours, and each printing only the first and last
pages — the middle pages having already been run off.[54] Then, since
the unit on which most printing charges were based remained 250, it
is almost certain that newspapers were printed in quantities of, say,
500 or 750 or 1,000.[55]

In the first week of 1644, when there were a dozen competing papers,
probably the new weeklies had an approximate circulation of 250, the
established ones of 500, and the front-runners, such as *Britanicus* and
A Perfect Diurnall, of 750 or 1,000. The average for most papers in the
1640's was, in all likelihood, 500. This meant that when twelve papers
were in business — assuming that each copy had four or five urban
readers — the adolescent newspaper could claim almost half the literate
males in metropolitan London for its audience. The newspaper had
thus become an important force in molding public opinion, as well as
a source of profit to the publishers. These two considerations do much

to explain why the editors were so careful not to call down the poised hand of the powers that were or might be.

Throughout the first half of 1644 those weeklies owned by comparatively experienced publishers and compiled by increasingly professional editors were generally stable in their output and in their adherence to an established style and content. During the second half of that year, however, the struggles within the Parliamentary coalition began to drag the press a little more deeply into partisan entanglements. Though such struggles and entanglements had existed since the start of the Civil War, they became more bitter and ensnaring after Cromwell's triumph at Marston Moor in July signified that the Royalists would not win the war.

During the six months before that battle *Aulicus* continued to heckle anti-Royalists and the London press; and in the first number of his 1644 series Birkenhead looked forward to a Royalist victory and the day when there would be no newsbooks in England.[56] Yet despite his aggressiveness, one can sense that Birkenhead knew his barricade was no longer plush-lined. From January on he persistently denied allegations of dissensions at Oxford. With the sixth number of this second series, and intermittently thereafter, he reduced the size of his paper from twelve to eight pages. Twice in June he felt compelled to deny rumors that *Aulicus* was dead or dying.[57] He also, throughout the last four of these six months, progressively decreased the space allotted to refuting the London press, increasing that given over directly to propping up the Royalist cause. Finally, after the king's departure from Oxford in June 1644, the news in *Aulicus* became less coherent, more scattered, for Oxford could no longer even try to rival London as a capital and news center. Meanwhile Birkenhead had probably been temporarily replaced as editor, either to provide a local scapegoat or to substitute for him a man more closely in touch with the peripatetic king.[58]

In spite of this shift toward the defensive, *Aulicus* did not stop being a hard-stinging gadfly. In one number Birkenhead or his replacement apologized for having omitted the adjective "pretended" in describing Parliament; in another he noted a rise in the suicide rate among supporters of Parliament and signers of the Covenant; and in a third he showed how wrathful God was against those who were hunting down "His Anointed." [59] Nor did the editor's skill in using divisive tactics slacken. Further, though the London press got a smaller share of space, he was still effective in mocking it, now both individually and collectively.[60] *Britanicus* was his favorite target. Its voice is, he wrote, the real voice of Parliament, and when it calls for the treatment of the king as a rebel, it is expressing the sentiments of those radicals who are leading England down the path to ruin. Dillingham of *The Parliament Scout* was his second favorite butt. In one number Birkenhead or his successor flourished the accusation that Dillingham was a pensioner, a mouthpiece, of the Earl of Manchester; in the next number, that Dillingham, along with certain other London editors, was trying to get a subsidy of £500 for continuing to spew forth anti-Royalist propaganda.[61] *Aulicus* and its cause may have been slipping, but neither was down, much less out.

Britanicus remained the London weekly most involved with *Aulicus*. For three weeks in January 1644 Audley and Nedham did not put out their paper; then they re-entered the arena with this announcement, almost certainly written by Nedham:

> I tooke up my pen for disabusing his Majesty, and for disbishoping and dispoping his good subjects, and for taking off the vizards and vailes and disguises which the Scribes and Pharisees at Oxford had put upon a treasonable and popish cause, and I laid it down as freely; but I feel the generation is restless, alwaies plotting and printing; I see Aulicus will be . . . comming abroad still. . . .[62]

So Nedham again took up his pen. But the running fight between *Britanicus* and *Aulicus* sometimes suggests a married couple for whom constant bickering is at once angrily destructive and sportingly competitive. On at least one occasion, however, a corespondent entered the ménage when a person or persons unnamed cleverly counterfeited *Britanicus*: he or they imitated its style and typography, even its pagination, while loading it with anti-Parliament news items.[63]

Nedham took this in stride and continued to refute *Aulicus*. In addition, he delighted in telling of his rival's vicissitudes: Digby, the king's friend, was supplanting Birkenhead; Birkenhead had been fired; Birkenhead was journalistically dead — and Nedham printed a vulgar obituary, including a urinalysis.[64] Thereafter *Britanicus* gave less space to attacking the Royalist press, more to boosting the cause of Parliament, and in June Nedham thus cockily proclaimed the shift:

> I shall now at the expiration of Aulicus make it my task to give you the faithfullest and most politicke Relations of the times I can, and to the best advantage of the Cause; and since the victory sits upon my Pen, I hope my Paper will be hereafter more acceptable to the Kingdom, for I have by an excellent and powerfull Providence led the people through the labyrinths of the enemies Plots, through all their Jesuiticall windings and turnings, through the Episcopall and Prelaticall pretences; I have taken off the Calumnies from a Parliament, the scandalls from an Assembly, and I have wiped

off the aspersions from every honourable Member and Agent in this Cause, from the House of Commons to the house of Lords, from thence to the City, from the City to the Armies, from the Armies to Scotland. . . . I have brought the secrets and sins of the Court abroad, from her Majestie to Mistris Crofts her very maid of honour, and from his Majesty to his very Barbour. . . . And if another rise up in the disguise of a Court Intelligencer . . . I shall never do him the honour hereafter to put him in the fore leafe of my booke, but behinde me, and there let him wait at the back door of my Intelligence.[65]

Yet Nedham's gloating self-confidence included elements of competitive bickering, personal aggrandizement, and whistling in the dark. *Aulicus* was not dead, and England was still deep in both "the labyrinths of the enemies Plots" and the fissures within the Parliamentary coalition. Moreover, Nedham failed to mention that *Britanicus* was becoming identified with the extremists of the day, the more militant Independents.[66] And he nowhere hinted that he had become involved in one of the touchier political cases of early 1644, a case relevant to the history of press-agentry, if not directly to the history of journalism, and one that casts some light on the tangled politics of that tangled era.

Nathaniel Fiennes was the son of Lord Say, the most militant Independent in the House of Lords. The son had risen to a high position in the Parliamentary coalition, and in 1643 he was made governor of Bristol. In July he surrendered the city to Prince Rupert in an action that was probably justified militarily but certainly a few days premature. In December 1643 he was tried and condemned to death, then promptly pardoned.[67] Meanwhile, before his trial both he and the justification he had written were violently attacked by Prynne and Prynne's friend Clement Walker. Then in February 1644 Prynne's *A Checke to Britannicus* went after Nedham for supporting Fiennes. Fiennes, though he was later to be a victim of Pride's Purge, was at this time identified with the war party; not only was he his father's son, but the court-martial which condemned him, and which was under the thumb of the army high command, had almost certainly arranged for his immediate pardon. Hence Prynne and Walker, alarmed at the revolutionary direction in which the war was heading, were using the Fiennes case to belabor the militants in Parliament and army. It was into this beehive that the chief writer of *Britanicus* did not stumble but stepped. Though Nedham gave almost no space to Fiennes' ups and downs in his paper, he presumably became his press agent at the time of his trial, and in February he emerged into the open with *A Check to the Checker of Britannicus*.[68] For reasons of money and prudence Nedham was taking a stand that the immediate future lay with the leaders of the army and with the Independents. He was right.

But politics invariably becomes simpler with hindsight. Early in 1644, after the death of Pym, the alliance between the Parliamentary Independents and the coming leaders of the army was only beginning to take shape. The less militant Presbyterians and Erastians continued to maintain their majority in the House of Commons, a majority which was not liquidated until Pride's Purge late in 1648. Yet the connection between neophyte journalism and complicated politics can be seen not only in Nedham's simultaneous efforts in behalf of Fiennes and *Britanicus*, but in the attempt by one of Nedham's comparatively prominent contemporaries, Durant Hotham, to set up a rival paper.[69] This intruder, *The Spie*, lasted from January to June 1644, and for part of this period it tried to shove *Britanicus* aside while it took over the job of answering *Aulicus*.

Hotham died at the age of seventy-four in 1691, having published, in the 1650's, a life of Jacob Boehme.[70] But early in 1644 he did not seem to be an excellent actuarial risk or the future biographer of a German mystic. In 1643 both his father, the man who had prevented the king's seizure of Hull at the start of the Civil War, and his brother had sunk into official disgrace for negotiating with the Royalists; and both men were executed early in 1645, despite the opposition of many moderates in Parliament. Whether Durant Hotham started *The Spie* to display his own anti-Royalism or to win good will for his family or to show off his wit — or for any other reason — is impossible to determine. But for six weeks he was more deeply embroiled with Audley and Nedham than with Birkenhead, his ostensible target. Intermingled with the clash of personalities in this early newspaper war was, again, the larger struggle of potential moderate versus potential extremist.

From the start Hotham, a Cambridge graduate and a member of the lesser aristocracy, presented his anti-Royalism with a new twist: the pretense that he himself went to Oxford to get the latest news. He also managed a rollicking style, modeled on Birkenhead's, which periodically bordered on true wittiness.[71] The following quotation, from *The Spie's* second number, illustrates both this stylistic zest and the dangerous path which Hotham was temporarily to pursue:

Gentlemen . . . Our Spie . . . sweares now never to leave hackneying it to Oxford, and vowes to turn an errant Jockie for your sakes, till his very posteriors become Parchment and fret and peele like the scalp of any Courtier. I protest I think he is a pretty towardly Thing to fetch and carry Newes; and I dare say, a Whelp of as right a strain as Britanicus, though not so curst.[72]

And Hotham proceeded to belabor *Aulicus*, using the same techniques as *Britanicus*.

The next four numbers of *The Spie* also continued to heckle *Britanicus*, though the bulk of their space was reserved for attacks on *Aulicus* and his cause. When, for instance, Hotham commented on Royalist sexual aberrations, the content and manner were those of Nedham, with Hotham possibly having a more sprightly touch.[73] It was, however, the barbs which Hotham tossed at Audley and Nedham that made *The Spie* distinctive and, in the context of its own time, exciting. Hotham accused the editors of *Britanicus* of garbling the Oxford news, of being plodding and unoriginal, and — most cutting — of losing readers to *The Spie*.[74] Within a few weeks Audley and Nedham were replying in kind. Referring to *The Spie* as a snarling and barking "little Beagle," the editors of *Britanicus* went on to make the more serious charge that Hotham was a secret Royalist.[75]

Such a charge carried extra weight for two reasons: Parliament, as well as the London press, had long been viewing with alarm the leakage of secrets to Oxford; and Audley and Nedham had influential friends. Their accusation brought quick results. The sixth number of *The Spie* mentioned its enemies at home; in the following week it stopped insulting *Britanicus*; and a month later, under official pressure, it moved its day of appearance closer to the end of the week. Consequently from early March until its demise at the end of June *The Spie* echoed but did not mock *Britanicus*. When Hotham left journalism it may have been because he realized that he had not helped his father and brother, but it was probably because the men in Parliament and army who were responsible for anti-Royalist publicity felt that one weekly, not *The Spie*, was sufficient to handle *Aulicus*.[76] In any event, Hotham then disappeared from newspaper history.

Not so *The Scotish Dove*, which hovered over the scene until December 1646. Like other London weeklies, with the exception of *Britanicus* and *The Spie*, the *Dove* paid little direct attention to *Aulicus*.[77] Smith continued to display his strong anti-Royalism and anti-Catholic piety. But what distinguished his paper during the early months of 1644 were its quasi-editorials. On the extremely likely assumption that Smith had edited *The Compleate Intelligencer* of the previous November, it is not surprising that he should shift its most prominent feature to his more successful newspaper. Thus the editorial queries and answers which had ended each issue of *The Compleate Intelligencer* were transformed, in December 1643, into the opening paragraphs of *The Scotish Dove*. These editorials, to give them the benefit of the doubt, were almost always garrulous, pious,

and noncommittal, and Smith was obviously against sin. He believed
in God and God believed in Parliament; he did not believe in factional-
ism and was against Royalist atrocities and the king's evil advisors;
and justice was, he felt, better than injustice.[78] Bland and safe as these
openings were — and Smith carried extra insurance in the form of a
close adherence to a biblical vocabulary and sentence structure —
they do represent a personal touch. Though Smith as yet here took
no stand on the partisan issues of the day, he was potentially enlarg-
ing the scope of the newspaper.

At the same time, he occasionally did take a stand in his paragraphs
of news. This news was predominantly military, with a sporadic
emphasis on the activities of the Scottish army. Smith, in fact, sometimes felt compelled to apologize because the Scots had not been more
active;[79] and it was, of course, safer to handle news of battles than
news of Parliament.[80] Even so, Smith was not always able to suppress
his Presbyterian leanings. In one number he assailed the decentraliza-
tion implicit in religious Independency, using the dissensions in New
England as an example of what happens when autonomous churches
rear their heads.[81] In a few instances he indulged in open praise of a
Presbyterian church settlement.[82] Still, despite the fact that he kept
on visualizing his paper as a blunt instrument of reform, Smith usually
wielded it carefully. As in the following passage, he would rather
insult his readers than offend any of the powers that be:

> I know most men are of itching eares, and are desirous to hear all newes;
> but I finde few industrious to informe themselves of the rise and cause of
> that which daily happeneth, which induced me to undertake this taske, de-
> sirous to informe men's judgements, and to undeceive the seduced and
> inconsiderate —

and he launched into an editorial against sin.[83]

Besides being garrulous and garbled, *The Scotish Dove* had an un-
pleasantness that differed from the comparatively lusty and open
scurrility of *Aulicus* and *Britanicus*, as well as from the usual anti-
Royalist asides in the London press. In one number Smith carried his
dislike of the king's cause to the extreme of seeming almost pleased that
the queen had had a miscarriage, and of commending an English captain who, in cold blood, had drowned some Irish prisoners.[84] Then, too,
Smith's piety was more exhibitionistic and calculating than that of
most of his contemporaries, as this implied deal between the editor
and his God indicates:

> From the North we have happie newes, a good return for our last weekes
> thanksgiving: I pray remember that our Dove told you last weeke that the

thankfulnesse to God for one mercy was a kinde of engaging God to bestow a second; let us bee more thankefull for the second, and God will yet do greater things for us.[85]

It is, in a sense, refreshing to move from Smith and his *Dove* to Dillingham and his *Parliament Scout*. In contrast to the *Dove*'s unctuousness, the *Scout* continued to display a naïve frankness that makes its political gropings and relatively outspoken asides seem both informative and engaging. Also, Dillingham still displayed an occasional tendency to lean to the left that was rare in the newspapers of the mid-1640's. Moreover, as he moved farther away from tailoring, he became a more competent editor. By the spring of 1644 *The Parliament Scout* was climbing to the level of *A Perfect Diurnall*, so much so that a contemporary accused Dillingham of being a "confederate" of Pecke and of agreeing with him "to utter nothing but perfumed breath, and to make no narration but what shall be pleasing" to the junto ruling England.[86]

Stylistically Dillingham's increased competence became evident in *The Parliament Scout* during the first half of 1644. Though still long-winded, he revealed a better control of paragraphing and continuity, a more effective use of personal asides; and though he still neglected any consistent breakdown of the news by place or date, he achieved a more coherent coverage. Thus the accounts of military affairs which filled the bulk of his paper were made livelier by his more frequent semi-anecdotal and humanizing touches, and his weekly paragraph or two of foreign news became clearer and more relevant than before.

Yet it is on what can be called the periphery of *The Parliament Scout* that Dillingham's personality shines through most clearly. In January he took over from Smith the practice of placing certain editorial queries at the end of his paper. In these and in his sporadic comments one can see him become increasingly anti-Royalist and, in so doing, more pro-Independent. Parliament's cause was white, the king's black, but within Parliament the grays were beginning to intrude. Early in 1644 Dillingham recommended the new-modeling of the army, a stand supported by the prominent Independents. At the same time he still cited those risks of religious toleration which the Presbyterians were loudly proclaiming.[87] By spring his sympathies were more clearly with the militants, and by then he had moved to the left on the issue of religious toleration.[88]

In Dillingham's case this move seems to have been based on changing conviction rather than on caution, for the evidence suggests that he was becoming progressively concerned with the lot of the common man. In one number of *The Parliament Scout* he mentioned the need for better housing in London, in another he advocated pensions for veterans, and in a third he implied that there was a need for some form of democratic conscription.[89] He also made it explicitly clear that he viewed low birth as no discredit.[90] In a few instances his humanitarianism even peeped through his anti-Royalist tirades.[91] Thus Dillingham, by the summer of 1644, had become a more competent journalist and a more exposed Independent, though he managed to retain at least some of his engaging naïveté.

During these seven months *Mercurius Civicus* also became a slightly better newspaper, even if its title-page woodcuts and off-rhymed headlines remained unchanged. By concentrating on military news and by developing his skill in the arts and crafts of political caution, the editor was able to suppress most signs of his inclination toward the Presbyterian party.[92] He also continued intermittently to emphasize London news, especially news of London regiments in battle, going to the extent of having two or three regular correspondents report to him from these detachments.[93] As a result of the intense competition among newspapers in the mid-1640's a weekly had to be either competent or distinctive in order to survive. *Mercurius Civicus* generally chose competence.

So, too, did the other established London papers. *The Kingdomes Weekly Intelligencer*, in all probability like *Civicus* still edited by Richard Collings, tried to give the news coherently, reliably, and inoffensively. Both his weeklies devoted large amounts of space to military items, though in *The Kingdomes Weekly Intelligencer* news of Parliament frequently took the place of stories about Londoners in *Mercurius Civicus*. Even so, Collings managed to cling to careful neutrality.[94] Blatant anti-Royalism, including getting closer to direct attacks on Charles, had by the spring of 1644 become a safe and standard routine for the London press to adopt, and Collings adopted it.[95] Yet he was now especially cautious concerning the factions within the Parliamentary coalition, as the following not untypical passage eloquently testifies:

> I was in hope to have given you the particular relation of the Battel neer Yorke [Marston Moor]: But in regard the relation thereof is not yet come to the hands of the Parliament, under the hands of the three Generalls, I shall be silent, lest . . . affection or other respects may occasion a slip of the pen in commendation of one Commander before another. . . .[96]

If carried to an extreme, such an ideal of ostensibly objective journalism would end up in the publication of blank sheets. Collings, however, found enough comparatively safe news weekly to fill two eight-page papers.

Daniel Border now only had eight pages to fill, *The Kingdomes Weekly Post* having faded from the scene in January. In his surviving paper, *The Weekly Account*, he treated the Westminster and military news of the day with the superficial fullness of most London editors. But he was not entirely typical, for he could be conspicuously (and simultaneously) cautious and flowery, platitudinous and purple, in his personal asides. No other editor of that era, including Smith and Dillingham, would have thus begun a May number of his newspaper:

> Walking this morning forth into the Wood alone, I know not well whether to increase or allay my Melancholly by the beautie and musicke of the Spring; there I might behold . . . the youthful windes struggling with the flowers. . . . The musick was placed on every tree, the Oake chanted to the Elme, the Hazle answered the Hawthorne. . . . But tell me Readers, is not this a lazie and ungratefull speculation to regard the delights of Peace when Warre hath almost covered this Nation with fire and bloud? [97]

But despite any feelings of defensiveness or guilt he may have had, Border was turning out an adequate newspaper.

Among the two or three relatively superior London papers of the first half of 1644 was *The True Informer*. Since, in all probability, it was still edited by Walley, the licenser of the press, it was able to stick close to the non-party line: the line, that is, least likely to offend either the Presbyterian majority in Parliament or the Independents, who were on the threshold of taking over command of the army. This adherence to a knowledgeable neutrality is evident in *The True Informer*'s normally straightforward and functional presentation of the news and in its avoidance of sensitive and controversial problems. It is also evident in the pious and hortatory editorial openings which, starting in February, usually graced the first page. Less unctuous and rambling than Smith's exhortations, their content was similar to his. When Walley urged the Parliamentary soldiers to be unlike the Cavaliers and to become "souldiers of Christ" he was being both proper and safe, just as he was when he took a strong stand against hypocrisy.[98]

In the spring *The True Informer* failed to come out for two weeks, a gap which the editor explained by saying that he wished to avoid "unnecessary repetitions." [99] This was not, however, the repetition of being both an editor and a censor, for in April Parliament replaced Walley as licenser of the newsbooks with John Rushworth, a clerk of the House of Commons.[100] *The True Informer*, true to form, neither mentioned nor reflected this change.

During the first half of 1644 *A Perfect Diurnall* also skipped a number, which Pecke justified by alleging that the little news of that week had been adequately dealt with elsewhere.[101] But between then and late 1649 it missed no weeks. Thus, in addition to being the most competent newspaper of the 1640's, *A Perfect Diurnall* was the most regular. Pecke, like Walley, relied on official reports and semiofficial leaks. Westminster was still the major source of news for all London journalists, but Pecke's coverage of Parliament read very much like an official Journal of one of the Houses, and his military news was almost always either a transcript or a précis of an official report. Hence the style of *A Perfect Diurnall* was a little duller and fuller of jargon than that of most of Pecke's competitors. But Pecke remained conscientious in collecting and trying to confirm the news; [102] and, more consistently than his fellow editors, he saved space by omitting official proclamations already in public circulation. The net result was that his crowded pages (and he sometimes regretted that he could not squeeze in more news) [103] provide the fullest journalistic picture of the official events of that hectic era.

Pecke's paper also kept to the middle of the Puritan road. Often this caution impelled the editor to avoid the controversial, even if this meant eliminating a big story, though he sometimes compensated for this by calling attention to his own prudence.[104] Caution, however, could have a positive side, and Pecke frequently strove to achieve impartiality, not just safety. At this stage of *A Perfect Diurnall's* career such impartiality showed itself mainly in two ways: the comparatively fair reporting of Royalist military victories, and the maintenance of an exact mid-point between the Presbyterian and Independent loci.

But both caution and the current London concept of impartiality precluded neutrality in the Civil War, and Pecke was as vociferous as other editors in his anti-Royalism. Indeed, he could wave the Irish red herring as strenuously as could Smith and Dillingham and Border, and his accounts of Laud's trial contained all the standard derogatory comments on the archbishop. Pecke even blamed the massacre of some Virginia colonists by the Indians on a Royalist-inspired plot.[105] Nor did he take a back seat to his fellow journalists in his outspoken anti-Catholicism. In the context of 1644, Pecke's careful politics were another sign of his competence.

So, too, was his probable connection with a second newspaper during the early months of 1644, one with which he had earlier almost certainly been involved.[106] *A Continuation of certain Speciall and Remarkable*

Passages, after several penultimate gasps, had expired in October 1643. Revived in December, it missed a couple of numbers in January 1644, sank into a two-month coma in May, and came back to brief life in July. It then disappeared for more than a year before it re-entered the scene. Assuming that Pecke managed to grab the editorship of this fleeting paper from January to May, his opening statement in this capacity offers an interesting sidelight on what a practicing journalist thought about the recent history of the newspaper:

> Not onely the variety of Relations in, but multiplicity of, Pamphlets have beene principall causes of the intermission of my weekly Continuation, which uncertainty of expressing the proceedings of the times have done much hurt in this Kingdome, not onely in abusing the moderate and the wise by frivolous fallacies related with intention to deceive, but deluding the ignorant and simple, by which many inconveniences have occurred to both parties, both suffering alike in that generall abuse of Pamphleteering; but since a lucky and provident restraint . . . is effected, so that now the common . . . Redundancy of stories or tales (for indeede so they may be more fitly called than relations) is much abated, and the overflowing streames of fictionate observations almost dryed up, and those things for the most part that now remaine weekely related of better credit. This onely and chiefely is the cause that moved me againe to revive . . . the Continuation, in which I shall bee ever carefull to observe that nothing passe my Pen that may be fallacious, or dishonorable to God, or hurtful to the State and Common-wealth.[107]

Regardless of its authorship, this passage indicates a growing sense of responsibility on the part of an experienced journalist. Perhaps this was why *A Continuation* contained one of the few references at that time to a newspaper's worth to future readers, for it could "perpetuate to all posterity the miraculous preservation of this Kingdome from the malice of all the inveterate Enemies of the same." [108]

In its own day *A Continuation* was a somewhat personalized version of *A Perfect Diurnall*. The editor was here more willing to indulge in a few stylistic romps: in one number he inserted a passage about Yorkshire, his "native Countrey"; in another he gave a glimpse of himself hanging around Westminster in an attempt to pick up the latest military news; in a third he ventured an ironic comment on the fact that *The Scotish Dove* was thought to be "so harmlesse and innocent a creature." [109] Considerably less professional than *A Perfect Diurnall*, *A Continuation* none the less suggests the guiding hand of a capable editor.

One other paper, *Certaine Informations*, also survived from 1643, but not for long. Having moved into a more openly pro-Presbyterian position, it exhaled its pious last breath in February 1644. As before, however, when one paper died, others took its place. During most of the 1640's there was an interested and partisan enough public in London for the journalistic birth rate slightly to exceed the death rate, though the Malthusian facts of life prevented any long-term increase in the weekly population.

The first new newspaper of 1644, *Occurrences of Certain Speciall and remarkable Passages in Parliament*, followed, under several different titles, a generally safe and pedestrian path from January 1644 to the dead end of the governmental decree of October 1649.[110] It was an average newspaper in the worst sense of the word: cautious, impersonal, dull; its piety conspicuous but undistinguished; its anti-Royalism standard; and its crowded pages well ordered but lacking in highlights. In fact, only in terms of its excessive anti-Catholicism did it show any signs of individuality, and such an item as its report that the Pope might have been poisoned by the Jesuits because of his Puritan leanings was unique.[111]

The second new newspaper of 1644 led a briefer but livelier existence. Its first number appeared in mid-January under the short title of *Mercurius &c.*, with the reader being left to choose the rest.[112] Then, with number three, the publisher chose for him: *Mercurius Veridicus* — the Truthful Mercury. During its short first life (it came to a temporary end in April after nine numbers) its pro-Presbyterian editor stuck closely to the standard news of the day. Despite this, he tried to achieve a rapidity of tempo and a personal touch remotely reminiscent of such Elizabethan pamphleteers as Thomas Nashe. But when *Mercurius Veridicus* was revived a year later even this distant echo had vanished.

The third new newspaper had an even shorter life — only six numbers — but in them its editor managed to display a few marks of distinction. In the first place, *The Military Scribe* by both its title and its emphasis on military news was deliberately "fitted . . . to these times of bloody War and dismall Enmity."[113] In the second place, the editor regularly gave about one-tenth of his space to military news from abroad, on the basis that

Forraigne Newes is so little welcome to the Plebeian or Vulgar sort of People, because they doe not comprehend how much the present affaires of Christendome are interwoven and connected . . . yet the meanest capacity may gather good fruit from the Results, and see the evident hand of God in the Actions and motions against the Protestants enemies.[114]

In the third place, he was relatively skillful in sprinkling the news with classical allusions, as well as with pious asides. Finally, he made the most explicit statement of his day on the potential value of the newspaper as an historical record: journalistic honesty is necessary, he claimed, in order "to leave true Memorials of our present affaires to all succeeding generations, that Posteritie may see the truth of their forefathers actions." [115]

Three months after the founding of *Mercurius Veridicus* and *The Military Scribe*, *A Diary, or an Exact Journall* arrived on the streets of London.[116] Published by Matthew Walbancke, a man relatively inexperienced in the newspaper game, it attempted to be the *Perfect Diurnall* of the end of the week. With adequate competence and impartiality it divided its crowded pages approximately equally between Westminster and military news. Apparently this course paid, for *A Diary* lasted from May 1644 to March 1646, without fireworks and almost without intermission.

An even less pyrotechnical but more durable paper got its start in June 1644. *Le Mercure Anglois*, which survived until the end of 1648, had the major distinction of being the first foreign-language weekly published in England. As such it was intended more for export than for sale among the French-speaking inhabitants of London. In fact, the day before its third number came out, a handbill containing the following notice was distributed in the city — probably the earliest example of a newspaper promoting itself by external advertisement rather than by self-praising squibs in its own pages:

These are to signifie, that all merchants and others that are desirous weekly to impart beyond seas the certain condition of affairs here and of the proceedings of the war, they shall have it weekly published in print and in the French tongue.[117]

The handbill went on to announce that any potential buyer could purchase the paper at Master Bourne's shop. Nicholas Bourne was temporarily back in the newspaper business.

Presumably *Le Mercure Anglois* was his idea. In any case, during its first half-year Bourne, either in partnership or alone, was the publisher. Though he did not print the paper, he apparently backed it financially and took care of its distribution.[118] John Dillingham was probably the editor, a job more nominal than real since most of the work was done by an underling who could speak French.[119] And even this man did not have to be an expert in the nuances of the language, for *Le Mercure Anglois* consisted of only four pages, and they were invariably filled with condensed officialese.

Le Mercure Anglois was distinctive in one other respect: to supplement its promotional handbill the publisher put out the equivalent of trial or preparatory numbers. The first issue, dated June 7, 1644, largely consisted of a summary of the state of realm; Number 2, the following week, then began with a summary of the first number. After a gap of three weeks, Numbers 3 and 4 repeated the process of opening with an abridgment of the previous issue; and a number early in August supplied a brief survey of recent Irish history.[120] Thus the overseas reader was gradually eased into the habit of buying the newspaper in order to keep up with events.

In contrast to the pre-1642 newsbooks, English news was the sole ostensible *raison d'être* for *Le Mercure Anglois*. Usually written in short and disconnected paragraphs and employing simple French, it devoted itself mainly to military affairs, with some news of Westminster thrown in. Throughout, its pro-Parliament bias was, of course, clear, though it studiously avoided any reference to the intricacies of intra-Parliament politics. But the foreign reader had to pay up to a shilling in postage for this primer among English newspapers.

The last of the nonephemeral weeklies to get started during this period was *The Court Mercurie*, which began its four-month career early in July 1644.[121] In spite of a lengthy discussion in its opening number of the implications of its title, it quickly gave up any pretense of concentrating on news of the king or having a special pipe-line to Oxford, and by August it had become typical of most of its fellows. Without unduly stretching a point, its adequacy as a purveyor of news can show the influence and competition of Pecke, the stridency of its anti-Royalism the influence and competition of Nedham.

Between January and July 1644 eight additional newspapers made quick entrances into, and quick exits from, the early equivalent of Fleet Street.[122] Two, which between them reached a total of three numbers, were given over to refuting *Aulicus*.[123] For three issues *The Weekly Newes from Severall parts beyond the Seas* tried to revive the journal devoted exclusively to foreign affairs.[124] Four papers, attaining a combined total of ten numbers, were brief replicas of their more durable London brethren; [125] while one weekly, *The Flying Post*, in its single issue did put forward a distinct innovation: the attempt to present the news, in English, to the interested continental reader.[126] Neither quantitatively nor qualitatively, however, did these journalistic fruit flies perform any significant function in the genetics of the early English newspaper.

Throughout the history of the newspaper, in every country, the most decisive part has, in fact, been played by nonjournalists. In modern times Hitler, no newspaperman, throttled the German press for a dozen years, while Mussolini, an ex-newspaperman, muzzled the Italian press for twice that length of time. But such extrinsic men and events need not be negative, and the Crimean War, to cite only one example, did much to further the growth of a strongly independent press in England. Some two centuries earlier, Cromwell's impact on the newspaper, as well as his role in the larger fight for civil liberties, is harder to assess, and he remains one of the central anomalies of the Interregnum. A dictator who ruled by the sword, he was also often an harassed proponent of individual rights. In both capacities his influence on the English newspaper would soon be felt.

But in the summer of 1644 Cromwell was just beginning to move to the front of the stage of history. On July 4, two days after Marston Moor, he wrote a letter to his brother-in-law which included this sentence about the military defeat of the Royalists: "It had all the evidences of an absolute victory obtained by the Lord's blessing upon the godly party principally." [127] That it was "an absolute victory" meant that the Civil War would now shift further from military battling, closer to political in-fighting. That this victory redounded to "the godly party principally" — the Independents — meant, in turn, that this political in-fighting would become increasingly complex and, within the Parliamentary coalition, more intense and overt. Consequently, beginning in the later months of 1644, Cromwell's triumph at Marston Moor would have its delayed reaction on the London press.

CHAPTER V

EARLY ADOLESCENCE II

August 1644 to July 1645

MARSTON Moor shattered Royalist military power, but it was not until eleven months later, in June 1645, that what was left of that power was buried at the battle of Naseby. By then the Parliamentary army, which had failed to gather many of the fruits of its victory at Marston Moor, had been remodeled, until it was able to function as the sword of an Independent God and an Independent Cromwell. It was this "new modeling" of the army, opposed by the Presbyterians and moderates and supported by the Independents and the war party, which provided the major political issue of the second half of 1644 and the first half of 1645. During much of this time the debate at Westminster on the New Model spilled over around campfire and street corner, and into pulpit, pamphlet, and newspaper.

Yet between August 1644 and July 1645 the major development in the London press was a continued growth in competence, and the journalistic reaction to Cromwell's triumph at Marston Moor was both delayed and muffled. This, in turn, was the result of indirect rather than direct intimidation. In April 1644 John Rushworth had replaced

Walley as censor of the weekly newsbooks. Rushworth was capable, and under his jurisdiction the weekly press, except for minor harassments coming chiefly from the House of Lords, was relatively free. A product of this freedom was a high degree of stability among the London newspapers.

The last chapter in the story of *Aulicus*, however, was a saga of instability — or of the stability of a man hanging by his teeth. Yet the paper showed only a few tremors, until in September 1645 it vanished, leaving behind a bill for £90 which the printer tried to collect from Charles II after the Restoration.[1] During most of this final year Birkenhead served as editor.[2] That his hand had not lost its touch is indicated by his persistent skill in sowing seeds of dissension. Unfortunately for him, though the seeds fell on fertile soil, their growth was too slow to save the Royalist cause. *Aulicus* now shed tears over its former bête noire, the Earl of Essex, since he was about to be demoted by the newly organized high command of the army, and it bemoaned the plight of those Lords still sitting at Westminster.[3] But more predictable were Birkenhead's recurrent efforts to exacerbate the grievances between Presbyterian and Independent, Parliament and army, England and Scotland, not to mention his attempts to add fuel to a variety of personal feuds. With a certain amount of foresight he reserved some of his strongest epithets for Cromwell, referring to him as a coward, bully, boor, and tyrant. Here is a typical example:

The Cathedral at Lincolne hath lately been prophaned by Cromwell's barbarous crew of Brownists: who have pulled down all the brave carved workes there . . . and (for which all Christians will ever abhorre them) have filled each corner of that holy place with their own and horses dung. . . .[4]

Birkenhead was ready and able not only to use Independent dung but whatever other materials came to his hand: the rumor, the loaded anecdote, the counterstory, the truth. But as his cause grew more desperate, the atrocity story with divisive overtones became his favorite weapon. The desecration of churches and the murder of patriotic Royalists were bad enough, but they were less heinous than the militants' increasing disrespect for the king, even the growing possibility that they might contrive his murder.[5] Nor did Birkenhead fail to draw the most sinister conclusions from the execution of William Laud, Archbishop of Canterbury, in January 1645.

On the surface, then, *Aulicus* remained what it had been when the cause for which it was set up to plead looked rosier. Yet one is aware of cracks in this bold façade. Throughout its final year *Aulicus* contained comparatively little news of Oxford or of the over-all status of

English Royalism. Consistently, indecisive skirmishes became major Royalist victories. Further, the paper's London edition appeared less frequently, and attempts to smuggle copies into the metropolis were increasingly less successful — so much so that, just before *Aulicus* expired, *Britanicus* claimed it was rare enough to cost sixpence a copy.[6] At intervals *Aulicus* did not appear at all. From November 23 to December 29, 1644, there was a gap, and in each of the first four months of 1645 *Aulicus* skipped an issue. In June, after a lapse of two weeks, it came out with this plaintive explanation:

> The Rebels' New Modell hath (for once) forced us to publish two weekes together — for . . . Sir Thomas Fairfax, Philip Skippon, Oliver Cromwell, and Richard Browne have lyen round the Printing House, so as till their departure Mercurius Aulicus could receive or communicate little Intelligence.[7]

During its final three months, when Oxford was again under intermittent siege, *Aulicus* appeared only three times.[8] Nevertheless, Birkenhead maintained his bravado, not only by what he had to say but by a typographical trick: he so numbered his pages that they seemed to be gapless, thus suggesting that the reader, not *Aulicus*, had skipped certain weeks.

But neither tricks nor threats were enough to keep the paper going. In its final few numbers one can detect a stridency that connoted strangulation.[9] Still, the last issue of *Aulicus*, dated September 7, 1645, was a close descendant of the first issue of January 1643. One of Birkenhead's final stories was a gloating report of Montrose's capture of Edinburgh. But for the next three months there were to be no such stories in the weekly press: first, because there was little news that could be interpreted as pro-Royalist; second, because there was no Royalist newspaper in which that little could be reported.

The history of *Mercurius Britanicus* during this period remained closely interwoven with that of *Aulicus*. Since *Britanicus* was probably the most popular and certainly the most rambunctious of the London newspapers, its history also remained closely interwoven with that of intra-Parliamentary politics. In both these involvements, however, Nedham lost neither his footing nor his voice. One illustration of this was the rumor, current in late 1644, that *Britanicus* had even frightened the king. As one London paper put it,

> [Charles] hath sent Secretary Nicholas . . . to Master Aulicus to require him to forbeare writing any more, till his Majesties pleasure be further knowne: the reason of this I cannot give you: It cannot sure be to save the 30. pound per Annum, the stipent His Majesty allowed him for writing his

weekly pamphlet: It is done rather to silence Britanicus, who hath so plentifully laid open the vices at court, and who took the liberty to do so because Aulicus did so abuse the Parliament. . . .[10]

But Birkenhead continued to abuse the Parliament, while Nedham kept answering in kind. Moreover, a note of regret crept into *Britanicus* whenever *Aulicus* failed to appear, one of relief when it reappeared.[11] Even when Nedham reached a crescendo of invective one can sense a feeling if not of camaraderie at least of zestful competition between him and Birkenhead:

But harke ye, thou mathematicall liar, that framest lies of all dimensions, long, broad and profound lies, and then playest the botcher, the quibling pricklouse every weeke in tacking and stitching them together; I tell thee (Berkenhead) thou art a knowne notorious odious forger: and though I will not say thou art (in thine owne language) the sonne of an Egyptian whore, yet all the world knowes thou art an underling pimpe to the whore of Babylon, and thy conscience an arrant prostitute for base ends. This is truth, not railing.[12]

Yet the running battle between these journalistic brothers under the skin usually seemed more fratricidal than fraternal. Many of the counterstories in *Britanicus*, particularly those concerning Royalist dissensions, were vitriolic, and its defense of Laud's execution, including its insulting epitaph for the archbishop, was foul.[13] The name-calling between the two weeklies even involved the American colonies. In the summer of 1644 *Aulicus* twice noted that the people of New England were shocked by the language of *Britanicus*. As part of its evidence it cited a published letter from a Massachusetts divine that placed some of the blame for God's wrath against England on Nedham and company.[14] Three times Nedham replied to this charge, putting most of the onus on Birkenhead and an alleged Oxford plot to discredit *Britanicus*.[15]

But more interesting than this routine squabbling is Nedham's display of political tightrope walking between Marston Moor and Naseby. (Audley now had little to do with *Britanicus*: in the late spring of 1644 he was writing an occasional piece for *The Kingdomes Weekly Intelligencer*, and in September he became a deputy licenser of the press under Rushworth.)[16] Nedham, in his agile acrobatics, first tried to reduce the distance he might have to fall — or at least to prepare a cushion to land on — by showing himself more aware of Presbyterian sensibilities. Between August 1644 and March 1645 he supported the Solemn League and Covenant, praised certain generals who were noted for their Presbyterian leanings, and even implied his approval of a

Presbyterian church settlement.[17] He also employed a few negative items to soften any accumulated conservative resentments against himself: several times he came out against freedom of speech, and intermittently he questioned the principle of religious toleration by warning against the dangers implicit in sectarian preaching.[18]

Yet Nedham knew which way the political winds were blowing, and by the spring of 1645 he had adjusted his stance accordingly. Since its first number *Britanicus*'s chief function had been to counter *Aulicus*, and in its repeated assaults on various Royalist positions it had necessarily expressed certain radical if negative opinions. Then at the end of 1644, despite his sops to the Presbyterians, Nedham resumed his comparatively open pro-Independent position. In the dispute between Cromwell and the more cautious Manchester, Nedham's public sympathies leaned toward the former.[19] He also strongly advocated the new-modeling of the army.[20] But it was in his treatment of the king that Nedham's current political alignment best showed itself. As late as November he was still stressing the theme of the king's evil advisors, but in January 1645 he shifted his attack so that it was recurrently and directly aimed at the king himself. Charles, said Nedham, was a conspirator, possibly a traitor, and it would be well for England if his son took over the throne.[21] In June these accusations reached a temporary climax in the lengthy and detailed charge that the king was an active agent of the Catholic cause.[22] Two months later, when Nedham printed a facetious notice calling for the arrest of Charles, he went too far: he, not the king, almost ended behind bars.

Before Nedham thus momentarily lost his balance he had leaned farther in the direction of the militants, for his attacks on the king carried with them a series of controversial opinions: that additional negotiations between Parliament and Charles would be futile, that the monopoly of the Merchant Adventurers was evil, and that the well-being of the people was the supreme law of the land.[23] (The phrase "salus populi suprema lex" was rapidly becoming a slogan paraded by all groups, regardless of their political coloration, but in certain contexts, including *Britanicus*, it could have distinctly radical implications.) The now more pugnacious Nedham also took it upon himself to reply directly to two pamphlets of early 1645 which had been, to say the least, unflattering in their portraits of the London press: John Cleveland's *The Character of a London Diurnall*, and George Wither's *The Great Assises Holden in Parnassus by Apollo and His Assessors*.[24] Finally, Nedham made it a point, in June 1645, to inform his readers that he was not being told by Parliament what to write, that he was his own boss; and two weeks later he assured them that he had not been suppressed the previous week, during which *Britanicus* had failed to appear, for being too bold against the king.[25] Though technically he may have been telling the truth, the slap on the wrist of being forced to skip a week signified that Nedham could go only so far on his own. He was the sort of man both to take his cue from persons in or near authority and to risk being conspicuous in order to raise the price for his services. Consequently in July he had to explain away another skipped week, this time by claiming that he was so busy helping to decipher some of Charles's letters captured at Naseby that he did not have time for his newspaper.[26]

Nedham thus differed from other London editors, all of whom during this period kept their feet on the ground. With the exception of *Aulicus* and *Britanicus*, the newspapers of the second half of 1644 and the first half of 1645 displayed little partisanship and much caution. Most of them were probably making a small profit, and though few new entries joined the competition for readers, almost no established weeklies left it. Further, since the Presbyterians were in nominal control of Parliament and the Independents in actual control of the army, the safest course was to antagonize neither. As a result the London press became less differentiated and, journalistically, more conservative.

In terms of caution *Le Mercure Anglois*, from its first number in June 1644 to its last in December 1648, remained outstanding. Because it was the one newspaper designed for export, its middle-of-the-road position may well have been justified. When, infrequently, it did take a stand, this usually represented the median of those taken by other weeklies. And regardless of Dillingham's role in this paper, he or the publisher was aware that the foreign office and the French ambassador, along with the regular censor, were looking over the translator's shoulder. Consequently *Le Mercure Anglois* concentrated on military news whenever such news was available. It invariably treated the forces of Parliament, whether on the battlefield or in the halls of Westminster, as praiseworthy. It also viewed the Royalists as evil, and those sects to the left of Independent congregationalism as boorish and dangerous.[27] Such issues as the dispute between Cromwell and Manchester or the propriety of the Self-Denying Ordinance (a preliminary to the new-modeling of the army) *Le Mercure Anglois* dealt with as suitable for brief mention, unsuitable for analysis or side-taking.[28] Even then, occasionally, the writer of the paper stubbed his toe on a problem of translation: apparently such words as "Hierarchie" and "Liturgie" were difficult to put into correct and noncontroversial French.[29] Moreover, while anti-Royalism was safe and proper in England, it could not imply any disapproval of the young Louis XIV, whom, wrote the editor, he admired.[30] Predictable, too, was the paper's general avoidance of French news. Less predictable, however, were its internal troubles. Its first issue in 1645 did not appear until March 6, its second seven weeks later. A new printer took over, Bourne temporarily ceased to be publisher, and Dillingham spent most of February in jail. Whatever maneuvers then occurred for the control of *Le Mercure Anglois*, its subsequent regularity suggests that it too had become profitable.

A Perfect Diurnall also stayed in the middle of the road, and Pecke continued to keep his feet dry by being both cautious and representative of normative Puritanism. One passage in particular from *A Perfect Diurnall* can exemplify the Puritanism of the Puritan Revolution in the same way that Marie Antoinette's probably apocryphal remark "Let them eat cake" can exemplify the *ancien régime*:

There hath beene a custome in the Church of Twicknam . . . upon Easter Sunday to have two great Cakes broken in the Church, and to be given to the young people of the Parish, but that being a superstitious Relique, it was ordered . . . that these Parishioners should forbeare that Custome, and instead thereof to buy loaves of Bread for the poore of that Parish with the money that should have bought the Cakes.[31]

Other examples of Pecke's caution and representativeness are ubiquitous. Typical is this report of a day's work by the House of Commons; it could offend no one but it could let an initiated reader know something of what had happened:

A great part of this dayes businesse . . . was matter of reconciliation of some private differences lately happened betwixt some Major Generalls and the Committee of certain Counties, which the Parliament have taken such a course to settle as the Countrey shall not sustaine the wrong, nor occasion such differences as formerly happened.[32]

Pecke was always especially careful in his reports of Parliamentary debates on religion. If any such debate struck him as unusually touchy, he fell back on self-censorship, merely saying, for instance, that there were "divers particulars . . . not convenient to be published at this time." [33] He also tended to be neutral and evasive in his coverage of the Cromwell-Manchester dispute and of the negotiations between Parliament and king, as well as in his treatment of the more sensitive areas of England's foreign relations.[34] He was equally discreet in delaying his support of the New Model until the lay of the land was clear. Yet Pecke could be positively rather than negatively impartial. Twice in this period he reported on depradations by Parliamentary soldiers, and his account of Laud's execution, including a full transcript of the archbishop's speech from the scaffold, was a fine example of early journalism at its best.[35]

The news-filled pages of *A Perfect Diurnall* also provide an excellent contemporary picture of the House of Commons: a very busy place that was gaining efficiency as its committee system matured; an aggregation of individuals whose personal and political loyalties were almost daily being stretched and re-formed; a governing body constantly preoccupied with raising money, and then more money. Such events as the parleying with the king at Uxbridge or the rise in the west of the Club-men, a large group of yeomen and peasants who with club and pitchfork tried to assure their neutrality, emerge from *A Perfect Diurnall* in at least two-dimensional fullness.[36] Even Pecke's occasional items of foreign news usually dealt with the significant rather than the trivial. By 1645, too, the paper's utilization of short news summaries on the title page had become eminently functional.[37] Finally, Pecke was now more willing to use sporadic personal touches to enliven his weekly. In one number he went from bad to good news via the transition "I shall not leave you in the dumps," and in June 1645 he spoke of Leicester as a city "of whose lamentable condition and miseries" he had not had "the least part in sorrow." [38]

Though Pecke was slightly superior to his fellow journalists as a purveyor of straight news, like them he consistently beat an anti-Irish, anti-Catholic drum, going so far as to approve of an ordinance calling for the death of all captured Irish rebels.[39] Like his colleagues, too, he could be a dupe for a sensational apparition story or an apparent devotee of stronger censorship of the press.[40] And he stayed in step in his treatment of the king, moving from objectivity toward a pro-Presbyterian peace petition of September 1644 to a direct attack on Charles in the spring of 1645.[41] In one number Pecke praised himself for his plainness, brevity, and ability to get the news.[42] In the context of the mid-1640's he qualified for such praise, but so, to an almost equal degree, did several London editors.

One such editor was Henry Walker, about whom fairly much is known except the date when he entered journalism. In the 1630's he had been an ironmonger who presumably went bankrupt; then, after a brief period at Cambridge, he was ordained a deacon.[43] In the early 1640's he set up as a bookseller and writer of anti-Royalist pamphlets. In both capacities he was soon in trouble with the authorities, rising to a climax in January 1642 when he was arrested for hurling a copy of his pamphlet, *To Your Tents, O Israel*, into the king's coach.[44] Then toward the end of 1644 this round-faced, red-haired Puritan almost certainly took a part in editing *Perfect Occurrences of Parliament*, a weekly which, under the title of *Occurrences of Certain Speciall and Remarkable Passages*, had been duly and dully appearing since January. Though Walker did not then acknowledge his connection with this paper, internal evidence and a scrawled notation by Thomason indicate that by late 1644 Walker was beginning to compete with Pecke.[45]

Assuming that Walker began his connection with *Perfect Occurrences* in the autumn of 1644, he at first had little impact on the paper. It remained pedestrian, impersonal, and violently anti-Catholic. The original editor had recently climbed to a peak of caution by telling his readers that he had been "commanded" to remind them to pray for "poor distressed Ireland," and "commanded" to warn those who had custody of some Jesuits to be stricter.[46] Gradually, however, *Perfect Occurrences* improved. The writing grew firmer and less monotonous, the editorial asides more vigorous. In December the editor implied that his weekly, which came out on Friday, was the proper complement to Monday's *A Perfect Diurnall*, a claim that was no longer farfetched.[47]

In 1645 the similarity between the two papers became more marked, especially insofar as *Perfect Occurrences* more and more placed its emphasis on Westminster; indeed, its editor became more explicit than Pecke in his concern with semiofficial news. At the start of the year he wrote that news of Parliament must be "deliberately read and seriously considered"; in March that he would omit a story about some ships being sunk "because these are private mens matters, and do not concerne the State"; and in April he tossed a controversial item to *Britanicus* as being the more "sutable" agent to reply to it.[48] Likewise, he no longer treated caution as a direct command but in a Peckean way referred to various touchy matters as, for instance, "not yet fit to be published."[49] Also, both papers several times expressed the complaint that they did not have enough room for all the printable news. Finally, *Perfect Occurrences* developed a certain adroitness in achieving impartiality rather than excessive evasiveness in regard to the Presbyterian-Independent squabbles of 1645.

The two papers differed in that Walker's wore its piety more conspicuously, included more attempts to impress its readers with the editor's learning, and printed more stories of apparitions and other astrological tidbits.[50] Moreover, *Perfect Occurrences* was usually more vitriolic in its anti-Royalism. On the credit side was Walker's infrequent but skillful insertion of human-interest items: two exciting pages on a London murder trial; the story of a cruel creditor having the corpse of a debtor thrust into his shop; the anecdote of the postman who got so drunk he mistook Wales for Ireland.[51]

In addition to Walker, a second man of importance to the history of the early newspaper entered the field in the mid-1640's. Between his appointment as licenser of the press in April 1644 and his becoming secretary to Sir Thomas Fairfax, the commander of the New Model Army, about a year later, John Rushworth probably lent his services to two long-run newspapers. Trained as a lawyer and equipped with a bent for history, he was by education and temperament well-suited for journalism.[52] Then, too, his experiences as assistant clerk to the House of Commons, as one of Parliament's chief messengers, and as censor gave him both access to and insight into the upper reaches of contemporary politics.

The first of these newspapers was *A Diary*, which since May 1644 had been presenting the news competently and impartially. During the winter of 1644–45, and possibly thereafter, Rushworth probably exerted some editorial supervision over it, though during this period the paper showed little change.[53] Except for an occasional diatribe against "rebels" and Catholics and an equally occasional flight into anecdotal rhetoric,[54] it pursued its functional and comparatively subdued course. Even its anti-Royalism was less strident than that of most papers, while its precision in navigating between the Presbyterian Scylla and the Independent Charybdis was superior. One can perhaps hear the voice of the censor in this explanation of why the editor was omitting a controversial piece of Westminster news:

I thank God I have so much grace that I will not venture to impart it to you, nor be a companion with those sawcy persons who will intrude into the weighty affaires of State, which for some great considerations are not fit to be knowne, or being knowne are not fit to be made legible to the world. There is a secret Ambition in some men to make the world believe that they alone have all the Interest or knowledge . . . but with these men I will mingle neither Braine nor Brest.[55]

If not by Rushworth, now often in the field with the army, such a statement still suggests a man who viewed himself primarily as a civil servant, only secondarily as a newspaperman — and Rushworth's reputation rests on his skill as a historian, not on his connection with journalism.

His potential as a journalist was, in fact, no more evident in the second long-run newspaper with which he was probably involved at this time. *The London Post* entered the world in August 1644, left it in March 1645, and re-entered it for two months in the winter of

1646–47.[56] During its first life it was similar to *A Diary* though with a heavier stress on military news and a larger display of devoutness. But Rushworth's "sub-Author" and probable co-editor of this paper, Gilbert Mabbott, showed a flair for colorful prose that augured well for his future in journalism.[57] Thus Mabbott often added a flourish to an otherwise dull military item, as in this report of a siege:

> It is in vaine to trust in Forces, Forts, or Castles, or Towers high as Heaven, for where neither the power of Men nor the showers of Bullets can enter, the leane hand of Famine and the pale Armie of Disease may. . . .[58]

Rushworth and Mabbott also reprinted letters conveying non-London news more frequently than did other editors. This may have been because they were both busy, since in March 1645 Mabbott became Rushworth's deputy licenser of the weekly press.[59] In any event, it seems likely that another "sub-Author" had a hand in *The London Post* almost from its foundation. In one case this third editor — or substitute staff — expressed a belief in astrology out of keeping with the views of the hard-headed Rushworth and the secular-minded Mabbott, in another he bothered to reply to Cleveland's and Wither's attacks on the London weeklies.[60] And he was probably responsible for one of the strangest stories to appear in a seventeenth-century English newspaper.

The corantos and newsbooks of the 1620's and 1630's had printed infrequent minor items concerning Jewish groups in Europe and North Africa, and a reference to a Jew or Jews had occasionally cropped up in the weeklies of the early 1640's.[61] Then on April 1, 1645, the following comparatively lengthy story appeared in *The London Post*:

> We have indeed received remarkable newes concerning the Jewes, which is that (by the judgement of God) being scattered over the whole face of the earth, they have now sent letters to collect themselves into one Body, and withdrawing out of every Country, to return unto the land of Jury. I doubt not but the same Power which doth reduce them into one Body will reforme them all into the truth and light of one Religion. Others may comment on it as they please, but (some other mighty changes being weighed with it), it appeares to me to be as a morning star before the day of the Resurrection.

Almost certainly based on unfounded rumor, this story died a-borning. *The London Post* did not follow it up, and no other paper mentioned any purported in-gathering of the exiles. At the same time, the story illustrates one idea that floated in the Interregnum air: the imminence of the Second Coming, an event which, according to certain millenarians, could happen only after the Jews had been converted. Consequently the author of this account could be sympathetic to Zionism, though his reasons were, from any Jewish point of view, decidedly unorthodox. Yet Christ did not return, and nothing that can be labeled Jewish news appeared in the English press until 1649.[62]

By this date Mabbott had achieved the distinction of being at once chief censor of the press and an editor noted for his radicalism and his dislike of censorship. But during the period from 1644 to 1649, as new men rose in English journalism, certain old practitioners dropped out. Henry Walley, Rushworth's predecessor as censor, joined this group of ex-journalists when, in February 1645, he apparently severed his connection with *The True Informer*.[63] Before then it had continued to give the news in a generally clear and straightforward manner. A little less professional than *A Perfect Diurnall*, *The True Informer* included more pious interjections, naïve obiter dicta, and reports that favored the Presbyterians.[64] Yet Walley's account of Laud's execution, complete with a half-page woodcut of the archbishop, was as full and controlled as that in Pecke's paper.[65] But both the strengths and weaknesses of *The True Informer* — and of many other papers — were shown by what happened when Walley stopped being editor: very little. After February its pages reveal an increase in credulity: a report of thirty-eight witches in Ipswich, thirty-seven of whom admit "they have one or two paps on which the Devill sucks," was not the sort of item Walley would have printed.[66] Perhaps, too, the paper showed a decline in political awareness. Yet on the whole *The True Informer* remained a first cousin of *A Perfect Diurnall*.

The withdrawal of the editor would have had a greater impact on *The Kingdomes Weekly Intelligencer* and *Mercurius Civicus*. Both were still compiled by Richard Collings, though any reader who bought the *Intelligencer* on Tuesday would have usually found it worth his while to pick up *Civicus* on Thursday.[67] The first of these now modeled itself more closely on *A Perfect Diurnall*; and that Collings was aware of the competition offered by Pecke is indicated by such an aside as this from the summer of 1644:

> I am resolved hereafter to give you an accompt (though briefly) of every particular thing of noat . . . though others should publish much thereof before I come to your view; it shall be [my purpose] to enlarge a Truth, or confirme it where it is certain, as neere as the best and most certaine Intelligence can direct me.[68]

In carrying out this aim Collings remained cautious and careful, commenting in one number that he would avoid "tart language" and stick

to "simply a narration of affaires," in another that he preferred describing actions to discussing intentions.[69] In his consequent concen-
tration on military reports and on the surface of Westminster news
he managed to conceal his Presbyterian inclinations and to achieve a
balanced impartiality. Thus stories and asides which could be interpreted as supporting the Presbyterians became neutralized by equivalent stories and asides which favored the Independents.[70] Then, as
the New Model moved from a gleam in the eye of certain militants
to a political reality and thence to a victorious force, Collings tended
to replace any pro-Presbyterian remarks with high praise for the men
who conceived and led this army. Nor did this necessarily involve any
hypocrisy. Since the day when he had first gone off to the wars, he
had consistently been more anti-Royalist than pro-Presbyterian. Hence
when he wrote that "a Civill War can admit of no Neutrality," [71] he
was confirming the fact that to himself, as well as to most journalists,
the defeat of the Royalist armies was more vital, if only for the time
being, than any intra-Parliamentary feuding.

But the Collings who peeps through the lines of *The Kingdomes
Weekly Intelligencer* and *Mercurius Civicus* differed from his colleagues in being more of a pragmatist. This pragmatism, which was
not quite the same thing as expediency, can be seen in Collings' view
of his own job and in the nature of his anti-Royalism. It can also be
seen in his answer to the conservative argument against the Self-
Denying Ordinance that the radicals would thereby gain too much
power in the army. To this Collings replied by claiming that such a
contingency would be neither good nor bad, but unlikely.[72] Or, a
more philosophical but equally amoral example, here is Collings justifying the suppression of the Book of Common Prayer:

> Suppresse it for a time, and you will afterwards heare no more of it. The
> difficulty is in breaking off a People from Custome (a second Nature),
> which once done they seldome think of returning to their flesh-pots more.
> Many of our Malignants are now so convinced of their former errors in
> that particular, that should that Service be taken up againe, they would be
> as great Non-conformists as any.[73]

Collings' pragmatic and professional sanction for *Mercurius Civicus*
was still its concern with London news. Though such news continued
to fill little space, he frequently mentioned his interest in metropolitan
affairs and he printed some items that other weeklies omitted or
slighted: three pages on the execution of a London criminal; a full
account of a riot in the Strand; and, because it was a London story, a
lengthy remonstrance from some prisoners-for-debt.[74] *Civicus* also

during this period retained its second trade-mark, its now well-worn title-page woodcuts.

Politically, *Civicus* stayed close to *The Kingdomes Weekly Intelligencer*. In 1644 its reports and remarks that had a Presbyterian slant outweighed those that were pro-Independent; and in 1645 it too balanced its political scales, with praise for the New Model likewise giving the Independents a slight advantage.[75] Yet *Civicus*, possibly because it appealed to a less sophisticated group of readers, became more vitriolic in its attacks on the king than did the *Intelligencer*. Except for *Britanicus*, no other newspaper of the mid-1640's could match this paragraph from a July number of *Mercurius Civicus*:

> And then if Popery and Protestantism can be contracted into one Religion, if regall tyranny and the subjects Liberty can be both at once defended, if the invitation of forraine forces to come over to destroy his Majesties subjects and the abhorring of the mentioning of an intention to bring forrainers in may be termed expressions of one signification and involved under one notion, if the repealing of all Lawes against Papists and the putting them in execution against them may both be executed by one Sword: in a word, if light and darknesse can be brought together, then may they reconcile His Majesties words with his actions, his pretences with his intentions, his publick declarations with his private resolutions.[76]

Collings could, as this passage shows, sometimes wield an effective pen. He could also display his journalistic conscience by printing unfavorable news, including a report of a minor mutiny in the Parliamentary army.[77] Usually, however, he remained cautious, and, like his colleagues, he often excused himself by stating that premature or sensitive news would aid the enemy.[78] But more than other journalists he relied on regular correspondents, so that he functioned a bit more fully in the role of a modern editor.[79] Finally, he could in a few instances be appropriately blunt, as in this passage:

> The Cavaliers about five daies since, taking the opportunity of the insobriety, or (in plaine English) the drunkennesse of some of our forces . . . fell upon them and took forty horse and prisoners.[80]

In sober contrast, Collings violated his normal policy concerning non-English news when he included in *Mercurius Civicus* the longest report of American affairs yet to appear in an English newspaper. For this reason, and because it viewed colonial events through Puritan eyes, the news "from Virginy" warrants extended quotation:

> We are still troubled with the Indians upon the frontier part of the Country, and therefore wee are now providing three forts in the middle of

the Country, being in the Kings Territories, which is not far from us, that so we may have a power amongst them able to destroy them and to deprive them of their livelihood. They lately in a treacherous manner cut off 400 of our people; they have not courage to doe it otherwise; we take this course now that so wee may follow our businesse in the summer. How ever the crops we make now cannot be so great as they have bin, and I think we shall be at the charge of halfe our labours to maintaine these forts, and the Souldiers at the middle plantation, which is a narrow passage the Indians have into the Forrest; this is onely our charge that dwell on the Northside of Jameses River, the people on the other side are to deale with the Indians there. This way though chargeable is thought most convenient to extirpate and subdue this people that doe much annoy us: they are so cowardly that ten of ours will make an hundred of them run away. We are at peace among our selves and have beene so ever since the massacre; Sir William Barclay [Berkeley] went for Bristoll and left Master Kempe his Deputy and is not yet returned: It is my opinion that the massacre (though a judgement) did divert a great mischiefe that was growing among us by Sir William Barclay's courses; for divers of the most religious and honest inhabitants were mark't out to be plundered and imprisoned for the refusall of an Oath that was imposed upon the people, in referrence to the King of England. It was tendered at mens houses, the people murmured, and most refused to take it. Those few that tooke it did it more for feare than affection; so that it is the opinion of judicious men that if the Indians had but forborne for a month longer, they had found us in such a combustion among our selves that they might with ease have cut of[f] every man if once we had spent that little powder and shot that we had among our selves. . . .

Since the massacre because men should not be disabled to defend themselves, and their Plantations, it was thought fit to make a Law that no mans servant, his corne, or Ammunition should be taken in execution; but when it shall please God [that] we shall suppresse our enemy, this Act will be repealed. . . .

I should now leave the forraigne newes were it not that upon the day of execution of the massacre upon the Christians by the Indians there hapned a great wonder, which to many may seeme incredible, and the rather for that it is related at so great a distance from this Kingdome; and indeed there are some people so criticall that they will believe no more than they see of the affaires of this Kingdome, and much lesse further of[f]: yet for the satisfaction of such as are desirous, I shall onely set down the words of the Letter comming from an honest and knowne hand in that Plantation, to a person of good repute in this City: Gods goodnesse hath beene lately very eminent in delivering me and my family from the Indian massacre. Upon the first day of April my wife was washing a bucke[t] of clothes, and of a sudden her clothes were all besprinkled with blood from the first beginning to the rincing of them, at last in such abundance as if an hand should invisibly take handfuls of gore blood and throw it upon the linnen. When it lay all of an heape in the washing-tub, she sent for me in, and I tooke up one gobbet of blood as big as my fingers end, and stirring it in my hand it did not staine my fingers nor the linnen. Upon this miraculous premonition and warning from God, having some kinde of intimation of some designe of the Indians (though nothing appeared till that day), I provided for defence, and though we were but five men and mistrusted not any villany towards us before, yet we secured our selves against 20 savages which were three houres that day about my house. Blessed be the name of God.[81]

Despite the credulity which Collings displayed in reprinting this final paragraph, he was usually a hard-headed newspaperman — and even today apparitions and miracles are a journalistic staple. Perhaps here too he was giving the public what it wanted. In any event, he was now able to report that *The Kingdomes Weekly Intelligencer* and *Mercurius Civicus* were "prosperous beyond the line of many others." [82] At least in retrospect Collings deserved to make money out of his profession.

So did John Dillingham. During the first half of 1644 he had fashioned *The Parliament Scout* into a relatively competent newspaper, but one which was slightly more radical and naïve than other weeklies. For the next six months, however, his comparative frankness often landed him in trouble, and as early as August he felt sufficiently menaced to present this prolix apologia:

We are informed that there is exceptions taken at our Scout; we are very sorry that any should take offence; our care hath been not to give just offence to any; we tooke up the thing to satisfie some friends whose tempers we know; it was not to satisfie such as, Athenian like, heare and tell, and to passe their time away, as too many do, reade over more bookes of newes than they make prayers or reade Chapters: if these be offended, it is at they know not what; nor did we intend to please the Parliaments enemies, for we count them Gods enemies . . . nor did we intend the satisfaction of the seeming friends of the Parliament . . . if any of these be displeased, we shall not be thought the worse of for these. We have sometimes modestly hinted the errours of our friends, given our enemies their due praise, presented our victories with the least, rather than over, and is this an offence? We have chosen rather to intimate what were good to be done (than to fill up a side of papour with the names of prisoners taken at such a place, and such a place . . .) and is this offensive? when its probable our advice hath been from as good heads as any in Christendome. . . .[83]

And he concluded by threatening to leave journalism if he was again criticized. He was but did not. Three months later, to give only one more example of Dillingham defending Dillingham, he was censured for not reporting the Battle of Newbury as a major victory for Parliament. In angry reply he cited the fact that *Aulicus* was being circulated in London, while he, "a true friend to the Parliament," was not allowed "nakedly" and truthfully to give the news.[84]

But "the truth," especially when it is clumsily presented, can irritate. In one number of *The Parliament Scout* Dillingham stated the oft-repeated case against the men then ruling England, though he did so on the tacit assumption that it was obviously false:

> Some complain that Malignants were favored, and that the well-affected beare the burden of the war, and many Committee men thought fit it should be so . . . and that there was much partiality in our Committees, that every one almost did seek his own [or] had a friend to favour, that few preferred the publique weal before their private . . . that sins were not punished, the Justices minding other businesse. . . .[85]

Then in October he had the lack of tact to report that certain soldiers were deserting from Manchester's army and joining the king's forces so that they could better fight for liberty of conscience.[86] And in January 1645, when Presbyterian-Independent friction was generating much heat, he made this comment on the problem of church settlement:

> And we pray also that the people of England may not . . . thinke that discipline in Religion, and Presbitery or Independency, is godlinesse. . . . [We should] adde to this shell, or sheath, or barke, or superficies of religion, the power of godlinesse, holy life, &c. which is as far surpassing the other as the kernell the shell, the knife the sheath, the tree the barke, or the soul the carcasse.[87]

Such oil did not calm troubled waters.

Besides showing Dillingham's lack of tact, these quotations indicate that his political sympathies were still tinged with red, his prose with purple. That he then leaned to the left is also suggested by his plea that all monarchies be severely limited by "known laws," that Cromwell and his colleagues be favorably judged for their efforts in behalf of religious toleration, and, in passing, that the divorce laws be eased.[88] Further, he continued to take a strong and persistent stand in favor of militant prosecution of the war. Yet Dillingham did not stray too far from the journalistic pattern of his day, and he often hedged his political bets. He came out against the right of an uneducated or sectarian preacher to occupy a pulpit; he was evasive on the issue of setting up a modified Presbyterian system; he usually managed to side-step the Cromwell-Manchester dispute; and he became adept at straddling the fence on the question of religious toleration.[89] Even so, he continued to suggest his own liberalism in sporadic asides which were social rather than political. He could be quite graphic about the horrors of war as experienced by the individual soldier or the displaced civilian.[90] He followed the Puritan line in his disapproval of celebrating Christmas, but he was able to add the plaintive remark that children would miss this day of play.[91] And there is a hint of both Charles Lamb and Jeremy Bentham in his comment on the decision to have the monthly holiday for apprentices fall on Thursday:

> It were to be wished Monday were the day, because then Sunday cloathes need not be laid up; besides a Monday is the Masters preparing day for the servants labour the week following, and then for the servant to play is best, but the matter is not very great.[92]

The Parliament Scout was set off from most weeklies in two other respects. First, it was both explicitly and implicitly directed to a rural audience, though the bulk of its readers were obviously in London.[93] Second, while *The Parliament Scout* was typical in devoting more than half its space to military news, Dillingham went on giving the impression that he was intelligently interested in the actual logistics of running an army and in the rugged realities of tactics. The result was that many of his military reports were more knowledgeable and immediate than those of his competitors.

These competitors, however, did not need to be concerned with their inferiority in this respect for long. Early in February 1645 Dillingham was imprisoned by the House of Lords, not so much for his naïve utterances, though they had some influence, but because what turned out to be the final number of *The Parliament Scout* had a slighting reference to the recently demoted Essex.[94] The Lords took this safe way of showing their disapproval of the new-modeling of the army, and thus Dillingham was more a victim of others' politics than of his own.

He spent no more than a month behind bars. In March his substitute for *The Parliament Scout* began its four-and-a-half-year career of still providing for the Thursday newspaper buyer. *The Moderate Intelligencer* exhibited Dillingham's recently acquired competence as a journalist and his even more recently acquired determination to stay out of jail. Hence it was both a better and a worse newspaper than *The Parliament Scout*. Its assets included a more coherent arrangement of the news, a higher degree of impartiality, and a little less garrulity, but these were balanced by a loss of personality and frankness. Now, as in Collings' two papers, Presbyterian and Independent items approximately equalized each other.[95] Dillingham also adopted the technique of inserting a few asides to show that he was not a radical: an occasional attack on the sects, for instance, or the statement that he was against the king's evil advisors, not against the monarchy.[96] As in *The Parliament Scout*, but now more frequently, *The Moderate Intelligencer* suppressed certain reports on the basis that they might aid the enemy or provoke unseemly discussion.[97]

But Dillingham did not completely eliminate his former self. Three times he came to his own defense as an honest and unintimidated newsman.[98] In one number he not only told of a plundering expedition by some of Cromwell's soldiers but he commented on the bravery of certain captured Royalists.[99] Occasionally, too, a socially liberal aside still cropped up, such as the editor's plea for better medical treatment for the wounded on both sides.[100] Finally, Dillingham's realistic handling of military news remained a feature of *The Moderate Intelligencer* during its early months. It is therefore strange to find this weekly momentarily anticipating a racist organ, for it was the first English newspaper to carry an anti-Negro story. Though the story was intended to reflect on the Catholics, it demonstrates how slightly the basic ingredients of racial prejudice have changed in more than three centuries:

There [near the Portuguese Ambassador's house] gathers many hundreds of men, women, maids, and boyes together, then comes Negers, and others of like rankes; these make sport with our English women and maids, [and] offer [i.c., kiss] in the Venetian manner, by way of introduction to that used in their Stewes [i.e., brothels]: why these black men should use our English maides and women . . . in that manner we know no reason for: but the truth is that the fault is wholly in those loose people that come there, and in the Officers of the Parish where it is done.[101]

Less strange is one hyperbole in *The Moderate Intelligencer* which points up the fact that Dillingham's intellectual background was popular rather than literary. In commenting on the number of lies told by the king's sympathizers, the editor claimed that they "would make as great a volume as *Esops Fables*, *Guy of Warwick*, *Bevis of Southampton*, and *St. George for England*" all rolled into one.[102] Since this list probably represented Dillingham's preference in books, it indicates that an ex-tailor with ordinary tastes was as well suited to speak to and for the early newspaper-reading public as a man with loftier qualifications. And Dillingham's career in journalism, if not notably successful financially, was durable.

So, too, was that of Daniel Border, a former scrivener, who, when he finally stopped editing, turned to medicine.[103] His paper, *The*

Weekly Account, during the second half of 1644 and the first half of 1645 stayed on the course it had earlier pursued. Border consistently avoided taking a stand on controversial political or religious issues, and his anti-Royalism was of the standard variety. Several times he called attention to his intra-Parliamentary impartiality, even in one instance putting in a bid for the thanks of posterity.[104] Occasionally a flourish of undisciplined rhetoric obtruded, and one gets the impression that the editor was neither so accurate as he claimed nor so informed as other editors.[105] It is inviting to speculate that he was addressing the less sophisticated part of the London public, the ancestors of the buyers of today's *Reader's Digest* — and in one number Border included a half-page digest of that week's news at the request, so he alleged, of his readers.[106] In terms of its quality, and possibly of its intent, *The Weekly Account* had become the poor man's *Perfect Diurnall*.

If the ancestors of the *Reader's Digest* audience read *The Weekly Account*, the people whose descendants today read the pulps probably purchased *The Scotish Dove*, for Smith more than ever seemed to be addressing himself to the lowest common denominator of London reader, as well as to a rural audience.[107] The defects of the *Dove* of early 1644 thus became more apparent, both absolutely, as Smith let himself go more often, and relatively, as other papers improved. To give him the credit that is his due, his weekly continued to give adequate coverage to military events, news of which filled about half its space, and he kicked a little more vigorously than his fellows against the Independent pricks.

But in his support of conservative Presbyterianism Smith took a morbid relish in wearing the oppositionist's hair shirt. In the summer of 1644, after bragging that he had been in business forty-five weeks, he noted that "the times and men are nocent: there is a snare in everything." [108] A month later he added that his *Dove* was "maligned, and endangered by every Bird of prey"; and in October he called attention to the fact that he, a gentle bird, was being unjustly persecuted.[109] Intermittently thereafter he supplied his readers with hints that the world was out to get him. If so, the world, at least the small part of it to which Smith addressed himself, had some provocation. At one point he referred to his mission "to inform a stupid people, and to give light to the understanding of a seduced nation"; [110] at another he thus patronizingly described his own weekly efforts:

I never kept any Diary of the daily occurrents; only for the better information of my Readers, I mingle something (of my own thoughts) in observation upon some particulars; especially for the satisfaction of my Country Friends, for whose sakes I chiefly send out my weekly Dove, that once writing may save all, and save me labour in writing severall letters to many severall friends.[111]

In keeping with this attitude Smith recurrently told his public that his function was not so much to present the news as to guide people on the proper path.[112]

Besides wearing a hair shirt, Smith clothed himself in a flashy toga of piety. Frequently and long-windedly he announced that he was both God-fearing and in close communication with the deity. In fact, he was close enough to bargain with Him. For instance, if Londoners followed the divine commands, Smith, so he claimed, would be able to give them nothing but good news.[113] Also, like the Royalist caricature of a Puritan, he was delighted when Christmas happened to fall on a day of fasting; and of course he approved the execution of fourteen witches as the only right action in man's warfare against the devil.[114]

Running through his pious asides and irregular editorial openings was a noticeable anti-Independent motif that was only slightly modified by belated praise of the New Model.[115] Smith went so far as to pray for the king's preservation, "unlike a Church-gathering Independent," and to state that a Presbyterian form of church government was the only arrangement agreeable to the theory and practice of the apostles.[116] Several times he took an outspoken stand against religious toleration, and he was courageous or naïve enough to hope that Essex would be appointed commander of the remodeled army.[117] Though *The Scotish Dove* indulged in most of the evasions and omissions of other London papers, it was still the most partisan; and Smith, though he usually wrapped his partisanship in a mantle of piety and a haze of generality, was obviously not too pleased by Cromwell's victory at Naseby.

Of the two remaining newspapers which had been established before August 1644, one, *The Court Mercurie*, was not around long enough to say anything about Naseby. After a gap in September, it died in mid-October, having deviated little from its summer role as an adequate and typical London weekly. The editor diverted his Presbyterian sympathies into attacks on *Aulicus*; and he indirectly confessed his lack of journalistic zeal by admitting that he got most of his news, not by brain- and leg-work, but from his friends.[118] Perhaps the death of *Aulicus* left him with too much space for his friends to fill. The second of these newspapers was a revival. *Mercurius Veri-*

dicus had come to an end in April 1644. When it came back a year
later it had lost the little stylistic sparkle which had briefly distinguished
it. Generally cautious and impartial, its editor now saved a little room
by cutting down on anti-Royalist items, then used this space for
stories which had some flavor of human interest.[119] Otherwise, *Mercurius Veridicus* was merely typical.

Between the death of *The Court Mercurie* and the rebirth of *Veridicus* a man who later played a small part in English journalism published
a vigorous and well-written plea for freedom of the press. John
Milton's *Areopagitica*, however, received little notice when it appeared
in November 1644, and its full impact was delayed until the nineteenth
century. But, except for a passing animadversion on *Aulicus*, Milton's
pamphlet had nothing explicit to say about the weekly newspapers; and
he was therefore not necessarily inconsistent when, in 1651, he became
a licenser of the newsbooks.

A month before *Areopagitica* slipped into the world, so did a new
newspaper — and with equal lack of fireworks. *Perfect Passages of
Each Dayes Proceedings in Parliament*, possibly edited by Henry
Walker, was a good run-of-the-mill journal from its inception in
October 1644 to its demise in March 1646. Like *Perfect Occurrences*,
a paper with which Walker was almost certainly connected, *Perfect
Passages* modeled itself on *A Perfect Diurnall*, the various "perfects"
being the result more of competition than of adjectival honesty. In
the manner of Pecke, *Perfect Passages* neglected crime stories, giving
as its reason that "they have no relation to the Parliament nor the
affaires of the Army." [120] Then, too, the editor was judicious, both in
the items he did not print and in those he skirted rather than embraced.
Finally, he had occasional access to Westminster, in one instance giving an account of a conference between the two Houses that indicates
he was on hand.[121]

But *Perfect Passages* is of interest politically because it shifted to a
pro-Independent position, if a subdued one, earlier than other neutral-
ist weeklies — another hint of Walker's possible editorship. By February 1645 such an aside as the following did not seem out of place in
its pages; and despite the patronizing tone, it represents what might
have been considered a premature display of tolerance:

> These are the men [Cromwell's soldiers] (meaning the Independents as
> we call them) that the other day many would have . . . turned out of the
> Army; you see how they submit to authority, and to be obedient, and how
> orderly they are, and readie to do service for the publike; and we had more
> need to fall downe upon our knees to pray them to stay in the Army; and
> truly for my part, I never tooke them for friends that went about to make

divisions between us and them in the Army, for however they differ in something in judgement from us, yet we cannot be ignorant that they have been as active for the Parliament both in purse, person, and prayers as any in the Kingdome.[122]

Politically interesting too, but certainly accidental, is the fact that *Perfect Passages* attacked two points of view that were later closely identified with the Levellers. In an early number it went after a sermon preached by a Cavalier minister in which certain "blasphemous" mortalist doctrines were uttered — and mortalism was a heresy associated with Richard Overton, who became the most scathing of Leveller propagandists.[123] Then in March 1645 *Perfect Passages* accused those in the army who were demanding full pay for the soldiers of being "Jesuiticall" plotters — and subsequent appeals by the Levellers for the army's back pay became their most potent lure in gaining military proselytes.[124]

Perfect Passages also represents one of the few papers of its day to be literally moved by its publisher's or editor's piety. Because the official monthly day of thanksgiving came on Wednesday, once a month the paper shifted its day of appearance to Tuesday, though the factor of sales had something to do with this.[125] A similar mixture of piety and salesmanship is evident in the paper's repeating an anecdote which, in a variety of forms, had been reported in other London weeklies: the devil suddenly appeared among a group of toast-drinking Cavaliers and carried off one of the more boisterous and blasphemous of the imbibers.[126]

In the case of the second new newspaper of this period devils played a more prominent role; and in one instance the editor of *The Parliaments Post* devoted four of his eight pages to a discussion of Satan and his ghostly and ghastly henchwomen.[127] Perhaps there is a positive correlation between credulity and political myopia: *The Parliaments Post*, despite its title, left most news of Westminster to be covered by such men as Pecke, while it concentrated on military matters and pious exempla.[128] When John Lilburne, the future leader of the Levellers and a man with a genius for self-publicity, was arrested, the paper's only comment was the more-than-half lie that it was "absolutely forbidden" to give any details.[129] Such credulity and caution, when combined with a pronounced lack of zest, could not be profitable. In October 1645, after a short life of twenty-one numbers, *The Parliaments Post* returned to oblivion.

The third new newspaper of late 1644 and early 1645, *The Exchange Intelligencer*, had an even shorter life, lasting only from mid-May to mid-July. The brevity of this span is, however, another proof of the public's desire for English news, since *The Exchange Intelligencer* devoted from one-third to one-half its space to foreign affairs. The fact that it lasted only eight numbers also indicates that the merchants of London were not interested or numerous enough to support a newspaper directed to them. Yet the opening paragraph of the first number — what would now be called its prospectus — shows that the editor thought he knew his history of journalism and was calculating accordingly:

> We had (some yeares agone) no diurnals of our own affaires in England. We did live then in so blessed a time that wee were onely curious and desirious to heare Forraigne newes. . . . And now by a strange alteration and vicissitude of times wee talke of nothing else but of what is done in England, and perhaps once in a fortnight we hearken after newes sent out of Scotland. It is true our owne domestique affaires are of a greater concernment than forraigne business; but yet we may looke farther than home, partly to comfort us when we heare that although our neighbours are not imbroyled with civill warres as we are, yet they are so well imployed and so farre ingaged . . . one against another that they cannot very well frame any grand designe against us. . . . Besides, it is requisite for Marchants and for those that travell beyond sea . . . to know . . . what forces are upon the seas, and where the armies quarter, that they may prevent many dangers, shun the meeting of foes, and seeke to joyne with their friends. These reasons have moved me to undertake this weekly labour. . . . The best of the French and Dutch coranto's shall be imparted to you, besides many other things out of marchants and gentlemens letters. . . .[130]

It is then interesting to watch the editor trying to select the foreign news at least partly on the basis of its applicability to English businessmen, and to see him debating with himself whether England should play balance-of-power politics in Europe or for the time being follow a policy of nonintervention.[131] Less interesting, however, is his superficial, pious, and dutifully anti-Royalist treatment of English news.

Between August 1644 and July 1645 only two additional short-lived newspapers and two incipient magazines set up in business. In October 1644 the busy John Rushworth probably had a hand in an undistinguished paper which lasted two numbers.[132] Early in 1645 *The Monthly Account* tried to summarize four weeks of English news. It also survived for two numbers. Then at the end of March *The Generall Account of The Proceedings in Parliament* more closely anticipated today's news magazines by attempting in its sixteen pages to give the gist of the news at home and abroad for the preceding month; it lasted one number. Finally, in April, Rushworth or his deputy Mabbott was probably responsible for *The Weekely Post-Master*.[133] This paper, despite its well-written asides and careful distinction between "Certain Intelligence" and "Reports," survived only four weeks. This can be partly explained by the opinion of the editor that unconfirmed news was something "begotten of ayre and some thinne appearances . . . like so many clouds which doe hang upon the evening of truth." [134] Probably such an attitude was and is more appropriate to the historian than to the journalist. In any case, a month after the demise of *The Weekely Post-Master* Royalist military power was eclipsed at Naseby; but whether this battle signified the evening or the morning of truth was a problem that the newspapers of London would have to cope with for the next four years.

CHAPTER VI

GROWING PAINS

August 1645 to May 1646

PARADOXICALLY, the defeat of the Royalists at Naseby made the king the most important man in England. In May 1646 he fled to the Scots, but before and after that inept flight he was the shifting center in a series of negotiations among Presbyterian and Independent groups, each bidding for his elusive support. In the course of these negotiations Charles whistled away much prestige and some bargaining power by failing to recognize his own weakness or the strength of his opponents. Yet he remained the most important man in England.

The newspapers between August 1645 and May 1646 reflected this high-stake game of hide-and-seek in two ways: directly, as news; indirectly, as policy, as the attempt by most editors to anticipate changes in the domestic balance of power or just to keep their footing amid the political crosscurrents. Since a by-product of the king's maneuvers was an extension of the newspapers' period of comparative freedom, their editors still had enough rope to hang themselves or to range farther afield.

Nedham temporarily hanged himself. Indeed, the final chapter in the story of *Mercurius Britanicus* can graphically illustrate both the hazards and the stimuli to which the adolescent weeklies were exposed, especially those which practiced open partisanship — and since the spring of 1645 *Britanicus*'s attacks on the king had increased in frequency and venom. Early in August, Nedham included an announcement in which the tone of facetiousness no doubt added to the shock, for it is particularly iconoclastic when one blasphemes with a grin:

If any man can bring any tale or tiding of a wilfull King, which hath gone astray these foure yeares from his Parliament, with a guilty Conscience, bloody Hands, a Heart full of broken Vowes and Protestations: If these marks be not sufficient, there is another in the mouth: for bid him speak, and you will soon know him [Charles stuttered]: Then give notice to Britanicus, and you shall be well paid for your paines. So God save the Parliament.[1]

The repercussions of this "wanted" notice were prompt. The House of Lords immediately objected to it, and Robert White, the printer of *Britanicus*, found himself in the Fleet prison. White then blamed Audley, who for a long time had been acting as Rushworth's deputy with the specific job of licensing *Britanicus* — one of the signs of the paper's special status. Audley put the blame on Nedham, who, he said, had rejected his suggestion that the offending passage be altered. But Nedham was let off with an official reprimand, while Audley was sentenced to a brief stint in the Gatehouse.[2] Meanwhile Nedham helped to preserve his own liberty by writing a humble *Apologie* within a week of his editorial indiscretion.[3] Yet the strangest published fruit of this entire contretemps was a pamphlet which appeared two days after Nedham's retraction: *Aulicus His Hue and Cry Sent forth after Britanicus*. This clever reply to the attack on the king and to Nedham's *Apologie* was almost certainly by John Birkenhead, but it was duly entered in the Stationers' Register and hence published with some kind of official sanction.[4]

Nor was this quite the end of the story. On apologizing to the Lords, Audley was released after a week, with the proviso that he not license any more newsbooks; and Mabbott's imprimatur began to appear on *Britanicus*. Yet three months later Audley was again licensing this weekly.[5] The censorship arrangements of 1645 were at least blessed with carelessness and inconsistency. Knowing this, and knowing that he had the backing of certain Independents, Nedham kept on with *Britanicus*, until in May 1646 he again transgressed, this time without the alibi of Audley's ostensible license.

But in August 1645, after missing only a week as a result of his blunder, Nedham was back at his old stand, attacking *Aulicus*, the Royalists, the king, and quickly claiming that any criticism of his paper was a mark of "Malignancie." [6] In September his final full-fledged diatribe against *Aulicus* came out, followed a week later by a railing notice of his rival's demise, though it was an obituary that contained a note of regret.[7] Thereafter *Britanicus*, without an Oxford punching bag, temporarily became more like other London newspapers, and by padding the news from Westminster it managed to be more superficial than most. Though Nedham was too astute an observer to avoid an occasional pregnant aside, he was also too smart to take a firm stand at just this time on the squabbles between Presbyterian and Independent. As an astute observer, he was one of the first editors publicly and lengthily to express his worries about a breach with the Scots. As a man temporarily above intra-Parliamentary disputes, he was able to don the mantle of a sage and, in four consecutive numbers toward the end of 1645, skillfully explain why no foreign countries were likely to aid the cause of Charles.[8] Even in this second role, however, Nedham got into a spot of trouble. In going out of his way to bestow ardent praise on Parliament, he questioned the right of the people to influence their rulers by means of petitions; and immediately several London papers came to the defense of their readers by assailing Nedham.[9]

This time Nedham was rescued, if rescue he needed, by a new "Mercurius Aulicus" which for three months enabled him to fill many of his pages with counterattacks against a safely Royalist opponent. At the same time he was again becoming convinced that an Independent wave of the future had begun to crest. In one number he even came to the support of the notorious radical, Lilburne,[10] and he now recurrently expressed the conviction that the defeat of the Royalists should be total: that any peace negotiations should be as militantly conducted as the later stages of the war had been. In March 1646 Nedham warned the Independents to be wary of Royalist support and entrapment.[11] In May, after the king had fled to the Scots, Nedham said that he was not surprised and that revenge must be taken against the promoters of the war, "that a strict accompt be required for the blood of all the Saints." [12] In what turned out to be the final number of *Britanicus* (May 11–18, 1646) he continued to berate the king, using language and concepts that were still almost two years premature. Nedham and Audley were brought before the House of Lords. Audley disclaimed any responsibility for this number of *Britanicus*, which had not been properly licensed, and was released. This time Nedham went to jail.[13]

Technically and legally his arrest could be justified, but why did it now occur? Probably because Nedham's backers realized that, in the jockeying for political position, blatant anti-Royalism could be neither a safe nor a consistent policy. If Cromwell and the king were to make a deal, then the Independents might be able to arrange a limited monarchy which would be tolerant in matters of religion and pliant in meeting the political demands of the army. Nedham, as the noisiest spokesman against the king, might turn out to be, if not dangerous, at least inconvenient. But his employers were not ungrateful for his past services. Instead of having him spanked, they saw to it that once again he only received a slap on the wrist. After less than two weeks in jail Nedham was released. He had, however, to post bail of £200 for good behavior, predictably his promise not to write political pamphlets or edit a newspaper.[14] For a year he turned to medicine; then in 1647 he came back to journalism, now on the side of the king. Perhaps the leading Independents, regardless of their ostensible foresight, should have seen to it that Nedham served a longer term, or none at all.

In respect to his contribution to early English journalism Nedham deserved reward, not punishment. *Britanicus*, despite its faults of distortion, hitting below the belt, inconsistency, and redundancy, had made the pioneer newspaper more personal and sinewy. For at least eighty of this weekly's 130 numbers Nedham had been the chief author.[15] If, as one of his Royalist opponents charged, he was paid £3 a week for editing *Britanicus*, his services to the militants in Parliament and army earned him this salary.[16] He was also owed a small debt by other journalists for deflecting to himself some of the official heat which might have singed them.

Five months before he was temporarily withdrawn from journalism, Nedham had, in turn, a chance to deflect his own and others' heat to *Mercurius Academicus*. Edited by a clergyman named Richard Little, this Oxford weekly attempted to revive *Aulicus*.[17] More restrained and resigned than its predecessor, it tried to carry on the job of splitting the Parliamentary coalition, and any innovations Little introduced were the result of political rather than journalistic developments. On occasion he almost sounded like an Independent, the king's flight to the Scots not yet having shown on which side the Royalist bread was to be buttered. *Academicus* flattered Lilburne, blamed the war on the Presbyterians, and warned the Independents that their opponents were scheming against the congregational churches.[18] Little also probed at a variety of other cracks in the Parliamentry edifice, railed at anti-Royalists of whatever shade of opinion, and sneered at the London press, especially *Britanicus*. Like Birkenhead, he was shocked at the revolutionary forces unleashed by the assault on traditional authority, and he pointed with horror at the 180 religious sects which, he alleged, were then active in London.[19] But in March 1646, after fourteen numbers, and after the defeat of the remnant of the king's army, *Academicus* closed shop.

The changing conditions that caused the departures from journalism of Nedham and Little had less effect on the editors of more neutral newspapers, though in March 1646 five of the shakier long-run London weeklies left the field. During the preceding six months, as a prelude to their departure, both Houses of Parliament had now and then growled a reminder to all editors that their freedom was by no means absolute, their right to stay in business by no means guaranteed. Even if one were not a Nedham or an Oxford propagandist, the job of editing a weekly was no sinecure.

It remained closest to that enviable status for the translator of *Le Mercure Anglois*. Unfortunately he could not long enjoy this office, for he died in November 1645.[20] His place was probably taken by John Cotgrave, a diffident man who, a year earlier, had edited *The Court Mercurie*.[21] At the end of 1645, too, Nicholas Bourne briefly resumed the job of publisher. Neither substitution made any noticeable difference. *Le Mercure Anglois* continued down the exact middle of the road, still exhibiting the superficiality deemed appropriate for a foreign audience. To give only one example, the new translator, just as his predecessor would have done, reported only the bare news that the king had sought refuge with the Scots.[22] Also, as before, the paper whenever possible made the most of military news. With the virtual end of the war this became difficult, though there were usually skirmishes in Scotland and Ireland, news of which could fill up some space. One number of *Le Mercure Anglois* doubled its length to eight pages to make room for an official declaration to the States General of Holland.[23] This deviation was one of the few that the staff allowed themselves.

Of the fourteen newspapers available during most weeks between mid-1645 and early 1646 *Le Mercure Anglois* would probably be the least satisfactory to today's reader, *A Perfect Diurnall* probably the most. Yet he would have to read it differently from, say, his *New York Times*. Because Pecke, like his fellows, was always conscious of a potential censor breathing down his neck, he was cautious, superficial, evasive. Further, his concept of news did not normally include the private, the local, or the sensational; and he assumed that his contemporaries could, if they wanted, find much between the lines. If, three centuries later, one also reads between the lines, he will discover that the events of 1645–46 are amazingly contemporary insofar as they signify decisive and sophisticated maneuvers in the struggle for political power.

During that year, however, *A Perfect Diurnall* communicated this struggle in a largely negative manner. In August 1645 Pecke reminded other journalists of the requirement that their products be licensed, and he cited the case of an editor who had been reprimanded by Parliament for neglecting this procedure.[24] If possible, Pecke would not be similarly reprimanded. Not only was his paper consistently licensed, but it covered such inflammable issues as the negotiations with the king and the settlement of the church with a circumspection that utilized the devices of self-censorship, extreme brevity, and deliberate vagueness.[25] In addition, throughout most of this period Pecke, when in doubt, praised Parliament and denied reports of its disunity.[26]

None the less he was a good journalist. The intermittent items of foreign news in *A Perfect Diurnall* remained, on the whole, terse and relevant to England. The paper's coverage of Westminster, if thin, was inclusive and accurate.[27] Accounts of by-elections, a topic which Pecke considered within his province, were more available than in most London weeklies. And finally, beneath the sugar-coating of Pecke's statements about harmony among the anti-Royalists, one can sometimes chip a tooth on the hard facts of political life. Thus in November 1645 the editor implied that the Scots might be a real threat to Parliament, and by the following spring he was ready to acknowledge that there were major differences between Presbyterian and Independent, between England and Scotland.[28] No bellwether in this respect, he was also no mute, as his handling of the negotiations between the Scots and Parliament in the spring of 1646 can illustrate. When the subject was taboo, Pecke avoided it; when Parliament made certain papers public, he gave them a great deal of space.[29]

Yet *The Kingdomes Weekly Intelligencer* is almost as good a lantern to light up that distant but unremote era. Collings continued to submerge his inclinations toward Presbyterianism in his anti-Royalism; and regardless of his underlying political coloration, he was delighted by the New Model's victories. In October he commented, "Now let all the Souldiers in Christendome shew us so many strong holds taken in any part of Europe in six yeares as we have taken in this Kingdome in six moneths"; and in the spring he took obvious delight in composing a "Cavaliers Letanie" that had for its refrain "Our horses and heeles deliver us." [30] He even went so far as to praise Captain Swanley, the man notorious for deliberately drowning some Irish prisoners.[31] But where Pecke's neutrality in intra-Parliamentary disputes seems inherent, Collings' seems the result of a balance between his opposing viewpoints. His militancy against the Royalists, rather than against the king, was now balanced by his conservativism, tokens of which were frequent in the pages of *The Kingdomes Weekly Intelligencer*. In the argument between Prynne and Lilburne, Collings was emphatically on the side of the former; he referred to any denial of the Trinity as a "horrid crime"; and he called on England to "lay aside babes meat" and thoroughly reform the church along Presbyterian lines.[32]

This internal balance, in combination with the fear of suppression which all editors shared, is visible in the vaporous editorials that Collings began composing early in 1646.[33] Like Smith's effusions, those of Collings were vague, platitudinous, safe, but lacking in Smith's oiliness. One example will suffice, not only for Collings but for innumerable offspring that have served as innumerable fillers in innumerable English and American dailies:

. . . Liberty is a precious enjoyment, for which we have all this while fought, and [are] now neer obtaining; but if not bounded and limited, it will run into exorbitancies. . . . God hath given limits to the Ocean; without Government . . . Confusion follows. We are not to do what we will, but what we ought. It is imbecility to yield unto evils, but it is folly to nourish them.[34]

Generally cautious in his news and invariably cautious in his editorials, Collings was willing to offend one group that was neither Royalist nor Catholic: certain London editors. Several times he made derogatory remarks about Dillingham's *Moderate Intelligencer* and at least once he insulted Smith's *Scotish Dove*.[35] Occasionally he exhibited a sympathy for astrology, though this may have been a sop to the tastes of his readers.[36] Or perhaps he now looked to the stars for comfort because he was finding it hard to be both a moderate Presbyterian and a militant anti-Royalist at a time when the conservative group in Parliament was flirting with the king. In any case, by the spring of 1646 *The Kingdomes Weekly Intelligencer* had shown a slight decline, one partly signified by the editor's forced optimism that he and his country would somehow be extricated from the horns of their dilemma.[37]

During the last half of 1645 and the first half of 1646 Collings' other paper, *Mercurius Civicus*, echoed the suppressed politics, including the whistling in the dark, of *The Kingdomes Weekly Intelligencer*. Here too there was a slight falling off in vigor, a slight piling on of extra caution. In one number Collings complained that *Civicus* came out at the end of the week, for "the World is now crowded with such a throng and multiplicity of upstart Scouts, Posts, Mercuries, and other Intelligencers, that coming forth so neere the Reare . . . I must onely content my selfe with the Crums and Gleanings of Information. . . ." [38]

For two months at the end of 1645 the paper dropped its woodcuts, the editor explaining that he hoped his readers would not "refuse to buy the Booke for the omission of a shaddow, when the same information for substance" was still available. [39] Apparently the readers did object. By January 1646 the pictures were back, including a new one of Charles, without a crown. [40] But the clearest sign of Collings' current discomfort was a lengthy aside in commemoration of the coronation of Queen Elizabeth. [41] Running through it was the motif that if the Stuarts had been Tudors, England would not be suffering the religious, political, and economic ills fluttering and weakening the national pulse.

Yet *Mercurius Civicus* retained its few distinctive qualities, among them the editor's ability to insert a touch of humor and to give local color to certain London stories. In telling of the king's flight to the Scots, for instance, Collings was partly concerned with communicating the tension which it excited in the metropolis. [42] He also showed a Dillingham-like interest in a scheme to set up workhouses for the poor in London and "to educate their children in Handicrafts." [43] Finally, *Civicus* continued to be militantly anti-Royalist, though such a policy was now divorced from any approval of Independency. [44] That this divorce was not easy is implicit in almost every issue of Collings' two newspapers; sometimes, as in this late 1645 number of *Civicus*, it was explicit:

But in regard some particulars therein [a case involving a Worcester Catholic] may prove offensive, I shall say no more of it at present, lest this, as some other things which have been lately published out of zeale and affection to the Parliament and publike good, be misconstrued, and the publisher for his good service receive a check (or worse usage) from those who (perhaps) are faulty, but must not be told on't. [45]

Maintaining any kind of balance was also complicated by the fact that throughout late 1645 and early 1646 rumbles of an impending tightening of the censorship kept emanating from Parliament. To them Collings responded with a mixture of resentment and relief. If resentment is apparent in the above quotation, relief at the ostensible security of being under a tight rein is apparent in this quotation from *Civicus* early in the spring:

We heard also of something concerning the weekly Pamphlets, which are now to be regulated, or (if you please) in a better sence, to be contracted into a shorter number. It is a good worke, and it will coole the heate of the blood, and the Ring-worme of any who shal for private gaine have a desperate itch to infect and abuse the Kingdome.[46]

Neither of Collings' newspapers, however, was among the five long-run papers that were eliminated in March when the weekly press was "contracted into a shorter number."

Nor was Dillingham's *Moderate Intelligencer* among them, though the ex-tailor briefly returned to the less restrained attitudes of his earlier venture, *The Parliament Scout*. One indication of this was his more frequent rebuttal of criticisms coming from official bodies and other editors.[47] Yet in most ways *The Moderate Intelligencer* remained a typically competent purveyor of straight news. Dillingham kept his hard-headed interest in military events, and whenever possible he devoted much space to battles and skirmishes anywhere in the British Isles. He was also still concerned with such matters as the soldiers' back pay and the bad condition of their shoes, as well as with retaining his rural circulation.[48] And he outdid all other editors in his ability to sprinkle his pages with platitudes and proverbs, until at times one is reminded of Sancho Panza.

But at times one is also reminded of Don Quixote. Starting in July 1645 Dillingham began his weekly with a short but hardly ever terse editorial. Here, if he seldom couched his lance against giants, he at least tilted against windmills. Yet behind his circumlocutions and platitudes, one can sense that he was genuinely trying to shape and clarify his own views on the major issues of the day. Therefore his inner wrestling match can provide glimpses of the impact of an incipient revolution on the man-in-the-street, even if one has to witness that wrestling match through such clouds of rhetorical smoke as: "We have usually begun with somewhat we conceive necessary to be prosecuted, or with diswasion from what we understood was on foot that might prolong these Kingdomes miseries or terminate them in an unsound peace" — and then, after a generalized appeal for compromise and reason, Dillingham changed the subject to "Martiall actions" which, he wrote, "go smooth." [49]

None the less, his editorials and editorial asides are instructive, especially when they touched on the question of religious toleration. In general, Dillingham now took a liberal, sometimes a radical, stand in favor of freedom. He could ironically comment,

Forty-three victories since June last, Ergo root out all Sects and

Schismes: God hath been pleased to borrow a poor Armie wherein are twenty severall opinions, yet all agree in fundamentals . . . Ergo root them out of the Kingdome, for they are not of one mind in all things, or rather, they differ in discipline.[50]

He later went so far as to recommend that Papists be spared persecution, though, like Milton, he hedged by not wishing to grant them political power.[51] One can, in fact, see two strands building up in Dillingham's confused pleas for toleration: first, a sort of naïve Cambridge Platonism that tried to find a broad common denominator in religion while it put aside differences in matters of organization and ritual;[52] second, a tentative Erastianism that incorporated the view that Parliament, since it was both wise and representative, should control the church.[53] Though often contradictory, both views tended toward the secularization of religion and hence, in the seventeenth century, toward toleration. Yet most of the powerful and vocal Presbyterians of the day were Erastians, a convenient doctrine when they had a majority in Parliament. Consequently one of Dillingham's problems — and it was by no means peculiar to him — was to equate liberty with a state-run church. The practical solution, and a course appropriate to a journalist who wanted to stay in business, was the advocacy of a mild form of Presbyterianism which might appease the orthodox and not antagonize the Independents. Such a path was tricky to follow, but Dillingham managed to stumble along it during much of the period in question. In doing so he was rubbing elbows with most of his urban contemporaries.

He was also probably typical of the man on the city street in his gradual move toward accepting a larger voice for the people. Like Nedham, Dillingham attacked the presumption of petitioners who took it upon themselves "to tell the Parliament they understand not what is best and when it is best," and he cited recent French history to show that the magistrate, not the multitude, should have real power.[54] But Dillingham's Erastianism consistently had a democratic orientation, he upheld Lilburne as a "stiffe defendor and eminent Martyr for the Liberties and Birth-Right of the Subject," and he attacked certain excise taxes in the manner of a twentieth-century liberal fighting a sales tax on food (though the following week he felt compelled to apologize for this stand.)[55]

Starting in February 1646 *The Moderate Intelligencer* expanded from eight to twelve pages. Despite a probable increase in price, this move was almost certainly designed to boost sales. It also gave Dillingham more room to take a stand on both sides of many controversial issues. At the same time, this extra space provides today's reader with a larger canvas on which to observe a seventeenth-century editor muddling through. Hence *The Moderate Intelligencer* probably ranks first as a journalistic mirror, though not as a record, of this specific period in English history.

Daniel Border, the editor of *The Weekly Account*, was in all likelihood as much a John Doe (or Bull) as Dillingham, though far less open and articulate. Indeed, in respect to being cautious and non-committal his paper was rapidly catching up with *Le Mercure Anglois*. Border more and more employed such phrases as "whereof more hereafter," and then dropped the matter completely. Recurrently he announced that national unity was necessary, but always without specifying how it was to be attained. Even after Charles's flight to the Scots, the editor gave the impression that Anglo-Scottish relations were still harmonious; and he reached a high peak of caution in this *non sequitur*: "The Commons were this day resolved in a Grand Committee about the Church, and therefore I shall pass to field intelligence." [56] One of the few instances in which Border seemed about to express himself on a controversial issue was a story about Lilburne that began with praise; then came the equivalent of "on the other hand," and Border concluded by reprimanding Lilburne for getting involved in politics.[57] Though the pages of *The Weekly Account* continued to be filled with an adequate quota of news, the editor's calculated caution, in harness with his long-windedness and self-conscious piety, made his weekly dull and comparatively uninformative — either as record or mirror.

Two other long-run weeklies survived the March "contraction." One of them, *Perfect Occurrences*, while not quite so complete or functional as *A Perfect Diurnall*, gave almost as much and as accurate news as Pecke's paper. Yet to this Peckean journal Walker added a touch of Nedham.[58] From January to March 1646 he eagerly devoted up to one-quarter of his space to scornful attacks on *Mercurius Academicus*. He also followed in Nedham's footsteps, and his own, by expressing sympathy with the Independents. This was usually carefully watered down, but it still came through in enthusiastic compliments to certain leading Independents and in an Erastianism that was secularized enough to be anti-Presbyterian.[59]

Perfect Occurrences also diverged from *A Perfect Diurnall* in that it was more concerned with London news, especially with the alleged need for local magistrates to take stronger measures against Royalist plots. (Appropriate stories and warnings were then appearing in all papers, but in *Perfect Occurrences*, as well as in *Mercurius Civicus*, they were lengthier and more urgent.) But Walker's most distinctive characteristic, and one that first became conspicuous at this stage, was his showing off his classical learning. Again, however, this was a distinction of degree, not kind. All London editors used an occasional Latin tag or allusion to Greek and Roman history to show they were not illiterate, but in Walker's case classical quotations and references swelled from a trickle to a stream.

Walker also tried to display other signs of sophistication. For instance, he mentioned that chess had become popular at Charles's wandering court, then went on to say:

> I am sure the Queene hath stragled so farre on the one side, and the Rookes on the other after their Wanton Bishops, that not onely the Knights have many of them lost themselves, but the Carelesse Pawns have suffered us to give the Royall Check severall times, which if we gain once more, beware a mate.[60]

Or he made a punning reference to a minister who had "wasted his lungs by his painfull preaching"; and he cryptically concluded one number with "Sir Thomas Fairfax is marching away upon a designe, but ——." [61]

Fundamentally, *Perfect Occurrences* remained the *Perfect Diurnall* of the end of the week, and Walker compensated for his divergences from Pecke by crowding his pages to such an extent that he had room for both asides and most of the news then thought fit to print. He also had room on occasion to speak for the government, as when he denied certain charges against a high-ranking officer or when he begged his readers to send warm clothes to the soldiers.[62] Then, too, Walker was enough of a journalist to point up his objectivity by printing a few stories of Parliamentary errors and of atrocities committed by the New Model; and his coverage of a case of bribery in a Norfolk by-election was full and honest.[63]

The other long-run weekly that survived the March "contraction," *The Scotish Dove*, is the best illustration, along with *Mercurius Britanicus*, of the hazards and stimuli to which the newspapers were then exposed. Smith escaped liquidation despite the fact that his journalistic personality, his politics, and the course of events all indicated that his *Dove* was due to be coted. More than any other editor of this time Smith gave vent to his conservative political and religious views. He continued to cloak them in generalization and piety, but even so his opening editorials and his sporadic commentary were hostile to the Independents. Usually by indirection, sometimes by direction, he made it clear that only the Presbyterians could preserve national and religious unity, that the Independents were radical and divisive.[64]

Such views, especially the recurrent suggestion that certain non-Presbyterian leaders of Parliament were indulging in graft, brought down on his head an assortment of brickbats flung by other editors, and by spokesmen for various Parliamentary committees tarred with Smith's brush. Smith throve on these attacks, wallowing week after week in paragraphs of self-pity and whining martyrdom.[65] He was at his worst, however, when he forsook prose for poetry. Luckily, one example can serve to show his politics, paranoia, and prosody:

The mourning Doves Complaint

The God of all, that all of nothing made,
One world destroy'd when grieved, thus he said:
Mans heart is evill, stain'd with concupiscence,
The earth corrupt, and fill'd with Violence;
Ambition, Malice, Oppression, and Pride
Breed discords, and whole Countries doe divide
Among them: in all Townes and Cities
Th' opprest cry 'gainst their corrupt Committees;
The sheepe complaine their shepheards seeke the fleece,
And doe divide, where they are bound to peece.
Selfe-love and Pride procure indignation
Against the Covenant for Reformation.[66]

In both prose and verse Smith continued to view himself as a reformer rather than a newspaperman. Not only did his weekly contain the smallest quantity of news of any of its contemporaries, but its editor committed the journalist's sin of sins by devoting a lengthy piece to the theme that there is nothing new under the sun.[67] Moreover, Smith remained a blue-nose, a Puritan in the worst sense of the word. One's hackles can still rise, for instance, at the *Dove*'s inclusion of a delighted account of some soldiers breaking up a Royalist wake.[68] Finally, Smith's exhibitionistic piety had a tendency to get in his way even when he was not writing about God or religion. Thus when he wanted to advocate the choice of conservative M.P.'s to fill various vacancies in the House of Commons, his advice was so general and devout that no one, then or now, could tell how Smith wanted him to vote. Also, Smith's reaction to Charles's flight was so colored by wishful thinking that it stands out from all the other forcedly optimistic accounts of May 1646.[69] Despite his claim that the *Dove* had been seen by the Pope,[70] his repeated shifts in the paper's day of publication, and his attempt to appeal more directly to a conservative audience, *The Scotish Dove* more than ever seemed aimed at the lowest common denominator of reader.

Smith disapproved of, among other things, freedom of the press, and in March 1646 he happily announced that Parliament had shut down about half of the city's newspapers.[71] He of course avoided giving the reason for this action: that the Scottish commissioners, resentful of the generally unfavorable publicity their "secret" negotiations with Parliament were receiving, had succeeded in bringing enough pressure to secure a muzzling of the press.[72] But the muzzle which Parliament applied, while it restricted the movement of editorial jaws, did not strangle the newspaper. Nine weeklies were allowed to stay in business, though Parliament resolved to regulate the day of appearance of these survivors. Again, but again briefly, order was imposed on the London press.

Among the seven newspapers that perished were five old-timers. Of these the most to be regretted is *Mercurius Veridicus*. Either because of a change in editors or because the regular editor himself changed, this paper during the six months before its shut-down developed a rare smoothness of style. Relatively brief and shallow in his coverage of Westminster, the editor none the less did the best job of his day in tying the news together by means of skillful transitions and in showing that he was personally interested in the paper's over-all readability. In one case, for example, he was concerned about the tedium of a story; and he used increasingly the device of pretending that he was going from place to place to get the news: "in our passage we met with one who . . ." or "diverting our course, hasting toward Nottingham, we. . . ." [73] In one number he even worked around to praise of Parliament by means of dialogue.[74] Indeed, the editor's promise that "his weekly Mercury shall not be disjoynted" was almost fulfilled.[75]

In achieving this readability, however, the editor of *Mercurius Veridicus* usually felt he had to suppress his tendency toward conservatism and straddle all political and religious fences. In partial contrast, *The True Informer*, which had been carefully neutral, now sidled toward the Presbyterian fold. In fact, in March, on the last page of its last number, the editor happily reported that the House of Commons had "absolutely agreed . . . that the Presbyteriall Government shall be established" [76] — an overstatment that he would never repeat in print. As a sign of this move to the right, *The True Informer* carried the most blistering attack of the mid-1640's on Lilburne, a man beginning to be identified as the noisy voice of a no longer quiescent democratic movement. Anticipating by two years the conservative partyline against the Levellers, this attack gave graphic expression to those fears that the Presbyterians and their allies were experiencing as the Puritan Revolution began to gather an unexpected momentum. The radicals, said the editor, are those who, to set up a phantasticall Utopia of their owne, would ruine the Church, State, and Kingdome, blast the honour and justice of the Parliament, banish Religion, destroy the unitie and Lawes of the Land, and introduce an Anarchy, and confusion of all estates, that they might the better fish in that troubled Sea, to repaire their owne desperate conditions, and build themselves a name upon the Dunghill of their own odious and accursed villanies.[77]

Carlyle was never more vehement. Further, the editor tried to prevent the shooting of any democratic Niagara by advocating with comparative explicitness the election of properly pious men to fill any vacancies in Parliament, and by reprinting a letter from a Massachusetts clergyman which underlined the dangers of toleration.[78]

Like Smith, whose views he seemed to share (including a strong sympathy for the Scots), the editor of *The True Informer* was a Puritan in the derogatory sense of that word. In his first number in 1646 he "explained" that his paper had not appeared the previous week because of the "prejudice of the vulgar" who insisted on celebrating Christmas, and a month later he featured a strong attack on Valentine's Day.[79] Despite the weekly's shift toward conservatism and prudery, it remained not unlike other London papers, both those that survived and those that were shut down. It can therefore serve to raise one problem that often crops up in the history of the early newspaper: is the humor in certain items intentional or unintentional? *The True Informer* contained a paragraph on the death of the Emperor of Russia: apparently knowing that he was about to die, the Emperor made and had published a lengthy speech, and thus, said the editor, "Died in print." [80]

The same fate met *A Diary*, a weekly which, either with or without the editorial guidance of John Rushworth, had gone on giving the news with relative fullness and clarity. It was probably closed at the request of Rushworth, then still censor of the newsbooks, to show his own impartiality. Presumably this step involved little sacrifice: because *A Diary* was almost never mentioned by pamphlets and newspapers of the day, it could not have had much prestige or circulation.

A fourth paper of those closed in March 1646 met its doom at least in part as a result of its politics. *Perfect Passages* since the summer of 1645 had been drifting in a direction counter to that of *The True Informer*. Still an adequately complete newspaper and one that did its best to step around the cracks in the Parliamentary coalition, it now more and more distinguished itself by a militant anti-Royalism. Henry Walker, almost certainly the editor, was at this time a moderate Independent, but he displayed his dislike of the king and the king's cohorts with approximately the same frequency with which he displayed his own classical learning. These persistent attacks on Charles contained enough vitriol to be if not alarming at least irritating to the men maneuvering to stay in power or gain new power. For this reason Walker, after March 4, had to be satisfied with earning his living by, and venting his views in, *Perfect Occurrences.*

The fifth of the old newspapers shut down was the resilient *A Continuation Of certaine Speciall and Remarkable Passages.* After an intermittent life in 1643 and the first half of 1644, it was revived in September 1645, closed down at the end of February 1646, and again briefly resuscitated in 1647. Pecke may have been the editor, since the paper during its penultimate five months was competent enough to suggest his hand.[81] *A Continuation*, though not quite so orderly or complete as *A Perfect Diurnall*, was at least average in its accuracy and comprehensiveness, and above average in its political tightrope-walking. The editor gave equal space and approval to Presbyterians and Independents; [82] and none of his views was overtly partisan enough to explain why *A Continuation* was put out of business. In any case, the paper was around long enough to bequeath an interesting letter to posterity. In February 1646 the editor claimed that the Royalist cause had grown so desperate that he seconded the advice given to a Cavalier to leave England and start a plantation in the West Indies. *A Continuation* then printed a letter from there telling the fugitive what to bring. The list included a small frying pan, two pairs of linen drawers, £500, and, if possible, three or four "labouring men." [83]

Any man who was in London at the time this letter was published could have purchased his paper from a field of sixteen weeklies. Indeed, in terms of the total number of separate newspapers 1645 was the most prolific year in the history of pre-Restoration journalism; and between the beginning of that year and March 1646 the average week saw fourteen newspapers for sale.[84] When this number was temporarily reduced, it may have been a relief not only to the printers and publishers allowed to stay in business, but to the buyer tempted by competing yet similar papers and accosted by their noisy hawkers.

Prior to this "contraction" *The Parliaments Post*, which had begun life in May 1645, voluntarily returned to oblivion in October after twenty-one numbers. But it improved before expiring. The editor was still preoccupied with devils, and he even made the semi-serious claim that all witches were pro-Royalist.[85] He also continued to slight Westminster news and to concentrate, whenever possible, on military affairs, not to mention pious exempla. Yet his style gradually became firmer and more vivid, and he developed proficiency in spinning a lengthy anecdote.[86] In addition, several late numbers of *The Parliaments Post* displayed one unique quality: an anti-Royalism so assured that the editor could appear almost indifferent to what happened to Charles.[87] Presumably, however, neither improvement nor indifference were guarantors of success, even of survival.

Of the new newspapers of late 1645 the longest lived was the best. Begun in August with the title *Heads of Some Notes Of the City Scout*,[88] in October it became *The City-Scout*, and in December, for its final three numbers, *The Kingdomes Scout*. Under each title the *Scout* stressed military news and oriented its politics toward the army. Consequently the editor, while remaining ostensibly neutral, gave his anti-Royalism an Independent tinge. He also toyed with the device of marginal notes to explain or comment on various items, a technique he handled more capably than Nedham had in *Britanicus*. But his most valuable contribution was a stylistic finish that the writer of *The Parliaments Post* was only approaching. The author of the *Scout* could on occasion be both lively and learned — or even epi-grammatic, as in this terse description of the king: "The Parliament have his power, the Queene his heart, and the Oxford Juncto his person." [89] This author, in the paper's next-to-last number, also pub-lished an elegy good enough to be included in an anthology of eighteenth-century graveyard poetry.[90] But the *Scout* also withdrew from the fray before Parliament could inter it.

One of the two new newspapers to have its life cut short by the Parliamentary ax was *The Kingdomes Weekly Post*, which got under way in October 1645 and changed its name in December to *The Citties Weekly Post*.[91] Under both titles the paper showed how the sheer task of writing a weekly compilation induced an editor to improve, es-pecially if, as here seems likely, he was new to journalism. Consistently anti-Royalist, pious, and credulous, as well as excessively concerned with military matters, he managed to become more selective in his coverage, more controlled in his style, and less jumbled in his organ-ization.[92] In one instance, in fact, history seems to have co-operated with him in organizing the news, for the editor joyfully pointed out that the Parliamentary armies were capturing Royalist strong points in almost alphabetical order: after Chester and Dartmouth, Exeter and Falmouth.[93] Whether history would have continued to co-operate is a question that, at this point, could not be answered: in March the *Weekly Post* was silenced.[94]

So, too, was a second new weekly, *The Moderate Messenger*, which lasted such a short time it does not provide enough bulk to show whether its editor was improving.[95] In his case, however, improvement was not so necessary. Usually competent and cautious, in his fourth number, perhaps anticipating that this was his final week, he made the clearest statement concerning the separation of church and state yet to appear in an English newspaper:

> As sacred things prohibit polluted fingers, so matters of State are very unseasonable in Priests hands; Prayer is the Church-mans onely weapon, and divine things should be the substance of his preaching; he ought neither to lift up his hand to reforme, nor his voice to reprove, in secular affaires.[96]

In the last half of 1645 and the first half of 1646, as in almost every other segment of the 1640's, at least one newspaper tried to avoid all problems of church and state by devoting itself exclusively to foreign news. In this instance the name of the paper was *The Phoenix of Europe*; the date, mid-January 1646; the presumed audience, statesmen and merchants; and the duration, one number. Had it been around, it probably would have survived the March "contraction," which was by no means permanent or very vigorous; nor were the contents of those newspapers allowed to stay in business noticeably affected. *Mercurius Britanicus* kept going until May, and long before the end of 1646 new weeklies were creeping back onto the streets of London. Within two months of Parliament's censorial foray, one new newspaper had already appeared: *Generall Newes, From all parts of Christendome*. Given over to foreign news, it was more successful than *The Phoenix of Europe*. Indeed, it lasted four numbers before its publisher, Nicholas Bourne, became convinced that the public was interested only in the rush of events near home.[97]

Essentially the public was right. Between early 1646 and late 1648 what had been a civil war to determine who among various elites would wield political power changed into an incipient revolution that might transform the structure of English society. By early 1649 the king, though potentially still the most important man in England, had had his head chopped off, and the country ceased to be a monarchy. The newspapers of these three years, despite recurrent efforts at censorship by Parliament and army, told and reflected these revolutionary developments. Understandably, therefore, the London public was not greedy for general news from other parts of Christendom.

CHAPTER VII

LATE ADOLESCENCE

June 1646 to September 1647

THE period from June 1646 to September 1647 was an exciting moment in the sweep of English history. How aware of this the man on the street was cannot be computed, but many Londoners became involved in and excited by the flurry of events, many sniffed the smell of change. Indeed, one of the qualities that the 1640's share with the modern world is the rapid rate of change. Though the march of history now proceeds at a gallop, in the 1640's it had accelerated to a trot. To cite only one example, during the second half of 1646 and the first half of 1647 the Levellers grew from a small group of leftist individuals to an organized party able to apply heavy pressure toward making England a democracy.[1]

While this first relatively massive democratic party was being set up on street corners and around campfires, as well as in the seventeenth-century equivalent of smoke-filled rooms, Charles was playing the part of both king and pawn. In January 1647, after a series of circular negotiations between him and the Scots, the Parliament, and the army, he was returned to the English, and the Scottish army marched home.

The First Civil War was over. But the problem of the English army remained, an army that refused to disband until it had received some guarantee of a satisfactory national settlement. The demands of the army were complicated by the pressure of Leveller propaganda, by the matter of the soldiers' back pay, by the maneuvers of the king, and by the struggle for power between a Parliament dominated by conservative Presbyterians and Erastians and an army led by men who were being pushed deeper into Independency and innovation. In June 1647 a minor officer kidnapped the king for his military superiors, and in August the New Model occupied London. Charles, though he did not know it, was on his way to the scaffold; Cromwell, though he may not have known it, was on his way to the saddle of power. In September the high command of the army took over the censorship of the newsbooks, in fact if not in name. The Second Civil War was only eight months away.

In contrast to the turbulence of events, their chroniclers, the London weeklies, experienced a period of relative stability. But when the army tried further to tighten the censorial vise that Parliament had begun turning in March 1646, this apparent stability came to an end. In the autumn of 1647 a Royalist press sprang up in London, and the army soon found itself too busy elsewhere to be as effective an agency of censorship as Parliament had been — and Parliament had not been ineffective. Between the spring of 1646 and September 1647 fewer separate weeklies than at any time since 1643 were published, though those that survived appeared with a high degree of regularity. In a typical week only seven or eight papers were now available; in May 1647, six. The shadow of the Parliamentary censor loomed large over even the most durable editors, and the sparks struck by the clash of groups and personalities were reflected only faintly in the weekly press. It was a more exciting period than the worn pages of the early newspaper indicate.

It certainly was more exciting than the pages of *Le Mercure Anglois* suggest. Its compiler maintained the policy of printing only what was "digne de votre observation," [2] and his definition of this precept was as far from that of Hearst or Beaverbrook as it is possible to be. On rare occasions the paper mentioned the split between Presbyterians and Independents, and with equal rarity the editor implied that his sympathies were with the former.[3] The foreign reader also had to be content with a style that was still heavily official and impersonal. For three months in the spring of 1647 he had to be content with nothing, for without explanation *Le Mercure Anglois* temporarily abandoned him.[4] When it returned in July, no perceptible changes had occurred.

In contrast, the reader of *A Perfect Diurnall* had much to be content with, and Pecke never abandoned him. Moreover, the actual rapidity of events, the sheer bulk of news, sometimes induced a liveliness of style that made *A Perfect Diurnall*, as well as some of its competitors, sound less like semiofficial gazettes. This cascade of news went on receiving its fullest and most accurate coverage in Pecke's paper. Yet to fulfill this function was never easy. Take, for instance, the immediate repercussions of Charles's flight to the Scots. At the start Pecke handled the story straightforwardly, with adequate fullness and without comment. But in June 1646 he printed a letter from Charles that hinted the king was dealing off both sides of the deck.[5] Official London had become increasingly fearful of the army, increasingly hopeful of a rapprochement with Charles. Pecke was therefore accused of siding with the Independents.[6] He responded by announcing that "we are not willing to medle too far in businesses of this nature (least we give offence) and will say the lesse, leaving others to consider . . . as to peace."[7] He then began to devote a little more space to foreign affairs, and to be even more neutral, if possible, in his handling of Westminster items. Yet in October he and one of his publishers, along with a few other journalists, were reprimanded by the House of Commons for being too full in their reporting of the negotiations between Parliament and the Scots.[8] In telling of this reprimand Pecke climbed to a pinnacle of impersonality by not mentioning his own name. Shortly thereafter the harassed editor understandably pleaded for a relaxation of tension:

The generall inquiry now is, whether we shall have peace or a new War, for most think the old quarrell at an end; and what then will be the subject of a new: why? between Presbiters and Independents, in the generall opinion; we will have uniformity, sayes one. . . . Another pleads Liberty of conscience. . . . A sad thing if this should occasion a quarrel. And is there none can be found to speak a word in season to reconcile these two —

At which point Pecke spoke his own word in behalf of a Presbyterian-Independent reconciliation.[9]

Gradually, however, he moved toward a less neutral position. He was shrewd enough to foresee the victory of the Independents, and in all likelihood his sympathies now lay with them. Further, as a journalist Pecke doubtless felt that he would have more freedom under the Independents than under the Presbyterians. In spite of what happened in the next decade, he was right, for in the 1640's it was the army that preached and sometimes practiced a democracy two centuries ahead of history's time-table. By early 1647 Pecke was beginning to show an only partially concealed hostility to the Presbyterians, a sporadic affection for the leaders and aims of the New Model.[10] But this affection did not include any approval of democracy. Pecke supported, or pretended to support, a strong censorship. Never did he wince or frown at the prospect of governmental control of the newspapers, and he went so far as to warn Parliament that, "if they let such eminent Trespassers as these [certain printers who had published "too much" concerning the negotiations with the Scots] . . . passe without exemplary punishment, they must expect to have the Presses open against them." [11] In addition, he did not trust the people. To cite one of many examples, he criticized a Presbyterian petition because the mere process of getting signatures was itself dangerous and wrong.[12]

Pecke's shift toward Independency, his suspicions of democracy, and his professional caution were all reflected in *A Perfect Diurnall's* balanced treatment of the rise of the Levellers. References to Lilburne and his followers were almost always brief, stripped, neutral. In the spring of 1647, partly at Leveller instigation, the army established its own semi-legislative council, about half of whose members were common soldiers selected by their respective regiments. In describing the activities of these "Agitators," Pecke remained impartial and as terse as the now greater importance of such news would allow him to be.[13] Thus by continuing to deal only with the surface of events, by ignoring their causes and implications, Pecke was able to give most of the news, but in the same sense that a temperature reading gives the weather. Moving toward Independency but not toward democracy, he found it safe and functional to treat each week's news as if it were largely discontinuous, as if events had neither a past nor a future. When the political weather was rough, even storm warnings could be dangerous.

In the summer, after a London mob had forced Parliament to rescind certain pro-Independent votes, the army occupied the city without bloodshed and re-intimidated Parliament. Again Pecke's reports were short and bare. The reasons for the army's move were given only after they had been made public in official explanations. No commentary or analysis marred the pages of *A Perfect Diurnall* at this hectic time, though it did call — or whisper — for national unity and indulge in generalized praise of England's fighting men.[14] Indeed, one of Pecke's few hints at the magnitude of events was that he once expanded his paper from eight to twelve pages to accommodate that week's crowded budget of news.[15]

Yet the last eight months of 1647 were the heyday of *A Perfect Diurnall*. During much of this period it appeared in two slightly variant editions, a sure sign that one press could not supply the weekly demand. Probably its circulation had climbed beyond 2,000. Nor are the reasons far to seek. First, Pecke's caution had paid off: his weekly now had the prestige that comes from durability. Second, his policy of full if superficial coverage had harvested a large crop of readers: when there was an abundance of exciting news, commentary and embellishment were unnecessary. Third, *A Perfect Diurnall* did not have to compete with as many papers as it had the year before. An additional factor that may have contributed to this popularity was Pecke's typicality, though to accuse anyone of being typical is at best impressionistic. Even so, his expedient attitude toward the rise to power of the army, his generally middle-of-the-road politics, and his acceptance of limited religious toleration all seem, in retrospect, typical of the majority of literate Londoners. Consequently, despite all its faults, *A Perfect Diurnall* must have seemed a respectable and permanent institution to many Englishmen during the crowded weeks of 1647. The young newspaper had come of age.

If not quite so grown-up as *A Perfect Diurnall*, *The Kingdomes Weekly Intelligencer* was a little more interesting, for Collings was less impersonal than Pecke. Also, he tried for a time to paddle against the contemporary political current. How he came close to capsizing but never did more than ship a little water can best be seen in the editorials which were an irregular feature of the *Intelligencer*. During the seventy weeks from June 1646 through September 1647 Collings twenty times omitted any editorial opening, and twenty times he began with a paragraph or two against sin or in favor of God. Of the other thirty, eight had to do with the weather, a safe topic at any time or place, and five were conventionally anti-Royalist. Two, written at the moment when the army was actually occupying London, praised the New Model; and three questioned the right of the public, including journalists, to pry into state secrets. So far Collings was keeping an even keel. But in the remaining dozen editorials, scattered throughout these sixteen months, he took a stand on the side of the Presbyterians and conservatives. In June 1646 he wrote that a well-ordered church "confirmes men in obedience" to the established government; and in subsequent editorials he urged the king to take the Covenant, thereby restoring peace and harmony to an England that would be ruled by a limited monarchy and a Presbyterian church.[16] He also attacked the "inconstant multitude" and its dangerously democratic aspirations, as well as those religious sects which were, he said, threatening national unity and morality.[17]

In most of these dozen relatively controversial openings Collings displayed a mixture of caution and defiance. To give a single example, one of his longer and more forceful editorials moved from sly obsequiousness to probably the most explicitly pro-Presbyterian statement to appear in any newspaper of 1646–47:

> I had an intent in the Preface to this Intelligence to acquaint you with what is THAT which hath rays'd a coyle in the Army. . . . I should have told you of the admirable care and patience of the Generall, I should have cleered the common Souldier. I should have extolled many Officers, I should have acquainted you with what subtile boldnesse some men drive on their designe to oppose those Worthies by whose Authority they have acted and performed great and glorious things. I should have represented the sad condition wherein wee are, but having spoken something of LIBERTY the last week, lest I might be mistaken for a Libertine, I will begin this weeke with something concerning RELIGION.
>
> For this is the Bond by which we doe oblige our selves to God in a commanded obedience for the performance of holy Duties according to his Will and Word. I say commanded obedience, for should we fancy a Divine worship of our own, there would be as many Religions as men. . . . We should not therefore trust to our own darke and false and misguiding lights, but in submission unto order apply our selves to such Pastors and teachers, who presume not too much on private inspirations, but take paines to receive their light from the Counsels and Doctors of the Church, who for the suppressing of Ignorance and superstition have been famous in their Generation, and shall be forevermore.[18]

Even more pugnacious were a few anti-Independent asides which Collings inserted in the news, especially during the second half of 1646. He made it clear, if in passing, that he approved of the Scots' attempt to pressure the king into signing the Covenant and that he had faith in their good intentions and probity.[19] He also went out of his way to point out the merits of a Presbyterian settlement of the church.[20] Moreover, *The Kingdomes Weekly Intelligencer* gave a little more space to news that favored the Presbyterians than did *A Perfect Diurnall*. Then in the summer of 1647 Collings suddenly but briefly displayed a sympathy for the king — in strong contrast to his earlier militant anti-Royalism and to the growing clamor in the army for the punishment of Charles, that "man of blood." The editor reminded the soldiers to take proper care of the "Royall Person"; three times he included stories and comments that made much of the king's popularity; and once he advocated that Charles be returned to power.[21] At the same time he permitted himself a few criticisms of the New Model, including support for the eleven M.P.'s recently purged by the army high command.[22]

But Collings did not always paddle against the current. He not only wrote two editorials in praise of the army for occupying London, but most of his comments and asides pertained to events that were not the subject of immediate debate. For instance, he avoided any obiter dicta on the army's seizure of the king or its advance toward London, he was cautious when dealing with controversies inside Parliament, and his news items on the growing power of the Levellers were consistently straightforward. This expediency received striking articulation in August 1647, when even the most myopic crystal-ball-gazer could see the omens of renewed civil war:

> Peace now beginning to hover over us and to cover us againe with her silver wings, there can but little Action be expected; I have thought it therefore an expedient method . . . to give unto you day by day the most memorable Passages of other Kingdomes.[23]

And Collings followed this up with three pages of foreign news. Thereafter, however, the editor seldom sought any such escapist refuge.

Whether as an offshoot of his courage or his caution, Collings was one of the few editors to be recurrently and openly proud of himself. He pointed to his coherent and objective narration of a complicated political story, and he several times mentioned the importance of the events he was describing, simultaneously implying that his description was appropriate.[24] He suggested his own praiseworthy restraint by ending one issue with the remark that "wee will not this week touch pitch," and his own ability by beginning another with a boast that, if by no means unique, was more outspoken than those customarily uttered by his fellow journalists:

> There were never more pretenders to Truth than in this Age, nor ever fewer that obtained it. It is no easie matter in such a variety of actions and opinions to deliver exactly to the world the proceedings of these present times which, as they aske sound judgement, so withall they desire an extraordinary Intelligence. . . .[25]

Also, Collings' prose developed an added firmness, and sometimes a sparkle, usually lacking in other weeklies. In October 1646 Pecke, perhaps aware of this improvement, alleged that Birkenhead, "the trade of writing Aulicus at Court failing," had become "journey man to the Kingdomes Intelligencer." [26] Collings promptly denied this,[27] and there is no evidence to substantiate the charge. Even so, his style began to show a further gain in control and liveliness. From the mixings of one of his metaphors one can even learn something about the effervescence of seventeenth-century beer: the rumors spread by the Royalists, he wrote,

> can be resembled unto nothing better than the Beere in bottles which they [the Cavaliers] drinke: they bounce and fly up with the Corke, and of themselves extreamly run out, they foame and they froth; and if you have but the least patience to attend the event you shall find all their loud promises nothing but vapours. . . .[28]

Collings could now pen a graphic and gripping page about a multiple murder in London, another about an Anabaptist mother in Kent who killed her child — an action one might expect of a member of such a wild sect.[29] He also transmitted one of the better anecdotes of the Interregnum. Preceding it with the account of a drunk who drowned at Stratford, the editor shifted into more euphuistic prose to provide what is probably the earliest analogue to the first chapter of Thomas Hardy's *The Mayor of Casterbridge*:

> The other [story] was of a Yeoman not farre from Warwick who for want of discretion or other discourse would sell his wife to his Companion. He asked what he would take for her. The Yeoman answered five pound. The other looking on her (for she was present) and conceiving with himselfe that a good wife is worth gold, he thought that she was worth five pound . . . whereupon he presently layd down the money, and tooke his purchase in his Armes and kissed her. Not a quarter of an hour after, the Yeoman repented of his bargaine, and offered to restore the money, and desired to have his wife returned. His companion left it to her choyce, not without some intimation that he was loath to leave her. The good woman assured him that she was well content to live with him and had rather goe with the buyer than the seller, and accordingly expressing a courteous farewell to her Husband, she went along with his Companion. The poore Yeoman who (on better consideration) had rather lose his life than lose his wife, hath since made his complaint to all the Justices in that County, and because he cannot get her by love he is resolved to try if he can get her by law, and with extreame impatience attends the approach of the Tearme, intending at the very first sitting, if he can, to have his cause heard in Westminster Hall before the Judges of the Common Pleas.[30]

To find out what happened to the Yeoman one must turn to Hardy; Collings never told his readers what the Judges of the Common Pleas decided.

But he did reveal something about how an editor functioned. After the king's flight to the Scots news from the north was of particular importance. Heavy rains, however, marked the autumn of 1646, and on several Mondays, the day the post from the north was due, one can see Collings worrying about whether it would arrive before he had to put his paper to bed.[31] A year later, after the demise of *Mercurius Civicus*, the editor, to increase his depleted income, began to print an occasional advertisement, the first being a notice about three stolen horses.[32] He probably also made a few shillings by including now and then an item vindicating an individual or a private group, for which, like his colleagues who did the same thing, he almost certainly received a fee.[33] Moreover, Collings took a professional and sympathetic interest in the fact that Charles was often concerned about public relations. In two consecutive numbers *The Kingdomes Weekly Intelligencer* described how Buckley, the king's printer, first moved his press from York to Newcastle, and then was given space in the king's own residence, presumably so that his ear could be near the royal mouth.[34] Thereafter Collings added other details about Charles, such as his interest in the flowers at Holmby;[35] and each of these items suggests that the editor was sympathetic to the king and responsive to Royalist press-agentry.

Meanwhile, from June to December 1646, Collings continued to have a hand in *Mercurius Civicus*, though it progressively came to seem only his left hand. Politically his two papers followed the same general line, but in *Civicus* the editor's views were given less prominence. Here he indulged in fewer asides and comments and almost never in full-fledged editorials. During these six months, too, an increasingly tired quality permeated his second newspaper. One of the final numbers of *Civicus* was copied almost entirely from that week's *Intelligencer*,[36] and earlier the Thursday paper had leaned ever more heavily on its Tuesday companion. By the end of the year even the woodcuts on the title page, especially the oft-used picture of Charles, had a worn look.

But back in June 1646 *Civicus* was still very much alive. One number from that summer revived Collings' pastime of flinging mud at Dillingham, "the Man that ariseth with a thimble on his finger"; another poked fun at Henry Walker, who, Collings implied, was upside down in his thinking.[37] In fact, until its final month *Civicus*, better than the *Intelligencer*, showed that its editor had glimmerings of a sense of humor, and his anti-sectarian account of the rebaptism of a Hartfordshire woman is still amusing.[38] Moreover, *Civicus* continued to print more London news than other weeklies, its detailed accounts of the steps taken to control the plague in the city being timeless examples of good journalism.[39] Collings may even have reached the journalistic peak of his day in *Civicus*'s obituary on Essex, a piece that was at once nostalgic and dignified, personal and stately.[40] It appeared in September 1646. Three months later, after a steady decline, *Civicus* joined the former general.

The paper's demise had, however, an aura of mystery. In November, Collings thus concluded the news of the week:

I have travailed with my pen to satisfie the Kingdome, and let no man throw more durt upon me, which will be inhumanely done, for I have found the way (by so many yeares travaile) to be deep and troublesome enough, neither doe I hope will my old host be angry (although I hear he intends to stop my passage) if hereafter I shall lodge at the Heart, or the signe of the Kings-Head. But Signes are signes, and Hearts are hearts.[41]

Deciphered this passage probably means three things: that Collings or the publisher of *Civicus* was planning to shut down the paper before it was shut down; that Parliament ("my old host"), or some of its agents, had been threatening the editor; and that Collings was announcing his underlying allegiance to the monarchy.[42] The next number was the almost verbatim copy of *The Kingdomes Weekly Intelligencer*; then came a normal issue, followed by a gap of two weeks, and in December the final number.[43] This began with a statement that the editor was again "in health" (whether physical or journalistic was not specified) and that it was a "faire day"; it ended with a routine listing of recently appointed sheriffs. From now on Collings would have only one paper in which to speak his piece. *Mercurius Civicus*, the first illustrated and first pseudo-metropolitan newspaper, was dead, almost certainly a victim of induced suicide.

The Scotish Dove, after several vigorous shoves, also impaled itself on the suicide's sword at the end of 1646. But up to and including its final number the *Dove* continued to flap its wings, and one can detect much courage in Smith's efforts to reform a world he never made. Yet his paper did not cease to be windy, pietistic, confused, and smug, its smugness now more than ever that of the self-conscious martyr. In September, Smith was ordered by the House of Lords to apologize to the French ambassador for some slighting references to the king of France, and a copy of his paper was officially burned by the common hangman.[44] During the same month the editor found himself in trouble with the House of Commons, this time for his recurrent animadversions on various Parliamentary committees.[45] Thereafter he more frequently proclaimed that the age was dangerous and blasphemous.[46] A rise in the threats against him in November only confirmed his feeling of being persecuted.[47]

A martyr requires both persecution and a sense of mission. Smith to the very end viewed his newspaper as an instrument of reform,[48] and almost every number of *The Scotish Dove* during the last six months of 1646 devoted at least two pages to an editorial. Despite the garrulity, murkiness, and religiosity of these editorials, Smith made it clear that he opposed not only sin and disunity, but religious toleration and political innovation. To reinforce these views, he perforated his superficial accounts of the doings at Westminster with anti-Independent asides. Even so, the final number of *The Scotish Dove*, which came out near Christmas after a month's hiatus, announced Smith's exit from journalism with more of a whimper than a bang. What bang there was consisted of a comparatively brief (for Smith) bragging apologia and a fairly lengthy (for anyone) reiteration of his views against Parliamentary graft, sectarian heresies, and Independent politics. The whimper consisted of bits of self-pity, of a long passage commiserating with the *Dove* for having to compete not only with a hostile *Zeitgeist* but with many weeklies, and of several pages of breast-beating over the plight of good men in a sinful world. From now on, that sinful world would no longer have Smith to invoke and provoke it. As an editor he had been consistently mediocre, and he was more a leech than a gadfly on the body politic. Yet his departure would create a small gap in the evolution of early journalism.

John Dillingham, having had his *Parliament Scout* shot from under him, was not, if he could help it, going to follow George Smith into silence. Consequently the contents of his remaining paper, *The Moderate Intelligencer*, came progressively closer to living up, or down, to the title. In the summer of 1646 Dillingham was still moving parallel to and on the left of the political fence, not straddling it. But that he was about to was hinted in this opening paragraph of a June issue:

So much exceptions are taken by one or other that we know not what to say, or hardly what to narrate. One while the Presbyterians threaten, then the Independents and others. In time of this nature its not good to hold Argument, only ask Questions. How long that will be is uncertain. Some guess by the end of next winter the sharpest of winds will have blown . . . away.[49]

Though "some" guessed incorrectly, Dillingham for the next five numbers followed his own advice and asked questions, before returning to intermittent editorials. From June to September the questions and then the editorials still tended toward Independency, but they became increasingly less outspoken. In November, discussing the controversial issue of tithes, the editor neatly balanced the pros and cons; and in the following year he had the effrontery, or its exact opposite, to claim that the actions of Parliament were not his concern.[50] But the best evidence that Dillingham was now tailoring a more cautious newspaper was the greater space he gave to foreign news. In July 1646 he once devoted five of his twelve pages to non-English affairs.[51] By the end of the year this had risen, on occasion, to seven or eight; and in August 1647 he set a record for the newspaper of domestic news: approximately ten pages of overseas material.[52]

In addition, Dillingham became more proficient in hedging. Apparently he was criticized for commenting on the evils of free quarter for certain regiments; he responded by praising the army and justifying its needs.[53] He now more carefully qualified his belief in religious toleration and his vague hopes for a broadly based form of government, justifying his shift toward conservative journalism with this remark on the worries of an editor:

No man . . . but will be apt to speake the most and best of what he likes and conceal the worst, and . . . though men readily affirme where there is nothing to ground, yet they will often adde, which if made publique and falling into the hands of men either disaffected to the thing or publisher, they presently grow angry with him. . . .[54]

And Dillingham went on to suggest that the newspaper's function was to purvey only ascertained news — in time of trouble the equivalent of official news. Under the pressure of circumstances he had contracted a severe case of respectability.

Yet *The Moderate Intelligencer* retained a few flashes of the old Dillingham. For instance, in commenting on the negotiations for the departure of the Scottish army, he remarked that "Mony answers all things," and that if the men were paid they would gladly go home.[55] (He later anticipated Samuel Johnson by mentioning the Scots' natural reluctance to leave "bonny England.") [56] Despite his interest in maintaining his non-London circulation, Dillingham made a sharp comment on the lack of political sophistication among rural Englishmen: "Tell a country man, here's a Petition that you may have this good [established] or that evill taken off, he swallows the pill in that sugar." [57] Moreover, the editor was often more concerned than his colleagues about such mundane matters as the price of corn; nor did he seem at all perturbed that Charles, now a prisoner of the army, missed having a tennis court.[58] But the most poignant number of *The Moderate Intelligencer* is the one that appeared on August 12, 1647, after skipping its first week in more than two years, for it vividly if indirectly shows the old Dillingham being swallowed up by the new. The paper opened dramatically: "And why not last week! was it a time to write or to pray and weep? They that live a few years may possibly say such a week was ominous. . . . Was it not easy to see, yea to foresee, what would come?" Then followed a brief and breathless account of the army's occupation of London, an account suggestive of tension and excitement, and also of the fact that Dillingham was shocked at the spectacle of naked power on the march. But the remaining seven pages dwindled into a summary of events on the other, less turbulent, side of the English Channel.

Even more poignant is the short story of Daniel Border's temporary demise in the summer of 1647. At the end of March a new weekly, *The Perfect Weekly Account*, was licensed to appear on Wednesday, the day on which Border's *The Weekly Account* had been coming out. In May and June, Border tried to meet this competition by adding "Perfect" to his title and issuing his weekly without a license. But in July he was briefly pushed from the journalistic scene, remaining in the wings until October. A probable victim of the censors' jitters, he was at that time neither sufficiently skillful nor courageous to deserve such officially endorsed competition.

From June 1646 through April 1647 *The Weekly Account* had gone on being second-rate. Border's few quasi-editorials were noncommittal and he recurrently sought refuge in facile optimism. His treatment of the Levellers, for instance, was markedly brief and neutral; and he could seem to praise the king without antagonizing the anti-Royalists: "We shall for brevity sake omit the number of people that resorted to his Majesty for cure of the Evill." [59] The editor also frequently omitted items that might have been hard to handle, a habit which was not the result of ignorance, since he seems to have had occasional entry into Westminster.[60] It is therefore difficult to explain why any censor wished to silence him; nor do the two months during which his paper came out under an expanded title supply an answer. Border made no significant alterations in his version of *The Perfect Weekly Account*, which at the end of June, without any preliminary death rattle, slid into oblivion.[61]

Yet this minor mystery is complicated by two factors. The first is that a 1649 Royalist referred to the editor of the licensed *Perfect Weekly Account* as B.D., perhaps a cruelly ironic reversal of Border's initials.[62] The second is that B.D.'s paper was essentially like Border's. The intruder had the advantage of bearing the censor's imprimatur, and it provided a slightly fuller coverage of official news. Otherwise it too was noncommittal, glibly optimistic, and generally characterless. After Border had dropped out of the unfair competition, however, it began to show a few signs of personality and increased competence, even if by September it had not graduated from mediocrity. Then in October 1647, to bring the wheel full circle, Border for three months took over, or had a hand in, the editorship of this rival *Perfect Weekly Account*.[63]

There is also a slight mystery concerning the editorship of *Perfect Occurrences*. In January 1647 it changed its full title, though "Perfect Occurrences" remained the key words, and added the statement that it was edited by Luke Harruney.[64] But "Luke Harruney" turned out to be an anagram for Henry Walker; and Walker, in October when the paper

again underwent a minor change in title, acknowledged his authorship.[65] Yet as Luke Harruney he denied having had any role in the
earlier *Perfect Occurrences*.[66] Since Walker was not noted for his
honesty, since technically "Luke Harruney" was a "new" editor, and
since the paper displayed a high degree of continuity, it is extremely
likely that Walker was merely disguising the fact that he was carrying
on at his old stand. In any case, the paper's content, political orientation,
and style remained largely unchanged, though the editor now showed
less inclination to lard his prose with classical allusions. The dominant
characteristic of *Perfect Occurrences* was still its crowdedness, which
enabled it to give almost as much news as *A Perfect Diurnall*, plus a
variety of items that Pecke saw fit to omit.

In these nonofficial items, particularly certain local and human-interest
stories, there is also a strong suggestion of continuity, as well as of a
sharp nose for news. Thus *Perfect Occurrences* achieved two journalistic "firsts": the first newspaper to refer to golf (the king at Newcastle
enjoying new clothes, books on religion, and hitting a ball toward a
hole); and the first to contain a hit-and-run story ("A Surly Drayman
with his Dray bruised a child in Woodstreet. . . . He ran away, and
left Horse, Cart, and Barrels . . ."; the child, reported the following
number, recovered).[67] Walker also included the story of some Parliamentary cannon at Bristol firing at glowworms, and the anecdote of a
sad little apothecary who was knighted by Charles and whose wife
asked, "Have they no body to make a fool on but my husband?" [68]
Moreover, *Perfect Occurrences* printed one of the more intriguing
pieces about contemporary theatrical productions, in this case that
plays, in the spring of 1647, were being acted in the London suburb of
Knightsbridge. Such notices were not rare, but this one implied, probably unwittingly, that part of the audience was made up of officers from
the New Model.[69] Then, too, Walker could go out of his way to set up
a pun: a presumably buxom woman, "being pressed to tell what her
bosome sin was," smote the man who asked and replied "Anger." [70]
Finally, *Perfect Occurrences* may indicate Walker's guidance in its
skepticism toward stories of witches and miracles, a skepticism which
the editor had recently been displaying with more consistency than
most of his colleagues. In one number, for example, he mentioned that
the witch-hunters of Hereford were interested in blood, not in suppressing sin; and he suggested that the Kentish practice of throwing
alleged witches into a river to see if they would drown was foolish.[71]

Notwithstanding these scattered spots of warmth and sophistication,
a generally colorless style and conventional content kept Walker's
weekly typical. Also typical was its political tiptoeing. The editor's

inclinations toward Independency became subdued until the actual approach of the army toward London; for in the winter of 1646–47, even if one anticipated an Independent victory, he had to recognize that the city mob, as well as the majority in Parliament, were generally zealous in their support of Presbyterianism. In addition, three times that winter and early spring the House of Lords took an ominous interest in Walker's paper.[72] As a result, he now played things safe, though he did allow himself an occasional dig at the Presbyterians, including one reference to their party in Parliament as the "Herastians." [73] He also, without ever going too far, gave the Levellers more space than any other immediately contemporary editor. In so doing he stayed nonpartisan but basically sympathetic to Lilburne and his cause.[74] On the other hand, he had little good to say about sects, and much bad about the impropriety of delving too far into state secrets and disseminating officially unwelcome news.[75] Further, as the political tension mounted, Walker indulged in fewer asides and comments. When he did venture an opinion, even after the army had occupied London, it was likely to be more muted than it would have been a year earlier.[76]

A Perfect Diurnall for years had occupied the Monday niche, so Friday's *Perfect Occurrences* was not in direct competition with Pecke. But for about three months in the autumn of 1647 the enterprising Walker, or an editor remarkably like him, attempted to encounter Pecke head-on. This competing newspaper, *A Perfect Summary Of Chief Passages in Parliament*, was sufficiently similar to the now muted *Perfect Occurrences* to suggest either the same editorial hand or the hand of a man equally resolved to stay in business. The result was a relatively colorless but crowded and efficient compilation of largely official news. On October 6, after eleven numbers, *A Perfect Summary* left the Monday field to Pecke.[77]

If Walker or his equivalent could compete with Pecke on Monday, so might Pecke or his equivalent compete with Walker on Friday. This explains why *A Continuation of certaine Speciall and Remarkable Passages* once again appeared on the streets of London. Possibly edited by Pecke, the eight numbers between mid-July and mid-September 1647 which constituted this paper's last gasp relied on official and semi-official handouts. By means of omissions and platitudes the editor avoided both the controversial and the personal. *A Continuation* may have been resilient, but it now had little bounce.

The heavy pressures toward conformity during the first three-quarters of 1647 are even more clearly revealed in a newcomer that also survived less than three months. In December 1646 Thomas Audley re-entered the fray in a weekly entitled *Diutinus Britanicus*, which, after two numbers, pointedly changed its name to *Mercurius Diutinus* (*not Britanicus*).[78] For its first eight issues this was a zestful paper consisting of half opinion and railing, half news. Often vigorous, personal, even semi-facetious, it briefly takes one back to the days when *Aulicus* and *Britanicus* were pommeling each other — and Audley's anti-Royalism here measured up to Nedham's. Audley also achieved the most Rabelaisian moment of his day when he described the vast menu purportedly consumed by the Russian ambassador to the Netherlands.[79] Then came the hangover. For its final three numbers Audley's newspaper joined the herd, and as a straight newsman the editor turned out to be pedestrian. Despite the fact that "Diutinus" means long-lasting, this mercury, without fanfare or loss, slipped out of the picture in February 1647.

Its course, as well as its life-span, was approximately duplicated by another brief revival: *The London Post*, the first number of which appeared in December, the seventh and last in February. For two issues it managed to be comparatively lively, then it too subsided into typicality. In fact, the editor, probably the same man who in late 1645 and early 1646 had gained journalistic experience as the author of *The Citties Weekly Post*, was well aware that independence — with a small "i" — would be difficult to attain. He started out confidently enough in the opening paragraph of *The London Post*'s first number:

> Thus wet and weary as he is, the CITY POST doth againe present himselfe unto you. You see him in his old Garbe still: His habiliments though coarse . . . are sound: His language still the same, neither in the change of time can he change his Temper. After almost a years absence he comes on his old Errand, which is to bring you weekly Intelligence, and this (for the most part) being . . . elaborately sought, he doth hope will prove more acceptable. . . .

But the second number did not come out until three weeks later, during which time the editor claimed he was suffering from a fever, a sickness which "doth much represent the Estate in which this Kingdome is." [80] And then, in the most cogent analysis of the journalist's plight yet to appear, he thus concluded his diagnosis of England's sickness:

> But the present times are not so fit for Relations, and this is one reason that hath much discouraged me from undertaking this Taske, for the Warres being happily concluded, which before yeilded Theame enough, I doe find that whosoever undertakes to write weekly in this nature, undertakes to sayle down a narrow Channell, where all along the shore on each side are Rocks and Cliffs that threaten him; and though for the present one side seems not so full of sands or Dangers as the other, and therefore many of us (whether out of love or conscience I know not) do seem to lean to that side most,

yet who knows not but that new tides may rise, and the rolling sands may remove unto the other shore. He onely is the happy steersman that can keep his course in the middle of the channell. . . .[81]

Thereafter he did his best to stay in mid-channel, being especially careful not to steer too close to those Presbyterian sirens for whose embraces he seemingly yearned.[82] Despite such cautious navigation, and despite the editor's newly acquired skill in presenting the news functionally, *The London Post* stayed afloat only two months.

Between June 1646 and September 1647 only one other nonestablished London newspaper managed to keep its head above water for as many as seven numbers. *The Moderne Intelligencer*, which came out during August and September 1647, used the life preserver of devoting from one-half to two-thirds of its space to foreign news. Moreover, the editor plugged his ears against the allurements of Royalist voices, though he never sang out loudly against them.[83] Relying more on omission than compression, he was able to achieve a moderate and unassuming tone as well as an adequate résumé of home news. But even this *via media* was not easy to follow, and he complained that news from the continent was "for the most part delivered with so much difficulty and paine that the interpreter himselfe knowes not many times what it is, [and] needs a Midwife to expound [it] unto the world." [84] It is tempting and not implausible to see here the hand of Nathaniel Butter, in difficult times trying again to be a "moderne intelligencer."

And the times were difficult. Some established papers, such as *The Scotish Dove* and *Mercurius Civicus*, disappeared, while others fell into step. Five new or revived weeklies each had a life expectancy of a mere two or three months. Moreover, during this period only nine additional newspapers tried to gain a hearing, and the longest lived lasted three issues. Yet the publishers and editors of most of these newcomers intended them to have a long life, and consequently they were usually properly staffed, licensed, and emasculated.

In June 1646 the first of these abortive births, *The Packet of Letters*, sought the anonymity of a reliance on letters, including one from London. The paper came out once.[85] The next two attempts to found a newspaper took place in October. *A Continuation of Papers from the Scotts Quarters* had one editorial point to make, that the Scots should leave England and go home; and one way to make it, a variety of letters from the north of England showing why.[86] That the lot of even a quasi-correspondent for a London newspaper was not a happy one is made clear in one of these letters:

Wee writ so much about the sufferings of our Country that we have writ our selves both out of work and out of credit, out of worke because wee have writ so much before that we cannot well write any more now, out of credit because what we supposed to be true [the burden of the Scots on northern England] . . . is hardly yet beleeved by many.[87]

This letter-writer would, in any case, soon have been out of work as a journalist: in mid-November, after three numbers, *Papers from the Scotts Quarters* was discontinued. The second October entry, *The Military Actions of Europe*, lasted only two issues, though it carefully divided its pages between a summary of foreign news and a superficial account of events at Westminster.[88]

In November a weekly named *Mercurius Candidus* appeared once. It featured a bitter attack on drink and women, praise of Fairfax, and a story from France which showed that Shakespeare was an inferior playwright.[89] In January 1647 it tried again, this time giving more news though still retaining outcroppings of the editor's contentious personality. This number had no successor. In the same month two undated issues of what can scarcely be called a newspaper were put out — and then, almost certainly, put out of business by the censor. *Englands Remembrancer of Londons Integritie. Or Newes from London: Of which all that fear God or have any desire of the Peace and safety of this Kingdome ought to be truely Informed* in a sense adhered to its title. The first number, in eight over-size pages, assailed the Independents and equated Presbyterianism with patriotism. The second, in twelve normal-size pages, kept to the same course, adding an attack on other newspapers and a violent diatribe against sects. Having spoken his piece, the editor was probably glad to receive the satisfaction of being suppressed.

None of the four remaining short-run newcomers attempted to flout or entrap the authorities. In February a paper again and appropriately named *The Moderate Messenger* bowed out after a single inoffensive issue. For four months no new weekly appeared, until in June 1647 a different *Mercurius Britanicus* briefly tried the journalistic stream. Generally neutral, if with a slight pro-army slant, this adequate weekly seemed to have as much buoyancy as most established papers. Yet after only three weeks it sank. So did the properly cautious *The Armies Post*, which rose to the surface on a lone Thursday in July. Finally, at the end of that month *A Diarie* for two numbers resurrected the unaggressive *Diary* that had quietly expired early in 1646.

In September 1647 the picture changed. The army, now in control of London, was being pushed to the right by the Presbyterians in Parliament and on urban and rural street corners, and pulled to the left by the radicals in the army and on urban street corners. When Fairfax, in the name of the New Model, took over censorship of the press, the high command was in a precarious position. Cromwell in particular was exposed to noisy criticism from both right and left, and he did nothing to placate his critics by persisting in devious negotiations with Charles. Under the circumstances military control of the press might well be indecisive and ineffective.

CHAPTER VIII

COMING OF AGE

September 1647 to June 1648

ON September 20, 1647, Fairfax sent this tactfully firm letter to the Speaker of the House of Lords:

> I have sent inclosed some Printed Pamphlets, that are not only very scandalous and abusive to this Army in particular, but indeed to the whole Kingdome in general. My Desire is, That these and all of the like Nature may be suppressed for the future; and yet, That the Kingdom's Expectation may be satisfied in relation to Intelligence, till a firm Peace be settled . . . That (if the House shall see fit) some Two or Three Sheets may be permitted to come out Weekly, which may be licensed, and have some Stamp of Authority with them; and in respect the former Licencer Mr. Mabbott hath approved himself faithful in that Service of Licence, and likewise in the Service of the House and of this Army, I humbly desire that he may be restored and continued in the said Place of Licencer.[1]

The Lords saw fit, and on September 30 Mabbott was appointed chief censor of the press, a job which he held until May 1649. From the start it was a ticklish position. He owed his place to the army, was appointed by the Lords, and was held responsible by the Commons.[2] Moreover, ex-newspaperman Mabbott developed a dislike of censorship and soon became a leading spokesman for the Levellers. Not only were Fairfax's instructions loose in not demanding a complete suppression of news, but his candidate for licenser turned out to be a misfit.

Seven months before Mabbott's appointment the Commons had set up a committee to stem the flood of "scandalous and abusive" pamphlets.[3] It failed, as did similar committees, for in 1647 and 1648 about 2,500 pamphlets, most of them concerned with politics, were published.[4] Meanwhile, in March 1647, Rushworth and his deputy Mabbott had been dismissed as censors. Then at the end of September Parliament passed a new ordinance to regulate the press. It defined the new censor's responsibilities and provided him with punitive powers. These included heavier fines and sentences for transgressing editors, printers, publishers, and booksellers, while any hawker caught peddling an unlicensed newspaper could be "whipt as a Common Rogue." [5] The breakdown of this ordinance is evident in the saga of London journalism from September 1647 to June 1648. By then the New Model was again shooting at Royalists and moving north to battle the Scots. By then Cromwell was much closer to being elevated to power, Charles to being lowered to the executioner's block.

On the fringes of England's march toward renewed civil war an active game of cops and robbers went on, the censors playing the part of cops, the gang of new Royalist weeklies that of robbers. In fact, one of the reasons for Fairfax's letter was that shortly before he wrote it the first of these flamboyant Royalist weeklies, *Mercurius Melancholicus*, was for sale on the streets of London. Probably costing two pence because of the danger of selling it, *Melancholicus* was the earliest of many mercuries that, by thumbing its nose at the government, irritated Parliament and army, then made inevitable the full crackdown on the press in the autumn of 1649. Until that time the story of the Royalist weeklies is confusing and exciting. Repeatedly an editor would be caught and jailed, then escape and return to his job. Meanwhile a crony or competitor would continue his paper. Nor were counterfeiting and cutthroat rivalry among these pro-Royalist journalists eliminated because they shared the same general views and specific risks. Even so, most of them were adroit in preserving their anonymity, and their small presses were easy to hide. Consequently the cops had a hard time.

Mercurius Melancholicus got the game started, though the paper's first number was by no means clear-cut. One of its opening paragraphs was scarcely calculated to please the Cavaliers, and it was sure to offend the anti-Royalists:

The King now shall enjoy his owne againe and the Royall throne shall

be arraied with the glorious presence of that mortall Diety, but first let him
beare his charge, for 'tis said, his armies having lost the field, theil now
charge him home: there's a trivial thing called the innocent blood of three
kingdomes is first to be required and a few more such sleight matters and
then let him enjoy it if he can. . . .[6]

The ambiguous editor of this first issue was a Presbyterian minister,
John Hackluyt.[7] Whether or not he was descended from the Elizabethan geographer, he had recently crossed his own Rubicon: a chaplain
in the Parliamentary army, like many of his co-religionists he turned
Royalist when the revolution seemed to be getting out of hand.[8]

  Mercurius Melancholicus was promptly counterfeited, if "counterfeit" can apply to anything as protean as the Royalist press during the
later 1640's. Often, too, it was not written by Hackluyt but by Martin
Parker, the most famous ballad-writer of the period.[9] Parker probably
objected to Hackluyt's appropriation of his already famous phrase
"When the King Enjoys His Own Again"; he certainly objected to
Hackluyt's qualified Royalism. So did a second ballad-writer, John
Crouch, who also put out a *Mercurius Melancholicus*.[10] Though for
most of the paper's thirteen-month existence there was only one weekly
claimant to the title, during eight scattered weeks there were two, and
on a few occasions three. In all likelihood Parker more and more frequently took over as Hackluyt reconsidered his position or languished
in jail. But between September 1647 and June 1648 they seem to have
split the job, with Parker writing those numbers that were most violently anti-Scot and anti-Presbyterian, as well as those that showed
some literary dexterity. Hackluyt could not, for instance, have penned
this epitaph for the Westminster Assembly:

> Here lyes a whore, he's a knave does deny it,
> The worme of Conscience makes her lye unquiet:
> A villanous enemy to my Lord Mitre,
> But an intimate friend of Sir John Presbyter;
> Geneva begat her, being young she grew pocky,
> And after was married to a blithe lad call'd Jocky:
> One daughter she had (be it spoke to her glory)
> Just like to her mother, call'd Directory;
> But ere she was borne, the wanton began
> To be enamour'd of a Parliament-man;
> He loved her well, and fed her with Mammon,
> Till from all modesty she grew to be common;
>   So she lived in sin, and dyed unsound,
>   And now Mrs. Synod doth stinke above ground.[11]

Despite any change in editors, the content and format of *Melanchol-*

icus, and of its counterfeits, remained fairly constant. Usually it began with a rhymed lament for the good old days. Then came half-a-dozen pages of negative news and scurrility, much of it in purple prose, interspersed with bits of verse and Latin. Generally the paper concluded with a plea for the return of the king to power and the church to respectability. That *Melancholicus* was often pitched to a shriek and always sloppily printed are both understandable, since it was constantly on the run. Hackluyt was caught and jailed late in 1647, and in the spring and summer of 1648 he again found himself behind bars. Yet he and Parker took delight in taunting their pursuers, in one case expressing ostensible indignation that only £20 was offered for the capture of "Melancholicus." [12] Among the more zealous of these pursuers was Henry Walker, a man who consistently exacerbated the Royalist journalists.

Though Parker and Hackluyt, and on occasion Crouch, accused each other of being inept interlopers, they agreed on the targets of their dislike, including Walker.[13] First on their list were the Independents, with Cromwell bearing the brunt of their contumely, and increasingly bearing it on his nose — one of the favorite butts of Royalist mud-slinging.[14] Second were the Levellers, those fiery partisans of religious anarchy and political egalitarianism:

> No more a beggar under bush,
> No more a lowzie-Varlet:
> The Pedler now shall praunce in Plush,
> And Scoundrel march in Scarlet.[15]

Indeed it was they, *Melancholicus* reiterated, who with their fellow conspirators in the army were contriving to murder the king. Third on *Melancholicus*'s list was Parliament, closely followed by the Westminster Assembly and by London. In Parker's numbers the Presbyterians and sometimes the Scots were not far behind. The editors regularly tried to play off these groups against each other, using atrocity stories, personal attacks, innuendo, exaggeration, and alarm, and several times calling on the people to rise up and smite the army. Consistency was not a virtue in this disruptive campaign, and Parker and Hackluyt were willing to sleep with such bedfellows as Lilburne and Fairfax whenever it seemed functional.

The second of the three "grand" Royalist weeklies of 1647–48 was *Mercurius Pragmaticus*, which first appeared on September 21. It was edited by two minor poets and by the most professional of Interregnum newspapermen. Marchamont Nedham was back in journalism. Though politically antipodal to *Mercurius Britanicus*, *Pragmaticus* resembled it in that it too was a product of collaboration. Samuel Sheppard, a writer of verse and satires and at one time a member of the clergy, lent a regular hand and was probably responsible for starting the paper.[16] John Cleveland, a more famous poet, worked with Sheppard, though he was sufficiently well known to have to lie especially low.[17] In 1645 Cleveland's attack on the weekly press, *The Character of a London Diurnall*, had angered Nedham; now times had changed. After his arrest in 1646, Nedham turned to the practice of medicine, but when he picked up his scalpel he did not drop his pen. In that summer he wrote a refutation of two of the more reactionary anti-tolerationists; and, a year later, two Hobbesian pamphlets, one a clever plea showing why various groups should ally themselves with the Independents, the other a resounding justification of the army.[18] And for sixteen months he kept his promise to stay out of journalism. Then, probably having been personally reconciled with the king and having arranged adequate financial sponsorship, Nedham became the Royalists' most effective propagandist.[19] (The style and skill of *Pragmaticus* indicate that he was its chief contributor during its first year; and his publication in 1661 of *A Short History of the English Rebellion* confirms his role, for 252 of its 256 four-line stanzas were taken from the title-page poems that adorned the paper.) The articulate Nedham always had evidence to show his allegiance to whatever cause he espoused.[20]

Now he espoused Charles, and with the aid of Sheppard and Cleveland he made *Pragmaticus* a thorn in the sides of Parliament and army. The thorn festered, for Nedham had a pipeline to Westminster that supplied him with information not only from the floor of the House of Commons but from cloakroom and caucus.[21] For this reason *Pragmaticus* is probably the newspaper of the later 1640's most valuable to historians, and it can dispel any notion that the politicians of three centuries ago were unsophisticated.

Superficially *Pragmaticus* resembled *Melancholicus*, especially those numbers edited by Parker. Both papers were defiant, scurrilous, and hasty — and both were bothered with counterfeits.[22] *Pragmaticus*, however, contained more news, was sprightlier, and adhered to a negative party line more regularly. Nedham and his colleagues, though willing to praise anyone who went after the Independents, never showed any real liking for the Presbyterians; and when the editors saluted the Scots with one hand, they held their nose with the other. *Pragmaticus* often indulged in praise of the Levellers, but made it clear that it had no enthusiasm for democracy, and that should Lilburne ever stop battling the Grandees, the editors would throw him to the dogs — where he belonged.[23] A title-page poem of one of the early numbers thus glibly summed up the paper's conservative view of recent English history:

> A Scot and Jesuite, joyn'd in hand,
> First taught the world to say,
> That Subjects ought to have Command,
> And Princes to obey.
>
> These both agreed to have no King,
> The Scotch-man he cries further,
> No Bishop; 'Tis a godly thing
> States to reforme by Murther.
>
> Then th' Independent, meeke and slie,
> Most lowly lies at Lurch,
> And so to put poore Jockie by
> Resolves to have No Church.
>
> The King Dethron'd! The Subjects bleed!
> The Church hath no aboad;
> Let me conclude, They're all agreed,
> That sure there is No God.[24]

But since *Pragmaticus* was uncensored, had access to Westminster, and little to lose, it gave its readers more than a barrage or scurrility; and Nedham was the editor of the day best equipped to play the role of an anti-Puritan Cassandra. He knew what was going on and was shrewd and experienced enough to predict with a high degree of accuracy what was in the offing. For instance, his commentary on Cromwell's impending disposal of the Levellers and their associates, the army "Agitators," was penetrating:

And thus his [Cromwell's] dear Democraticks being left all in the suds, his face is now more toward an Aristocracie than Zion, which hath raised a deadly feud betwixt him and the Adjutators, who looke upon him as fallen from grace; especially since he hath used all his wit and power in the Army to suppresse them, now that he has served his ends upon them.[25]

As early as October 1647 Nedham was cynically but accurately predicting Pride's Purge and Cromwell's subsequent troubles with Parliament:

But Mr. Crumwel hath them [Parliament] in the Mill, and grind they must, seeing that they are at his Beck who holds a Whip and a Bell over their guilty Heads. . . . So that when he hath used them long enough under the name of a Parliament, then (perhaps) they shall be disbanded severall waies, that the Sword-men may stand for ever. . . .[26]

Nedham also anticipated the Second Civil War and the events of the early 1650's, as in this prophecy in the spring of 1648:

Yet I believe that Scots will be right honest . . . touching the person of the King; but I feare they may put a Slur upon us in this after-Game, in laboring to foist in their Presbytery, with its Appurtenances. . . . Then let the English looke to themselves . . . for if it bee to bee brought in upon his Majestie's shoulders, upon pretence of restoring him, I suppose his Crowne and dignity is but in little more danger now he remaines in Caris-brooke Castle [as a captive of the English army] than if his person were in Edinburgh. . . .[27]

Then, too, Nedham gave his readers a good many peeks at the machinations of a successful political faction. *Pragmaticus* told how the Independents used private pressures to get an impressively large at-tendance at certain sessions of the House of Commons; how they practiced open intimidation, clever delay, and blackmail to win a Par-liamentary majority; and how, to sell their case to the public, Cromwell and his cronies employed sermons, troop movements, and manufactured plots.[28] The resultant if inadvertent impression of political skill on the part of the Independents was substantiated by Nedham's scathing vi-gnettes of their leaders.[29] If one looks at the London scene of 1647–48 through the lens of *Pragmaticus*, he sees a grimy landscape flecked with graft, violence, and cruel ambition. It is a distorted view, but it was well drawn and included objects and shadings that no other journal could manage.

The third long-run Royalist weekly of the later 1640's, *Mercurius Elencticus*, got under way November 5, 1647. Edited by a pugnacious astrologer, George Wharton, its prophecies were far less reliable than Nedham's. Wharton was assisted by Samuel Sheppard and other Royal-ist journalists, especially in the spring of 1648 when the editor was caught and jailed.[30] Indeed, only in giving vent to the excitement of the chase was *Elencticus* as lively as *Melancholicus* and *Pragmaticus*. Wharton explained a gap of four weeks by the fact that the censorial dogs were hot on his trail, and he abruptly concluded one issue by announcing that he had suddenly been "forced to slip aside." [31] He also provided some graphic details about the government's efforts to catch offending writers and printers: thirty spies, Wharton reported, had been appointed by Parliament to track down hostile books and news-papers, and for this they were paid £52 10s. a week, or, he added almost correctly, £2756 a year.[32] But despite the thrill of the hunt, *Elencticus* was at first dull. It could be as vigorous as *Melancholicus* and *Pragmat-icus* in its denunciations of Cromwell and as reverential to the king, and it too could display divisive anecdotes and ugly vignettes. Yet it had no pipeline to Westminster, and Wharton's style was long-winded, his poetry feeble, and his classical lore intrusive. Often he filled his pages with polemical astrology, sometimes being more concerned with derogating the star-gazers associated with Parliament than with supporting Charles. For instance, Wharton predicted that June 28, 1648, would be a fatal day for the anti-Royalists; then when it came around he had to engage in nimble footwork to show he had not really been wrong.[33] Wharton was also interested in genealogy, and he made the most of the low pedigrees of the New Model leaders.[34]

Melancholicus, *Pragmaticus*, and *Elencticus* quickly spawned a host of imitations, most of them short lived, plus an even shorter-lived smattering of anti-Royalist replies. (Appendix E is a list of those newspapers from September 1647 to the end of 1648 that lasted fewer than five numbers.) In September 1647 the one number of *Mercurius Anti-Melancholicus* happily called down a plague on all houses, but a lesser one on the Royalists; while *Mercurius Clericus* in its single issue gloomily turned to the cause of Charles as the only cure for England's ills. In the same month *Mercurius Morbicus*, possibly edited by Henry Walker, used most of its two numbers to attack *Melancholicus*, rail at Royalists, and indirectly support the army. In October *Mercurius Medicus*, also possibly by Walker, devoted its two issues to castigating Royalist editors. In November a revived *Mercurius Rusticus* put the onus for the plight of rural England on the army, and in December its second and final number pleaded for lower taxes. Toward the end of the year *Mercurius Populus* filled its eight pages with a history of oppression from Roman times to November 11, 1647, winding up with a class-conscious defense of democracy. *Mercurius Insanus Insanissimus* in March and April 1648 for three weeks berated Parliament and army, achieving unconventionality mainly in its title. In April the one number of a resurrected *Mercurius Academicus* gave loaded details of a Parliamentary visitation of and on Oxford. And in April and May *Mercurius Veridicus* briefly reappeared on the streets of London, this time on the Royalist side.

The spring and early summer of 1648 represented the high point of Royalist journalism. Nine separate anti-government weeklies appeared in May, eight in June. Of these *Mercurius Gallicus* was distinctive because it identified the cause of French Protestantism with that of English Royalism; *Mercurius Poeticus* because its one number attempted to rhyme its news and views; *The Parliaments Scrich-Owle* because, after one issue entirely in verse, the editor had the good sense to shift partly to prose in his two remaining weeks; and *Westminster Projects* because its two numbers suggest the hand of Nedham. Meanwhile the anti-Royalists were not silent. *Mercurius Anti-Mercurius* in three scattered issues dissected leading Royalist editors. Twice in May *Mercurius*

Honestus tried dialogue to convey its anti-Royalism. And in June *Mercurius Censorius* used irony to deflate the Royalist weeklies. Such were the short-lived offspring of *Melancholicus*, *Pragmaticus*, and *Elencticus*.

But they also produced a litter of more durable children, two of them illegitimate, four of them legitimate. The first of these journalistic bastards, *Mercurius Anti-Pragmaticus*, came out nine times between October 1647 and February 1648. Edited by a man who claimed to be an Oxford graduate,[35] it patterned itself on the Royalist mercuries and devoted almost half its space to noisy refutation of *Pragmaticus*. Yet in the remaining pages the editor walked carefully, doing his best to alienate neither Presbyterian nor Independent and attacking the king's evil advisors rather than the institution of monarchy and the person of Charles. Moreover, he viewed the Levellers, now often the recipients of lukewarm Royalist embraces, with conservative horror, a horror which he tried to transmit to his fellow citizens:

> For John Lilburne hath new designes on foot to split all in pieces, for he is resolved to appeale to all the Commons of England . . . to set them to cutting throats again, and to see what the private souldiers of the Army, the hobnails and clouted shoes, will do for him; for this grand incendiary, finding not his wishes accomplished, will attempt with Cataline to fire the city about our ears, and to give his undertakings the fairer glosse, he furbisheth them continually with exclamations against the Parliament and the Officers of the Army.[36]

The second illegitimate offspring, *Mercurius Britanicus*, also modeled itself on *Aulicus*'s successors, just as its namesake had modeled itself on *Aulicus*. For thirteen numbers from May to August 1648 the new *Britanicus*, complete with title-page poems and scattered verse, attacked the Royalist press and the supporters of Charles.[37] Edited by John Hall, a graduate of Cambridge and according to contemporary gossip a dissolute young fellow,[38] it achieved a peak in the hyperbole of refutation when it characterized Henry Marten, a member of Parliament equally notorious for his republicanism and whore-mongering, as the "English Brutus." [39]

If *Britanicus* could be resurrected, so could *Aulicus*. But before this happened John Birkenhead also rejoined the living, now as editor of one of the four longer-lived legitimate offspring of the "grand" Royalist mercuries. *Mercurius Bellicus* was clever and belligerent, and its two dozen numbers between November 1647 and July 1648 displayed Birkenhead's touch in setting the components of the Parliamentary coalition at odds.[40] The editor was still adept in using the lie, the half-truth, the antiradical horror story, and — more frequently than he had in *Aulicus* — the sudden change whereby one week a group was praised, the next week excoriated. Thus Birkenhead sometimes treated the Scots as villains, sometimes as heroes. Better than his colleagues he could spin a mean anecdote, promote tears for Charles, and invoke traditional feelings of snobbism. *Bellicus*, for instance, included a portrait of certain Independent M.P.'s as men "to whom fond Theollogie is a riddle inexplicable, Rhetorick fallacious and Logicke needlesse disputes, to whom Poesie is pernicious and Prose tedious, who read Calvin with more applause than Austen [Augustine], and prefer Hollingshead to Livie. . . ." [41] In addition, Birkenhead, possibly through the co-operation of Nedham, had sporadic access to the inner recesses of Westminster, as shown, for example, in his circumstantial account of a case of Parliamentary embezzlement.[42] Finally, he had not lost his skill in putting on a show of optimism, and the reader is sometimes induced to forget the execrable type and paper that characterized *Mercurius Bellicus*, as well as its surreptitiously printed parents and brothers.

From early February to mid-May *Bellicus* was ably seconded by the revived *Mercurius Aulicus*.[43] Edited almost certainly by Samuel Sheppard, it too tried to conquer by dividing, alternating blandishments and insults and quickly switching from screams of alarm to the laughter of ostensible optimism. Sheppard contributed to social history the allegation that Hugh Peters, one of Cromwell's right-hand men, had imported his whore from New England, and to political history a few of the juicier anti-Marten anecdotes.[44] The editor also could run the rhetorical gamut, going from carefully balanced clauses ("And now whilst the old Lord Commons are making new Lawes at Westminster, the new Lord Mayor is breaking old Lawes at London. . . .") to heaped-up hyperbole:

> Fetch me a quill pull'd from the wing of some sad croaking Raven, clapping with his owne wings his funerall obsequies, to pensill out a Trayterous perjur'd Parliament. Give me some Inke that's mixt with Gall and Vinegar, such as they gave my Lord and King to drink. Yet more Gall. So now 'tis well.[45]

Sheppard was kept busy dodging Mabbott's agents and accumulating journalistic experience. In January 1648 he wrote the two numbers of a Royalist paper entitled *Mercurius Dogmaticus*, and in the spring, when Wharton was jailed, he became the chief contributor to *Elencticus*.[46] Meanwhile, he served as editor of *Aulicus*. As soon as it shut down, Sheppard launched a similar weekly, *The Parliament Kite*, which managed to stay aloft until the end of August.[47] Shortly thereafter he expended his energies writing an imitation of Spenser called *The Fairy King*, part of it composed in prison. But in *The Parliament Kite* he indulged in smut that would have brought a blush to the cheeks of Acrasia: the story, for instance, of the anti-Royalist who buggered a stone jug, or the account of the house of Miles Corbet, one of the regicides-to-be, where prices were lower than in other London brothels.[48] As he had been in *Aulicus*, Sheppard was free with his purple prose, and he now increased the amount of undiluted invective. The former minister and writer of pastorals thus began one number:

> Panders, Pimps, Villanes, Roagues, Bastards, Traytors, Thieves, Murderers, Cheaters, Juglers, Canniballs, Tyrants, Parliament-Men, Canters, Committees, Pick-pockets, Sequestrators, Generals, Colonells, Sectaries, Scribes and Pharisees, Hypocrites, Devills, what shall I call yee?

And he went on to refer to the English body politic as a "stinking Carcasse" redeemed only by the Christ-like Charles.[49] Sheppard also tried to support the king by printing such wildly optimistic rumors as that Cromwell had died (complete with an indecent panegyric) or that Fairfax was a gout-ridden corpse.[50] *The Parliament Kite* was as long-winded, shrill, repetitious, defiant, scurrilous, and unreliable as its progenitors, sometimes more so.

Mercurius Psitacus, the fourth legitimate offspring of *Melancholicus*, *Pragmaticus*, and *Elencticus*, survived for seven numbers — from June to August 1648. It too was a chip off the Royalist block, a little less smutty than *The Parliament Kite* and fuller of tears for the king. The editor, who had just escaped from jail, was a marked man.[51] In one number he announced that he was being so closely pursued by the "state-Bloodhounds" that *Psitacus* was full of errata and evasive in its day of publication; in another he bragged about how the censorial agents had missed him by an eyelash.[52]

Often, however, they did not miss. By the end of summer the wave of the short-run Royalist weekly had broken, though the three "grand" mercuries managed to keep going. That they survived for another two years, even if intermittently, was the result of their informal system of rotating editors, the laxity of the prison in which these men were usually confined, and the friendliness of many Londoners which made it harder to track down their portable presses.[53] Both individually and collectively, therefore, the Royalist newspapers provoked and frustrated the censors. They had a similar effect on the editors of the six established London weeklies.

As might be expected, this effect was minimal on the staff of *Le Mercure Anglois*. Having to dodge no Parliamentary pursuivants, it regularly provided its readers with the surface of the news in demotic French officialese. Leveller agitation received small notice, the splits between Independent and Presbyterian less. But one can sense a slight lessening in the paper's anti-Royalism. It now gave a proportionately large share of space to stories about the king and to incidents in which the militant Independents looked inept. Even so, any hostility to Cromwell was indirect, and *Le Mercure Anglois* seemed unmindful of the political and journalistic turmoil surrounding it.

The case was different for *A Perfect Diurnall*, now more than ever the leading newspaper. From the autumn of 1647 to the summer of 1648 it consistently appeared in two editions, and its publishers had to employ two printers.[54] Its weekly circulation, since there were fewer licensed papers for sale, probably approached 3,000. Understandably Pecke was willing to affix his initials to the title page and adhere to all the other provisions of the new licensing regulations. He also assembled the rudiments of a staff, for a pamphlet of late 1647 contained the first reference to an English newspaper woman: Pecke's "she-intelligencer." [55] Then, too, *A Perfect Diurnall*'s large circulation may have enabled the editor to charge more than the normal sixpence for the advertisements which, beginning in the spring of 1648, he irregularly included.[56]

By this time Pecke had achieved an almost monotonous competence, and the style of his short paragraphs would have received the blessings of Thomas Sprat. Pecke's concern was still with Westminster and the headquarters of the New Model, and he rarely allowed overseas affairs to intrude.[57] Such central events as the army debates at Putney in the autumn of 1647, when the Levellers almost succeeded in getting Fairfax and Cromwell to superimpose democracy on England, received full coverage. So did all the official news of the day, even though it increasingly reflected the tensions between Independent and Presbyterian as civil war again became imminent. But in reporting this news Pecke was careful to gauge the political weather accurately and to do nothing to offend the leaders of the army. Here, for instance, is his account of the end of the Putney debates:

The debate discovered so much resolution & integrity in the Generall and [his] officers, that it produced severall votes, and it is believed some of those officers who were chief actors in this business [i.e., those whose sympathies were with the Levellers] will be made exemplary . . . and this much is certain, that of this party which make such a noise there will not be found above 400 of 21000. The Officers appeared to do like religious and conscientious men, and so did most of the Agitators; there is not that division in the army our friends feared and enemies hoped for.[58]

Thereafter, the editor showed little sympathy for the Levellers.[59] When the Royalist weeklies praised Lilburne, Pecke responded with silence or with brief mention of the actions taken against him.

The Kingdomes Weekly Intelligencer displayed a similar expediency, though Collings was still torn between his desire to stay in business and his dislike for what was happening on the national scene.[60] Again the lure of journalism was greater than the pull of political principle. But Collings' conflicting views remained sufficiently unconcealed for his paper to be both more and less informative than *A Perfect Diurnall*. He ignored a slightly larger number of controversial items than did Pecke and he more frequently substituted foreign for Westminster news. Sometimes, too, his caution was excessively self-conscious. In one issue Collings first summarized the Leveller "Agreement of the People," then a "Remonstrance" from the Parliament of Scotland, concluding his condensation of these antipodal documents with no other comment than "I leave them both to the judicious to consider of them." [61] On other occasions he felt compelled to titillate then balk his readers, as in this instance:

> This day the House of Commons being sate an expresse order was given that none should be suffered to come up into the outward Lobby, neither were any in the House suffered (unless upon an extraordinary occasion) to goe down, so close were their debates; I must therefore desire you to excuse me if I cannot for the present communicate what they debated on unto you.[62]

Yet he sometimes let his political prejudices seep into print. *The Kingdomes Weekly Intelligencer* included several stories on the plight of the king, now under close imprisonment on the Isle of Wight. Some were poignant, especially one that described Charles as being "overgrown with grief and hair." [63]

As a result of such minor indiscretions Collings found himself in trouble. In December 1647 he began a number by announcing that, despite his current difficulties, he would give the particulars of that week's news, "not from others, but as I have collected and digested them by my selfe"; and he concluded the paper with this explanation:

> The writer of this Intelligence was on the last Saturday brought before the Committee of Examinations, being accused of writing that outrageous Pamphlet called *Pragmaticus*, but he so cleerly and so fully vindicated himselfe that the honourable Committee immediately discharged him, not without hopes of reparation for his disgrace and losse.[64]

But Collings was not completely in the clear. In May 1648, for example, he again called attention to his own vicissitudes, this time hinting that the government harassing him was by no means popular:

I know not by what misfortune it comes about, but wheresoever I doe turn, I observe the greatest part disaffected to the Parliament and those who derive their powers from them, and doe reflect it upon others to be made the subjects not onely of disregard but of contempt, and so distempered are their judgements that amongst many of them it is enough to condemn this Paper for no other reason but because it is licensed.[65]

Even so, Collings clung to his editor's uneasy chair.

He may have clung to it partly for the sake of having an outlet for his prose. Many times during these nine months Collings let himself go in a way that would have gladdened the heart of Carlyle. Indeed, his account of a riot in Norwich was the most lurid piece of reporting of the 1640's:

. . . In this confusion being led by too many heads, they [the rioters] found none at all. Armes were wanting as much as reason, and therefore to supply themselves with armes, in great noyse and tumult they throng to the Magazine, and to increase their unhappines it is not enough that they have inflamed themselves with choler unlesse withall they inflame the city. The Magazine is broken open, some provide themselves with halberts, some with pikes, others with muskets; they hold a lighted match in one hand, and breake open a barrell of powder with the other, when by chance (a broken coale of match accidentally falling upon some of the loose powder) behold a dreadfull blaze (not from the clouds, but ascending to them) doth breake into the ayre with a voice louder than thunder, and that with so suddain a terror as if it were rather an object of the memory than of the eare or eye. The frighted temples startle, the walls of the city tremble as if shaken with a mighty earthquake, the stones fall down; the men fly up, but suddainly come downe againe, all but their soules excepted, which being now at peace will no more be conversant on earth amongst the thunders and the tempests of Warre. In the mean time three troopes . . . doe enter and secure the city, whiles many of the Inhabitants amazing in feare doe resort to this afflicting spectacle, and with troubled eyes they behold their ruines and themselves, heavy as the heart of grief and sad as the face of desolation.[66]

Collings could also ride a metaphor a long distance, as in this sad review of recent events:

This Island hath been for seven long years too fruitfull in her own Sorrows. Too often she hath conceived in Cruelty and brought forth Destruction. She hath lately been delivered of one unnatural warre, and now behold she is big with another. And it were well if she had not twins within her. When shall this Island rejoyce in safety? When shall there be no more struggling of her children in her wombe? When shall they make happy the hands of the midwife, and be born with the white thread of Peace about their wrists, and not with the crimsin one of warre? [67]

Sometimes his preference for personification and the pathetic fallacy even more strongly suggests the style of a Pre-Romantic:

The Ayre doth still continue its sighes and the cloudes their teares, and that in such repeated stormes as if they did strive to expiate the polluted Earth, or as if the Firmament would dissolve in compassion for those men who will have no compassion on themselves. In the mean time Rage is the Gallant and all in fashion with this Age, which desperately drives on to invite and increase new Dangers, whiles Destruction it selfe stands amazed, and Nature doth tremble at the progresse of unnaturall wars. In this fiery time of active horror, sorrow is too tame a subject.

At which point Collings, probably aware that he was getting beyond his depth, shifted to an attack on the Royalist mercuries, that "minstralsie of the Fiddle . . . who . . . will finde a time to dance when all the world should mourn." [68]

In addition, Collings, stylistically the most flexible of the licensed editors, showed some knowledge of earlier English literature and a greater concern than his fellows for news of the stage. *The Kingdomes Weekly Intelligencer* contained the only reference to Chaucer to appear in an Interregnum newspaper.[69] It also had several stories on attempts to revive the theater, including one account of "sixscore Coaches . . . in Golden lane" bringing their occupants to see the players at the Fortune.[70] Yet plenty of drama existed outside the Fortune, and Collings usually suppressed his political conservatism, as well as his tendency to unbridle his Pegasus, so he could go on writing a weekly that the authorities would not shut down.

Henry Walker was also interested in what happened on and to the stage, and his *Perfect Occurrences* ran one of the fuller accounts of a raid:

A stage-play was to have been acted in Salisbury Court this day (and bills stuck up about it) called A King and no King, formerly acted at the Black-Fryers, by his Majesties servants, about 8. yeares since, written by Francis Beaumont and John Fletcher.
The Sheriffes of the City of London with their Officers went thither, and found a great number of people, some young Lords, and other eminent persons; and the men and women with the Boxes (that took monies) fled. The Sheriffes brought away Tim Reade the Foole, and the people cryed out for their monies, but slunke away like a company of drowned Mice without it.[71]

Yet Walker was even more interested in the melodrama of tracking down Royalist editors. Several times he gloatingly referred to the arrests of their printers, and he took sporadic delight in attacking Hackluyt and his associates.[72]

With the rise to power of the Independents, Walker felt more secure. In March 1648 he changed printers and probably became publisher as well as editor of *Perfect Occurrences*.[73] Apparently the former printer did not like this arrangement and for two weeks he issued a counterfeit. He next made a deal with Walker so that he and the new printer either worked together or printed the paper on alternate weeks. Probably *Perfect Occurrences* was profitable enough to warrant such maneuvers, and a few times both printers were employed to bring it out in two editions.[74] Moreover, the advertisements it contained, though infrequent, were more numerous than in its competitors.

Even if it made money, *Perfect Occurrences* during this period declined from being the *Perfect Diurnall* of the end of the week. It was still crowded with news, now often including the London bills of mortality, and at the end of many issues Walker added a functional summary. But he outdid Pecke in sticking to official jargon, and he fell behind him in his ability to select the news and condense a story. Also, Walker still liked to show off. Beginning in the spring of 1648 he weekly displayed his knowledge of Hebrew by taking the name of some prominent leader and constructing its Hebrew etymology.[75] Between nonjournalistic politicking, aid to Mabbott's agents, and philology Walker was too busy to edit a first-rate newspaper.[76] He was not too occupied, however, to see that *Perfect Occurrences* remained inoffensive to the powers that were or might be. It was properly antiradical, moderately unsympathetic to the king, and encomiastic toward the leaders of the army; and it periodically featured items best labeled "Puritan," such as a pleased notice that one hundred ale houses had been closed in the area of Westminster.[77]

Despite its faults, *Perfect Occurrences* was more readable than *The Perfect Weekly Account*. Border, who had been briefly pushed aside when his *Weekly Account* was forced out of business, came back in October 1647 to help edit the paper that had supplanted his.[78] His return made little difference. *The Perfect Weekly Account* remained a cautious, choppy, and impersonal compilation which relied heavily on already published documents. In January 1648 it vanished, reappearing late in March unimproved by its vacation. Border, if possible, was not again going to be on the outside looking in, and to make things more certain he stopped writing editorials and editorial asides.

Dillingham, displaying similar resolution and care, kept his *Mod-*

erate Intelligencer alive, though in June he almost lost it to Mabbott. But Dillingham was hard-headed enough to survive this attempted coup and to put out a competent paper. The chief feature of *The Moderate Intelligencer* remained its length, though usually eight of its twelve pages consisted of foreign news, most of it routine. (Two exceptions were a letter from a Frenchman who had been traveling in Africa, and the story of a duel between two ladies of Aix.) [79] In the other four pages the editor almost always presented the news from Westminster in the form of summaries of what had been accomplished, not of what was pending. He maintained a strict neutrality, occasionally bending over backward to prove that he was no longer radical. Increasingly he eliminated signs of his own personality, both in his style and in his avoidance of domestic news that was at all irregular. No editorials and very few obiter dicta intruded, their place being partly taken by such phrases as "that no offense be taken, no more shall be said." The editor's comment on a controversial pamphlet put out by the Levellers can epitomize the new Dillingham:

> Great discourse hath been this week about . . . *The Case of the Army*; some say it is the sence of the Army, others that it will be; some that a Jesuit was the principal Agent or Promoter, others that it is not so; some say that the Army have taken in so many ill-affected that they, besides the undoing of the country, are like to undo themselves and all their friends. Some say, most are for Anarchy, others say for Monarchy, and others say they will fall in with the Parliament and be conformable, which is very probable and most likely; one cries, if we agree we are undone; others, if we do not we are undone.[80]

True and functionally written as it was, this comment was calculated to irritate no one in or on the threshold of power. It came from a hand that had gained much experience but, in so doing, had lost not only its thimble but most of its individuality.[81]

The story of the defiant Royalist mercuries and of the six timid established newspapers illustrates the contention that when a system of censorship is not watertight, those who defy it do so with abandon, those who obey it do so slavishly. The second part of this generalization can be further illustrated by the new licensed weeklies which Mabbott and his agents allowed to appear. The first, *Heads of Chiefe Passages in Parliament*, came out for three numbers in January 1648, then modified its title and lasted another eight weeks. Edited by former censor Walley, it played the game according to the rules.[82] Eschewing the personal and sticking close to official hand-outs, it signaled the coming party line by being slightly more anti-Royalist a little sooner than its fellows.

Equally subservient was the contemporaneous *The Kingdomes Weekly Post*, the ten numbers of which came out between early January and March. Edited by Border, it resembled his *Perfect Weekly Account*, as it did Walley's newcomer.[83] Despite the claim in the opening issue that it would print news that other papers missed or misrepresented, it contained the normal jargon-filled version of official news, though in a few nonsensitive stories Border allowed himself flashes of purple prose, even an occasional comment. Its next-to-last number, however, included an item indicating both Charles's awareness of public relations and the importance of the early newspaper: the captive king was said to be complaining that he did not have "a free accesse of Intelligence." [84] If he had been granted this access, *The Kingdomes Weekly Post* would have been barely adequate to keep him informed.

It would have been more adequate than the third new licensed paper of 1648, *Packets of Letters from Scotland*. Almost certainly conceived and edited by Walker, it was a specialized journal, for it dealt only with events in the north.[85] From March to November it appeared three or four times a month, functioning as a supplement particularly to *Perfect Occurrences* but generally to other established papers. It probably sold well, since the letters which filled it covered a series of Royalist uprisings and the Scottish preparations for war, then the war itself. Walker made little effort to rewrite or integrate these letters, but some of them have an immediacy absent from more carefully filtered reports. Then, too, speedier posts were now bringing the news to London, so that items from the Scottish border might be only two days old when they appeared in *Packets of Letters*.[86] As an editor Walker was slipshod, but he had connections in high places which he exploited to the full.

Gilbert Mabbott was equally enterprising, and as chief censor he had his own links with leading Independents. The son of a Nottingham cobbler, he had managed to climb high.[87] Nor did he tumble after the Restoration: partly through the influence of General Monck he received a remunerative patent from Charles II to sell "Wine and strong waters in Ireland." [88] Mabbott, in fact, was a censor who grew to dislike censorship,[89] a man of principle who employed the tricks of the time-server, and a radical who was trusted by Fairfax and Cromwell and rewarded by the king whose father he helped to kill.

In June 1648 Mabbott decided to return to journalism. As a stepping stone he used the fact that a month earlier Dillingham had included the phrase "Dieu nous donne les Parlyaments briefe, Rois de vie longue" in *The Moderate Intelligencer*.[90] Mabbott made this an excuse to refuse to license the paper; and with the co-operation of White, its printer, he appropriated the title and numbering of Dillingham's weekly.[91] For three numbers *The Moderate Intelligencer* came out in two series, one by Dillingham and a new printer, the other by Mabbott and White. Dillingham petitioned the House of Lords against this theft and, despite the opposition of Mabbott and White, managed to regain exclusive right to his title, as well as the right to be licensed and to keep his Thursday publication day.[92] Consequently, on a Tuesday in the middle of July, Mabbott brought forth the first number of a newspaper entitled *The Moderate*. With this misnamed weekly another chapter in the history of early English journalism began.

CHAPTER IX

MATURITY

July 1648 to January 1649

MABBOTT picked his time well for returning to journalism. The founding of *The Moderate* was preceded by a series of local uprisings which helped to cement the Royalist-Presbyterian coalition. In June 1648 the Scots, after elaborate but disunified preparations, began to march south, the New Model to move north. These maneuvers were counterpointed by a revolt in Wales and a mutiny in the Parliamentary navy. In August, after the Scots had been defeated at Preston and Colchester had fallen, the Second Civil War came to a virtual end. The disciplined troops under Cromwell had seen to it that the revolution would not be reversed, and that, after this additional and perhaps needless blood-letting, the losers would be made to suffer. In September and October the victors, now bargaining more toughly, again tried to negotiate with the king. The negotiations failed. The army had meanwhile formulated its own demands. The result was Colonel Pride's purge of a still balky Parliament in December, and the trial and execution of Charles in January 1649. Mabbott would have no dearth of news. He would also have no censor to contend with, since he continued to be chief licenser of the weekly press. And he would have plenty of political grist to grind in his mill: along with the New Model and the Scots, the Levellers were behaving militantly, and by early fall *The Moderate* was trumpeting the slogans of John Lilburne.

But the paper got off to an inauspicious start. Wearing the disguise of *The Moderate Intelligencer*, its first three numbers each consisted of twelve pages, of which more than half were devoted to foreign news. The opening number began with the lie that the editor had given up his "former Title of Moderate Intelligencer" and was now calling himself "The Moderate," though the paper's name, numbering, and pagination were not changed.[1] In July, after the House of Lords for political rather than moral reasons had ruled against him, Mabbott changed the paper's title, still blessing it with his own imprimatur. He also reduced the size to eight pages, claiming that a single sheet would be easier to mail to the country, and using the same reason to justify the paper's shift from Thursday to Tuesday.[2] Then for five numbers, until the middle of August, Mabbott kept *The Moderate* typical of the better newspapers. He showed a practiced hand in making an occasional anecdote vivid, he had access to eye-witness accounts of the siege of Colchester, and he was on the side of the Independent angels. But with Number 5 he began more fully to reveal his own politics, among other things praising the concept of a truly representative Parliament. With Number 6 *The Moderate* became the first newspaper consistently to preach a radical program, as well as the first to become the organ of a functioning political party. (Because Royalism was an attitude espoused by a variety of groups whose aims were negative or vague, the Royalist mercuries were not the megaphones of a party. The Levellers, in contrast, had a positive and specific program and an apparatus to implement it, complete with mass meetings, precinct fund-raisers, a widespread organization, and a caucus.) For ten months Mabbott preached the Leveller program. To do so effectively he usually discarded foreign news and packed his opinions into lead editorials of one or two pages. And as he became more outspoken, his style grew more direct.

Between the defeat of the Scots and the execution of Charles, Mabbott gave vehement voice to a series of radical proposals. At the time of Preston he was already attacking the Presbyterians, not only for their connivance with the king but for their lack of a properly spiritual religion.[3] Simultaneously he excoriated Charles, not a man surrounded by evil advisors but a person responsible for the blood of thousands, a liar, and a symbol of tyranny. Charles, wrote Mabbott, wanted a treaty only so he could cut the throats of the Independents.[4] With heavy irony he referred to those who kiss "the Kings Majesties most pure hand that was never imbrued in any Saints blood," and then, without irony, to the corpses of 300,000 who had "never bowed the knee to Baal." [5] From mid-summer Mabbott was positive as well as negative in his radicalism. His editorials, his scattered comments, and his selection of news were all designed to help the Leveller cause. Lilburne's activities, whether he was demanding reparations or fighting with Prynne or playing the part of a vociferous martyr, got their full share of space. In September when the Levellers presented a petition backed by 40,000 signatures Mabbott printed it in full.[6] Subsequently he supported its twenty-seven propositions whereby England was to be transformed into a republic.

In this campaign Mabbott, in concert with Leveller propaganda, followed an increasingly democratic line. At the end of September he opened one number with the declaration that, "Where the peoples judgements are rectified, the Traytors purposes are prevented" — [7] and as Smith had done in *The Scotish Dove*, though with opposite aims, Mabbott proceeded to rectify his readers' judgments. A few weeks later, after briefly reviewing recent history, he concluded an editorial with two implied syllogisms. The first was not out of line with what other editors were saying: the king can err, when he does he forfeits the people's trust, the people therefore can wage war against him. The second was out of line: Parliament too can err, can forfeit the people's trust, and hence justify a people's war against it.[8] *The Moderate* was now against king and Parliament and for the army, provided the army kept on implementing the will of The People.

To illustrate this popular will Mabbott gave much space to left-wing demands. In October, for instance, his paper summarized a strongly anti-monarchical petition from Oxford, quoted from public letters from four different army units in support of the Leveller program, mentioned petitions from York and Newcastle which pleaded for a republic, and praised a variety of informal radical requests. In its pages the slogan "Salus populi suprema lex" had indeed become a leftist battle-cry. *The Moderate* also featured certain Leveller shibboleths, such as the need to rescue the law from French and Latin so that the common people would no longer be victimized, and the equal need to relieve England from other burdens of Norman domination.[9]

In actively preaching democracy Mabbott was smart enough to realize that his message had to be simple. This was especially true in late 1648 when *The Moderate* was, almost certainly, being distributed in London and the hinterlands by Leveller agents, with the result that in some weeks its circulation probably exceeded that of *A Perfect Diurnall*. Consequently many of Mabbott's editorials anticipated the oversimplifications in today's tabloids, such as this plea for government of the people:

> The laws and Government of this land, being Tirannous and Arbitrary, and destructive to the freedome of the people, may be lawfully taken away by the people . . . and till that be done, the people of this Nation are slaves, and not Free-men. . . . All Powers and Authorities, either by King or Parliament, acting against . . . the people are void by the Laws of God, man and nature: the people . . . give these powers and Authorities, expecting they should not abuse their Trust in acting against the good of their Electees (their Lords and Masters), to whom they ought to give an account for breach of their Trust, because the servant cannot be above his master, nor the creature above his maker. . . .[10]

If Mabbott and the Levellers were right, the Civil War had been fought, not to achieve an accord between a limited monarch and an oligarchic Parliament, but to superimpose a late-nineteenth-century constitutional settlement on seventeenth-century England. It took another six months, however, before Mabbott and the leading Levellers were willing to acknowledge that they might be too far ahead of history's schedule.

Meanwhile *The Moderate* kept pounding away in its editorials and news items to change that schedule. In November it played to the hilt the murder of Colonel Rainsborough, one of the most articulate and glamorous of the Levellers. It also called for the dissolution of Parliament and its replacement by a more representative body, and demanded that Charles be brought to trial for mass murder.[11] In November, too, Mabbott expanded the paper to twelve pages, probably better to compete with *The Moderate Intelligencer*, though unlike Dillingham he gave less than half his space to foreign news. In December *The Moderate* vigorously supported Cromwell, justified Pride's Purge, and called for the death of Charles, "the person called the King."[12] Half a dozen editorials at the end of the year and the beginning of 1649 then employed slightly more sophisticated language and arguments to attack the idea of monarchy; and in a few numbers the editor colored the news from France so that the Fronde seemed a democratic popular front battling against kingly absolutism. By January, Mabbott had welded rather than linked the Presbyterians to the Royalists, announcing, for instance, that their "proud flesh must [go] down with Monarchy, the one being equall in Tyrannie with the other."[13] He also called for the abolition of the House of Lords, an immoral and archaic bastion of privilege. Just before Charles's trial the editor culminated his attack on England's hereditary institutions with an irreverent account of the king's sex life.[14]

The next three numbers of *The Moderate*, from January 9 to 30, gave most of their domestic news to an objective and full report of Charles's indictment and conviction before a special High Court of Justice. Mabbott surrounded his account with enough anti-monarchical petitions and comments to impress upon his readers that the country's leading criminal was receiving his just deserts, and receiving them by due process of law. Number 30 then summarized the final proceedings against the king and the preparations for his execution, and devoted two pages to a dignified narration of his performance on the scaffold. The editor made it clear that "not Death, but the cause, makes a Martyr," but he went beyond effective partisanship by reporting that Charles had left behind a pregnant mistress.

Yet Mabbott was more than a wild-eyed partisan or starry-eyed idealist; he was a competent journalist. From June 1648 to January 1649 *The Moderate* included enough straight news, crime stories, and varied fillers to make it competitive with the long-established papers. One of its fillers was the first article on flying to appear in an English weekly. In this case Mabbott was taking advantage of contemporary interest in the possibilities of human flight, as well as of newspaper-readers' chronic thirst for pseudo-science.[15] Thus it was smart journalism to print this letter from Warsaw, with its mixture of mythology and embryonic physics, of naïve credulity and sharp skepticism, of awe for the past and hope for the future:

. . . [I] do now make bold to represent unto you that strangest and never heard of before invention of flying in the air, which, I doubt not, will, for curiosity and finenesse of the conceit, be a matter of delight and pleasure unto those that are learned, especially that have studyed the Mathematicks; and although this subject may be a matter of laughter and be despised amongst . . . the vulgar [who do] not believe any thing whatsoever any further than they can apprehend the same, never considering what likelyhood or probability there is for the effecting thereof. The thing is thus:

There is at this present in this Court a certain man lately come from Arabia, who is come hither to the King of Poland, to whom he proffereth his head for security of that which he propoundeth, which is that he hath brought from that Countrey the invention of a Machine, being Airie & of a construction so light, nevertheless so sound and firm, that the same is able to bear two men, and hold them up in the Air, and one of them shall be able to sleep, the whiles the other maketh the Machine to move, which thing is much after the same manner as you see represented in the old Tapistry hangings [of] the Dragons flying, whereof this same takes its name: I do give you them for patern or modell of this invention, [it] being a thing much in question and to be doubted concerning these flying Dragons, whether any be alive; likewise it is questioned by many of the truth of being any Unicorns, Griffins, Phoenix, & many other like things, which by many wise, understanding men are deemed to have little or no reality in them, but all imaginary; neverthelesse we beleeve this upon the credit of Antiquity and the report of many who know more. There are few in this Court but have got a pattern of this Machine, and [I] do hope to send you one likewise, in case that the project takes some good effect and proves to be as true as rare in its invention; the forms of it which he hath made, and afterwards presented here, with the many strong reasons he gives for to maintain his Proposition, seeme to be so strong and so likely to be true that there is great hopes conceived thereof; and although he undertakes that the Celerity or swiftnesse of this Airie post shall go far beyond that of our ordinary Posts, seeing he promises to go with the same in 24 hours 40 Leagues of this his Country, which will make of English miles near 240, which thing seemeth so strange to many that therefore they fal off from him & so give little credit to it, although he hath brought with him good Certificates, how it hath been approved by many in other places where he hath made experiment thereof to his great Honour and credit and the Admiration and great amazement of the beholders; besides, it may well be thought that a man of Honour, as he seems to be, would not set so little by his life as to lay it at stake about a businesse of that nature, except he had some good grounds for it, and had some experimentall knowledge of the same, seeing he must hazzard his life two severall wayes: the one in case he did not make a triall of what he had promised, and so proved to have come hither as an Imposter, to have cheated this Court, who upon discoveries of like businesses will not make it a jest or a thing of small moment; and the other time of danger is when he begins to take his flight, which he is to do above the highest Towers or Steeples that are, and without his dexterity and certain knowledge therein would run into an utter ruin and destruction.

Whether it be true or no, there are Commissioners appointed who are to examine the businesse and so, accordingly as they finde it, to make their report; and [he] is appointed to make an essay and shew a piece of his skill in their presence before he is suffered to act it publickly, that if in case his businesse doth not prove according to expectation, they that have given credit to it and him may not be exposed to open shame and derision; even as it happened once in the City of Paris, where a stranger, having gathered together neer the Louvre many thousands of Spectators, in whose sight, as a man void of sense and reason, having taken his flight from the top of the highest Tower thereabouts, which is between the Louvre and the River of Seine, this miserable wretch fell down upon the ground, broke his neck, and his body [was] torn in pieces. Whilest every one is expecting the issue of this, there are many great wagers laid about it; yet take this by the way, that there hath been severall great consultations made with the Mathematicians about this, who have all declared that the putting it in execution is very difficult, but for the thing it self do not count [it] impossible; and to this purpose there was a true information brought of a prisoner, who having tied very fast about his Coller and under his Arms a long Cloak, whereunto was made fast a Hoop to keep the spread out and round, casting himself from the top of a high Tower, where a small River ran at the foot thereof, wherein he thought only to have faln, it happened otherwise, for he was carried on the further side of the water, and came there save and sound; this Cloak, which stood him instead of a sail, did bear up the weight of his body, and so parted the air by degrees that he had time to descend easily to the ground, without receiving any hurt by the fall; and not to bring here that fabulous History of *Dedalus*, the most famous Artist . . . *Archites Tarentin* made a wooden Pigeon, who fled very high into the air; as also an artificiall Eagle [was made] at Nuremberg, at the . . . great Reception which was made by that City unto *Maximillian* the Emperor; although both of them were much heavier and yet not so big as a childes bable, these two things being raised a great heighth into the Air, being only held with a Packthred. But another Ingineer had not so good successe, for having raised himself into the Air by means of an Engine much like to this we speake of, before he had raised himself so high as he intended, the Wiers did break in pieces, whereby he fell to the ground sooner than he was willing, and by the fall broke his thigh, and was in great danger of his life; yet by this we may gather thus much: That the thing may possibly be done; moreover, experience daily shews us that nothing is impossible unto man, but that through labour and industry the most difficult things at length may be obtained; only in this point concerning the possibility or impossibility of things, wise men do seem to be most slow in giving their opinion about it; there are also examples of birds, and those that swim, whereby we may judge by their swiftnesse that the Air may do the same operation upon other subjects, according as the Artist can accommodate . . . [him] self to it.[16]

Unfortunately Mabbott never let his readers know how the Warsaw experiment turned out, and no other English newspaper of the period mentioned this, or any, attempted flight. A partial explanation may be that licensed journalists thought it necessary to keep both feet on the ground during the winter of 1648–49.

In this they continued to differ from the editors of the Royalist mercuries. Nedham, the chief contributor to *Pragmaticus* until the end of 1648, was still getting inside stories from Westminster, and he even bragged about " a deep designe" being plotted against him by a member of Commons, who allegedly announced in Parliament that *Pragmaticus*

comes abroad more exact and perfect than . . . ever . . . and relates all passages and whatever we say in the House. And truly except some course be taken to prevent this . . . I conceive we shall quite lose the freedom and privacy of our debates. And for my part, Mr. Speaker . . . I suspect one of our own clerks, a drunken-debauched fellow with a red face. . . .[17]

Whether or not Nedham's informant drank too much and had a red face, he did a good job of informing his employer. For example, *Pragmaticus* was able to describe the narrow margin by which, in one instance, the Independents gained a majority:

For, the house being divided . . . and finding there were 57. on one side, and seven and fifty on the other, it was urged to Mr. Speaker that he should declare himself. . . . Not knowing whether it were safe yet to quit the Army Faction, he paused a while and opened his mouth leisurely . . .

thereby, Nedham added, throwing a brief scare into the "Saints Vote-drivers." [18] Not only did the radicals have party whips, but according to *Pragmaticus* they knew how to filibuster.[19] Nedham also secured some of the details of an Independent caucus suddenly convened at 6:00 A.M., and on several occasions he was able to purvey both the substance and flavor of Parliament's allegedly most secret discussions.[20]

Moreover, he continued to display his political sophistication. In July his paper was still openly, often bitterly, against the Presbyterians. In August it became less unfriendly, and in November it began to praise their program and their leaders, though not their theology. *Pragmaticus* showed similar agile footwork in regard to the Levellers. In the summer Nedham was promoting a bout between good John Lilburne and bad Oliver Cromwell; in the fall he was castigating the Levellers as the worst of rebels; toward the end of the year, while still trying to divide them from the leaders of the army, he was violently disapproving of both. They can, Nedham wrote, "as soon combine as fire and water . . . consider that the Levellers aim . . . at pure democracy, or a Government of the many headed rabble, and the design of Oliver and his Grandees [is] for an Oligarchy in the hands of himself." [21] Then, as Charles's fate became clearer, Nedham more and more preferred oligarchy to democracy. *Pragmaticus* increasingly reviled the aspirations of the London masses, "the dregs of the People," "the rascall Multitude . . . the Prophane vulgar." [22] One number included this stanza in its title-page poem:

No God above, nor Gods below,
  Our Saints (I see) will owne;
Allegiance is Rebellion now,
  Treason to weare a Crown.

And the editor went on to exclaim, "Good God, what a wild thing is Rebellion!"[23]

Nedham had other well-tested tricks. Like Birkenhead, from whom he had learned much, he minimized the New Model's victories and exaggerated into success any skirmish in which the Royalists were not routed. During the negotiations between the victors and the king, Nedham portrayed the former as Machiavellian subversives, the latter as a saintly martyr for English institutions.[24] He exploited wild rumors at a time when there were many, such as the story that Cromwell, with the connivance of two Lords, was planning to take over London and chop off twenty designated heads.[25] The editor recurrently blamed the decay of trade — except, as he noted, that of preaching — on the dislocations caused by the rebels; and he usually pointedly ignored the licensed weeklies.

Nedham and his collaborators also did their best to ignore the censorship. For fifteen weeks during the second half of 1648 *Pragmaticus* flouted it by appearing in a twelve-page version.[26] But the last of these expanded issues came out after a gap of a week and with the agents of the government hot on its trail. The next week, for reasons of "security," the paper returned to eight pages. Despite its vicissitudes, it was salable enough to attract counterfeits, and at least five times during this period an inferior *Pragmaticus* tried to cut into Nedham's market.[27] Early in 1649, when the army, fearful of the public reaction against the king's trial and execution, tightened the censorial screws by sending more trackers into the alleys and byways of London, *Pragmaticus*'s troubles increased. It failed to appear during the first three weeks of February, and hence did not cover the beheading of Charles, though for the last two of these weeks counterfeits were again for sale.[28] Meanwhile the paper had become more strident, until by early 1649 lamentation and invective had generally replaced its incisive news. Indeed, its coverage of the king's trial was conspicuously lacking in detail and precision. Nedham had chosen this moment to desert the sinking Royalist ship, and the fortieth number of *Mercurius Pragmaticus*, covering the two weeks from December 26 to January 9, as well as subsequent issues, was no longer the beneficiary of his clever touch.[29]

Nedham's decision to abandon journalism coincided with the last days of *Mercurius Melancholicus*, which ceased regular publication in October, managed one number in November, and two in January. But its demise was not so great a loss as Nedham's temporary desertion. To the end the paper remained bare of hard news and full of scurrility, wild rumors, and breast-beating. Then, too, its various editors became more heated in denouncing each other. Here, for instance, is Parker on Hackluyt:

. . . a Buffone scoundrel . . . I will not say Priest lest I more abuse that holy Function than he himself hath done by his vile incontinency, having more Wives, nay thrice as many to his bed as he hath suits to his back; and five times as many Lemmans as wives; and least you should mistake the beast, and think he is a Loyalist, pray understand that . . . he hath taken the Covenant, and been in actual Rebellion against his King; he is as religious as a Windmill, and turns which way the winde blowes, a person so treacherous, and courteous also, that were the King here disguised, for 6 pence he would kisse him and say Hayle Master, and deliver him up to his crucifiers at Westminster. . . .[30]

And Hackluyt, then in jail, fought back by informing on Parker and Sheppard.[01] The last days of *Melancholicus* were further enlivened because at least six times between July and September it came out in two competing editions. Yet all issues agreed that the men opposing the king were murderers, grafters, liars, hypocrites, and incendiaries.[32] Cromwell, an "Atheisticall Leveller," bore the brunt of these insults, closely followed by Henry Marten, a licentious Leveller. Unlike *Pragmaticus*, *Melancholicus*, regardless of who was editing it, frequently threw mud at Mabbott, Walker, and Pecke, especially toward the end of its career. Its two final numbers achieved a peak of shrillness, and one of the last items was a shocked outcry at the Grandees for planning to permit religious toleration.[33] It was a bad moment for Royalist editors.

Mercurius Elencticus underlined their plight. Wharton complained in December that the "Blood-hounds were . . . hot in the chase," [34] and for four weeks early in 1649 he was unable to put out a paper. But back in July *Elencticus* had cheerfully reported that "the Saints have all the Symptomes of dying-men"; and as late as November, Wharton had zestfully related, if in the third person, how he had recently escaped from jail.[35] Now, however, the fight seemed lost and Royalist editors increasingly quarreled with one another. In October, for instance, Wharton or his temporary replacement mentioned that *Elencticus* had been criticized by its colleagues, but that, until it was disclaimed by the king, the editor would carry on with his "old drudgery." [36]

"Drudgery" was not quite the right word. The paper continued to be concerned with astrological lore, and Wharton inserted even more shreds and patches of Latin; but he had grown more skillful. He now included enough coherent anti-Independent news for *Elencticus* to fall between the invective-filled *Melancholicus* and the often penetrating *Pragmaticus*. He had also become agile in supporting monarchism without offending the Presbyterians, and better than other journalists he could put across the idea that anti-Royalism was vastly unpopular. At one point he showed that 75 per cent of the people of England were against those who opposed the king, at another that only thirty M.P.'s were "down-right for the Army." [37] Wharton was aided by Sheppard, whose most distinctive contribution was a revised short section of the Fifth Book of Spenser's *Faerie Queen*, with the anti-Leveller implications made clear.[38]

It was the future Baronet Wharton who, of all Royalist editors, was consistently most shocked by the democratic threat in an Independent victory and in Leveller aspirations. The Independents are, he wrote, "Beggers, Bratts, and mere upstarts"; the Levellers, proponents of communism, anarchy, and atheism; and those who do not realize this are, among other things, "cowardly Cuckolds." [39] In diametric contrast to the report of Rainsborough's funeral in *The Moderate*, Wharton stressed the low-class, unsavory aspects of the crowd, ending up with a scurrilous epitaph on the man whom Mabbott was then celebrating as a martyr for English liberties.[40] Shortly thereafter the two numbers of *Elencticus* that appeared in January were properly aghast at the preparations for Charles's trial, and Wharton added to his predictable exclamations of horror a reiterated emphasis on the low birth of the regicides, together with a few asides on the ominous configuration of the planets.[41] This was followed by four weeks of silence, until early in February *Elencticus* reappeared in two separate numbers. The one by Wharton contained a long and excited account of the king's trial and execution, concluding with the sentence that the saintly Charles had "yielded up his spotlesse soule with that Alacrity, Courage, Constancy, Faith, Hope and Charity which becam the Justice of the Cause he dyed in, and the Greatnesse of his Royall Spirit." [42] And Wharton, despite his star-crossed eyes, proceeded to proclaim Charles II king of England. Unlike Nedham, he was not deserting the sinking ship, not even directly acknowledging that it was going down.

Except for *Pragmaticus*, now carrying on without Nedham, no other Royalist mercury was around to echo *Elencticus*'s defiance. By then the swarm of Royalist weeklies that had flourished in the summer of 1648 were all silenced. A few, however, had managed to make a fitful contribution to English journalism, if not to the cause of Charles. In July *A Wonder, A Mercury without a Lye in's Mouth* stated that God disliked rebels as much as he did witches. Starting at the end of that month and continuing for five numbers, *The Royall Diurnall*, edited by Sheppard, searched for anti-Independent straws in the wind, often pausing to attack the apathy of Londoners and the lack of apathy of Hackluyt.[43] For two issues in August, both bearing the same date, *The Colchester Spie* concentrated on pro-Royalist news of the siege of that city, a very temporary topic. A resurrected *Aulicus*, probably still by Sheppard, put in a brief appearance in August, as it, too, did its best to goad the inhabitants of London out of indifference.[44]

In September the number of short-lived Royalist mercuries declined. But a Catholic priest, taking advantage of the recent flurry of journalistic activity and the laxity of the censors, published *Mercurius Catholicus*. Its single number, complete with cross and rosary on the title page, presented the editor's point of view on the true church, a subject which scarcely comes under the head of current events. In the same month *The Parliament-Porter* assailed Independents and Levellers. The last of its four numbers even came to the defense of actors, a group being persecuted in the same manner and for many of the same reasons as the newsgirls on the streets of London.[45] In December the last of these Royalist fireflies deserving of mention, *Mercurius Impartialis*, gave most of its space to attacking Leveller journalists.

During the waning months of 1648 a few fly-by-night anti-Royalist weeklies also continued to flit across the scene. In August *Hermes Straticus* spent most of its one number berating *Elencticus*. Two months later *Mercurius Anti-Mercurius* returned for a week to assail Royalist editors and to help the Puritan cause with smutty verse. In November *The True Informer, Or Monthly Mercury* anticipated today's biased news magazines by devoting its twenty-four pages to a zestful pro-Leveller summary of recent events. And in December *A Declaration*, possibly by Walker, for three numbers heavy-handedly supported the army and looked forward to a republic, at one point commenting on the imminent death of the House of Lords with a sardonic "Sic transit gloria mundi." [46]

But the newspaper of late 1648 that gave the clearest proof that England was in a state of rapid transit was *Mercurius Militaris*, which came out five times in October and November. It was written by John Harris, a former actor, present Leveller, and future burglar, who was currently displaying his polemical talents as editor of *Mercurius Anti-Mercurius* and *The True Informer*.[47] In 1646 he had had a hand in one or two anti-Royalist weeklies, and more recently he had contributed, under the pseudonym of Sirrahniho, two pamphlets to the cause of the Levellers.[48] An outspoken cynic and radical, Harris now turned his sharpened pen against the enemies of Lilburne. In so doing he showed that those who attacked the government from the left could fulminate in the same manner as those who attacked it from the right — and then expect the same repercussions. The title-page poem of the final number of *Mercurius Militaris* made this dramatically clear:

> Who ever dares discover knaves in power
> Must not enjoy his next succeeding hour;
> The Crimes of State, if any Crimes dare call,
> He but prepares for his own funerall.
> Last week even twenty Beagles from the State
> Pursued this Mercury with mortal hate.
> Where's that Rogue (said they) who dares speak Reason?
> When Cries for Justice are voted Treason?
> Where is that Villian thats so politick?
> That gives a just account of each State Trick?
> Who dares the people tell of their hard fate,
> In being slaves to two, the King and State?[49]

Censorship, as well as politics, makes strange bedfellows: Harris, like Nedham and Wharton, was dodging Mabbott's agent, and at the same time supporting Mabbott's party and castigating *Pragmaticus* and *Elencticus*.

He was also imitating these papers in his emphasis on the negative, exploitation of invective, and use of facile verse. Harris' opening statement in the the first number of *Mercurius Militaris* might have appeared in any of the Royalist weeklies. He here announced that he would concentrate on news of the army in order to "tell you of their Councels and Designs . . . and you shall judge whether they levell right at Freedome" — [50] though his concept of "Freedome" raised the hair of those Royalist editors who took notice of him. Further, Harris mocked Charles with a maximum of irreverence, as in his comments on the story of the king's spittle supposedly curing a sick child.[51] He also flung the Levellers' favorite political brickbats: that until England became a democracy, it would remain a degenerate captive of Norman institutions; and that those who opposed this progress were "sycophants," "tyrants," and, in the case of members of Parliament, men who had "designed a perpetuall reign for themselves." [52] In addition, Harris criticized Fairfax, viewed lawyers as "Horse-leeches," and heaped praise on "Honest Jack Lilburne." Finally, in Harris' as in Mabbott's hands, the murder of Rainsborough and his impressive funeral became a smashing attack on all enemies of the people.[53]

Harris, by attacking Charles, Parliament, Cavaliers, Grandees, Scots, religious zealots, and political neutrals, probably irritated everybody but the Levellers. Walker followed a different course in the last short-run weekly of 1648, *Heads of a Diarie*.[54] Its six numbers in December and January stuck close to the official Journals of the House of Commons and gave the news in such a way that no one in power could be irritated or offended. Walker, in contrast to Nedham, was being especially careful because his access to leaders of Parliament was undisguised. He had meanwhile continued to bring out *Packets of Letters* three or four times a month, until the end of November when the news from the north could no longer compete with what was happening in London. His desire to stay in business was most evident, however, in his major weekly, *Perfect Occurrences*, and in his dispute with Mabbott in the summer of 1648 concerning its control. Back in March, Walker had made a half-hearted effort to get the House of Lords to grant him a monopoly in dispensing the news.[55] In July he was impressed by the face that White, Dillingham's printer, had put up a strong case for retaining the title of *The Moderate Intelligencer*; that, if it had not been for the hostility the Lords felt for Mabbott, the printer would have controlled the paper's fate. Consequently in August, Walker petitioned the Upper House to make sure that Mabbott did not poach on his territory.[56] The petition was granted and *Perfect Occurrences* remained Walker's property, at least temporarily inviolate against the encroachments of any ambitious printer or radical censor.

This Friday paper, despite its decline in quality, remained a valuable holding, and two printers still alternated in printing it. But more than ever it was crowded and cautious, its choppy paragraphs full of official jargon, its brief asides platitudinous, its Hebrew anagrams intrusive.[57] It used a few more letters from scattered correspondents than other papers, and it continued printing with some regularity the city's bills of mortality. Walker now sometimes employed self-contradiction to make sure he stayed in step. In the summer of 1648 he reported that Cromwell had sent the king to the Isle of Wight to save him from Lilburne, then a week later denied this explanation.[58] He also included a short account of an attempt to bribe a member of a Parliamentary committee by means of six sugar loaves, then the following week withdrew the charge.[59] In other ways, too, the editor was careful. He gave the murder and funeral of Rainsborough only cursory attention,[60] and avoided comment on the king's trial. But in his lengthy coverage of this event Walker tied together many of the developments between 1642 and 1649 by mentioning that the king had just received a new wardrobe.[61] One of the threads that links the start of the Civil War with the last act of its first major phase was Charles's inveterate short-sightedness and self-induced optimism; and no man could possibly need more than one new suit for his own beheading.

Six weeks before the king's execution *Le Mercure Anglois*, still wearing its old clothes, came to a far less significant end. Dillingham's tenuous relation to this paper, now that he was involved in his own troubles, probably became looser, while the translator continued subtly to betray his conservative sympathies by inserting a few more anti-Independent items than was usual for this four-page weekly. Sometimes, too, a stray adverb or adjective indicated a preference for the Presbyterian point of view: the Prince of Wales had "hereusement" arrived in Holland; the political demands of one regiment were expressed in "termes sy hauts." [62] But *Le Mercure Anglois* remained overwhelmingly careful, impersonal, and superficial. Its final number, in mid-December, consisted entirely of the surface of the news of that hectic week, told without dramatics or comment. Nor did it contain any hint that for eighteen months cross-Channel readers would have no French weekly to keep them half-abreast of what was going on in England.

Assuming that Dillingham was responsible for supervising the translator of *Le Mercure Anglois*, this job helped to teach him two things: a smattering of French and a great deal of caution. The ex-tailor in his *Moderate Intelligencer* now inserted a few obiter dicta in French and saw to it that this, his prime journalistic concern, would remain one of the established newspapers. He not only fought back successfully against White and Mabbott but showed that he was a journalist fit to survive in the dangerous environment of late 1648 and early 1649. In the previous summer he nine times informed his readers that his was still the true *Moderate Intelligencer*, and from then on he understandably suppressed any sympathy he might have felt for the Mabbott-endorsed program of the Levellers. The struggle for survival was rough, but it lacked such modern refinements as a Gestapo: *The Moderate Intelligencer* continued often to bear the imprimatur of Gilbert Mabbott.

Dillingham's survivability was most evident in his increasingly careful competence. He was still able to fill his twelve pages with a coherent summary of public events at home and abroad, usually devoting slightly less than half his space to domestic news.[63] But he now more than ever resembled other licensed journalists in his concern not to offend any official or group who might be able to retaliate. In fact, he could approach absolute innocuousness: the dateline on an item about a complaint against high taxes on September 30 was completed with the phrase "From a Place"; a call for revenge against the Royalists was merely labeled "From a County." [64] Unlike Walker, Dillingham was not yet completely certain that the Independents would gain control. Consequently in the autumn of 1648 he frequently fell back on such an inoffensive and diluted summary as ". . . when it comes to the question whether the distinction of Ecclesiasticall or Civill, whether Monarchicall, Aristocraticall, Democraticall, Episcopall, Presbyterian, or Independent Government be Jure Divino, it's disputed strongly on both sides. . . ." [65] Dillingham was becoming an expert in expediency.

As such he began to give lip-service to the belief that power is self-justifying. In September he implied that the government and the public quite properly operated in different spheres.[66] In December he deserted his tolerationist position and conceded that the magistrate should have at least restrictive powers in the field of religion.[67] And in January 1649, in three consecutive opening editorials, Dillingham climbed aboard Leviathan. The first editorial, written in a tone of nostalgic sadness, included the central clause that "alteration in the Persons or Governours must not be understood as an alteration of power or government"; the second emphasized that it was not the form of government but the nature of the men in power that determined the excellence of a state; and the third urged England to accept her new rulers on the grounds that they were in power.[68]

Dillingham's expediency was a product not only of the times but of his own hard-headedness. It was reflected in his self-censorship and political flexibility, as well as in repeated asides that the country's troubles would be solved if the soldiers were properly paid. Occasionally it was tinged with humor, as in this comment: "There were chosen for Common-Councell-men so many Souldiers, that they may almost serve for a Councel of War." [69] The week after Pride's Purge, a story Dillingham had covered briefly and deftly, he thus began *The Moderate Intelligencer*:

The Souldiers continued their management of the House of Commons. . . . It's said by many, can the courses of the Army be justified? It's answered, Let them not complain who encouraged the Apprentices . . . besides, looke upon former times: when did a Parliament decree but in favour of the conqueror? . . . Parliaments are principally assembled to take off the grievances of the subject, and provide against future miseries, which, if this hath, there lies no complaint.[70]

Dillingham would not, if he could help it, be among those who publicly complained.

This would not be easy. During the second half of 1648 he had often avoided harshly anti-Royalist items and muted his praise of the army. He had even inserted a notice from Wharton that a story in a counterfeit *Elencticus* concerning the nefariousness of Charles and the death of Wharton was untrue.[71] Also, at the start of the king's trial Dillingham had printed a lengthy letter from Amsterdam which argued that Charles should not be executed.[72] Now, in reporting on the trial and beheading, Dillingham was fair and full, and between his lines one can sense sympathy for the chief character in "the famous tragedy . . . drawing to a period." [73] Indeed, the two numbers of *The Moderate Intelligencer* covering the final week in January and the first week in February mingled caution and compassion in such a way that Dillingham achieved a truly impressive objectivity. He deserved to survive. Even so, he still had to play the game according to the rules set down by the army — and now by himself. In mid-January he reported, with dangerous logic, that "[today] being Seboth day, the Pulpits rang against the Army and their proceedings"; the next week he apologized.[74] He delayed printing the king's last speech because to have published it promptly might have been dangerous.[75] Early in February he began an epitome of the Thirty Years' War that for two months would help him safely to fill space. Dillingham had joined Pecke as London's most competent noncontroversial journalist.

In attaining this level Dillingham passed Collings, a man slightly less expedient in subduing his personal inclinations. Consequently, early in 1649, when *The Kingdomes Weekly Intelligencer* got fully in step with the march of history, the change was more noticeable than it was in *The Moderate Intelligencer*. Back in July, in one of his irregular lead editorials, Collings had commented: "The discourse of the Kingdome is indeed concerning Peace . . . but the practice of the Kingdome is the [en]listing of more men. . . . The voyce is Jacobs voyce, but the hands are the hands of Esau." [76] For a while Collings was able to fill much of his space with military news, but even then he frequently implied that peace was the only real cure for England's ills — and "Peace" could easily suggest disapproval of Cromwell and his cohorts. In August and September *The Kingdomes Weekly Intelligencer* contained scattered asides and selected news indicative of the editor's view that a treaty between Parliament and king would be healthful, popular, and nonradical.[77] Collings then hinted that the breakdown in negotiations was the fault of the radicals, not of Charles.[78]

But in the winter of 1648–49 Collings got a tighter grip on his sentiments. He still allowed himself to be against the Levellers, usually by minimizing their activities and underplaying news that might be favorable to them. Rainsborough's funeral, for example, merited only three lines.[79] Even this was not an entirely safe course, and Collings in one instance felt compelled to justify himself: "I have been demanded by some why in this Intelligence I have made no greater mention of the large Petition [of the Levellers] . . . nor of other Petitions in the same Nature. . . . The Answer is as ready as the Complaint: Because the

Parliament hath layd them all aside." [80] This was true; it was certainly not convincing. Collings, however, was careful not to offend Mabbott. When the chief censor presumably threatened him with setting up another Tuesday newspaper, Collings replied to Mabbott (as well as to Dillingham) only with the restrained remark that "I will say no more nor undervalue another to raise my own Intelligence, but will leave to the world to judge if this be not moderate Intelligence, and whether this may not give to reasonable men as full satisfaction, and be as acceptable as that, or any other." [81]

Restraint combined with experience meant that Collings survived and continued to put out a competent weekly. He retained the conviction that news was good if it was hot, and on at least one occasion he held up printing his paper until the last possible minute.[82] He also included a few tidbits missed by other editors, such as the pregnancy of a seventy-one-year-old woman in Scotland, and the information that attendance in Commons was highest between 10:00 A.M. and noon; and he provided the decade's most complete newspaper account of a raid on the theaters.[83] Like Dillingham's, his reporting of the king's trial achieved a high level of impartiality, coherence, and fullness, even sometimes of drama. And running through it were a few compassionate touches that made both Charles and Collings seem more human: "The King carryeth himself very resolutely and looketh well, although he hath no great reason for it, for he hath not bin in bed these two nights"; or, on the day that Charles was beheaded, "This Day it did not rain at all, yet it was a very wet day in and about the City of London by reason of the abundance of affliction that fell from many eyes." [84] Probably Collings dropped a tear or two, if not for the king then for himself, a journalist who had helped to bring the new order into being and then lost his enthusiasm for it.

In all likelihood Border did not weep. His Wednesday paper, *The Perfect Weekly Account*, remained an adequate but second-rate production, barely sufficient unto the day in its coverage of permissible news. More and more frequently the editor fell back on such phrases as "time will tell" in order to avoid giving an opinion or hinting an attitude. The few times he ventured a prediction it was usually inaccurate, as in his expectations that the king would sign a treaty with Parliament.[85] Occasionally, too, he inserted homely and noncontroversial asides, such as the remark that corn prices were much higher in London than only twenty-seven miles away, where it sold for five shillings a bushel.[86] Border also included the second Zionist story to appear in an English newspaper: a report of a petition from two Amsterdam Jews who wanted help in sending their people to Palestine.[87] But generally *The Perfect Weekly Account* stuck to official jargon and public events, giving the Levellers, for instance, enough space to placate them without angering the conservatives, and covering the trial of Charles with just enough fullness to avoid warmth, offense, and incompleteness. In the course of the trial Border began one number with this explanation:

> But . . . in these our dayes the meanest sort of people are not only able to write &c. but to argue and discourse on matters of highest concernment; and thereupon do desire that such things which are most remarkable may be truly committed to writing and made publique. . . .[88]

It was to the "meanest sort of people" among the newspaper-reading public that Border now seemed to be addressing himself.

Enough of their superior brethren were still buying *A Perfect Diurnall* for it to go on appearing in two editions. (Its relatively large circulation is corroborated by the fact that it now carried more advertisements than any other weekly, among them one of the first medical ads — apples and frankincense as a fine remedy; and it sometimes included as many of three separate book notices, at a fee of sixpence each.) [89] Pecke was shrewd in his flexible neutrality, and the developments which he carefully covered but even more carefully failed to comment on represent a roster of the major controversies between June 1648 and January 1649. For instance, when the army marched on London, Pecke merely reprinted the official declaration justifying this intimidation of the city, then gave four lines to the troops' arrival.[90]

Yet he was still the best straight journalist of the era. His reports on the siege of Colchester were clear, condensed, sometimes graphic. He was realistic, if impersonal, about the probable failure of negotiations between king and Parliament. And behind his façade of objectivity one can sense that he knew that nothing would stop Cromwell and the disciplined New Model.[91] Pecke could also placate certain men in power without undue flattery. Cromwell, of course, received a full share of encomia. But Pecke was also sympathetic to Mabbott, and several times he went out of his way to praise the influential William Lilly, an astrologer whose stars boded well for the Independents.[92] Indeed, Pecke very possibly climbed to the journalistic pinnacle of his day in his dispassionate account of Charles's execution. Here is how it began:

> This day the King was beheaded, over against the Banquetting house by White-Hall. . . . He was brought from Saint James about ten in the morning, walking on foot through the Park, with a Regiment of Foot for his guard, with Colours flying, Drums beating . . . with some of his

Gentlemen before, and some behind bareheaded . . . to the Gallery in Whitehall, and so into the Cabinet Chamber, where he used to lye, where he continued at his Devotion, refusing to dine (having before taken the Sacrament), onely about 12. at noone he dranke a Glasse of Claret Wine and eat a piece of bread. From thence he was accompanyed by Dr. Juxon, Col. Thomlinson, Col. Hacker, and the Guards before mentioned, through the Banqueting house adjoyning, to which the Scaffold was erected. . . . The Scaffold was hung round with black, and the floor covered with black, and the Ax and Block laid in the middle of the Scaffold. There were divers companies of Foot and Horse on every side the Scaffold, and the multitudes of people that came to be Spectators very great. . . .[93]

As he wrote these words Pecke may have wondered when the ax of the new order would descend on his paper. Eight months later he had his answer.

CHAPTER X

DECLINE AND FALL

February to October 1649

THE governmental ax did not fall on the journalists of London until autumn 1649, though it had long been hovering over their exposed and nervous necks. But when it descended its blow was not completely fatal. Cromwell could be both a military dictator and a believer in civil liberties, for he and the men around him had battled bishops and Presbyters largely on the grounds of freedom of conscience.[1] Also, the publication of news on a comparatively massive scale was still morally and politically a new problem for any government to cope with. During the late 1640's and the 1650's, therefore, the story of censorship is inconsistent, and often the barks of the censors were worse than their bites. Yet they could bite when occasion and their masters demanded, as both did at the start of 1649 and again in September.

Earlier they had growled. In the summer of 1648 Mabbott asked for more power to deal with the rash of Royalist mercuries.[2] A month later Parliament partly granted his request by appointing a provost marshal and twenty underpaid deputies to aid in sniffing out subversive printers and authors.[3] In January red-coated soldiers joined the hunt, while

Mabbott, probably against his wishes, was assigned two fellow censors. At this time, too, the Stationers' Company, ostensibly purged of its anti-Independent elements, contributed its men and knowledge to the enforcement of the licensing laws.[4] Nor was the House of Commons remiss, for it stepped in to suppress reports of the king's trial.

Early 1649 was a tense moment in English history. In January the Lower House declared that "the People are, under God, the Original of all just Power," and that their representatives in Parliament are supreme.[5] Immediately after Charles's death the kingship and House of Lords were abolished and England became a Commonwealth — but not a republic. Real power lay in the hands of a small and unrepresentative House of Commons and in a politically homogeneous Council of State, both of them creatures, though never completely housebroken creatures, of the high command of the army. By summer Cromwell was leading part of the army to Ireland, there bloodily to put down the rebellion that had again flared. Meanwhile sparks of revolt were burning in England, the London crowds were restive, and a group of Leveller-led soldiers mutinied. In May and July stringent Treason Acts were passed, and at the end of September consolidated and put into effect. By mid-October every licensed London newspaper had been silenced, many of them forever. Thereafter, except for a few fitful months, a relatively free weekly press was, if not dead, moribund.

Preliminary signs of rigor mortis, though evident in all newspapers of 1649, were most clearly exhibited by three weeklies that early in the year entered the arena. The first lasted only five numbers, starting life in January as *The Armies Modest Intelligencer*, then promptly substituting "Weekly" for "Modest." Its first two numbers were noisily polemical. They followed the Leveller line by demanding an end to Norman tyranny, ungodly tithes, and imprisonment for debt, and by approving the fact if not the manner of the king's trial and execution. But beginning with his third number the editor subdued his radical inclinations, and his final issue emasculatedly supported the Commonwealth's efforts to preserve itself.

The second new newspaper of 1649 survived from late January to October 1. That it did so was another indication of the decline of journalism. *A Perfect Summary of Exact Passages* underwent several changes in title but was edited throughout by Theodore Jennings, a man who had served in the New Model and more recently as a glorified errand boy for some of the leading Independents.[6] Concurrent with his entry into journalism he was appointed Mabbott's deputy censor. In this capacity he was lax, as editor laxer.[7] *A Perfect Summary* consisted of short paragraphs dealing with the surface of the news and written in a style that was heavily official and verbose. Their arrangement was careless, and even the editor's brief concluding summaries were not always accurate. Jennings' paper was no rival to *A Perfect Diurnall*, though it too appeared on Monday. Yet its actuarial expectations were as good as those for Pecke's paper, since Jennings hewed to the government line with absolute tenacity. From his first number, when he praised a non-monarchical system, to his last, when he approved of the acts to stifle the press, he never criticized the actions of the Commonwealth. Often, too, he glossed over the news so that no one else would find fault with the Rump, the Council of State, and the New Model. The abolition of the kingship received one line, the new Leveller "Agreement of the People" four lines, and the storming of Drogheda less than half a page; [8] and one of the final items in the last issue of *A Perfect Summary* was the apologetic announcement that "those appointed to license (when this Copy was writ) not being concluded as then who should license, I hope it will not be offensive that I as well as others before me have for this one week put out my Summary. . . ." [9]

The third new newspaper of 1649, *The Kingdomes Faithfull and Impartiall Scout*, was also undistinguished. During its eight months' existence from February to October it was edited by Border, now one of the more experienced journalists and a man who had learned to hold his head above water by floating with the current and, if necessary, by kicking.[10] He managed to give the semiofficial news in a straightforward manner, usually with much unobtrusive self-censorship, and he was trained enough to supply periodic relief by personal touches. His acquired professionalism can be seen in his treatment of the Levellers, a group that as Cromwell turned against them grew increasingly disaffected with the Commonwealth. Over and over the editor inserted mildly anti-Leveller comments in his descriptions of their pleas, uprisings, and punishments. But at the same time he never lost his subdued admiration for the courage of their leaders and for a few of their aims which were not openly hostile to the government. In telling of the funeral of Robert Lockyer, the one Leveller executed for mutiny, Border observed that its "Solemnity . . . surpassed any that hath been in London many yeers . . . he was but a private Trooper, but a most heroick Spirit." [11] And in a brief anecdote from Paris about two American Indians who had expressed democratic opinions, Border commented, "a worthy expression of two Heathen Levellers." [12] He showed similar control in his account of the Diggers, a small band who in the spring of 1649 tried to establish communism on a hilltop in Surrey.[13]

Yet Border could kick, not against the government but against one of its spokesmen, Henry Walker. The squabble began in March when

Border imitated Walker's exhibitionistic use of Hebrew (though he later shifted to Latin and Greek) and took over from Walker the habit of reprinting the London bills of mortality. From April on, Border stole a march on his rival by including William Lilly's monthly pro-government prognostications. Then early in June *The Kingdomes Faithfull and Impartiall Scout* featured a full and sympathetic account of Mabbott's resignation as censor. At this point the squabble momentarily became rough and tumble. The following week Walker's *Perfect Occurrences* contained this statement:

> I am desired to insert something here in behalf of Mr. Whaley [the man who, with Jennings, had been appointed deputy censor] . . . whose name was last week printed to not onely malignant lyes of newes from beyond Seas in the Pamphlet called The Weekly Scout, but of his Imprimatur to some ridiculous vaine absurd propositions therein, in the name of Mr. Mabbot, as that licensing is a monopoly, and his judgement . . . that every one may print what he list, and the like.[14]

Walker went on to flatter the government and to hint his own regret that he had neither the power nor the perquisites of a censor. A week later the *Scout* replied by attacking Walker for his greed, knavery, background, and incompetence.[15] Walker's turn was next, and he let Jennings pinch-hit:

> I [Jennings] desire all people to take notice that I denie to give any authority to a Pamphlet called The Kingdomes Scout, because the Common-wealth hath been so abused by it, by Robert Wood of Grubstreet [the publisher of the *Scout*], who contrives false inventions at an Alehouse to adde to it what he fancies as news, after M. Border the author hath write it, and the Licenser perused it, and thus he hath abused the Judge Advocate [Whaley] and my selfe and the Common-wealth; and the Author . . . doth now disclaim it, refusing any more to write it for him; and if he be so impudent still to publish it, I desire all those whom it concernes to suppress it that the people may not be cheated by it.[16]

Jennings' complaint reveals two matters of more importance than the contretemps between Walker and Border. The first is its evidence of carelessness and confusion in the censorship: who was to license what paper? what happened if material was added after a paper had been approved? who was to blame if a properly censored issue contained items offensive to the government? what happened if a weekly was not licensed at all? The brief history of *The Kingdomes Faithfull and Impartiall Scout* answers each of these questions: no one quite knew. Most of the time the paper was licensed, occasionally not. When it was, first Mabbott supplied his imprimatur, then Jennings, and once or twice

Whaley; and Jennings continued to "approve" the *Scout* after his charges against its publisher.[17] Moreover, like other established papers, it contained comments and late news added after an issue had been officially approved. The government cracked down only if it considered a paper dangerous, and then an imprimatur was no guarantee of safety. In short, until October 1649 censorship was effective as a threat; in its day by day operations it was slipshod. But Jennings' complaint also reveals an attempt to divide publisher from editor. Despite Dillingham's earlier success in retaining the title of *The Moderate Intelligencer*, the printer or publisher normally controlled a paper. The editor was his employee and probably had no vested interest in the weekly, though in such long-run relationships as that between Pecke and his printers some sort of profit-sharing scheme may have been set up. In the case of the *Scout*, however, Wood and Border rebutted Jennings by not splitting up.

They also continued to squabble with Walker. At the end of June they defended the loyalty of the *Scout* and accused Walker of being a "schismatical Conventicler" who was trying to make money by getting a friend appointed official hangman. In addition, they pointed out that Jennings regularly approved of *Perfect Occurrences* without, as he admitted, reading it in full.[18] Thereafter the squabble faded away. If there was a winner, it was probably Wood and Border, for Walker began in July to supplement his Friday's *Occurrences* with a Tuesday paper, and thus he no longer put all his journalistic eggs into direct competition with the *Scout*. Yet Wood and Border now saw to it that their paper was more cautious and subdued than ever. An item like the report that between 700 and 800 people had died of hunger in Lancashire was treated as if it had no connection with the politics or economics of England.[19] Even the editor's bits of humor assumed a more subservient cast, as in his comment on the rumor that natives of Florida lived two or three centuries: Florida would therefore be a good place to send those heretical Englishmen who believed the soul died with the body.[20] Florida might also have been a good spot for *The Kingdomes Faithfull and Impartiall Scout*, which early in October was silenced by the suddenly firm hand of the government.

So were all the established weeklies, though only *The Moderate* failed to exit quietly. From February to May 1649, while Mabbott was still at least nominally chief licenser, it emphasized two motifs: the justice of the Leveller program, and, as a sort of counterpoint, the economic distress that was making radical reform more necessary. But these two themes occupied only a small share of the weekly's twelve pages. Mabbott's customary three to five pages of foreign news were adequate, his correspondent from Edinburgh particularly well informed and coherent, his coverage of semiofficial news almost as capable as Pecke's, and some of his opening editorials as safe and platitudinous as those of his colleagues. Mabbott was even willing to immerse himself in the primitive credulity of many of his contemporaries, as when he reprinted a letter from Scotland that drooled over a local witch-hunt.[21] Even so, the approximately 10 per cent of the paper given over to controversy sharply distinguished *The Moderate* from other weeklies and kept it the voice of organized if disintegrating radicalism.

Between the death of the king and his own resignation from the office of censor Mabbott went on supporting the aims and slogans of the Levellers. He advocated the abolition of the House of Lords and of certain undemocratic ceremonial oaths, as well as of various traditional honors and stipends. He urged that the law be simplified, the judiciary decentralized, and class distinctions before the law eliminated. He spoke up for a more equitable redistribution of land and the end of tithes. He was against imprisonment for debt and in favor of a truly representative Parliament; and he castigated religious persecution while pleading for the right of free speech. Nor is this list complete, for Mabbott attacked other forms of "Norman tyranny." Further, he usually reprinted at least one pro-Leveller petition each week and called attention to the many for which he did not have space. Early in March, in one of two numbers that he expanded to sixteen pages, the editor gave half his paper to Lilburne's impassioned defense of his right to criticize the government.[22] In April, Mabbott again produced a sixteen-page paper, this time to defend the four imprisoned leaders of the Leveller party and to print their self-justifying *Manifestation*.[23] He recurrently made much of their vicissitudes and the agitation in their behalf, and he refused to be horrified at a Leveller-inspired mutiny in the army.[24] He even included, without any derogatory comment, a "Declaration" from the Diggers in support of their attempt literally to sow the seeds of English communism.[25]

Cromwell and the regicides had themselves been labeled as radicals, and many of the aims and slogans of the Levellers — though not of the Diggers — were espoused by the more militant Independents. Hence Mabbott was not jailed, not even dismissed from his licensing job; nor was *The Moderate* suppressed, though it was threatened. But Cromwell did have the problem of ruling a disturbed and disaffected country, one surrounded by hostile foreign powers. No Robespierre or Stalin, he was willing to permit *The Moderate* to clamor for reforms to which he and the men around him had at least given lip service.

These men, however, were not willing to let it or any other voice become an active threat to the government. Lilburne and his fellow leaders of the Leveller party were not acquitted and released from the Tower until the end of 1649, and then were told not to engage in politics. Meanwhile in May the army mutiny was quickly and effectively suppressed.

Yet the second motif that Mabbott emphasized, England's economic distress, makes the survival of *The Moderate* more surprising, and it underlines some of the anomalies and problems of England's transition to a quasi-republic. Matters of the pocketbook have usually been more effective than larger ideological issues in moving men to action, as Mabbott, a contemporary of Harrington, was aware. Thus from February through May *The Moderate* stressed the economic plight of England. In almost every petition it reprinted were references to the dislocation and stagnation of trade. In editorials and asides, as well as in frequent letters, the editor and his correspondents called attention to poverty, unemployment, hunger. Sometimes he anticipated the conservative argument in behalf of Roosevelt's New Deal, as in the implied threat that, if the poor were not relieved, "their necessities will enforce them to be rich, and level what they never intended." [26] Sometimes he was more incendiary: "Must we still grind the faces of the poor, and maintain the mighty in their vain glory?" [27] Consequently the readers of *The Moderate* must have grasped the connection between the country's economic ills and the apparently high-handed and self-seeking activities of the Rump and the Council of State, a connection made even clearer by the paper's emphasis on the aims and sufferings of the Levellers.

But among these readers were certain persons high in the government who undoubtedly informed such apologists as Henry Walker that it would be appropriate to join the hue and cry against Mabbott. Early in May the Council of State threatened to suppress *The Moderate*,[28] and a few days later Parliament accepted the editor's resignation as censor. At the end of the month Mabbott got Pecke and Border to print the reasons for his resignation, reasons that have not yet become practically or ideologically obsolete:

1 Because many thousand of scandalous and Malignant Pamphlets have been published with his name thereunto, as if he had licensed the same (though he never saw them) on purpose (as he conceives) to prejudice him in his reputation amongst the honest party of this Nation.

2 Because that Imployment (as he conceives) is unjust and ilegall as to the end of its first Institution, viz. To stop the Presse for publishing any thing that might discover the Corruption of Church or State in the time of

Popery, Episcopacy, and Tyranny, the better to keep the People in Ignorance, and carry on their Popish, Factious, Trayterous and Tyranicall designes for the enslaving and distruction both of the bodies and Soules of all the free people of this Nation.

3 Because Licencing is as great a Monopoly as ever was in this Nation, in that all mens Judgements, Reasons &c. are to be bound up in the Licensers (as to Lycenceing), for if the Author of any sheet, Book or Treatise writ not to please the fancie, and come within the compasse of the Lycencers Judgement, then he is not to receive any stamp of authority for publishing thereof.

4 Because it is lawfull (in his Judgement) to print any Book, sheet, &c. without Lycencing, so as that the Authors and Printers do subscribe their true names thereunto, that so they may be lyable to answer the contents thereof, and if they offend therein, then to be punished by such Lawes as are or shall be for those cases provided.[29]

It would be tempting to see here the influence of Milton. But Mabbott's main inspiration came from his own experiences as censor, with an assist from the _humble Petition_ of the Levellers which five months earlier had steamed from the pen of Richard Overton.[30] Even if frustration was Mabbott's prime motive, his tolerance as licenser and his adherence to the Leveller cause suggest that principle then played some part in determining the actions of this man who in 1653 came back to the job of censor, and eight years later was granted a profitable monopoly by Charles II.[31]

But in the summer of 1649 these events were still in the future, and for three months _The Moderate_, blessed with the imprimatur of Jennings, trimmed its sails to the prevailing winds. Almost all its space was given over to the presentation of Westminster news, either in reprinted ordinances or in summaries of official acts, and to four or five pages of foreign news. Its sporadic editorials were tame and platitudinous, and what few anti-government asides intruded were sufficiently oblique to be inoffensive. Mabbott still allowed himself to be anti-Presbyterian, a stand which involved little risk, and to print more news of the fading Leveller cause than did his contemporaries. Yet he swung far enough to the right to approve the suppression of a tract justifying the Leveller mutineers.[32]

Then suddenly in September the final three numbers of _The Moderate_, lacking any censor's seal of approval, moved most of the way back to a position of radical defiance.[33] Number 61 began with the statement that the people, as a result of graft and high taxes, have started to "rage and cry out for a lawful Representative," and the next issue contained several items openly friendly to the Levellers.

The final number, covering the week of September 18–25, opened with an editorial leading to the conclusion that national unity and tranquillity required that the people "be totally Free, or absolutely tyed to Servitude." Embedded in the paper's straight news reports were three stories which conveyed regret, plus a touch of anger, at the now evident fact that the Leveller cause was vanquished. Finally, Mabbott was the only non-Royalist editor to criticize the new licensing act, pointing out that it was, if nothing else, cumbersome. It was, but not unworkable enough to permit *The Moderate* to rise again. For more than a century no newspaper in England so sustainedly called for the implementation of democracy, so vehemently pleaded the case for the dignity of all Englishmen.

If Mabbott in 1649 was controversial, Walker was contentious. He fought with Border and Mabbott, and he took special relish in harrying Royalist mercuries. But he was also enterprising, and his journalistic activities show that he was as much a businessman as a newspaperman. Until its demise in October, Walker used *Perfect Occurrences* not only to make money but to promote other ventures in which he had a financial stake. It contained the same number of advertisements as most other established papers — one or two a week — but twice Walker ran an embryonic advertising campaign. One took place in August, when *Perfect Occurrences* announced that an "office of Entries" was to be set up in London. This office, Walker's own project, was to handle notices, at four pence each, about lands and goods for sale or lease, jobs offered and wanted, shipping and coach schedules, and other commercial items; and it functioned on the theory that a centralized place of exchange would provide a cheaper and more efficient way of doing business than the old way of posting bills around the city.[34] The other campaign, also in the summer of 1649, involved Sir Balthazar Gerbier, an art dealer and semiprofessional man of the world. Gerbier had just opened an academy in London where young men were to be taught, for a high fee, all the arts of being a gentleman.[35] Though the academy did not prosper, Walker, either flattered by knowing a cosmopolite like Gerbier or having a financial interest in his venture, several times gave it glowing publicity.[36]

Nor did Walker stop there in his self-promotional schemes. The final three numbers of *Perfect Occurrences* contained notices of public Hebrew lectures to be given by the editor. Though free, these would no doubt add to his fame.[37] Just before then Walker began but promptly dropped another plan, the announcement of which is self-explanatory:

Those that desire to looke back upon what the Parliament have done from their first sitting shall have a briefe collection every week . . . and all such Gentlemen and others, who desire to lay the same by them till they have the whole, may cut out the two following leaves, and that halfe sheet will begin that Chronicle, and in time (if God permit) will meet with this latter part [i.e., catch up with *Perfect Occurrences*], and then they will have all complete.[38]

Then followed *Perfect Occurrences of Every daies journall in Parliament* . . . collected by Henry Walker, dated November 3 to December 4, 1640, and consisting of four pages of a day-by-day summary of those distant events. Walker, had he lived long enough, might have gone on to invent the crossword puzzle and the comic strip.

Entrepreneur Walker was of course careful to see that his major investment, *Perfect Occurrences*, stayed in business; consequently he hewed to the government line. He approved of various methods of tightening the censorship, gloated over captured Royalist editors, and on occasion went out of his way to be optimistic about England's republican future.[39] He gave the Levellers adequate and generally objective coverage, but could be hostile when it seemed appropriate. The editor advocated, for instance, the suppression of one of Lilburne's books, and he reported that had the Leveller mutineers been successful, they would have murdered all ministers and lawyers and communized all private property.[40] Walker was also voluminous. In February he expanded the paper to twelve pages, then to sixteen, and he invariably crowded them with choppy paragraphs of authorized news, usually leaving himself only one or two pages for foreign affairs. He was willing, however, to bid for the goodwill of his readers by such devices as pleading for lower food prices or including off-color anecdotes, such as the story of a soldier who tried to force a girl to steal a chamber pot.[41]

Walker's weekly continued to be successful. It was still printed on alternate weeks by separate printers, and at least once it was counterfeited.[42] Even so, it joined its fellows on their forced march into oblivion. The 145th and final number of *Perfect Occurrences* contained, along with its large quota of straight pro-government news, a plug for the editor's Hebrew lectures, an optimistic notice about the "office of Entries," and a page on the bloodthirstiness of the Irish (the previous week Walker had included a brief account of the capture of Drogheda). But the paper gave no hint that it was about to be silenced.[43]

Earlier Walker had also exhibited his resourcefulness by establishing *A Tuesdaies Journall* to supplement Friday's *Perfect Occurrences*. In March 1649 another post was set up to link London with the rest of the country,[44] and in July and August, Walker took advantage of it. His second newspaper was printed by his regular printer, Robert Ibbitson, and carried on its title page the coat of arms of the Commonwealth. Walker announced its arrival in *Perfect Occurrences*, giving the impression that he had been ordered by Parliament to supply this means for the public to get the true news twice a week.[45] Thus the eight-page *A Tuesdaies Journall* provided a condensed version of *Perfect Occurrences*, including plugs for Gerbier and the editor's Hebrew lessons.

Border also had two strings to his journalistic bow: Friday's *The Kingdomes Faithful and Impartiall Scout*, which had started in January, and Wednesday's *The Perfect Weekly Account*, with which he had been connected since late 1647. He concentrated his limited talents on the newer paper, and *The Perfect Weekly Account*, besides no longer being consecutively numbered, was duller and more cautious. For instance, the week after the *Scout* printed Mabbott's statement on his resignation, *The Perfect Weekly Account* had a paragraph on why these reasons were false.[46] At the end of September, just before both papers were shut down, Border concluded one number of *The Perfect Weekly Account* with the remark that ". . . this sheet was in the Press before the Act for regulating Printing was published . . . but for the future I shall be conformable to the Act, and do nothing irregular or without the License derived from thence." [47] It would have been difficult for anyone to view the paper as other than "conformable." [48]

In the early autumn Border mentioned that London alehouse keepers had been ordered to sell their best beer or ale at a penny a quart.[49] A foaming tankard might have seemed a better buy than either of Border's papers, but probably not than Dillingham's twelve-page *Moderate Intelligencer*; for during its final ten months it shared with *A Perfect Diurnall* the distinction of being England's best newspaper. Dillingham had come a long way professionally, but he had also traveled far politically and philosophically. His weekly continued to dispense news the government thought proper in a clear and comparatively full manner, and its foreign coverage, whether occupying one or nine pages, was almost always competent. He now gave somewhat more space than his competitors to what was happening in Ireland, and better than they he sensed the impending threat to the Commonwealth coming from Scotland. He could also still write safe but not necessarily flaccid editorials and show considerable skill in inserting interesting but noncontroversial fillers when there was a dearth of safe news. (The longest and, to an American, the most readable of these incipient feature stories is a detailed description of North Carolina.) [50]

Dillingham's professional development had been slow and steady. His shift to the political and philosophical right was more rapid and intermittent, but by mid-1649 he had completed his move from groping liberalism to an assured and expedient conservatism. This conservatism manifested itself in three ways. Most important was his articulate support of the government. Early in February he commented, "There's Kings gone, them and Lords in two dayes: how easie it is to pull down," and he directed his readers to turn to that part of II Samuel where the daughters of Israel are told to weep over Saul.[51] But even if Dillingham was distressed at how the mighty had fallen, he quickly changed his tune. Two weeks later his opening editorial supported the government and the high taxes necessary to maintain it, and contrasted peaceful England to war-torn Germany.[52] Then to underline this contrast and safely fill space, Dillingham included a serial history of the Thirty Years' War, beginning it in February and concluding it in April. Also, he was now openly hostile to the Levellers. In March, for instance, *The Moderate Intelligencer* contained this alarmist account of radical activities:

> We begin . . . to be in amazement to see what is done in this Town [London], and in severall parts of the Country, even upon the market days. . . . [Pro-Leveller] troopers coming with the late Printed papers and Petitions . . . affixing them upon posts, reading them at market places, making speeches to the people exhorting them to joyne with them, disswading them from paying excise before the faces of those that appeared to receive them. . . . They tell the people they will live and die with them in their deliverance from such like slaveries and this new Tyranny, naming the most eminent in the Army to the people as the causers of it; with these Troopers doe accompany many of the people . . . and some of the Militia; others underhand doe abet them. If those that governe doe not something to stop these proceedings, and by way of ease, troubles will undoubtedly arise. . . .[53]

Whenever the government did something to stop these proceedings, Dillingham supported it. In May and June he vigorously editorialized in favor of an iron fist to beat down the Irish, and he once recommended that settlers be brought from New England to make Ireland a more amenable colony.[54] Finally, he supported the government by inserting a few items reflecting on Charles II, including the allegation that the prince, like his father, was pro-Catholic.[55]

The second way in which the editor manifested his move to the right was his adherence to a generally conservative economic policy. In three consecutive weeks in the spring he mocked at utopian and single-package economic panaceas; he advised government officials and what was left of the nobility to get back into the habit of conspicuous consumption so that trade could be increased; and he stated that England's economic woes were largely the result of the middle class's fears for its own stability, though he added that he was against any form of price control to assuage these fears.[56] The following week he urged that the Commonwealth set up a plan to guarantee year-round employment for the poor.[57] This met with official disapproval, for the editor then wrote that he had been advised to drop such radical ideas, at which point he quickly changed the subject and accused the Levellers of interfering with the conquest of Ireland.[58] Three months later, after having largely avoided the touchy problem of economic reform, Dillingham took a neutral position on the need to end imprisonment for debt; and in September, on an issue that was receiving widespread publicity, he sided with the Earl of Rutland against the coal miners of Derbyshire.[59]

The third way in which Dillingham displayed his move to the right was by the intensification of his Hobbesianism. In February, though dubious about the abolition of the kingship and House of Lords, he decided that "a passive posture will have most comfort, least hazard." [60] Thereafter he several times recommended passive acceptance to any who might be disgruntled with the government. He also came fully around to the Erastian-Hobbesian view that the church should be, at least outwardly, the creature of the state.[61] He even extended to the field of domestic relations the concept that power justifies itself, reversing his earlier stand by announcing that he opposed any easing of the divorce laws and believed marriage should always require parental consent.[62]

During the final month of his paper's life Dillingham, aware that the end was near, allowed himself to brag about his new conservatism and old competence. He was proud of his ability unobtrusively to shun dangerous news; and he referred to himself as one of those "who set themselves with all their studies to speak and write the best they possibly can meet with in commendation of the Governours of this Commonwealth, among whom this Author apprehends himself to have equalled, if not exceeded, any who have done it, without fawning, lying or dissembling." [63] The next-to-last number of *The Moderate Intelligencer* concluded with the notice that, if it was ordered to cease publication, the editor would take "leave of his friends, with a wish that the succeeder, whoever, be as impartiall." [64] At the end of the 237th and final number, after a lengthy pro-English account of the massacre at Drogheda, he bade a cryptic farewell to his public:

> This work, for the future, is left for those whom Fame saith wants none. It's the opinion of most that a bowle without bias is best, others that a little bias is tolerable; some think a great bias is better than either . . . let it then be so, a la moade de France.[65]

For Dillingham, though he later very briefly returned to journalism, it was good-by, not au revoir. The saga of *The Moderate Intelligencer*, during its four-and-a-half-year life, shows that his departure would be a loss. It also shows that, in the seventeenth century, experience was the best school of journalism — and Dillingham had earned his degree the hard way.

So had Richard Collings, the durable editor of *The Kingdomes Weekly Intelligencer*; and during its last ten months he did his best to avoid the suppression that silenced him in October. Possibly in anticipation of this eventuality he inserted more comments on how to present the news than did other journalists. In June he noted that "the Generall Demand of the people is, What is your newes from Ireland? The sellers of the weekly sheets make answer, and cry aloud in the streets, Newes hot from Ireland." [66] And Collings shrewdly saw to it that the hawkers of his paper had plenty of Irish news to peddle. At the same time he continued to pride himself on his honesty and, as had been true since his first entry into journalism, on his adept handling of military news. Thus in August, when rumors of English successes in Ireland were being widely circulated, Collings warned and reassured his readers:

> And indeed in many Papers there have been such apparent contradictions and such a thwarting of the truth by an endeavour to inlarge the story, that whiles the Reader turns Sceptick and finds he hath reason to suspect something, hee therefore doth draw unto himselfe a wilde conclusion and will believe nothing —

but, he went on, his readers received reports that were not "defective or excessive," and which came from "honest hands." [67]

The reconquest of the Irish was, however, a far less dangerous topic than the reform of the English, and Collings trod a careful path in his generally impersonal and condensed coverage of the Rump and Council of State. Often he called attention to his concern for truth, but truth judiciously retailed. He would, he claimed, "omit nothing . . . worthy of . . . observance," and he would "truly and faithfully represent the sense and censure of the House of Commons." [68] Yet Collings' definition of "worthy" had become increasingly cautious, a process which he now sometimes went out of his way to rationalize, as in this passage in the summer of 1649:

> The Parliament this day not sitting, and therefore this present Wednesday being likely to have blanks enough, I had an intention to give you what other Pens doe so much in vaine overburden you with, and that is the Debates of the Parliament . . . but these (untill they are passed into orders or acts) being rather Subjects of discourse than of satisfaction, I doe purposely omit them. [69]

And in the next-to-last number of *The Kingdomes Weekly Intelligencer* Collings reviewed his journalistic past and his present plight:

> The businesse of this Pen being (as I have alwayes said) to declare unto you the actions in the field, I have for the most part waved the Parliament news, and shall so continue untill I am better satisfied with what safety . . . this Pen may walk upon this Paper, which I conceive was never more uncertaine than at this present. And truly for my owne part, if I had their [Parliament's] whole journalls lying by me, I should forbeare to give you the account thereof. [70]

Whether because of his forbearance or his industry [71] or his functional prose, Collings was able to claim in September that "the Prince (for all his Agents) is much streightened in his Intelligence, and I believe it to be the reason why he reads all our weekly Books of news, amongst which that which he gives most credit to (if I heare the truth) is this." [72]

The editor might have added that if Charles read *The Kingdomes Weekly Intelligencer* it may have been because he could detect sympathy for himself between, and occasionally in, its lines. Sometimes this sympathy was dimly reflected in Collings' use of light irony, as in this comment on the execution of three high Royalist officers: "And this week will make it selfe . . . famous. . . . In one Day you shall find executed a Duke, an Earle, and a Lord, which is more than ever England saw in the Court of Justice since she . . . by Commerce with other Nations hath been refined from fable and neglect. . . ." [73] Sometimes Collings let his sympathy for Charles seep to the surface, as in his account of the prince's grief at his father's death or in the story of the young man's reunion with his mother. [74] Collings was, of course, careful not to go too far, and even to draw back, as he did, for instance, when he promoted the rumor that Charles was about to turn Catholic. [75] But the editor also expressed sympathy by omission, by quietly avoiding boos for the Royalists and cheers for the Commonwealth.

Collings' care to escape the wrath of the Commonwealth and yet to flatter it as little as possible can be seen in his treatment of the Levellers. As a potential Burkean conservative he disapproved their long-run aims but approved their agitation against the Grandees. His account of Lockyer's funeral, for instance, was sympathetic without being overtly political.[76] He also claimed that the army mutineers, because they were willing to destroy property, were not really Levellers; and without in any way condoning them he proceeded to refer to the rebelling soldiers as "Dissenters." [77] Again in September, after a second Leveller-inspired mutiny had been crushed, Collings repeated these semantic antics, though the following week he acknowledged that the "Levellers so called, who were the hope and fear of the two parties in this divided Nation," had been "reduced to . . . obedience." [78]

Collings was his most cautious just as the end came. His only news of the capture of Drogheda was Cromwell's official letter justifying the massacre. The next week, ending October 9, the 332nd and last issue of *The Kingdomes Weekly Intelligencer* contained no sign of its editor's personality or views. Nine months later, however, the paper, under a slightly different title, returned to the journalistic hustings. It was again guided by the trained hand of "R.C." — a hand that had learned, among other things, how not to show itself.

After October the professional hand of Samuel Pecke played only a small part in the shaping of English journalism. Yet until then *A Perfect Diurnall* continued to be coherent, carefully impersonal, and relatively complete. During its final seven months it usually consisted of sixteen pages, with only two or three pages normally given over to foreign events. It remained successful, appearing in two separate editions, and along with *The Kingdomes Weekly Intelligencer*, getting twice as much income from advertising as most papers: two or three shillings a week. Moreover, for two weeks in July — shades of 1642 — Robert Wood published a rival *Perfect Diurnall*, which also came out on Monday.[79] Finally, unlike his colleagues, Pecke was careful to see that his paper was regularly entered in the Stationers' Register.[80] He had a good job and wanted to keep it.

More than ever Pecke was now a straight newsman, one who without fanfare seemed to approve of whatever group was in power. In September when the Leveller cause had been throttled, he shifted away from neutrality toward the radicals and made much of the alleged collusion between Levellers and Royalists.[81] Increasingly he relied on the official and semiofficial handouts that constituted the news of England, Ireland, and Scotland that the Council of State thought proper. In the autumn, when these items did not fill his weekly, Pecke borrowed a leaf from Walker and inserted "A Perfect Diurnall" of first two then four pages that began to cover the news of Parliament for 1640. All this could not save the day. On October 8, 1649, *A Perfect Diurnall* was shut down. In November it reappeared in a single issue of eight pages. Thereafter, for the first time since early 1642 no *Perfect Diurnall* from the pen of Samuel Pecke was for sale on the streets of London. Doubtless it was missed.

Prior to the extinction of the established press, several new weeklies tried to take advantage of any lessening in the censorial heat. In January and February the government used soldiers and agents of the Stationers' Company to ferret out hostile printers and writers. In April and May the leaders of the army, convinced that the war in Ireland would be popular, temporarily restrained their searchers; though in June, after Mabbott's resignation, they were again briefly let loose. Then until September, despite the fact that there were several censors each with his own area of jurisdiction, and despite the proliferation of acts and resolutions to control the press, enforcement was lax.[82] In general the harshness of execution depended on the attitude of the military high command, not on what was on the statute books, and that attitude could and did fluctuate.

These fluctuations were reflected by the varying number of new licensed weeklies that appeared during the spring and summer of 1649. From early March until mid-September *The Impartiall Intelligencer* risked suppression by going into business, but in no other way. Its twenty-eight issues were devoted to a bare summary of that news which was common to all licensed papers. If a story was not unanimous, the editor followed the majority, as when he joined the pack in July in attacking Border's *Scout*.[83] More than any other paper of 1649 it resembled the official Journal of Parliament.

A Modest Narrative of Intelligence began life in April and ended it in September. It too tempered itself to changes in the official wind, in keeping with its opening statement that it would print only what would "serve for all . . . [to] take notice of, either as to their duty in order to obedience, or to their good in order to their much desired quiet." This end-of-the-week paper was set up to take advantage of the newly established Saturday post from London; what it printed was therefore further watered down because it was partly addressed to a rural audience. The first dozen numbers opened with editorial attacks on the Levellers or on their alleged brothers under the skin, the Diggers. At the end of June the editor proclaimed the demise of the radicals, and consequently the end of his need to refute them. Then for three months he editorialized on such subjects as the goodness of altruism, the excellence of obedience, and the benefits of wisdom and religion. In September, in his two final numbers, he returned to attacking the Levellers. All his controversial editorials are significant not only because they reveal the thinking of a man who wanted to keep in step with the authorities, but because they indicate the lack of sophistication of the non-London public, for whom they seem mainly to have been written. His chief argument, though very possibly true, would probably not have appealed to a knowledgeable Londoner. If, he wrote, the Levellers had their way and a democratic election were held, then the Royalists would win; if the Royalists were excluded from the franchise, then the Presbyterians would win; therefore the Rump should not be dissolved and the Levellers should stop trying to divide the country by demanding an election.[84]

But the editor was not incompetent. He was skillful in scattering Latin quotations and bits of verse, and his handling of straight news was selective and coherent. Indeed, the final paragraph of the final number told what happened at Drogheda, before the news had a chance to grow cold or be twisted by second thoughts on the part of the government. *A Modest Narrative* managed to hang on for twenty-five numbers, and it once contained a notice that its advertisements, at least those for lost horses, had produced results.[85]

Continued Heads of Perfect Passages in Parliament was the third licensed weekly to take advantage of the relaxation of censorship in the early spring. Crowded, safe, impersonal, it survived only five numbers, its one distinction being that its editor twice inserted Old English proverbs in his platitudinous opening paragraphs.[86]

Five additional licensed weeklies soon bobbed to the surface. *England's Moderate Messenger* lasted from late April to early July, its eleven numbers achieving typicality in every respect but one: the large amount of space it gave to the Levellers before the May mutiny.[87] *Mercurius Brittanicus*, now with two "t"'s but without Nedham, for four numbers devoted more than half its space to detailed and scurrilous attacks on *Pragmaticus*, even including a reply to the Royalist assault on Cromwell's nose.[88] But the paper's last two numbers, in late May and early June, subsided into mediocrity. In May, too, *A Moderate Intelligence*, in the two weeks it survived, was totally undistinguished, as were the two numbers of *Mercurius Pacificus* and the one number of *Mercurius Republicus* at the end of the month.

In the summer, when the atmosphere for journalism was again a little less lowering, three more weeklies, each properly licensed, bid for their share of London's pennies. Late in June *The Moderate*

Mercury collected only a few. Its two numbers — in spite of the editor's claim that he would give his readers only what was "more remarkable and less common," and in spite of such personal touches as "I forgot to tell you . . ." — conformed to the pattern of all authorized weeklies. So did *The Moderate Messenger*, which at the end of July continued the paper that had been entitled *England's Moderate Messenger*, and which, with the aid of much borrowing from Walker and Border, hung on until September.[89] The third new authorized weekly of that summer changed its title and printer and came out three times in August. For one week, as the *Armies Painfull-Messenger*, it was undistinguished; for two weeks, as *Great Britaines Paine-Full Messenger*, it was equally so. In the autumn no publisher took the risk of starting a paper.[90]

Variations in the stringency of the censorship were more clearly reflected by the number of unlicensed papers, all but two of them Royalist, which were surreptitiously printed during 1649. The approximate box-score is instructive. In February and March only *Pragmaticus* and *Elencticus* appeared, and then only for a total of eight issues. In April six unauthorized weeklies rolled up a total of eleven issues. In May, when a high of twenty-six different papers were for sale, ten unlicensed ones amassed between them twenty-three numbers. In June, July, and August, four or five surreptitious weeklies achieved a monthly average total of fourteen issues. In September the number of unlicensed papers rose to six, their combined number of appearances to sixteen. In October these figures shrank to four and fourteen respectively, in November to three and seven. Finally, in December, *Mercurius Pragmaticus*, the lone survivor, came out twice.[91] Notwithstanding the crowded and jumbled maze that was seventeenth-century London, diligent censorial hounds could eventually sniff out even the best-hidden presses and most anonymous editors.

One of the two non-Royalist foxes in this hunt closed shop before he was detected. John Harris for three weeks in April and May again entered the political wars by reviving the pro-Leveller *Mercurius Militaris*.[92] He easily resumed his earlier stance, striking out lustily at Cromwell and the Grandees, and employing the techniques of the Royalist mercuries — from scurrilous verse to gay invective to smutty innuendo — to give force to his blows. No *Moderate*, *Mercurius Militaris* belabored the Levellers' highest-placed opponents, on the assumption that the Rump was subordinate to the Council of State and both were under the thumb of the Council of War.[93] Harris also found space for straight news, radical editorializing, and scattered attacks on journalists in both camps; and he managed to give the impression that the unpopular and tyrannical military government, riddled by graft, would soon fall before the democratic onslaught of the Levellers, England's modern Robin Hoods.[94]

Instead of spawning a successful counterrevolution, Harris' paper promptly called forth another *Mercurius Militaris*, a single-shot effort of late May which vituperatively assailed the Levellers and Royalist journalists. It included the statement that the editor was a friend of Jennings, who would, the following week, bestow his imprimatur on this newsless sheet. Jennings' new friend was John Hackluyt, the former editor of *Mercurius Melancholicus*. Arrested early in 1649, he was unable to escape; therefore he recanted and was released. *Mercurius Militaris* was part of his pay-off.[95] But only part: in June, Hackluyt edited two numbers of its continuation, bearing the strange title, in aggressively Protestant London, of *The Metropolitan Nuncio*. It received Jennings' seal of approval, probably because it attacked various Royalist editors by name.

Meanwhile the Royalist mercuries had bigger fish to fry and more dangerous antagonists to contend with than Hackluyt, and three of them managed to stay alive for many months. The most durable, *Mercurius Pragmaticus*, under different editors and with minor changes in title, even hung on until the middle of 1650. One of these editors was again Marchamont Nedham, who in the spring of 1649 decided that the ship he had deserted might not founder but sail on to a profitable harbor. Yet like Conrad's tale of the sinking but unsunk "Patna," *Pragmaticus*'s story is ambiguous, for the paper encountered a sufficient variety of counterfeits, most of them claiming to be the genuine article, to make it sometimes impossible to decide who was counterfeiting whom.

The last issue of the authentic *Pragmaticus* appeared on January 30, 1649. On February 13 and 20 counterfeit numbers came out, but in the intensity of their invective they were not inferior. For instance, the charge that the government now consisted of "a cursed Juncto of incarnate Devills and the Army of the very scumme and garbage of our People" could have appeared in any issue of *Pragmaticus*.[96] At the end of February the presumably authentic series resumed publication. From then until April it showed, if possible, an increase in the fervor of its attacks on the government, a decrease in its already slim content of news. It now embraced any and all who were battling the Commonwealth, and during some weeks it contained enough pro-Leveller items to suggest the hand of Mabbott or Harris.[97] Repeatedly it urged the Levellers and other disaffected groups to revolt. It encouraged them by reports of imminent foreign aid, by wild rumors (all Royalists were to be massacred, Cromwell was planning to make himself king, the quarrels among the Grandees were about to burst into flame), and by a note of optimism that was sometimes piercing enough to disguise the fact that it was forced.[98] This last was not easy, for *Pragmaticus*'s description of the attempts to suppress *Eikon Basilike* had just dramatized how dangerous life could be for those who wrote against the status quo, and the editor had recently been "routed out of his lodgings . . . by Parliament beagles and whole squadrons of rebellious Mermidons, & forc't to build his nest in another angle." [99] Despite these risks, which were only partly mitigated by the fact that *Pragmaticus* sold for two pence, at the end of April authentic-seeming counterfeits were twice secretly peddled on the streets of London.[100]

Concurrently with them *Mercurius Pragmaticus*, (*For King Charles II*) joined the attack on the Commonwealth. Its first number came out on April 24, two weeks before the regular *Pragmaticus* disappeared. Nedham was back.[101] This time he lasted only two months, his career momentarily terminated by the accident of being caught and jailed.[102] But it was an active two months. His *Pragmaticus* was like its immediate predecessor but slightly more effective. Nedham, for instance, skillfully portrayed Lockyer as a proper "Martyr for the Liberties of England," and he assailed the Treason Act of May in phrases that anticipated John Stuart Mill.[103] Better than other Royalist editors he could point a neat contrast: the pomp at Whitehall versus the poverty of the exiled Charles, or his deft oversimplification that "betwixt the two Factions we shall never be at rest; for all the week we are slaves to the Independents, and on Sunday to the Presbyter." [104] In what was probably the final number from his pen, Nedham put on a fine show of versatility, including among a variety of items a pious account of how the dead king's blood had cured the eyes of a young girl, together with several cynical references to New England as a sanctuary for the Grandees when they fled old England.[105]

For much of these two months Nedham's paper competed with another *Mercurius Pragmaticus*. (*For King Charls II*.), in all likelihood edited by one of the men, possibly Cleveland, who had earlier been his associate and replacement.[106] This man was an experienced propagandist, and there is little to choose between the two series. He coined the phrase "Purple Bumpkins" to describe the rich anti-Royalists of London; he could spin a dirty story as well as any of his colleagues; and he effectively rebutted Hackluyt.[107] When Nedham was imprisoned he kept on going, and until September *Pragmaticus* came out in a single series. The new editor also revealed flashes of political

The new tydings out of Italie are nt yet com.

Out of Weenen, the 6 November.

THe French Ambassadour hath caused the Earle of Dampier to be buried stately at Presburg In the meane vvhile hath Bethlem Gabor cited all the Hungerish States , to com together at Presburg the 5. of this present , to discourse aboute the Crovvning & other causes concerning the same Kingdom.

The Hungarians continue vvith roveing against these Lands. In like manner those of Moravia , vvhich are fallen uppon the Cossackes yester night by Hotteyn, set them on fire , and slaine many dead , the rest vvill revenge the same.

Heere is certaine nevves com , that the Crabats , as also the Lord Budean, are fallen unto Betlem Gabor.

The Emperour sends the Earle of Altheim, as Ambassadour to Crackovv in Polen, to appeare upon the same meeting-day.

Novv comes tidings, that Betlem Gabor is at Thurna, there doe gather to gether great store of States.

The Emper. Maj. hath appoynted heere a meeting-day upon the 1. of Decemb. thereupon should appeare the 4. Proclaimed States. The appoynted taxing shall bring up a great som of money.

Out of Prage , the 5 of November.

Three dayes agone are passed by, a mile from this Cittie 6000. Hungarians (chosen out Soldiers) under the General Redisferens, vvhich are gon to our Head-camp, & the Enimie lieth yet near unto ours by Rackonits , though the crie goeth, that the enimie caused all his might to com togither, to com this vvayes against Prage, if that comes to passe, it shall not run of vvithout blovves, the vvhich might be revealed vvith in sevv dayes.

It continues , that in the Satser Crais are gathered togither 10000 Contrie-men most high-dutch-men against Meitlen, & no Bohemians , they vvill help the King, to drive the enimie out of the Land. In like manner som certaine 1000 Contrie-men rebel in the Lentmaritscher Crais, but it is feared that those Countrie-men are starred up , through practise of the Adversarie , that the enimie in the meane vvhile might com to Prage. We understand, that Bucquoy hath not been in the Camp, but by the Duke of Saxen som certaine dayes , therefore vve are to looke to our selves, for feare of Trecherie. And it is thought that the Emperour vvill leave Austria to the Hungorians, & see to effect his intention only uppon Praghe.

Out of Ceulen, the 21. Novemb.

Writing from Marpurg in Hessen , that the Earle of the same Land, doth cause the foresaid Cittie to be strongly fortified , there on doe vvorke many 100 men dayly , and there is mustered in the Earlethip Zigenheym not long since 1.Governement of foote-men , & 6.Cornets of horse-men , the foote-men are sent to Marpurg & Rijnsels. But the horse-men are lodged in the Villages about the Cittie , & thereafter are also mustered the Duke of Saxen Lauvvenburgs Governement in Tries-Zigenheym, novv further vvhere they shallbe laid & used, is yet unknovvn. The sames Brothers Governement, there quarter is laid by Cassel , the Souldiers vvhich are taken on about Hamburg, Lubeck, in the Dukeship of Holsteen , & Meckelenburg, should also be mustered about Cassel , & be used vvhere neede shall require.

Since the last vve cannot enquire, that there is any thing of any importaunce passed betvvixt the Marquis Spinola & the Vnited Princes. We understand that the foresaid Spinola vvil lay his Souldiers in Garnisson vvith the first , & deale them unto divers places, on part to Oppenheym, Altzey, Ingelheym & Cruitsnach, the other part at Summeren & Bacharacht , the speech goeth that there shalbe layed vvith in Ments a good Company in Garnisson.

The Bishop at Halberstadt, Duke Christiaen at Bruynsvvyck, doth cause to be taken on 2000 Musquetters, to send to the Vnited Princes.

Heere is tydings , that bervveen the King of Bohemia & the Emperours solke hath beene a great Battel about Prage , but because there is different vvriting & speaking thereuppon , so cannot for this time any certainety thereof be vvritten, but must vvayte for the next Post. As also of the Cittie Pilsen , vvhich the Earle of Mansvelt (so the speech goeth) shonld have delivered into the Emperours hands.

From Cadan in Bohemia , 4. mile from Raconits, the 12. November.

From Solts is certaine advise that the Emperours folk have made them selves vvith all theire might out of theire Camp, & taken their vvay to vvards Praghe, like as they vveare then com to the long mile , but as the King understand such , he is broken up vvith his armey, and com to the log mile beforen the enimie, vvhere they have had a very strong Battelle & on both sides more then 6000 men slaine , though most on the Kings side , also hath the enimie gotten of the King som peeces of Ordenuaunce and vvaggens vvith amunitie, so that the King must retire back to Praghe , and the enimie to the Weissenberg . there he lies yet and roves from thence to the Leut Maritscher Crais unto Brix,

The first English newspaper (untitled), published by Pieter van den Keere in Amsterdam, December 2, 1620: recto of this single sheet of small folio size.

hath taken in, Trebnits, Pielan & Dux, alfo laid folk upon Leutmarifcher Slainer, and Launer paffages, that the Paffage upon Prage is vvholy taken avvay, and this day is com heere in a certain Perfon that brings tydinghs unto our Magiftrat, that bervvixt Sonnevveid and Patronit, vvhere the enimie hath lien are found fom certaine 1000 dead Bodies, & on the other fide there King lay alfo fom certaine 1000. dead bodies, vvhat is com to paffe bervvixt both vve fhal fhortly heare.

Out of Amberghe, in the Vpper-Pallatine, the 17. duo.

Here hath beene a greate crie, that the Duke of Beyeren fhould have taken in Praghe, and beaten our King out of the helde, but is not certaine, for the Carle of Solms vvrites out of Waltfaxfen of the 14 of this prefent, that the Duke of Beyeren vvas broken up with his camp very ftil, & marched in al haft to Prage, though they had left fom 100 men vvhich lay in theire quarter foom houres, vvhich made fires there in, that on vvoulde not have thought hut that the vvhole Armay had layen there ftill, but as ours underftood that they vveregon follovved they them prefently, though the Beyefens vverd com to Weiffenberge before but the 8 of this prefent have ours fett uppon the Beyerens by force, and fought the vvhole day togither, that on both fides are flaine aboute 8000 men, and very many fhould be hurt. Our King, vvith the Lord General the Earle of Hohenlo, alfo the vvhole army are vvith in Prage, & the Duke of Beyeren uppon the Weyffenbergh & Stem; vve hoope that they fhall fhortly be driven from thence Whatfurther is done betvvixt them, vve look for every houre to enquire further thereof & it feemes none can com from Prage, becaufe the paffages are every vvhere fhut.

Out of Ceulen, the 24 of Nouember.

Letters out of Neurenburghe of the 20 of this prefent, make mention, that they had advife from the Borders of Bohemia, that there had beene a very great Battel by Prage, betvveen the King & the Duke of Beyeren, & many 1000. flaine on both fides, but that the Duke of Beyeren fhould have any folke vvith in Prage, is yet uncertaine, there uppon under the Merchants vvith in Neurenberge are laid many 100. Florins that the Emperour, nor the Duke of Beyeren have no folke vvith in Prage. The caufe that here comes no certainty thereof, is this; That all paffages are fo befet, & fo dangerous to travaile, that it is to vvondered at, & not enough to be vvritte of, vvhat roveing, fpoyling and killing is done dayly uppon all vvayes.

Vppon the Schanfe Priefts cap is ftrongly buileed, & buy dayly much vvood lime & ftone, to make houfes there upon, and fo provide them felves for the vvhole vvinter. And are not long fince in the night 500 Souldiers paffed by Dure out of Gulik, fo the fpeech goerh, there meaning fhoulde be to build a nievv Sch. nrfe by Flammerfheym, to take avvay the paffag from the Marquis Spinola.

Imprinted at Amfterdam by George Vefeler, A₀. 1620. The 2. of Decemember.
And are to be foulde by Petrus Keerius, dvvelling in the Calverftreete, in the uncertaine time.

The first English newspaper (untitled), published by Pieter van den Keere in Amsterdam, December 2, 1620: verso.

April 17. *Numb.* 26.

THE CONTINVATION

of our former Newes from Aprill the 8. vntill
the 17. relating thefe particulars.

The holding on of the Diet of *Regenfpurgh*,
with the Duke of *Saxonies* refufall to appeare, his
letters to that purpofe vnto the Elector of *Cullen*.

The taking of the Citie of *Igla* in *Moravia* by the Marqueffe of
Iegerenfdorff, and other exploits of the Lord *Braians*, and the Baron
of *Rodern*, with other parts of the Armie of *Bethlem Gabor*.

The Emperours preparation to refift them.

The Duke of *Bavariaes* new levies alfo for himfelfe.

The late bootie taken by thofe of *Franckendale*.

The ftate of Religion in the Empire.

Together with

The chufing of *Chriftian* Duke of *Brunfwick* to be
Generall for the lower *Creitz* of *Saxonie*.

The taking of the Countie of *Schowenberg* by the forces
of Count *Mansfield*.

As alfo,

The preparations of the King of *Denmarke*, and the
Hanfe townes.

The bufineffe alfo of thofe of the other partie, Monfieur *Tillye*,
the Marqueffe *Spinola*, and others.

The warres of the *Grifons*, and the new league for the reco-
uerie of the *Valtoline*.

LASTLY,

Diuers other particulars from fundry places ; as the *Iefuites*
enterlude at *Rome*, the troubles of *Conftantinople*, &c.

LONDON,

Printed for *Nathaniel Butter*, *Nicholas Bourne*,
and *Thomas Archer*. 1623.

THE CONTINUATION OF OUR FORMER NEWES, Number 26, April
8–17, 1623: the title page of this Gainsford-edited twenty-four
page coranto. This and the rest of the newspapers of the period
were printed in quarto size.

*Numb.*92.

Mercurius Britanicus,
Communicating the affaires of great

BRITAINE:

For the better Information of the People.

From *Monday* the 28.of *July*,to *Monday* the 4. of *August*,1645.

WHere is King *Charles* ? What's become of him ? The *Ruimouri* strange variety of opinions leaves nothing certain : for *concern-* some say, when he saw the Storm comming after him as far as *ing the* *Bridgwater,* he ran away to his *dearly beloved* in *Ireland* ; yes, *King.* they say he *ran away* out of his own *Kingdome* very *Majestically* : Others will have him erecting a new *Monarchy* in the Isle of *Anglesey* : A third sort there are which say he hath hid himselfe. I will not now determine the matter, because there is such a deale of uncertainty ; and therefore (for the satisfaction of my Countrymen) it were best to send *Hue and Cry* after him.

If *any man can bring any tale or tiding of a wilfull King*,which Hue and *hath gone aftray thefe foure yeares from his Parliament , with a* Cry after *guilty Confcience, bloody Hands, a Heart full of broken Vowes and* him. *Proteftations : If thefe marks be not fufficient , there is another in the* * *mouth ; for bid him fpeak , and you will foon know him : Then* * Bos in *give notice to* Britanicus,*and you fhall be well paid for your paines :* lingua. *So God fave the Parliament.*

But now I think on't (Reader) I know not what to say to A Prince him ; for I have been *telling him his owne* this good while, irrecover- and yet no *amendment* at all : Nay, the dying *groanes* and ably loft.

MERCURIUS BRITANICUS, Number 92.
July 28–August 4, 1645.

pangs of this poor *bleeding Kingdom*, could never wring one *ſigh* or *Teare* from him ; but on the contrary, rejoyced in the *ruine* of his faithfull *Subjects*, falſly branding them for *Rebels* and *Enemies*, **No man** and cheerefully ſiding with the *known Enemies* and *Rebels* to his **of Con-** *Crown* and *Dignity* : What remedy then for ſuch obſtinacie ? **ſcience or** I have ſaid nothing here, which I have not already made apparent **Honeſty** out of his own *Letters* ; but the reſt behind ſpeak more plainly **but muſt** **condemne** and odiouſly, concerning *Ireland* ; eſpecially thoſe to the Marquis **him,** of *Ormond*, which whoſoever reades, will rather wonder he ſhould proceed ſo irreligiouſly, than that *Britanicus* dares write ſo boldly.

I ſhall proceed ſtill with the *Letters* in the ſame Order that they were *Printed*, not as they were dated. In a fourteenth *Letter* from the *King* to the *Queen*, dated *Daintrey*, Sunday, *June* 8. 1645. He writes thus,

Deare Heart :

A 14.th. " Since the taking of *Leiceſter*, my marching down hither to **Letter to** " relieve *Oxford* made the Rebels raiſe their ſiege before I could **the Queen** " come neare them, having had their Quarters once or twice bea-
" ten up by that Garriſon, and loſt four hundred men at an aſſault
" before *Boſtoll-houſe* ; at firſt I thought they would have fought
" with me, being marched as far as *Brackley*, but are ſince gone
" a ſide to *Brickhill*, ſo as I beleeve they are weaker than they
" are thought to be ; whether by their diſtractions, which are cer-
" tainly very great (*Fairfax* and *Browne* having been at cudgels,
" and his men and *Cromwel's* likewiſe at blowes together, where
" a Captaine was ſlaine) or waſting their men, I will ſay : Beſides,
" *Goring* hath given a great defeate to the Weſterne Rebels, but I
" do not yet know the particulars.

The King [Who do you think now wrote *Aulicus*, the *King* or *Berken-* **writes the** *head* ? This is part of the very ſame ſtuffe and language, which fil- **ſame In-** led up the laſt *Aulicus* : for he told of the *beating up of our quar-* **telligence** *ters at Oxford*, when more than a *Quarter* of the *Garriſon* were **with Auli-** out of their wits for feare, and an Alarm taken in all the Quarters **cus.** of their bodies : That we loſt four hundred men before *Borſtoll* ; then beſides the falſhood, let them take alſo the ſhame of being beaten by a ſmall *Army* : That our *Generalls* alſo were at *Cud-* *gels*, and the *Army* full of *diſtractions* ; yet ſee that our *Generalls* ſhould

The first two of eight pages of the anti-Charles number that got Nedham in temporary trouble.

MERCVRIVS Num. 17.
PRAGMATICVS:

Communicating Intelligence from all parts, touching all Affaires, Defignes Hu-Humours, and Conditions, throughout the K I N G D O M E.

Efpecially from *Weftminfter*, and the *Head-Quarters*.

From Tuefday, *Ianu.* 4. to Tuefday, *Ianu.* 11. 1648.

A glorious Prince *this Parliament*
   The King fhould be did fweare ;
But now we underftand they meant
   In Heaven, *and not here.*

Let them invade the Throne, *and part*
   His Crowne, *and vote his* Fate ;
Tet know in each true noble *heart,*
   He keeps his Chaire of State.

Princes *may be, like other men,*
   Imprifon'd, and kept under
A while, as Fire *in Clouds,* but then
   At length appeare in Thunder.

And as in hidden Caves the Wind
   Sad tremblings *doth create ;*
So Monarchs, *by their owye confin'd,*
   'Caufe Earth-quakes *in the* State.

     ——Nemo me impunè laceffit.

THe *Kingdome* fhall be fatisfied (they fay) ere long, why the *King* is made a *clofe prifoner*, as foone as the *Houfes* are deli-vered of their *Declaration :* But I thinke I had beft be beforehand
                R   wit

MERCURIUS PRAGMATICUS, Number 17,
January 4–11, 1648.

with them, and tell you one reason is, becaufe it is good-thriving up-on the *publique ftocke*. That's a maine reafon indeed; and in this kind of *Trafficke*, they will deale with any Cuftomers, but *Kings*, having ingroffed all the *Trade* betwixt themfelves and their *Com-mittees*, who turne and wind for them both in *City* and *Countrey*, and doe all the drudgery of *oppreffion*, and pay Tribute of all *Robbe-ries* to their Lords and Mafters, as the pick-pockets of *London* doe to their *Soveraign: Lady* MALL : And as fhe, when any of the *limbs* of her Trade are in queftion, was ever able to ftrike in with Mafter *Recorder* at the *Seffions*, to fave them harmeleffe ; fo what enor-mities foever their *Agents* commit abroad, the *Grandees* here can and will protect them againft the cries and complaints of the *op-preffed* : For the *Money-mills* muft goe, though they *grind* the faces of the poore to *powder*.

But for feare this world fhould not hold long, unleffe fome fur-ther fine *pretences* be fet on foot to foole us into *patience*, the *Com-mons* tooke feverall particulars into confideration : Firft, the prefent unfetled ftate of the *Kingdome*; which, becaufe the *Members* know this is no time for every *Tub* to ftand upon his owne *bottome*, muft needs be *hoop't* round with new *Fundamentals*, and from a glorious *Monarchy* be tranflated into a *Dutch* modell from the fubjection of a *King*, to the arbitrary vaffalage of a *free State*.

And therefore it was, that after the tedious *debate* of a whole day, it was put to the *Queftion* (night drawing on) whether *Candles* fhould be brought in ? And becaufe now was the time when the maine *ftroke* fhould be given at ROOT and BRANCH, *Harry Martin* brought on a whole Regiment of *New-Lights*, that what was long fince contrived in *darkeneffe* might be acted openly: which being cried downe by fome that were in their *wits*, alas, they were fuddenly quell'd, as foone as Mafter *Cromwell* difcovered the *tinder-box* of his *nofe*, and the *lightning* of his eyes, whereby the whole *Faction* fell fuddenly into a *flame*, and fo *Candles* were lighted pre-fently : And Alderman *Atkins* being *Groome* of the *Houfe*, was or-dered to make ufe of the *Snuffers*.

All things being thus prepared, the *Mortar-pieces* levell'd, and the *Engineers* holding *Match* to the *Traine* and the *Touch-hole*, up ftart foure principall *Fire-men* ; among whom Mafter *Herbert Morley* was moft confpicuous, as well for the *Wallet* which he alwayes car-ries about with him, as thofe other *good qualities*, which are ufually the *infeparable Adjuncts* of fuch kind of Anticks Of all *Coyne* this
Gen-

The first two of eight pages. A typical Royalist weekly,
but one which betrays Nedham's hand and eye.

The Moderate:

Impartially communicating Martial
Affaires to the KINGDOME of

ENGLAND.

From *Tuesday October* 24. *to Tuesday October* 13. 1648.

T's better to be unborn then untaught ; Ignorance being the mother of all errors, blinding the senses, and making the soul incapable of understanding, either Divine, or Morall ; she believes not what she sees, nor understands what she knows ; There can be no greater foe, saith *Lactantius*, then *her self*, because she destroys *self* for want of knowledge : Hence the Politians, and Royal Councels of the whole world ; have so much complied and hitherto Coacted for keeping the people in greatest of ignorance, well knowing, till that effected, they would not be enslaved, because too sensible of their own freedoms ; in prosecution hereof, the Laws of our Land must be in French and Latine, because the people should not understand them, or avoid the breach thereof, in being ignorant of them; though indeed there can be no trespasse against Law, where that Law declares the trespasse in the *known* language of the people. But by this snare of Satan, all the poor Commons of England must be catcht as a prey, to be devoured by the ravenous beasts, (the Lawyers,) whose hunger would soon be answered with famine, if the people might have knowledge of their own Laws and Freedoms. Is it not a pretty fallacy, to make the people believe that the Laws of this Nation are for their good and well-being, and afterwards to keep them ignorant of that good, in clothing them in an unknown language, though the breach hereof (which cannot possibly be avoided) must ruin them and their posterities for ever, so that the good intended them thereby, must turn to their utter ruine ? Can the people obey a Law, when they are ignorant of that Law they are to obey, and shall they notwithstanding be lyable to the penalties thereof when disobeyed? As if the Parliament of England should declare in Greek or Hebrew, That such as hereafter shall leavy war in this Nation without their Authority, and consent, are Rebels and Traitors, and shall die without mercy, and afterwards they execute all offenders thereof as Rebels and Traytors, though ignorant both of the Declaration it self, or penalties thereof ? Could ever Prince in Europe tyranize over a people, or would dare to infringe their Laws and Freedoms, if the people were made sensible of them ? Was not the ignorance hereof, the sole promoter, and long support of his Majesties Cause in this Nation ? For what true English-men, who knew themselves a free people, would draw their swords for him, who had endeavored ever since his coming to the Crown, to enslave them ? How could they be so unnaturall to fight against *Magna Charta*, or any other Freedom, which their fore-

Q   fathers

fathers blood did confirm as a legacy to them and their heirs for ever ? What base degenerate spirits would sell their Birthrights (without which we are in no other capacity then slaves) for a messe of Pottage, or the deceitfull smile of a perjured Prince ? How was it possible for the King to induce a belief in the people that he should fight for their Freedoms and good, when they know the people in all the world are now slaves to their Princes, and cannot be ignorant likewise, how for many Ages together this design hath been violently prosecuted against the free Commoners of this Nation ? Could it ever be expected that Christians should be so inhumane, and self destructive, to sheath their swords in their own bowels, and fight with their enemies against themselves, to make themselves slaves to their enemies and their posterities for ever, but that they were not sensible of their own freedoms, both by the Law of God, man, and nature, but deluded by false Prophets, who taught the works of the Law, and not of Grace, and preached the Kingdom of Antichrist, and not of Christ, making the people believe that all powers were ordained of God, and to resist these powers, though never so unlawfull, were to bring upon themselves Hell, and Damnation ? And lest there should be any of this seed yet left in the Nation, spreading abroad this Doctrine to deceive the people with these fallacies, I shall give them an explanation of the true sense of that Assertion.

1 God hath ordained all things in heaven and earth for the good and wel-being of man; and what power soever is contrary to, or acting against the same, is no power of God, but against his expresse will and pleasure, and in opposition to himself, and his eternall decree for that purpose, and therefore most lawfull to be disobeyed; and therefore the Parliament levyed war against the King, and disobeyed his pretended power.

2 Every Officer appointed for the good of the republique, and well government of the people, as the King, Parliament, Justices of peace, Constables, &c. is elected by the people; the King by three severall Voices, by way of consent and approbation of the people, before his Coronation; the Parliament by the severall Counties, &c.

3 The Kingly Office, as it is a great trust, so the people will not admit him to the execution thereof, without he swears to be faithfull, in performing the trust reposed in him, executing their Laws and Statutes, for their peaceable government, and wel-being, and not otherwayes; as by his Oath of Coronation appeares.

4 In case any of the Trustees, or electives of the people, shall forfeit their trust, in breaking their Oathes, violating the peoples laws, freedomes, and priviledges, leavying war against them, or inviting in a forraigne, or siding with a domestique enemy, to destroy them; the people are bound by the law of God, man, and nature, to disobey them, and bring them to speedy Tryall for breach of that trust which they reposed in them, as appeares by the Declaration of Parliament against his Majesty, and their Letter of encouragement to the Kirk of *Scotland*, to leavy war against the Parliament of *Scotland*.

5 It is lawfull for the people after such breach of trusts, to use all Coercive power for bringing to condigne punishment such trustees, and to fight with, kill, and slay all such as shall oppose them therein, as the Kirk of *Scotland* will bring their last Parliament to a tryall, by that which is to be chosen in January next.

If God hath ordained all things in heaven and earth for the good of the people; what earthly Principalities or Powers which the people have chosen for their good, can injoyn them to obedience in things destructive and unlawfull ? Is not *Salus populi suprema Lex*, The peoples safety the supreme Law ? And what Laws and Powers there are contrary hereunto, are not they all void, being against the supreme, and highest of all Laws, to which all other must give place and precedency, and all Kings and Parliaments vail to, and stand in fear of ? Do the people chuse themselves a King or a Parliament for their good and safety, and to perform the Trusts which they repose in them, and if they, or either, or both of them break their Trusts in leavying war against them, or inviting a forraign enemy to massacre and destroy

them,

The first two of eight pages. England's only
consistently left-wing newspaper.

(1383)　　　　　　　Numb: 288

A Perfect Diurnall

OF SOME
PASSAGES
IN
PARLIAMENT:

And the daily proceedings of the Army under his Excellency
the Lord Fairfax.

From Munday the 29. of Ianu. till Munday the 5. of Feb. 1648.

Collected for the satisfaction of such as desire to be truly informed.

Printed by E.G. and F.L. for Francis Coles and Laurence Blaiklock : And are to
be sold at their Shops in the Old-baily, and at Temple-bar.

Beginning Munday, Ianuary 29.

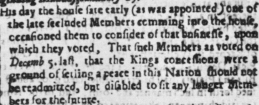

His day the house sate early (as was appointed) one of
the late seeluded Members comming into the house,
occasioned them to consider of that businesse, upon
which they voted, That such Members as voted on
Decemb 5. last, that the Kings concessions were a
ground of setling a peace in this Nation should not
be readmitted, but disabled to sit any longer Members for the future.

The Dutch Ambassadours had their audience in
the house, they read their instructions and Letters of
credence in French, but had no copies thereof in
English (as is usuall) but said copies should be prepared to morrow morning. Their desire was to intercede for the Kings life, and to keep and preserve a fair
correspondency between this Nation and the Estates of Holland ; but having no
Transcripts ready, and being unwilling to leave the Originall, the house at that time
could not proceed in debate thereof.

This day an Act passed for alteration of severall names and forms heretofore used
in Courts, Writs, Grants, Patents &c. and setling of proceedings in Courts of Law,
Justice, and equity within the Kingdoms of England and Ireland, Dominion of
Wales, and Town of Barwick upon Tweed, as followeth:

Be it Enacted by this present Parliament, and by Authority of the same, That in
all Courts of Law, Justice, or Equity ; and in all Writs, Grants, Patents, Commissions, Indictments, Informations Suits Returns of Writs ; and in all Fines, Re-
coveries, Exemplifications, Recognizances, Processe and proceedings of Law, Justice

130　　　　　　　　　　　　　or

her, gave her his bleſſing, and two ſeales that he had wherein were two Diamonds, ſhe wept bitterly. The P. Elector, D. of Richmond, and others, made ſuit to ſee him, which he refuſed. This night he lay at S. Jamea.

From Scotland they write, that the Miniſters of the Kirk, Preach againſt the Army in England, and the proceedings againſt their King, They ſay they are bound by their Covenant to preſerve Monarchy, and that in the Race of the preſent King. Their Parliament have paſſ'd ſeverall Votes. That thoſe that have been in the late Engagement againſt England ſhall not bear any office, as long as they live, except ſuch of them as were under age, and ſhall manifeſt their repentance. Such as ſate in Committees, and took their Oathes, ſhall not beare Office for ten yeare. Such as never evidenced their diſlike of their way by Petitioning, ſhall not beare Office for five yeers. Such as are prophane ſwearers, laſcivious perſons; and ſuch as do not worſhip God in their private houſes, are not to be admitted to any place of Truſt. An Act is paſt for citing all Officers of State to anſwer, if they appear not, they are to be diſcharged of their truſt. Earl Louderdale expreſſeth a readineſſe to give obedience to all decrees of Parliament, but that was not thought fit, and therefore he was ordered to appear by Writ, which was accordingly, a Committee is to conſider of him. The Earl of Glencarne having by Petition to Parliament made his way, his Petition being myſterious, as to that of owning them as a Parliament, its to be conſidered.

From Dartmouth Ian 26. thus, We had the other day a ſight of P. ince Rupert with about 14 Revolted Ships ſayling by our Coaſt, and bending towards Ireland: They drive the whole Channell before them, and ſeze upon many ſeverall Veſſels, but one of great value, laden with Cloath, worth 5000 l. We apprehend a great neglect in not having any Navy abroad. One of th ſet was driven in here the 26. where ſhe now remaines. The Maſter reports, that the Fleet is very poorly victualled, and worſe manned, having not 400 Marriners amongſt them.

Not any Poſt from Paris this week, nor the laſt; nor any Letters this week from Ireland.

Tueſday, January 30.

THis day the King was beheaded, over againſt the Banquetting houſe by White-Hall, The manner of Execution, and what paſſed before his death take thus.

He was brought from Saint James about ten in the morning, walking on foot through the Park, with a Regiment of Foot for his guard, with Colours flying, Drums beating, his private Guard of Partizans, with ſome of his Gentlemen before, and ſome behind bareheaded, Doctor Juxon late Biſhop of London next behinde him, and Col. Thomlinſon (who had the charge of him) the Gallery in Whitehal, and ſo into the Cabinet Chamber, where he uſed to lye, where he continued at his Devotion, refuſing to dine (having before taken the Sacrament) onely about 12. at noone, he drank a Glaſſe of Claret Wine, and eat a peece of bread. From thence he was accompanyed by Dr. Juxon, Col. Thomlinſon, Col. Hacker, and the Guards before mentioned through the Banquetting-houſe adjoyning, to which the Scaffold was erected, between Whitehall Gate, and the Gate leading into the Gallery from Saint James: The Scaffold was hung round with black, and the floor covered with black, and the Ax and Block laid in the midále of the Scaffold. There were divers companies of Foot and Horſe, on every ſide the Scaffold, and the multitudes of people that came to be Spectators, very great. The King making a Paſſe upon the Scaffold, lookd very earneſtly on the Block, and askre Col. Hacker if there were no higher; and then ſpake thus) directing his ſpeech to the Gentlemen upon the Scaffold.

King ___ I ſhall be very little heard of any body here, I ſhall therefore ſpeak a word unto you here; indeed I could hold my peace very well, if I did not think that holding my peace, would make ſome

men

Pages 1 and 3, of eight pages. Pecke's account
of the king's execution.

(482)

where she had not remained the space of half an hour, but she was accidentally accoasted by a a *young Gentleman*, who much pittying her languishing condition, that one so fair should want a *Mate*, boldly adventured to Court her; and after he came home, thinking of the Pleasure he enjoyed unexpectedly, in an *amorous* strain Writ on her this *Song* following.

AS th'ther day I chanc't to pass
   Th'rough *Flora's* glittering treasure;
I saw a fair and comely Lass
   Receiving *Flora's* pleasure.

My steps to her I did direct,
   I could not be confined,
By Complements I was not check't
   Untill our Lips had joyned.

Fair *Virgin* then to her I said,
   'tis pitty such a Center
Should tarry single in this shade,
   and not a man to enter.

She wept, and blusht, and then she cry'de
   (As modesty did moove her)
Fortune comitted homicide
   Upon her faithfull Lover,

Alas (said I) if that be all,
   Let peevish grief not starve you,
Pine not away for one mans fall,
   For I, my self, will serve you.

Then (like a faithfull *Amorist*)
   I, with my armes imbrac't her,
Her Rubie-Lips I often kist,
   Then on the ground I cast her.

Un-

MERCURIUS DEMOCRITUS, Number 61,
June 22–29, 1653.

Unwillingly, she seem'd to fall :
   at first she shun'd the motion,
But by and by she fell, for all
   her symptomes of devotion.

Then on her thighes, my hands did glide,
   which were as soft as Jelly,
The vale she drew, and then I 'spide
   the Suburbs of her belly.

(Imagine then how nigh I came
   To my intended Center,
I soon (with ease) found out the same :
   And sooner I did enter.)

For when I saw that Mossie Wall
   Wherewith the same was founded ;
I was resolu'd thereon to fall,
   on Courage firmly grounded.

I rush't the Wall down, and I threw
   My self more nigh the matter ;
She shently winc't, but yet I drew
   My nimble *Rapier* at her.

Then Leggs, and breasts, and face we joyn'd,
   For I lay just upon her,
I'le speak no more, you know my minde,
   and what it Cost me on her.

One Mr. *Resin*, a little great dapper *Lutenist* (that had the *Rams gutts* bequeathed to him for *Lute-strings*)taking a Chamber at *Islington* to teach, at quarter day , the roome being too hott, without leave of his *Landlord* he took *Ship* in *old Fish-street*, where for his *play* he Is fed with *gubbins*, on condition he will *grease Hobsons* overworn *wheels* , till the *Catts* hath caught the *Mouse* nabbing *Rowls* at the Barr.

Ppp 2   A

Pages 2 and 3, of eight pages. An example
of Crouch's ribald journalism.

Mares, Kyne and sheep, and found guilty thereof, by an assise, conform to his own Confession, was adjudged to be taken upon *May 3.* to the ordinary place of execution at *Glasgow,* there to bee strangled till he be dead, and afterward his Body to bee burnt to ashes, and his goods to be Escheat for the use of the Commonwealth; and the Mares, Kyne and sheep with whom he polluted himself, to bee searched for, killed and burnt.

Christian Mathie, convict of severall Adulteries with marryed men, she herself being a marryed Woman; *viz.* for adulteries committed by her with *Robert Hill* a marryed man, to whom she bare 3 Children; with *Patrick Hodge,* to whom shee bare one Child; with *Alexander Brackanrege* a marryed man, to whom she bear two children; shee was ordered to be hanged on Wednesday *May 7.*

John Buchanan accused of stealing sundry horses and Mares, was found guilty, and hanged at the ordinary place of execution, *May 8.*

Ayre, May 6, 1656.

David Old, and *Agnes Dick* his Wives brothers daughter for Incest with other, confest judicially, and found guilty thereof by an Assise, ordained on the first Wednesday of *June* next to the ordinary place of execution for the Burgh of *Air,* and there betwixt two and four hours in the afternoon, to be hanged till they be dead, and all their moveable Goods to be Escheat. The Commissioners at the
earnest

From Dantzick, June 21.

The Bores are up in *Samaytens*, and hinder the Posts passages from *Riga*, and doe much mischief. The *Moscovite* hath taken the field, and will hold his Rendezvouz about *Smolensko*, settle things, and then set forward his march; they of *Riga* are warned to ship away their wood, or else they will fire it. The eyes of all men are turned upon the *Holland*-fleet in the *Sound*; and what conjunction the Dane and *Moscovite* will make; the *Moscovite* having his Ambassador at Copenhagen, a short time will disclose.

Since my last, the English Merchants residing here, have received a small Answer from the Magistracy of this Town, That they must take an Oath of Fidelity to help to defend the Walls in person, pay Taxes, and all other military Duties; or, if they will depart, they must leave their Tenths behind them. Intelligence on both sides is very uncertain, this Towne it self sometimes in 5, or 6, Weeks time getting nothing of Newes, and yet have their Secretary constantly with the King of Poland for information; But the Countrey is so broken, that there is no travelling for Posts.

From Koningsberg, June 20,

Our Lord, the Elector of *Brandenburgh*, is now gone from hence, the Swede and he being agreed to unite Counsels and Forces. Nevertheless, the said Elector is, and will bee ready to doe all good offices:

Two of its sixteen pages, illustrative of Nedham's competence in handling domestic and foreign news.

A Vote concerning the Queen.
Her Plots have sail'd from Aberdeen.

Numb.3.

Mercurius Civicus.

LONDONS
INTELLIGENCER:
OR,
Truth impartially related from thence
to the whole Kingdome, to prevent mif-information.

From *Thursday*, *May* 18. to *Thursday*, *May* 25. 1643.

Thursday, *May*, 18.

THis afternoon his Excellency the Earle of *Essex*, attended
with Colonell *Hambden*, Colonell *Goodwin*, and Colonell
Stapleton, departed from hence towards *Redding*, resolving
t· advance with all speed, according to the request made unto him
by the Lords and Commons in Parliament, for the speedier expe-
diting whereof, 25000. pounds is since sent him for the payment
of the Souldiers under his Command : Also it was this day in-
C   formed

MERCURIUS CIVICUS, Number 3, May 18–25, 1643. The title page
of this eight-page weekly. England's first illustrated newspaper.

shrewdness (his analysis, for instance, of the possibilities of Leveller-Presbyterian and Leveller-Royalist coalitions), touches of liberalism (his denunciations of the censorship acts of July and September), and skill in inflating rumors (Danish aid to the Royalists was on the way; the Turks, when they heard of the execution of Charles, strangled the English Ambassador).[108] Then in September another *Mercurius Pragmaticus, For King Charls II* for two weeks contributed its noisy part to the Royalist chorus. Nedham's release in November caused no change in the anti-government tune. Having helped to purchase his freedom with a recantation that included placing the blame for his adventures in Royalist journalism on "secret whisperers," Nedham was now ready to contribute his decibels to swelling the praise of the Commonwealth.[109] Less than a year later he again became its leading weekly spokesman.

A second of the three "grand" Royalist mercuries also managed to endure through most of 1649, for *Mercurius Elencticus*, still edited by Wharton, resumed publication in May.[110] (In April, however, Samuel Sheppard, temporarily out of jail, had found time to write one number before being recaptured.)[111] At this point Wharton re-entered the fray, and until November *Elencticus*, skipping only one week, added its voice to the anti-Commonwealth choir. It was now a more highly trained voice. Wharton continued to improve both as newsman and as propagandist. He paid more attention to continuity, less to astrology, and unlike his Royalist brethren, he sometimes apologized for the dearth of news in his weekly and even tried to transmit a few unloaded reports. But he reserved most of his space for attacks on Cromwell and the Grandees, using invective, rumors, wild optimism, distortion. He defined "Royalists" as all those who, regardless of nationality, politics, and religion, were against "Tyrants and Traitors," and consequently he regularly embraced the Levellers as partners in the struggle for righteousness.[112] Wharton was still adept at making the Commonwealth seem extremely unpopular, claiming in one instance that 90 per cent of the soldiers were pro-Leveller, in another that foreign nations, Presbyterians, nobles, traditionalists, and most lawyers and merchants were solidly against the government.[113] He also became an expert character-assassin, and his dissections of Hackluyt and Colonel Pride rank among the most devastating of that era.[114] By October not only his Royalist convictions but his apparent confidence in himself caused him to cry out against the new censorship law, and then to regret that he no longer had a weekly organ in which to speak his piece.[115]

John Crouch, who had written a few "counterfeit" numbers of

Mercurius Melancholicus, edited the third durable Royalist mercury of 1649. *The Man in the Moon* rose in April, disappeared in November, returned in January 1650, and sank in June when Crouch was arrested. Shortly thereafter he came back to journalism, but by the backdoor; for Crouch, first with *The Man in the Moon*, then on a more lavish scale with his weeklies of the 1650's, proved himself the smuttiest news-man produced by the Puritan Revolution — a man whose stories and vocabulary could still hold their own in the club-cars and men's rooms of today's impuritan world. *The Man in the Moon* began by bragging about its editor's access to the inner circles of government and his willingness to write a fearless exposé, though its sustained lack of news indicates that he had no pipeline to Westminster or Whitehall.[116] But Crouch was addressing himself to a low-class and/or bohemian audience, and his paper, unlike most Royalist mercuries, sold for only a penny. The editor claimed he would be satisfied if he made enough to pay his printer.[117]

He probably did. His style, if windy, was usually lively and varied, his content often salacious. For instance, he described in gaily unappe-tizing detail three purported brothels run by and for supporters of the government, each with its prices and services adjusted to the income and interests of its customers.[118] Crouch also spiced up *The Man in the Moon* by dramatizing his own vicissitudes, sometimes humorously, as when he told of one of his female hawkers routing a group of soldiers, sometimes seriously, as when he made the most of his narrow escapes.[119] He was skilled in defamation and took much delight in excoriating pro-government journalists, especially Walker.[120]

Crouch's politics, though he almost always concentrated on per-sonalities rather than issues, were reactionary. He approved of Leveller agitation and revolt but made it clear that he despised the long-run aims of the radicals.[121] He equated religious freedom with heresy; and in one of his rare serious statements on political theory he justified the divine right of kings in terms that even the most ardent Royalist had discarded: "All just power is derived from God to the King, and from the King to the people; all other power is of the Devil, usurped, wicked, false." [122] In support of this view *The Man in the Moon* persistently flayed Cromwell, and twice ran extended reports to show that he was a Papist working hand-in-glove with the Pope and the Jesuits.[123] Crouch also exploited all kinds of anti-government rumors, and so played up England's economic discontent and official corruption that he sometimes gave the impression that no self-respecting king would want to be restored. In any event, Crouch's journalistic efforts did little to pave the way for the Restoration, though *The Man in the*

Moon and its successors anticipated the tone of the Merry Monarch's court.

But in 1649 the pot of gold of 1660 must have seemed extremely distant to the Royalists. Even so, in the spring, coinciding with the brief relaxation of censorship, three new weeklies joined the attack on the Commonwealth. It survived; each of them lasted only two weeks. The vehement and vituperative *Mercurius Philo-Monarchicus* managed one number in April, one in May. *Mercurius Elencticus*, (*For King Charles II*) came out twice in May, both its issues loaded with heavy irony and mediocre verse. At the end of May and the beginning of June *Mercurius Melancholicus, For King Charles the Second* admitted that it was a "melancholy time," but did its best to change the situation by all devices common to the Royalist press. Its editor, probably Martin Parker or John Taylor, also anatomized Hackluyt, ending with the observation that since he was not being paid enough by the government for turning his coat, he was ready to shift back to the cause of Charles. Thus even in its brief revival the editors, past and present, of *Mercurius Melancholicus* were fighting among themselves.

In the summer another covey of Royalist mercuries briefly fluttered onto the scene. In July *Mercurius Carolinus*, written by "Alethophilus, Basiluphilus, Britannophilus," survived only one number, despite its author's nom de plume. In August and early September *Mercurius Aulicus.* (*For King Charls II.*) lasted three times as long and seemed approximately twice as effective in its attempts to incite the government's numerous opponents. Finally, in September the last of the Royalist weeklies of 1649, *Mercurius Hybernicus*, optimistically announced in a poem "To Prag & Elencticus":

> Weekly our tragick Bells shall toule
> Sad Requiems to each Traytors soule,
> Nor shall our well-knit triple knot
> Be cut by an high Treason vote.

But by the next week the triple knot had become only double: the editor of *Hybernicus* was wrong about his own durability; he was right in anticipating "an high Treason vote."

On September 20 the leaders of the army, irritated by the virulence of such pamphleteers as Lilburne and by the raucousness of the Royalist mercuries, and possibly dubious about the public reaction to the massacre at Drogheda, got the Rump to pass the most stringent printing law of the Interregnum. Drawing on a long tradition of censorship, from Tudor proclamations to the recent Treason Acts, it forced all printers to post a bond of £300, prohibited the printing and circulation of scandalous and seditious matter, enlarged the powers and increased the degree of specialization of the licensers, and withdrew official approval from all weeklies then in operation.[124] The law's enforcement was turned over to the Stationers, but this group was now to be aided by the Lord Mayor, by a system of heavy fines, and potentially by any pressures which the government might apply. Despite an initial week or two of confusion, the new statute hit London journalism with the force of a sledge hammer, and the casualty rate among licensed weeklies was 100 per cent. *The Impartiall Intelligencer*, a relative newcomer, died on September 19. *The Moderate* breathed its last six days later. Two other licensed papers, neither of them old, also came to an end late in September: *The Moderate Messenger* and *A Modest Narrative of Intelligence*. Within two weeks the seven remaining authorized newspapers joined the dead: Jennings' *Perfect Summary* on October 1; Dillingham's *Moderate Intelligencer* on October 4; Pecke's *Perfect Diurnall*, though it came back for one number in November, on October 8; Collings' *Kingdomes Weekly Intelligencer* on October 9; and, during the next three days, Border's *The Kingdomes Faithfull and Impartiall Scout* and *Perfect Weekly Account* and Walker's *Perfect Occurrences*.[125] Even the ghostly figures of *Pragmaticus*, *Elencticus*, and *The Man in the Moon* which hovered over the scene added to the graveyard atmosphere.

Yet all was not completely dead, for Parliament by the act of September 20 had authorized two new newspapers, one to deal with Westminster news, the other with affairs of the army. In October these licensed pallbearers began their task, doing little, however, to dispel the charnel smell that now clung to English journalism. Though the air soon became less fetid, the early newspaper never regained that smell of health it had briefly acquired in the later 1640's.

CHAPTER XI

THE COMMONWEALTH
NEWSPAPER I

October 1649 to September 1651

THE early 1650's witnessed the continued decline of the English newspaper and the rise to greater power of Oliver Cromwell. Far more than his successors of the next three centuries Cromwell had dictatorship thrust upon him. Yet he was neither weak nor bashful, and if there had to be a personal center of power to prevent the Puritan Revolution from disintegrating, he was willing to supply it. When the Irish, the Scots, the Dutch, and the Rump got in the way, Cromwell saw to it that they were rebuffed or liquidated. A reluctant dictator, he was none the less efficient.

During the first years of the decade Cromwell's efficiency continued to be manifested chiefly on the battlefield, though he made sure his domestic fences were kept well mended. Between mid-1649 and mid-1650 he completed the conquest of Ireland in a campaign that is still having political repercussions from Belfast to Boston. The following year he took charge of the military subjection of Scotland, and at the Battle of Worcester the New Model shattered the strength of Scotch Presbyterianism and almost shattered Charles II, whom the

Scots had proclaimed king and then dragooned into taking the Covenant. In the spring of 1652 the economic competition between England and Holland oozed over into a naval war that terminated, after more sound than fury, in a stalemate late in 1653. Cromwell's quarrel with his fourth overt opponent, the Rump, had meanwhile come to an end with the dissolution of that hardy body in the spring. By then he and his military associates had, at least temporarily, established the safety and supremacy of England — and of themselves.

The weekly press was, in general, a victim of Cromwell's rise to power. From September 1649 to September 1651 the stringent "Act against Unlicensed and Scandalous Books and Pamphlets" was in effect, and after it lapsed a new law substantially re-enacted its provisions. Even so, the newspapers did not remain entirely lifeless. But English journalism was least lively, most deathlike, at the end of 1649; and the first two weeklies to come out under the act of September 20 had many of the characteristics of zombies.

A Briefe Relation of some affaires and transactions, Civill and Military, both Forraigne and Domestique started serving its bland menu on October 2, 1649, a service it continued for fifty-five weeks. The paper was both licensed and written by Walter Frost, the Secretary of the Council of State and a man who had long worked for the Independents as clerk, propagandist, and counterspy.[1] He had done a capable job in these roles, but he was no newspaperman. The third number of *A Briefe Relation* opened with the statement that "Through the goodnesse of God wee still can say we have not much Newes at home"; it concluded with one and a half blank pages prefaced with this explanation:

> The howerly expectation we had of some certayne newes from Ireland caused us to reserve these Pages . . . but that not comming, 'twas thought more fit to leave them blank . . . than to fill them up with that which signifies nothing, which hath beene the usuall Custome of those who heretofore have impos'd upon their Readers with the blotting of good paper to little purpose.

And from start to finish Frost adhered to the unjournalistic credo that no news is good news. Also, he filled at least three-quarters of his paper's usual sixteen pages with foreign news, sometimes approaching, and once achieving, complete saturation in cross-Channel material.[2] The remainder of his space was given over to non-London, and hence non-Parliamentary, items, most of them pertaining to Ireland and Scotland. Frost penned no editorials, and the few asides he allowed himself were always in praise of the Commonwealth. He had an easy job: his Irish and Paris correspondents were competent, and for the rest he generally relied on government handouts.

A Briefe Relation, however, furnishes a few items of interest to the historian of literature, such as a favorable notice of Milton's *Eikonoklastes*, an advertisement for the second edition of Thomas Browne's *Pseudodoxia Epidemica*, and some lists of recently published books.[3] For the historian of subliterature it provides an insight into how the newspaper of three hundred years ago got its reports from abroad. One of Frost's correspondents showed that the problems and techniques of digging up confidential diplomatic news have changed little since 1650:

> We are become horrible politique here [Breda], and things are kept under such secrecy as I know not what to affirm for the truth. The very favorites differ in their reports, whether to abuse us that are of the Tribe of Club-Intelligencers, or because they know not, I cannot determine; but the business [negotiations between Charles and commissioners from Scotland] is among a few, and a Supper or Bottle of Rhenish can do little now as to picking of locks. . . .[4]

A second method of getting overseas news has shown equally slight change: extracting items from local papers, in this case the use by Frost's Paris correspondent of printed French gazettes.[5] Frost also had to contend with a problem that still plagues modern publishing, the power of the printer. In one number, for instance, he red-facedly complained that his printer had deleted part of a story praising an army officer — and the editor could do nothing about it but apologize.[6] But despite these signs of modernity, *A Briefe Relation* marked a large step back to the newspaper in which home news was taboo.

The second official weekly authorized under the September act, *Severall Proceedings in Parliament*, concerned itself with news of Westminster, but it managed to intensify the caution and conformity that had emasculated most papers of the later 1640's. Even so, under various titles, it survived six years. At the start it too was licensed and edited by the same man. But Henry Scobell's job was easier than Frost's, for as official Clerk to the Parliament he was responsible for compiling its Journals, of which *Severall Proceedings* was merely a diluted digest. Its sixteen pages were made up entirely of news of or from Westminster, presented with a maximum of impersonality and in a heavily official style. What little foreign or general English news Scobell included consisted of items that had come to the House in the form of letters of which Parliament took public notice. The editor's most time-consuming task was probably soliciting advertisements; for his paper, in this era of slight competition, usually contained several announcements of books about to be published, plus a few paid notices of lost horses and strayed apprentices.[7]

Severall Proceedings was sanctioned by the government largely as a sop to the London public, now suddenly deprived of its mixed newspaper fare, rather than as an important vehicle of propaganda. Scobell's employers were careless enough to have the first three numbers come out on Tuesday, the same day as *A Briefe Relation*, before shifting, at the end of October, to Friday. Scobell was careful, however, to enter his paper in the Stationers' Register and to see that nothing unduly controversial appeared, regardless of how heated a debate might be among the still feuding members of the Rump. He covered the capture of Drogheda with a bare summary of the numbers slain, omitted news of Lilburne's trial, and on days when Parliament was not in session assumed that there was no news fit to print.[8] Indeed, almost the only sign that Scobell had any personality was an occasional plug for Walker's friend Gerbier.

Early in 1650 the paper shifted to Thursday and Walker became editor.[9] He was sufficiently busy being a minister of a suburban parish and handling publicity chores in behalf of the Commonwealth for his taking over to make little difference. Gradually he increased the number of advertisements and in 1651 he made a bid for more readers by including some crime news. Walker also occasionally betrayed his own personality by, for instance, vindictively telling how buyers as well as sellers of unlicensed papers would be punished.[10] Occasionally, too, he permitted politics to enter, as in the story that Charles was pleased by the defeat of the Scots at Dunbar; and a few times he inserted pieces of relatively sensational piety, such as a letter from New England on the pains and pleasures of converting the Indians.[11] None the less *Severall Proceedings* remained a watered-down version of Parliament's official Journal; and as editor, Walker, like Scobell, seemed merely a clerk.

On Monday, December 17, 1649, the paper specializing in army news promised by the act of September finally began to appear, a weekly habit it retained until the autumn of 1655. *A Perfect Diurnall of Some Passages and Proceedings Of, and in relation to the Armies* was also edited and licensed by the same man, in this case John Rushworth, the Secretary of the New Model. Equipped with journalistic experience, he was smart enough to hire Pecke as his assistant, and from the start Pecke presumably did most of the work.[12] Now, however, he had more time for pub-crawling, since this new *Perfect Diurnall*, too, consisted almost entirely of government handouts. Yet it was a better paper than *A Briefe Relation* or *Severall Proceedings*.

In the first place it was less restricted. Its opening statement announced that its mission was to tell of the "affaires of the Army," but slowly it lost its military emphasis. In the spring of 1650 it expanded from eight and sometimes twelve pages to sixteen. By then, though it continued to give much space to news of battles and garrisons, it had become generalized. It now consisted of two to four pages of foreign and shipping news, a few pages on the doings at Westminster, a variety of Scottish and Irish items, a half page of advertisements, and a few miscellaneous pieces — most of them having the characteristics of official press releases. In the second place, *A Perfect Diurnall*, in its arrangement of these ingredients and in its compression of certain involved stories, exhibited the hand of an editor better trained and more diligent than Frost or Scobell or Walker.[13] Yet that hand had now become almost completely automatized. Pecke's style was still functional, but it never became personal or lively, and no hint that all was not well ever smirched his paragraphs. Only in a few anecdotes intended to show that those who opposed the Commonwealth were wrong and in occasional human-interest and apparition stories can one see even a glimmer of the Pecke of the mid-1640's.[14] Consequently during its long career *A Perfect Diurnall* never came to life, and Pecke was now more than ever a ventriloquist's dummy for the military men ruling England.

From June 1650 to June 1651 he and his colleagues did not have the raucous catcalls of even one Royalist mercury to remind them of their subjection; and before then the Royalist voices, if shrill, had been few. Back in November 1649 only *Pragmaticus*, *Elencticus*, and *The Man in the Moon* had appeared, and then for a total of only seven issues. Crouch's three numbers were still vigorous, vituperative, scurrilous. So were the three November issues of *Mercurius Pragmaticus*, (*For King Charls II.*), which continued to berate the government and praise the Levellers, and which contained an attack on "that adulterous Rabby" John Milton.[15] Only *Elencticus* noticeably changed as a result of the new journalistic situation, devoting about half the space in its final three issues — two in October and one in November — to a point-by-point refutation of *A Briefe Relation*. In December *Pragmaticus*, temporarily the lone survivor, appeared twice, both times snarling at the Grandees for their crimes and sins, and reassuring its readers that foreign intervention would soon put the rebels in their place.

In the first half of 1650 *The Man in the Moon*, which emerged from hiding early in January, was the most durable of the Royalist mercuries: it skipped no weeks and it outlasted *Pragmaticus* by eight days. This was no mean feat. In January, Crouch indignantly lamented the arrest of his printer (and possibly brother), Edward Crouch.[16] In February he reported that among others hot on his trail was "Parliament Joan." This "fat woman . . . about fifty" was now the most effective ferret for the government and Stationers' Company, and one of her favorite tricks was to nose out Royalist editors and sympathizers by peddling anti-government papers.[17] In March, Crouch announced that John Harris, the former pro-Leveller editor, had joined his pursuers; and the following number of *The Man in the Moon* was at least partly written by a substitute, for Crouch went back into hiding.[18] But he managed to elude the hunters, and in May he mocked them for being unable to collect the £50 offered for his capture.[19] In June, however, someone should have been £50 richer: Crouch, despite the fact that he had been varying his paper's day of appearance, was caught and imprisoned.[20]

Possibly his silencing was worth this sum to the government. *The Man in the Moon* had continued to make Cromwell its major target, though Henry Marten was hit frequently enough for his piecemeal biography to suggest that he would have been more at home in the Montparnasse of the 1890's than in the London of the 1650's. Also well spattered with the editor's dirt were Walker and Frost.[21] Crouch kept on attacking the government by salaciousness, defiance, the exploitation of rumors that ranged from the sublime to the ridiculous, and the re-iterated assertion that the tyrants were about to fall. In his campaign he claimed to have two staunch allies: his dog Towzer, and his God, both confirmed Royalists. Though £50 was a large sum, Crouch's paper was so negative, cocky, and distorted that it could have functioned only as an irritant, not a threat, to the Commonwealth.

The editor of *Pragmaticus* was worth a bigger reward. His weekly, if as vituperative and zestful as *The Man in the Moon*, was less smutty and more telling. It did a better job of rallying the opponents of Rump and army, and it effectively exhorted the Levellers to join the Presbyterians, even the Catholics, to help bring down "The Junto." [22] It also regularly depicted the economic, political, and moral bankruptcy of England, and it pointed out that the alleged crime and anarchy in London were an inevitable offshoot of a decade of rebellion.[23] The editor, too, was more consistent than the freer-swinging Crouch. He expressed un-changing horror at "sectarian abhominations," mocked at various acts for relief of the poor, and considered the members of the Rump "Jewes" in every derogatory sense of the word.[24] Though in April he admitted that his pen was not "usually thus bitter," [25] he did not cease to cut and slash at the government, especially Cromwell, and to abuse its pub-licists, especially Walker. In May he utilized title-page poems, lengthy laments, and so-called news stridently to urge the people to rouse them-selves and strike down tyranny. At the end of that month, however,

"Pragmaticus" himself was struck down: though not arrested, he must have felt that his capture was imminent enough for him to lie low.[26] For a year he did.

Meanwhile from the end of February to the end of April another Royalist mercury, *The Royall Diurnall*, joined the negative chorus. It sang in harmony with *The Man in the Moon* and *Pragmaticus*, for it was as violent, vindictive, and verbose as they. Though it contained slightly more news, it gave ample space to denouncing the government as illegitimate, the governors, especially Cromwell and his cronies, as bastards. When it dropped out, its place was taken by *Mercurius Elenticus*, now spelled with only one "c." [27] Authored by one of the more experienced Royalists — but not by Wharton, again behind bars — it also achieved a high pitch of denunciatory vehemence, even if its voice was more monotonous than that of its fellows.[28] The editor coined or retailed the word "Lyurnall" to describe the licensed press; and he told the anecdote, suggestive of Book I of *Gulliver's Travels*, about a man who wrote to a friend concerning a plot of land and was promptly arrested for a plot against the state.[29] The final number of *Elenticus* kept on urging the Royalists not to be discouraged: Charles was about to land in Scotland and a restoration was imminent.[30] But by the time Charles did land in June 1650, the editor had joined the author of *Pragmaticus* in hiding. A few days later, with the arrest of Crouch, the opposition press was silenced, and for a year the authorized periodicals could sing their muted hosannas uninterrupted by Royalist catcalls.

Shortly after Crouch was jailed, the two longest run weeklies of the Interregnum got their start. The first lasted approximately five hundred numbers, the second four hundred. The first was the most professional weekly of the seventeenth century, the second a rehash in French of the news from London. The first immediately became the government's most effective organ of publicity, the second an incidental means of promoting the cause of the Commonwealth on the continent. The first was edited by Marchamont Nedham.

As editor of *Pragmaticus* Nedham had been arrested in June 1649; he escaped and was re-arrested in August. Three months later, after the probable intervention of William Lenthall and John Bradshaw, both high in the government, he was freed. Within seven months he had been paid £50 by the state for services rendered, promised the high annual salary of £100, and made editor of the new official weekly, *Mercurius Politicus*.[31] In return Nedham promised to change sides; and to show his good faith, in the spring of 1650 he wrote a lengthy pamphlet entitled *The Case of the Common-Wealth of England Stated*. This persuasive tract opened with the straightforward statement that the author had again shifted his position. It then learnedly and readably supported the government, addressing itself first to the "Conscientious man," then to the "Worlding," and in both sections justifying the Commonwealth on grounds that were expedient rather than idealistic. Nedham was undoubtedly the best propagandist the leaders of England could have secured thus to state their case, and then to restate it weekly in the pages of *Mercurius Politicus*. He was, in fact, so well qualified to edit the major official newspaper that the traditional argument that Milton must have helped him is groundless.[32]

The evidence that Nedham did the job on his own can be divided into three categories: the testimony of his contemporaries; the professional manner in which *Mercurius Politicus* handled, and occasionally manhandled, the news; and the paper's editorials. The statements of half-a-dozen Londoners, as well as Nedham's high salary, constitute the first category.[33]

The second category is the fact that *Mercurius Politicus* was the slickest and most competent Interregnum newspaper. Though it was the mouthpiece of the government and never ceased to live the life of an echo, Nedham did a good job of disguising the fact that he was neither the master of his journalistic fate nor the captain of his journalistic soul. Both the style and content of his paper were such that they gave — and still give — an impression not only of mastery but often of independence and freshness. No circulation figures survive, but it is extremely likely that *Politicus* had as many readers as *A Perfect Diurnall* had in its heyday, and more influence in shaping public opinion.

On May 8, 1650, the Council of State authorized Nedham's salary. A month later he submitted to the Council a prospectus for his new weekly. It was to be published "in defense of the Commonwealth, and for Information of the People," and, in order to be "cryed up," was to be written in a "jocular way." The prospectus concluded with the request that the editor be supplied with "the best Intelligence of State." [34] On the following Thursday, June 13, the first number was for sale, probably, because of its sixteen-page length, at a cost of two pennies. Regardless, Nedham informed his readers that they were getting their money's worth, for the paper opened with this self-confident announcement.

Why should not the Common-wealth have a Fool, as well as the King had? . . . . But you'll say, I am out of fashion because I make neither Rimes nor Faces, for Fiddlers pay, like the Royal Mercuries. Yet you shall know I have authority enough to create a fashion of my own, and make all the world to follow the humor.

Nedham went on to assure his public that, though it was "a ticklish time to write Intelligence," he would be honest and fearless. In subsequent issues he boosted *Politicus*, until he apparently felt certain that it had become accepted and popular. In June he called attention to the fact that both ladies and Cavaliers liked it because of its "true English" style; in July he boasted that his was "the only State-Almanack to tell what [the] Weather is in the Commonwealth"; and in August he managed simultaneously to apologize for and brag about his allegedly misspent youth.[35]

In keeping with his prospectus Nedham frequently added a jocular touch. For instance, until the Scots invaded England he periodically attacked Charles — "young Tarquin" — with a mixture of mild invective and patronizing raillery; and with delightful but scathing facetiousness he expressed sympathy for the imprisoned Royalist poet-playwright William Davenant.[36] But the editor's experienced touch was most evident in his ability to condense lengthy official reports and to support the government without seeming a hack or a toady. In urbane and controlled prose he could show the folly of Presbyterians, Scots, Royalists, Levellers, and neutrals by reporting their exploits in a negative manner. Similarly he could praise the Commonwealth by quietly emphasizing the wisdom of its acts and activities.

As a man with access to the Council of State, Nedham was able to get large quantities of reliable news, which he could, if occasion demanded, sift and color. He was also able to count on the services of at least two capable correspondents in Scotland, one of them connected with the army, the other with the diplomatic staff. In addition, he had two, sometimes three, able and knowledgeable men writing letters from Paris, and a first-rate correspondent in The Hague. Consequently the foreign news in *Politicus* was the most expert of that era. Yet Nedham did not overload his paper with cross-Channel items but varied their quantity in inverse ratio to the amount of printable British news. Sometimes, therefore, he might devote more than half his space to continental affairs, though usually they occupied three or four pages.

Nedham displayed his professional touch in other ways. One was his foresight. Early in 1651, for instance, he featured several unfriendly stories about the Dutch, in anticipation of Anglo-Dutch hostilities the following year.[37] A second was his ability to create suspense. During the summer of 1651 he handled the preliminaries to the Battle of Worcester and the battle itself with enough drama so that even in reading the accounts today, when the outcome is no longer in doubt, one is anxious to discover what happened. To add to the suspense Nedham had the artistic and political judgment now to treat Charles as a menacing villain, not a foolish youth. The editor was also skillful in insinuating rather than declaring an attitude. To give only one example, he was able to suggest that clericalism was evil, but neither in his news nor in his asides did he directly reflect on the Independent clergy.[38] Finally, Nedham displayed his professionalism in his ability to secure a relatively large number of advertisements.

The third category of evidence that proves Nedham's responsibility for *Mercurius Politicus* consists of the editorials with which, until August 1652, the paper almost always began. For its first fifteen numbers *Politicus* opened with a breezy page or two attacking Royalists or Presbyterians or Scots and sticking up for the Commonwealth and Nedham.[39] All these lead articles had in common a tone of flippancy and a touch of Hobbes. Then with Number 16, at the end of September, the flippancy vanished and the touch of Hobbes became an embrace. For the next forty-four weeks, until October 1651, each issue featured a serious editorial, some so serious that they have been attributed to John Milton.[40]

Nedham was indeed plagiarizing, not from Milton but from his own works; for almost every one of these forty-four pieces was gently lifted from *The Case of the Common-Wealth of England Stated*. Sometimes, it is true, Nedham added material or made minor revisions, but by and large the readers of *Politicus* were getting a fragmented and rearranged version of that tract by which he had helped to earn his editorship. Whether they read the pamphlet or the paper, they were also getting a heavy dose of expediency. Furthermore, when the resourceful Nedham had finished cannibalizing *The Case*, he utilized the next forty-four editorials, with only minor revisions and deletions, to make up a pamphlet published in 1656 as *The Excellencie Of A Free State*. In one instance, one of the more "Miltonic" bits first appeared in *The Case*, next in *Politicus*, and wound up in *The Excellencie*.[41] Nedham could be expedient in more ways than one.

Though he was secret about his self-plagiarism, he was open about his view that power is its own justification. Nedham seldom upheld the Commonwealth on ideological or idealistic ground; rather, he strongly defended it on the basis of *Realpolitik*, back to normalcy, live and let live. He was well read in political theory, including Machiavelli, and had a wide knowledge of history. A few samples from his first series of editorials can show why, in terms of his background, politics, and style, Nedham was well suited to be the Commonwealth's Hobbes. In October 1650 he justified the Junto by pointing out that "if a King may . . . by the Right of warr lose his Share and Interest in Authority and Power, being conquered; then on the other side, by Right of warr, the whole must needs reside in that part of the people which prevailed over him. . . ." [42] A month later Nedham added another buttress to this pragmatic edifice by stating that "ipso facto the Sword creates a Title for Him, or Them, that beare it, and installs them with a new Majestie of Empire." [43] Then early in March 1651 he enlarged his focus in order to justify England's playing imperialistic balance-of-power politics: "I look upon England, in the posture it now stands in, as a mighty Animal indeed, if it knew its own strength; and such a one as might make it self (if not Master, yet) grand Arbitrator of Affairs in Europe." [44] In June, at the end of *Politicus's* first year, Nedham glorified the government he served in accents reminiscent of Volpone's hymn to gold in Ben Jonson's most cynical play:

> Was it the Sword then that did thus enslave us from time to time, and shall we not free our selves now we have the Sword in our own hands? Must Usurpers ride in triumph, with the Sword by their sides, over the heads of the people? And shall not the Patriots of England, adorned with all the Priviledges and Liberties of the people, take occasion to secure themselves, and settle us, with much more reason, by the Power of the Sword? The Sword is the great Engin, used by the hand of God, in erecting, altering, and establishing all the Frames of Government of the world. It is the main spring that moves all the wheels of Providence in these sublunary things: and if there be any thing under the sun that holds Jure Divino it is the Sword. . . .[45]

Finally, in the next to last editorial he lifted from *The Case* Nedham seemed to be preaching the program of the Levellers, but on close examination it turns out to have been diluted and postponed. However, it sounded good, especially the peroration:

> True Freedom . . . consists not in a license to do what ye list, nor in an exemption from such Taxes as are necessary for your safety, but in these few particulars: First, In having wholesome Lawes suited to every mans state and condition. Secondly, In a due and easie course of Administration, as to Law and Justice, that the Remedies of evill may be cheap and speedy. Thirdly, in a power of altering Government and Governors upon occasion. Fourthly, in an uninterrupted course of Successive Parliaments. . . . Fifthly, in a free election of Members to sit in every Parliament, when the Rules of Election are once established.[46]

Cumulatively these editorials argued cogently for submission to the government, and they effectively wooed moderate Royalists, Presbyterians, and Levellers. Nedham made the program of the Independents seem neither radical nor reactionary, and the Caesar to whom he asked his readers to render homage appeared the image of patriotism, justice, security, and efficiency. Both as pamphleteer and journalist he had made a convincing case.

In so doing, Nedham needed no help, and Milton's role in *Mercurius Politicus* was nominal. During much of 1650 he was concerned with his eyesight, answering Salmasius, and justifying the ways of the Commonwealth to continental diplomats and intellectuals. He probably approved the idea of a readable pro-government newspaper, and possibly was consulted on the hiring of Nedham. Milton may even have contributed a few ideas to *Politicus*, including the suggestion that its editorials become serious. But the only tangible evidence for any connection at that time between him and Nedham is that from March 1651 to January 1652 he officially licensed *Mercurius Politicus*.[47] In return, and because it was news, Nedham on ten occasions in 1651 printed stories from abroad concerning Milton, most having to do with the success of *Defensio Pro Populo Anglicano* and the discomfiture of Salmasius.[48]

It is extremely likely, however, that Milton had more to do with the second long-run paper that was started in the summer of 1650. In July *Nouvelles Ordinaires de Londres* began its eight-year task of retailing authorized news of England to a foreign audience.[49] Written in French, it was the Commonwealth version of *Le Mercure Anglois*, as safe and dull but a bit more professional. The editing and printing were done by William Dugard, who, possibly for European consumption, here signed himself Guillaume Du-gard. In 1648, after four years as headmaster of the Merchant Taylors' School, he had set up a private printing press, and shortly thereafter printed *Eikon Basilike* and Salmasius's attack on the regicides. As a result, early in 1650 Dugard was arrested, but a few weeks later, very possibly after the intervention of Milton, he was released. Dugard then assumed the title of "printer to the Council of State" and for ten years made a success of his business. Three of his publishing efforts, shortly after he shifted to the cause of the Commonwealth, were Milton's "First Defense," a French version of *Eikonoklastes*, and *Nouvelles Ordinaires*.[50] Probably Milton helped to start this paper: he seems to have known Dugard, and he was certainly aware that Royalist exiles had lately been virtually monopolizing the dissemination of English news on the continent, even if mainly by word of mouth.[51]

But Dugard, too, soon needed little or no outside help — except for the government press releases which in raw or digested form constituted the diet of his weekly. The opening paragraph of the first number stated (in French) that the editor "deemed it not unacceptable to foreign nations to impart, in a language that extends and is understood throughout Europe, all the most signal and remarkable happenings [in England]." As in *Le Mercure Anglois*, these signal and remarkable happenings were the official actions at Westminster, military news, and the government's version of what was going on in Scotland and Ireland. Very occasionally an item of foreign news was included, provided it impinged directly on the affairs of the Commonwealth. This adequate but superficial survey, written in an impersonal and official-sounding style, was chiefly addressed to a Paris public. But *Nouvelles Ordinaires* could be bought in London, until the end of 1650 at three establishments, then only at the shop of Nicholas Bourne. It had some additional circulation outside France, for in 1651 Dugard complained about a counterfeit published at The Hague; and he may have envisioned a fairly large readership among foreign merchants, though not until 1654 did he regularly include reports aimed at them.[52]

Nouvelles Ordinaires lived up to its title, for its news, condensed into four pages, corresponded to what other authorized weeklies were peddling. No controversial items sullied Dugard's neatly printed sheet, and only on an average of once a month did he find room for a human-interest story. Even these usually redounded to the credit of the Commonwealth: a young girl was to be whipped for falsely accusing a man of being a delinquent; Princess Elizabeth plaintively passed away; several soldiers were properly punished for unruliness and criminality; a Jewish Arab was convicted of sodomy.[53] Perhaps Dugard's more sophisticated readers found some of his translations into French interesting: Cromwell became "My Lord Général," Parliament often "La Maison," and whenever he was not sure of himself Dugard fell back on similar literal translations.

Yet he contributed, at least in embryo, two innovations to early journalism: the extra and the continued story. Between consecutive Thursdays in September 1650 an extra edition came out entitled *Nouvelles Extraordinaires*, consisting of Cromwell's letter to Parliament on the victory at Dunbar. A few weeks later, unable to finish reprinting another letter from Cromwell, the editor continued it in the following issue.[54] Despite such devices, *Nouvelles Ordinaires* remained conformist and dull; and certainly Cardinal Mazarin, one of its irregular readers, had better sources of information.[55]

Not so most Londoners, even if by the summer of 1650 they had a larger selection of weeklies to choose from. At that time the government, desirous of popular support in the war against the Scots and aware that the official press was not a very convincing propaganda instrument, permitted several new papers to get started. Some were durable, others short-lived, but all were printed by bonded printers and, though not entered in the Stationers' Register, sanctioned by the Council of State.[56] For this they gave weekly thanks by parroting the official line.

In June, Border re-entered journalism via *The Impartial Scout*. Made up mostly of official news, much of it concerned with events in Scotland, plus a smattering of foreign items, the paper did an adequate job for the nine numbers it lasted.[57] Border's hand is visible in its platitudinous editorials and tendency to emphasize the anti-Presbyterian aspects of the government's position. As he had done in 1649, he also supplied his readers with Lilly's monthly prognostications and the London bills of mortality.

So did Walker, who in July supplemented *Severall Proceedings in Parliament* with a new weekly, *Perfect Passages of Every Daies Intelligence*. Both papers, the second under various titles, survived until the autumn of 1655, for Walker was not a man to invest in a losing proposition. Nor did *Perfect Passages* require much of an investment. It too relied on government handouts, and the editor repeatedly went out of his way to derogate the Scots and to heap praise on the men, especially Cromwell and sometimes Walker, who were leading England to victory, righteousness, and stability. The tone of such praise was set in the opening paragraph of the first number:

All things have their time, and rare effects attend humane affairs. There was a time when the Pen that sets now to Paper was had in choice esteem, a time when the hand that guides it held up the sword for defence of the Parliament; and a present time of freedom wherein he may once more serve his Country, impartially communicating Intelligence (without flattery. . .).[58]

But Walker, even on a part-time basis, was not incompetent. Interspersed among his authorized letters and reports (and flattery) were enough pious asides and crime stories to please and titillate the godly, while his platitudinous opening sentences could have displeased only those in favor of sin. Then, too, Walker was more strenuous than his colleagues in securing advertisements.

The easing of censorship, the re-entry of Border, and the starting of a second newspaper by Walker gave a superficial *deja vu* appearance to the summer of 1650; and particularly in July the journalistic scene briefly resembled old home week. For two weeks Pecke accompanied his work for Rushworth by reviving his own *A Perfect Diurnall*, an adequate but undistinguished effort.[59] Border added to the nostalgic atmosphere by supplementing *The Impartial Scout* with a resurrected *Perfect Weekly Account*, which came out twice in July, once in August, and once in September. In the first number the editor mentioned the paper's "Antiquity" and assured his readers that it would continue to be the sort of journal that "was never the least kind questioned for scandal or falsehood." [60] From the government's point of view, there was no reason why it should be. Collings, too, returned, and the one July number of *The Weekly Intelligencer of the Commonwealth* made much of the fact that the editor was a man of experience:

Having been almost sick unto death, and lain above halfe a yeare speechlesse, upon a little recovery I have made bold (but not without permission) to take the aire again. What though I look pale? If you find Truth in my Intelligence, and a lively complexion in my lines, I hope I shall passe again for a sound Intelligencer.

And Collings went on to say that, as before, he would be honest and impartial, though because of "wild Informers" and Royalist propaganda, this would not be easy.[61]

Nor was it. After this one attempt *The Weekly Intelligencer* disappeared until October; then after four numbers it again vanished, this time until the end of December. But when it came back, it was for almost five years of continuous existence. *The Weekly Intelligencer* earned this long life, for, with the exception of *Politicus*, it was London's best paper. Collings seems to have relished this pre-eminence. Several times during 1651 he called attention to his ability to collect and arrange the news, pointing out that he was gratifying his readers' desire for unadorned, honest reports — that it was "Intelligence and not the melancholy of Contemplation" they wanted and he would provide.[62] He was even sufficiently confident to reprimand his public when they asked more of him than he could, according to his own cautious standards, deliver:

Your Generall Inquiry is, What is the News from the North? Why Gentlemen, what News can be expected from that Climate at this time [early March], when Winter lyes always on beds of Snow, and Thule [is] covered with mists, where the discontented Day makes no where a shorter abode, and where it is thought that weary Nature did faint away. . . .

He was confident enough as well thus to denounce his competitors, actual and potential:

Why, let them print a thousand Intelligencers . . . and bring them forth upon the Tuesday. Let them counterfeit this Title, and continue to abuse their Readers and themselves. . . . This Intelligence hath been . . . drawn up almost ten years together, and now lives by its own strength, as it hath flourished in the acceptation of the Readers. . . .[63]

Collings could afford to brag. *The Weekly Intelligencer*, though it followed the official line, was more readable and reliable than its fellows, excluding Nedham's weekly. Collings' style was clear and disciplined, but it was also varied and flexible. He was concerned with transitions, and he could shift key when appropriate; from, for instance, the blunt language of "[the man was] hanged for Pederasty, in plain English buggery," to the rolling cadence of:

The great Expectation and Discourse of the greatest part of Christendome is, what are the proceedings in the great Assembly at the Hague, and the great discourse of many at the Hague is, what are the proceedings of the Armies in Scotland: on these two hinges the Door of this Intelligence now must move; in which I shall be carefull in the first place to give you all the truest News I can collect, and in the last, all the choicest I can learn.[64]

In addition, Collings was more selective than his colleagues in choosing what constituted significant news, labeling unfounded reports as such, and printing only those foreign items of immediate interest to the English public. Of all authorized editors, again with exception of Nedham, he was now the least credulous. Thus he gave a natural explanation for a "plague of frogs"; he remarked that the sayings of some Somersetshire prophets were "fitter for a Ballad than [for] this Pamphlet"; and he once went in person to check on a ghost story, concluding his somewhat eerie narrative with a few skeptical comments.[65]

Border was now almost as hard-headed as Collings when it came to his profession. At the beginning of 1651, three months after the demise of his *Impartial Scout*, Border tried again, this time with *The Faithfull Scout*. It survived, with a few gaps and changes in title, until, along with most other weeklies, it was suppressed by the Protectorate late in 1655. The first number opened with the commonplace announcement that the paper was worthy of survival:

I had long before this time appeared to the World, had not the World appeared to me in the shape of misfortune, and frightned me from my intentions. I confess the petulancy of these times (which are able to swell a word into a volume) have been sufficient adversaries to my designes; but now having put on the Armour of Resolution, I intend (by the assistance of the Almighty Power) to encounter falshood with the sword of truth. I will not endeavour to flatter the world into a belief of things that are not; but truly to inform them of things that are, and not make my own conceits my Intelligencer, as many in these times. . . .[66]

Thereafter it was a typical Border product, and consequently fit, though by no means fittest, to survive. *The Faithfull Scout* was properly God- and government-fearing. Its pages were lightened by a few human-interest vignettes and a scattering of inoffensive asides, and loosely held together by sporadic transitions. From early January to the end of June the paper began with platitudinous editorials on such subjects as immortality, piety, honest governors, and self-discipline. But maybe even such topics were too nerve-racking for the editor to deal with or the government to countenance: for five weeks in the summer of 1651 *The Faithfull Scout* did not appear, and when it came back it had dropped its editorials. Border, however, retained the weekly feature of the bill of mortality and the monthly circulation-builder of Lilly's predictions, now partly justifying the latter on the basis that "some men are so covetous of news that they are desirous to know the event of things before time can bring them to pass." [67] Temporarily the editor suppressed his inclinations to derogate the Presbyterians, except in official stories, and he settled down to put out a weekly that was adjusted to "the petulancy of these times," not a reflection of them.

Border's former rival and partner, "B.D.," came to a similar decision. In January 1651 he too was willing to risk another try at journalism, and his paper, *A Perfect Account*, also lasted until late 1655, in the process skipping several weeks. Like *The Faithfull Scout*, *A Perfect Account* was crowded, cautious, Commonwealth. Both showed some selectivity in condensing trivial items and in summarizing involved events; both gave approximately one page to foreign affairs; and both contained a smattering of advertisements and colorful nonpolitical stories. B.D. sometimes cited Lilly, though he did not feature his prophecies; nor did *A Perfect Account* regularly begin with an editorial. It also differed from Border's paper in being more hackneyed and sometimes betraying antisectarian sentiments.[68] These, however, were never blatant enough to suggest that B.D. was not playing safe.

Two reasons for the survival of a paper like *A Perfect Account* were, first, the willingness of the government to have its story told by several organs, presumably on the theory that, even if they were similar, their multiplicity would make them more convincing; and second, the habit many Londoners had acquired of wanting to get the news every day. From early 1651 to late 1655 this was possible, for the authorities usually allowed seven newspapers to appear. (*A Briefe Relation* went out of business in October 1650, and *Nouvelles Ordinaires* had a small enough English circulation to avoid competing with other Thursday weeklies.) On Monday an eager reader could buy the Rushworth-Pecke *A Perfect Diurnall*, on Tuesday Collings' *Weekly Intelligencer*, and on Wednesday B.D.'s *Perfect Account*. Thursday he had a choice between the Scobell-Walker *Severall Proceedings* and Nedham's *Mercurius Politicus*. Friday was probably a better day for Walker, for then his *Perfect Passages* competed with Border's *Faithfull Scout*. Thus the journalistic scene bore a superficial resemblance to what it had been in the late 1640's, but it was a faded likeness.

Not only were these authorized newspapers less free than their predecessors, but they had fewer short-run newcomers to goad them into liveliness. From July 1650 to the end of 1651 only eight additional pro-government and two Royalist weeklies dared raise their heads, and their average life was only two numbers.[69] For three weeks in the summer of 1650 *True Intelligence From The Headquarters* concentrated on news from Scotland, transmitting it with a mixture of clumsiness and immediacy that gave an air of authenticity to its semiofficial reports. In August *The best and most perfect Intelligence* joined the "deare brethren of the Waste-Paper Fraternitie" and devoted its single issue to an ardent defense of Cromwell and the Independents. For two weeks in September *The Moderne Intelligencer*, published by "Parliament Joan" and edited probably by Walker, properly purveyed proper news, as did its single number a year later.[70] Perhaps enjoying creating rather than destroying newspapers, Joan, probably again with Walker's assistance, revived the title *Mercurius Anglicus* for one week in October. It too was conformist except for its especially vigorous denunciations of Charles.

Then for eight months no new newspaper appeared, until in June 1651, a year after the founding of *Politicus* and *Nouvelles Ordinaires*, *Pragmaticus* and *Elencticus* scurried on and off the scene. For one number *Mercurius Pragmaticus Revived* gave two-thirds of its space to quasi-news, only one-third to straight invective, and included the apologetic admission that the editor's "Comical fancy hath contracted its self in some measure from that licentious Nimbleness and Sphere it formerly rambled in." During the next three weeks the paper came out as *Mercurius Elencticus*, the first issue concluding with the quatrain,

> Pythagoras, thy Transmigration's good:
>   As in my Melancholy Muse I stood,
> I felt the change, and change is oft with us;
>   For Prag has slipped into Elencticus.

Prag had not had far to slip. All four numbers gaily if somewhat frenziedly loaded the news against the Commonwealth, cursed the Grandees, and found rays of Royalist sunshine in the activities of the dour Scots. But on July 1 Prag-Elencticus went back into hiding. Or did he? For herein lies a minor mystery. On July 8 the printer he had used, James Moxon, produced the single issue of a paper entitled *Mercurius Scommaticus* (the Jeering Mercury).[71] Written with a good deal of vigor, it commented that the times were troubled and the world in decay. But the author was willing briefly to serve the Commonwealth with his wits. In so doing he attacked the Scots and Presbyterians, conveyed some news, and secured two advertisements. Very possibly Prag-Elencticus was trying to earn a little money to cushion his hiding place.

A month later, in August 1651, there was no mystery about two papers full of official news that appeared, each for a single number: *The Armies Intelligencer* and *The true Informer: Of the Actions of the Army*.[72] And in September the longest lived of these ephemeral weeklies of the early 1650's began its six-issue career. *The Diary*, taking advantage of the public's desire to find out what happened to Charles after his flight from the Battle of Worcester, gave his escape a comparatively big play, though here, as in the rest of its news, it relied almost exclusively on official reports.[73] When the king's story was completed by his arrival in Paris, *The Diary* ceased to be kept. In this respect it differed from the authorized papers that continued in business.

CHAPTER XII

THE COMMONWEALTH
NEWSPAPER II

October 1651 to April 1653

FROM autumn 1651 to spring 1653 the London weeklies generally
played the part of a kept press. Theoretically the act of September 1649 lapsed after two years; actually its provisions remained in effect
until early 1653. The government was not strict in enforcing it, but the
threat of harshness was always present, and despite the fact that very
few persons were prosecuted, almost no newspapers stepped out of
line.[1] In May 1652 Parliament began debating in a slow but heated manner a statute to replace it, and eight months later passed a new censorship
law.[2] It differed mainly in giving to the Council of State some of the
enforcement powers previously allotted to the Stationers' Company, but
until Cromwell inaugurated his own system of control in 1655 the
newspapers underwent little change. In the spring of 1653, when he
finally dismissed the Rump, there was a brief flurry of comparative
freedom; then the weekly press again subsided into almost total acquiescence.

Throughout this period eight long-run papers were usually available
each week. On Monday the Rushworth-Pecke *A Perfect Diurnall* con-

tinued to be the standard purchase. Early in 1653, probably to emphasize its prestige, it changed its name to *The Perfect Diurnall*. Its sixteen
pages went on giving the surface of important news, but when foreign
affairs began to play a larger role in the politics of the Commonwealth,
Pecke gave about half his space to cross-Channel events. He also increased the number of advertisements, and by 1653 the paper usually
ran half-a-dozen announcements of new books, patent medicines, lost
articles — at a charge of a shilling each.[3] The editor remained adept in
playing up significant news, provided it was not too dangerous. Thus
Charles's plight after the Battle of Worcester was given prominence;
whenever news arrived of the Commonwealth's military maneuvers in
the West Indies it received full treatment; and the tensions between
England and Holland, as well as the war, were given competent coverage. (All authorized papers devoted much space to this war, an accom-
plishment made easier because most dispatches from Holland were
censored by neither the Dutch nor the English governments.) Pecke
displayed his skill, too, in a few well-told human-interest items, of which
probably the most indicative of current morality, at least in Scotland,
was the account of unnatural relations between an Edinburgh man and
his horse: apparently caught *flagrante delicto*, both were sentenced to
be executed.[4] Finally, Pecke showed his professionalism by his caution.
On one occasion he accused a printer of publishing a rival *Diurnall*,
then apologized because this man was a favorite of Cromwell's.[5] When
the Rump was dissolved, Pecke gave the story five lines, and followed
it with three pages of the official declaration justifying Cromwell's
move.[6]

Unlike Pecke, Collings had not become completely impersonal and
obedient. On those scattered occasions when he wrote about himself he
praised his own careful selectivity and diligence.[7] In one instance he
spoke briefly of his poverty, a condition confirmed in a contemporary
Royalist attack on him.[8] He deserved to be better off. Not only was *The
Weekly Intelligencer* one of the most functional London newspapers,
but it printed an average number of advertisements, and it seems to have
achieved a fairly large rural circulation.[9] Collings also continued to be a
capable editor. His paragraphing was intelligent, his allocation of space
judicious. Usually he gave about three pages to foreign news, the other
five to Westminster, Irish and Scottish items, along with a smattering of
human-interest stories and pro-government asides. But his love for the
Commonwealth was not wholehearted. When Lilburne was exiled in
1652, the editor gave his saga broad and neutral coverage; and he recurrently included stories about another exile, Charles II, generally
treating him with sympathetic irony, as in this instance: "It was objected

by some in my last that the inserting of the titular Scots King playing at Nine-pins was a subject too low for the height of his personage, and for the Gravity with which this sheet is constantly attended." [10]

Yet Collings almost always played safe, and a few times he took out extra insurance by praising *Mercurius Politicus*.[11] Like his fellows, he was extremely careful not to disclose "high" news, this example from the summer of 1652 being typical:

> But what say you if yet we shall have peace with Holland? The News indeed may seem as strange as it is good. For the present therefore I shall but onely name it, and leave it to knowing men . . . to conjecture it, to you to discourse it, and to Truth and Time to confirm it.[12]

Also Collings, probably deliberately, now struck a balance between skepticism and credulity in his stories of witches, apparitions, and strange events, sometimes appearing to smile, other times to gape.[13] A few times, however, he seemed lazy or careless. Early in 1653, after a five-week gap, *The Weekly Intelligencer* opened with the phrase "Having slept some weeks in this sloth of Winter," a statement that was probably more than figurative, though the new censorship act may have had something to do with the paper's lapse;[14] and in March 1652 one number included an attack on "the damned opinion of Predestination."[15] The next week Collings offered this explanation:

> This sheet (I know not by what misfortunes) being drawn up the last week by the hand of an unknown Gentleman, I shall leave him to give satisfaction concerning what was there spoken of Predestination, which not without the deepest reverence I have always numbered Inter Arcana Dei. It hath been . . . my business in this weekly Paper to give you matter of Intelligence, and not to declare my Judgment, or to trouble your own with the mysteries of Divinity, which I leave to the Divines.[16]

Thereafter he saw to it that no unknown Gentleman upset his apple cart.

Collings was still, with the exception of Nedham, the best stylist among English journalists. Usually stripped and impersonal, his writing sometimes had a touch of Keatsian lyricism, as when he referred to "the laughing Spring riding on the back of the Western winds, and April under every Hedg, walking with her disshevelled hair"; sometimes a touch of the 1890's:

> How black is this flower in my hand, which yesterday was sweet as the morning, and fairer than Beauty it self. Just so are Cities which to Day are flourishing in all their glory, and to morrow trembling at the voice of the Canon, and ugly as the face of Ruine.[17]

Collings was superior, too, in retailing certain anecdotes which have retained their poignant humor: the story of a man crying "very sad News," and then, when Londoners came to buy his papers, announcing that there were many poor people; or the account of a London coal-seller who advertised his price at four-pence a bushel — in Amsterdam.[18]

Between December 1651 and May 1652 Collings was faced with direct competition from a Tuesday paper, *The French Intelligencer*. Its editor, possibly Border,[19] presented a strange mixture. Generally dull and careless, he showed touches of skill and discrimination. Never openly opposed to the Commonwealth, he was sympathetic to Lilburne and Charles, and he held some of the views of the Fifth Monarchists, that group which believed the kingdom of God was about to be established in England and were busy getting ready for the rule of the saints. Often credulous, he occasionally revealed a sharp strain of skepticism. Also, his paper's title was not entirely accurate: though the weekly usually began with a paragraph of French news and even a few times delayed publication until the foreign posts arrived, it devoted fewer than half its eight pages to non-English news, with the rest being a potpourri of official and miscellaneous items.

From January to April 1652 this potpourri had an anti-government aroma. But from the start *The French Intelligencer* was slightly out of step, and three of its earliest numbers contained stories that were unusual: a warning to a bankrupt London heir that, if he did not stop being extravagant, the editor and all his fellows would "so characterize him to the world that his Landress shall not give him the credit for the washing of his shirt"; a reference to the Dutch massacre of English settlers at Amboyna in 1624, probably an anticipatory bit of government-inspired propaganda; and a prophesy that Cromwell would conquer Rome in 1656.[20] Then the editor's pro-Royalism began to intrude, and a mid-January issue ended with the words "GOD SAVE THE KING," a slogan which he justified by saying that it was uttered in France.[21] Two weeks later he ran a lengthy story about a servant robbing his master, but told in such a way that it applied to England's recent history.[22] And in March, commenting on a solar eclipse, the editor remarked,

> I am sure that no man more commpassionates the misfortunes of that Star-crossed Gentleman [Charles] than the Author of this Weekly sheet; and I desire that his condition may be a lively example to those, whether Soldier or Magistrate, who rule over their Fellow Commoners; and let them know that their greatness being built only upon the uncertain breath of that suspicious, humorsom, skittish Creature, the people, is very uncertain, and subject to various vicissitudes. . . .[23]

Not quite so outspoken but still not concealed was the editor's favorable view of Lilburne, a man whose concept of "the people" was remote from his own. Each week from mid-January to the end of March *The French Intelligencer* contained an item or items sympathetic to the Levellers. In one instance the editor even looked with favor on a proposal for a single levy, an embryonic income tax, to finance the government.[24] He also predicted that the Fifth Monarchy would begin in England in 1655.[25] Certainly political consistency was not one of the paper's virtues. Nor was astrological consistency: after a statement that many of Lilly's predictions had proved wrong, the editor twice reprinted the astrologer's monthly prophecy.[26] But late in April the tone of the paper changed. It now printed four or five pages of foreign news and avoided all comment on controversial domestic happenings. A few weeks later it printed nothing.

Now, however, it was Pecke's turn to worry; for *The French Intelligencer*'s successor, edited by the same man, shifted to Monday and lasted eight months. *The French Occurrences* from May until September displayed few Royalist symptoms, though it contained an increasing number of references to ancient prophecies, several of which had anti-Commonwealth overtones.[27] The editor continued to give about half his space to foreign affairs, mostly French and Dutch; and in one number he acknowledged that his news from France came in the form of an "Abstract of the French Letters, translated into English," apparently an incipient press service to which other journalists subscribed.[28] But even in these early numbers the paper leaned toward a monarchical point of view. It favored items that supported the French king against his own rebellious subjects, and at least twice gave cryptic backing to opponents of the Commonwealth.[29] Then in the later months of 1652 *French Occurrences* became open in its sympathies. Three times in large letters resembling a modern headline it printed "GOD SAVE THE KING" or its equivalent, and once "LORD, WHERE'S OUR MONEY GONE," though each time the editor set up an alibi by claiming that the phrase came from abroad.[30] Again he carried a series of items that played up Lilburne and the Levellers; [31] and he increasingly if indirectly conveyed the idea that the Commonwealth was weak, its enemies strong and growing stronger. But on January 3, 1653, Pecke — and Cromwell — could stop worrying about *The French Occurrences*: on that date it quietly expired.

B.D., the editor of Wednesday's *A Perfect Account*, had no normal competition to worry about. He remained adequately clear, selective, and cautious, and his paper continued to get an average return from advertising, though it failed to come out ten times during this period.

B.D. slightly distinguished himself by being less credulous than most of his contemporaries, and if he cited Lilly to help to explain an eclipse of the sun, he mocked at astrology.[32] The editor also became very interested in crime news. *A Perfect Account* ran several stories on James Hind, the day's most famous highwayman; it told of a man who stabbed his wife and child and then himself, concluding with the comment that thus "we may see as in a Glasse what man is when he is left to himself"; and it noted that some Edinburgh surgeons were trying to secure the body of a man executed for pretending to be a woman.[33] Finally, one of B.D.'s asides is especially revealing of the generally patronizing attitude most Londoners had toward their rural compatriots: he justified anglicizing a French name by stating that this was the only way his "Countrey friends" could know whom he meant.[34]

On Wednesday the newspaper-buyer had only B.D. and Crouch to choose between; but on Thursday he had Walker's *Severall Proceedings*, Dugard's *Nouvelles Ordinaires*, and Nedham's *Mercurius Politicus*. The first was, however, as undistinguished as B.D.'s weekly and now less competently edited. Walker was still busy, and he filled his sixteen pages with items probably in the order in which they came to his desk or pocket, only being careful to eliminate anything offensive to the government.[35] The result was that half his paper consisted of semi-official reports, the other half of foreign news, with the latter having the dubious advantage of being more varied than in other weeklies. Except for an occasional blast at disobedient editors and publishers, Walker's personality remained almost invisible.[36] Indeed, his paper's major asset was its unmitigated regularity: like *A Perfect Diurnall*, *Severall Proceedings* skipped no weeks.

Nouvelles Ordinaires also appeared uninterruptedly, and even brought forth one extra, a *Nouvelles Extraordinaires* telling of Admiral Blake's victory.[37] Dugard still relied on official letters and printed very little non-English news, though often he commented on the shortage of space in his four-page weekly and on the fact that he was forced to continue reports in the following number. Despite a few descriptions of crimes, fires, duels, and prodigies,[38] Dugard bent most of his editorial efforts to being careful. He made his inoffensive journal especially innocuous by, for instance, delaying telling of Charles's escape and arrival on the continent, by treating Lilburne's exile in one noncommittal paragraph, and by devoting only four lines to the dissolution of the Rump.[39] Presumably Nicholas Bourne made very little money out of his now exclusive London distributorship of this paper.

Mercurius Politicus, in contrast, was England's most popular and profitable weekly, and Nedham continued to do an excellent job of purveying all the news he could without jeopardizing his position. Moreover, he was assisted by consistently capable correspondents at home and abroad. Thus in handling the Anglo-Dutch war he not only gave full coverage to naval battles, but managed to interweave the economic and political aspects into his continued story. Sometimes, too, when dispatches were coming in as the paper had to come out, that story had the elements of a thriller.[40] *Politicus* was, of course, strongly nationalistic, but never to such an extent that its bias unduly distorted the news. Probably for this reason and because of the paper's large circulation, the government occasionally used it as a trial balloon. Both early and late in the war Nedham printed reports from abroad concerning peace feelers, presumably so the Council of State could sample London's reaction.[41]

By and large, *Politicus* remained a subtle rather than blatant instrument of propaganda. Recurrently it featured items about the rise in England's power and prestige overseas flattering to Englishmen of all shades of opinion.[42] Nedham enjoyed deriding the Scots and their kirk, but again he was appealing to English nationalism and hinting that the Commonwealth had given England a stability still absent from Scotland, as well as a way of life that did not include the torturing and burning of witches.[43] The editor did not stop praising the Rump and the Council of State, but he avoided the manner of sycophant; nor did he cease to attack their opponents, though seldom in the manner of a hatchet man. *Politicus*'s few references to Lilburne in exile were patronizing rather than vindictive, and its regular comments on Charles usually made him seem petty and puny. For instance, a report from Amsterdam noted in passing that Lilburne was finding "but small encouragements" to stay there; and of Charles, Nedham wrote, "The King and his family are said to be great Readers and Admirers of Playbooks and Romances; but truly as that is little honour to them, so the worst part of the scene is that themselves are become not onely Actors, but real Tragedies and Romances to the world"; and, later, that "the little Court linger at St. Germans building Castles in the air."[44] When attacking Charles's pro-Catholicism, Nedham could be more vituperative, but he seemed to prefer mocking the king's poverty and the debauchery and intrigue that surrounded him.

Nedham was also an effective propagandist in terms of what he omitted. By concentrating on foreign, Scottish, and Irish news, as well as on nonpolitical home news, he left little space for what was happening at Westminster or Whitehall, and his reports of Parliament were bare and brief. But Nedham was at his best in the forty-four editorials, most of them about four pages long, with which from October

1651 to August 1652 *Politicus* opened. The first editorial in this series appeared the week after Nedham concluded his borrowings from his own *Case of the Common-Wealth*, and five years before this second series, with some deletions and rearrangements, came out as *The Excellencie Of A Free State*.[45] As before, Nedham revealed his familiarity with history, especially that of republican Rome and allegedly republican Venice, and with political science and scientists, especially Machiavelli.[46] Shrewdly and clearly Nedham came to the defense of an English republic, pointing out the virtues of a semidemocratic system, answering objections to it, and showing the weaknesses of other forms of government. In supporting the political theory of the Commonwealth he was both practical and now sometimes idealistic. Regularly he preached such democratic doctrines as the right of the people to have a say in their government, the need for a separation of powers, the wisdom and piety of a nontheocratic state. He also varied his style so that it moved from gentle cajolery to rhetorical barrage, from a bare statement like a Commonwealth "is in a setled state when fully established and founded, and when all men are supposed friends to its establishment," to the oratorical ring of "Liberty . . . is like the Golden Fleece or the Hesperian fruit, watcht by Argus his hundred eyes, or by ever-waking Dragons." [47] Toward the end of this series Nedham compellingly pleaded the case for an enlightened public, a case which needs as much defending now as then. The people, he wrote, should know what freedom is,

and have it represented and enjoyed in all its lovely Features, that they may grow zealous and jealous over it; but that it may be a Zeal according to knowledge and to good purpose, it is without question most necessary that they be made acquainted and throughly instructed in the means and rules of its preservation, against the adulterous wiles and rapes of any projecting sophistes that may arise hereafter. And doubtless this endeavour of mine, in laying down the rules of preserving a Free State, will appear so much the more necessary if we consider that all inconveniences that . . . have hapned . . . to embroile or ruin it have proceeded . . . from the peoples neglect, or rather ignorance, of those means and rules that should be communicated unto them, both for practise and observation.[48]

Thus the former editor of *Pragmaticus* and the staunch Tory-to-be could eloquently espouse the establishment of real if limited democracy in England.

Yet Nedham was a publicist, never, if he could help it, a martyr. When this series of editorials came to an end, he replaced it with foreign news. The Commonwealth seemed secure and, if it was not democratic, there was no reason to remind people of what they might be missing. In any case, the Anglo-Dutch war was providing plenty of news, as well as an outlet for popular resentments. In May 1652, two months before his final editorial, Nedham translated and Dugard published John Seldon's *Mare Clausum*, brought up to date by the inclusion of Nedham's preface and notes showing that the Dutch were encroachers.[49] He also properly handled such incidental chores as seeing that *Politicus* was licensed, with John Thurloe succeeding Milton as licenser, and that it was sometimes entered in the Stationers' Register. Nedham also made sure that his salary from the government was supplemented by an adequate income from advertisements. In short, he was on top of the journalistic world, and in a few years he would have no other editor clambering up the sides of his pinnacle.

In the early 1650's Walker, if not at the top, was resting on his own comfortable summit. He supplemented *Severall Proceedings*, a paper overshadowed by *Politicus*, with Friday's *Perfect Passages of Every Daies Intelligence*.[50] Somewhat better edited than his Thursday effort, it showed that Walker was devoting at least a little time to journalism. Until the end of 1652 he regularly opened with a platitudinous and verbose paragraph or two in praise of virtue, honesty, wisdom, God, in the process displaying his classical learning and an increasing tendency toward expediency. Moreover, in *Perfect Passages* Walker did a better job of selecting foreign news with an eye to its relevance to England. He also handled crime news more dramatically, as in his account of the trial of a woman with fifteen husbands, or his report of a split jury casting lots and thereby acquitting the defendant in a rape case.[51] Possibly he was learning something from Nedham, for Walker managed to achieve suspense in a few of his war stories and to treat Charles with a certain amount of derogatory condescension.[52] (On the other hand, he sometimes gave the royal exile excessive credit for successful intervention in Europe's dynastic quarrels.) [53] Finally, Walker or his printer may have added to the paper's income by charging an extra fee for the use of conspicuous type in certain advertisements.

Regardless of any minor improvements, the old Walker predominated. He retained his trademarks of the London bills of mortality and Lilly's prophecies, though when the astrologer got in trouble Walker joined the hue and cry.[54] He was still vindictive against his less secure competitors, in one case announcing that the author of a "false" report would be punished, presumably at Walker's instigation.[55] A few times he carelessly insulted his non-London readers, the most notable instance being a story from Somersetshire about the natives signing a blank petition.[56] But he was not careless vis-à-vis the authorities. On the last day of 1652, in anticipation of the new censorship act, *Perfect Passages* even shut up shop. But not for long: within a few weeks Walker's lengthy career as a loyal and circumspect spokesman for the Independents paid off. On January 21, 1653, the Friday newspaper-buyer could pick up Walker's continuation of *Perfect Passages, The Moderate Publisher of Every daies Intelligence*, a weekly which lasted, after another change in title, until late 1655. Strangely enough, however, Cromwell's dissolution of the Rump seems momentarily to have thrown the editor off stride, for in his one-paragraph report he included the cryptic phrase, in large type, "Rouze up sad Hearts, Win Gold, and wear it"; and the same number included a brief plea for redress of the people's grievances.[57] But by the following week *The Moderate Publisher*, now containing more foreign news, was back in step, nor did it thereafter break ranks.

Border's *Faithfull Scout*, Walker's Friday competition, though it never marched in a direction contrary to that of other authorized papers, now often got out of step. Twice late in 1652 the editor and his printer were questioned for allegedly offensive articles, and Border may have spent the first few days of the new year behind bars.[58] The reason for his troubles is clear in the crowded pages of *The Faithfull Scout*: he was openly, if somewhat clumsily, moving to the left. Yet on the surface the paper showed little change. It included the bills of mortality and Lilly's prophecies, though when the astrologer got in hot water Border was not unsympathetic.[59] Its one to four pages of foreign news were still adequate, its coverage of Westminster cautious and choppy. The editor now dug up a few facetious items, such as the story of the constable who refused to "commit" a man who claimed his name was "Adultery." [60] He even printed some humorous semi-political anecdotes, including the remark to Parliament of the Danish ambassador that his beard was as old as their state.[61] Border also ran some sensational bits that other editors missed or ignored, like the account of the body of a giant found in Sussex, or a series of adventures in which James Hind was involved.[62] He or his printer also arranged for the first illustrated advertisement to appear in an English newspaper, a notice of two lost jewels with an accompanying picture.[63] Finally, he was the one editor of the day to feature a weather story, a big summer rainstorm in London.[64]

Such signs of life on Border's part were largely incidental; the major change was that his intermittent editorials and frequent editorial asides were, in late 1651 and in 1652, often written in pink-tinged ink. Several times he beat the radicals' favorite whipping boy, the professional lawyers;[65] and he repeatedly and pointedly went after the Presbyterians, attacking their theology, politics, and hangers-on. In so doing he even indulged in some heavy-handed humor, as when he told of a session of a Scottish court where 1,000 persons were accused of adultery, but where, since each of the accused claimed only one bastard, it was "counted a very small fault in the Scotch Creed."[66] In addition, Border's account of Lilburne's conviction and exile was friendly, as were his scattered references to left-wing petitions, persecuted sects, and the oppressed poor.[67] Among the projects for which he briefly crusaded were a plan for rotation in office and a scheme for peace between the Dutch and English so that both could fight Spain.[68]

Yet Border was not the editor Mabbott had been. Several times he undercut his tolerationist views by speaking out against innovation and heresy, and he periodically diluted his democratic class-consciousness by praising the Commonwealth for some of its most undemocratic manifestations. Moreover, he now vitiated his effectiveness as a spokesman for any cause by a notably uncritical credulity: wild miracles and apparitions, witches who had an extra teat to give the devil his due, and Merlin's prophecies all marred the pages of *The Faithfull Scout*. Border also had more explicit troubles. Once he was faced with a counterfeit; once he got involved in a squabble with Collings; and several times he traded blows with Crouch and with the pro-Presbyterian editor of a revived *Mercurius Britannicus*.[69] During the first five weeks of 1653 no *Faithfull Scout* appeared. It then returned for six weeks, disappeared for another five, was temporarily replaced at the end of April by *The Armies Scout*, and came back in June, this time for twenty-seven months. In more ways than one Border had gradually acquired a certain amount of bounce, despite the fact — if Crouch is to be trusted — that *The Faithfull Scout* never secured many readers.[70]

Dillingham briefly re-entered journalism at the end of 1652, and for three weeks in December he edited a revived *Moderate Intelligencer*. Typical and undistinguished as the paper was, he made much of his comeback:

Awaken'd once more by the sadnesse of the Times, I presume to thrust my impartial Mercury upon the Stage of the World again. The abuses of the Intelligence are such that my wearied Pen could no longer forbear to run the hazard of its Truth and castigate the looser transgressions of the Presse. . . . But the Age is so desperate an adorer of Novelties that it embraces newes in any language, or under any colour. . . . As therefore I am no Tymist to flatter the exorbitancy of any side, so likewise I am no Romance-monger to present the world with Tragi Comedies of my own invention. . . . I professe my self no Satyr, but a man passionately grieved at the stupid blindnesse of the people; my Title shall preserve me modest, as formerly; and my Conscience a clear dispencer of the sincerity of Relations.[71]

Such a derogation of the press echoed the tone, even the phrases, of many similar attacks. What is surprising is that Border, when *The Faithfull Scout* came back in February 1653, extensively plagiarized from Dillingham's diatribe in order to announce his own return.[72] In that month and in March, Dillingham, despite his professed scorn, edited the five numbers of *The Moderate Messenger*, a somewhat jumbled and unselective weekly that seemed to support the Commonwealth and only indirectly hinted that all was not well. Then Dillingham again withdrew from journalism, this time permanently.[73]

He had not been the only returnee. Under the new censorship act an "agent for the army" was to be appointed licenser of military news. Mabbott, apparently reconciled to the facts of seventeenth-century life, got the job and held it for almost three years.[74] Meanwhile John Crouch had also come back, and from the spring of 1652 to the autumn of 1655 he wrote a series of weeklies given over to parody and pornography. At the crest of English Puritanism, when public morality was an avowed concern of the government, Crouch's papers were not only permitted but, in all likelihood, not unprofitable.

Crouch had been arrested in June 1650 for his scurrilous antigovernment blasts in *The Man in the Moon*. He was released sometime before April 1652, by which date *Mercurius Democritus* had begun its ribald life. Calling itself a "Perfect Nocturnall," the subtitle went on to announce that the paper would give the "Wonderfull News Out of the World in the Moon, The Antipodes, Tenebris, Faery-Land, Egypt, Green-land, and other adjacent Countries," and that it was "Published for the right understanding of all the Mad-merry People of Great Bedlam." The title-page poem of the first number then announced Crouch's facetious prospectus:

> Of Wonders great I here shall tell,
>   More strange did ne'er come out,
> In Lil-lyes Progg. nor Mandivel,
>   Diurnall or the Scout.

> Their Lies are now grown too too stale,
>   Alas the more's the pitty,
> They should commixt with Yest and Ale
>   Besot both Town and Citie. . . .

Perhaps you'll say these are but Lies,
   Why should I this deny,
Lies are all truths i' th' Antipodes,
   Read on, Ile tell you why.[75]

Any reader who read on found that Crouch did a thorough job of avoiding politics and seriousness in order to "create laughter." Occasionally the editor allowed an item of news to creep in, and behind his irreverence one can detect a strong feeling of nationalism, and, possibly, a tinge of Royalism. But the overwhelming bulk of his material consisted of caricature and smut. Chiefly he parodied other papers, especially *The Faithful Scout*, and by extreme exaggeration he tried to show how credulous and unreliable Border and his ilk were. In *Democritus* prophecies became absurdly fantastic, as did such alleged news reports as, to cite only one, the story of a Dutch admiral who recruited an army mounted on 16,000 sea horses.[76] Crouch also poked fun at advertisements, in one case running a notice about a lost Presbyterian horse.[77] Though Border was his favorite target, all editors were peppered with his pellets, and he claimed that the only honest news in any London paper was the bill of mortality.[78] As to Crouch's pornography, it was either Rabelaisian, such as his account of a gigantic fart, or Aretinesque, such as some of his love and drinking songs.[79]

In the mid-summer of 1652 *Democritus*, after twenty-one numbers, apparently gave offense to someone high in the government, and for two months its place was taken by the almost identical *Laughing Mercury*. Gay, irreverent, smutty, it was a little more inclusive in heckling "Grubb-street liers," and it gave more space to attacking sects, not sex. Borrowing his fantastic tales, salacious anecdotes, and off-color puns from a variety of sources, Crouch told many stories still current at stag parties.[80]

In November *Mercurius Democritus* replaced the *Laughing Mercury*, again without much change. The editor now did a little more with phony ordinances and allowed a stronger strain of anti-Presbyterianism to infiltrate his parodies. He also printed more fake advertisements, including one for a lost maidenhead.[81] Then, too, his exaggerations became still more fantastic. Almost always giving precise figures, Crouch told, for example, how the devil mustered 173,000 witches for a conclave on Salisbury Plain.[82] He even, in one instance, supplemented a story with a picture: the last will of a gamecock was accompanied by an illustration of two fighting cocks.[83] Yet Crouch could be delightful, and some of his lyrics, including a few printed as prose, have a persistent charm:

So cold, cold, cold, so wonderous cold, and through the Bush the Winde blowes cold; Where are our Coals ye young Knaves, old; for through the Bush the Winde blows cold? (But where be our great Fleets of Coals?) One knave, two Knaves, three too old, and thorow the Bush the Winde blowes cold: cold, cold, cold, and wonderous cold, and thorow the Bush the Winde blowes cold.[84]

But whether he was being clean or dirty, Crouch was banking on two assumptions: that the government would agree that the man who is merry "seldom hatcheth treason," and that the journalists he attacked could not retaliate effectively. Until October 1655 these assumptions proved correct, and Crouch went on giving voice to some of the seamier facets of the Puritan Revolution.

Among other things, he supplied a running comment on the weekly press, not so much on the established papers, except for Border's, as on various short-run periodicals. Crouch had an adequate supply of grist for his satiric mill because between the end of 1651 and the spring of 1653 a dozen journals entered the field. Collectively they indicated that hope, at least in the breasts of journalists, springs eternal, and that the government, even when it was heading toward dictatorship, could be lax and unvindictive. Indeed, the fact that the cast of journalistic characters remained fairly permanent shows that the authorities' punishment of transgressing editors and publishers was usually mild and temporary.

Two papers avoided Crouch's comments, the first by being printed in Scotland, the second by appearing before he returned openly to journalism. *Mercurius Scoticus*, Scotland's first newspaper, was published in Leith and lasted twenty-one numbers, from July to December 1651. Directed to Cromwell's soldiers, it dispensed proper military news.[85] But very possibly Crouch would have remarked favorably on the four issues of *Mercurius Bellonius* that appeared early in 1652. Its poems, flashes of ridicule, and erratic but cautious presentation of news all suggest that it was written by Crouch, perhaps as a Nedham-like payment for being released from jail.[86] On the next newcomer, *The Dutch Spy*, which managed three numbers in the spring, he did comment.[87] Edited probably by Border, it concentrated on Dutch news for only one number, and even then surrounded it with four pages of Fifth Monarchy prophecies. Nor did the next two issues show much improvement. The third new weekly of 1652, *Mercurius Phreneticus*, probably aroused an ambivalent reaction in Crouch: admiration for its facetious news and advertisements, its parodies and bawdy verse; and resentment at the competition its three numbers offered *Democritus*.[88]

In each Samuel Sheppard, almost certainly the editor, showed that his training in scatological journalism had not been forgotten.

In May he revived *Mercurius Pragmaticus*. But times had changed. Sheppard had been released from jail in the summer of 1650 as a result of the intervention of Thurloe and after promising to stay neutral, for shortly thereafter he penned this epigram:

> Most strange it seemes unto the Vulgar rout,
> That that which thrust me in should guard me out,
> My Soule with no engagement's clog'd, but thus
> My gaining life strook dead Elencticus.[89]

Then in the first number of the new *Pragmaticus* he attacked, not the government but other newspapers:

> By your leave M. Mercuries, by what pitiful stiles or appellations soever distinguished, from what corner soever of the Compass, squeaking out your abortive trash and nonsensical quibbles into the bosom of the nauseated World, to sneak a livelihood: such is the restless noise of your roaring sub-sizers through the whole city that Gentlemen even in their own defense are constrained to buy up your pamphlets to prevent the hazard of being struck deafe with the lamentable cries of the paper-mongers.[90]

In the ensuing five issues Sheppard attacked other editors, especially Crouch and Border (both of whom replied in kind), and paid reluctant tribute to the public's thirst for news. He also made it clear that his readers, particularly any former Cavaliers, should expect no "Ranting in the old Aulical phrase." [91] The result was a weekly that consisted of approximately half straight news, half jest book. The editor avoided political controversy, was safely anti-Dutch and anti-Scot, and donned motley only to ridicule journalism and emulate Crouch. For two numbers, in fact, he did at least as well as his rival, making much of a facetious petition that asked, among other things, that London children resemble their fathers, not those who begot them.[92] But early in July, Sheppard became bored or alarmed, for the next issue of *Pragmaticus*, labeled number one, claimed that its predecessor was a counterfeit and inserted a few cryptic but unmistakable pro-Royalist remarks. This the government would not allow, and no second number appeared.

Concurrent with the last days of *Pragmaticus*, one of the strangest periodicals of the era thrice raised its bowed head. *Mercurius Heraclitus, Or, The Weeping Philosopher* sadly bemoaned the iniquity of the age: its crimes and sins, wars and plagues, profaneness and impiety. The editor put a black border around his title-page poems, told a

series of melancholy anecdotes, and reveled in his own lugubrious-
ness. From the end of June to the middle of July any Londoner for
a penny could, to paraphrase the paper's subtitle, have his eyes moist-
ened, heart saddened, and mind perplexed by this professional Cassandra.

Also strange was what happened to a revived *Mercurius Britannicus* (with two "n's") that appeared in 1652. For five numbers in July
and August this sixteen-page paper was in all likelihood edited by
Nedham, a supposition substantiated by the sprightly style, competent
handling of news, nonslavish support of the Commonwealth, and a
bad pun on "Need 'um." [93] Then he went back to his other propaganda
chores, and in October, Cottrell, the printer of the paper, again revived
the title. This time it lasted two months, but it was now a very different
weekly. It garbled the official news that filled most of its eight pages,
while it gave whatever space remained to supporting Presbyterianism
— this in a sheet entitled *Britannicus*! The editor vigorously defended
tithes and an orderly hierarchy, attacked Independent and sectarian
preaching, and castigated Lilly for impiously misreading the future.[94]
So ardent was his shock at the government's policy of toleration that
he often recoiled into Royalism. Sometimes, too, his indignation spilled
over into poetry:

> Must judgment rouze us from our sleep,
>   To works of Peace and Piety?
> Jonah! can nothing but the Deep
>   Convince thee of the Deity? [95]

But the favorite target of abuse of this "blue-apron'd Mercury" was
Border's *Scout*. Border quoted extensively from *Britannicus* in order
to refute its orthodoxy, while its editor struck and bit back. In December both papers were suppressed, and Cottrell spent a few days in
jail.[96] The Commonwealth could be lenient with noncontroversial
weeklies, not with unseemly squabbling.

Cottrell's short imprisonment points up one development in the
newspapers of the early 1650's: as they became more docile, the power
of the printer or publisher over them increased. Earlier the public
had closely identified a paper with its editor, and accordingly purchased the product of a Pecke or a Collings. Now that identification
was harder to make. Pecke, for instance, was more than ever shrouded
in anonymity, Dillingham apparently had not been missed, and only
Nedham consistently blew his own horn. There was even a good deal
of confusion about the name of the writer of *The Faithfull Scout*.
Crouch at one time referred to him as George and gave him a friend

named Jenny; at another time he hinted that Jenny, or another friend, was doing the leg work for *French Occurrences*.[97] Border and the editor of *Britannicus* traded punches without, presumably, knowing each other's name; and it was Cottrell who was called to account for his editor's zeal. Since 1642 the publisher had been responsible for hiring the editor and establishing a paper's policy, and he had been the one to bear the losses or reap the profits. But from late 1649 on, the power and prestige of most editors shrank; and the scorn which such men as Sheppard and Crouch felt for them was more justified than it would have been the preceding decade.

The most devastating expression of that scorn to appear in a newspaper was written by Sheppard and filled the one number of *Mercurius Mastix*.[98] Printed in August 1652 by Cottrell, a chronic non-conformist, it consisted of a series of exaggerated accusations which reveal both the weakness and strength of the early press.[99] Sheppard first commented that newspapers appeared almost every day, "as if they were playing at Leap-frog," and that they were inaccurate, distorted, and padded. Even so, he acknowledged, they held some sway in rural England:

. . . if they finde any thing that has the least probability of truth, first they give you it at large, and with a solemn preface. Well, it goes merrily down that week, and is authentically dispersed in City and Country: but by your leave, when the Carryer comes up again, he findes nothing but the self-same thing abridged or in another dress; and the Parson, when he returns, complains that he is cheated of his money.

Sheppard then mentioned that the fate of most weeklies was "to be intom'd in a Privie"; yet he also admitted that some people thought highly enough of them to keep a file of back numbers. He went on to berate the stupidity of the public, at the same time hinting at the hold the London press had on its urban readers:

. . . and the snivelling Puppies will endeavour to be serious. Then they talk of decay of Religion or of decay of Trade, the more lamented loss of the two: the good Citizen himself is caught with this snare; and when he hears a thing which so much concerns his particular, he cannot chuse but put a finger in the money-box and buy it, gravely putting it up . . . that he may read it to his simpering wife after supper.

Sheppard concluded by attacking fly-by-night weeklies. But even in his peroration he admitted that many people read several papers and that the press might have a significant impact on public opinion. Perhaps that was why he recurrently turned up as an editor.

Sheppard's derogatory remarks were particularly relevant to the last two short-lived newspapers of 1652. In August *Mercurius Cinicus* devoted one page of its one number to news, the other seven to pornography. At the end of the year, in antipodal contrast, *The Flying Eagle* gave most of its space to self-righteous piety. Though his paper appeared on Saturday, the editor objected to any profanation of the sabbath eve, and he fulminated against celebrating Christmas. His handling of news was inept, and at the end of his fifth and final number he confessed that it was too cloudy for his eagle, but that at some future date he would perhaps fly back "with more heavenly intelligence." [100]

In the spring of 1653, when Cromwell's dissolution of the Rump was imminent, two newcomers took advantage of a relaxation in the censorship and of the public's increased appetite for Westminster news. Both *Moderate Occurrences* and *The Faithful Post* were published by George Horton, one of the more energetic printer-booksellers of the 1650's and the man in whose journalistic stable Border often resided. *Moderate Occurrences* lasted from March to May, dispensing an adequate and cautious cross-section of the news interspersed with a few personal asides. Horton was not extravagant, and for these two months many of the items in Tuesday's *Moderate Occurrences* were repeated in Friday's *Faithful Post*. When the former went out of business, Horton either turned the *Post* over to another publisher, an unsavory character named Robert Eeles, or had it temporarily stolen from him by Eeles.[101] Before then, however, Horton had so numbered and paginated the paper that it seemed a continuation of Border's *Faithfull Scout*, and he had his editor claim that this was the authentic *Scout*, Border's the counterfeit.[102] But Horton's chief means to promote sales were the paper's illustrations, three of them, including a three-quarter-page woodcut of a Dutch admiral, decorating the first two numbers.[103] In addition, in his use of large type he came closer than any of his contemporaries to modern headlines. The first issue of the *Post* headed a story of an earthquake with "BEHOLD AND WONDER"; the third led into the news of Holland with "EVERY MAN FOR HIMSELF, AND GOD FOR US ALL"; and the fourth blazoned the ousting of Parliament with "CHANGE OF GOVERNMENT." [104]

One result of this change of government was a rise in the number of newspapers. Since the end of 1651 ten or twelve had been available most weeks, eight of them regularly so. With the Rump dissolved and the immediate future of England murky, the number rose to fifteen, then gradually shrank. Collectively they continued to play the part of a kept press until Cromwell dismissed them in September 1655.

CHAPTER XIII

THE NEWSPAPER UNDER
THE PROTECTORATE

May 1653 to September 1655

CROMWELL dissolved the Rump on April 20, 1653, a step that was widely praised. Starting in July, the Nominated or Barebones Parliament occupied 140 of the seats in Westminster until December, when Cromwell dismissed this zealous but inexperienced group. Thereafter he served as England's "Protector" under a new and written constitution, the Instrument of Government. In name as well as fact Cromwell was now virtual dictator, but he padded his fist by continuing to believe in freedom of conscience and in limited liberty for speech and press. He also tried to cling to historical continuity by maintaining a Parliament, and for four months at the end of 1654 Cromwell permitted the First Parliament of the Protectorate to question the constitution under which it sat. Then he dismissed it, ruling for almost two years without parliamentary help. That rule seemed stable and secure. Peace had been concluded with the Dutch, England's prestige was high, and various localized uprisings were easily suppressed. Even the most widespread, Penruddock's Rising in the spring of 1655, was put down without much trouble, though it served as an excuse for tightening security measures and establishing the rule of the Major Generals.

Until the autumn of 1655 the newspapers operated under the act of January 1653. Mabbott was censorial agent for the army, the Council of State was responsible for the law's enforcement, and the Stationers continued to play a lesser role, as the extreme irregularity of entries in their Register testifies. In the fall of 1654 Parliament ordered that no news of its activities be printed without a license from its Clerk, and *Politicus* was the only weekly so blessed.[1] Though other newspapers did not strictly adhere to this order, they remained docile, and no offender was punished. Parliament and the Council of State might be ineffective as censors, but Cromwell had the army with him — and his hand was heavy enough for editors and publishers not to want to get slapped.[2]

Any Londoner who during these two-and-a-half years read every newspaper would have received a limited view of current history. Yet that view showed some variations, depending on which weekly supplied the lens. *The Perfect Diurnall* was the clearest, and by 1653 it was sufficiently established to discourage any regular Monday competition. It continued to use about half its sixteen pages for foreign news, including brief items about Charles's travels, the rest, except for an average of half-a-page of advertisements, for official events in the British Isles and a scattering of crime news. It hewed to the Protectorate line, heaped praise on Cromwell, and tried to guarantee its durability by being circumspect. In the spring of 1653, for instance, when Lilburne melodramatically returned from exile and won acquittal in an exciting trial, Pecke's coverage was sparse and cool; late in 1654 he stayed in step by temporarily obeying Parliament's order and printing no Westminster news; and in 1655, amid a flurry of anti-government uprisings, he managed skillfully to belittle the opponents of the Protectorate by the unhysterical and ostensibly neutral tone of his reports. Moreover, the paper's correspondents were capable, though one in Scotland hated the place;[3] and Pecke's style, if impersonal and unvaried, was clear.

During its final year and a half *The Perfect Diurnall* made a bid to attract more lawyer and merchant readers. From May to November 1654 it included an intermittent series of legalistic and generally noncontroversial proposals for reform of the law. Almost certainly not by Pecke, this feature was directed to professional lawyers and to the many amateurs who felt qualified to discuss the laws of England. Then, from the end of 1654 on, the paper printed a paragraph of shipping news of immediate interest to London merchants, a service that was more regular and often more detailed than its equivalent in other weeklies. But even if Pecke or his publisher had visions of establishing a seventeenth-century *Wall Street Journal*, the government was not co-operative. On September 24, 1655, the 302nd and last issue of *The Perfect Diurnall* appeared. It represented approximately the 800th paper that Pecke had edited since late 1641 (about 10 per cent of the output of the weekly press between that date and the Restoration), and it contained no hint that his days as a journalist were over.[4] The paper's final item was an advertisement for two lost horses.

Most Londoners who wanted to read current history on Tuesday probably bought *The Weekly Intelligencer of the Commonwealth*. Collings now usually provided an equal mixture of foreign and safely antiseptic domestic news. When the Nominated Parliament was dismissed he had only this to say:

> This day there was a Debate concerning the Ministers and their maintenance, for which the Lord General and a great part of the House have much declared themselves, but the House this Day not agreeing, and the honour of the Church being of great concernment, it was thought fit the Parliament should be dissolved, which accordingly was done.[5]

A year later, when the first Protectorate Parliament was also dissolved, Collings delayed his account for a week, "in the discretion of a safe silence," then printed the official handout justifying Cromwell's action.[6] The editor never criticized the government directly; nor, except for a few signs of neutrality toward its opponents, did he allow himself the luxury of indirect criticism. Near the end of his career he even managed to make an asset of his caution by claiming that, since the authorities were chary about what could be printed, an eight-page paper was likely to be less padded and more honest than one of sixteen pages.[7]

As before, Collings retained certain characteristics that marked him as one of the better editors. (On the other hand, he now printed a few more unverified rumors than had been his wont: for instance, that the Queen of Sweden was coming to England to plead the cause of Charles; that eighty whales had fought in the Dundee River; that Charles was dead.)[8] In the first place he betrayed signs of compassion where most other journalists were callous, as in his sympathetic account of a group of persecuted Quakers, or his remark on the plight of the Irish that, "although they are the most barbarous in the world, I cannot make mention of it [famine and pestilence] without some humanity of compassion."[9] (Collings could, however, speak of the death of his printer in tearless terms: perhaps the paper would now have fewer typographical errors.) [10] Second, he intermittently showed a nose for news that would qualify him to be a feature-writer on a tabloid. An eye-witness account of the execution of a criminal was probably the best to appear in any Interregnum paper, and, along with several other editors, he wrote up what may well be the goriest single-crime story on record: the account of a jealous wife in Kent who cut out her rival's vulva and served it to her unfaithful husband.[11] Collings' nose for the peculiar and pathetic had likewise become sharper, and he seemed to find relish in telling of the London ladies of pleasure who were off to Virginia where they would no doubt be reformed; of the brewer and his girl who got so involved in a kiss that they fell into the brew vat and drowned; of a synagogue in Hackney; and of a lost child who was found — dead.[12] He also ran two graphic items that showed Charles's ability to keep a poker face under the most trying of circumstances.[13] His was the first newspaper to contain an advertisement for a cookbook; and an equally modern touch, suggestive of World War II, was his comment on Penn's activities in the West Indies that "these times have made us all Cosmographers." [14] Third, Collings' style, if now more subdued, still showed a superior range and flexibility, as well as an occasional sparkle of humor. With a straight face he referred to an indictment of a lawyer that filled a sheet nine yards long, and in his next-to-last number he commented on himself and his colleagues: "It is with your Writers of Intelligence as with a pack of Beagles hunting in the field, if one puppy doth make but a faint discovery, the whole Pack will be ready to clap in, and in a ful cry run themselves out of breath. . . ." [15]

A week later, on September 25, 1655, Collings was out of the hunt. The final number of *The Weekly Intelligencer* opened with the statement that "I love Oxford well, and I have reason for it"; it closed with the story of a London fanatic who wanted to assemble the dispersed Jews and lead them to Palestine. The Jews did not go to Palestine and Collings did not retire to Oxford; instead, in all probability, he went back to selling books and pamphlets from a stall somewhere in London.

From July to December 1653 he had been faced with the minor competition of a Tuesday weekly, *Several Proceedings of Parliament*. Printed by Parliament's official printer, it digested the Journals of the House without embellishment or comment. Since this did not fill its customary sixteen pages, the anonymous editor used foreign news and a few advertisements to occupy the rest of his space, though in one number he left a page blank. When Cromwell dissolved the Nominated Parliament, *Several Proceedings* lost its *raison d'être* and quietly vanished.

More serious for Collings was the rivalry of a paper that in April 1654 adopted the title *The Weekly Post* but that earlier had been edging into the Tuesday niche. In the spring of 1653 Horton lost or yielded *The Faithful Post* to Eeles. In either case, from June to August, Horton resumed publishing a *Faithful Post* but shifted its day to Tuesday. Eeles, meanwhile, put out his *Post* on Friday, from the end of May to September, in the process taking over Horton's numbering system so that his version would seem the authentic continuation. Of the two, Horton's paper was a little more sprightly and personal, while Eeles's production was better printed and organized; and the latter did preserve the story of a man aged eighty-nine committing adultery with a woman of fifty-six.[16]

In November and December, after Eeles presumably left journalism, Horton came back with three numbers of a weekly called *Great Brittain's Post*, a commonplace sheet except for its typographical variety and a story about a tax collector in Wales who hung a padlock on the "private parts" of a lady with whom he had had an affair.[17] Then in January 1654 Horton issued one number of *The Politique Post*. It was distinguished by the fact that one-quarter of its space was filled with three pictures and two maps, so that it more closely resembled a modern layout than did any other Interregnum weekly. He followed this with a Tuesday paper, *The Grand Politique Post*, that lasted until April.[18] Border may have been the editor, though signs of any editorial guidance were sparse. The *Post* was obedient, unselective, and heavily overloaded with prophecies and witches. Twice Horton's publishing touch was evident in the use of pictures, while Border's part-time hand seems visible in a few purple passages and pink-tinged asides. (One aside, whether or not by Border, anticipated Carlyle by praising the governor of Barbados for being vigorously anti-Negro.)[19] The paper also ran one of the more spiteful personal advertisements ever to appear: ". . . there is a young man in love with a Widow that hath two bastards by her last husbands son before he married her, and two more in the time that she was his wife."[20]

In April 1654 *The Weekly Post* replaced *The Grand Politique Post*, and, except for twenty-two weeks in which it failed to appear, competed with Collings until the autumn of 1655.[21] For most of this period Horton was the publisher, though Wood for several months joined or supplanted him. The London public probably preferred Collings' weekly, but the *Post* had certain attributes that now make it interesting. More frequently than his contemporaries, the editor, almost certainly Border, called attention to what he was not printing. Moreover, though he remained volubly pro-government, he increasingly allowed a few disguised but unmistakable anti-Cromwell allusions to creep in. In some instances even Border's circumspection had an anti-Protectorate flavor: for example, to the story of one of Cromwell's general's being attacked by a dog the editor appended the comment that it was "dangerous meddling with state affairs"; of his own cryptic reports of what was going on at Westminster he remarked that it was "good sleeping in a whole skin"; and he pointed out that certain things could be said in France but not in England.[22] In addition, the paper sometimes nipped at the flanks of the government by pleading for the release of various prisoners, among them Lilburne, who had been jailed for political reasons.[23] On the other hand, *The Weekly Post*, especially during its final year, was vitriolic in attacking extreme sects and vilifying Quakers.

This crowded, confused, and inconsistent weekly also experimented with a few innovations. Among its many advertisements was the first to illustrate an incipient trademark — a picture of a package of throat lozenges — and the first to promote the services of a pious ghost-writer:

If any young Preachers want any new Sermons, let them repaire to Ralph Walker . . . and there they may have Manuscripts of his own making, and receive Directions how to confute all Errors and Heresies for 40 years past, and 40 yeares to come; provided alwayes, that they are such men as are well approved.[24]

Twice the paper contained news pictures, and Horton again used large type to create semi-headlines.[25] Toward the end of its career the *Post* emulated *The Perfect Diurnall* by printing shipping news, while Border went back to his earlier habit of mixing large doses of piety in his stories of witches, prophets, prodigies, and apparitions.[26] The final two numbers even included two "characters," one of a pickpocket, the other of a government stool pigeon.[27]

In certain respects, then, *The Weekly Post* was different from other papers; B.D.'s *Perfect Account* was, in contrast, extremely typical. This Wednesday sheet divided its eight pages between foreign and official home news and almost never departed from standard items. When it was declared illegal to print news of Parliament, *A Perfect Account* neglected Westminster; when such news became customary, B.D. presented it circumspectly and briefly.[28] Even the paper's fillers were derivative, and the editor borrowed freely from most of his colleagues, picking up, for instance, some of Collings' gory crime stories, Border's credulous tales, and Pecke's shipping news, not to mention a few reports from Pecke's Scotland-hating correspondent. All papers of the 1640's and 1650's utilized the same major sources, all extensively borrowed from one another. B.D. was merely less original than most, and even his rare asides now had the quality of an echo. Yet his paper, on the evidence of its longevity, regularity (during its final thirty months it skipped only ten weeks), and normal quota of advertisements, seems to have been moderately successful.

One reason why it and most other weeklies were not more successful was the persistent competition from relations and news ballads. These ephemeral publications could be bought on the streets of London almost as soon as a newspaper whenever there was a crime or off-color story juicy enough to interest an author and printer. Several of the advertisements in *A Perfect Account*, in fact, promoted "books" that dealt with incidents which had been covered in recent issues, and at least once the paper plugged a book telling a story that week being concluded in its own pages.[29] *A Perfect Account* is also instructive concerning the vagaries of the censorship under the Protectorate. Early in 1654 one of its female hawkers was arrested, not for peddling anything subversive but because the paper had not been licensed that week, an oversight B.D. and his fellows frequently indulged in.[30]

One of the few journalists from whom B.D. borrowed little was Crouch. *Mercurius Democritus* had been available for pilfering until November 1653, when Crouch was jailed.[31] He was promptly released, and in January and February 1654 *Democritus* reappeared for four zestful issues. From then until June, Crouch was silent or silenced, but again came back, this time with a paper entitled *Mercurius Fumigosus, Or The Smoking Nocturnall*. It survived, with only a few gaps, until October 3, 1655, thus outlasting all other weeklies except Dugard's and Nedham's. *Fumigosus* showed few changes from *Democritus*. The most evident was that it usually printed approximately half a page of straight news, having been ordered to do so. On occasion, however, the editor violated even this mild requirement, casually announcing that there was no news.[32] *Fumigosus* also exhibited a slight increase in the employment of four-letter words, Swiftean scatology, and diatribes against Quakers. But on the whole it was as nonpolitical, irreverent, smutty, and facile as its predecessor. As a parodist Crouch still went after other editors as liars and fools, with Border again bearing the brunt of the attack. In Crouch's pages the Dundee River whales spawned hundreds of monstrous progeny, many lurid crimes stories were burlesqued and over-burlesqued, and some of the witches featured in other weeklies were clad in motley or salaciously disrobed. As a poet Crouch was usually vulgar, sometimes tender, and a Maypole could be, in his hands, a phallic or a festive symbol.

He could also be an effective raconteur, as in his story of a near-sighted Peeping Tom or his anecdote about a preacher who said that

Jonah was swallowed by a quail and, when corrected, claimed his version represented a greater miracle.[33] Often Crouch flavored his tall tales and dirty stories with parodies of journalism, as in his Beggar's-Opera account of the low-class reception of a "Welsh Ambassador," or his semitechnical analysis of a bride's "articles of surrender." [34] Sometimes these parodies had a broader and only partially concealed contemporary reference. Toward the end of its career, for instance, *Fumigosus* ran several stories on a female assembly that blended Rabelaisian vigor, sexy innuendo, and mockery of Cromwell's emasculated Parliaments. Crouch's readers must have chuckled at identifying his innumerable cuckolds, whores, pimps, cheaters, crooks, hypocrites, usurers, and misers with men and women prominent or notorious in London life.

Crouch's facetiousness also continued to sparkle in his fake advertisements, and to his notices about lost maidenheads he added requests for information about mislaid prostitutes and wandering drunks. But a few times he inserted complaints about his own poverty,[35] and to mitigate it he ran some serious advertisements. He also followed the lead of Horton and included a few pictures, one of them of "Don Fumigosus" sardonically smoking a pipe.[36] In all these ways he managed to suggest what was going on behind the city's closed doors and at its bustling street corners, especially after dark. If he usually modeled himself on Rabelais, he also knew the works of Ben Jonson and, in all likelihood, those of Shakespeare.[37] Though Crouch was lazy, glib, and harassed, he was not a dull observer of the passing scene, and his pages provide today's reader with a whiff of the life of three centuries ago. If the odor was not that of incense or roses, it was pungent, and it was a smell that was to hang over the Restoration court and to pervade our own era.

No such pungency emanated from Thursday's *Nouvelles Ordinaires*. It kept on printing adequate digests of official news, never straying into the personal or the controversial. Involved or loaded incidents like the dissolutions of various Parliaments, Lilburne's vicissitudes, and the rise and fall of Royalist plots were all handled with brevity and caution. Understandably, Cromwell dominated the news, and the initials "S.A.," standing for "Son Altesse," appeared in about half of the thousands of short paragraphs that made up Dugard's four-page weekly. The editor now less frequently stumbled over problems of translation, and starting at the end of 1654 he included more shipping and diplomatic news of specific interest to continental merchants. Under the Protectorate, when the news seemed more orderly and hence more easily packaged, he was able to cut down his use of continued stories, but three times he found it profitable or expedient to put out extras.[38] Now with even greater rarity did items of human interest appear: a paragraph about a French-

Walloon church in London, a brief story from Bristol about the wreck of a Virginia-bound ship, an account of a fanatic who plotted to kill all M.P.'s.[39] In short, Dugard consistently tried to put out a weekly inoffensive to the authorities and appropriate to a largely Parisian audience. That he succeeded is indicated by the paper's longevity, by Nicholas Bourne's continued role as its distributor, and by the fact that the government excluded it from the crackdown on the press. Consequently from October 1655 to early 1658 only Dugard was able to share with Nedham the honor of being England's practicing journalists.

The lion's share of that honor belonged to Nedham. As a result of his ability and preferred position he was the most prominent and popular, but by no means the best liked, newspaperman of the day, and *Politicus* dominated the Thursday scene. Dugard offered little competition, and Walker's *Severall Proceedings* remained a relatively dull compendium, though it now showed greater competence in varying its quantity of foreign news, sometimes giving it two pages, sometimes as many as eleven.[40] Under all circumstances Walker remained loyal to the Protectorate, and he generally followed the rule that the more politically pregnant an item, the shorter the report on it. Sometimes this meant no report at all. Of Parliament's heated debate concerning the Instrument of Government, he wrote, "Some have presented a Petition judged dangerous" — end of story.[41] A conservative Independent and self-conscious Puritan, Walker ignored Christmas and often berated the Quakers as disruptive and ungodly.[42] But usually his views were implied rather than stated. Once or twice he mentioned his antisectarian inclinations; a few times he allowed himself to speculate, in very general terms, on foreign policy; and once he attempted an expanded self-justification. It speaks for itself:

> I am told that there are some who pretend to godlinesse that are offended with my so freely owning and declaring for this present Government. . . . My answer is, that though they stand not with it, yet the Lord stands with it, and therefore I can comfortably blesse God for it; not that I flatter greatnesse, for it is well known that most of the Prisons in London are witnesses of my sufferings . . . and hardly escaping with my life, though I never sought for Place, Preferment, or any reparations for my suffering. . . .[43]

Walker had long had the reputation of being a Judas, toady, and self-seeker, as well as a few less printable names. That it may have been justified was hinted at in *Severall Proceedings* during its last months. Here he showed an almost morbid interest in local crimes, especially those involving unnatural deaths and fires. The final issue, which came out on September 27, 1655, included a series of "sad accidents," among them a smashed workman and three slaughtered children: one run over, one drowned, and one killed by a bear. Before then, for about a year, Walker had been viewing with alarm, mingled with a dash of sly relish, the spread of crime and perversion. He had also probably been viewing with alarm the decline in the number of advertisements in *Severall Proceedings*, though early in 1655 it carried one of the longest paid announcements of the day: two and a half pages on the symptoms and cure of smallpox.[44]

Almost certainly the decline in Walker's revenue can be attributed to the success of *Politicus*. But *Politicus* also cut into Dugard's profits, for Nedham mentioned the fact that it had its own overseas readers, and at least once an English ambassador abroad complained about the paper's inaccuracies.[45] Even assuming the ambassador was right, Nedham's coverage of foreign affairs remained first-rate. He retained good correspondents in France and Holland, and *Politicus*, like most weeklies, got full reports on Whitelocke's embassy to Sweden from a member of the entourage. Nedham's handling of the massacre of the Piedmontese Protestants was excellent, and he found room for strange and remote items from such places as China and central Turkey.[46] He also took full advantage of the increased efficiency of foreign posts, in one story boasting that it took only nine days for news, in winter, to come from Rome to Paris.[47] Frequently he ran short accounts of Charles and his coterie, usually making the wandering court seem feeble and inept, sometimes ridiculous.

When, for a short period, *Politicus* was the only paper regularly to carry news of Parliament, Nedham's reports were clear, bare, brief, and confined to *faits accompli*. Dangerous items received only a few judicious lines. For instance, Nedham wrote that Cromwell was cured, not having mentioned that the Protector had been sick; and when Venables and Penn returned from the West Indies without proper orders, their story, including their commitment to the Tower, rated two lines.[48] A few times, but less often than most of his colleagues, Nedham showed that his soul was where it should be by attacking the Quakers. Moreover, he struck a proper note of enthusiasm in his articles and asides in praise of Cromwell and the Protectorate without sounding like a sycophant or dupe.

Nedham's professionalism was also displayed in his ability to play up a crime so that it had much of the suspense and gore of today's detective novels.[49] Or he could anticipate a Saki short story, as in the anecdote of a Highland laird whose cook was captured and who was willing to go to great lengths to get him back.[50] One of the most interesting pieces in

Politicus is an account of a strike in Newcastle, further proof that an embryonic labor movement existed in seventeenth-century England. In London, Lilburne had agitated for higher wages and better working conditions, in the west there had been scattered miners' strikes, and in a few seaports dockside arrangements were conducive, then as now, to strikes and strike-breaking. Apparently this was especially true of Newcastle:

> We have had a great stop of Trade by our Keel-mens pretence of too small wages from their masters; they all as one man stood together, and would neither worke themselves, nor suffer others, though our Mayor used all possible means to satisfie them; whereupon he made a Proclamation, but all was to no purpose. And now though a Company of foot and a Troop of Horse be drawn into Town, yet they continue in their obstinacie, notwithstanding that some of their Leading men have been apprehended. The Justices intend to meet and try if they can compose the busines.[51]

Other bits and pieces of *Politicus* sound equally modern: an advertisement for a medicine called "The Countess of Kent's Powder"; several pseudo-scientific articles on a mechanical ship being built in Rotterdam, which later turned out to be a hoax engineered by a French inventor; an occasional commercial item that reads like the prospectus for a speculative stock.[52]

Because of his access to the government and his many contacts, Nedham was in a better position to utilize improvements in the English postal system than were other editors. They, however, did not have much of a chance, for a month after Thurloe applied his expert hand to the mails, Nedham's competitors were all out of business.[53] Nedham made no comment on their mass demise but shortly thereafter raised his charge for a single advertisement from sixpence or a shilling to half a crown.[54] Not one to gloat over his monopoly, he was energetic to see that it paid him proper dividends. For four more years it did.

Walker, too, continued energetic, but at a lower rate of return and not so much in journalism as in writing books, doing semisecret publicity chores for the Protectorate, and preaching. Even so, he went on supplementing Thursday's *Severall Proceedings* with Friday's *Moderate Publisher of Every daies Intelligence*, an eight-page paper that early in 1654 changed its name to *Certain Passages of Every dayes Intelligence*. Earlier Walker had tried to make this the livelier of the two; now, during its last two years, he let it relax into mediocrity. Like *Severall Proceedings* it was choppy and official, lacking in personal touches and transitions, and extremely cautious; and during its final year it too displayed a sometimes morbid interest in crime and violent death. Yet from its crowded pages one gradually acquires the impression that Walker really believed everything he said in favor of the government and fully approved of not saying what was unauthorized or dangerous.[55]

Walker's Friday paper differed from his Thursday effort in two respects. First, it was more pious and credulous.[56] In addition to a heavy dose of devout stories, in 1655 it resumed the habit of printing Lilly's monthly predictions, along with a sprinkling of astrological "news." Second, it purveyed a few more London stories than were common in most weeklies, including *Severall Proceedings*: for instance, a race between a butcher and a footman, of course satirized by Crouch; or the petition of a man who wanted to be hangman because the current executioner was clumsy.[57] Yet this Friday paper was, at best, run-of-the-mill, its two to four pages of foreign news average, and its anti-Quaker, anti-Royalist, anti-Leveller remarks typical in quantity and quality. Probably this was why the number of advertisements Walker printed on Friday also declined. Yet he seems to have been indifferent. *Certain Passages* was conspicuous, even then, for poor typography and confused numbering and pagination.[58] Walker opened one number by announcing that, since there was so much news, it did not matter where he began; eighteen months later, equally casually, he reprinted a letter commenting on the fact that all weeklies were "so barren of news." [59] When at the end of September 1655 he was shoved out of journalism, he almost certainly left with a shrug of the shoulders.[60]

Border, in contrast, probably was frustrated and disgruntled when his career was interrupted. His *Faithfull Scout* had come to a temporary end in March 1653. Then, after five weeks, its place was taken by *The Armies Scout*, published by Wood and, in all likelihood, edited by Border. Crowded, superficial, pious, it survived six weeks. Its final number announced that Wood was joining forces with his sometime rival, sometime collaborator, Horton, "it being thought most expedient for all contestations to be brought to a period." [61] Horton's *Faithful Post* and Wood's *Scout* were therefore merged, and on June 10, 1653, *The Faithfull Scout*, edited by Border, was back in business. From then until September 28, 1655, it provided Walker with competition on Friday, in the process skipping only one number.

As a competitor Border was no Nedham. His handling of news, both foreign and domestic, tended to be haphazard and impersonal, often extremely credulous.[62] He could be as indifferent as Walker, as evidenced by his extensive borrowing from his own news and fillers in Tuesday's *Weekly Post*.[63] But it was in Border's divergences from Walker and other editors that the few merits of *The Faithfull Scout* reside. Nor were these merits wholly unrecognized in the mid-1650's:

as the number of advertisements in Walker's Friday paper fell, those in Border's rose, and during its final nine months the *Scout* averaged a page of paid notices.[64] Moreover, during the first half of 1654 Horton and Wood resumed quarreling over who was to print this presumably profitable paper, with Wood finally winning.[65] Regardless, Border seems to have been just a hired hand, and at least once he inserted a reference to his poverty.[66] Yet to the end he continued to speak his mind, and though he usually whispered, the noises he made were more audible than those coming from other editors.

Even so, Border was fully aware of the rules under which he had to operate: "More I could say," he wrote, "but the Scout loves not a prison"; or "Truth is not to be spoke at all times say some; therefore I must be silent." [67] During 1655 he also sowed the paper with anti-Quaker references. But more frequently than in *The Weekly Post* he went out of his way to be friendly to Lilburne and his lost cause. Sometimes Border's support was mild and indirect, as in his regrets that Lilburne was still in jail or that the prisoner needed warmer clothes; sometimes outspoken, as in his comment on the arrest of a group of pro-Leveller apprentices that Bridewell was a fit place for "Vagabonds," not for upholders of English liberty.[68] Border also worried about other prisoners, whether behind bars for debt or politics, and he often expressed sympathy for all who were suffering the ravages of poverty. Intermittently, too, he showed his approval of the Fifth Monarchists.[69] What is more significant, he was willing to criticize the government and to display a certain ambivalence toward Cromwell. Late in 1653, when the Nominated Parliament was dissolved, *The Faithfull Scout* ran a two-page analysis of why.[70] So startling was Border's temerity that two weeks later a counterfeit *Scout* was printed to justify Cromwell's action and to answer the questions Border had raised.[71] Nor in at least half the issues of his Friday paper could he resist including an editorial paragraph or two. Invariably platitudinous, whenever they pertained to current events they seemed to support the government; but over and over they mentioned the dangers of tyranny, sometimes striking close to home. On occasion, too, an unmistakable note of irony crept in, for Border had finally become adept at verbal hide-and-seek.

In addition, in a scattering of asides he took a stand against the Council of State by advocating the abolition of tithes. Several times he commented unfavorably on high taxes, and despite his attacks on the Quakers, he supported the concept of broad religious toleration.[72] Then during the *Scout*'s last year Border began to snipe at Cromwell. Remarking on the Protector's recovery, he wrote "Well! — I wish the late deliverance may be attributed to Gods mercies"; and when Cromwell was again sick, Border prefaced the news with a paragraph on the fall of princes.[73] Intermittently he implied that Cromwell had not kept his word, and in the final number he drew a distinction between king and tyrant, followed by a story concerning Charles's generosity and by two pro-monarchical prophecies.[74] On the other hand, Border often seems to have genuinely approved of the Protector and Protectorate. When *The Faithfull Scout* was shut down, its editor was probably still groping; hence, in all likelihood, his frustration and disgruntlement.

Yet Border must have become accustomed to having his journalistic horses shot from under him. From May to August 1653 it was probably he, not Dillingham, who edited *The Moderate Intelligencer*, a Monday paper printed by Wood.[75] For a dozen numbers it split its space between foreign news and obedient reports of national affairs, though it gave a good deal of sympathetic linage to Lilburne's trial. It then quietly expired, returning in February 1654 with a different subtitle and on Wednesday, but almost certainly with Border again at the editorial helm.[76] It was now printed by Horton, who had probably collaborated with Wood in the earlier series, and it lasted until May.

In the first two numbers of this revived *Moderate Intelligencer* the editor heaped praise on the Protectorate, but Border showed his hand by emphasizing the government's potential role as a guarantor of freedom and justice.[77] Also, he twice exhorted the authorities to release political prisoners, and twice he included remarks conspicuously friendly to Lilburne.[78] The second is interesting as one of the clearest acknowledgments that certain political leaders were willing to use trial balloons to gauge public opinion:

> Strange and various are the Reports from the Isle of Jersey touching Mr. John Lilburne, so that I shall endeavor to reduce my Pen from inserting any thing that may prove obnoxious or disconsonant from the Rules of Verity; onely thus much, that . . . 'tis made out that he is mortus est. But whether it be under the notion of feeling the pulses of the people or alienating . . . their affections from the present Government, I cannot administer Antidote. . . .

In addition, Border showed his hand by a comment on his own poverty, a kindly story about a man who wanted to liberalize the law, and two references to his reluctance at having to be cautious.[79] He also served briefly as a shuttlecock between Horton and Wood: Wood once printed a counterfeit *Moderate Intelligencer*, and sporadically he may have taken over from his rival and/or partner.[80] Border, who had started as a scrivener, found time during his busy journalistic career to pick up some knowledge of medicine, and by late 1655 he had certainly received plenty of bruises to nurse.[81]

In May 1654, at the same time that *The Moderate Intelligencer* became silent, a relatively long-lived newcomer entered the scene. *A Perfect Diurnall: Or, Occurrences of Certain Military Affairs* chose to compete with Pecke both in name and in Monday publication day, and it survived for six months.[82] Whatever success it had may have been due to the fact that it sold for a penny, Pecke's sixteen-page paper for two.[83] Besides calling his customers' attention to this saving, the editor pointed out that they were getting "the sum of the whole Weeks Intelligence" in his eight-page version.[84] He was speaking the truth. His *Diurnall's* foreign and domestic news generally duplicated, if in condensed form, that in Pecke's paper, and both shared the anti-Scot correspondent in Scotland.[85] This impersonal weekly also garnered two or three advertisements each issue. Yet Pecke's *Perfect Diurnall* outlasted it by a year. Possibly the London public was willing to pay twice as much for the illusion of getting twice as much news; possibly, too, Pecke had built up a clientele loyal enough to say "hang the expense."

Whether because of the expense or the threat of hanging, the period from May 1653 to September 1655 was comparatively barren in terms of new newspapers. Only in the spring and summer of 1653 after the dissolution of the Rump, and again in the early months of 1654 after the demise of the Nominated Parliament, did various publishers take advantage of any incipient confusion and relaxation of the censorship. In May and June 1653 *Mercurius Britannicus* managed three numbers, two published by Horton, one by Eeles, and all marked by extreme caution and garrulous piety. *Mercurius Pragmaticus* appeared six times in the early summer. Despite the fact that it employed the format and scattered verse of earlier Royalist weeklies, it seemed loyal to the government, if a little harsh in its attacks on Levellers and tolerationists. But beneath the surface the editor displayed enough irony to hint at his pro-Charles views. Thus, for instance, by means of a story allegedly from China, he pointed out the weaknesses of republicanism.[86] He also acknowledged that he had been accused of being a Cavalier, but promptly denied the charge.[87] Perhaps the government was not convinced: in July *Pragmaticus* came to an end. Concurrently another editor thrice pounded away at corruptions and abuses in the administration of justice. A diatribe rather than a newspaper, *Mercurius Radamanthus* also expired in July.

Meanwhile in June *The Daily Proceedings* had belied its title by appearing for only one undistinguished number. In July *The Impartial Intelligencer* came out for three equally undistinguished issues. Its editor claimed he was new to journalism,[88] but if so, it made little difference: the content and form of what could be printed had become sufficiently well defined to eliminate most distinctions between experienced and inexperienced journalists. In August *The Newes*, modern only in its title, came out once, its subtitle and its emphasis on an English naval victory suggesting that it may have been an old-fashioned relation. In the same month Horton published *The Loyal Messenger*, a typical effort that, despite its plea for "Elbow room . . . in these tottering times," lasted just one week, though its title was briefly revived in April 1654.[89]

More durable but equally run-of-the-mill was *The True and Perfect Dutch Diurnall*. Either it came out very irregularly or Thomason was careless about collecting it. Of its dozen extant issues, two date from July 1653, three from January 1654, and the remaining seven from the spring of 1654. If Thomason was negligent in this instance, he can be excused. The paper was impersonal and unselective. Except for a few gory crime stories, it stuck close to authorized news, praised the Protectorate, and in spite of its title gave the Anglo-Dutch war merely the most typical coverage.

In January 1654, after four months in which no new weekly appeared, the energetic Horton published *The Loyal Intelligencer*, its one issue ("Number 13") being average enough to fill a niche in any of his journalistic ventures. A second publisher who was also busy with a variety of subliterary enterprises, Thomas Lock, printed two numbers of a mediocre paper, one labeled *The True Informer*, the other *The true and Perfect Informer*. In February, Horton brought out a weekly with an equally unoriginal title, *Perfect Occurrences*. Edited probably by Border, its second and final number concluded with the notice that it was "thought meet that these Occurrences be forthwith printed and published and dispersed in all Cities, Towns, and Corporations, throughout England, Scotland, Ireland, and Wales." [90] Presumably no such windfall occurred, but two months later another publisher revived the title and hired another editor. This *Perfect Occurrences* came out five times, and it achieved uniqueness only in giving a disproportionate amount of space to news concerning Scotland.

In March three newcomers briefly poked up their heads. For one or two numbers *Mercurius Poeticus*, written entirely in prose, gave a heavily pro-government version of the news.[91] For two weeks *Mercurius Nullus* mixed a little moral indignation with a great deal of smut. And for three numbers *Mercurius Aulicus* reappeared, now a far cry from its original namesake. The two lines with which it opened revealed that a weekly, if it followed the proper course, did not have to worry too much about the niceties of censorship:

> That Paper that great Cromwell's name doth bear,
> Ye all will grant needs not a Licenser.[92]

The editor went on to flatter the Protector both by his version of the news and by an effusive poem. He then began his second issue with:

> A Licenser! thou piece of ignorance!
> In my Lord's name fearless, my Book, advance.

This was followed by a sad bit of autobiography to the effect that the editor's father had lost £13,000 by supporting the king, and that the editor, a destitute orphan, had been helped by Cromwell. *Aulicus* was his partial repayment, but whether Cromwell accepted it as legal tender is not known. In any case, no fourth number appeared, probably much to the relief of Birkenhead.

In May and June 1654 *Perfect and Impartial Intelligence* divided the space in its three numbers between conventionally handled news and an unconventional commentary on the life of Julius Caesar that had distinctly anti-Cromwellian implications.[93] In the summer only one newcomer bobbed up: for two weeks *Mercurius Jocosus*, written and printed by Thomas Lock, mixed one part news with three parts humor. Less smutty than Crouch's, Lock's verses and anecdotes showed signs of a wit that might have qualified him to write Restoration comedies. The author of the last short-lived weekly of this period also displayed some wit, but of a more contentious variety. On October 31 and November 7, 1654, the sixteen-page *Observator* concentrated on attacking those who attacked the Protectorate. In the process it derogated anti-government pamphleteers as a gang of Sir Politick Would-Be's who ought to be condemned to the galleys, not just to the privies.[94] If, as was probably the case, *The Observator* was written by Nedham, his desires were partially gratified. No other new weekly appeared, and in September 1655 seven established papers were closed down, though *Mercurius Fumigosus* managed to hang on for an extra week. Faced only with the meager competition of Dugard, Nedham for three-and-a-half years would have the journalistic field almost to himself.

CHAPTER XIV

THE END

October 1655 to June 1660

AT THE end of August 1655 Cromwell ordered that the laws against the press be put into effect, and three newly appointed commissioners, among them the Lieutenant of the Tower, went to work. Within a month these men, armed with specific instructions and backed by the army, had done their job.[1] After October 3, Thomason, who did not bother to collect *Nouvelles Ordinaires*, had only to buy Nedham's subsidized paper to maintain his remarkable collection. In retrospect, however, the years from 1655 to 1660 have a certain inevitable quality, similar to the late 1930's, as if events were moving toward a predetermined outcome. From the vantage point of three centuries, though not from that of the people who were then trying to shape their own destinies, these years might be considered newsless, in the sense that the future loomed larger and more pregnant than the present. Regardless of when the Restoration was conceived, its gestation was clearly visible during the later 1650's.

From mid-1655 to the end of 1656 Cromwell's eleven Major Generals supervised English politics and morals with an efficiency and rigor that had never been approached. The unpopularity of their rule was reflected in the persons chosen in the summer of 1656 to sit in the Second Parliament of the Protectorate. Despite the fact that one-third of its members were excluded by the army, those allowed to serve, especially the republicans, gave voice to the widespread dislike of military rule. Not even the declared war against Spain that occupied a small portion of the country's energies and resources from 1656 to 1659 was able to arouse enough nationalism to overcome the recurrent problems of deficit financing and the army's interference in England's political life.

In the spring of 1656 Cromwell almost bowed to the demand for a return to tradition by accepting the crown. But then, alarmed at the anger of the republicans and moved by the distaste for this step felt by most of his old comrades in arms, he refused, though he continued to hold the reigns of government more tightly than James or Charles ever had. Early in 1658 he dissolved his last Parliament. From then until his death in September, unimpeded by any debates in Westminster and only mildly disturbed by repeated threats and minor uprisings, he governed England through an obedient Council of State. Probably the clearest proof of his ability was what happened to his son and successor, Richard Cromwell. Those men whom Oliver had kept in check and who had served him zealously and well, on his death became confused, self-seeking, and — as soon became obvious — self-destroying. In the spring of 1659 Richard was pushed out, and the Rump came back to Westminster. Half a year later Monck and his army, now the only disciplined force left in the British Isles, marched from Scotland to England, and in April 1660 the Convention Parliament completed arrangements for the king's return. On May 25 Charles II landed at Dover and was greeted by a large and enthusiastic crowd. The Good Old Cause was dead, the Restoration had begun. As a postscript, early in 1661, exactly twelve years after the execution of Charles I, Cromwell's corpse was exhumed, and his head chopped off and exhibited before a jeering mob.[2] Very possibly both the jubilant throng at Dover and the irreverent throng at Tyburn had been visible to the farsighted in 1655, including Oliver Cromwell.

In any case, he tried to postpone these events by, among a great many other actions, limiting to Nedham the task of dispensing news. To make things doubly safe Nedham was almost certainly supervised by Thurloe, Cromwell's Postmaster General, Secretary of State, and master of counterespionage.[3] Nedham was the logical choice: experienced, judicious, and trustworthy — as long as the government remained strong and his income adequate. Starting with the first week in October 1655 he brought out *Mercurius Politicus* in two sixteen-page editions: under its own title on Thursdays, and as *The Publick Intelligencer* on Mondays. Both were usually printed by Thomas Newcomb, since 1649 one of London's more successful printers, both were totally regular in their publication, and both were duly entered in the Stationers' Register.[4]

Nedham, though he was energetic, was not profligate, and from the start the overlap in these two editions was considerable. Soon, in fact, almost all the domestic news and more than half the advertisements in the *Intelligencer* became verbatim repetitions of items in *Politicus*, as did almost half the foreign news. Consequently any patient reader needed to buy only one weekly — and that could be either one — while his impatient brother would encounter at least a 50 per cent duplication.[5] Even then most of the differences between the two papers can be accounted for by the fact that the editor used some of his letters from foreign correspondents on Monday, others on Thursday; but over any extended period the non-English news in *Politicus* and the *Intelligencer* was extremely similar. Since Nedham probably charged two pence a copy, promptly raised his fee for advertisements, and was still subsidized by the government, he did very well for himself — according to a contemporary source, better than £500 a year.[6] He had a sizable stake in the preservation of the Protectorate.

By and large he earned his keep. He was effusive but hardly ever ridiculous in his praise of Cromwell and Cromwell's close associates. To cite only one example, his obituary on the Protector may have been a panegyric, but it contained a great deal of truth:

. . . His first undertakings for the Publick Interest, his working things all along, as it were out of the Rocks, his founding a Military Discipline in these Nations such as is not to be found in any example of preceding times . . . his Wisdom and Piety in things divine, his Prudence in management of the Civil Affairs, and conduct of the Military, and admirable Successes in all, made him a Prince indeed among the people of God. . . .[7]

Nedham also adeptly supported the government, from the acts of the Major Generals to the farflung depredations against Spain. Then, too, he was trenchant in his attacks on the opponents of the Protectorate, whether Quakers, Fifth Monarchists, Royalists, or republicans. For instance, when Edward Sexby, an ex-Leveller who was caught plotting to assassinate Cromwell, died in jail, Nedham stressed his near insanity and his confession and repentance, then went on to give a clinical description of Sexby's final illness — probably to forestall any rumors that he had been murdered.[8] The editor also used his paper for occasional announcements that the government wanted publicized; and shortly before Cromwell was offered the crown *Politicus* sent up a trial balloon to see how hard the antimonarchical winds were blowing.[9]

Nedham remained careful negatively as well as positively. Such items as the arrest of the intransigent republican Sir Henry Vane or the dissolution of Parliament or the recall of the Rump received only a few bare lines.[10] When Parliament was in session Nedham printed only stripped reports, again sticking to legislation that had been enacted and avoiding comment on debates. Moreover, week in and week out both editions were more than half-filled with cross-Channel affairs, so that sometimes he had only a page or two to load with English news. But despite the fact that *Politicus* and the *Intelligencer* were not spurred by competitors, their foreign coverage was extensive, coherent, and in its own day reliable, though the editor was no longer especially concerned to see that it was relevant to England. He cut down on the number of stories about Charles, and during the later 1650's those he included contained more vitriol and less tolerant amusement than they had in the early years of the decade. As the Restoration became a more imminent threat, Nedham further reduced the space allotted to the man whose exile was nearing an end.

He was still competent in filling any leftover space with noncontroversial local and crime stories and a few somewhat tongue-in-cheek accounts of miracles, apparitions, and prodigies.[11] In such items, as well as in more official reports, he told, for instance, about the negotiations between Cromwell and Menasseh ben Israel for the admission of Jews to England; about the persecution of a deluded Messiah, James Naylor, whose punishment the Protector tried to mitigate; about the departure, after several months in London, of the "Ambassador from the King of Florida"; about the "Opera" at Drury Lane.[12] One story (from Breslau) reads like the archetype of Byron's *Mazeppa*, another (from Surat) like Kipling in its plea that the English colonize India.[13] Closer to home, Lilburne's funeral in the autumn of 1657 received one graphic page, Cromwell's, a year later, three resplendent pages.[14]

But probably the most interesting bits in *Politicus* and the *Intelligencer* are the advertisements. Some of them are still poignant: a notice about a lost mute, another about a vanished child, a third concerning two abandoned infants, and a fourth requesting information on two runaway girls.[15] Some are still beguiling: a report of a stolen Van Dyke painting, another concerning a man "who went from his keeper." [16] One notice about some escaped convicts anticipated Dickens' descriptive touches:

. . . Walter Frick, a little fellow aged about 22 years, flaxen haired, whitely faced, in a gray cloth sute trimmed with black Ribbon, and a large gray hat edged on the brim with a silk and silver edgeing; and John Smith, a middle sized man with fair hair, a sad coloured Searge sute, with two rows of black hair buttons down the breeches, a stuffe sad coloured large coat with sleeves, a large pair of boots, and a sad gray hat, with a freckled face and a thin sharp nose. . . .[17]

Some of these advertisements sound even more modern: a plug for a treatise on how to attain "Peace . . . of Minde"; the first advertisements for tea and beer; a notice about a new kind of fire extinguisher, another about an improved bed for the sick; an announcement from a man that he would not be responsible for his wife's future debts.[18] Sometimes they employed the hard sell, particularly some of the longer notices of new books and a three-and-a-half-page promotion of stock in the East India Company.[19] On a few occasions an advertisement might be unintentionally humorous, like this announcement from a seventeenth-century Colonel Blimp:

> These are to advertise those persons who have printed the Catalogue of the Names of the Members of the present Parliament that they ought to correct it in severall places, and particularly in Suffolk, where for the County they have printed Thomas Barnardiston Esq, instead of Sir Thomas Barnardiston Knight.[20]

Book advertisements were Nedham's staple, and in one issue he ran nineteen,[21] though seven or eight was the average. The authors promoted in *Politicus* and the *Intelligencer* ranged from Milton to men whose names have vanished. Closely behind plugs for new books came medical advertisements. The result was that Nedham usually filled one page of each of his papers with profitable insertions, probably much to the consternation of those men now excluded from journalism.

Despite their absence, he continued to show signs of superiority that justified Cromwell's choice. Apparently he could take shorthand,[22] so that some of his reports were fuller and more accurate than they would have been in the pages of less skilled editors. He was also on occasion still a master of suspense and drama.[23] And in five consecutive numbers of *Politicus* in the spring of 1657 he returned to a "jocular style" in lead editorials, which were not repeated in the *Intelligencer* nor again attempted in *Politicus*. Four were datelined "From Utopia," one "From Oceana," and Nedham began by criticizing those "afflicted with an infectious Itch of scribbling political discourses." Among the infected he included Hobbes, Harrington, and himself.[24] He went on to attack the right of the people to discuss politics, and from there proceeded, only in part facetiously, to recommend a semi-Hobbesian utopia in which security ranked far above liberty, and a king, provided he was the right man, might well be the best leader.[25] Thus Nedham gave voice to the fact that the Puritan Revolution was grinding to a halt. In May 1659, just after the Rump had been reseated at Westminster, he was ousted from his editorship, his place temporarily filled by John Canne, a Baptist minister who ten years earlier had been one of the Levellers' more vociferous opponents.[26] Nedham's monopoly was broken, and very briefly he found himself on the outside looking in.

But before then his monopoly had not been quite complete. From the middle of May to the end of September 1657 *The Publick Adviser* rubbed shoulders but did not compete with *Mercurius Politicus* and *The Publick Intelligencer*. This sixteen-page weekly, which sold for a penny, consisted entirely of advertisements and was part of a somewhat grandiose commercial venture. Eight offices were set up in London to function as employment agencies, exchange shops, and places of investment, with *The Publick Adviser* publicizing the services and products available. Probably Nedham was involved in this venture; [27] in any case, the fees charged by the *Adviser* seem to have been set so that it did not cut into his income from advertising. Most of them were high, ranging from five shillings for four insertions of a book advertisement to ten shillings for four insertions of a medical advertisement. Even so, the *Adviser* was able to parade a series of notices which give an insight into the daily life of that time and place; and they show, among other things, that it had shifted toward orderly respectability. Coffee and chocolate were here advertised for the first time; wet and dry nurses offered their services; a language teacher wanted a job; so did "a pretty young man"; a barber needed an apprentice; some people wanted to "purchase Annuities for life"; others had "barren lands to be improved"; and one young lad yearned to go to sea. Just as today it is possible to visualize the life of a city by reading the want-ads, so the life of seventeenth-century London can be at least partly reconstructed by examining the notices — from the qualifications of a butler to the price of a middle-class apartment — that filled *The Publick Adviser*.

Yet the scheme of which this paper was the central organ did not flourish. The managers promptly reduced the number of offices and rotated the days they were open so that only two clerks were needed, and the organization quickly found itself in legal difficulties. Oliver Williams, a man who soon rose to some importance in journalism, challenged the company's right to charge fees, even to exist, and set up a rival scheme.[28] Then for a week in July he boosted his own agency in *The Weekly Information From The Office Of Intelligence*, a paper of advertisements and self-promotion almost identical with *The Publick Adviser*.

Nedham was then in a position to ignore Williams, and he could not have been much disturbed by the competition of *Nouvelles Ordinaires*. Dugard, during this paper's last two years, considerably increased the amount of foreign news, including a few items from such distant places as Boston and the land of the "Cham de Tartarie," as well as news of concern to merchants engaged in overseas trade. When Parliament was in session *Nouvelles Ordinaires* continued to supply the gist of its completed actions. Now that the news was more predictable and because he was borrowing heavily from *Politicus*, Dugard ran very few continued stories, and only twice felt compelled to put out extras.[29] Even his rare accounts of crime and violence — a robber caught in a "cabaret á biére," an explosion in Ratcliff, a murder in Plymouth — were dull and lifeless.[30] Moreover, Dugard fell deeper and deeper into the habit of beginning his paragraphs with the phrase "Le Lettres . . . disent." Since he garnered very few advertisements (about six book notices in two years), his paper had no more impact on Nedham's revenue than on his circulation. At the end of January 1658, after 400 issues, *Nouvelles Ordinaires* quietly expired.[31] Though continental readers would now have to get their news of England by means even more second-hand, presumably they did not complain; and not until 1667, when the *Gazette de Londres* began to provide a twice-weekly translation of the *London Gazette*, were they regularly able to buy a paper concerned with English affairs.[32]

Nedham might ignore Williams and Dugard, but he was extremely aware of events that impinged directly on his own career. By the spring of 1659 he was no doubt convinced that his bed of roses would become increasingly thorny. The signs of an impending Restoration were clear, and one of them was the fact that his near-monopoly was coming to an end, for other journalists were reading the handwriting on the wall.

Probably the first to do so and return to journalism was Border: on a Friday at the end of April 1659 a revived *Faithful Scout* was for sale. Published and printed by Horton, it had many links with the earlier *Scout*. Still credulous, Border again found room for Lilly's prophecies and other supernatural data; and still haphazard as an editor, he again presented the news without much finesse. But now, having had more than three years in which to mull over his political philosophy, he was temporarily an ardent republican. He berated the concept of one-man rule, attacking both Cromwell and Charles and supporting the republican-dominated Rump. In an early number he even espoused certain democratic proposals put forward by the remnants of the Leveller party and urged all who believed in this cause to meet weekly at Lilburne's tomb.[33] In a sense this was an appropriate spot, for there was a quality at once nostalgic and desperate in Border's pleas that the Good Old Cause not be forsaken. He had begun the revived *Scout* by declaring that not "harsh-sounding Discord but well-intentioned Harmony" was his aim.[34] Yet there was a stridency in his assaults on such antirepublicans as Prynne, as well as an urgency in his defense of the Rump, that could not have inspired much harmony — or confidence.

In July, Horton altered the name of the paper, for one number to *The National Scout*, then, until its demise in the opening days of 1660, to *The Loyall Scout*. It showed little change, though starting in the summer of 1659 it and its fellows went through the formalities of being licensed. It kept on giving one-fourth of its space to foreign news, and about half a page to advertisements, many of them quack medical notices. Its domestic news remained somewhat garbled, though almost all of it was written in official-sounding language. Yet *The Loyall Scout*, in its omissions and evasions, as well as in its platitudinous editorials, became much less republican, much more soft-spoken. In the late summer Border seemed extremely upset by Royalist uprisings; in October he urged a firm settlement of the government, without specifying what form it should take; in November he let it be known that he was not against the king, just against tyrants.[35] Discouraged by the shortsightedness of the leaders of Rump and army and aware that the squabbling between them would put an end to the power of both, Border, from late 1659 on, seems to have awaited the Restoration, if not with eagerness, at least with resignation.

His movement away from intransigence can also be seen in the second weekly he edited: a revived *Weekly Post*, the opening number of which came out early in May 1659, the last on the first Tuesday in 1660. Also published by Horton, it was as crowded and credulous as the *Scout*. Border's sloppiness was slightly more conspicuous in the *Post*, one issue of which, for instance, made much of the national turmoil caused by Booth's Rebellion, but then undercut whatever drama the news contained by a paragraph on the "perfect tranquility" in London.[36] Until late autumn, however, Border stayed consistent in his republicanism, sturdy in his opposition to one-man rule. But again there was the suggestion of a lost cause: how else explain an editorial extolling the virtues of Alfred's England?[37] By November, Border was editorializing in behalf of peace and obedience, and in the *Post*'s final number he attacked John Lambert and supported Monck.[38] The writing on the wall was being duplicated in the weekly press.

While many of London's leading intellectuals and politicians were busy adding to the national instability by drawing up paper constitutions, some of their humbler colleagues returned to journalism. Probably the second to so do was Crouch, and for five or six numbers in May and June *Mercurius Democritus* peddled nonpolitical parodies and pornography. The years had brought little change, though Crouch now had a broader range of advertisements to satirize. (One of the enterprises he facetiously boosted was an office where chastity could be insured.) [39] Apparently unchanged, too, was the author's poverty, to which he again referred.[40]

The third editor to make a comeback was, in all likelihood, Collings, for from May to December 1659 *The Weekly Intelligencer of the Common-Wealth* was again available on Tuesday.[41] Now an even more chastened man, Collings allowed almost no hint of his views to protrude from or between his lines. By seeming to approve of whatever happened at Westminster or in the meetings of the high army officers, he managed to give the impression that all was going well and that he, for one, did not want to interfere. He relied very heavily on official and semiofficial reports, and when they were lacking, he wrapped his own style in official phrases. He also frequently fell back on pious asides and wishful thinking. But he was still a competent editor. He could, for instance, be terse and graphic in his account of an insane woman murdering her grandchild, or Carlylean in describing a hailstorm; and he could, on rare occasion, insert a trenchant aside, such as his comment that the nub of England's problem was that the people did not know whom to trust.[42] He was able to handle transitions well, and to add skillful and not too patronizing explanations for the benefit of his rural readers.[43] Yet after thirty numbers *The Weekly Intelligencer* slipped back into oblivion.

The fourth editor to re-enter journalism had never really left it. Nedham was expelled from his editorship of *Mercurius Politicus* and *The Publik Intelligencer* in mid-May. He immediately retaliated by trying to compete with *Politicus* by means of an eight-page Thursday paper, *The Moderate Informer*.[44] Cautious and undistinctive, it closed, or was closed, after two weeks. Nedham then turned his energies to writing a pamphlet that came out in August. In the fifty-five pages of *Interest Will not Lie* he capably enunciated the thesis that the restoration of Charles would benefit only Papists; that Presbyterians, Baptists, neutrals, soldiers, M.P.'s, Londoners, even most Royalists, would all be better off spiritually, economically, and politically if England stayed a republic. Nedham's expedient argument and expediency again paid off: the Rump promptly gave him back the editorship of *Politicus* and the *Intelligencer*.

Under Canne, meanwhile, they had remained largely unchanged.

Their foreign correspondents were the same, and by the time Canne took over, their domestic news was so dominated by official reports that the editor's job was more than ever a matter of wielding a scissors and a pot of paste, not a pen. Between May and August, Canne further reduced the number of items about Charles, in a few of his encomia on the Rump he went farther than Nedham would have, and he whistled in the dark a little more shrilly than his predecessor.[45] But these differences were minor, and Nedham's return caused little alteration, though he himself was now a somewhat changed person. Knowing that he had been so long identified with the cause of Cromwell that he could not be embraced by the Cavaliers, Nedham kept up his fight against the monarchy even after the Restoration became a sure thing, and for a few months he gave the impression of being a man of principle.

The evidences of his brief battle for a lost cause are clear though infrequent in the pages of *Politicus* and the *Intelligencer*. In November he included in his obituary on Bradshaw high praise for this "Noblest Friend" who had so well and wisely presided over the court which condemned Charles I.[46] Several times at the end of the year Nedham took pot shots at Monck, identifying him with Charles II; and he opposed the readmission to the Rump of those now pro-Royalist M.P.'s who had been excluded in 1648.[47] In December he printed an antimonarchical statement in the *Intelligencer*, then in *Politicus* defended, if halfheartedly, his right to take such a stand.[48] Gradually, however, he reefed his sails and began to navigate with the prevailing winds. Accounts of Charles appeared more often, and in them he was shown as a potential king, not a wandering minstrel. During the early months of 1660 story after story acknowledged the growth of sentiment for a return of kingly government. By this time, too, Monck dominated the news, and Nedham now treated him as a sympathetic and intelligent, though tight-lipped, figure. The editor was still restrained enough so that, if — miraculously — republicans and army leaders had co-operated to prevent the Restoration, he would have kept his job; and in March he was, almost certainly, the author of a short, cryptic, antimonarchical tract, *News from Brussels*.

But the tract was anonymous and *Politicus* and the *Intelligencer* were now completely circumspect and inoffensive. Their foreign news continued to be competent and extensive, though at times when English affairs were tumbling around at a rapid rate it occupied only a few pages. None the less, Nedham's sun was setting: his subsidy from the government had come to an end in 1659; the circulation of his papers had shrunk, mainly because of renewed competition, but partly because of their loss of vigor; and the number of advertisements in them showed a falling off. Late in March 1660 the Council of State ordered him to cease and desist, though he managed to hang on for two weeks.[49] The final numbers of both his papers were full of foreign events, and each, strangely enough, contained a few more advertisements. Not so strange were their resigned stories about various prominent Londoners who were busy denying any past actions against the monarchy. The end had come. The last number of Nedham's *Publick Intelligencer* appeared on April 9, of *Mercurius Politicus* on April 12.[50] Certain Royalists were saying that hanging was too good for him, and he fled to Holland.[51] A few months later, "for money given to an hungry courtier," he was granted a pardon and came back to England. There, until his death in 1678, he combined the "practise of physic" with pamphleteering. In 1676 rumor had it that he was paid £500 by Charles II for writing against the king's Parliamentary opposition.[52] To the end Nedham showed that a professional pen, if not mightier than the sword, could be an effective and remunerative instrument.

On a lower level it could be the same thing for some of his colleagues, a few of whom, after the fall of Richard Cromwell in the spring of 1659, also came back to journalism. In June *The Weekly Account* returned, its one undistinguished number possibly edited by B.D. "Prag" also rejoined the paper war, on the side that was about to emerge victorious. For one number in June he gloated over the plight of the Good Old Cause and in rollicking and scurrilous fashion attacked Parliament and Presbyterians. In September *Pragmaticus* again briefly emerged, this time diluting its Royalism with some straight reporting, because, as the editor admitted, he needed money, and people would pay for news, not for wit and poetry. (He also implied that they might be buying his sheet for toilet paper, a fate he seemed to regret.)

The most active returnee was Oliver Williams, who in 1657 had fought *The Publick Adviser* and tried to set up a rival scheme. As Williams several times made clear, he did not like or trust Nedham,[53] but he borrowed a few leaves from Nedham's book, particularly the practice of writing a paper that came out in two separate editions. At the end of June 1659 Williams started a Friday weekly, *A Particular Advice*, then promptly supplemented it with Tuesday's *Occurrences From Forraigne Parts*. Both concentrated on making money, and dispensing news was only incidental. Williams repeatedly boosted his "Office of Intelligence," not a news bureau but a place where services and products could be exchanged. He also pleaded with anyone who had anything to buy or sell to advertise in his papers. But his venture was again unsuccessful. Williams had rivals and enemies, and he once hinted that his project had been sabotaged.[54] Nor did advertisers flock to his pages. Though sometimes as much as one-third of his space was filled with advertisements, often he was able to secure very few, once sinking to one, once hitting zero.[55] Moreover, he had trouble getting a regular printer, and at least six different men at one time or another printed his two weeklies. Finally, Canne, who had briefly occupied Nedham's editorial chair, may have tried to grab a share of whatever profits Williams was making.[56]

Almost certainly these were small, though Williams, by interlocking his numbering system and pagination, as well as by splitting the news between *A Particular Advice* and *Occurrences From Forraigne Parts*, made it hard for the eager reader not to buy both. Nor, except in the advertisements, was the amount of overlap between them large. Because the number of advertisements varied and because Williams sometimes published eight pages, sometimes sixteen, he often had much space that he had to fill with news. This he did by concentrating on foreign affairs and sticking like a leech to official reports on domestic happenings. Occasionally he allowed himself an editorial paragraph, but then mostly for the sake of showing off his classical and Hebrew learning, and invariably he dodged comment on anything controversial.

Early in 1660 *Occurrences From Forraigne Parts* came to an end and Williams changed the name of *A Particular Advice* to *An Exact Accompt*. No longer half of a biweekly venture, it lasted until July. Still impersonal and careful, it averaged one page in eight of advertisements and about four of foreign news. Until the Restoration was only a few weeks away, it shunned stories about Charles; but when he returned, *An Exact Accompt* indulged in all the proper eulogies, all the expected attacks on those who had opposed the monarchy. Like Nedham, at whom he continued to snipe, Williams would try not to get caught off base; and as late as 1670 he was still experimenting with various advertising schemes in London.[57]

Early in 1660, shortly after the demise of *Occurrences From Forraigne Parts*, he exhibited his resourcefulness by founding England's first daily paper, *A Perfect Diurnal Of every dayes Proceedings in Parliament*. Between February 21 and the final dissolution of the Rump on March 16 it appeared twenty-one times, skipping only those days on which Parliament did not sit.[58] Not really a newspaper, its eight pages were devoted exclusively to digesting the resolutions, orders, bills, proclamations, and lists of appointees emanating from Westminster.[59] The editor never commented or analyzed, never included a word of transition or explanation, and England's first daily contained no gene likely to develop into a Beaverbrook or Hearst production.

After Nedham's news monopoly came to an end in the spring of 1659, the London newspaper-buyer regularly had a choice among Nedham's two papers, those edited by Border and Collings, and after June, Williams' various efforts. But at the end of 1659 and the beginning of 1660 this choice was reduced when both Border-edited papers, *The Loyall Scout* and *The Weekly Post*, along with Collings' *Weekly Intelligencer*, closed down.[60] The old order was ending, and the dawn of a different day was heralded by two journalistic developments. The first was trivial but symptomatic. In December *The Faithfull Intelligencer*, printed and published in Edinburgh, made it clear that the editor, an officer in Monck's army, came of higher rank than that suitable to a mere "Diurnal-Writer." Predictably he devoted his opening number to attacking the London press and supporting Monck's conservative moves and aims.[61] The second and more significant development occurred at the end of that month. Henry Muddiman, the most important journalist of the early 1660's, began to write the two weeklies with which he was long connected. Skilled and energetic, as well as a trusted friend of Monck's, he was the first newspaperman openly to leap aboard the Restoration bandwagon.[62]

He started his profitable career as spokesman for the revived monarchy at the end of 1659 with *The Parliamentary Intelligencer*, a sixteen-page weekly that changed its name to *The Kingdomes Intelligencer* at the beginning of 1661 and survived until 1663. Starting with the first Thursday in 1660 Muddiman supplemented this Monday paper with *Mercurius Publicus*, which also lasted until 1663. Like Nedham, whom he was in the process of gloatingly supplanting, Muddiman made these two papers essentially one by having them duplicate each other — even more extensively than had *Politicus* and *The Publick Intelligencer*. At the start he was cautious and impersonal, though praise of Monck dominated his pages. Muddiman stuck to official reports, gave one-third of his space to foreign events, and garnered a slightly above average number of advertisements. Then in the spring he filled his pages with news of Charles's triumphal return and with vilification of any stray upholders of the Good Old Cause.

In June and July, Muddiman briefly squabbled with Williams, who had temporarily resurrected *Mercurius Politicus* and *The Publick Intelligencer* for the purpose of selling advertisements rather than purveying news. Muddiman won, and the Privy Council ordered that all papers except his *Parliamentary Intelligencer* and *Mercurius Publicus* be suppressed.[63] They then dutifully supported the Restoration by printing only what the government wished. In November 1660 Birkenhead was appointed licenser of what was left of the weekly press.[64] Muddiman gave him no trouble.

Prior to the establishment of Muddiman's monopoly, Interregnum journalism gave a few feeble kicks. In February 1660 Horton published one commonplace number of *Londons Diurnall*. Between January and August, Crouch wrote eight scattered issues of *Mercurius Fumigosus*, the last two of them adding to their smut and parodies vituperative attacks on the Good Old Cause, as did his one-number revival of *The Man in the Moon*.[65] (At the end of 1660 a paper calling itself *The Wandring Whore* briefly surpassed Crouch by making its pornography more factual and less fanciful.) In March four Royalist papers took advantage of the collapse of the Commonwealth to rear their heads, each for probably only one number. Wharton may have been the author of one, *Mercurius Honestus*, which gave one-third of its space to open and energetic pro-Royalism, two-thirds to straight news — but with that news exuding a confidence that the cause for which the editor had long fought was triumphing. The other three were more concerned with gloating than reporting, and their titles reveal how quickly times had changed: *A Perfect Diurnall: Or The Daily Proceedings In The Conventicle of the Phanatiques, Mercurius Phanaticus*, and *The Phanatick Intelligencer*. In May *Merlinus Phanaticus* attacked antimonarchists and astrologers and chuckled over Nedham's flight to Holland. In the late spring, in a final flurry, five or six weeklies, most of them lasting only one or two numbers, supported the monarchy and castigated its opponents, some of them using official reports, others employing the rollicking prose and verse their editors had practiced ten years earlier under different circumstances. Times had changed — much more than their titles: *Mercurius Aulicus, Mercurius Civicus, Perfect Occurrences, Mercurius Veridicus, Mercurius Democritus*.[66]

At the end of June the Convention Parliament passed a resolution that no Parliamentary proceedings could be reported without the consent of the Lower House. Thereafter all newspapers, including Muddiman's, were deprived of what had usually been their most regular nourishment.[67] *The Votes Of Both Houses*, the one issue of which came out on June 20, 1660, was in a sense the last product of Interregnum journalism, and it was a dull and official account of what happened that week in Westminster.

By then the Restoration was complete. Order, if not in the court, at least in the censorship and on the streets of London, had been reimposed. England, though it would never go back to the *status quo ante*, was rapidly returning to normalcy. Beginning in May 1660 *Mercurius Publicus* ran a series of toothpaste advertisements which suggested that the good citizens of London, with smiling faces and sweetened breath, were ready to welcome the dawn of a more tranquil if less exciting era:

. . . most excellent Dentifrices to scour and cleanse the Teeth, making them white as Ivory: Preserves from the Toothach, fastens the Teeth, and sweetens the Breath, and preserves the Gums from Cankers and Imposthumes. . . .[68]

Cankers and imposthumes in the body politic would now no longer be revealed by the weekly papers, which for almost twenty years Londoners had been able to buy — at a cost only one-twelfth of that for a packet of dentifrice.

CHAPTER XV

CONCLUSION

THE straightjacketed press of the 1660's and most of the 1670's announced that the storms of the Interregnum were over but never registered the building up of new ones. Though the Good Old Cause was officially dead, its ghosts continued to stalk the land, and the England of the Restoration was a very different place from the England of 1641. Indeed, the Interregnum was far more than a parenthesis in English history, and its two decades were more crammed with significant events and seeds of change than were the twenty years that preceded or followed it.

The newspapers from 1641 to 1660 told — even if superficially — the story of these significant events. What, however, did they have to say about seeds of change? Here the answer is not clear-cut, since seeds are hard to see until they begin to sprout; but the reader of today can discover much in the early weeklies that was invisible to their contemporary audience. In particular he can find many characteristics of modern mass journalism.

From the start most newspapers were set up and maintained to make money. In the seventeenth century, as in the twentieth, profits were usually more important than principle, though it was pleasant when the two went hand in hand. The authorized papers of the 1640's and 1650's hung on by not antagonizing the government, while certain Royalist weeklies managed to compensate for the rigors of search and seizure by means of private subsidies and a higher sales price. More- over, in the late 1640's advertisements began to be an important source of income, though advertisers never gained any influence over the early press. Finally, gathering momentum throughout the Interregnum was the power of the publisher or printer, the entrepreneur, so that in the 1650's the role of such men as Pecke and Border and Collings was largely that of a hired hand. Journalism had quickly become a busi- ness and a job, not a hobby.

By definition journalism has always been concerned with news, and from Butter to Beaverbrook the bulk of that news has consisted of public events. In England during World War II when papers were thinner, the percentage of such news rose, that of features and fillers shrank, with the result that a daily of 1944 was not too dissimilar in content from a weekly of 1644. On the other hand, the newspapers of Milton's era were beginning to feel their way toward greater diversi- fication and potential thickness, as well as toward limited specializa- tion. From Gainsford on, editors included some human-interest items, ranging from the weird and gory to the local and poignant. Walker's Hebrew etymologies and reprinting of the news of 1641 were a short step toward today's many-sectioned papers, and Crouch's ribald efforts can be viewed as the embryo of the comic page. Then, too, certain weeklies tailored themselves to a partially specialized audience: *Civicus* made an attempt to appeal specifically to metropolitan readers, a few short-run papers were edited to win a rural hearing, and Pecke's ship- ping news of the mid-1650's was designed to attract merchants. Politi- cal specialization was more conspicuous. Royalist, Presbyterian, and Independent papers can be easily distinguished, and *The Moderate* was not only co-ordinated with Leveller propaganda, but its sales were, in all likelihood, pushed by Leveller agents. Thus the journal- ists of the Interregnum were both reporters and, in the modern mean- ing of the word, editors.

As reporters the majority felt some sort of duty to inform the small world of their readers. Pecke and Collings did the best their abilities and the authorities permitted to transmit accurate reports. Dillingham became proficient in the straightforward presentation of news, and such men as Border and B.D. stumbled toward competence. A paper like *A Perfect Diurnall* could, in fact, have carried on its masthead the slogan "All the News That's Fit to Print," though its definition of fitness would have been far more restricted than that of *The New York Times*.

As editors several pioneer newspapermen viewed their weekly efforts as instruments of reform. Part of their motivation was no doubt mercenary: to gain circulation or to please their employers. Yet many partisan editors were also moved by conviction. Smith's laments, Mabbott's resignation as censor, the vicissitudes of Sheppard and Wharton and Cleveland, all indicate that editors (and publishers) were willing to suffer for their beliefs. While such suffering did not include martyrdom, it sometimes involved a few months in jail and the temporary loss of a job or a business.

In summary, then, the Interregnum press anticipated not only today's features and fillers but today's concept of the newspaper as an instrument of information and/or reform. Pecke's semiofficial reports and Smith's editorial breast-beating were remote from the services of the Associated Press and the incisive commentary of a columnist like Walter Lippmann; but given a little time to adjust, Pecke and Smith would probably feel at home in Times Square or on Fleet Street. Nedham certainly would.

These men and their publishers, like their modern counterparts, made three basic assumptions about the public. One is that people were interested in news. Another is that they could be influenced by how that news was presented. A third, though less evident, is that the dissemination of news was itself good. Even those early journalists who scoffed at the public for wanting news, repeatedly gave it to them. Such men as Cleveland and Sheppard were vociferously antidemocratic; Nedham could equal Hobbes in supporting a semidictatorial state; and not even Mabbott was consistent in his espousal of radical views. Yet each tried to inform and influence the largest audience he could. Despite the fact that there was often a good deal of patronizing or Machiavellian condescension in so doing, most early publishers and editors were concerned with getting to and at large numbers of people. So, in much the same way, are their journalistic descendants, though the arts of communication and salesmanship have made giant strides. Thus more than three hundred years ago the seeds, both good and bad, of today's mass circulation dailies were planted. The Restoration slowed their growth; it did not kill them. In the eighteenth century they budded slowly and unevenly; in the nineteenth and twentieth they blossomed. They have not yet been fully harvested.

Besides indicating the origins of the modern press, the newspapers of the Interregnum, viewed en masse, have much to say about their own period. Most of what they reveal consists of the significant public events, the commonplaces, of mid-seventeenth-century history. Except for a few behind-the-scenes stories in *Aulicus* and *Pragmaticus*, the official Journals of Parliament tell almost as much about Westminster as do the newspapers. Enough records of battles exist so that the military historian could skip the weekly press without much loss, while the scholar interested in continental affairs could also find fuller and more accurate sources. Even many of the sensational human-interest and prodigy stories were duplicated in ballads and broadsides. Further, there are certain lively problems in English history to which the press contributes no final solution. For instance, one can take almost any stand on the role of the gentry in the 1640's and find support for it in contemporary newspapers, though the word "gentry" seldom cropped up. Equally indecisive is the press's contribution to the chronic controversy about Cromwell: in the weeklies of his era one can find evidence that he was a Hitler, Napoleon, Winston Churchill, Abraham Lincoln, not to mention various combinations of angel and devil, radical and reactionary, visionary and crook.

There are, however, two facets of Interregnum history on which the press collectively can cast some new light. The first is the importance of London. The early weeklies give the overwhelming impression that the role of the metropolis was closer to that of Paris in eighteenth-century France than most historians have assumed. London was the capital, in every sense of the word, of England's economic, political, social, and cultural life.[1] The increasing productivity and fluidity of English society were there most evident. It was there that decisions were made and financed, that men with ambition came, that the effervescence of change was most exhilarating. A letter from Leicester dealing with a local by-election began by referring to London as "the Sea of news, from which small rivulets often flow to us in the Country, but that we should be able to make return of any thing new to you is news indeed." [2] Most journalists patronized their rural readers, who, after all, did not have the advantage of being at the center of things. The vast majority of weeklies were addressed to Londoners, permanent and transient, for it was only in the city that enough people, interest, and news existed to justify printing a newspaper.

The second facet is the extent to which the "Puritan Revolution" was secular rather than religious. The durability of Crouch is merely the most conspicuous journalistic example that the tastes of the age were not Puritan, that the devout Presbyterian Richard Baxter was right when he wrote that "the rabble [here a synonym for "the multitude"] hate both Magistrates and Ministers that would bring them up

to piety," and that "they are bitterly distasted against the serious diligent practice of religion." [3] Baxter could have gone beyond the rabble.
If one adds up the names supplied by various polemical papers of those
allegedly suffering from venereal disease, he would expect most middle-
and upper-class Englishmen of the next generation to be born idiots.
Yet almost every weekly gave some space to pious asides and exhortations, and God was often actively in the news. None the less, one
gets a strong feeling that most devout bits and pieces in the Interregnum press were sops and clichés, inserted mainly for reasons of
propriety. As in the editorial comments that decorate American papers
on the Fourth of July, habit and platitude, not conviction, predominated.
By and large, the problems and interests of three hundred years ago,
as revealed in the press, were as variegated and mundane as today.
The price of beer was of more concern than the price of salvation, a
fact of which editors were aware. All groups and factions claimed
God as an ally, none openly blasphemed; but most Interregnum publi-
cists used the deity as a slogan rather than a mystery, and God's place
in the early newspaper, though sometimes broad, was almost never
deep. In short, the press of that day was more revolutionary than
Puritan.

The weeklies of the 1640's and 1650's can also make two contribu-
tions to the history of English literature. The first is that Restoration
prose did not wait until 1660. Such men as Collings and Nedham wrote
paragraphs, even pages, that would have been approved by the Royal
Society, and both could display the functionalism of Sprat and the
rhetorical clarity of Dryden when the latter were still in their teens.
One can even find anticipations of the female-oriented journalese of
the early eighteenth century, and if one looks closely, foreshadowings
of Wilkes and Carlyle.

The second contribution is the evidence provided by the weekly
press that the line between skilled professional and genius is thin and
often crossed. During the Interregnum men normally precluded from
authorship entered the arena and wrote for an audience still relatively
unaccustomed to the written word. Under the pressure of competition
and the sheer task of compiling eight or more pages a week, many of
them quickly became adept. Dillingham moved from tailoring to first-
class journalism within a few years; Collings early displayed a flexibility and firmness of style; and Britanicus-Pragmaticus-Politicus Nedham wrote well enough for some of his prose to be attributed to Milton.
One could, in fact, compile an anthology from the pioneer newspapers
that would seem to include such writers as Bacon, Browne, Milton,
Bunyan, Butler, Dryden, Defoe, and Addison and Steele. Yet all these

selections would have been written by men who were, for the most part, lacking in formal education and who were writing as part of their daily jobs. Amid the chaos of civil war and incipient revolution the professional man of letters — a category that contains the hack — largely replaced the dilettante.

That he did so was important to England's literary and political future. The thousands of newspapers printed between late 1641 and mid-1660 increased the number of people interested in reading for information and served as a training school for men who could gratify this enlarged public. The journalistic outpouring also meant that many citizens became habituated to wanting to know what was going on and to participating in politics. The barrier to a return to the *status quo ante* was thus considerably strengthened by the small pages of the weeklies that for two decades fluttered from the presses of London. Pecke and his colleagues, in spite of all their caution, were pointing to the future. What they had started their descendants would carry on, often ineptly and viciously, sometimes well and proudly. The English, and consequently the American, newspaper had been launched on its exciting journey.

Some of the More Significant Attacks on Journals and Journalists between 1625 and 1632

In 1625 Abraham Holland, a minor poet who died in 1626, concluded *A Continu'd just Inquisition of Paper-Persecutors* with this free-swinging attack on Butter & Company:

> But to behold the wals
> Butter'd with Weekly Newes compos'd in Pauls,
> By some decaied Captaine, or those Rooks,
> Whose hungry braines compile prodigious Books,
> Of Bethlem Gabors preparations, and
> How termes betwixt him and th' Emperor stand:
> Of Denmarke, Swede, Poland, and of this and that,
> Their Wars, Jars, Stirs, and I wote not what:
> The Duke of Brunswicke, Mansfield, and Prince Maurice,
> Their expeditions, and what else but true is:
> Yea of the Belgique State, yet scarcely know,
> Whether Brabant be in Christendome or no:
> To see such Batter everie weeke besmeare
> Each publike post, and Church dore, and to heare
> These shamefull lies, would make a man, in spight
> Of Nature, turne Satyrist and write
> Revenging lines, against these shamelesse men,
> Who thus torment both Paper, Presse, and Pen.

In the following year, approximately contemporaneous with Jonson's *The Staple of News*, *The Fair Maid of the Inn*, partly written by John Fletcher, contained a brief but Jonsonesque portrait of "a lying stationer . . . a new Mercurius Gallo-Belgicus" (Act IV, Scene 2), as well as some to-be-expected puns on the name Butter.

In 1631 Richard Brathwait in his *Whimzies: or, a New Cast of Characters* was equally abusive though more detailed in his character of a "Corranto-Coiner":

. . . [He] is a State newesmonger; and his owne genius is his intelligencer. His mint goes weekly and he coins monie by it. Howsoever the more intelligent merchants doe jeere him, the vulgar doe admire him, holding his novels oracular; and these are usually sent for tokens . . . betwixt city and countrey. Hee holds most constantly one forme or method of discourse. He retaines some military words of Art, which hee shootes at randome; no matter where they hitt, they cannot wound any. He ever leaves some passage doubtfull, as if they were some intimate secrecies of State, closing his sentence abruptly with, hereafter you shall heare more. Which words, I conceive, he only useth as baites, to make the appetite of the reader more eager. . . . Some generall-erring relations he pickes up as crummes or fragments, from a frequented ordinarie; of which shreads he shapes a coat to fit any credulous fool that will wear it. . . . Paules is his walke in winter; Moorfields in summer. Where the whole discipline, designes, projects, and exploits of the States, Netherlands, Poland, Switzer, Crimchana and all, are within the compass of one quadrangle walke most judiciously and punctually discovered. But long he must not walke, lest he make his newes presse stand. Thanks to his good invention he can collect much out of a very little; no matter though more experienced judgments disprove him; hee is anonymous and that will secure him. To make his reports more credible; or, (which hee and his stationer only aymes at) more vendible, in the relation of every occurrent hee renders you the day of the moneth; and to approve himself a scholler, he annexeth . . . "veteri stylo," "novi stylo." Palisados, parapets, counterscarfes, forts, fortresses, rampiers, bulwarks, are his usual dialect. . . . Hee has now tyed himself apprentice to the trade of minting, and must weekly perform his taske, or (besides the loss which accrues to himselfe) he disappoints a number of no small fooles, whose discourse, discipline and discretion is drilled from his state-service. These you shall know by their Monday's morning question . . . Stationer, have you any newes? Which they no sooner purchase than peruse; and, early next morning (lest their countrey friend should be deprived of so rich a prize) they freely vent the substance of it. . . . Hee would make you believe that hee were knowne to some foreine intelligencer, but I hold him the wisest man that hath the least faith to beleeve him. For his relations he stands resolute, whether they become approved, or evinced for untruths. . . . Hee holds especially concurrence with two philosophicall sects, though hee bee ignorant of the tenets of either; in the collection of his observations he is peripateticall, for hee walkes circularly; in the digestion of his relations hee is Stoicall, and sits regularly. Hee has an alphabeticall table of all the chief commanders, generals, leaders, provinciall townes, rivers, ports, creekes, with other fitting materials to furnish his imaginary building. Whisperings, muttrings, and bare suppositions are sufficient grounds for the authoritie of his relations. . . . You shall many times find in his . . . corrantos miserable distractions; here a city taken by force long before it bee besieged; there a countrey laid waste before ever the enemie entered. . . . He is the very landskip of our age. He is all ayre, his eare alwayes open to all reports, which, how incredible soever, must passe for currant, and find vent, purposely to get him currant money, and delude the vulgar. Yet our best comfort is his chymeras live not long; a weeke is the longest in the citie, and after their arrival, a little longer in the countrey; which past, they melt like *Butter*, or match a pipe, and so *Burne*. . . . Some have held him for a Scholler, but, trust mee, such are in palpable error, for hee never yet understood so much Latine as to construe Gallo-Belgicus. . . . [This "character" is given in full in The Times, *Tercentenary Handlist*, pp. 9f.]

Another character-writer, Donald Lupton, thus depicted the early newspapers and their editors:

These commonly begin with Vienna and end with Antwerp. The Spanish & French affairs must not be left out. . . . Ordinarily they have as many Leyes [lies] as Lines. . . . They are new and old in five days. They are busie fellows, for they meddle with other mens Affaires. No Pope, Emperour, or King but must bee touched by their pen. . . . They have used this trade so long that now every one can say, it's even as true as a Currantoe, meaning that it's all false. Now Swedens and the Emperors War in Germanie is their Store-house, with how Lubecke, Hamburgh, Leipsich, Breame, and the other Hans. Townes affect the Kings Majesties proceedings. If a towne be beleagured or taken, then they never care, but how they may send their Leyes fast enough, and far enough. Well, they are politicke, not to be descried, for they are ashamed to put their names to their Books. If they write good Newes of our side, it is seldom true; but if it is bad, it's always almost too true. I wish them either to write not at all, or lesse, or more true; the best newes is when we heare no Newes. [From *London and the Countrey Carbonadoed and Quartered into severall Characters*, 1632.]

Finally, to end this sampling on a less secular note, an Oxford minister allegedly prayed in 1632 that Christ would "inspire the currantomakers with the spirit of truth, that people might know when to utter praises for the King of Sweden's victories, and when to pray for him in distress. They often did both these and then found out that the supposed causes did not exist" (quoted in Dahl, *Bibliography*, p. 23). Hence Butter and Bourne were even accused of wasting God's time.

All these complaints, with only minor variations, were repeated throughout the Interregnum.

APPENDIX B

A Chronological List of English Newspapers
from November 1641 through May 1642

Note: For the first eight weeks I do not significantly diverge from the descriptive bibliography in Coates, *D'Ewes*, pp. 404–406. I have ended this list in May because beginning in June the entries in the *Catalogue of the Thomason Collection* are almost complete. The five papers of foreign news which Butter issued during this period are not included. For further details on the two or three papers reprinted in Edinburgh, see W. J. Couper, *The Edinburgh Periodical Press*, I, 163–166.

1641

Nov. 22–29, *The Heads of Severall Proceedings In This Present Parliament* (John Thomas).

Nov. 29–Dec. 6, *The Heads of Severall Proceedings in both Houses of Parliament* (John Thomas).

Dec. 6–13, *The Diurnall, Or, The Heads of All the Proceedings in Parliament* (John Wright and Thomas Bates).

Dec. 13–20, *Diurnal Occurrences, Or, The Heads of severall proceedings in both Houses of Parliament* (Thomas and Bates).

Dec. 13–20, *The Diurnall, Or, The Heads Of All the Proceedings in Parliament* (Wright).

Dec. 13–20, *The Diurnall Occurrances: Or, The Heads of Proceedings in Parliament* (Bates and Francis Coules).

Dec. 20–25, *Diurnall Occurrances, Touching the dayly Proceedings in Parliament* (John Hammond).

Dec. 20–26, *The Diurnall, Or The Heads Of All the Proceedings in Parliament* (Wright).

Dec. 20–27, *Diurnall Occurrences: Or The Heads of severall proceedings in both Houses of Parliament* (Thomas).

1642

Dec. 27–Jan. 2, *Diurnall Occurrences in Parliament* (William Cooke).

Dec. 27–Jan. 3, *Diurnall Occurrences: Or The Heads of severall proceedings in both Houses of Parliament* (Butter and Thomas).

Dec. 27–Jan. 3, *The Diurnal Occurrances, Touching the dayly Proceedings in Parliament* (Hammond); reprinted in Edinburgh.

Jan. 2–10, *Diurnall Occurrences in Parliament* (Cooke).

Jan. 3–10, *Diurnall Occurrences: Or The Heads of severall proceedings in both Houses of Parliament* (Butter and Thomas).

Jan. 3–10, *The Diurnal Occurrances, Touching the daily proceedings in Parliament* (Hammond).

Jan. 3–10, *The Diurnall Occurrances in Parliament* (Coules and Bates).

Jan. 3–10, *The Passages in Parliament* (Butter).

Jan. 8–17, *The Diurnal Occurrences, Or Proceedings in the Parliament the last weeke* (John Burroughes).

Jan. 10–17, *Diurnall Occurrences: Or, The Heads of all the severall Proceedings and passages in both Houses of Parliament* (Thomas).

Jan. 10–17, *Diurnall Occurrences in Parliament* (Cooke).

Jan. 10–17, *Diurnal Occurrences: Or, The Heads Of The proceedings in both Houses of Parliament.*

Jan. 10–17, *A True Diurnall Of The Last Weeks Passages In Parliament* (Humphrey Blunden).

Jan. 10–24, *A Continuation Of The True Diurnall Occurrences in Parliament* (Robert Bryson?); reprinted in Edinburgh.

Jan. 17–24, *Diurnall Occurrences: Or, The Heads of all the severall Proceedings in both Houses* (Thomas).

Jan. 17–24, *A True Diurnal or the Passages in Parliament* (Humphrey Tucker), no. 2. (This and the two following entries represent the first domestic newspapers to begin numbering consecutive issues.)

Jan. 17–24, *A Continuation of the true Diurnal Passages in Parliament* (Blunden), no. 2.

Jan. 17–24, *The Diurnall Occurrances in Parliament* (Coules and Thomas Banks), no. 2.

Jan. 24–31, *A True Diurnall Occurrences* (Francis Leach and George Thompson), no. 3.

Jan. 24–31, *A True Diurnall of the Passages in Parliament.*

Jan. 24–31, *A Perfect Diurnall of the Passages in Parliament.*

[Feb. 3], *Irelands True Diurnall, Or A Continued Relation of the cheife passages that have happened there since the 11th. of January . . .* (William Bladen).

Jan. 31–Feb. 7, *The True Diurnal Occurrances Or, The heads of the Proceedings of Both Houses in Parliament* (Hammond).

Jan. 31–Feb. 7, *A Continuation of the true Diurnall of Passages in Parliament*, no. 4.

Jan. 31–Feb. 7, *The Diurnall Occurrances in Parliament* (Coules and Banks), no. 4.

Feb. 7–14, *Diurnall Occurrences, Or, The Heads of all the Proceedings in Parliament* (Thomas), no. 6.

Feb. 7–14, *A Continuation of the True Diurnall Occurrences in Parliament;* probably reprinted in Edinburgh.

Feb. 7–14, *A Continuation of the True Diurnall of Passages in Parliament*, no. 5.

Feb. 7–14, *The True Diurnal Occurrances Or, The heads of the proceedings in Parliament* (Hammond).

Feb. 7–14, *Diurnal Occurrences. Or, The Heads of the Proceedings in both Houses of Parliament* (J.G.), no. 6.

Feb. 14–21, *The Continuation of the Diurnall Occurrences. Or, The Heads of all the Proceedings in both Houses of Parliament* (Thomas), no. 7.

Feb. 14–21, *The Diurnall Occurrences in Parliament* (Coules and Banks), no. 6.

Feb. 14–21, *A Continuation of the true Diurnall of Passages in Parliament*, no. 6.

Feb. 21–28, *A Continuation of the True Diurnall of the Passages in Parliament*, no. 7.

Feb. 21–28, *A Perfect Diurnall of the Passages in Parliament*.

Feb. 28–Mar. 7, *A Continuation of the true Diurnall of all the Passages in Parliament*, no. 8.

Feb. 28–Mar. 7, *A Continuation of the true Diurnall of Passages in Parliament*, no. 8.

Feb. 28–Mar. 7, *A Perfect Diurnall of the Passages in Parliament*.

Feb. 12–Mar. 8, *A true Diurnall: Or A continued Relation of Irish Occurrences* (Bladen).

Mar. 7–14, *A Perfect Diurnall of the Passages in Parliament* (Cooke), no. 9.

Mar. 7–14, *A Continuation of the true Diurnall of Passages in Parliament*, no. 9.

Mar. 7–14, *A Continuation of the true Diurnall, of all the Passages in Parliament*, no. 9.

Mar. 7–14, *A Continuation of the true Diurnall of Proceedings in Parliament*, no. 9.

Mar. 14–21, *A Perfect Diurnall of the Passages in Parliament* (Cooke), no. 10.

Mar. 14–21, *A Continuation of the true Diurnall, of all the Passages in Parliament*, no. 10.

Mar. 14–21, *A True Diurnall of the Passages in Parliament*, no. 10.

Mar. 14–21, *A True Diurnall of the Passages in Parliament*, no. 10 (not identical with the above number).

Mar. 14–21, *A Continuation of the true Diurnall of Proceedings in Parliament*, no. 10.

Mar. 21–28, *A Perfect Diurnall of the Passages in Parliament* (Cooke), no. 11. (This number appeared in two slightly variant forms.)

Mar. 21–28, *A Continuation of the true Diurnall, of all the Passages in Parliament*, no. 11.

Mar. 21–28, *A Continuation of the true Diurnall, of all the Passages in Parliament*, no. 11 (not identical with the above number).

Mar. 21–28, *A Continuation of the true Diurnall of Passages in Parliament*, no. 11.

Mar. 21–28, *A Continuation of the true Diurnall of Passages in Parliament*, no. 11 (not identical with the above number).

Mar. 21–28, *A Continuation of the true Diurnall Occurrences and passages in both Houses of Parliament*, no. 11.

Mar. 21–28, *Diurnall Occurrences in Parliament*, no. 11.

Mar. 28–Apr. 4, *A Perfect Diurnall of the Passages in Parliament*, no. 12.

May 12–20, *Many Remarkable Passages from Both Houses of Parliament* (Thomas Ryder).

May 23–30, *The Heads of All The Proceedings In Both Houses of Parliament* (John Smith and Andrew Coe).

A Chronological List of the Various Issues of
A Perfect Diurnall of the Passages in Parliament
from June through December 1642

Note: Only if the title varies from the above is it given; the personal names are those of the printer or publisher.

JUNE

June 13–July 4, no printer given, nos. 1, 2, 3.

JULY

July 4–18, William Cooke, nos. 4, 5.
July 18–25, William Cook, unnumbered.
July 25–Aug. 1, William Cooke, no. 7.

July 4–11, William Rogers, unnumbered.

July 11–18, Robert Williamson, unnumbered.

A Perfect Diurnall Or The proceedings in Parliament:
    July 11–19, no printer, unnumbered.
    July 18–25, John Thomas, unnumbered.

July 18–Aug. 1, Thomas Cook, nos. 6, 7.

July 18–25, J.G. and R.W., unnumbered.
July 25–Aug. 1, Robert Wood, unnumbered.

July 25–Aug. 2, John Johnson, unnumbered.

AUGUST

Aug. 1–15, William Cooke, nos. 8, 9.
Aug. 22–Sept. 5, William Cooke, nos. 11, 12.

Aug. 1–7, Thomas Cook, no. 8.
Aug. 8–15, Thomas Cook, no. 9.

Aug. 1–8, Robert Wood, no. 8.

Aug. 8–15, Thomas Fawcet, unnumbered.

SEPTEMBER

Sept. 12–19, Walter Cook and Robert Wood (here and in the next two entries I am normalizing the spelling: Cook once added an "e" to his name, and Wood once appeared as "Woodner," once as "Woody"), no. 14; three different issues, each numbered "14" and none identical.

Sept. 19–26, no. 15; two different issues, each numbered "15" and not identical.

Sept. 26–Oct. 3, no. 16.

Sept. 12–Oct. 3, Francis Coles (or Coules), nos. 14, 15, 16.

Sept. 26–Oct. 3, Francis Cole, unnumbered.

A Perfect Diurnall of the Proceedigns [sic] in Parliament:
  Sept. 12–19, Robert Wood and William Cook, unnumbered.
  Sept. 19–26, William Cooke, unnumbered.

Sept. 26–Oct. 3, William Cooke, no. 15.

Sept. 26–Oct. 3, William Cooke, no. 17.

OCTOBER

Oct. 3–24, Walter Cook and Robert Wood, nos. 17, 18, 19.

Oct. 3–10, Walter Cook and Robert Wood, no. 18; probably a forgery.

A Perfect Diurnall of the Proceedigns in Parliament:
  Oct. 3–10, William Cooke, unnumbered.

Oct. 3–17, Francis Coles, nos. 17, 18.

Oct. 10–17, William Cooke, unnumbered.

Oct. 24–31, Printed by T.F. for William Cooke, no. 17.

NOVEMBER AND DECEMBER

Oct. 31–Dec. 12, Cook and Wood, nos. 21, 22, 23, 24, 25, 26.

Dec. 19–Jan. 2, 1643, Cook and Wood, nos. 28, 29 (the series did not stop here).

Oct. 31–Dec. 12, no printer, but "Collected by the same hand that formerly drew up the Coppy for William Cook," nos. 21, 22, 23, 24, 25, 26.

Dec. 19–Jan. 2, 1643, printed by John Okes and Francis Leach and sold by Coles, nos. 28, 28 [sic] (the series did not stop here).

A Chronological List of English Newspapers Between September 1647 and the End of 1648 that Lasted Fewer than Five Numbers

1647

Mercurius Anti-Melancholicus, one number, Sept. 18–24; a plague on both houses but slightly Royalist.

Mercurius Morbicus, two numbers, "1, 2, 3," Sept.; no. 4, Sept. 20–27; anti-Royalist, possibly by Walker.

Mercurius Clericus, one number, Sept. 25; Royalist.

Mercurius Medicus, two numbers, Oct. 11, Oct. 15–22; anti-Royalist, possibly by Walker.

Mercurius Populus, one number, Nov. 11; pro-Leveller.

Mercurius Rusticus, two numbers, *ca.* Nov. 12 and Dec. 10; anti-army.

Mercurius Vapulans, two numbers, probably late November; Royalist.

1648

Mercurius Dogmaticus, two numbers, Jan. 6–13, Jan. 27–Feb. 3; Royalist, probably by Sheppard.

Mercurius Insanus Insanissimus, three numbers, mid-March, Mar. 28, Apr. 24; Royalist.

Mercurius Brittanicus, one number, Mar. 31–Apr. 7; anti-Royalist.

Mercurius Anti-Mercurius, three numbers, Apr. 4, Sept. 12–19, Sep. 26–Oct. 2; anti-Royalist, almost certainly by Harris.

Mercurius Critticus, two numbers, Apr. 6–13, Apr. 27–May 4; Royalist, probably by Cleveland.

Mercurius Academicus, one number, Apr. 10–15; Royalist.

Mercurius Veridicus, three numbers, Apr. 14–May 8; Royalist.

Mercurius Militaris, one number, Apr. 21–28; Royalist, possibly by Cleveland. (The title was revived by Harris in October and November in behalf of the Levellers.)

Mercurius Urbanicus, one number, May 2–9; Royalist.

Mercurius Poeticus, one number, May 5–13; Royalist.

Mercurius Publicus, three numbers, May 8–29; Royalist.

Mercurius Gallicus, probably one number, though the extant issue is labeled 3, May 12; Royalist.

Mercurius Honestus, two numbers, May 19 and 25; anti-Royalist.

Mercurius Censorius, three numbers, June 1–20; anti-Royalist, possibly by John Hall.

Mercurius Domesticus, one number, June 5; Royalist.

Westminster Projects, probably two numbers, though the extant ones are labeled 5 and 6, June 6 and 23; Royalist, possibly by Nedham.

The Parliaments Vulture, one number, June 15–22; Royalist.

The Parliaments Scrich-Owle, three numbers, June 29–July 14; Royalist.

A Wonder [,] *A Mercury Without A Lye in's Mouth*, one number, July 6; Royalist.

Mercurius Scoticus, one number, July 19; Royalist, possibly by Wharton.

Mercurius Anglicus, one number, July 27–Aug. 3; Royalist.

Mercurius Aquaticus, one number, Aug. 4–11; Royalist.

The Colchester Spie, two numbers, both dated Aug. 10–17; Royalist.

Hermes Straticus, one number, Aug. 17; anti-Royalist.

Mercurius Fidelicus, two numbers, Aug. 17–31; Royalist.

The Parliament-Porter, four numbers, Aug. 28–Sept. 25; Royalist.

Mercurius Catholicus, one number (?), Sept. 15; pro-Catholic. (According to Williams, *English Journalism*, p. 240, a second number came out in December.)

The Treaty traverst, one number, Sept. 19–26; Royalist.

Mercurio Volpone, two numbers, Sept. 28–Oct. 12; Royalist.

[*The True Informer, Or Monthly Mercury*, one number, Oct. 7–Nov. 8; a pro-Leveller twenty-four-page monthly, probably by Harris.]

Mercurius Pacificus, one number, Nov. 8; Royalist, by John Taylor.

Mercurius Militans, one number, Nov. 14; Royalist.

Martin Nonsense, one number, Nov. 20–27; Royalist.

A Declaration, Collected out of the Journalls of Both Houses, three numbers, Nov. 29–Dec. 20; anti-Royalist, pro-Independent, possibly by Walker.

Mercurius Impartialis, one number, Dec. 5–12; Royalist, possibly by Wharton.

BIBLIOGRAPHY

No newspapers are included in this listing since they are conveniently itemized in Dahl's *Bibliography of English Corantos and Periodical Newsbooks* and in the *Catalogue of the Thomason Collection*, As far as I know, however, every English newspaper between November 1641 and June 1660 is mentioned in my text, notes, or appendices, and is included in the index. The following arrangement is alphabetical, except that seventeenth-century works are listed under their author's name in chronological sequence. Also, London is the place of publication for all items before 1700. Those books and articles whose contribution has been mainly bibliographical are followed by "(B)."

Abbot, Wilbur C. "The First Newspapermen," *Proceedings of the Massachusetts Historical Society*, LXVI (1936–1941). Boston: Published by the Society, 1942, 32–52.

—— *The Writings and Speeches of Oliver Cromwell.* 4 vols. Cambridge: Harvard University Press, 1937–1947.

Alger, J. G. "A French Newspaper in London, 1650–58," *Notes and Queries*, Eighth Series, IX (1896), 286.

Allen, Eric W. "International Origins of the Newspapers: The Establishment of Periodicity in Print," *Journalism Quarterly*, VII (1930), 307–319.

Altick, Richard D. *The English Common Reader: A Social History of the Mass Reading Public, 1800–1900.* Chicago: University of Chicago Press, 1957.

Ashley, Maurice. *Cromwell's Generals.* London: Jonathan Cape, 1954.

—— *The Greatness of Oliver Cromwell.* London: Hodder and Stoughton, 1957.

Aubrey, John. *Brief Lives*, ed. Oliver Lawson Dick. London: Secker and Warburg, 1950.

Barbour, Violet. *Capitalism in Amsterdam in the Seventeenth Century.*

Baltimore: The Johns Hopkins University Studies in Historical and Political Science, Vol. LXVII, 1950.

Bastide, Charles. *The Anglo-French Entente in the Seventeenth Century.* London: The Bodley Head, 1914.

Baugh, Albert C. *A History of the English Language.* New York: Appleton-Century, 1935.

Baxter, Richard. *The Autobiography of Richard Baxter*, ed. J. M. Lloyd Thomas. London: Dent, 1931.

Beller, Elmer A. "Milton and 'Mercurius Politicus,'" *The Huntington Library Quarterly*, V (1941–42), 479–487.

—— *Propaganda in Germany during the Thirty Years War.* Princeton: Princeton University Press, 1940.

Berdan, John, ed. *The Poems of John Cleveland.* New Haven: Yale University Press, 1911.

Beveridge, Sir William, and others. *Prices and Wages in England from the Twelfth to the Nineteenth Century.* Vol. I. London: Longmans Green, 1939.

Birch, Thomas, ed. *The Court and Times of Charles the First.* London: Henry Colburn, 1848.

—— ed. *The Court and Times of James the First.* London: Henry Colburn, 1848.

Birkenhead, John. *Aulicus His Hue and Cry Sent forth after Britanicus*, 1645.

—— *The Assembly-Man*, 1647 (reprinted 1662).

—— *Two Centuries of Pauls Church-Yard*, 1659.

—— *Cabala*, 1663.

Blagden, Cyprian. "The Stationers' Company in the Civil War Period," *The Library*, Fifth Series, XIII (1958), 1–17.

Bond, Richmond P., ed. *Studies in the Early English Periodical.* Chapel Hill: The University of North Carolina Press, 1957.

Bourne, H. R. Fox. *English Newspapers, Chapters in the History of Journalism.* 2 vols. London: Chatto & Windus, 1887.

Brathwait, Richard. *Whimzies: or, a New Cast of Characters*, 1631.

Brett-James, Norman G. *The Growth of Stuart London.* London: Allen & Unwin, 1935.

Brown, Louise F. *The Political Activities of the Baptists and Fifth Monarchy Men in England during the Interregnum.* Washington: American Historical Association, 1912.

Bruner, Helen M., compiler. *Catalogue of English Pamphlets in the Sutro Library.* Part II. San Francisco, 1941 (B).

Brunton, D., and D. H. Pennington. *Members of the Long Parliament.* Cambridge: Harvard University Press, 1954.

Bücher, Carl. *Industrial Evolution*, trans. from the 3rd German ed. by S. Morley Wickett. New York: Henry Holt, 1909.

Bush, Douglas. *English Literature in the Earlier Seventeenth Century, 1600–1660.* Oxford: Clarendon Press, 1946 (B).

Cambridge Bibliography of English Literature, The, ed. F. W. Bateson. 4 vols. Cambridge: The University Press, 1940 (B).

Catalogue of the Pamphlets, Books, Newspapers, and Manuscripts Relating to the Civil War, the Commonwealth, and Restoration, Collected by

George Thomason, 1640–1661. 2 vols. London: The British Museum, 1908 (B).

Chalmers, George. *The Life of Thomas Ruddiman.* London, 1794 (B).

Cheynell, Francis. *Aulicus his Dream,* 1644.

—— *Aulicus his hue and Cry,* 1645.

Clarendon, Edward Hyde, Earl of. *The History of the Rebellion and Civil Wars in England.* 7 vols. Oxford: The University Press, 1839.

Cleveland, John. *The Character of a London Diurnall,* Oxford and London, 1645.

—— *The Committee-Mans Complaint,* 1647.

—— *The Character of a Moderate Intelligencer,* 1647.

—— *The Character of Mercurius Politicus,* 1650.

—— *The Second Character of Mercurius Politicus,* 1650.

—— *A Character of a Diurnal-Maker,* 1653.

Clyde, William M. "Parliament and the Press, 1643–7," *The Library,* Fourth Series, XIII (1932–33), 399–424; XIV (1933–34), 39–58.

—— *The Struggle for the Freedom of the Press from Caxton to Cromwell.* London: Printed for St. Andrews University by Humphrey Milford, 1934.

Coates, Willson, ed. *The Journal of Sir Simonds D'Ewes From the First Recess of the Long Parliament to the Withdrawal of King Charles from London.* New Haven: Yale University Press, 1942 (B).

Collins, D. C. *A Handlist of News Pamphlets, 1590–1610.* London: South-West Essex Technical College, 1943 (B).

Copy of a Letter Written from Northampton, The, 1646.

Couper, W. J. *The Edinburgh Periodical Press.* 2 vols. Stirling: Eneas Mackay, 1908 (B).

Crane, R. S., and F. B. Kaye. *A Census of British Newspapers and Periodicals 1620–1800.* Chapel Hill: University of North Carolina Press, 1927 (B).

Dahl, Folke. "Amsterdam — Cradle of English Newspapers," *The Library,* Fifth Series, IV (1949–50), 166–178.

—— "Amsterdam — Earliest Newspaper Centre of Western Europe," *Het Boek,* XV (1938–39), 161–197.

—— *A Bibliography of English Corantos and Periodical Newsbooks, 1620–1642.* London: The Bibliographical Society, 1952 (B).

—— *Dutch Corantos, 1618–1650, A Bibliography.* . . . The Hague: Koninklijke Bibliothek, 1946 (B).

—— with Fanny Pettibon and Marguerite Boulet. *Les Debuts de la Presse Francaise — Nouveaux Aperçus.* Göteborg: Wettergren & Kerber, 1951.

Davies, Godfrey. *Bibliography of British History Stuart Period, 1603–1714.* Oxford: Clarendon Press, 1928 (B).

—— "Charles II in 1660," *The Huntington Library Quarterly,* XIX (1956), 245–275.

—— *The Early Stuarts, 1603–1660.* Oxford: Clarendon Press, 1949.

—— *The Restoration of Charles II, 1658–1660.* San Marino: The Huntington Library, 1955.

Dialogue between Thomas Scot and Marchamont Nedham, A. 1660.

Dictionary of National Biography, The.

D'Israeli, Isaac. *Curiosities of Literature*. London: George Routledge and Sons, no date.

Diurnall Occurrences [for the Parliament of 1629], 1641.

Diurnall Occurrences, Or Dayly Proceedings of Both Houses . . . From the third of November 1640, to the third of November 1641, The, 1641.

Downefall of Mercurius Britannicus-Pragmaticus-Politicus, The, 1660.

Escott, T. H. S. *Masters of English Journalism*. London: T. Fisher Unwin, 1911.

Fair Maid of the Inn, The, 1626.

Featley, Daniel. *Sacra Nemesis, Or The Levites Scourge*, 1644.

Firth, Charles H. *The House of Lords during the Civil War*. London: Longmans, Green, 1910.

―――― *The Last Years of the Protectorate, 1656–1658*. 2 vols. London: Longmans, Green, 1909.

―――― "London during the Civil War," *History*, New Series, XI (1926–27), 25–36.

―――― *Oliver Cromwell and the Rule of the Puritans in England*. Oxford: The University Press, 1953.

―――― and Godfrey Davies. *The Regimental History of Cromwell's Army*. 2 vols. Oxford: Clarendon Press, 1940.

―――― and R. S. Rait. *Acts and Ordinances of the Interregnum, 1642–1660*. 3 vols. London: His Majesty's Stationery Office, 1911.

Frank, Joseph. "An Early Newspaper Reference to Chaucer," *Notes and Queries*, New Series, III (1956), 298.

―――― "An Early Newspaper Allusion to Shakespeare," *Shakespeare Quarterly*, VII (1956), 456.

―――― "England's First Newspaper Article on Flying," *The Huntington Library Quarterly*, XX (1957), 185–189.

―――― *The Levellers*. Cambridge: Harvard University Press, 1955.

―――― "News from Virginny, 1644," *The Virginia Magazine of History and Biography*, LXV (1957), 84–87.

Fraser, Peter. *The Intelligence of the Secretaries of State and Their Monopoly of Licensed News, 1660–1688*. Cambridge: The University Press, 1956.

French, J. Milton. *The Life Records of John Milton*. 5 vols. New Brunswick: Rutgers University Press, 1949–1958.

―――― "Milton, Needham, and 'Mercurius Politicus,'" *Studies in Philology*, XXXIII (1936), 236–252.

Fresh Whip For all scandalous Lyars, A, 1647.

Gabler, Anthony J. *Check List of English Newspapers and Periodicals before 1801 in the Huntington Library*. Cambridge: Harvard University Press, 1931 (B).

Gainsford, Thomas, *The Secretaries Studies*, 1616.

Gardiner, Samuel Rawson. *The Constitutional Documents of the Puritan Revolution, 1628–1660*. Oxford: Clarendon Press, 1889.

―――― *Cromwell's Place in History*. London: Longmans, Green, 1902.

―――― *History of the Commonwealth and Protectorate, 1649–1656*. 4 vols. London: Longmans, Green, 1903.

―――― *History of England from the Accession of James I to the Outbreak of the Civil War, 1603–1642*. 10 vols. London: Longmans, Green, 1895.

—— *History of the Great Civil War, 1642–1649.* 4 vols. London: Longmans, Green, 1893–1898.

—— *Oliver Cromwell.* London: Longmans, Green, 1901.

Greg, W. W. *Some Aspects and Problems of London Publishing between 1550 and 1650.* Oxford: Clarendon Press, 1956.

Griffith, R. H. "The Second Newspaper of English News," *The Times Literary Supplement,* Dec. 4, 1924, p. 823.

—— "Some Unrecorded Newsbooks," *The Times Literary Supplement,* Dec. 11, 1924, p. 849.

Haller, William. *Liberty and Reformation in the Puritan Revolution.* New York: Columbia University Press, 1955.

Handlist of Seventeenth Century Newspapers in the Guildhall Library. London, 1954 (B).

Handover, P. M. *Printing in London from 1476 to Modern Times.* London: Allen & Unwin, 1960.

Hanson, Lawrence. "English Newsbooks, 1620–1641," *The Library,* Fourth Series, XVIII (1937–38), 355–384.

Harris, John. *The Grand Designe,* 1647.

—— *The royall Quarrell,* 1648.

Hatin, Eugéne. *Histoire Politique et Littéraire de la Presse en France.* Vol. I. Paris: Poulet-Malassis et de Broise, 1859.

Heath, James. *A Brief Chronicle of the Late Intestin Warr,* 1663.

Hemmeon, J. C. *The History of the British Post Office.* Cambridge: Harvard University Press, 1912.

Herd, Harold. *The March of Journalism.* London: Allen & Unwin, 1952.

Herford, C. H., and Percy Simpson, eds. *Ben Jonson.* 11 vols. Oxford: The Clarendon Press, 1925–1952.

Hexter, J. H. *The Reign of King Pym.* Cambridge: Harvard University Press, 1941.

Historical Manuscripts Commission, Sixth Report, Appendix; Seventh Report, Appendix.

Holland, Abraham. *A Continu'd just Inquisition of Paper-Persecutors,* 1625.

Hotson, Leslie. *The Commonwealth and Restoration Stage.* Cambridge: Harvard University Press, 1928.

Hudson, Derek. *British Journalists and Newspapers.* London: Collins, 1945.

Hutchinson, Lucy. *Memoirs of the Life of Colonel Hutchinson,* new ed. revised by C. H. Firth. London: George Routledge & Sons, 1906.

Jackson, Mason. *The Pictorial Press, Its Origin and Progress.* London: Hurst and Blackett, 1885.

Jackson, William A. *Records of the Court of The Stationers Company, 1602 to 1640.* 2 vols. London: The Bibliographical Society, 1957.

James, Margaret. *Social Problems and Policy During the Puritan Revolution, 1640–1660.* London: George Routledge, 1930.

Jaryc, Marc. "Studies of 1935–1942 on the History of the Periodical Press," *The Journal of Modern History,* XV (1943), 127–141 (B).

Jonson, Ben. *News from the New World,* 1620 or 1621.

—— *The Staple of News,* 1626.

Journals of the House of Commons, The.

Journals of the House of Lords.

Keeler, Mary F. *The Long Parliament.* Philadelphia: American Philosophical Society, 1954.

Klarwill, Victor von, ed. *The Fugger News-Letters.* 2 vols. London: John Lane, 1924 and 1926.

Lefler, Hugh Talmadge. "A Description of 'Carolina' by a 'Well-Willer,' 1649," *The North Carolina Historical Review,* XXXII (1955), 102-105.

Letter of Address To The Protector, A, 1657.

Lilburne, John. *An Answer to Nine Arguments,* 1645.

——— *Londons Liberty In Chains discovered,* 1646.

Lilly, William. *An Introduction to Astrology.* London: George Bell and Sons, 1884.

Lupton, Donald. *London and the Countrey Carbonadoed and Quartered into severall Characters,* 1631.

Madan, Falconer. *Oxford Books.* 3 vols. Oxford: Clarendon Press, 1895, 1912 (B).

Manwaring, G. E. "Journalism in the Days of the Commonwealth," *The Edinburgh Review,* CCXLIV (1926), 105-120.

Masson, David. *The Life of John Milton.* 7 vols. 2nd ed. London: Macmillan, 1881.

Mathews, Joseph J. *Reporting the Wars.* Minneapolis: University of Minnesota Press, 1957.

Matthews, George T., ed. *News and Rumor in Renaissance Europe (The Fugger Newsletters).* New York: Capricorn Books, 1959.

McClure, Norman, ed. *The Letters of John Chamberlain.* 2 vols. Philadelphia: The American Philosophical Society, 1939.

McCutcheon, Roger P. "The Beginnings of Book-Reviewing in English Perodicals," *PMLA,* XXXVII (1922), 691-706.

——— "Americana in English Newspapers, 1648-1660," *Publications of the Colonial Society of Massachusetts: Transactions,* XX (1917-1919), 84-96.

Merewether, Henry A., and Archibald J. Stevens. *The History of the Boroughs and Municipal Corporations.* 3 vols. London: Stevens, 1835.

Milford, R. T., and D. M. Sutherland. *A Catalogue of English Newspapers and Periodicals in the Bodleian Library, 1622-1800.* Oxford: Printed for the Oxford Bibliographical Society, at the Oxford University Press, 1936 (B).

Miller, Edwin H. *The Professional Writer in Elizabethan England.* Cambridge: Harvard University Press, 1959.

Milton, John. *Areopagitica,* 1644.

Morison, Stanley. "The Bibliography of Newspapers and the Writing of History," *The Library,* Fifth Series, IX (1954), 153-175.

——— *The English Newspaper — Some Account of the Physical Development of Journals Printed in London between 1622 and the Present Day.* Cambridge: The University Press, 1932.

Mott, Frank Luther. *American Journalism.* New York: Macmillan, 1941.

Moxon, Joseph. *Mechanick Exercises on the Whole Art of Printing,* ed. Herbert Davis and Harry Carter. London: Oxford University Press, 1958.

Muddiman, J. G. (see also his pseudonym, J. B. Williams). *The King's Journalist 1659-1689.* London: The Bodley Head, 1923.

—— "The Licensed Newsbooks, 1649 and 1650," *Notes and Queries*, CLXVII (1934), 113–116.

Nedham, Marchamont. *A Check to the Checker of Britannicus*, 1644.

—— "Preface" to Lilburne's *An Answer to Nine Arguments*, 1645.

—— *Mercurius Britanicus, His Apologie To all Well-affected People*, 1645.

—— *Independencie No Schisme*, 1646.

—— *The Case of the Kingdome Stated*, 1647.

—— *The Lawyer of Lincolnes-Inne Reformed*, 1647.

—— *The Levellers levell'd*, 1647.

—— *Loyalty speakes Truth*, 1648.

—— *An Answer To A Declaration of The Lords and Commons . . .* , 1648.

—— *The manifold Practices And Attempts of the Hamiltons . . . To get the Crown of Scotland*, 1648.

—— *The Reverend Alderman Atkins . . .* , 1648.

—— *The Solemn League and Covenant*, 1648.

—— *A Plea for The King, and Kingdome*, 1648.

—— *A Most Pithy Exhortation*, 1649.

—— *Digitus Dei*, 1649.

—— *Certain Considerations tendered in all humility*, 1649.

—— *The Case of the Commonwealth of England Stated*, 1650.

—— *Of the Dominion, Or Ownership of the Sea*, 1652.

—— *The Excellencie Of A Free State*, 1656.

—— *The Great Accuser cast down*, 1657.

—— *Interest will not Lie*, 1659.

—— *News from Brussels*, 1660.

—— *The Citties Feast To The Lord Protector*, 1661.

—— *The True Character Of a Rigid Presbyter*, 1661.

—— *A Short History of the English Rebellion*, 1661.

—— *A Discourse Concerning Schools and School-Masters*, 1663.

—— *Medela Medicinae*, 1665.

—— *A Pacquet of Advices*, 1676.

—— *A Second Pacquet of Advices*, 1677.

—— *Honesty's best Policy*, 1677.

—— *The Pacquet-Boat Advice*, 1678.

—— *Christianissimus Christianandus*, 1678.

Newton, Arthur P. *The Colonising Activities of the English Puritans*. New Haven: Yale University Press, 1914.

Notestein, Wallace. *Four Worthies*. London: Johnathan Cape, 1956.

—— *The Winning of the Initiative by the House of Commons*. London: British Academy, 1927.

—— with Francis Relf. *Commons Debates for 1629*. Research Publications of the University of Minnesota, Studies in the Social Sciences Number 10. Minneapolis: University of Minnesota, 1921.

Ogg, David. *England in the Reign of Charles II*. 2 vols. 2nd ed. Oxford: Clarendon Press, 1955.

Overton, Richard. *The humble Petition*, 1649.

Parker, Henry. *Humble Remonstrance of the Company of Stationers*, 1643.

Parliamentary History of England, The. Vol. III (1642–1660). London: T. C. Hansard, 1808.

Patrick, J. Max. "The Arrest of Hugh Peters," *The Huntington Library Quarterly,* XIX (1956), 343–351.

Plant, Marjorie. *The English Book Trade, an Economic History of the Making and Sale of Books.* London: Allen & Unwin, 1939.

Plomer, Henry R. "An Analysis of the Civil War Newspaper 'Mercurius Civicus,'" *The Library,* Second Series, VI (1905), 184–207.

—— *A Dictionary of the Booksellers and Printers Who Were at Work in England, Scotland and Ireland from 1641 to 1667.* London: The Bibliographical Society, 1907.

Porritt, Edward. *The Unreformed House of Commons.* 2 vols. Cambridge: The University Press, 1909.

Press Club, London, The. *Catalogue of an Exhibition Illustrating the History of the English Newspaper.* Cambridge: The University Press, 1932.

Presse full of Pamphlets, A, 1642.

Prynne, William. *A Checke to Brittanicus,* 1644.

Radin, Paul, ed. *An Annotated Bibliography and Summary of F. Cole's "A Perfect Diurnall of the Passages in Parliament."* Sutro Branch, California State Library, Occasional Papers, English Series No. 2, San Francisco, 1939 (B).

Remonstrance of London Occurrences, A, 1643.

Robinson, Howard. *The British Post Office, a History.* Princeton: Princeton University Press, 1948.

Rogers, Nathaniel. *A Letter discovering the cause of Gods continuing wrath against the Nation,* 1643.

Rollins, Hyder E. *Cavalier and Puritan — Ballads and Broadsides Illustrating the Period of the Great Rebellion, 1640–1660.* New York: New York University Press, 1923.

—— "Samuel Sheppard and His Praise of Poets," *Studies in Philology,* XXIV (1927), 509–555.

Rope for Pol, A, 1660.

Rostenberg, Leona. "Nathaniel Butter and Nicholas Bourne, First 'Masters of the Staple,'" *The Library,* Fifth Series, XII (1957), 23–33.

Roth, Cecil. *A History of the Jews in England.* Oxford: The Clarendon Press, 1941.

Rushworth, John. *Historical Collections.* 8 vols. London: D. Browne, 1721–22.

Sabine, George H. *A History of Political Theory.* New York: Henry Holt, 1937.

Salmon, Lucy M. *The Newspaper and the Historian.* New York: Oxford University Press, 1923.

Schlatter, Richard. *Richard Baxter & Puritan Politics.* New Brunswick: Rutgers University Press, 1957.

Scott, Thomas, *Vox Populi,* 1620.

Shaaber, Matthias A. "Forerunners of the Newspaper in America," *Journalism Quarterly,* XI (1934), 339–347.

—— "The History of the First English Newspaper," *Studies in Philology,* XXIX (1932), 551–587.

—— *Some Forerunners of the Newspaper in England, 1476–1622.* Philadelphia: University of Pennsylvania Press, 1929.

Sheppard, Samuel. *The Famers Fam'd*, 1646.

—— *The False Alarum*, 1646.

—— *Animadversions upon. . . Londons Liberty*, 1646.

—— *The Weepers: or, the bed of Snakes broken*, 1652.

Siebert, Fredrick S. *Freedom of the Press in England, 1476–1776.* Urbana: University of Illinois Press, 1952.

—— "Regulation of the Press in the Seventeenth Century — Excerpts from the Records of the Court of the Stationers' Company," *Journalism Quarterly*, XIII (1936), 381–393.

Singer, Charles, with A. R. Hall and Trevor I. Williams, eds. *A History of Technology.* 5 vols. Oxford: Clarendon Press, 1954–1958.

Sirluck, Ernest. "Shakespeare and Jonson among the Pamphleteers of the First Civil War: Some Unreported Seventeenth-Century Allusions," *Modern Philology*, LIII (1955), 88–99.

—— "'To Your Tents, O Israel': A Lost Pamphlet," *The Huntington Library Quarterly*, XIX (1955–56), 301–305.

Skelton, R. A. "Pieter van den Keere," *The Library*, Fifth Series, V (1950), 130–132.

Speeches and Passages Of This Great and Happy Parliament: From the third of November, 1640, to this instant June, 1641, 1641.

Stewart, Powell. *British Newspapers and Periodicals 1632–1800* [at the University of Texas]. Austin: The University of Texas, 1950 (B).

Taylor, John. *The Whole Life and Progresse of Henry Walker*, 1642.

—— *Mercurius Aquaticus*, 1643.

—— *Rebels Anathematised and Anatomized*, 1645.

—— *Works of John Taylor, the Water Poet, not included in the Folio Volume of 1630.* 5 vols. in 4. Manchester: The Spenser Society, 1870–1878.

Tercentenary Handlist of English & Welsh Newspapers, Magazines & Reviews. London: The Times, 1920 (B).

Thompson, Elbert N. S. "War Journalism Three Hundred Years Ago," *PMLA*, XXXV (1920), 93–115.

Thompson, James Westfall. "The Origin and Development of the Newspaper," *Rice Institute Pamphlet*, XVII (1930), 141–156.

Thurloe, John. *A Collection of the State Papers of John Thurloe.* 7 vols. London: F. Gyles, 1742.

Transcript of the Registers of the Worshipful Company of Stationers; From 1640–1708 A.D., A. 3 vols. London: privately printed, 1913–14.

True Character of Mercurius Aulicus, The, 1645.

Van Stockum, W. P., Jr. *The First Newspapers of England Printed in Holland, 1620–1621.* The Hague: Nijhoff, 1914.

Varley, Frederick J. *Mercurius Aulicus.* Oxford: Basil Blackwell, 1948.

Walker, Henry. *A Terrible Out-Cry Against the Loytering Exalted Prelates*, 1641.

—— *Corda Angliae*, 1641.

—— *The Prelates Pride*, 1641.

—— *An Answer To A Foolish Pamphlet . . . by John Taylor*, 1641.

—— *Taylors Physicke*, 1641.

——— *The Churches Purity*, 1641.

——— *To Your Tents, O Israel*, 1642.

——— *Ecce Homo; The Little Parliament unbowelled. . .* , 1644.

——— *A Sermon, Preached In the Kings Chappell at White-Hall*, 1649.

———*A Collection of Several Passages concerning . . . Cromwell*, 1659.

——— *Serious Observations lately made touching his Majesty*, 1660.

Webb, Henry J. "Military Newsbooks during the Age of Elizabeth," *English Studies*, XXXIII (1932), 241–251.

Weber, H. H. "Check List of English News Pamphlets, 1641 to 1666, in the Harvard College Library on July 1st, 1934," unpublished (B).

——— "The 'Mercurius Bellicus' of 1643," *Notes and Queries*, CLXV (1933), 345–347.

——— "The Mercurius Poeticus of 1660," *Notes and Queries*, CLXIX (1935), 354f.

Webster, John. *The Picture of Mercurius Politicus*, 1653.

Wedgwood, C. V. *The Common Man in the Great Civil War*. Leicester: Leicester University Press, 1957.

——— *The King's Peace, 1637–1641*. New York: Macmillan, 1955.

——— *The King's War, 1641–1647*. New York: Macmillan, 1959.

——— *Poetry and Politics under the Stuarts*. Cambridge: The University Press, 1960.

——— *The Thirty Years War*. London: Jonathan Cape, 1938.

Weed, Katherine K., and Richmond P. Bond, *Studies of British Newspapers and Periodicals from Their Beginning to 1800, A Bibliography*. Chapel Hill: University of North Carolina Press, 1946 (B).

Weill Georges. *Le Journal: Origines, Evolution et Rôle de la Presse Périodique*. Paris: La Renaissance du Livre, 1934.

Wilkins, John. *Mathematical Magick*, 1648.

Williams, J. B. (pseudonym of J. G Muddiman). "The Beginnings of English Journalism," *The Cambridge History of English Literature*. New York: G. P. Putnam's Sons, 1911. Vol. VII, pp. 389–415.

——— "The Early History of London Advertising," *The Nineteenth Century and After*, LXII (1907), 793–800.

——— "Henry Walker, Journalist of the Commonwealth," *The Nineteenth Century and After*, LXIII (1908), 454–464.

———*A History of English Journalism to the Foundation of the Gazette*. London: Longmans, Green, 1908.

Williamson, Hugh Ross. *The Day They Killed the King*. New York: Macmillan, 1957.

——— *Four Stuart Portraits*. London: Evans Brothers, 1949.

Wing, Donald G. *Short Title Catalogue . . . 1641–1700*. 3 vols. New York: Index Society, 1945–1951 (B).

Wither, George. *The Great Assises Holden in Parnassus by Apollo and His Assessors*, 1645. Reprinted at Oxford for the Luttrell Society by Basil Blackwell, 1948.

Wood, Anthony à. *Athenae Oxonienses*. London: Tho. Bennet, 1691.

——— *Life and Times*, ed. Llewelyn Powys. London: Wishart, 1932.

Wood, James Playsted. *The Story of Advertising*. New York: Ronald Press, 1958.

Wright, Louis B. *Middle-Class Culture in Elizabethan England*. Chapel Hill: University of North Carolina Press, 1935.

Yale University Library. "Annotated List of Newspapers in the Yale University Library," unpublished (B).

Yule, George. *The Independents in the English Civil War*. Cambridge: The University Press, 1958.

NOTES

I

THE UN-ENGLISH ENGLISH NEWSPAPER
1620-1642

Bibliographical Note: My evidence for this chapter is based on a reading of more than half the approximately 360 extant corantos and newsbooks dealing with foreign news which came out between 1620 and 1642. The figure of 360 is derived from Folke Dahl's *Bibliography of English Corantos and Periodical Newsbooks, 1620-1642* (London, 1952), which lists 404 separate items, not counting duplicates and near-duplicates. Of these about sixty are lost and are known only through entries in the Stationers' Register or by references to them in contemporary newsletters and other newsbooks. Since the publication of Dahl's book, a few scattered issues have turned up, but his list is so full and careful that they necessitate little change in his arrangement or conclusions. Two secondary articles are also relevant to this chapter: Folke Dahl, "Amsterdam — Cradle of English Newspapers," and Matthias Shaaber, "The History of the First English Newspaper." Lawrence Hanson, "English Newsbooks, 1620–1641," is an adequate summary, though it has been superseded by Dahl's *Bibliography*.

1. See, for instance, James Henry Breasted, *A History of Egypt*, 2nd ed. (New York: Charles Scribner's Sons, 1921), p. 109.

2. Sir Richard Jebb, *Essays and Addresses* (Cambridge: The University Press, 1907), pp. 159f; and Carl Bücher, *Industrial Evolution*, pp. 218–220.

3. For a survey of the early newsletter, see Bücher, *Industrial Evolution*, pp. 221–236; and for probably the earliest London newsletter, see Stanley Morison, "The Bibliography of Newspapers and the Writing of History," p. 155. In the early eighteenth century "Dawks's News-Letter" was still set in a type meant to look like handwriting.

4. Two volumes of *The Fugger News-Letters*, edited by Victor von Klarwill, were published in 1924 and 1926, and *The Letters of John Chamberlain*, edited by Norman McClure, appeared in 1939. (Wallace Notestein, *Four Worthies*, gives a chapter to Chamberlain.) Two collections edited by Thomas Birch are

full of contemporary newsletters: *The Court and Times of James the First,* and *The Court and Times of Charles the First.*

5. The best account of the predecessors of the newspaper is Shaaber, *Some Forerunners of the Newspaper In England, 1476–1622.*

6. D. C. Collins' *Handlist of News Pamphlets, 1590–1610,* lists 270 English items for these twenty years, the majority of them dealing with continental news; and Henry J. Webb, "Military Newsbooks during the Age of Elizabeth," pp. 241–251, itemizes thirty-one, of which seven came out in 1602. All were concerned with foreign news, though they contained repeated references to English troops serving overseas.

7. A copy of this incipient magazine is described in The Press Club, *Catalogue of an Exibition Illustrating the History of the English Newspaper,* p. 1. For further information on *Mercurius Gallobelgicus,* see Shaaber, *Forerunners,* pp. 310f, and Williams, *English Journalism,* pp. 11f. Among a host of seventeenth-century allusions to this semiannual compilation was one by John Cleveland, who referred to it as the "original sinner" in the evolution of the newspaper (*The Character of a London Diurnall,* 1645, p. 1).

8. The actual place and date of what can be called the first newspaper is disputed, though the area of disagreement is small. I am following the consensus: see, for instance Bücher, *Industrial Evolution,* p. 237; Morison, "Bibliography of Newspapers," p. 155; Marc Jaryc, "Studies of 1935–1942 on the History of the Periodical Press," pp. 130f; Georges Weill, *Le Journal: Origines, Evolution et Rôle de la Presse Périodique,* p. 21; and Eric W. Allen, "International Origins of the Newspapers: The Establishment of Periodicity in Print," pp. 307ff. For the first Dutch newspapers see Dahl, "Amsterdam — Earliest Newspaper Centre of Western Europe," p. 167. ("The English Mercurie" of 1588, reporting on the defeat of the Spanish Armada, has been conclusively proved to be a nineteenth-century forgery, as has "The Weekely Newes" of 1606.)

9. Dahl, "Amsterdam — Earliest Newspaper Centre," pp. 161–197; and Violet Barbour, *Capitalism in Amsterdam in the Seventeenth Century,* pp. 66f. Many of the corantos of the 1620's testified to Amsterdam's importance in the early history of journalism, though Venice remained a close second as a key point in the transmission of news.

10. Bücher, *Industrial Evolution,* p. 238. See also Peter Fraser, *The Intelligence of the Secretaries of State and Their Monopoly of Licensed News, 1660–1688,* pp. 37, 45.

11. Dahl, "Amsterdam — Earliest Newspaper Centre," p. 195. The first newspaper to be published in France had to wait eleven years, until 1631. (See Folke Dahl, Fanny Petibon, Marguerite Boulet, *Les Debuts de la Press Francaise — Nouveaux Aperçus,* pp. 7ff.) The first American newspaper did not appear until the end of the century.

12. See the short article on van den Keere by R. A. Skelton. Very possibly van den Keere brought out a newspaper in English earlier in 1620, though the issue dated December 2 is the earliest that has survived (Dahl, *Bibliography,* p. 31).

13. Dahl, "Amsterdam — Cradle," pp. 168f.

14. These earliest English corantos have been reproduced by W. P. Van Stockum, Jr., *The First Newspapers of England Printed in Holland, 1620–1621.*

15. For the historical background in England from 1603 to 1642 the ten volumes of Samuel Rawson Gardiner's *History of England from the Accession of James I to the Outbreak of the Civil War* have been my rod and staff. My chief guide through the maze of the Thirty Years' War has been C. V. Wedgwood's *The Thirty Years War.* With the start of that war in 1618 the number of relations published in England dealing with German events showed a marked rise.

16. Dahl, *Bibliography,* pp. 42–46.

17. *Ibid.,* p. 22.

18. *Ibid.*, and his *Dutch Corantos, 1618–1650, A Bibliography*, p. 23.

19. See, for instance, Richard Brathwait's *Whimzies: Or, a New Cast of Characters* (1631), where the author mentioned the use of old newspapers to stop mustard pots and wrap herbs.

20. *Corante, or newes from Italy, Germanie, Hungarie, Spaine, and France*, July 3, 1621, printed by Broer Jansz, one of van den Keere's Amsterdam competitors. A contemporary glimpse of the passions and horrors of this war can be caught in the engravings reprinted in Elmer A. Beller, *Propaganda in Germany during the Thirty Years War*.

21. Dahl, *Bibliography*, pp. 33f; or see Jansz's seventh number, which also deleted a reference to King James.

22. Fredrick S. Siebert, *Freedom of the Press in England, 1476–1776*, pp. 61f. William M. Clyde, *The Struggle for the Freedom of the Press from Caxton to Cromwell*, pp. 295–297, reprints this decree of 1637.

23. *Tercentenary Handlist of English & Welsh Newspapers, Magazines & Reviews*, p. 9.

24. Siebert, *Freedom of the Press*, p. 150.

25. Dahl, *Bibliography*, pp. 49f; Hanson, "English Newsbooks," p. 363.

26. Siebert, *Freedom of the Press*, p. 151.

27. *Ibid.*

28. Dahl, *Bibliography*, pp. 51–54.

29. Shaaber, *Forerunners*, p. 288; Hanson, "English Newsbooks," pp. 379f; Dahl, *Bibliography*, p. 51; and Henry R. Plomer, *A Dictionary of the Booksellers and Printers Who Were at Work in England, Scotland, and Ireland from 1651 to 1667*, pp. 40f. For biographical details see Leona Rostenberg, "Nathaniel Butter and Nicholas Bourne, First 'Masters of the Staple.'"

30. From May to October 1622 twenty-two newsbooks were published by Nicholas Bourne and Thomas Archer, fourteen by Butter, either alone or with another publisher, and three by various other booksellers (Dahl, *Bibliography*, p. 55). See also Shaaber, "First English Newspaper," pp. 553–556.

31. E.g., *Newes from the Palatinate*, March 1622; *Good newes for the King of Bohemia*, Apr. 17, 1622; *The safe arrivall of Christian Duke of Brunswick*, July 3, 1622; *A continuation of more news from the Palatinate*, July 26, 1622; and *A True relation of the affaires of Europe*, Oct. 4, 1622.

32. *More newes from the Palatinate*, March 1622, quoted in Dahl, *Bibliography*, p. 57.

33. E.g., *Good newes from Alsatia and the Palatinate*, June 5, 1622; *The late proceedings in all troubled parts of Christendome*, June 25, 1622; *Mansfeilds arrivall in the Dukedome of Brabant*, Aug. 27, 1622; and *The King of Bohemia's welcome to Count Mansfield*, Apr. 1622.

34. *A true relation of the affaires of Europe*, Oct. 4, 1622.

35. *The strangling and death of the Great Turke*, July 15, 1622 (and at the end of this paper the editor invited his readers to come back the next week for more news); *A true relation of the affaires of Europe*, Oct. 4, 1622; and *Newes from the Palatinate*, March 1622.

36. *The certaine newes of this present weeke*, Aug. 23, 1622; *A continuation of more newes from the Palatinate*, July 26, 1622.

37. E.g., *Two great battailes. . .*, Sept. 2, 1622; *A relation of many memorable passages*, Sept. 14, 1622. In a slightly later newsbook (*March 12 [1624]. Numero 17 Newes of Europe*) the editor specified that he had three letters sent from Brussels on March 5: one from a soldier, one from a burgher, and one from the agent of a London merchant. Usually, however, he did not have that variety of sources for a single story. For a brief discussion of the increased use of letters written by Englishmen abroad, see Hanson, "English Newsbooks," p. 380.

38. For further details see Shaaber, "First English Newspaper." pp. 560ff; Hanson, "English Newsbooks," pp. 368ff; and Dahl, *Bibliography*, pp. 86f.

39. Of the twelve extant newspapers published by Archer between September 1624 and August 1628 I have seen only four, all of them similar to the contemporaneous sheets put out by Butter and Bourne. One number (*A certaine and perfect relation*, Nov. 1625) provides a graphic account of some of the vicissitudes involved in getting out the news: if storms did not interfere with the cross-Channel posts, there were always the pirates who operated out of Dunkirk. For further details see Shaaber, "First English Newspaper," pp. 560–563, and Dahl, *Bibliography*, pp. 86f. Sometime in 1624, too, one Thomas Locke set up a scheme for the establishment of an official English newsbook (Williams, *English Journalism*, pp. 23f), but apparently nothing came of it.

40. *Novem. 7. 1622. Numb. 6. A coranto; Novemb. 21. 1622. Numb. 8. The continuation of the former newes.*

41. C. H. Herford and Percy Simpson in their edition of *Ben Jonson* identify Gainsford with "the Captain" in *The Staple of News* and thence with the editor of the first numbered series of newsbooks (Vol. II, pp. 173–175). See also Shaaber, "First English Newspaper," pp. 578f. The case for Gainsford is strengthened by a handbook he wrote on how to compose certain kinds of letters (*The Secretaries Study*, 1616), the last twenty pages of which consist of "Letters of Newes." These "Letters" display a competent hand as well as a nose for news.

42. *Novemb. 16. 1622. Numb. 7. A continuation of the newes of this present weeke.* For a similar comment, this time directed at the continental journals, see *January the 31. Numb. 16. Weekely newes.*

43. *Aug. 29. Numb. 46. Ital: Gazet. Nu. prio. More newes from Europe.*

44. *October 2. Number 50 Our last newes;* and *Aprill 17. Numb. 26. The continuation of our former newes.*

45. See, for instance, *Aprill 24. Numb. 28. The continuation of our former newes,* where Amsterdam was referred to as "that Mart of newes." At least two numbers in this series (18 and 19) included several pages still in Dutch.

46. E.g., *May 26, 1623. Numb. 33. A relation of Count Mansfeilds last proceedings; Feb. 28. Numb. 20. The newes of forraine parts.*

47. E.g., *May 30. Number 34. The last newes.*

48. Dahl, *Bibliography*, p. 114.

49. Herford and Simpson, *Ben Jonson*, II, 175, note 2.

50. Here is one such typical reply:
"Gentle Reader: By this time I hope your selves will justify my simplicity or innocency, that I acquaint you with nothing but what is extracted out of true and credible Originals; that is to say, either Letters of justifiable information, or Corantos published in other Countries . . . and these you know are either publiquely brought over by the posts from Amsterdam and Antwerp, or privately sent to such friends and Gentlemen as do correspond with understanding men in forraigne parts. . . . I will still keepe my selfe within the same limitation, and . . . will proceede to give you the same satisfaction which you your selves confesse you received. . ." (*Decemb. 13. Number 7. Weekly Newes from Germanie*).
See also, for example, Gainsford's opening remarks in *February 24. Number 14. The affaires and generall businesse of Europe,* and in *July 3. Numb. 30. Late newes or true relations;* and *Aprill 20. Numero 21. The newes of Europe.*

51. *Novemb. 20. Numb. 4. The affaires of Italy.*

52. *March 19. Numero 18. Newes from Europe.*

53. E.g., *Septemb. 11. Numb. 32. The continuation of the weekely newes;* and *Decem. 4. Numb. 43. The continuation of our weekly newes,* which included one paragraph from France on the marriage of Prince Charles, and, on the last page, a list of English soldiers drafted to help Count Mansfield — one of the very rare items of home news to appear in an early newspaper.

54. *September 16. Number 33. The continuation of the weekly news.* (The "advertisement" is given in full in Dahl, *Bibliography*, p. 125.) In an earlier number (*April 21* [*1623*], *Numb. 27. The continuation of our weekely newes*) had appeared what might, with a slight stretching of the imagination, be considered an advertisement: a reference by Butter and Bourne to a book they were bringing out which would supplement the news in that issue of the paper. Early in 1625 a more obvious advertisement appeared, a notice of a pamphlet describing Charles's marriage to Henrietta Maria (*Februar. 1. Numb. 6. The continuation of our weekly newes*). It is this notice which James Playsted Wood in *The Story of Advertising*, p. 32, credits with being the first advertisement, and which Roger P. McCutcheon claims was the first book advertisement to appear in a newspaper ("The Beginnings of Book-Reviewing in English Periodicals," p. 698).

55. Similarly, though considerably earlier, Bishop Hall in 1605 had used "Mercurius Gallobelgicus" as a pseudonym in publishing his satire *Mundus Alter et Idem* (Shaaber, "First English Newspaper," p. 564).

56. Herford and Simpson, *Ben Jonson*, II, 169.

57. For details concerning both the threats and actualities of censorship from 1621 to 1632 see Siebert, *Freedom of the Press*, pp. 153–156; and for the recurrent harassments of Butter, Bourne, and Archer, see William A. Jackson, *Records of the Court of The Stationers' Company, 1602 to 1640, passim*.

58. "Two-pence a Sheet" was mentioned in Jonson's *The Staple of News*, Act I, scene v, line 65. Also, a surviving copy of *The continuation of our weekely newes* for June 8, 1627, has written in the margin on page 10 in a contemporary hand the figure "2d" (Dahl, *Bibliography*, p. 153). Five years later, *The Continuation of our Swedish intelligence*, Sept. 1, 1632, has the figure "3d" written on the title page, also in a contemporary hand (Dahl, *Bibliography*, p. 214).

59. See especially the data on book-printing costs for this period in Marjorie Plant, *The English Book Trade: An Economic History of the Making and Sale of Books*, pp. 220f.

60. *Ibid.*, pp. 221f.

61. *July 16* [*1630*]. *Numb. 9. The continuation of the most remarkable occurrences*, quoted in Dahl, *Bibliography*, pp. 167f.

62. *November 19* [*1628*]. *Num. 22. The continuation of our weekly newes.* For the full story of this failure see Vol. VI in Gardiner's *History of England*.

63. Dahl, *Bibliography*, p. 182, and the brief article on Watts in *The Dictionary of National Biography* (hereafter cited as *DNB*).

64. E.g., *Septemb. 2* [*1631*]. *Numb. 37. The continuation of our forraine avisoes.*

65. E.g., *Novemb. 9* [*1631*]. *Numb. 46. The continuation of our weekely newes; November 22* [*1631*]. *Numb. 49. The continuation of our weekly avisoes; September 1* [*1632*]. *Numb. 42. The continuation of our weekely avisoes; September 4* [*1632*]. *The continuation of our Swedish . . . newes.*

66. Siebert, *Freedom of the Press*, p. 155, and his "Regulation of the Press in the Seventeenth Century — Excerpts from the Records of the Court of the Stationers' Company," pp. 383f. The full story of this ban is given in Dahl, "Amsterdam — Cradle," pp. 173–175; Siebert, *Freedom of the Press*, p. 156, points out, however, that the order came from the King's Council, not from Star Chamber.

67. Dahl, "Amsterdam — Cradle," pp. 176f; Siebert, *Freedom of the Press*, p. 157.

68. Siebert, *Freedom of the Press*, pp. 157–159.

69. Dahl, *Bibliography*, p. 280.

70. The thirteen numbers of this potential magazine bear the following titles and dates:
The Swedish Intelligencer, The First Part, Jan. 1632.
The Swedish Intelligencer, The Second Part, July 1632.

The Swedish Intelligencer, The Third Part, Feb. 1633.
The Swedish Intelligencer, The Fourth Part, Feb. 1633.
The Continuation of the German History, The Fifth Part, Oct. 1633.
The History of the present Warres of Germany, A Sixt Part, June 1634.
German History Continued, The Seventh Part, Nov. 1634.
The Modern History of the World, The eighth part, Nov. 1635.
Numb. 1. The Principall Passages of Germany, Italy, France. . . , Feb. 1636.
The Continuation Of The Actions, Passages, and Occurrences. . . , Apr. 1637.
Diatelesma. Nu. 3. The Moderne History of the Worlde. . . , Oct. 1637.
Diatelesma. The Second part of the Moderne History of the World, 1638.
Diatelesma: The Fifth Part Or Number, Feb. 1639.

Watts seems to have been an adequate editor, and Miss Wedgwood several times cites him in her *Thirty Years War*. In places, too, he anticipated the military analyst of the Hanson Baldwin variety. (For a brief discussion of Watts as a writer on military affairs, see Joseph J. Mathews, *Reporting the Wars*, pp. 34–36, 261–265.) Finally, as Shaaber points out ("First English Newspaper," pp. 583f), this series is interesting, for it shows that "what was intolerable to the government once a week seems to have been unobjectionable twice a year."

71. Siebert, *Freedom of the Press*, pp. 158f; and Shaaber, "First English Newspaper," p. 584. The first number Butter and Bourne then issued (December 20, 1638) was a book rather than a newspaper, since it consisted of ninety-six pages of accumulated stories. If one does consider it a newspaper, it was the first in England to be illustrated, for on page 9 is a picture of a volcano erupting in mid-ocean.

72. Siebert, *Freedom of the Press*, pp. 142, 159.

73. *Cent. 3. Numb. 48. The continuation of the forraine occurrents.* This passage is also given in Dahl, *Bibliography*, p. 251, and in Siebert, *Freedom of the Press*, p. 160.

74. For instance, on January 1, 1639, they issued four separate four-page newspapers, each with a different title and each containing different items of news.

75. *Century 3. Numb. 20. The newes for this week from Norimberg, Frankford, and Holland*, quoted in Dahl, *Bibliography*, pp. 246f.

76. *The continuation of the most remarkable passages*, June 4, 1642, also quoted in Dahl, *Bibliography*, p. 265.

77. *The most remarkable passages from most parts of Christendome*, May 1642, p. 50. The phrase was used in connection with a story from Dunkirk that mentioned the rebellion in Ireland.

78. *Britanicus Vapulans*, no. 1, Oct. 27–Nov. 4, 1643.

79. Plomer, *Dictionary*, p. 41.

80. *A continuation of more news from the Palatinate*, July 26, 1622.

81. To cite only an early and a late example of these horrifying vignettes, see *May 7, 1623. Numb. 30. A relation of the Duke of Brunswicks march* and *The ordinary weekly curranto from Holland*, May 22, 1639.

82. See, for example, *July 29. [1623] Numb. 42. More newes of the . . . Duke of Brunswicke* (as well as the next two numbers in this series); *Decemb. 13 [1623]. Number 7. Weekely newes from Germanie*; and *Novem. 15 [1624]. Numb. 41. The continuation of our weekly newes.*

83. *October 20 [1631]. Numb. 44. The continuation of our late avisoes.*

84. E.g., *Aprill 14 [1625]. Numb. 17. The continuation of our weekely newes.*

85. Roughly one-tenth of these early newspapers contained some sort of apparition, vision, or monstrous-birth item. The most remarkable Swiss cow comes from *The most remarkable passages*, May 1642.

86. *Aprill 28 [1632]. Numb. 20. The continuation of our forraine avisoes.*

87. *Aprill 14 [1632]. Numb. 18. The continuation of our forraine avisoes.*

88. *Septemb. 19 [1631]. Numb. 39. The continuation of our forreine newes.*

89. *The suprisall of two Imperial townes,* July 19, 1622; *Febru. 8* [*1625*]. *Numb. 7. The continuation of our weekely newes; July 4* [*1623*]. *Numb. 38. The relation of our last newes.*

90. *Numb. 72. The ordinary weekely curranto from Holland,* May 27, 1639; e.g., *Novemb. 28* [*1622*]. *Numb. 9. Briefe abstracts out of diverse letters of trust; A true relation of the proceedings,* July 11, 1622.

II

THE FIRST ENGLISH NEWSPAPERS
November 1641 to January 1643

Bibliographical Note: My evidence for this chapter is based on a reading of almost every newspaper that appeared between November 1641 and January 1643. Because Thomason missed collecting a few in this period, my total is a trifle larger than the 171 separate issues of newspapers which the *Catalogue of the Thomason Collection* lists for 1641 and 1642. For the historical background of the 1640's the four volumes of Gardiner's *History of the Great Civil War, 1642–1649,* are, I think, still unsurpassed, though C. V. Wedgwood's *The King's Peace, 1637–1641,* and *The King's War, 1641–1647,* are well-written supplements. So, too, is J. H. Hexter's *The Reign of King Pym,* and his analysis of the political maneuverings in the Long Parliament during the first two years of the Civil War is extremely enlightening. Wallace Notestein and Francis Relf, in their critical edition of the *Commons Debates for 1629,* have provided much information on the immediate ancestry of the newspaper concerned with English news.

1. See, for instance, Godfrey Davies, *The Early Stuarts 1603–1660,* p. 22, and Gardiner, *History of England,* IV, 117f.

2. I have been unable to find any conclusive evidence for the existence of such newsletters prior to 1628. But Ben Jonson in his *News from the New World,* probably produced in 1620, possibly in 1621, has the "Factor of News" boast of the 1,000 to 1,200 letters of news he sends out each week. Even if we discount Jonson almost entirely, he does suggest that the professional newsletter writer was off to a relatively large-scale start.

3. Notestein and Relf, pp. xx–xxii, lii–liii.

4. *Ibid.,* p. xxxii.

5. *Ibid.,* pp. xxxiv–xxxv.

6. *Ibid.,* p. xxxvi.

7. *Ibid.,* pp. xvii, xlii–xliii.

8. Three bits of evidence, among many, for this statement are the large rise during 1641 in the number of printed Parliamentary speeches, the increased circulation of inexpensive pamphlets which contained several speeches by one man or the reports of certain Parliamentary committees, and a variety of pamphlets attacking any discussion of current events.

9. Siebert, *Freedom of the Press,* pp. 165–167; Cyprian Blagden, "The Stationers' Company in the Civil War Period."

10. The first of these books was entitled *The Diurnall Occurrences, Or Dayly Proceedings of Both Houses . . . From the third of November 1640, to the third of November 1641*; the other, *Speeches and Passages Of This Great and Happy Parliament: From the third of November, 1640, to this instant June, 1641.* Though Thomason does not supply a date for their appearance, almost certainly they were published in mid-November 1641, for on November 18 the House of Commons

ordered its committee on printing to "suppress the diurnal occurrences of Parliament." The discrepancy between Parliament's professed policy and its actual practice was underlined shortly thereafter by the assertion of Sir Simonds D'Ewes on January 6, 1642, that it was "the highest treacherie . . . for any member of that howse [of Commons] to witnes or reveale what was done or spoken in that howse" — an assertion that appeared in a speech which D'Ewes then had printed and circulated. (For further details, see Willson Coates, ed., *The Journal of Sir Simonds D'Ewes From the First Recess of the Long Parliament to the Withdrawal of King Charles from London*, p. xxi.) The impending publication of *Speeches and Passages* was also noted unfavorably by Parliament, in this case in June 1641 (*The Journals of the House of Commons*, II, 168). A third book of relevance to the English newspaper also came out in November 1641: a *Diurnall occurrences* covering the activities of the 1629 Parliament.

11. The three papers which were competing with each other by the third week in December were: *Diurnall Occurrences, Or The heads of severall proceedings in both Houses of Parliament*, published by John Thomas and Thomas Bates; *The Diurnall, Or, The Heads Of All the Proceedings in Parliament*, published by John Wright; and *The Diurnall Occurrances; Or, The Heads of Proceedings in Parliament*, published by Thomas Bates and Francis Coles. Of these, the first was moderately accurate, the latter two somewhat garbled and very similar. In the case of these and all subsequent newspapers I am following their own imprints in determining who was the publisher and who the printer, except in those rare instances where there is conclusive evidence contradicting the imprint. Thus when a weekly was printed *for* X, X was the publisher; when it was printed *by* X, X was the printer. (See also W. W. Greg, *Some Aspects and Problems of London Publishing between 1550 and 1650*, p. 85).

12. Other weeks in early journalistic history are equally confusing. *A Presse full of Pamphlets*, a satire on the pamphlets and newsbooks of the day, claimed in April 1642 that a single week could "at one prodigious birth" produce fifteen different newspapers.

13. John Thomas' *Diurnall Occurrences*, no. 6, Feb. 7–14, 1642, contains the only newspaper reference to anyone's being officially questioned at this time for printing the weekly news.

14. *Commons Journals*, II, 324, 387, 402; William M. Clyde, "Parliament and the Press, 1643–7," pp. 399–401; and Coates, *D'Ewes*, p. xx. The two issues of *A Continuation of the true Diurnall of Passages in Parliament*, no. 11, Mar. 21–28, 1642, contained references to this action by the House of Commons, but provided few details and no comment. Earlier, two numbers of *The True Diurnal Occurrances* (Jan. 31–Feb. 7 and Feb. 7–14, 1642) had indicated on their title pages that they were licensed, but in neither case do the initials of the man by whom that number was "averred" seem to belong to any official licenser.

15. Siebert, *Freedom of the Press*, p. 205; *Commons Journals*, II, 500f.

16. For further details, see Stanley Morison, *The English Newspaper — Some Account of the Physical Development of Journals Printed in London between 1622 and the Present Day*, pp. 14–24.

17. Williams, *English Journalism*, p. 36; *Tercentenary Handlist*, p. 21; and Howard Robinson, *The British Post Office, a History*, pp. 29f.

18. Henry R. Plomer, "An Analysis of the Civil War Newspaper 'Mercurius Civicus,' " p. 187. Statements in many papers of the 1640's confirm Plomer's figure of a penny.

19. See, for instance, Sir William Beveridge, and others, *Prices and Wages in England from the Twelfth to the Nineteenth Century*, I, 163–165.

20. For instance, two papers for March 21–28, 1642, both labeled "Numb. 11," were identical except for minor typographical variations: *Diurnall Occurrences in Parliament* and *A Perfect Diurnall of the Passages in Parliament*. Here and in

earlier instances there was either blatant plagiarism or the control of a single person. Note also the interchange of titles as shown in Appendix B.

21. For further details see Coates, *D'Ewes*, p. 406.

22. *Diurnall Occurrances in Parliament* (William Cooke), Jan. 2–10, 1642. For the full dramatic story of this royal fiasco, see Gardiner, *History of England*, X, 107–151.

23. *Diurnall Occurrences: Or The Heads of severall Proceedings* (Butter and Thomas), Jan. 3–10, 1642.

24. For an early example see *The Diurnall Occurrances: Or, The Heads of Proceedings in Parliament* (Bates and Coles), Dec. 13–20, 1641. This number included a report on Irish atrocities and a summary of a speech by Pym in which he charged that the Irish called themselves "The Queenes Army." See also Wedgwood, *King's War*, p. 54.

25. *A Continuation Of The True Diurnall Occurrences in Parliament*, Jan. 10–24, 1642; e.g., *The Diurnall, Or The Heads Of All the Proceedings in Parliament* (Wright), Dec. 20–26, 1641; *A Perfect Diurnall of the Passages in Parliament*, Feb. 21–28, 1642; *A Perfect Diurnall of the Passages in Parliament* (Cooke), no. 10, March 14–21, 1642; and *A True Diurnall of the Passages in Parliament*, March 14–21, 1642.

26. The first English newspaper to be concerned with home news referred to the fact that London crowds had offered to "attend" the House of Commons, and almost without exception every newspaper between then and March 1642 contained at least one story having to do with a pro-Parliament petition. Some of these petitions were allegedly signed by thousands, a fact which no doubt increased their value as news, and one from Salop claimed 10,000 signatures (*A Perfect Diurnall of the Passages in Parliament*, no. 9, Mar. 7–14, 1642). Also, one newspaper (*The True Diurnall Occurrences*, Jan. 31–Feb. 7, 1642) mentioned three women's petitions to Parliament, the first reference I know of to organized female political activity during the Civil War period.

27. *A Presse full of Pamphlets*, 1642, Sig. A3.

28. *A Fresh Whip For all scandalous Lyars*, 1647, p. 2. There are brief biographies of Pecke in Williams, *English Journalism*, pp. 38f, and in Wilbur C. Abbott, "The First Newspapermen," pp. 40f. See also *Journals of The House of Lords*, V, 533.

29. *A Fresh Whip*. p. 3.

30. Siebert, *Freedom of the Press*, p. 186; and *A Transcript of the Registers of the Worshipful Company of Stationers; From 1640–1708 A.D.*, I, 59.

31. Siebert, *Freedom of the Press*, pp. 205f.

32. Hexter, *Reign of Pym*, pp. 31–99; Gardiner, *History of England*, X, 169f, and *Great Civil War*, I, 9–19.

33. By October 1642 almost every issue of every newspaper contained at least one reference to Royalist atrocities, and by the end of the year the name of Prince Rupert had appeared often enough to make him a bogey man to the London public.

34. *A Continuation of certain Speciall and Remarkable Passages*, 23, Dec. 12–15, 1642.

35. *A Perfect Diurnall Of the Passages in Parliament* (William Cooke), 23, Nov. 13–20, 1642.

36. Charles almost certainly had nothing to do with *A Diurnall and Particular*. But despite his political ineptitude, he did have some awareness of the need for favorable publicity, and he was periodically concerned with having a sympathetic printing press under his direct control. Thus, late in 1642 the royal press was moved from Shrewsbury to Oxford. (See, for instance, *England's Memorable Accidents*, Dec. 19–26, 1642, p. 125.)

37. The following is a chronological list of the newspapers from June to

December 1642 which apparently lasted only one number, exclusive of papers named *A Perfect Diurnall.* (For the bibliography of this interlocking series of newspapers, see Appendix C.)

Remarkable Passages in Parliament, May 30–June 6.
True Intelligence from Ireland, June 9–20.
A true and perfect Diurnall Of all the chiefe passages in Lancashire, July 2–9.
A Currant, July 12.
A Diurnall and Particular of The last Weekes daily Occurents, July 16–26.
Some Speciall Passages From Hull, Anlaby, and Yorke, Aug. 1.
Some Speciall Passages From London, Westminster, Yorke, Aug. 1–9.
A Continuation of the true Diurnall of Passages in Parliament, Aug. 8–15.
Some Speciall and considerable Passages, Aug. 9–16.
A True Relation of Certaine speciall and Remarkable Passages, Aug. 15–19.
Speciall Passages from divers parts, Aug. 16–23.
Certaine Speciall and Remarkable Passages, Aug. 22–26.
An Exact and True Diurnal, Aug. 29–Sept. 5.
A True and Perfect Diurnall Of the passages in Parliament, Aug. 29–Sept. 6.
Remarkable Passages, Or a perfect Diurnall Of . . . proceedings, Sept. 5–12.
A Perfect Relation, or Summarie, Sept. 19–29.
A Continuation of true and speciall Passages, Sept. 22–29.
Speciall and Late Passages From The Most Eminent Places, Oct. 6.
Weekly Intelligence From Severall parts (one or two numbers), Oct. 4–18.
A Collection of Speciall Passages and Certaine Informations, Oct. 17–Nov. 1.
A Continuation Of certaine Speciall and Remarkable Passages, Nov. 17–24.
A Grand Diurnall Of The Passages in Parliament, Nov. 21–28.

38. During the second half of 1642 the active printer-publishers were Humphrey Blunden, Francis Coles, Francis Leach, Thomas Cook, Walter Cook, Robert Wood, and Stephen Bowtell. Of these, usually one or two were out of the newspaper picture during any given short period.

39. As shown in Appendix C, publishers appropriated each other's numbering systems as well as titles. All this infighting did not make the competing journalists very happy. In one number of one *A Perfect Diurnall* (printed by Okes and Leach and sold by Coles, no. 28, Dec. 19–26, 1642), for instance, the publisher announced that the "Courteous Reader" should beware of "a false & counterfeit Diurnall . . . printed & fashioned . . . by a company of Grub street mercenary fellows" — while the alleged counterfeit countered with the claim that it was printed "to prevent all false copies." Two weeks later, Okes and Leach, in what was probably their final number of *A Perfect Diurnall*, included a long lament about the alleged imitation put out by Cook and Wood. In the course of this lament they asked the reader to compare the rival copies to see which was "the most approved one." This reader tried and found no significant differences. During the final months of 1642 there were many charges and countercharges concerning which was the true series of *A Perfect Diurnall*, a situation complicated by the shifting of editors from one series to another. These shifts were indicated by notices that one paper was now being edited "by the same hand that formerly drew up the Coppy" for another *Perfect Diurnall. Speciall Passages and certain Informations* also became mixed up in the game of counterfeits by claiming that Humphrey Blunden's *Speciall Passages* was not the authentic series.

40. Two early attempts at continuous pagination, one before and one after the March suppression, were *A Continuation of the true Diurnall Passages in Parliament,* which began to number its pages continuously in February 1642; and the paper which, after two numbers, stabilized its title in August as *Speciall Passages and certain Informations from several places.*

41. *A Continuation of certain Speciall and Remarkable passages,* which lasted from September 1642 to January 1643.

42. *A Collection of Speciall Passages and Certaine Informations*, Oct. 17–Nov. 1, 1642.

43. Thomas Underhill's *Special and Late Passages From the Most Eminent Places in Christendome*, Oct. 6, 1642. Other papers of the day contained bits and pieces of foreign news; but except for Butter's half-dozen efforts in 1642, Underhill's was the only one to devote itself to cross-Channel items.

44. Humphrey Blunden's *Speciall Passages From divers parts of this Kingdom*, 2, Aug. 16–23, 1642.

45. Three of the infrequent instances during 1642 in which Elsing's name appeared were *A Perfect Diurnall* (Robert Wood), July 25–Aug. 1; *A True Relation of Certaine Speciall and Remarkable Passages*, Aug. 15–19; and *Certaine Speciall and Remarkable passages*, Aug. 22–26. One additional device, if it can be called that, was the occasional arrangement of the news by place rather than chronologically: e.g., *Speciall Passages From divers parts of this Kingdom*, 2, Aug. 16–23, 1642; and *Speciall Passages and certain Informations from severall places*, 9, Oct. 4–11, 1642 — both of which papers, incidentally, normally appeared on Tuesday.

46. This phrase was part of the full title of *The Daily Intelligencer*, a run-of-the-mill paper whose only number came out on Jan. 30, 1643.

47. *Speciall Passages and certain Informations*, 4, Aug. 30–Sept. 6, 1642.

48. *A Continuation of certaine Speciall and Remarkable Passages*, Nov. 17–24, 1642.

49. *A Diurnall and Particular*, July 16–26, 1642; *England's Memorable Accidents*, Nov. 14–21, 1642, p. 83.

50. *Speciall Passages And certain Informations*, 10, Oct. 11–18, 1642; Lucy Hutchinson, *Memoirs of the Life of Colonel Hutchinson*, pp. 101f.

51. The public's desire for authentic news was also suggested by the use of such phrases as "Collected for the satisfaction of those that desire true information" and "Collected for the use of all that desire to be truly informed" in the subtitles of various papers. Note, too, the frequency of such words in newspaper titles as "true" and "perfect."

52. E.g., *England's Memorable Accidents*, Oct. 3–10, 1642, p. 38, and Nov. 7–14, 1642, pp. 74f.

53. E.g., *ibid.*, Oct. 10–17, 1642, p. 43; Dec. 26, 1642–Jan. 2, 1643, p. 133.

54. E.g., *ibid.*, Oct. 31–Nov. 7, 1642, p. 72; Nov. 21–28, 1642, p. 93; and Nov. 28–Dec. 5, 1642, p. 100.

III

CHILDHOOD
January to September 1643

Bibliographical Note: My evidence for this chapter is based on a reading of slightly more than 90 per cent of the newspapers published in England between January and September 1643. *Mercurius Aulicus*, alone among Interregnum weeklies, has rated a modern monograph: F. J. Varley's *Mercurius Aulicus*, a functional if somewhat thin summary; while *A Perfect Diurnall* has merited its own descriptive bibliography: *An Annotated Bibliography of F. Cole's [sic] "A Perfect Diurnall of Some Passages in Parliament,"* edited by Paul Radin. Plomer's article on *Mercurius Civicus* provides a brief account of England's first illustrated newspaper.

1. Gardiner, *Great Civil War*, I, 81f; Hexter, *Reign of Pym*, pp. 105–107.

2. Varley, *Aulicus*, pp. viii–ix; Plomer, *Dictionary*, p. 88.

3. Varley, *Aulicus*, p. xi. There are biographies of Birkenhead in Anthony à Wood's *Athenae Oxoniensis*, pp. 475–477, and in *DNB*. A few of Birkenhead's approximately half-dozen pamphlets are also enlightening: *Two Centuries of Pauls Church-yard* (probably written in the mid-1640's but printed in 1659) was a witty satire on the Assembly of Divines, though not so violent as his *Assembly-man* penned in 1647. Probably by Birkenhead was a tract of 1663 entitled *Cabala*, an attack on the nonconformists and a retrospective derogation of the Good Old Cause. In each of these works Birkenhead showed his mastery of the facetious, but also his tendency toward long-windedness and conspicuous exaggeration.

4. John Aubrey, *Brief Lives*, pp. 23f.

5. See, for instance, *Aulicus*, 8, Feb. 19–26, 1643, p. 97.

6. E.g., *Aulicus*, 5, Jan. 29–Feb. 5, 1643, pp. 65f.

7. Bowtell in the next-to-last number of *England's Memorable Accidents* (Jan. 2–9, 1643) had an interesting aside in which he attacked the powers held by the king of France.

8. *Speciall Passages*, 25, Jan. 24–31, 1643.

9. See, for example, Wedgwood, *King's War*, p. 162.

10. Williams, *English Journalism*, pp. 42f; Siebert, *Freedom of the Press*, p. 206; and Clyde, "Parliament and the Press," p. 405. *A Continuation*, 26, Jan. 2–6, 1643, contained the story of this petition, which it handled straightforwardly and inoffensively but without the denunciation found in most other papers.

11. E.g., *A Continuation* (Cook and Wood), 31, Feb. 9–16, 1643.

12. Williams, *English Journalism*, p. 45, names William Ingler as its editor, the only editor besides Pecke then to enter his name in the Stationers' Register.

13. Williams, *English Journalism*, p. 45. Also, starting with no. 229 (Oct. 5–12, 1647) the title page of *The Kingdomes Weekly Intelligencer* bore the phrase "Collected by R. C." Since the paper seems to have been edited by the same man throughout its long life, it is probably safe to assume that Collings was the editor from the start.

14. E.g., *Kingdomes Weekly Intelligencer* (hereafter cited as *KWI*), 5, Jan. 24–31, 1643, pp. 37, 40.

15. *Ibid.*, p. 40. In a later number (March 21–28, 1643) Collings even risked a semi-facetious headline: "William a Conquerer" — in reference to a victory won by the Parliamentary general William Waller.

16. *Ibid.*, 9 and 10, Feb. 21–Mar. 7, 1643.

17. *Ibid.*, 17, Apr. 25–May 2, 1643.

18. *Ibid.*, 16, Apr. 11–18, 1643, p. 128.

19. See, for instance, *ibid.*, 14, Mar. 28–April 4, 1643, p. 112. Almost every paper had its letter-writers, but Collings' man in Wales seems to have worked under a more regular arrangement.

20. In *A Continuation* (Cook and Wood), 37, Mar. 16–23, 1643, the editor expressed the suspicion that *Aulicus* (the "Oxford Diurnall") was being printed in London. There is overwhelming evidence to show that this was the case by September, including an allusion thereto in *Aulicus* (38, Sept. 18–25, 1643) and a note to this effect by Thomason on an October number of *Aulicus*. Falconer Madan's *Oxford Books*, II, 491, mentions that *Aulicus* was reprinted in London four times in 1643, fifteen times in 1644. (See also Milton's complaint about *Aulicus* in *Areopagitica*, Nov. 1644.) Finally, in a later newspaper — *Perfect Occurrences*, 19, May 7–14, 1647, p. 152 — there is a cryptic reference to the secret Royalist press in London on which, presumably, *Aulicus* had long before been reprinted. Except for slight differences in format and wording, those London reprints of *Aulicus* that I have seen are very close to the Oxford originals. Thus *Aulicus* was the first English newspaper to appear in two editions, discounting

those early weeklies that had one or two numbers reprinted in Edinburgh (see Appendix B).

21. One of the first of these attacks appeared in *KWI*, 16, Apr. 11–18, 1643, p. 128. Besides the newspaper replies to *Aulicus*, about a dozen pamphlets went after Birkenhead between the spring of 1643 and the summer of 1645. (These are listed in Madan, *Oxford Books*, II, 496.)

22. E.g., *Aulicus*, 15, Apr. 9–16, 1643, pp. 190f; see also no. 26, June 25–July 2, 1643.

23. *Ibid.*, 23, June 4–11, 1643, p. 307.

24. E.g., *ibid.*, 14, 19, 21, 23, 24, from early April to mid-June 1643, especially pp. 172, 239, 279, 297, 302, 314.

25. See especially *ibid.*, 23, June 4–11, 1643, pp. 297–303, where Birkenhead expressed loud alarm at Pym's threat, Marten's radicalism, and the alleged utilization of "Waller's Plot" by the war party to increase its power.

26. See, for instance, *ibid.*, 17–19, Apr. 23–May 14, 1643, *passim*. *Aulicus's* earliest references to Cromwell occurred in nos. 9 and 10, Feb. 26–Mar. 12, 1643, and one of the first mentions of him in a London weekly appeared in *A Perfect Diurnall* (Cook and Wood), 38, Feb. 27–Mar. 6, 1643.

27. In particular, see *Aulicus*, 17, Apr. 23–30, 1643, p. 210.

28. A second regular post was probably not established until late 1647. Since London was the source of almost all national news, incoming posts had little effect on the newspapers; and foreign news, being subject to the vagaries of weather, probably arrived in the metropolis on no fixed day.

29. *KWI*, 22 and 23, May 30–June 13, 1643.

30. For instance, with no. 23 (June 19–26, 1643) G. Bishop and R. White took over the printing of *Certaine Informations*; and there seems to have been some shifting of printers between the two series of *A Perfect Diurnall*.

31. Williams, *English Journalism*, pp. 47f; Siebert, *Freedom of the Press*, pp. 209, 211. In October 1643 the London Common Council took steps to suppress these hawkers.

32. *KWI*, 17, Apr. 25–May 2, 1643, p. 129.

33. See, for example, *ibid.*, 15, Apr. 4–11, 1643, pp. 117ff — where Collings displayed his knowledge of recent history in depicting the evils of the Royalist cause.

34. *Perfect Diurnall*, 53, June 12–19, 1643. For Pecke's and his publishers' release from jail see Siebert, *Freedom of the Press*, p. 206.

35. Pecke infrequently — but more than other editors at this time — called attention to items he was not printing, such as the details of an anti-Parliament plot which were "not as yet ripe for discovery."

36. *A Continuation* (Leach and Coles), 48, June 1–8, 1643.

37. The editor of *A Continuation* (Cook and Wood) in its next-to-last week (no. 44, May 4–11, 1643) referred, for instance, to a message to Parliament from the king as being a "matter too high for him to argue against," and to a decision of the Council of War involving Essex as "too deep a secret for men to pry into."

38. *Speciall Passages*, 41, May 16–23, 1643, p. 331.

39. See especially *ibid.*, 39, May 2–9, 1643, pp. 315f.

40. The first twenty-one numbers of *Mercurius Rusticus* appeared between May 20, 1643, and March 16, 1644. Four more numbers followed in the next two years, and the entire series was published in one volume in 1646. (For further bibliographical details, including the significant re-issue of this volume in 1685, see Anthony J. Gabler, *Check List of English Newspapers and Periodicals before 1801 in the Huntington Library*, p. 29.) Bruno Ryves, the editor, was a clergyman, and after the Restoration he became Dean of Windsor (Williams, *English Journalism*, p. 45). One number of a paper with the same title appeared in October 1643: written by George Wither, it was not pro-Royalist. Mention

should also be made of a single-issue paper of foreign news, *A Coranto from beyond Sea*, June 9, 1643. It is interesting in that its last paragraph recommended the blocking of the mouth of the Elbe by the English navy in order to prevent Danish aid from getting to the Royalists. To underline this recommendation, the editor dedicated his paper to the Earl of Warwick, the admiral of the Parliamentary fleet, thus making *A Coranto* the only Interregnum newspaper to be equipped with a formal dedication.

41. The first picture was of the queen, who was prominent in that week's news. No. 11, Aug. 3–11, 1643, contained a woodcut illustration on page 4: a picture, which had previously appeared on the title page, of a spiked weapon called a "Round-head." With one possible exception (see above, Chapter I, note 71), this was the first picture to appear in the text of an English newspaper.

42. E.g., *Civicus*, 5, June 8–16, 1643, p. 40, where the editor went after *Speciall Passages*.

43. Williams, *English Journalism*, p. 44, mentions Collings as the editor of *Civicus*, though he supplies no supporting evidence.

44. Clyde, "Parliament and the Press," pp. 400f.

45. Siebert, *Freedom of the Press*, p. 206.

46. Williams, *English Journalism*, pp. 44f.

47. Clyde, "Parliament and the Press," pp. 401f; Williams, *English Journalism*, pp. 44–46; Siebert, *Freedom of the Press*, pp. 186–188, 207. The full act is given in C. H. Firth and R. S. Rait, *Acts and Ordinances of the Interregnum, 1642–1660*, I, 184–187. The first licenser for "small Pamphlets," the category which included newspapers, was Henry Walley, the Clerk of the Stationers' Company.

48. E.g., *Perfect Diurnall*, 5 and 6, July 24–Aug. 7, 1643, and 9, Sept. 11–18, 1643; for the Battle of Newbury, see no. 10, Sept. 18–25, 1643, pp. 79f.

49. *Ibid.*, 9, Sept. 11–18, 1643, p. 72.

50. *Ibid.*, 7, Aug. 28–Sept. 4, 1643, p. 52. No. 9, Sept. 11–18, 1643, p. 70, did, however, contain a bit of what might be considered skillful propaganda: a warning to the French not to aid the Royalists, partly because of the attendant dangers of another Protestant revolt in France.

51. *Ibid.*, 4, July 17–24, 1643, p. 25; 10, Sept. 18–25, p. 73.

52. *KWI*, 31, Nov. 7–14, 1643, p. 235.

53. *Civicus*, 12, Aug. 11–17, 1643, p. 93; 18, Sept. 21–28, 1643, p. 143. During October these pro-Presbyterian indications became a little more marked and frequent.

54. *Ibid.*, 9, July 20–28, 1643, p. 66; e.g., 7, July 6–13, 1643, pp. 51, 53.

55. At least two numbers of a paper probably representing a continuation of *Speciall Passages* and called *Wednesday's Mercury* came out during July and August. The first, dated July 19, 1643, is interesting in that it contained a notice that those who wished to sign a petition in favor of militant prosecution of the war come to the hall of the Merchant Tailors. The second extant issue (no. 4, Aug. 2, 1643) had this apologetic self-advertisement: ". . . our tyred post having . . . a bad horse, is not able to give you his intelligence so soone as others, but although he comes last, yet by going and riding softly, he heares, sees, and observes what many times others for hast[e] omit. . . ." Yet there is no evidence in either number that the editor had any inside information, and presumably then as now old news was not very salable.

56. *A Continuation*, 51, July 20–27, 1643.

57. For a fuller discussion of this aspect of the Interregnum, see Frank, *Levellers*, pp. 256f.

58. G. E. Manwaring, "Journalism in the Days of the Commonwealth," pp. 105ff.

59. *The Parliaments Scouts Discovery*, June 9–15, 1643, immediately preceded *The Parliament Scout* and was thus, in a sense, its first number. Probably also

edited by Dillingham, it concentrated on military news and was distinguished by many heavy-handed personal transitions as well as by a fancy title page.

60. *Parliament Scout*, 2, June 29–July 6, 1643, p. 12.

61. See, for instance, *ibid.*, 3, July 6–13, 1643, p. 19.

62. E.g., *ibid.*, 6, July 27–Aug. 3, 1643, p. 41; and the graphic account of the death in battle of the Marquis de Vivelle in no. 14, Sept. 22–29, 1643, pp. 105ff.

63. *Ibid.*, 7, Aug. 3–10, 1643, p. 50; 8, Aug. 10–17, 1643, p. 63; and 7, p. 55. The women's petition was treated very differently in contemporary issues of, for instance, *Mercurius Civicus* and *Certaine Informations*. The latter is worth quoting as a stirring example of seventeenth-century antifeminism aroused by the spectacle of women having the gall to interfere in politics: "Yesterday in the afternoone, two or three hundred Oyster wives, and other dirty and tattered sluts, tooke upon them the impudency to come to the Honourable House of Commons, and cried for Peace and Propositions, and they so filled the staires that no man could passe up or downe, whereupon a man upon the top of the staires drew his sword, and with the flat side strook some of them upon the heads, which so affrighted them that they presently made way and ran downe . . ." (no. 30, Aug. 7–14, 1643, p. 231).

64. *Parliament Scout*, 3, July 6–13, 1643, p. 21.

65. *Ibid.*, 4, July 13–20, 1643, p. 25.

66. It was immediately preceded by two similarly titled papers, though there seems to be no direct connection between them and *The Weekly Account*: *A Weekly Accompt*, one number only, July 3–10, 1643, published by Robert Wood and John Greensmith; and *A Weekly Accompt*, one number only, July 27–Aug. 3, 1643, published by Bernard Alsop. At the start Border's weekly was published by Philip Lane, then in May 1644 Alsop took over.

67. *Weekly Account*, 1, Sept. 6, 1643, p. 1. See also the concluding paragraphs of no. 2.

68. E.g., *Aulicus*, 26, June 25 July 2, 1643, p. 344; 30, July 23–30, 1643, p. 406; and 36, Sept. 3–10, 1643, p. 502.

69. E.g., *ibid.*, 39, Sept. 25–Oct. 1, 1643, p. 543; and 34, Aug. 21–28, 1643, p. 458, where Birkenhead claimed that there were then only sixty in attendance at the House of Commons.

70. *Ibid.*, 28, July 9–16, 1643, pp. 371ff; 36, Sept. 3–10, 1643, p. 501. (The letter from the soldier's wife is given in Varley, *Aulicus*, pp. 51f.)

IV

EARLY ADOLESCENCE I
September 1643 to July 1644

Bibliographical Note: Here and subsequently my account is based on a reading of more than 95 per cent of the English newspapers published within the period covered by each chapter.

1. The title page of the first number proclaimed that it was licensed; and it was entered in the Stationers' Register on September 5, 1643. In February 1645 it was re-entered under the sponsorship of Essex, and shortly thereafter, though Essex was now dead, it was still published "by warrant from the late Lord General." (For further details see Clyde, "Parliament and the Press," p. 416.) It seems likely that Essex's connection with *Britanicus* long predated 1645 and extended back to the paper's founding.

2. *The Spie*, 4, Feb. 13–20, 1644, p. 32. The case for the multiple authorship

of early numbers of *Britanicus* is corroborated by internal evidence, and hinted at in subsequent official investigations of the paper.

3. *Mercurius Anti-Britanicus*, 3, *ca.* Aug. 18, 1645, p. 23.

4. *Ibid.* See also Williams, *English Journalism*, pp. 53f.

5. Clyde, "Parliament and the Press," pp. 418f. Shortly after his service as a deputy licenser Audley got back into journalism by editing *Mercurius Diutinus* (November 1646 to January 1647). During 1644 he probably contributed some pieces to *KWI.*

6. There are articles on Nedham in the *DNB* and Wood's *Athenae Oxonienses.*

7. *Mercurius Anti-Britanicus*, 3, *ca.* Aug. 18, 1645, p. 25.

8. *Ibid.*

9. Wood, *Athenae Oxonienses*, III, 1180.

10. *Mercurius Britanicus* (hereafter cited as *Brit.*), 4, Sept. 12–19, 1643, p. 25.

11. *Ibid.*, 4 and 5, Sept. 12–26, 1643, pp. 26, 35.

12. E.g., *ibid.*, 5, 6, 8, Sept. 19–Oct. 3, Oct. 10–17, 1643, *passim.*

13. *Ibid.*, 4, Sept. 12–19, 1643, p. 28.

14. A good case can be made for the fact that shortly after Pym's death both the war party and the Independents rapidly gained in strength. (See, for instance, George Yule, *The Independents in the English Civil War*, pp. 30, 44.) Pym's death was not, of course, the cause of this shift in power, but the absence of his restraining hand — a hand remarkably like that wielded by Lyndon Johnson in the United States Senate during the 1950's — undoubtedly helped to accelerate the change.

15. This number of *Brit.* (Dec. 7–14, 1643) called forth a reply from John Taylor entitled *Mercurius Aquaticus; Or, The Water-Poets Answer To All That Hath or shall be Writ by Mercurius Britanicus* (reprinted in *Works of John Taylor, the Water Poet*, Vol. V). Taylor first reprinted this sixteenth number of *Brit.*, then refuted it item by item, concluding with, "And so having cost my Reader halfe an hower, and my selfe an afternoone . . . I leave you as I found you, fit only to write verses on the Death of Mr. Pym." *Brit.*, 21, Jan. 29–Feb. 5, 1644, contained a reply to Taylor.

16. *Aulicus*, 49, Dec. 3–10, 1643, p. 703. Actually Pym died of cancer of the lower bowel (Wedgwood, *King's War*, p. 277).

17. E.g., *Aulicus*, 42, Oct. 15–22, 1643, pp. 590, 595.

18. E.g., *ibid.*, 43, Oct. 22–29, 1643, p. 601.

19. *Ibid.*, 51, Dec. 10–17, 1643, p. 722; *Brit.*, 19, Dec. 28, 1643–Jan. 4, 1644, p. 145.

20. See his opening remarks in *KWI*, 31, Nov. 7–14, 1643.

21. *Ibid.*, 35, Dec. 5–12, 1643, p. 273, where Collings hoped that the English Parliament, like the Scot Parliament, would make an example of those who refused to sign the Covenant.

22. E.g., *Perfect Diurnall*, 16, Oct. 30–Nov. 6, 1643, p. 123.

23. *Ibid.*, 17, Nov. 6–13, 1643, p. 131.

24. *Ibid.*, 12, Oct. 2–9, 1643, p. 96.

25. E.g., *ibid.*, p. 91; 23, Dec. 25, 1643–Jan. 1, 1644, p. 183.

26. See, for instance, *Civicus*, 19, Sept. 28–Oct. 6, 1643, p. 146 (the editor's vigorous support of the Covenant); 23, Oct. 26–Nov. 2, 1643, pp. 181f (his boost of another new book by Prynne).

27. E.g., *ibid*, 21, Oct 12–19, 1643, p. 165; 24, Nov. 2–9, 1643, p. 185; 25, Nov. 9–16, 1643, pp. 193f.; 27, Nov. 23–30, 1643, p. 309; 30, Dec. 14–21, 1643, p. 334; and subsequent numbers in 1644.

28. *Parliament Scout*, 24, Dec. 1–9, 1643, p. 210.

29. E.g., *ibid.*, 20, Nov. 3–10, 1643, p. 174; 26, Dec. 15–22, 1643, p. 223.

30. *Ibid.*, 20, Nov. 3–10, 1643, p. 177; 26, Dec. 15–22, 1643, pp. 219f. Though in

a later aside (no. 36, Feb. 23–Mar. 1, 1644, p. 307) Dillingham said that he was not a soldier, he may once have seen military service.

31. *Ibid.*, 24, Dec. 1–8, 1643, p. 203.

32. *Weekly Account*, 7, Oct. 11–18, 1643.

33. Its apparently irregular appearance during the summer of 1643 may have been the result of Thomason's failure, for a rare change, to collect all the newspapers of his day. *The Catalogue of the Thomason Collection* has no entries for *Certaine Informations* between mid-July and mid-October. The Sutro Collection, however, has three numbers from this period, and Harvard has four — two of which are duplicates of the Sutro items. Probably *Certaine Informations* came out with something less than weekly regularity during these three months.

34. E.g., *Certaine Informations*, 35, Sept. 11–18, 1643, p. 271, where the editor "proved" God's dislike of the Royalists by telling how many Cavaliers were sick; and 42, Oct. 30–Nov. 6, 1643, p. 327, where the editor claimed that at Oxford it was treason to be against Popery.

35. Appropriately enough, *The Kingdomes Weekly Post* carried on its title page a woodcut of a postman blowing his own horn.

36. Williams, *English Journalism*, p. 51.

37. *True Informer*, 11, Nov. 25–Dec. 1, 1643, p. 82. See also the opening paragraph of no. 7, Oct. 28–Nov. 4, 1643.

38. *Perfect Diurnall*, 20, Nov. 27–Dec. 4, 1643, p. 159; *True Informer*, 12, Dec. 2–9, 1643, p. 96.

39. For Smith's account of Smith, see the final issue of *The Scotish Dove*, unnumbered and undated, but picked up by Thomason in December 1646.

40. This first number was entitled *The Scottish Mercury*, but the opening remarks of *The Scotish Dove* of the following week (no. 1, Oct. 13–20, 1643) repeated the same sentiments. The *Cambridge Bibliography of English Literature*, I, 755, lists a paper entitled *The Scotch Intelligencer*, which may or may not have appeared for two weeks in October 1643.

41. As early examples see *Scotish Dove*, 5, Nov. 10–17, 1643, pp. 34–37; and 7, Nov. 24–Dec. 1, 1643, pp. 49f.

42. This clause is from *Scotish Dove*, 7, Nov. 24–Dec. 1, 1643, p. 49, but the opening, in its entirety, of the fourth number expressed the same purpose.

43. *Ibid.*, 9, Dec. 8–15, 1643, p. 66.

44. The opening paragraph of its only issue (Oct. 7, 1643) is a fine example of Smith's sanctimoniousness:
"Christian Reader, I spoke to thee in these godly notions towards the end of thy weeke, hopeing thou wilt be at leasure after reading the daily stories to thinke and observe with me; I can allow thee to turne thy selfe from one Diurnall to another, and to weary thy selfe, and refresh thy selfe with the witt and relations of all; only in a Christian regard to thy condition and the time, spare one serious thought to looke backe upon all, and see the worke of a Diviner hand."

45. Williams, *English Journalism*, p. 56.

46. Such queries and answers were commonplace in the pamphlets of the period, though new to the newspaper.

47. *Britanicus Vapulans*, 1, Oct. 27–Nov. 4, 1643; continued for a second number as *Mercurius Urbanus*, Nov. ?, 1643. For a brief discussion of the first number see Ernest Sirluck, "Shakespeare and Jonson among the Pamphleteers of the First Civil War: Some Unreported Seventeenth-Century Allusions," pp. 91f. *Vapulans* was merely one of many attacks, in pamphlets and newspapers and coming from several political directions, that then began to criticize *Britanicus* for its alleged excesses and improprieties.

48. For further details see the opening statement of its only number, Nov. 3, 1643.

49. These three numbers covered the period from Oct. 21 to Nov. 11, 1643.

50. Also, *The Scotish Dove*, 23, Mar. 15–22, 1644, p. 177, referred to certain readers "who *possibly* reads [*sic*] not many other Relations of this kind" (my italics).

51. See in particular Norman G. Brett-James, *The Growth of Stuart London*, pp. 495–515. One of the rare contemporary references to London's population was a statement in *The Moderate Intelligencer*, 100, Jan. 28–Feb. 4. 1647, p. 900, that the number of people within the so-called line of communication was 60,000. But this is also inconclusive in regard to any accurate total for greater London.

52. There are also no hard figures on the literacy rate in the mid-seventeenth century. Albert C. Baugh's *History of the English Language*, p. 246, estimates that from one-third to one-half of the adults in the London of Shakespeare's time could read. Almost certainly this percentage was higher in the 1640's.

53. *Mercurius Elencticus*, 29, June 7–14, 1648, p. 222, has the following aside, the only instance I know of in which a fairly precise circulation figure is given: "But John Hall appears againe under the name of Brittanicus, in a fourth number (the third I never saw, for there were but 200. in all printed for his own use, which he ran a begging with amongst the Members) . . . ." Since the context of this aside is derogatory, and since the *Brittanicus* here referred to was a short-run revival of a strongly anti-Royalist paper, *Elencticus's* figure was almost certainly exaggerated low.

54. Again this figure is partly speculative, though it is based on the following pieces of semicircumstantial evidence:

   1) It has been estimated that two men, each working for eight hours, could print 1,000 sheets on a seventeenth-century hand press (Plant, *English Book Trade*, p. 89). About 1730 one of the large Dutch printing firms was able to turn out 3,000 sheets in one fourteen-hour day (Charles Singer, A. R. Hall, and Trevor I. Williams, eds., *A History of Technology*, III, 404). This figure is relevant because printing methods in the early eighteenth century differed little from those in the mid-seventeenth century, nor was there much difference between English and Dutch techniques.

   2) It is very probable that the political pamphlets of the Interregnum, many of them almost identical in size and format with the weekly newspaper, were normally issued in quantities of 1,000 to 1,500, provided they were addressed to a nonspecialized audience; and in at least one instance in the mid-1640's this figure went as high as 10,000 (Frank, *Levellers*, p. 95).

   3) At intervals during the 1640's *A Perfect Diurnall* appeared in two editions. They differed slightly in size and in minor matters of typography, not in content, thus indicating that the paper was printed on two separate presses. Presumably one press was not enough consistently to satisfy the demand; and what was true of *A Perfect Diurnall* may well have been true of other papers. (*A Diary*, 58, June 19–26, 1645, mentioned a typographical error in "some sheets" of *A Perfect Diurnall*, again suggesting that it was turned out on more than one press, since a newspaper run was usually not taken off the press in order to correct typographical errors. At the same time, the issue here referred to dealt with the Parliamentary victory at Naseby and consequently may have had an unusually large circulation.)

   4) My own mathematics, based on a variety of sources, show that it was necessary for a publisher to sell about 500 copies of his paper at one penny each in order to make a decent profit.

55. Plant, *English Book Trade*, pp. 221f.

56. *Aulicus*, 1, Dec. 31, 1643–Jan. 6, 1644, p. 762.

57. *Ibid.*, 24, June 8–15, 1644, the final paragraph; 26, June 22–29, 1644, the opening entry.

58. *Brit.*, 27, Mar. 11–18, 1644, pp. 209ff. One of the many ironies of early English journalism is that Birkenhead's accounts of the military threats to Oxford make particularly good reading — e.g., *Aulicus*, 22, May 25–June 1, 1644.

59. *Aulicus*, 12, Mar. 16–23, 1644, p. 887; 19, May 4–11, 1644, p. 972 (these morbid statistics were repeated in other numbers); 23, June 1–8, 1644, the first item under date of June 4.

60. In February, Birkenhead claimed with only slight exaggeration that twenty-one anti-Royalist papers were then being published in London (*ibid.*, 7, Feb. 10–17, 1644, p. 835).

61. *Ibid.*, 23, June 1–8, 1644, p. 1009; 24, June 8–15, 1644, p. 1021.

62. *Brit.*, 21, Jan. 29–Feb. 5, 1644, p. 161.

63. *Ibid.*, 28, Mar. 18–25, 1644. Numbers 27 and 29 also came out in counterfeit editions, but both were similar to the regular *Britanicus*, including their dedication to refuting *Aulicus*.

64. *Brit.*, 25, Feb. 26–Mar. 5, 1644, p. 191; 27, Mar. 11–18, 1644, p. 209; 36, May 13–20, 1644, p. 279.

65. *Ibid.*, 39, June 10–17, 1644, p. 304.

66. Not only was *Britanicus* coming under heavier attack from many groups for being too outspoken, but the paper itself now more frequently took a stand that could be identified with the radical elements in Parliament and army: see, for instance, in the first half of 1644, 20, Jan. 4–11, p. 160 — praise for an Independent book; 22, Feb. 5–12, p. 176 — the suggestion that the public needed more, not less, information; 41, June 24–31 [*sic*] — a plea for religious toleration; also scattered attacks on the king which were phrased in the language of what was then left-wing democracy. In one instance (no. 38, May 27–June 3, p. 302) Audley or Nedham went so far as to hint at treachery among certain Parliamentary generals, presumably those who were not sufficiently militant.

67. For further details see the article on Fiennes in the *DNB*; Gardiner, *Great Civil War*, I, 179; and Wedgwood, *King's War*, pp. 232–234, 273.

68. This thirty-page booklet was dated by Thomason February 29, 1644. It is a restrained, apparently objective, and effective defense of Fiennes, and one which shows Nedham's considerable knowledge of the law. Prynne's attack on him had opened by harking back to the three-week silence of *Britanicus* in January 1644: "Wee are informed that Brittanicus during his last weekes silence hath been visiting Nath. Fiennes." Prynne then went on to say that Fiennes had "bribed Brittanicus to trumpet forth his unknowne eminent deserts and publicke vertues to the people. . . ." If true, Nedham was one of the first professional press agents in the subhistory of English literature.

69. That Hotham edited *The Spie* is based on Thomason's notation to this effect on the title page of the fifth number, Feb. 20–27, 1644.

70. There is a short biography of Hotham in the *DNB*.

71. The subtitle of *The Spie*, "Communicating Intelligence from Oxford," was also derived from *Aulicus*.

72. *The Spie*, 2, Jan. 30–Feb. 5, 1644, p. 9.

73. E.g., *ibid.*, 4, Feb. 13–20, 1644, p. 28.

74. *Ibid.*, 3, Feb. 5–13, 1644, p. 24; 5, Feb. 20–27, 1644, p. 33; 4, Feb. 13–20, 1644, p. 32.

75. *Brit.*, 24 and 25, Feb. 19–Mar. 6, 1644, pp. 183, 191. The relevant passages can also be seen in Williams, *English Journalism*, pp. 56–58.

76. George Wither's *The Great Assises Holden in Parnassus by Apollo and His Assessors* (Feb. 1645) mentioned that *The Spie* "Forbidden objects has presum'd to see,/ And therefore merited in law, and sence,/ His eares to forfeit, for his eyes offence."

77. In the first seven months of 1644 *The Scotish Dove* contained only about

a half-dozen passages given over to attacking *Aulicus,* though Smith frequently tossed it brief hostile glances.

78. Nos. 12 through 40 of *The Scotish Dove* (January to July 1644) generally served up some sort of editorial stew made up mainly of one of these stock topics but seasoned with the others.

79. E.g., *ibid.,* 15, Jan. 19–26, 1644, p. 120.

80. In *ibid.,* 31, May 10–17, 1644, p. 247, Smith underlined this by saying that it was the function of *A Perfect Diurnall,* not of the *Dove,* to give full coverage to events at Westminster.

81. *Scotish Dove,* 17, Feb. 2–9, 1644, pp. 135ff. As the tension between Presbyterian and Independent mounted, the newspapers and pamphlets increasingly referred to New England as an example of what whoever was doing the writing wanted to prove. Thus the theological problems of Massachusetts were cited by both factions to show that toleration was good or bad.

82. E.g., *ibid.,* 27, Apr. 12–19, 1644, pp. 210f.

83. *Ibid.,* 31, May 10–17, 1644, pp. 242f; see also no. 30, May 3–10, 1644, p. 236.

84. *Ibid.,* 32, May 17–24, 1644, pp. 250, 254.

85. *Ibid.,* 27, Apr. 12–19, 1644, p. 215. Smith also had a conspicuous tendency to credit certain Parliamentary victories overwhelmingly to prayer (e.g., no. 25, Mar. 29–Apr. 5, 1644, p. 199).

86. Cleveland, *Character of a London Diurnall* — also given in Williams, *English Journalism,* p. 49.

87. E.g., *Parliament Scout,* 32, Jan. 26–Feb. 2, 1644, p. 276. For a similarly ambiguous stance see the queries at the end of no. 35, Feb. 16–23, 1644.

88. See especially *ibid.,* 43, Apr. 11–18, 1644, p. 360; 44, Apr. 18–26, 1644, p. 370; 46, May 2–9, 1644, pp. 386f.; 48, May 16–23, 1644, p. 399; and 53, June 20–27, 1644, p. 427, where Dillingham concluded a black-and-white review of recent history by sticking up for both Independents and sectaries. As to *Aulicus*'s accusation that Dillingham was a mouthpiece for the Earl of Manchester, probably it was partly true — at least so Dillingham implied in no. 52, June 13–20, 1644, p. 418. (See also his pro-Manchester remarks in no. 54, June 27–July 4, 1644, p. 436.) But supporting Manchester in the spring and summer of 1644 was still not incompatible with taking a position on the side of the Independents.

89. *Ibid.,* 42, Apr. 4–11, 1644, p. 354; 36, Feb. 23–Mar. 1, 1644, pp. 307f; 44, Apr. 18–26, 1644, p. 368.

90. E.g., *ibid.,* 48, May 16–23, 1644, p. 403.

91. E.g., *ibid.,* 46, May 2–9, 1644, where Dillingham, with a touch of gentleness, wished that the queen had been as loyal to her country as to her husband; no. 51, June 6–13, 1644, p. 412, where he commented, somewhat wryly, that it was an easy descent to Purgatory from the bogs of Ireland, a less harsh sentiment than the standard fire-and-sword approach to things Irish; and no. 56, July 11–19, 1644, where he pitied the many slain Royalist noblemen, though he wished that they had not allowed themselves to be "so corrupted and Poperized."

92. Collings' suppressed Presbyterianism and his unsuppressed caution are epitomized in this reference to a discussion in the Assembly of Divines concerning freedom of the press, a reference which also illustrates the double standard of that day concerning civil liberties: ". . . [the discussion] was not after the Archbishops manner, but for the calling in and suppressing of all lascivious, idle, profane and scurrilous books, formerly printed with license" (*Civicus,* 56, June 13–20, 1644, p. 548).

93. See, for example, *ibid.,* 59, July 4–11, 1644, p. 565.

94. This neutral course can be illustrated by the nice balance Collings preserved in the following items that appeared in *KWI* in the first half of 1644: 41, Jan. 23–30, pp. 315f — praise of the younger Sir Henry Vane; 43, Feb. 7–14, pp. 329f — praise of the Council of State; 55, May 14–21, p. 447 — praise of Essex.

If viewed in their immediate historical contexts, the first of these encomia can be considered pro-Independent, the second precisely neutral, the third pro-Presbyterian. However, in at least one instance Collings, as chief editor, failed to take into account the extreme sensitivity of the House of Lords. In June, White, the printer of *KWI*, was called to the bar of the Upper House for having cast some aspersions on one of its members. White claimed that Audley had written the defamatory passage, and apparently the case was dropped. (See also Siebert, *Freedom of the Press*, p. 210.)

95. See, for instance, Collings' direct attack on Charles in *KWI*, 59, June 11–18, 1644, p. 476, and his unusually strong language in the account of a Royalist atrocity in no. 65, July 23–30, 1644, p. 520. *Civicus* was at this time sticking more closely to the traditional theme of the king's evil advisors.

96. *KWI*, 62, July 2–9, 1644, p. 500.

97. *Weekly Account*, 37, May 8–15, 1644.

98. *True Informer*, 23, Feb. 17–24, 1644, p. 166; 31, May 4–11, 1644, pp. 217ff. Walley was also being proper and safe in his anti-Royalism, which, though vigorous, steered clear of direct attacks on the king.

99. *Ibid.*, 31, May 4–11, 1644, p. 217.

100. Siebert, *Freedom of the Press*, p. 209. Birkenhead, more than a year earlier, had mentioned Rushworth as a journalist who had easy access to the leaders of Parliament (*Aulicus*, 13, Mar. 26–Apr. 2, 1643, p. 167).

101. *Perfect Diurnall*, 32, Mar. 4–11, 1644, p. 249.

102. See, for instance, *ibid.*, p. 255, where Pecke mentioned his efforts to find out the exact whereabouts of the Scottish army.

103. E.g., *ibid.*, 27, Jan. 22–29, 1644, p. 216; 47, June 17–24, 1644, p. 376.

104. E.g., *ibid.*, 29, Feb. 5–12, 1644, p. 229; 43, May 20–27, 1644, p. 337.

105. *Ibid.*, 47, June 17–24, 1644, p. 374.

106. One of the two publishers of *A Continuation* was Francis Leach, a man with whom Pecke had long had a professional connection.

107. *A Continuation*, 1, Dec. 29, 1643–Jan. 5, 1644.

108. *Ibid.*, 12, Mar. 14–21, 1644.

109. *Ibid.*, 2, Jan. 3–10, 1644; 12, Mar. 14–21, 1644; 3, Jan. 10–17, 1644. The Yorkshire reference may indicate that Pecke was not then the editor, as he later mentioned Leicester as his "native Countrey."

110. From January 5 to April 19, 1644, its title was *Occurrences of Certain Speciall and remarkable Passages in Parliament;* then for two or three weeks this became *Perfect Occurrences of Parliament*, followed by two weeks as *Perfect Occurrences Of Some Passages in Parliament*. From the end of May 1644 to March 1646 it bore the title of *Perfect Occurrences of Parliament*, and for the remainder of 1646, *Perfect Occurrences Of Both Houses Of Parliament*. Finally, from January 1647 to its demise it settled down with the name *Perfect Occurrences of Every Dayes journall in Parliament.*

111. *Perfect Occurrences of Parliament*, 25, May 24–31, 1644.

112. The first number had this subtitle: "Upon my life new borne and wants a name. Troth let the Reader then impose the same. Veridicus — I wish thee, if not so bee — Mutus — for wee Lyers enough doe know." This was changed in the second number to: "not — Veridicus, nor yet — Mutus. But Cambro — (or if you please) — honest Britannus." Presumably the hawkers used the short title.

113. *Military Scribe*, 1, Feb. 20–27, 1644, p. 1. See also the opening of no. 2.

114. *Ibid.*, 2, Feb. 27–Mar. 5, 1644, p. 16.

115. *Ibid.*, p. 9.

116. Its first number, entitled *An Exact Diurnall*, appeared on Wednesday, May 22, 1644. Thereafter, under the title of *A Diary*, it came out on Thursday or Friday, missing only two weeks during its twenty-two months of life.

117. Quoted in Williams, *English Journalism*, p. 50.

118. Numbers 1 through 21 (June 7–Nov. 14, 1644) were printed for Robert White and sold by Nicholas Bourne. With no. 22 Bourne's name disappeared, reappearing for three months (November 1645 to February 1646) as that of the publisher. In March 1646 Bourne presumably severed his connection with *Le Mercure Anglois*. Meanwhile, a year earlier, Thomas Forcet had become the paper's printer, a job which he retained for the remainder of its existence.

119. Williams, *English Journalism*, p. 49, credits Dillingham with the idea for a newspaper in French, though Bourne strikes me as a more likely nominee. Dillingham probably was the nominal editor: there are several distinctive parallels between *Le Mercure Anglois* and *The Parliament Scout* (and later with *The Moderate Intelligencer*), and Dillingham seems to have known a little French. Also the printer, Robert White, was for six months connected with both *Le Mercure Anglois* and *The Parliament Scout*.

120. *Mercure Anglois*, 7, Aug. 1–8, 1644, pp. 25f.

121. Its first number was dated June 22–July 2, 1644. Williams, *English Journalism*, p. 228, mentions John Cotgrave, the probable translator of *Le Mercure Anglois*, as the editor, though there is, as far as I know, no evidence to corroborate this possibility — or to refute it.

122. I have omitted one semiperiodical from the text, "A Continuation of True Intelligence." Somewhere between an established and a fly-by-night production, its final issue was labeled as the seventh number, though possibly only five came out (two in June, two in July, and one in August). Moreover, "A Continuation" was concerned almost entirely with news of Manchester's army in the north, and its title changed with each issue. It was, therefore, a "relation" rather than a newspaper.

123. *Anti-Aulicus*, Feb. 6 and 8, 1644; *Mercurius Aulicus-Mastix*, Apr. 12, 1644.

124. Its three numbers came out on May 1, 6, and 13, 1644.

125. *Mercurius Anglicus*, three numbers in February 1644; *Britaines Remembrancer*, three numbers, two in March and one in early April 1644; *A True and Perfect Journal*, two numbers in April 1644; and *Cheife Heads of Each Dayes Proceedings in Parliament*, two numbers in May 1644. The first two of these weeklies were a little out of the ordinary: *Mercurius Anglicus* in the effusiveness of its praise of Parliament; and *Britaine's Remembrancer* in its contentiousness, which included casting a few slurs at *Britanicus* as well as at *Aulicus*.

126. Its one number, which appeared on May 10, 1644, had a title-page picture of a mounted post-boy similar to that which had graced *The Kingdomes Weekly Post*, though the editor of *The Flying Post* was probably not Border. Whoever he was, he not only announced his concern with the European reader but helped him along. Thus to a story about York he appended a brief description of the city so that the non-English reader would be better able to follow the report.

127. Wilbur Cortez Abbott, *The Writings and Speeches of Oliver Cromwell*, I, 287.

V

EARLY ADOLESCENCE II

August 1644 to July 1645

1. Varley, *Aulicus*, p. ix.

2. For a few numbers in 1644 Peter Heylin probably took over as editor, a job he had previously held in August and September 1643. Sir Edward Nicholas

and George Digby at various points contributed items, advice, and directives to Birkenhead. For further details, see Madan, *Oxford Books*, II, 491.

3. E.g., *Aulicus*, Feb. 2–9, 1645, p. 1366; Apr. 13–20, 1645, p. 1571. (Starting in January 1645 the issues of *Aulicus* ceased to be numbered.)

4. *Aulicus*, 38, Sept. 14-21, 1644, p. 1168. See also, in particular, the diatribes against Cromwell in three numbers in 1645; Apr. 27–May 4, May 4–11, and May 25–June 8.

5. E.g., *ibid.*, Apr. 13–20, 1645, p. 1543.

6. *Brit.*, 95, Aug. 25–Sept. 1, 1645, p. 852. For some of the difficulties attendant on smuggling *Aulicus* into London and there peddling it, see for instance *KWI*, 91, Mar. 11–18, 1645, p. 732; *Civicus*, number 79, Nov. 21-28, 1644, p. 729; and *Parliament Scout*, Dec. 12–19, 1644, p. 625. *The True Character of Mercurius Aulicus*, 1645, claimed that a copy of *Aulicus* sold for as much as 18 pence just before the paper's extinction.

7. *Aulicus*, May 25–June 8, 1645, p. 1603.

8. The dates for these three final numbers of *Aulicus* were July 13–20, Aug. 10–17, and "last of August" to Sept. 7, 1645.

9. E.g., *ibid.*, Aug. 10–17, 1645, pp. 1702, 1705.

10. *KWI*, 83, Nov. 26–Dec. 3, 1644, p. 666. Other London papers retailed the same rumor; and one of them, *Perfect Passages of Each Dayes Proceedings*, 7, Nov. 27–Dec. 4, 1644, p. 49, so doctored it that the king intended to put an end to *Aulicus* because of its "Notorious lies."

11. E.g. *Brit.*, 60, Dec. 2–9, 1644, p. 471; 62, Dec. 16–23, 1644, p. 489; 65, Jan. 6–13, 1645, p. 511; and 76, Mar. 24–31, 1645, p. 607.

12. *Ibid.*, 69, Feb. 3–10, 1645, p. 547.

13. *Ibid.*, 68, Jan. 27–Feb. 3, 1645, n.b. p. 539.

14. *Aulicus*, 29, July 7–14, 1644, p. 1090; 32, July 28–Aug. 4, 1644, p. 1114. The letter in question was written by Nathaniel Rogers — *A Letter discovering the cause of Gods continuing wrath against the Nation*. According to Thomason it was published in December 1643. For further details see Roger P. McCutcheon, "Americana in English Newspapers, 1648–1660," p. 87.

15. *Brit.*, 46, July 29–Aug. 5, 1644, p. 361; 47, Aug. 12–19, 1644, p. 367; and 49, Aug. 26–Sept. 2, 1644, p. 387. Number 47 also included a rejoiner to Daniel Featley's *Sacra Nemesis, The Levites Scourge* (August 1644), which had tried to "discipline" *Britanicus* and *Civicus*, and which, unintentionally, had paid tribute to the power of the press.

16. *Clyde*, "Parliament and the Press," pp. 407, 416.

17. E.g., *Brit.*, 48, Aug. 19–26, 1644, p. 382; 51, Sept. 23–30, 1644, p. 403; 55, Oct. 21–28, 1644, p. 433; 68, Jan. 27–Feb. 3, 1645, p. 539; 72, Feb. 24–Mar. 3, 1645, p. 579; 80, Apr. 21–28, 1645, p. 731.

18. E.g., *ibid.*, 54, Oct. 14–21, 1644, p. 428; 59, Nov. 18–25, 1644, p. 469; 85, May 26–June 2, 1645, p. 770; 86, June 9–16, 1645, p. 783.

19. *Ibid.*, 60, Dec. 2–9, 1644, p. 474.

20. E.g., *ibid.*, 61, Dec. 9–16, 1644, p. 482; 63, Dec. 13–20, 1644, p. 502; 65, Jan. 6–13, 1645, p. 514.

21. E.g., *ibid.*, 64, Dec. 30, 1644–Jan. 6, 1645, p. 510; 72, Feb. 24–Mar. 3, 1645, p. 576; 74, Mar. 10–17, 1645, p. 591; 79, Apr. 14–21, 1645, p. 728.

22. *Ibid.*, 88, June 23–30, 1645, pp. 793, 796.

23. *Ibid.*, 72, Feb. 24–Mar. 3, 1645, pp. 581f; 84, May 19–26, 1645, p. 767; 74, Mar. 10–17, 1645, p. 594. As another indication of Nedham's lean to the left, in January 1645 he contributed a one-and-one-half page preface to Lilburne's *An Answer to Nine Arguments*. In it he praised Lilburne and added some words in behalf of religious toleration.

24. Nedham's reply appeared in *Brit.*, 70, Feb. 10–17, 1645, pp. 549, 565. Cleveland's attack was a generalized diatribe against the London press. Though written

with some vigor, the "character" that emerges is distorted, vague, and too indiscriminate to be convincing. Wither's *Assises* was a lengthy and conventional poem which dealt with the Parnassan trial of London's leading editors, plus "Aulicus." The charges brought against them boiled down to the allegation that each was wordy and/or a liar. By and large Wither (almost certainly the author, though he also appeared as a juror in the poem) treated these early journalists gently, despite the fact that he was a bit rough on "Britanicus" and "Aulicus." This may account for the fact that Nedham, in reply, accused Wither of aiming mainly at himself. Other journalists answered Wither; and Cleveland's *Character* called forth at least three pamphlets, one of them written by the publishers of *A Perfect Diurnall*, Coles and Blaikelocke. (Number 88, Mar. 31–Apr. 7, 1645, p. 702, contained an advance notice of this pamphlet.) According to one newspaper, Wither's *Assises* was printed in a run of 1,500 copies because its author's motive was greed, not reform (*Perfect Passages of Each Days Proceedings*, 17, Feb. 12–19, 1645, p. 130).

25. *Brit.*, 85, May 25–June 2, 1645, p. 771; 86, June 9–16, 1645, p. 777.

26. *Ibid.*, 90, July 14–21, 1645, p. 809. The only other weeks which the paper skipped during this period were between September 9 and 23, 1644, a gap which the editor never did explain.

27. E.g., *Mercure Anglois*, 18, Oct. 17–24, 1644, p. 71; 21, Nov. 7–14, 1644, p. 81; 35, Apr. 24–May 1, 1645, p. 141; 39, May 22–29, 1645, p. 158.

28. To cite only one example, see *ibid.*, 24, Nov. 28–Dec. 5, 1644, p. 95.

29. E.g., *ibid.*, 9, Aug. 15–22, 1644, p. 35.

30. E.g., *ibid.*, 10, Aug. 22–29, 1644, p. 37.

31. *Perfect Diurnall*, 88, Mar. 31–Apr. 7, 1645, p. 699.

32. *Ibid.*, 58, Sept. 2–9, 1644, pp. 460f.

33. E.g., *ibid.*, 70, Nov. 25–Dec. 2, 1644, p. 553.

34. E.g., *ibid.*, 71, Dec. 2–9, 1644, p. 563 (later Pecke took a pro-Cromwell position — see, for instance, no. 86, Mar. 17–24, 1645, p. 684); 64, Oct. 14–21, 1644, p. 511; 87, Mar. 24–31, 1645, p. 693.

35. *Ibid.*, 82, Feb. 17–24, 1645, pp. 649f, and 86, Mar. 17–24, 1645, p. 679; 76, Jan. 6–13, 1645, pp. 603ff. (Most of this number is reprinted in Bruner, *Catalogue of . . . the Sutro Library*, pp. 20–25.)

36. For the Uxbridge negotiations see *Perfect Diurnall*, 78–82, Jan. 20–Feb. 24, 1645; for the Club-men, 84 and 85, Mar. 3–17, 1645, pp. 666, 674f. The Club-men had been receiving intermittent and usually brief mention in the London press for more than two years; probably the first item concerning them appeared in *KWI*, 9, Feb. 21–28, 1643, pp. 69f.

37. E.g., *Perfect Diurnall*, 98, June 9–16, 1645: the title-page summary of the news from Naseby.

38. *Ibid.*, 71, Dec. 2–9, 1644, p. 566; 97, June 2–9, 1645, p. 768.

39. *Ibid.*, 65, Oct. 21–28, 1644, p. 516

40. E.g., *ibid.*, 69, Nov. 18–25, 1644, p. 548; 77, Jan. 13–20, 1645, p. 612.

41. From, e.g., *ibid.*, 60, Sept. 16–23, 1644, pp. 476ff, to, e.g., 93, May 5–12, 1645, p. 739.

42. *Ibid.*, 72, Dec. 9–16, 1644, p. 567.

43. Williams, *English Journalism*, p. 71. For fuller and even more loaded details see John Taylor, *The Whole Life and Progress of Henry Walker the Ironmonger*, 1642 (reprinted in Vol. I of Taylor's *Works*). There are several snarling pamphlets in the Taylor-Walker quarrel of 1642, most of them not very informative. Two of the first newspapers of English news contained stories of Walker's early vicissitudes: *Diurnall Occurrences*, Dec. 20–27, 1641; and *Diurnall Occurrences*, Jan. 3–10, 1642.

44. For full details see Ernest Sirluck, " 'To your Tents, O Israel': A Lost Pamphlet," pp. 301–305.

45. Thomason's notation appears on the title page of *Perfect Occurrences of Parliament*, 15, Nov. 15–22, 1644, where he scrawled the names of Walker and of the astrologer Partridge. Earlier (no. 4, Aug. 30–Sept. 6, 1644) the editor had gone out of his way to praise Walker, perhaps a hint that he was acquiring him for a colleague.

46. *Ibid.*, 3, Aug. 23–30, 1644; 7, Sept. 20–27, 1644 — both these being numbers in a new series.

47. *Ibid.*, 20, Dec. 20–27, 1644.

48. *Ibid.*, 1 (in another new series), Dec. 27, 1644–Jan. 3, 1645; 11, Mar. 7–14, 1645; 14, Mar. 28–Apr. 4, 1645.

49. E.g., *ibid.*, 24, June 6–13, 1645.

50. A few times, however, the editor expressed a healthy skepticism about visions: e.g., *ibid.*, 18, Apr. 25–May 2, 1645.

51. *Ibid.*, 22, May 23–30, 1645; 1, Dec. 27, 1644–Jan. 3, 1645; 31, July 25–Aug. 1, 1645.

52. Rushworth receives a relatively lengthy biography in the *DNB*.

53. The major bit of evidence identifying Rushworth with this paper is the opening statement in no. 30, Nov. 28–Dec. 5, 1644, which seems to link *A Diary* with *The London Post*, a weekly with which Rushworth was then almost certainly connected. In addition, *A Diary* was the sort of careful and neutral paper to attract and reflect a man like Rushworth.

54. E.g., *Diary*, 10, July 25–Aug. 2, 1644, p. 74; 13, Aug. 15–22, 1644, pp. 98f.; 43, Mar. 6–13, 1645.

55. *Ibid.*, 57, June 12–19, 1645. See also no. 58, the following week, and no. 62, July 17–24, 1645.

56. Rushworth's connection with *The London Post* is derived in part from a statement in *The Man in the Moon*, 26, Oct. 17–24, 1649, p. 218. Prior to its revival in 1646–47, *The London Post* was probably continued for four numbers in April and May 1645 under the title of *The Weekely Post-Master*.

57. For Mabbott's connection with *The London Post*, see *The Man in the Moon*, 26, Oct. 17–24, 1649, p. 218; and R. T. Milford and D. M. Sutherland, *A Catalogue of English Newspapers and Periodicals in the Bodleian Library, 1622–1800*, p. 82.

58. *London Post*, 3, Aug. 27, 1644. See also no. 7 (incorrectly labeled no. 5), Sept. 24, 1644: the account of Fairfax during a retreat.

59. Siebert, *Freedom of the Press*, p. 210.

60. *London Post*, 21, Jan. 21–28, 1645; 23, Feb. 11, 1645 — in reply to Cleveland; 24, Feb. 18, 1645 — in reply to Wither.

61. See, for example, *Military Scribe*, 4, Mar. 12–19, 1644, pp. 27f: the story of a Jew exiled from Lisbon for an allegedly anti-English libel.

62. In August 1646 *Le Mercure Anglois* (no. 35) and *Perfect Occurrences* (no. 34) each gave a little space to praise of a book published in Amsterdam on the laws of the Jews and written by Menasseh ben Israel, a man who would return to the news in the 1650's. This praise was, I suspect, more in the nature of an advertisement than a story that can properly be labeled "Jewish news."

63. Prior to this *The True Informer* had skipped four issues: two in September, one in December, and one in January. When it did return to action, after a gap of two months, its first number was called *A Perfect Declaration of The Proceedings in Parliament*, Apr. 26, 1645. In the following week it reverted to its original title.

64. E.g., *True Informer*, 47, Sept. 21–28, 1644, pp. 346–348; 53, Nov. 2–9, 1644, p. 400; 55, Nov. 16–23, 1644, p. 416; 59, Dec. 21–28, 1644, p. 448; 66, Feb. 8–15, 1645, pp. 498f.

65. *Ibid.*, 61, Jan. 4–11, 1645.

66. *Ibid.*, 14 (in the revived series), July 19–26, 1645, pp. 108f.

67. *KWI*, 88, Jan. 7–14, 1645, p. 710, suggested that one advantage of non-Monday publication was that the post from the north usually arrived on Monday.

68. *Ibid.*, 68, Aug. 14–20, 1644, p. 543.

69. *Ibid.*, 69, Aug. 20–27, 1644, p. 551; 104, June 10–17, 1645, p. 833. See also no. 81, Nov. 12–19, 1644, p. 657.

70. The following references are to some of the instances in which Collings praised leading Presbyterians, a Presbyterian church settlement, or Presbyterian restraints on non-Presbyterians: in 1644 — *KWI*, 67, Aug. 6–14, p. 538; 70, Aug. 27–Sept. 3, p. 566; 71, Sept. 3–10, pp. 568–570; 74, Sept. 24–Oct. 1, p. 594; 83, Nov. 26–Dec. 3, pp. 663f; in 1645 — 89, Jan. 21–28, pp. 715f; 99, May 6–13, pp. 795f. On the other side, the following represent a sampling of his pro-Independent remarks: in 1644 — 84, Dec. 3–10, pp. 675f; in 1645 — 91, Mar. 11–18, pp. 731f; 108, July 8–15, p. 864; 110, July 22–29, p. 879.

71. *Ibid.*, 100, May 13–20, 1645, p. 804.

72. *Ibid.*, 85, Dec. 10–17, 1644, p. 682.

73. *Ibid.*, 106, June 24–July 1, 1645, p. 845. See also *Civicus*, 88, Jan. 23–30, 1645, pp. 803f, where Collings advanced essentially pragmatic arguments in behalf of Parliament's right to control the church. Collings also raises a pragmatic problem for the historian of the early newspaper. On March 11, 1645, after a gap of five weeks, *KWI* reappeared. In this issue (no. 90, p. 726) he mentioned the news from the north as coming to him via the "Weekly Post," which was, he said, printed at York. *Aulicus* and its successor were printed at Oxford, and an occasional earlier weekly had been reprinted at Edinburgh. But Collings' reference to this presumed York paper is the only tangible evidence I know of for the existence of a provincial press. My guess is that he was here referring to a newsletter, and that the "printed" was an error on his part.

74. *Civicus*, 91, Feb. 13–20, 1645, pp. 823–825; 101, Apr. 24–May 1, 1645, pp. 903f; 103, May 8–15, 1645, pp. 920–922. During the period under consideration *Civicus* skipped no weeks, while *KWI*, in addition to the gap of five weeks between the end of January and the beginning of March 1645, missed three.

75. For a sampling of the pro-Presbyterian passages in *Civicus*, see nos. 69, Sept. 11–19, 1644, p. 653; 70, Sept. 19–26, 1644, p. 661; 85, Jan. 2–9, 1645, pp. 777f; 86, Jan. 9–16, 1645, p. 786; 91, Feb. 13–20, 1645, p. 829; 112, July 10–17, 1645, p. 998; 113, July 17–24, 1645, p. 1001. On the Independent side see, for instance, nos. 91, Feb. 13–20, 1645, pp. 827f; 97, Mar. 27–Apr. 3, 1645, pp. 875f; 104, May 15–22, 1645, p. 928.

76. *Ibid.*, 11, July 3–10, 1645, p. 984. See also the following week, p. 997, where the editor gloated over Charles's fallen condition.

77. *Ibid.*, 97, Mar. 27–Apr. 3, 1645, p. 874. In June 1645 Collings found himself briefly in trouble with the House of Lords for including in *Civicus* a letter reflecting on the Dutch ambassador — a contingency he may have foreseen (Clyde, *Struggle for Freedom*, p. 86).

78. E.g., *Civicus*, 78, Nov. 14–21, 1644, p. 722; 114, July 24–31, 1645, p. 1011.

79. E.g., *ibid.*, 85, Jan. 2–9, 1645, p. 776.

80. *Ibid.*, 97, Mar. 27–Apr. 3, 1645, p. 877.

81. *Ibid.*, 104, May 15–22, 1645, pp. 929–931. This "News from Virginny" has been reprinted in full in *The Virginia Magazine of History and Biography*, LXV (1957), 84–87. (*Perfect Passages of Each Dayes Proceedings*, 29, May 7–14, 1645, p. 228, had a shorter account of the massacre.) Since 1642 the London papers had carried intermittent reports of events in the Western Hemisphere: e.g., an account of an anti-Spanish revolt in the West Indies, a New England petition asking that poor children from England be allowed to come there, the rumor that Laud was to be punished by being sent to New England, praise of the northern colonists for their loyalty to Parliament. Yet such reports were usually brief, unsubstantiated, and colored by the politics of the paper in which they appeared.

82. *Civicus*, 76, Oct. 31–Nov. 7, 1644, p. 703. Collings also announced that he would leave journalism when a true peace was established (no. 83, Dec. 19–26, 1644, p. 766). Perhaps he was aware that the newspaper has always thrived on tension and violence.

83. *Parliament Scout*, 58, July 25–Aug. 1, 1644, p. 468.

84. *Ibid.*, 73, Nov. 7–14, 1644, p. 585.

85. *Ibid.*, 65, Sept. 12–19, 1644, pp. 517f.

86. *Ibid.*, 70, Oct. 17–24, 1644, p. 558.

87. *Ibid.*, 81, Jan. 2–9, 1645, p. 647.

88. *Ibid.*, 59, Aug. 1–8, 1644, p. 474; 68, Oct. 3–10, 1644, p. 546; 77, Dec. 5–12, 1644, p. 615.

89. *Ibid.*, 74 (misnumbered 73), Nov. 14–21, 1644, p. 591; e.g., 75, Nov. 21–28, 1644, pp. 598f; e.g., 76, Nov. 28–Dec. 5, 1644, pp. 606f; 83, Jan. 16–23, 1645, p. 665, and 84, Jan. 23–30, 1645, pp. 670f.

90. E.g., *ibid.*, 70, Oct. 17–24, 1644, p. 560; 75, Nov. 21–28, 1644, p. 598.

91. *Ibid.*, 79, Dec. 19–26, 1644, p. 636.

92. *Ibid.*, 81, Jan. 2–9, 1645, p. 648.

93. E.g., *ibid.*, 73, Nov. 7–14, 1644, p. 588; 78, Dec. 12–19, 1644, p. 630; 81, Jan. 2–9, 1645, p. 652; 82, Jan. 9–16, 1645, p. 660. Dillingham also usually reserved his final paragraph or two for foreign news, possibly another sign of his interest in non-London readers.

94. Clyde, "Parliament and the Press," pp. 415f; Manwaring, "Journalism in the . . . Commonwealth," pp. 110f.

95. E.g., *Moderate Intelligencer*: no. 1, Feb. 27–Mar. 6, 1645, p. 4, vs. no. 2, Mar. 6–13, 1645, p. 10; or the balanced opening of no. 3, Mar. 13– 20, 1645.

96. E.g., *ibid.*, 4, Mar. 20–27, 1645, p. 27; 10, May 1–8, 1645, p. 76; 16, June 12–19, 1645, p. 122.

97. E.g., *ibid.*, 15, June 5–12, 1645, p. 120.

98. *Ibid.*, 5, Mar. 27–Apr. 3, 1645, p. 33; 9, Apr. 24–May 1, 1645, p. 71; 18, June 26–July 3, 1645, p. 137.

99. *Ibid.*, 17, June 19–26, 1645, p. 134. See also no. 22, July 24–31, 1645, pp. 172f.

100. *Ibid.*, 17, June 19–26, 1645, p. 136.

101. *Ibid.*, 7, Apr. 10–17, 1645, p. 53.

102. *Ibid.*, 11, May 8–15, 1645, p. 84.

103. Williams, *English Journalism*, p. 51.

104. *Weekly Account*, 31, July 31–Aug. 6, 1645. Border went on to say that "Intelligence like a key unlocks and opens unto you a Cabinet, in which you may sit at home and behold the great affaires of the 3 Kingdomes abroad." For examples of his cautious impartiality, see no. 5, Jan. 29–Feb. 5, 1645; 11, Mar. 4–11, 1645; and 17, Apr. 23–29, 1645.

105. E.g., *ibid.*, 62, Oct. 31–Nov. 6, 1644, pp. 492f; 4, Jan. 22–28, 1645; 7, Feb. 13–20, 1645; 19, May 7–14, 1645; 27, July 2–9, 1645. (In January 1645 Border started a new series of this paper, one lacking in continuous pagination. During both series in the eleven-month period under consideration *The Weekly Account* skipped six scattered weeks.)

106. *Ibid.*, 62, Oct. 31–Nov. 6, 1644, p. 495.

107. E.g., *Scotish Dove*, 55, Nov. 1–8, 1644, p. 426; 61, Dec. 13–20, 1644, pp. 473f; 65, Jan. 10–17, 1645, p. 505.

108. *Ibid.*, 46, Aug. 23–30, 1644, p. 361.

109. *Ibid.*, 49, Sept. 27, 1644, p. 377 (the comment appeared in reference to the fact that the paper had just skipped two weeks, the *Dove*'s only gap between August 1644 and July 1645); 52, Oct. 11–18, 1644, pp. 401f. Smith also had the gall to answer Wither's *Great Assises* by saying that the *Dove* "loves Laconick brevity the best" (no. 70, Feb. 14–21, 1645, p. 548).

110. *Ibid.*, 55, Nov. 1–8, 1644, p. 426.

111. *Ibid.*, 61, Dec. 13–20, 1644, pp. 473f.

112. E.g., *ibid.*, 56, Nov. 8–15, 1644, p. 440; 65, Jan. 10–17, 1645, p. 505; 92, July 18–25, 1645, p. 723.

113. *Ibid.*, 92, July 18–25, 1645, p. 723.

114. *Ibid.*, 61, Dec. 13–20, 1644, p. 479; 93, July 25–Aug. 1, 1645, p. 732.

115. E.g., *ibid.*, 80, Apr. 25–May 2, 1645, pp. 631f; 91, July 11–18, 1645, pp. 716–718.

116. *Ibid.*, 59, Nov. 29–Dec. 6, 1644, p. 462; 67, Jan. 24–31, 1645, p. 527.

117. E.g., *ibid.*, 62, Dec. 20–27, 1644, p. 485; 63, Dec. 27, 1644–Jan. 3, 1645, p. 491; 66, Jan. 17–24, 1645, p. 517; 68, Jan. 31–Feb. 7, 1645, p. 530; 70, Feb. 14–21, 1645, p. 546; 76, Mar. 28–Apr. 4, 1645, p. 597; 93, July 25–Aug. 1, 1645, p. 735.

118. *Court Mercurie*, 11, Sept. 25–Oct. 4, 1644. John Cotgrave, its probable editor, in all likelihood became the translator for *Le Mercure Anglois* in November 1645.

119. E.g., *Mercurius Veridicus*, 6, May 17–24, 1645, p. 50; 7, May 24–31, 1645, pp. 51f.

120. *Perfect Passages*, 8, Dec. 4–11, 1644, p. 60.

121. *Ibid.*, 22, Mar. 19–25, 1645, p. 176.

122. *Ibid.*, 17, Feb. 12–19, 1645, pp. 131f.

123. *Ibid.*, 6, Nov. 20–27, 1644, p. 44.

124. *Ibid.*, 20, Mar. 5–11, 1645, pp. 153f.

125. Border's *The Weekly Account* also shifted its day of publication away from Wednesday on days of thanksgiving, though not so regularly as *Perfect Passages*, nor so self-righteously. (See, for example, the editor's praise of his own godly moves in *Perfect Passages*, 15, Jan. 29–Feb. 5, 1645, p. 113; 21, Mar. 12–19, 1645, p. 161.) But despite these moves, *Perfect Passages*, except for the month of December 1644, missed no numbers during this period. As to the factor of sales. *Perfect Passages*, 17, Feb. 12–19, 1645, p. 130, in its reply to Wither's *Great Assises*, mentioned that 500 copies of the poem were sold by "mercuries" — that is, hawkers. If these peddlers, most of them women, were at that time also selling newspapers, a public day of fasting would certainly have cut down their business on the streets of London.

126. *Perfect Passages*, 20, Mar. 5–11, 1645, p. 160.

127. *Parliaments Post*, 13, July 29–Aug. 5, 1645.

128. *Ibid.*, 1, May 6–13, 1645, announced that the editor was leaving Westminster news to "The Diurnall," a practice which he then usually followed.

129. *Ibid.*, 11, July 15–23, 1645. Lilburne's career can be followed in the bits and pieces concerning his vicissitudes that appeared in a variety of newspapers, starting in 1642 when he was captured by the Royalists and concluding with his death in 1657.

130. *Exchange Intelligencer*, 1, May 15, 1645; the passage is also given in Bruner, *Catalogue of . . . the Sutro Library*, p. 18.

131. E.g., *Exchange Intelligencer*, 7, July 1–8, 1645, pp. 50f.

132. *The Countrey Foot-Post*, Oct. 2, 1644; *The Countrey Messenger, Or The Faithfull Foot-Post*, Oct. 4–11, 1644. Williams, *English Journalism*, pp. 228f, mentions Rushworth as the editor, a distinct possibility since *The Countrey Foot-Post* claimed to come from the hand of man with journalistic experience. *The Countrey Messenger*, its continuation, achieved a moment of distinction by concluding with a long and horrified summary of current continental wars.

133. The connection of Rushworth or Mabbott with *The Weekely Post-Master* is based on its similarities with *The London Post*, which had recently expired.

134. *Weekely Post-Master*, 1, Apr. 8–15, 1645, p. 1.

VI

GROWING PAINS
August 1645 to May 1646

1. *Brit.*, 92, July 28–Aug. 4, 1645, p. 825.
2. See also Clyde, "Parliament and the Press," pp. 416–418.
3. *Mercurius Britanicus, His Apologie To all Well-affected People*, licensed by Mabbott on Aug. 9, 1645, dated by Thomason two days later, and printed by Robert White.
4. Tangential to this tussle were three numbers of a newspaper published at Oxford in August 1645 entitled *Mercurius Anti-Britanicus*. The first two numbers were largely given over to attacking *Britanicus* and defending the king, with particular regard to disputing Nedham's interpretation of the king's captured correspondence. No. 3, *ca.* Aug. 18, 1645, included a derogatory account of how *Britanicus* was compiled. Nedham did not bother to reply to this opponent until mid-September (*Brit.*, 97, p. 865). Several other attacks on Nedham were inspired by his flippancy toward the king.
5. Clyde, "Parliament and the Press," p. 419.
6. *Brit.*, 93, Aug. 11–18, 1645, p. 840.
7. *Ibid.*, 98 and 99, Sept. 15–29, 1645, pp. 874f, 881. After no. 100 there was a gap of a week, possibly because Nedham missed an Oxford target.
8. *Ibid.*, 101, Oct. 13–20, 1645, pp. 901, 904; 104–107, Nov. 3–Dec. 1, 1645, *passim*.
9. *Ibid.*, 106, Nov. 17–24, 1645, p. 937; 107, Nov. 24–Dec. 1, 1645, p. 945. Nedham replied to these attacks in no. 112, Dec. 29, 1645–Jan. 5, 1646, p. 985.
10. *Ibid.*, 116, Jan. 26–Feb. 2, 1646, p. 1021.
11. *Ibid.*, 120, Feb. 23–Mar. 2, 1646, p. 1051. After this number there was an unexplained gap of a week, conceivably the result of this item's tactlessness.
12. *Ibid.*, 129, May 4–11, 1646, pp. 1103, 1110.
13. Clyde, "Parliament and the Press," p. 419.
14. For further details, see the biography of Nedham in the *DNB*.
15. In his testimony before the House of Lords, Nedham acknowledged his authorship of the last eighty numbers of *Britanicus*. It is very likely that he also had a large hand in most of the preceding fifty issues.
16. *Mercurius Academicus*, 6, Jan. 19–26, 1646, p. 56.
17. Madan, *Oxford Books*, II, 499.
18. *Mercurius Academicus*, 5, Jan. 12–19, 1646, p. 44; 8, Feb. 2–9, 1646, p. 77; 9, Feb. 9–16, 1646, p. 82.
19. *Ibid.*, 11, Feb. 23–Mar. 2, 1646, p. 101. On the same page Little claimed that New England, because of its many religions, was more infidel than Turkey — in contrast to later allegations in the London press that it was infidel because of its persecuting conformity.
20. *Mercure Anglois*, 1 (in a new series), Nov. 13–Dec. 4, 1645, p. 1.
21. For Cotgrave's connection with *Mercure Anglois*, see *Man in the Moon*, 26, Oct. 17–24, 1649, p. 218.
22. *Mercure Anglois*, 20, Apr. 23/May 10–May 7/May 17, 1646, p. 80. (Starting in December 1645 the paper adopted this system of double-dating in order to include both old-style and new-style dates. Here, too, it took no stand.)
23. *Ibid.*, 52, Aug. 21–28, 1645.
24. *Perfect Diurnall*, 108, Aug. 18–25, 1645, p. 870.
25. E.g., *ibid.*, 136, Feb. 23–Mar. 2, 1646, pp. 1093f; 146, May 11–18, 1646, p. 1167.
26. E.g., *ibid.*, 123, Dec. 1–8, 1645, p. 985; 140, Mar. 30–Apr. 6, 1646, p. 1124.

27. One example of this accuracy was Pecke's apologetic correction of a mix-up in names in the preceding number (*ibid.*, 105, July 29–Aug. 4, 1645 p,. 838).

28. E.g., *ibid.*, 120, Nov. 10–17, 1645, pp. 954f; 143, Apr. 20–27, 1646, p. 1147.

29. E.g., *ibid.*, 142, Apr. 13–20, 1646, pp. 1140–1144.

30. *KWI*, 122, Oct. 14–21, 1645, p. 978; 140, Mar. 2–10, 1646, pp. 38–40.

31. *Ibid.*, 143, Mar. 24–31, 1646, pp. 57f.

32. *Ibid.*, e.g., 120, Sept. 30–Oct. 7, 1645, p. 966; 144, Mar. 31–Apr. 7, 1646, p. 71; 150, May 19–25, 1646, p. 113.

33. Collings had anticipated this practice in August 1645 by a lengthy dissertation, stated in very general terms, on whom not to vote for in Parliamentary by-elections (*ibid.*, 114, Aug. 19–26, 1645, pp. 912–914), and subsequently in his comments on a few election results (*ibid.*, 117, Sept. 9–16, 1645, p. 938, and 128, Nov. 25–Dec. 2, 1645, p. 1028).

34. *Ibid.*, 149, May 12–19, 1646, p. 105.

35. E.g., *ibid.*, 145, Apr. 7–13, 1646, p. 73; 148, May 5–12, 1646, p. 99.

36. E.g., *ibid.*, 149, May 12–19, 1646, p. 108. Astrological almanacs were then the best-selling books: in 1646 the sales of one such annual by Partridge hit 13,500, and another by him rose to 18,500 in 1648 (Richard D. Altick, *The English Common Reader: A Social History of the Mass Reading Public, 1800–1900*, p. 20). Since 1642 the newspapers had acknowledged this competition by printing occasional predictions and by confirming or denying the wisdom of contemporary astrologers.

37. Also, during the first five months of 1646 *KWI* skipped four numbers — this without any comment from Collings.

38. *Civicus*, 119, Aug. 28–Sept. 4, 1645, pp. 1047f.

39. Quoted in Plomer, "Mercurius Civicus," p. 190.

40. *Civicus*, 139, Jan. 15–22, 1646.

41. *Ibid.*, 130, Nov. 13–20, 1645, pp. 1136f.

42. E.g., *ibid.*, 153, Apr. 30–May 7, 1646, p. 2233.

43. *Ibid.*, 127, Oct. 23–30, 1645, pp. 1113f. Various social schemes had been intermittently put forward in the London newspapers, perhaps the earliest being a plan for county military academies proposed in *A Perfect Diurnall*, Aug. 29–Sept. 5, 1642.

44. E.g., *Civicus*, 139, Jan. 15–22, 1646, p. 2013; 148, Mar. 19–26, 1646, p. 2086.

45. *Ibid.*, 134, Dec. 11–18, 1645, p. 1171.

46. *Ibid.*, 145, Feb. 26–Mar. 4, 1646, p. 2062.

47. E.g., *Moderate Intelligencer*, 38 (the second week so numbered), Nov. 20–27, 1645, p. 207; 49, Feb. 5–12, 1646, p. 287; 50, Feb. 12–19, 1646, p. 304; 53, Mar. 5–12, 1646, pp. 327f; 60, Apr. 23–30, 1646, p. 417. See also the attack on Dillingham entitled *The Copy of a Letter Written from Northampton*, Feb. 1646.

48. E.g., *Moderate Intelligencer*, 37, Nov. 6–13, 1645, p. 196; 39, Nov. 27–Dec. 4, 1645, p. 207; 45, Jan. 8–15, 1646, p. 259; 62, May 7–14, 1646, p. 440; 65, May 26–June 4, 1646, p. 476. Dillingham was also concerned with the shortage of able preachers, and he substantiated his worries by stating that there were only 3,000 qualified men to occupy 9,000 pulpits (no. 42, Dec. 18–25, 1645, pp. 229f).

49. *Ibid.*, 54, Mar. 12–19, 1646, pp. 339f.

50. *Ibid.*, 36, Oct. 30–Nov. 6, 1645, p. 181.

51. *Ibid.*, 58, Apr. 9–16, 1646, pp. 387f.

52. E.g., *ibid.*, 29, Sept. 11–18, 1645, p. 232; 35, Oct. 23–30, 1645, p. 179; 38, Nov. 13–20, 1645, pp. 197f; 50, Feb. 12–19, 1646, pp. 295f; 52, Feb. 26–Mar. 5, 1646, p. 324.

53. E.g., *ibid.*, 33, Oct. 9–16, 1645, p. 159; 51, Feb. 19–26, 1646, p. 307; 53, Mar. 5–12, 1646, p. 330; 56, Mar. 26–Apr. 2, 1646, pp. 363f; 59, Apr. 16–23, 1646, pp. 395f, 400f.

54. *Ibid.*, 37, Nov. 6–13, 1645, p. 193; 44, Jan. 1–8, 1646, pp. 247f.

55. *Ibid.*, 52, Feb. 26–Mar. 5, 1646, p. 323; 59, Apr. 16–23, 1646, p. 406. The apology came the following week, on p. 417.

56. *Weekly Account*, e.g., 20, May 6–13, 1646; 40, Oct. 1–8, 1645.

57. *Ibid.*, 34, Aug. 20–26, 1645.

58. Walker in the summer of 1645 even tried to help Nedham by claiming that *Britanicus*'s facetious call for the king's arrest was a counterfeit (*Perfect Occurrences*, 32, Aug. 1–8, 1645).

59. E.g., *Perfect Occurrences*, 45, Oct. 24–31, 1645; 50, Nov. 28–Dec. 5, 1645; 51, Dec. 5–12, 1645; 3, Jan. 9–16, 1646; 11, Mar. 6–13, 1646.

60. *Ibid.*, 32, Aug. 1–8, 1645.

61. *Ibid.*, 1, Dec. 26, 1645–Jan. 2, 1646; 34, Aug. 15–21, 1645.

62. *Ibid.*, 51, Dec. 5–12, 1645; 49, Nov. 21–28, 1645.

63. *Ibid.*, 48, Nov. 14–21, 1645.

64. E.g., *Scotish Dove*, 94, Aug. 1–8, 1645, pp. 740f; 103, Oct. 3–10, 1645, p. 814; 110, Nov. 19–27, 1645, pp. 865f; 122, Feb. 11–18, 1646, pp. 965f; 123, Feb. 18–26, 1646, p. 575; 126, Mar. 11–18, 1646, pp. 596–599; 128, Mar. 28–Apr. 8, 1646, pp. 612f; 129, Apr. 8–15, 1646, pp. 619–622; 133, May 6–13, 1646, pp. 649–651.

65. E.g., *ibid.*, 108, Nov. 7–12, 1645, p. 855; 109, Nov. 12–19, 1645, p. 859; 125, Mar. 4–11, 1646, p. 590; 127, Mar. 18–28, 1646, p. 610.

66. *Ibid.*, 110, Nov. 19–27, 1645, p. 872.

67. *Ibid.*, 115, Dec. 24, 1645–Jan. 1, 1646, pp. 905–907. At least once Smith advised his readers to go to *A Perfect Diurnall* for news of Parliament (*Scotish Dove*, 130, Apr. 15–22, 1646, p. 630).

68. *Scotish Dove*, 94, Aug. 1–8, 1645, p. 743.

69. E.g., *ibid.*, 133, May 6–13, 1646, p. 655.

70. *Ibid.*, 104, Oct. 10–17, 1645, p. 819.

71. *Ibid.*, 127, Mar. 18–28, 1646, p. 606.

72. *The Parliamentary History of England*, Vol. III (1642–1660), pp. 441–444. See also Wedgwood, *King's War*, p. 547.

73. *Mercurius Veridicus*, 24, Sept. 27–Oct. 4, 1645, p. 166; 5, Jan. 24–31, 1646.

74. *Ibid.*, 7, Feb. 7–14, 1646.

75. *Ibid.*, 32, Nov. 29–Dec. 6, 1645, p. 244. See also the editor's opening statement in no. 27, Oct. 25–Nov. 1, 1645, p. 196.

76. *True Informer*, 45, Feb. 28–Mar. 7, 1646, p. 360.

77. *Ibid.*, 27, Oct. 18–25, 1645, pp. 211f.

78. *Ibid.*, e.g., 19, Aug. 23–30, 1645, pp. 146f; 44, Feb. 21–28, 1646, pp. 348–351.

79. *Ibid.*, 36, Dec. 27, 1645–Jan. 3, 1646, p. 281; 42, Feb. 7–14, 1646, p. 329.

80. *Ibid.*, 33, Nov. 29–Dec. 6, 1645, p. 259.

81. But contrary to this hypothesis was the editor's casual mention that he was born in Buckingham, not Leicester (*A Continuation*, 9, Nov. 14–21, 1645).

82. E.g., *ibid.*, 6, Oct. 24–31, 1645; 10, Nov. 21–28, 1645; 12, Dec. 5–12, 1645; 16, Jan. 2–9, 1646.

83. *Ibid.*, 21, Feb. 6–13, 1646.

84. For a yearly breakdown of the total number of separate newspapers during the Interregnum see *Catalogue of the Thomason Collection*, I, xxi.

85. *Parliaments Post*, 17, Sept. 2–9, 1645. See also the lengthy editorial on the power of the devil in no. 13, July 29–Aug. 5, 1645.

86. For the editor's new crispness of style see, for instance, his account of the Club-men in no. 14, Aug. 5–12, 1645; and for his recently acquired ability as a raconteur, see his story of the Catholic soldier confessing to a priest as if he were shooting a gun — no. 16, Aug. 19–Sept. 2, 1645.

87. E.g., *ibid.*, 16, Aug. 19–Sept. 2, 1645; 20, Sept. 23–30, 1645.

88. Its probable first issue, dated Aug. 19, 1645, claimed on the title page to be the fourth number.

89. *Kingdomes Scout*, 1, Nov. 25–Dec. 2, 1645.

90. *Ibid.*, 2, Dec. 2–9, 1645.

91. Despite the absence of any explicit statement to this effect in *The Citties Weekly Post*, it was almost certainly a continuation of *The Kingdomes Weekly Post*. The two papers had the same subtitle, the same day of appearance (Tuesday), and the same style and over-all content.

92. In *The Kingdomes Weekly Post*, Nov. 11–18, 1645, p. 42, the editor wrote that his paper's function was "onely to declare . . . the newes of the Field, and of the feats of Warre, for what belongeth to the high Councell of the Parliament or to the Assembly of Divines doth not so properly conduce to the . . . title of a Post." Even so, he regularly included some nonmilitary items, among them several astrological tidbits.

93. *Citties Weekly Post*, 8, Feb. 3–10, 1646.

94. This improving editor was, however, soon back in journalism: see above, Chapter VII, p. 131.

95. The first number of *The Moderate Messenger* was dated Jan. 27–Feb. 3, 1646; its fourth, after skipping a week, Feb. 24–Mar. 3, 1646.

96. *Ibid.*, 4, Feb. 24–Mar. 3, 1646.

97. The first number of *Generall Newes* was dated May 6, 1646; nos. 2 and 3, assuming they came out, are not extant; and the fourth and final number was dated May 21–26, 1646. *The Cambridge Bibliography of English Literature*, I, 757, lists two other items from this period, both of them probably relations rather than full-fledged newspapers: *The Westerne Informer*, one four-page number in March 1646; *An Exact and True Collection of the Weekly Passages*, two numbers in February and March 1646.

VII

LATE ADOLESCENCE

June 1646 to September 1647

1. Frank, *Levellers*, pp. 77–134.

2. *Mercure Anglois*, 38, Sept. 3/13–10/20, 1646, p. 149.

3. E.g. *ibid.*, 25, June 4/14–11/21, 1646, p. 171; 39, Sept. 10/20–17/27, 1646, p. 155; 43, Oct. 8/18–15/25, 1646, p. 171; 4, July 22/Aug. 1–July 29/Aug. 8, 1647, p. 16.

4. This gap extended from mid-April to the end of July 1647. Prior to that, between October 1646 and March 1647, the paper had skipped three issues, in each case reappearing in a number that tried to cover two weeks in four pages.

5. *Perfect Diurnall*, 149, June 1–8, 1646, pp. 1197f.

6. *Ibid.*, 150, June 8–15, 1646, p. 1200.

7. *Ibid.*, 151, June 15–22, 1646, p. 1211.

8. *Ibid.*, 168, Oct. 12–19, 1646, pp. 1347, 1349. See also Siebert, *Freedom of the Press*, p. 211.

9. *Perfect Diurnall*, 172, Oct. 26–Nov. 2, 1646, p. 1362.

10. E.g., *ibid.*, 185, Feb. 8–15, 1647, p. 1486; 188, Mar. 1–8, 1647, p. 1510.

11. *Ibid.*, 173, Nov. 16–23, 1646, p. 1389.

12. *Ibid.*, 175, Nov. 30–Dec. 7, 1646, p. 1406. See also Pecke's explicitly antidemocratic remarks in no. 171, Nov. 2–9, 1646, p. 1373.

13. E.g., *ibid.*, 198, May 10–17, 1647, p. 1590; 199, May 17–24, 1647, p. 1598.

14. E.g., *ibid.*, 210, Aug. 2–9, 1647, pp. 1688–1692.

15. *Ibid.*, 201, May 31–June 7, 1647.

16. *KWI*, 154, June 23–30, 1646, pp. 145f; 170, Oct. 13–20, 1646, pp. 265f; 186,

Feb. 2–9, 1647, p. 413; 188, Feb. 16–23, 1647, p. 429; 201, Mar. 16–23, 1647, pp. 461f; 225, Aug. 31–Sept. 7, 1647, p. 653.

17. *Ibid.*, 153, June 16–23, 1646, pp. 137f, and 159, July 28–Aug. 4, 1646, pp. 185f; 171, Oct. 20–27, 1646, p. 273, and 183, Jan. 12–19, 1647, p. 389.

18. *Ibid.*, 209, May 11–18, 1647, pp. 525f.

19. *Ibid.*, 153, June 16–23, 1646, p. 138; 156, July 7–14, 1646, p. 168; and, e.g., 163, Aug. 25–Sept. 1, 1646, p. 224.

20. E.g., *ibid.*, 166, Sept. 15–22, 1646, pp. 243f; 168, Sept. 29–Oct. 6, 1646, p. 258; 178, Dec. 8–15, 1646, p. 356.

21. *Ibid.*, 214, June 15–22, 1647, p. 567; 215, June 22–29, 1647, p. 579; 217, July 6–13, 1647, p. 596; 227, Sept. 14–21, 1647, p. 669. The suggestion that Charles be returned to power occurred in a short editorial in no. 225, Aug. 31–Sept. 7, 1647, p. 653.

22. E.g., *ibid.*, 211, May 25–June 1, 1647, p. 542; 214, June 15–22, 1647, p. 572.

23. *Ibid.*, 222, Aug. 10–17, 1647, p. 630. Almost as escapist was the editorial with which no. 202 (Mar. 23–30, 1647) opened: a paean to the currently glorious condition of England.

24. E.g., *ibid.*, 203, Mar. 30–Apr. 6, 1647, p. 481; 212, June 1–8, 1647, p. 556; 214, June 15–22, 1647, p. 565.

25. *Ibid.*, 153, June 16–23, 1646, p. 144; 172, Oct. 27–Nov. 3, 1646, p. 281.

26. *Perfect Diurnall*, 169, Oct. 19–26, 1646, p. 1356.

27. *KWI*, 171, Oct. 20–27, 1646, p. 280.

28. *Ibid.*, 165, Sept. 8–15, 1646, p. 233.

29. *Ibid.*, 166, Sept. 15–22, 1646, p. 248; 185, Jan. 26–Feb. 2, 1647, p. 408.

30. *Ibid.*, 230, Oct. 12–19, 1647, pp. 695f.

31. E.g., *ibid.*, 157, July 14–21, 1646, p. 176; 166, Sept. 15–22, 1646, p. 248; 167, Sept. 22–29, 1646, p. 256; 174, Nov. 10–17, 1646, p. 304.

32. *Ibid.*, 228, Sept. 21–28, 1647, p. 682.

33. The best example of such a vindication is *KWI*'s reply (no. 151, June 2–9, 1646, pp. 125f) to an attack in *The Moderate Intelligencer* on some respectable London women who took an excursion to Oxford to watch the siege. Dillingham, among others, probably picked up similar fees: see, for instance, his vindication of a certain Major Ormsbie, at the Major's request, in *Moderate Intelligencer*, 131, Sept. 16–23, 1647, pp. 1281f.

34. *KWI*, 174, Nov. 10–17, 1646, p. 299; 175, Nov. 17–24, 1646, p. 309. This move received passing mention in other papers, including *Mercure Anglois* and *Moderate Intelligencer*. For some of the earlier peregrinations of the king's press, see *Civicus*, 123, Sept. 24–Oct. 1, 1645.

35. *KWI*, 202, Mar.. 23–30, 1647, p. 471.

36. *Civicus*, 181, Nov. 5–12, 1646, and *KWI*, 173, Nov. 3–10, 1646.

37. *Civicus*, 160, June 18–25, 1646, pp. 2284, 2290. Collings also went after Walker in no. 163, July 16–23, 1646, p. 2320; and in September he pointedly referred to the fact that *The Scotish Dove* was not noted for its reliability (*Civicus*, 170, Aug. 27–Sept. 3, 1646, p. 2369).

38. *Civicus*, 177, Oct. 8–15, 1646, pp. 2114–2116.

39. *Ibid.*, 170, Aug. 27–Sept. 3, 1646, pp. 2365–2368; 171, Sept. 3–10, 1646, pp. 2372–2375.

40. *Ibid.*, 172, Sept. 10–17, 1646, pp. 2385f.

41. *Ibid.*, 180, Oct. 29–Nov. 5, 1646, p. 2442.

42. Between the lines there may be the implication that *Civicus* was in trouble for having been too full in its reports on the Parliament-Scot negotiations. Williams, *English Journalism*, p. 69, has a somewhat different interpretation, one that makes the editor, a "brave old fellow," an ardent martyr for the cause of Charles.

43. This last number was dated December 3–10, 1646. For post-Restoration revivals of "Mercurius Civicus" see Plomer's article, pp. 205–207.

44. Siebert, *Freedom of the Press*, p. 211; *Lords Journals*, VIII, 504; *Scotish Dove*, 152, Sept. 16–23, 1646, p. 43. The alleged insult to France probably occurred in no. 150, Sept. 2–9, 1646, p. 31.

45. Siebert, *Freedom of the Press*, p. 211; *Commons Journals*, IV, 664. The offending issue of *The Scotish Dove* referred to by the House was no. 146, Aug. 5–12, 1646. For Smith's attacks on certain Parliamentary committees see, for example, nos. 143, July 15–22, 1646, p. 733, and 148, Aug. 19–26, 1646, pp. 14f.

46. E.g., *Scotish Dove*, 156, Oct. 14–21, 1646, p. 17; 157, Oct. 21–28, 1646, p. 81; 161, Nov. 18–26, 1646, p. 117.

47. E.g., *ibid.*, 159, Nov. 4–11, 1646, p. 102.

48. Smith explicitly reiterated this view in, e.g., *ibid.*, 154, Sept. 30–Oct. 8, 1646, pp. 57f, and 162, Dec. 25 [?], 1646, pp. 2–5.

49. *Moderate Intelligencer*, 65, May 28–June 4, 1646, p. 467.

50. *Ibid.*, 90, Nov. 19–26, 1646, pp. 759ff; 124, July 22–29, 1647, p. 1200.

51. *Ibid.*, 69, June 25–July 2, 1646.

52. *Ibid.*, 126, Aug. 12–19, 1647.

53. *Ibid.*, 78, Aug. 27–Sept. 3, 1646, pp. 623f.

54. *Ibid.*, e.g., 82, Sept. 24–Oct. 1, 1646, pp. 663f; 87, Oct. 29–Nov. 6, 1646, pp. 723f; 121, July 1–8, 1647, p. 1155. The quotation is from no. 101, Feb. 4–11, 1647, p. 912.

55. *Ibid.*, 92, Dec. 3–10, 1646, p. 783.

56. *Ibid.*, 102, Feb. 11–18, 1647, p. 923.

57. *Ibid.*, p. 914. In 1642, when the signing of mass petitions was something new, Londoners showed an equal lack of political sophistication. (See, for instance, the account of a peace petition in *A Continuation of Certaine speciall and remarkable Passages*, Dec. 8–15, 1642, pp. 5f.) In April 1647 Cleveland derogated Dillingham in *The Character of a Moderate Intelligencer*, accusing him of being the "Countrymans chronicler," a liar, and a bundle of inconsistencies.

58. *Moderate Intelligencer*, 100, Jan. 28–Feb. 4, 1647, p. 881; 127, Aug. 19–26, 1647, p. 1235.

59. *Weekly Account*, e.g., 46, Oct. 28–Nov. 4, 1646, and 13, Mar. 24–30, 1647; 8, Feb. 17–24, 1647.

60. See, for instance, Border's ostensibly verbatim report of a speech by Fiennes in the House of Commons (*Weekly Account*, 42, Oct. 17–24, 1646); and his full account of the Lower House's decision to have a ballot box made, an item that the editor apparently thought harmless (*ibid.*). *A Perfect Diurnall*, 167, Oct. 5–12, 1646, p. 1342, and *Perfect Occurrences*, 42, Oct. 9–16, 1646, carried slightly varying reports on this scheme for a ballot box.

61. The fact that two series of *The Perfect Weekly Account* appeared during May and June 1647 raises a bibliographical problem. I am assuming that the one with which Border was connected consisted of nos. 19 (May 5–12) through 26 (June 23–29).

62. *Man in the Moon*, 26, Oct. 17–24, 1649, p. 218.

63. See the title page of *Perfect Weekly Account*, 41, Oct. 13–20, 1647.

64. *Perfect Occurrences*, 1, Jan. 1–8, 1647.

65. *Ibid.*, 39, Sept. 24–Oct. 1, 1647, p. 1. (See also Williams, *English Journalism*, pp. 75, 117f.) In an earlier issue (no. 9, Feb. 26–Mar. 5, 1647, p. 72) the editor inserted a denial that it was Walker who had thrown a pamphlet into the king's coach in 1642.

66. *Perfect Occurrences*, 1, Jan. 1–8, 1647, p. 1.

67. *Ibid.*, 25, June 12–19, 1646; 33, Aug. 7–14, 1646. Apparently Charles enjoyed golf enough to disregard the weather, for there is a reference to his playing the game in Scotland in October (*A Continuation of Papers from the Scotts Quarters*, 3, Nov. 5, 1646, p. 5).

68. *Perfect Occurrences*, 36, Aug. 28–Sept. 4, 1646; 40, Sept. 25–Oct. 2, 1646.

One example of unintentional humor is the opening of no. 49, Nov. 20–27, 1646: ". . . I desire you [the reader] in the last weekes Occurence, the 7. line of Mundayes passage, to blot out the word unconscionable and (with your pen) to make it inconceivable." The preceding week the misprinted adjective had modified "Godhead"!

69. *Ibid.*, 18, Apr., 30–May 7, 1647. See also Leslie Hotson, *The Commonwealth and Restoration Stage*, pp. 23f. References to closing the theaters appeared in the newspapers from the very beginning of 1642 to the Restoration, sufficient proof, as Hotson points out, that the drama, though often pushed underground, was never entirely extinguished during the Civil War period.

70. *Perfect Occurrences*, 7, Feb. 12–19, 1647.

71. *Ibid.*, 34, Aug. 14–21, 1646. See also nos. 30, July 17–24, 1646; 35, Aug. 21–28, 1646; 13, Mar. 26–Apr. 2, 1647, p. 104; 39, Sept. 24–Oct. 1, 1647, p. 267. At the same time, Walker could be very naïve, or perhaps all journalists at that time dropped their guard when it came to stories about America. In any case, *Perfect Occurrences*, 14, Apr. 2–9, 1647, p. 111, cited a letter from New England on the customs of the Indians. These allegedly included fines for adultery, for wearing long hair, and for killing lice by biting them — the fines being expressed in terms of English money.

72. Siebert, *Freedom of the Press*, p. 212; *Lords Journals*, IX, 37, 131, 142.

73. *Perfect Occurrences*, 35, Aug. 14–21, 1646.

74. E.g., *ibid.*, 28, July 3–10, 1646; 29, July 10–17, 1646; 39, Sept. 18–25, 1646; 11, Mar. 12–19, 1647, p. 84; 20, May 14–21, 1647, p. 130; 29, July 16–23, 1647, pp. 191, 193; 38, Sept. 17–24, 1647, p. 261. Once, however, Walker attacked Lilburne's pamphlet *Londons Liberty* (no. 45, Oct. 30–Nov. 6, 1646).

75. Also, in *Perfect Occurrences*, 21, May 21–28, 1647, p. 132, Walker leaned over backward to praise the Stationers' Company for its suppression of incendiary books. But despite his caution, he let one cat out of the bag. When the king was being escorted from his Scottish flirtation at Newcastle to Holmby House, Walker reported that his convoy was so arranged that "His Majesty passeth *as if* he had no forces about him, but his royall Guard onely." (My italics. This item is from no. 7, Feb. 12–19, 1647, p. 50.)

76. In the autumn of 1647 Walker began to insert an occasional advertisement. But what may have been one of the first book advertisements, rather than a friendly mention, had appeared half a year earlier: *ibid.*, 13, Mar. 26–Apr. 2, 1647, p. 102.

77. Its final number appeared on a Wednesday, the previous ten, starting July 26, 1647, on Monday. In February 1648 a similarly titled newspaper, though put out by a different publisher, survived for one unnoteworthy issue.

78. For Audley's role as editor see *Mercurius Diutinus*, 9, Jan. 20–27, 1647, p. 65, and Williams, *English Journalism*, p. 69.

79. *Diutinus Britanicus*, 2, Dec. 2–8, 1646, pp. 14f.

80. *London Post*, 2, Jan. 14–21, 1647, pp. 1f.

81. *Ibid.*, pp. 10f. (This one number consisted of sixteen pages.)

82. E.g., *ibid.*, 3, Jan. 21–28, 1647, p. 24; 4, Jan. 28–Feb. 4, 1647, pp. 26f.

83. E.g., *Moderne Intelligencer*, 3, Aug. 26–Sept. 2, 1647, p. 24; 7, Sept. 23–30, 1647, p. 56.

84. *Ibid.*, 5, Sept. 9–16, 1647, p. 33.

85. Williams, *English Journalism*, p. 232, mentions Pecke as the editor. I am very dubious.

86. *Ibid.* and ditto. It is possible, however, that *Papers from the Scotts Quarters* was intended as a supplement to *A Perfect Diurnall.*

87. *A Continuation of Papers*, 4 (there was, as far as I know, no number 1), Nov. 12, 1646, p. 2. This quotation is also useful to point out a characteristic of seventeenth-century spelling. "We" is here spelled indiscriminately with one

or two "e" 's. This was not the result of any system on the editor's part, but the product of the typesetter, who used this easy way to justify his lines of type. Thus an extra "e" could make a line properly tight, a single "e" could make room for another letter.

88. The publisher of this newspaper was Giles Calvert, who in the 1650's became one of the official printers for the Council of State and a leading publisher of Quaker books.

89. According to Williams, *English Journalism*, p. 232, the editor of this number of *Mercurius Candidus* (Nov. 11–20, 1646) was John Harris, a man who later became an apologist for the Levellers and an active journalist. For the paper's anti-Shakespeare item see Frank, "An Early Newspaper Allusion to Shakespeare."

VIII

COMING OF AGE

September 1647 to June 1648

1. *Lords Journals*, IX, 441. See also Clyde, "Parliament and the Press," pp. 54f, 57f.

2. Siebert, *Freedom of the Press*, p. 213. See also *Perfect Summarie of Chiefe Passages*, 11, Sept. 29–Oct. 6, 1647, p. 85.

3. Siebert, *Freedom of the Press*, p. 212.

4. *Catalogue of the Thomason Collection*, I, xxi. Only the two-year period 1642, 1643 saw a larger output of pamphlets: about 3,000.

5. Firth and Rait, *Acts and Ordinances*, I, 1022; Siebert, *Freedom of the Press*, p. 213.

6. *Melancholicus*, 1, Sept. 4–11, 1647, p. 1. The passage is given in Williams, *English Journalism*, p. 80.

7. For Hackluyt's connection with *Melancholicus* see, among other references, *Mercurius-Morbicus*, 1, 2, 3 (in one number), Sept. 1647; *Perfect Occurrences*, 37, Sept. 10–17, 1647, p. 250; 63, Mar. 10–17, 1648, p. 517; 73, May 19–26, 1648, p. 525; and 81, July 14–21, 1648, pp. 591f; *Melancholicus*, 21, Jan. 15–22, 1648, p. 120; and *Mercurius Anti-Mercurius*, 1, Sept. 12–19, 1648.

8. *Melancholicus*, 52, Aug. 14–21, 1648.

9. For Parker as a journalist see Rollins, *Cavalier and Puritan*, pp. 33–36, and the short biography in the *DNB*. For Parker's connection with *Melancholicus* see, for example, *Mercurius Morbicus*, 4, Sept. 20–27, 1647, and *Mercurius Anti-Mercurius*, Sept. 12–19, 1648, which hinted that Parker had recently stood in the pillory as a punishment for his Royalist editing. Parker is a good example of the close connection between ballad writing and anti-government journalism.

10. *Mercurius Morbicus*, 4, Sept. 20–27, 1647; *Perfect Occurrences*, 66, Mar. 31–Apr. 7, 1648, p. 474 (where his name is given as Edward Crouch); and Williams, *English Journalism*, p. 81. At various times, too, John Taylor, the Water Poet, probably lent a hand to *Melancholicus* (e.g., *Metropolitan Nuncio*, 2, May 30–June 6, 1649).

11. *Melancholicus*, 36, May 1–8, 1648, p. 220. For instance, on political grounds alone, it seems likely that Parker edited no. 23 (Jan. 29–Feb. 5, 1648), and that Hackluyt wrote no. 21 (Jan. 15–22, 1648). On literary grounds, it is probable that no. 26 (Feb. 19–28, 1648) was by Parker, no. 30 (Mar. 20–27, 1648) by Hackluyt. On those weeks when two issues of *Melancholicus* appeared, the attribution of one to Parker and the other to Hackluyt is not difficult.

12. *Ibid.*, 26, Feb. 19–28, 1648, p. 150. For the editors' harassment see, for

instance, no. 23, Jan. 29–Feb. 5, 1648, p. 133; 29, Mar. 13–20, 1648, p. 168; 40, May 22–29, 1648, p. 237; and 44, June 19–26, 1648, p. 265. As early as October 1647 one of the paper's printers was caught (*Perfect Occurrences*, 42, Oct. 15–22, 1647, p. 295).

13. E.g., the two early counterfeit numbers of *Melancholicus*, nos. 3 and 4, Sept. 11–24, 1647, and the non-counterfeit nos. 3, Sept. 11–18, 1647, p. 15, and 6, Oct. 2–9, 1647, p. 32.

14. E.g., *ibid.*, 41, May 29–June 5, 1648, p. 248.

15. *Ibid.*, 9, Oct. 23–30, 1647, p. 52.

16. *Metropolitan Nuncio*, 3, June 6–13, 1649. For a full account of Sheppard see Hyder Rollins, "Samuel Sheppard and His Praise of Poets."

17. *Mercurius Anti-Mercurius*, Apr. 4, 1648. John Berdan has edited *The Poems of John Cleveland*, and supplied a biography fuller than that in the *DNB*. In the mid-1640's many weeklies contained references to Cleveland's Royalist activities.

18. *Independencie No Schisme*, July 1646; *The Case of the Kingdome Stated*, June 1647; *The Lawyer of Lincolnes-Inne Reformed*, July 1647.

19. Wood, *Athenae Oxonienses*, p. 1180; *Mercurius Anti-Pragmaticus*, 9 (misnumbered 19), Jan. 27–Feb. 3, 1648.

20. Besides his contribution to *Pragmaticus* at this time, Nedham would have other evidence to prove his Royalism. At the end of 1647, under the pseudonym of Mercurius Pragmaticus, it was in all likelihood he who dashed off an anti-Leveller closet drama, *The Levellers levell'd*, a mixture of ragged verse and high-flying prose in which the allegory is clumsy but the conservatism clear. Nedham is also the best candidate for author of *Loyalty speakes Truth*, published early in 1648, a conversation among the three long-run Royalist mercuries about the sad state of England. Shortly thereafter he almost certainly wrote *An Answer To A Declaration . . .* , a secretly printed tract signed by Mercurius Pragmaticus which attacked Parliament and army from the point of view of a moderate Scot. In May 1648 Nedham, still preserving a certain amount of anonymity, wrote *The manifold Practises and Attempts of the Hamiltons . . . To get the Crown of Scotland*, in support of the "loyal" Scots. Probably by Nedham was an approximately concurrent publication, *The Reverend Alderman Atkins (The Shit-breech) His Speech. . . .* This alleged speech is full of malapropisms and deliberate errors (the army returned home "augmented" by the loss of 1,000 men), so that Atkins is made to conform to his epithet. Finally, sometime during the first half of 1648, Nedham in a signed two-page tract, *The Solemn League and Covenant*, warned the king against being embraced too closely by the Scots.

21. In *Pragmaticus*, 12, Nov. 30–Dec. 7, 1647, the editor bragged about his "familiar" who supplied him with information from Westminster. See also nos. 14, Dec. 14–21, 1647, and 27, Mar. 14–21, 1648. In October 1647 *Pragmaticus's* printer was arrested (*Perfect Occurrences*, 42, Oct. 15–22, 1647, p. 291), and in March 1648 a second printer was jailed (*KWI*, 251, Mar. 7–14, 1648, p. 871). In neither instance did *Pragmaticus* skip a week, possibly another indication of Nedham's connections in high places.

22. In September 1647 one counterfeit appeared, in November three, then none until August 1648. In the case of *Pragmaticus* "counterfeit" is an appropriate designation for these inferior imitations.

23. E.g., *Pragmaticus*, 12, Nov. 30–Dec. 7, 1647; 19, Jan. 18–25, 1648.

24. *Ibid.*, 5, Oct. 12–20, 1647.

25. *Ibid.*, 4, Oct. 5–12, 1647. For the historical context of this commentary see Frank, *Levellers*, pp. 135–147.

26. *Pragmaticus*, 6, Oct. 19–26, 1647.

27. *Ibid.*, 27, Mar. 14–21, 1648.

28. E.g., *ibid.*, 3, Sept. 28–Oct. 6, 1647; 6, Oct. 19–26, 1647; 11, Nov. 23–30, 1647; 17, Jan. 4–11, 1648; 19, Jan. 18–25, 1648; 23, Feb. 15–22, 1648; 28, Mar. 21–28, 1648; 1 (in a new series), Mar. 28–Apr. 4, 1648; 5, Apr. 25–May 2, 1648; 6, May 2–9, 1648.

29. E.g., *ibid.*, 6, Oct. 19–26, 1647 (Henry Marten); 9, Nov. 9–16, 1647 (Hugh Peters); 17, Jan. 4–11, 1648 (Henry Vane); 12, June 13–20, 1648 (a relatively full rogues' gallery).

30. There is a biography of Wharton in the *DNB*. See also Williams, *English Journalism*, pp. 88f. The editor's denial that he was Wharton (*Elencticus*, 11, Feb. 2–9, 1648, pp. 79f) is unconvincing, and his role in the paper is corroborated by nos. 16, Mar. 8–15, 1648, p. 119, and 31, June 21–28, 1648, pp. 237ff. In March 1648 Wharton was captured. He escaped in August, was recaptured in September, and again escaped.

31. *Elencticus*, 6, Dec. 29, 1647–Jan. 5, 1648, p. 42; 13, Feb. 16–23, 1648, p. 100. See also no. 23, Apr. 26–May 3, 1648, p. 174, and *Melancholicus*, 21, Jan. 15–22, 1648, p. 120.

32. *Elencticus*, 10, Jan. 26–Feb. 2, 1648, p. 76.

33. *Ibid.*, 21, Apr. 12–19, 1648, p. 159 (the prediction); 31, June 21–28, 1648, p. 237 (the nimble footwork).

34. After the Restoration, Wharton became a baronet.

35. *Mercurius Anti-Pragmaticus*, 4, Nov. 4–11, 1647.

36. *Ibid.*, 2, Oct. 21–28, 1647.

37. A single issue of *Mercurius Brittanicus* (with two "t"'s) came out on Apr. 7, 1648. The thirteen-number *Britanicus* kept to one "t" but adopted three different subtitles.

38. Hall was also, in all likelihood, the editor of *Mercurius Censorius* in June 1648. For his role in *Britanicus* see *Mercurius Bellicus*, 19, May 30–June 6, 1648; *Elencticus*, 29, June 7–14, 1648, p. 224, and 30, June 14–21, p. 233. *Elencticus* provided a derogatory biography of Hall (no. 34, July 12–19, 1648), perhaps because Hall had been hired by William Lilly, a pro-Parliament astrologer, to attack Wharton (J. B. Williams in *The Cambridge History of English Literature*, VII, 405). According to a current rumor Hall was paid £5 a week for editing *Britanicus*, not the more usual fee of half a crown (Rollins, *Cavalier and Puritan*, p. 44).

39. *Britanicus*, 5, June 13, 1648, p. 35.

40. For Birkenhead's connection with *Bellicus*, see *Mercurius Anti-Mercurius*, Apr. 4–11, 1648; *Mercurius Anti-Pragmaticus*, 4, Nov. 4–11, 1647. For a discussion of a similarly titled periodical see H. H. Weber, "The 'Mercurius Bellicus' of 1643," which describes how the five numbers of this early series gradually shifted from a relation to a quasi-weekly.

41. *Bellicus*, 12, Apr. 11–18, 1648.

42. *Ibid.*, 22, June 20–27, 1648.

43. *Aulicus*'s chronology is confusing. The first half-dozen numbers came out with weekly regularity from February 3 to March 9, 1648. The following issue, numbered "7, 8, 9," covered the four weeks March 2–30, the next number, "10, 11, 12," the ensuing three weeks. But this may have been a counterfeit, as no. "10, 11, 12, 13" (Mar. 30–Apr. 27) alleged. No. "12, 13, 14," possibly another counterfeit, was dated May 4–11, and the final issue in this series of *Aulicus*, no. 15, bore the date May 11–18. Throughout, the paper carried Sheppard's motto, "Quis me impune lacessit."

44. *Ibid.*, 1, Jan. 27–Feb. 3, 1648; e.g., 5, Feb. 24–Mar. 2, 1648.

45. *Ibid.*, 4, Feb. 17–24, 1648; "10, 11, 12, 13," Mar. 30–Apr. 27, 1648.

46. *Mercurius Anti-Pragmaticus*, Sept. 12–19, 1648. Sheppard also may have had an occasional hand in *Melancholicus*.

47. Sheppard's motto appeared in a few issues of *The Parliament Kite*, and his editorship is confirmed by internal evidence.

48. *Parliament Kite*, 6, June 16–23, 1648, p. 30; 10, July 20–27, 1648, p. 54.

49. *Ibid.*, 6, June 16–23, 1648, pp. 27ff. Sheppard had prepared himself for this sort of outburst by writing, in 1646, three violently anti-Leveller tracts: *The Famers Fam'd, The False Alarum,* and *Animadversions upon . . . Londons Liberty.*

50. *Parliament Kite*, "2, 3," May 16–June 1, 1648, p. 12; 5, June 9–16, 1648, p. 24.

51. *Psitacus*, 1, June 14–21, 1648 — the title-page poem. The editor had been jailed for his journalistic efforts in behalf of Charles.

52. *Ibid.*, 3 [*sic*], June 21–26, 1648; 4, June 21–July 3, 1648. The paper never did achieve a fixed day of publication.

53. For an account of this prison, Peters House, see Rollins, *Cavalier and Puritan*, pp. 38f. It is worth noting that during World War II many continental presses were able to elude the Nazis.

54. See *A Perfect Diurnall*'s title page, starting with no. 218, Sept. 27–Oct. 4, 1647. In one case Pecke referred to a mistake in one edition (no. 235, Jan. 25–31, 1648, p. 1692), and in several instances there were minor textual and typographical differences between the two editions.

55. *A Fresh Whip*, p. 3. See also *Man in the Moon*, 57, May 29–June 5, 1650, p. 426.

56. For the charge of sixpence see *Man in the Moon*, 57, May 29–June 5, 1650, p. 427, and Williams, *English Journalism*, p. 164. One of the earliest of these advertisements was for a book by an American, the first such notice to appear in an English newspaper (*Perfect Diurnall*, 242, Mar. 13–20, 1648, p. 1946; for further details see McCutcheon, "Americana in English Newspapers," p. 87).

57. When, for example, the Speaker of the House was unexpectedly ill and Commons did not sit, Pecke had quickly to find a space-filler. In one instance he used a letter from a German on the possibilities of peace in England; in another he reluctantly inserted half a page of foreign news (*Perfect Diurnall*, 228, Dec. 6–13, 1647, pp. 1883f; 241, Mar. 6–13, 1648, pp. 1941f).

58. *Ibid.*, 221, Nov. 18–25, 1647, p. 1779.

59. Pecke, for instance, claimed that he did not have space for the Leveller "Agreement of the People," though it was a document sufficiently short and newsworthy to merit reprinting (*Perfect Diurnall*, 226, Nov. 22–29, 1647, p. 1795). His account of Lilburne's arrest and official interrogation was also hostile (e.g., no. 234, Jan. 17–24, 1648, pp. 1884ff).

60. *KWI* missed the week of Sept. 28–Oct. 5, 1647. Then beginning with no. 229 (Oct. 5–12, 1647) the phrase "Collected by R. C." appeared on the title page, and through June 1648 the paper skipped no issues.

61. *Ibid.*, 233, Nov. 2–9, 1647, p. 722.

62. *Ibid.*, 241, Dec. 28, 1647–Jan. 4, 1648, p. 790.

63. *Ibid.*, 251, Mar. 7–14, 1648, p. 865. See also, for example, no. 234, Nov. 9–16, 1647, pp. 728ff.

64. *Ibid.*, 238, Dec. 7–14, 1647, pp. 757, 764.

65. *Ibid.*, 262, May 23–30, 1648, p. 953.

66. *Ibid.*, 258, Apr. 25–May 2, 1648, p. 925.

67. *Ibid.*, 260, May 9–16, 1648, p. 937.

68. *Ibid.*, 266 (the first of two so numbered), June 20–27, 1648, pp. 985f. For additional examples of Collings' rhetorical skill see in particular nos. 239, Dec. 14–21, 1647, p. 765, and 265, June 13–20, 1648, p. 977.

69. *Ibid.*, 241, Dec. 28, 1647–Jan. 4, 1648, p. 785: "It hath been the custome heretofore to passe away the sloth of these Winter nights with a Canterbury tale or two out of *Chaucer,* but the Gravity of these Times not admitting of such vanities, *Canterbury* hath been at this season so unhappy as to make a tale of herself." Then followed an account of rioters there looting shops on Christmas, and the next day demonstrating in favor of the king.

70. *KWI*, 244, Jan. 18–25, 1648, p. 816.

71. *Perfect Occurrences*, 40, Oct. 1–8, 1647, p. 281. The passage is quoted in Hotson, *Commonwealth and Restoration Stage*, p. 26.

72. E.g., *Perfect Occurrences*, 42, Oct. 15–22, 1647, pp. 291, 295; 63, Mar. 10–17, 1648, p. 517; 66, Mar. 31–Apr. 7, 1648, p. 474; 73, May 19–26, 1648, p. 525. As to Walker's editorship, his name was affixed to the end of no. 39, Sept. 24–Oct. 1, 1647, though thereafter it sometimes appeared as Luke Harruney. The Royalist mercuries of early 1648 contained many references to Walker as a sycophant and bloodhound. His popularity among the Royalists was not increased by the fact that in February he was paid £30 for writing an attack on the king and in March was responsible for the publication of *Vindiciae contra Tyrannos*. (For further details see Williams, *Cambridge History of English Literature*, VII, 400, and his "Henry Walker, Journalist of the Commonwealth," p. 459.)

73. *Perfect Occurrences*, 65, Mar. 24–31, 1648, p. 459.

74. E.g., *ibid.*, 75, June 2–9, 1648, p. 539: a reference to a mistake being corrected in "some" copies.

75. *Ibid.*, 63, Mar. 10–17, 1648, p. 516, had an advertisement for Hebrew lessons; the etymologies began the following week.

76. *A Fresh Whip*, 1647, paid inadvertent tribute to Walker's energy by claiming that he did much of his news-gathering at night and that he was concerned with promoting his paper's sales.

77. *Perfect Occurrences*, 66, Mar. 31–Apr. 7, 1648, p. 469.

78. Border's initials began appearing on the title page with no. 41, Oct. 13–20, 1647.

79. *Moderate Intelligencer*, 160, Apr. 6–13, 1648, *ca.* pp. 1260ff; 166, May 18–25, 1648, pp. 1350ff.

80. *Ibid.*, 136, Oct. 21–28, 1647, p. 1333.

81. But Dillingham had not entirely forgotten his old touch, and in one instance he mocked an astrologer by claiming that any informed person could have foretold the same events (*ibid.*, 134, Oct. 7–14, 1647, p. 1310).

82. The initials H. W. C. (Henry Walley, Clerk) appeared on the title page of this Wednesday newspaper, which changed its name after three numbers to *The Kingdoms Weekly Account of Heads of Chiefe Passages in Parliament*.

83. No. 1, Dec. 29, 1647–Jan. 5, 1648, had the initials B. D. on the title page, but with no. 2 these became D. B. G. (Daniel Border, Gentleman).

84. *Kingdomes Weekly Post*, 9, Feb. 22–Mar. 1, 1648, p. 72.

85. Walker's editorship is strongly indicated by the fact that *Packets of Letters* was printed by Robert Ibbitson, the man now most regularly used by him; also, Walker was the journalist most likely to have access to the letters which constituted this paper. In June 1648 it was probably he who was responsible for a single-issue paper, *A Perfect Diary Of Passages Of the Kings Army*, which devoted itself almost entirely to the siege of Colchester.

86. E.g., *Packets of Letters*, 6, Apr. 24, 1648: the letter from York dated Apr. 22. Normally, however, it took a week for news from Edinburgh to get into print in London (e.g., *Severall Proceedings*, 78, Mar. 20–27, 1651, p. 1185).

87. *Elencticus*, 44, Sept. 20–27, 1648, pp. 351f; *Man in the Moon*, 26, Oct. 17–24, 1649, p. 218. (In *The Moderate*, 12, Sept. 26–Oct. 3, 1648, p. 96, the editor denied his low birth, but he also added, unconvincingly, that he was not Mabbott.) A petition of Mabbott's asking that he be appointed chief censor mentioned his five years of service to the House of Commons (*Historical Manuscripts Commission*, Sixth Report, Appendix, p. 198). In July 1646 he was paid £20 for certain jobs he had done for Parliament (*Lords Journals*, VIII, 441), and in 1648, £40 as "agent for . . . Fairfax, for his good services in bringing up the articles for the surrender of Colchester" (*Historical Manuscripts Commission*, Seventh Report, Appendix, p. 52).

88. Williams, *English Journalism*, p. 151. Mabbott's long connection with the Holland family may have helped him to land on his feet (e.g., *Moderate*, 12, Sept. 26–Oct. 3, 1648, p. 94).

89. Among the irritations of being censor were the accusation that Mabbott was a stooge for Walker (*Melancholicus*, 17, Dec. 18–25, 1647, p. 98), and the forging of Mabbott's name to some of the more violent "malignant sheets" (*Perfect Diurnall*, 226, Nov. 22–29, 1647, p. 1800).

90. *Moderate Intelligencer*, 164, May 4–11, 1648, p. 1314.

91. Williams, *English Journalism*, p. 114; *Historical Manuscripts Commission*, Seventh Report, Appendix, p. 33.

92. *Lords Journals*, X, 345; *Moderate Intelligencer* (Dillingham's), 172, June 29–July 6, 1648, p. 1421, and 173, July 6–13, 1648, p. 1433.

IX

MATURITY

July 1648 to January 1649

1. *Moderate Intelligencer* (Mabbott's), 171, June 22–29, 1648, p. 1409.

2. This was the gist of the announcement repeated in the first seven numbers of *The Moderate*, July 11–Aug. 29, 1648.

3. E.g., *ibid.*, 7, Aug. 22–29, 1648, pp. 49f.

4. *Ibid.*, 6, Aug. 15–22, 1648, p. 45.

5. *Ibid.*, 10, Sept. 12–19, 1648, p. 80; 9, Sept. 5–12, 1648, p. 67.

6. *Ibid.*, 9, Sept. 5–12, 1648, pp. 69ff. See also Frank, *Levellers*, pp. 167–169.

7. *Moderate*, 11, Sept. 19–26, 1648, p. 81. See also no. 8, Aug. 29–Sept. 5, 1648, p. 57.

8. *Ibid.*, 14, Oct. 10–17, 1648, pp. 114f.

9. E.g., *ibid.*, 16, Oct. 24–31, 1648, p. 120; 17, Oct. 31–Nov. 7, 1648, pp. 137f.

10. *Ibid.*, 17, Oct. 31–Nov. 7, 1648, pp. 138f.

11. E.g., *ibid.*, 19, Nov. 14–21, 1648, p. 154.

12. *Ibid.*, 23, Dec. 12–19, 1648, p. 203. See also the derogatory account of Mabbott in *Mercurius Impartialis*, 1, Dec. 5–12, 1648.

13. *Moderate*, 25, Dec. 26, 1648–Jan. 2, 1649, p. 235.

14. *Ibid.*, 26, Jan. 2–9, 1649, p. 248.

15. An indication of this interest was the popularity of John Wilkins' *Mathematical Magick*, published in 1648: three of its chapters carried on the author's previously published speculations on how human beings might conquer the air.

16. *Moderate*, 23, Dec. 12–19, 1648, pp. 207f. For further details see Joseph Frank, "England's First Newspaper Articles on Flying."

17. *Pragmaticus*, 21, Aug. 15–22, 1648 — also given in Williams, *English Journalism*, p. 94. In the same number the editor boasted about his "Familiar" at Derby House, where the committee then ruling England held its meetings.

18. *Pragmaticus*, 18, July 25–Aug. 1, 1648.

19. *Ibid.*, 26, Sept. 19–26, 1648; 30, Oct. 17–24, 1648. In one instance the Independents used a filibuster to delay a vote until they had a majority, in another to secure an adjournment to a ticklish debate.

20. *Ibid.*, 27, Sept. 26–Oct. 3, 1648; e.g., 20, Aug. 8–15, 1648. Number 19, Aug. 1–8, 1648, contained the story of an egg merchant's paying £60 for a seat in Parliament.

21. *Ibid.*, 39, Dec. 19–26, 1648. See also, for example, nos. 25, Sept. 12–19, 1648, and 29, Oct. 10–17, 1648.

22. *Ibid.*, 28, Oct. 3–10, 1648; "36, 37," Dec. 5–12, 1648.

23. *Ibid.*, 35, Nov. 21–28, 1648.

24. E.g., *ibid.*, 24 (misnumbered 23), Sept. 5–12, 1648.

25. *Ibid.*, 17, June 18–25, 1648.

26. Numbers 18 through "32, 33," July 25–Nov. 14, 1648; no. 40, Dec. 26, 1648–Jan. 9, 1649, also consisted of twelve pages.

27. Numbers 20, 21, 22, 38, and 39 of *Pragmaticus* had to contend with counterfeits.

28. *Pragmaticus*, 44 and 45, Feb. 6–20, 1649, were spurious. The genuine no. 43, Feb. 20–27, 1649, began with a reference to these "counterfeits" and to the fact that the Parliamentary "Beagles" had forced the editor to lie low.

29. Nedham later acknowledged retiring after no. 41 (see below, Chapter X, note 101), but it is extremely likely that his connection with it and no. 40 was merely nominal. That he picked his time well is indicated by a report in *Perfect Occurrences*, 108, Jan. 19–26, 1649, p. 803, that "Pragmaticus" — probably Nedham's successor — had been arrested. Meanwhile, at the end of November, Nedham had displayed his clever touch by writing *A Plea for The King, and Kingdome*, a vigorous and pugnacious reply to the "Remonstrance of the Army."

30. *Melancholicus*, 52, Aug. 14–21, 1648.

31. See, e.g., *ibid.*, 48, July 17–24, 1648 — both the two issues so numbered and dated. That Sheppard had a hand in *Melancholicus* is implied by no. 51, Aug. 7–14, 1648. Hackluyt may have again escaped from jail, for he seems the most likely candidate for editor of no. 59, Oct. 2–9, 1648. See also the report of the arrest of Hackluyt in *Perfect Occurrences*, 81, July 14–21, 1648.

32. *Melancholicus*, 49, July 24–31, 1648, p. 296, refrained from railing long enough to name the members of both Houses and the London aldermen most violently opposed to Charles.

33. *Ibid.*, 3 (in a new series), Jan. 5–12, 1649, p. 20.

34. *Elencticus*, 55, Dec. 5–12, 1648, p. 525.

35. *Ibid.*, 32, June 28–July 5, 1648, p. 245; 50, Nov. 1–8, 1648, pp. 485ff. Wharton also used the third person to praise his own Almanac (no. 49, Oct. 24–31, 1648, p. 404).

36. *Ibid.*, 47, Oct. 11–18, 1648, p. 383.

37. *Ibid.*, 35, July 19–26, 1648, p. 273; 55, Dec. 5–12, 1648, p. 532.

38. *Ibid.*, 35, July 19–26, 1648, p. 276.

39. *Ibid.*, 37, Aug. 2–9, 1648, p. 289; e.g., 56, Dec. 12–19, 1648, pp. 534ff; 40, Aug. 23–29, 1648, p. 331.

40. *Ibid.*, 52, Nov. 15–22, 1648, p. 503.

41. *Ibid.*, 58 and 59, Dec. 26, 1648–Jan. 9, 1649, *passim*. Number 59, p. 563, also contained a brief report of a petition from some Amsterdam Jews asking that their banishment from England be repealed.

42. *Ibid.*, 1 (in a new series), Jan. 31–Feb. 7, 1649. (This number is reprinted in Williams, *English Journalism*, pp. 200–210.) The account of the king's execution in the "counterfeit" *Elencticus* was not so effective as Wharton's.

43. For Sheppard's editorship of *The Royall Diurnall*, see Rollins, "Sheppard and His Praise of Poets," pp. 526f, and Williams, *English Journalism*, p. 99.

44. Possibly Birkenhead edited the third of these three numbers, for *Aulicus*, Aug. 21–28, 1648, exhibits his divisive touch.

45. *Parliament-Porter*, 4, Sept. 18–25, 1648. Francis Bethen had just been appointed Provost Marshal to Parliament to aid in suppressing subversive pamphleteers, ballad writers, journalists, playwrights, and actors; and he was given twenty deputies to help him in his searches and seizures.

46. *A Declaration*, 2, Dec. 6–13, 1648, p. 11.

47. For more on Harris see *Mercurius Impartialis*, 1, Dec. 5–12, 1648, and Williams, *English Journalism*, pp. 106f.

48. *The Grand Designe*, Dec. 1647, and *The royall Quarrell*, Feb. 1648.

49. *Mercurius Militaris*, 5, Nov. 14–21, 1648, p. 33. The paper had skipped the preceding week.

50. *Ibid.*, 1, Oct. 10–17, 1648, p. 1.

51. *Ibid.*, 2, Oct. 17–24, 1648, pp. 9f.

52. *Ibid.*, 4, Oct. 31–Nov. 7, 1648, p. 28.

53. *Ibid.*, p. 30; 5, Nov. 14–21, 1648, pp. 37f.

54. Walker's editorship is based on internal evidence and the fact that Ibbitson printed *Heads of a Diarie*.

55. Clyde, *Struggle for Freedom*, p. 148.

56. This petition is given in *Historical Manuscripts Commission*, Seventh Report, Appendix, p 45. It was strongly anti-Mabbott and, among other things, accused him of making almost £100 a year out of his licensing activities. See also Clyde, *Struggle for Freedom*, pp. 147–149, and Williams, *English Journalism*, p. 107. At the end of August, Mabbott countered by proposing a more effective scheme to control the press, including a larger grant of powers to himself.

57. *Perfect Occurrences*, 95, Oct. 20–27, 1648, p. 705, contained a boost for lectures on Hebrew given by Walker.

58. *Ibid.*, 85, Aug. 11–18, 1648, p. 623; 86, Aug. 18–25, 1648, p. 422. (The paper's pagination, like that of many of its contemporaries, leaves much to be desired. In Walker's case the alternation of printers added to the confusion.)

59. *Ibid.*, 83, July 28–Aug. 4, 1648, p. 608; 84, Aug. 4–11, 1648, p. 475.

60. *Ibid.*, 97, Nov. 3–10, 1648, p. 717; 98, Nov. 10–17, 1648, p. 715.

61. *Ibid.*, 105, Dec. 29, 1648–Jan. 5, 1649, pp. 785f. Walker also called attention to the seventh anniversary of Charles's attempt to arrest the five leaders of the Parliamentary opposition (*ibid.*, p. 788).

62. *Mercure Anglois*, 60, Sept. 7/17–14/24, 1648, p. 237; 66, Oct. 19/29–Oct. 26/Nov. 5, 1648, pp. 261f.

63. *Moderate Intelligencer*, 182, Sept. 7–14, 1648, contained two particularly intriguing items of foreign news: an account of current happenings in China, and a story from Paris about the possibility of establishing an academy in England modeled on the ideas of Castiglione.

64. *Ibid.*, 185, Sept. 28–Oct. 5, 1648, p. 1567; 196, Dec. 14–21, 1648, p. 1793.

65. *Ibid.*, 182, Sept. 7–14, 1648, p. 1529.

66. *Ibid.*, 181, Aug. 31–Sept. 7, 1648, p. 1517.

67. *Ibid.*, 196, Dec. 14–21, 1648, p. 1790. A month later, in keeping with both the tolerationist views of the Independents and his readers' prejudices, Dillingham included this evasive item:
"There was also a Petition to repeale the Laws made against the Jews, who were . . . banished . . . because they ingrossed Trade and Riches to the prejudice of the Natives . . . and yet not before the people had like to have torne them in pieces; it's true they may be useful when the inhabitants, as in Poland, Spaine, and other parts, live in a way of gallantry . . . but in a countrey abounding with Merchants . . . they are as water to the shoos: This is not said as against their having their consciences" (no. 200, Jan. 11–18, 1649, p. 1848).

68. *Ibid.*, 199–201, Jan. 4–25, 1649, pp. 1825f, 1837f, 1849f. In no. 187, Oct. 12–19, 1648, p. 1689, Dillingham had editorialized to the effect that it is the execution not the form of the law that is important.

69. *Ibid.*, 197, Dec. 21–28, 1648, p. 1802.

70. *Ibid.*, 195, Dec. 7–14, 1648, p. 1777. The preceding week's account of Pride's Purge concluded with the wry understatement that "this dayes work" boded ill for unity between Parliament and army.

71. *Ibid.*, 173, July 6–13, 1648, p. 1435.

72. *Ibid.*, 198, Dec. 28, 1648–Jan. 4, 1649, pp. 1814f.

73. *Ibid.*, 201, Jan. 18–25, 1649, p. 1850.

74. *Ibid.,* 200, Jan. 11–18, 1649, p. 1839; 201, Jan. 18–25, 1649, p. 1855.

75. *Ibid.,* 203, Feb. 1–8, 1649, p. 1875.

76. *KWI,* 267, July 4–11, 1648, p. 1001.

77. E.g., *ibid.,* 270, July 25–Aug. 1, 1648, p. 1025; 272, Aug. 8–15, 1648, pp. 1045, 1047; 276, Sept. 5–12, 1648, p. 1073; 279, Sept. 26–Oct. 3, 1648, p. 1097.

78. *Ibid.,* 283, Oct. 24–31, 1648. The entire issue is a good example of how Collings could weave a few anti-Independent threads into a fabric of objective news.

79. *Ibid.,* 286, Nov. 14–21, 1648, p. 1157.

80. *Ibid.,* 281, Oct. 10–17, 1648, p. 1113.

81. *Ibid.,* 272, Aug. 8–15, 1648, p. 1048. Possibly Mabbott had started to implement his threat: a month earlier the paper had skipped a week — its only lapse during this period — and the following week (July 18–25) it faced the competition of a counterfeit *Kingdomes Weekly Intelligencer.*

82. *KWI,* 291, Dec. 19–26, 1648, p. 1194.

83. *Ibid.,* 294, Jan. 9–16, 1649, p. 1224; 279, Sept. 26–Oct. 3, 1648, p. 1102; 293, Jan. 2–9, 1649, pp. 1210f. (This account of a raid is reprinted in Hotson, *Commonwealth and Restoration Stage,* pp. 40f.)

84. *KWI,* 295, Jan. 6–13, 1649, p. 1232; 297, Jan. 30–Feb. 6, 1649, p. 1241.

85. *Perfect Weekly Account,* Nov. 15–22, 1648, p. 286. (The paper ceased to be numbered in October, though its pagination, beginning with page 233, then became continuous.)

86. *Ibid.,* 26, Sept. 6–13, 1648.

87. *Ibid.,* Jan. 10–17, 1649, p. 351.

88. *Ibid.,* Jan. 17–24, 1649, p. 357.

89. *Perfect Diurnall,* 261, July 24–31, 1648, p. 2102; e.g., 277, Nov. 13–20, 1648, *passim.* For the charge of sixpence see *Man in the Moon,* 57, May 29–June 5, 1650, p. 427. One of Pecke's lengthier book advertisements is quoted in McCutcheon, "Beginnings of Book Reviewing," pp. 698f.

90. *Perfect Diurnall,* 279, Nov. 27–Dec. 4, 1648, pp. 2337ff.

91. E.g., *ibid.,* 269, Sept. 18–25, 1648, p. 2168; 276, Nov 6–13, 1648, p. 2221.

92. E.g. *ibid.,* 266, Aug. 28–Sept. 4, 1648, p. 2142; 268, Sept 11–18, 1648, p. 2160.

93. *Ibid.,* 288, Jan. 29–Feb. 5, 1649, p. 2315. Such relations as *A Perfect Narrative* (Jan. 23, 1649) and *A Continuation of the Narrative* (Jan. 25, 1649) had functioned as the equivalent of extras, in order to give full and up-to-the-minute news of the king's trial; and other relations promptly covered his execution. Hugh Ross Williamson's *The Day They Killed the King* provides a dramatic though shallow narrative of what happened on January 30, 1649.

X

DECLINE AND FALL
February to October 1649

1. Probably the most dramatic testimony to Cromwell's civil-libertarian inclinations was his involvement in 1656 in the case of James Naylor, a Quaker who thought himself Christ. See, for instance, C. H. Firth, *The Last Years of the Protectorate, 1656–1658,* I, 84–106.

2. E.g., *Perfect Diurnall,* 266, Aug. 28–Sept. 4, 1648, p. 2140; Williams, *English Journalism,* p. 99.

3. E.g., *KWI,* 275, Aug. 29–Sept. 5, 1648, p. 1068, and 277, Sept. 12–19, 1648, p.

1083; Clyde, *Struggle for Freedom*, pp. 158f; and Chapter IX above, note 45. The Royalist mercuries had much to say about these "beagles."

4. Siebert, *Freedom of the Press*, p. 215; Clyde, *Struggle for Freedom*, pp. 159–164.

5. *Commons Journals*, VI, 111.

6. The nomenclature of *A Perfect Summary*, even disregarding its changes in subtitle, was wayward. No. 1, Jan. 22–29, 1649, was called *A Perfect Summary of Exact Passages of Parliament;* no. 2, *A Perfect Collection of Exact Passages of Parliament.* With no. 3 the paper returned to its original title, but in April it was changed to *A Perfect Summary of An Exact Dyarie of Some Passages in Parliament.* In August it resumed its first title, which it retained until the paper came to an end in October. For Jennings' military service see *Perfect Occurrences*, 16, Apr. 16–23, 1647, p. 127; and for his tie-in with certain leading Independents, see Williams, *English Journalism*, p. 115.

7. For Jennings' laxness as censor see, for example, Rollins, *Cavalier and Puritan*, pp. 13, 47.

8. *Perfect Summary*, 8, Mar. 12–19, 1649, p. 72; 15, Apr. 30–May 7, 1649, p. 142; 26 (the second week so numbered), Sept. 17–24, 1649, p. 216.

9. *Ibid.*, 27, Sept. 24–Oct. 1, 1649, p. 224.

10. The first number of this paper, Jan. 26–Feb. 2, 1649, was entitled *The Kingdomes Faithfull Scout;* with no. 2 it became *The Kingdomes Faithfull and Impartiall Scout.* Starting with no. 10, Mar. 30–Apr. 6, 1649, Border's name frequently appeared at the end.

11. *Kingdomes Faithfull and Impartiall Scout*, 14, Apr. 27–May 4, 1649, p. 110. See also, for example, nos. 8, Mar. 16–23, 1649, p. 61, and 16, May 11–18, 1649, pp. 121ff.

12. *Ibid.*, 11, Apr. 6–13, 1649, p. 84.

13. *Ibid.*, 13, Apr. 20–27, 1649, pp. 99ff.

14. *Perfect Occurrences*, 127, June 1–8, 1649, p. 1094.

15. *Kingdomes Faithfull and Impartiall Scout*, 20, June 8–15, 1649, pp. 154, 160.

16. *Perfect Occurrences*, 129, June 15–22, 1649, p. 1128. Jennings later attacked the *Scout* in his *Perfect Summary*, 29, July 16–23, 1649, p. 114.

17. Apparently Jennings did so reluctantly, for in the first number of *A Perfect Diurnall* to be licensed by him rather than by Mabbott (no. 304, May 21–28, 1649), he had Pecke include a notice that Jennings would "from hence forth upon good grounds" refuse to license the *Scout*.

18. *Kingdomes Faithfull and Impartiall Scout*, 22, June 22–29, 1649, pp. 170ff. Some data on the *Scout*'s squabble with Walker can be found in Clyde, *Struggle for Freedom*, pp. 179f, and Williams, *English Journalism*, pp. 117–119.

19. *Kingdomes Faithfull and Impartiall Scout*, 21, June 15–22, 1649, p. 162.

20. *Ibid.*, 30, Aug. 17–24, 1649, p. 229.

21. *Moderate*, 51, June 26–July 3, 1649, p. 591.

22. *Ibid.*, 34, Feb. 27–Mar. 6, 1649, pp. 334–342.

23. *Ibid.*, 40, Apr. 10–17, 1649, pp. 409, 416–421, 424.

24. E.g., *ibid.*, 44, May 8–15, 1649, pp. 498, 503f.

25. *Ibid.*, 41, Apr. 17–24, 1649, p. 433.

26. *Ibid.*, 37, Mar. 20–27, 1649, p. 375.

27. *Ibid.*, 39, Apr. 3–10, 1649, p. 406.

28. Clyde, *Struggle for Freedom*, p. 173.

29. *Perfect Diurnall*, 304, May 21–28, 1649, p. 2500; *Kingdomes Faithfull and Impartiall Scout*, 18, May 25–June 1, 1649, p. 143.

30. For further details see Frank, *Levellers*, pp. 185f.

31. Another indication that Mabbott could be a man of principle was his defense of a publisher's right to circulate the Koran in English (*Moderate*, 37, Mar. 20–27, 1649, p. 374.).

32. *Ibid.*, 58, Aug. 14–21, 1649, p. 676.

33. At this time, too, four months after his resignation, his imprimatur appeared on one issue of *KWI* (no. 328, Sept. 4–11, 1649).

34. *Perfect Occurrences*, 137, Aug. 10–17, 1649, pp. 1216f. See also Williams, *English Journalism*, pp. 162f.

35. There is a biography of Gerbier in Hugh Ross Williamson, *Four Stuart Portraits*, pp. 26–60. (For his Academy see pp. 50–52.)

36. E.g., *Perfect Occurrences*, 133, July 13–20, 1649, p. 1192; 135, July 27–Aug. 3, 1649, p. 1205. See also *Man in the Moon*, 15, July 25–Aug. 2, 1649, pp. 124f.

37. *Perfect Occurrences*, 143, 144, 145, Sept. 21–Oct. 12, 1649, *passim*. These lectures might also have included some promotion of the "office of Entries."

38. *Ibid.*, 139, Aug. 24–31, 1649, p. 1250.

39. E.g., *ibid.*, 126, May 25–June 1, 1649, p. 1051, and 127, June 1–8, 1649, p. 1080; 129, June 15–22, 1649, p. 1121; 125, May 18–25, 1649, p. 1059. Number 30, June 22–29, 1649, p. 1089, gave the impression that Walker was an official spokesman for the army.

40. *Ibid.*, 117, Mar. 23–30, 1649, pp. 934; 126, May 25–June 1, 1649, pp. 1053f.

41. *Ibid.*, 119, Apr. 6–13, 1649, p. 964; 121, Apr. 20–27, 1649, p. 999.

42. See *Ibid.*, 114, Mar. 2–9, 1649, p. 896.

43. The last few numbers of *Perfect Occurrences* were, however, reduced from sixteen to twelve pages. Walker may have been able to relax because his services to the Independents had just been rewarded with a benefice.

44. *Moderate*, 38, Mar. 27–Apr. 3, 1649, p. 396; *Perfect Occurrences*, 117, Mar. 23–30, 1649, p. 925; *Modest Narrative of Intelligence*, 1, Apr. 7, 1649, p. 1.

45. *Perfect Occurrences*, 133, July 13–20, 1649, p. 1192. *A Tuesdaies Journall* lasted from July 17 to Aug. 21, 1649.

46. *Perfect Weekly Account*, May 30–June 6, 1649, p. 505.

47. *Ibid.*, Sept. 19–26, 1649, p. 616.

48. Border, who had not been unsympathetic to the Levellers, for instance condemned the Diggers on theological grounds: private property was the result of Adam's fall, hence communism could not work among sinful men (*ibid.*, July 18–25, 1649, p. 552).

49. *Ibid.*, Sept. 5–12, 1649, p. 595. (The previous week Border mentioned, on p. 587, that the price of beer was ten shillings a barrel.)

50. *Moderate Intelligencer*, 215, Apr. 26–May 2, 1649, pp. 2018f. This account has been reprinted in Hugh Talmadge Lefler's "A Description of 'Carolina' by a 'Well-Willer,' 1649." A shorter but similar account appeared in *Perfect Diurnall*, 304, May 21–28, 1649, p. 2506, and it has been reprinted in Radin, *Bibliography and Summary*, p. 66.

51. *Moderate Intelligencer*, 203, Feb. 1–8, 1649, p. 1884.

52. *Ibid.*, 205, Feb. 15–22, 1649, pp. 1897f.

53. *Ibid.*, 208, Mar. 8–15, 1649, p. 1935.

54. *Ibid.*, 222, June 14–21, 1649, pp. 2097f.

55. E.g., *ibid.*, 227, July 19–26, 1649, p. 2178.

56. *Ibid.*, 207, Mar. 1–8, 1649, pp. 1921f; 208, Mar. 8–15, 1649, pp. 1933f; 209, Mar. 15–22, 1649, pp. 1945ff.

57. *Ibid.*, 210, Mar. 22–29, 1649, p. 1957.

58. *Ibid.*, 211, Mar. 29–Apr. 5, 1649, pp. 1965f.

59. *Ibid.*, 226, July 12–19, 1649, pp. 2155f; 233, Aug. 30–Sept. 6, 1649, p. 2250. In the first of these two numbers Dillingham again observed that "money answers all things" (p. 2166).

60. *Ibid.*, 204, Feb. 8–15, 1649, p. 1885.

61. E.g., *ibid.*, 232, Aug. 23–30, 1649, p. 2227.

62. *Ibid.*, 218, May 17–24, 1649, p. 2056.

63. E.g., *ibid.*, 235, Sept. 13–20, 1649, p. 2274; 233, Aug. 30–Sept. 6, 1649, p. 2242.

64. *Ibid.*, 236, Sept. 20–27, 1649, p. 2286.

65. *Ibid.*, 237, Sept. 27–Oct. 4, 1649, p. 2298. The last part of this passage was so badly printed that it is almost indecipherable.

66. *KWI*, 317, June 19–26, 1649, p. 1401.

67. *Ibid.*, 325, Aug. 14–21, 1649, p. 1465.

68. *Ibid.*, 319, July 3–10, 1649, p. 1417.

69. *Ibid.*, 320, July 10–17, 1649, p. 1428.

70. *Ibid.*, 331, Sept. 25–Oct. 2, 1649, p. 1518.

71. In *KWI*, 324, Aug. 7–14, 1649, p. 1457, the editor boasted that he had "set hours in every week to search after and to examine Intelligence." Later he became less diligent.

72. *Ibid.*, 328, Sept. 4–11, 1649, p. 1496. Collings also reported that the Royalists in France had little news from England except via the Royalist mercuries, "which makes them either to laugh or fight . . . at the variety of forced Languages in the beginning of some Pamphlets and the rudenesse of the dresse in which most of them come forth . . ." (no. 321, July 17–24, 1649, p. 1440).

73. *Ibid.*, 302, Mar. 6–13, 1649, p. 1281.

74. E.g., *ibid.*, 305, Mar. 27–Apr. 3, 1649, p. 1312; 320, July 10–17, 1649, pp. 1431f. In no. 317, June 19–26, 1649, pp. 1407f, Collings included an account of the death of Brandon, the man who allegedly beheaded Charles I; it was mutedly pro-Royalist.

75. *Ibid.*, 313, May 22–29, 1649, p. 1370.

76. *Ibid.*, 309, Apr. 24–May 1, 1649, p. 1344.

77. *Ibid.*, 311, May 8–15, 1649, p. 1353.

78. *Ibid.*, 328, Sept. 4–11, 1649, p. 1496; 329, Sept. 11–18, 1649, p. 1497.

79. The second of these two numbers contained a garbled report of an act "concerning New England . . . making the Island a Corporation. . . ."

80. Clyde, *Struggle for Freedom*, p. 179. *KWI* was not entered at all during this period, other papers only intermittently.

81. *Perfect Diurnall*, 319, Sept. 3–10, 1649, p. 2695. Back in May, Pecke had, for instance, printed a moderately sympathetic account of Lockyer's funeral (no. 301, Apr. 30–May 7, 1649, p. 2479).

82. For further details see Siebert, *Freedom of the Press*, pp. 221f; Clyde, *Struggle for Freedom*, pp. 163f, 177f, 180f; and Williams, *English Journalism*, pp. 110f. Scattered items in the licensed press and numerous angry laments in Royalist mercuries also had much to say about the censorship.

83. *Impartiall Intelligencer*, 21, July 18–25, 1649, pp. 164f.

84. *Modest Narrative*, 6, May 5–12, 1649, p. 41; see also nos. 8, May 19–26, 1649, pp. 57f, and 9, May 26–June 2, 1649, pp. 65f. A few of the editor's arguments were more convincing, such as the allegation that the Levellers were going around in a circle by failing to define what they meant by "the People" (e.g., no. 7, May 12–19, 1649, pp. 49f).

85. *Ibid.*, 15, July 7–14, 1649, p. 120.

86. *Continued Heads*, 1, Apr. 13–20, 1649, p. 1; 3, Apr. 27–May 4, 1649, p. 17.

87. *England's Moderate Messenger*, which came out on Monday, was probably edited by the person who in July authored the two rival issues of *A Perfect Diurnall*.

88. *Mercurius Brittanicus*, 4, May 15–22, 1649, p. 26. Despite the allegation in *Pragmaticus* (no. 4, May 8–15, 1649), Mabbott was probably not the editor of *Brittanicus*.

89. *England's Moderate Messenger* had come to an end with no. 11 on July 9. The first issue of *The Moderate Messenger* — "number 14" — appeared on July 30. It too was printed for R. W. and authored by "the same hand who formerly drew up the Diurnall." Also, this issue began with page 89, while the final page of *England's Moderate Messenger* had been numbered 88.

90. *The First Decade of Useful Observations* (June 25, 1649), which is listed in the *Catalogue of the Thomason Collection* under newspapers, was a political tract, not a weekly of news. I have not been able to see the one issue of *A Book without a Title* (June 12, 1649), which is mentioned in Williams, *English Journalism*, p. 245, but it was probably not a legitimate newsbook. Nor in all likelihood was *Mercurius Verax*, which appeared on June 4, 1649, and is listed in *The Cambridge Bibliography of English Literature*, I, 760.

91. Here, in tabular form, is this box-score:

Month	Number of Titles	Total Number of Separate Issues
February	2	4
March	1	4
April	6	11
May	10	23
June	4	16
July	5	14
August	4	13
September	6	16
October	4	14
November	3	7
December	1	2

92. For external evidence of Harris's editorship see *Royall Diurnall*, 1, Feb. 25, 1650.

93. *Mercurius Militaris*, 1, Apr. 17–24, 1649, pp. 5ff.

94. E.g., *ibid.*, 3, May 1–8, 1649, pp. 26ff.

95. See *Mercurius Melancholicus, For King Charles the Second*, 2, May 31–June 7, 1649, pp. 7f; *Mercurius Elencticus*, 9, June 18–25, 1649, p. 66. Further details are provided in Williams, *English Journalism*, pp. 112f, and Clyde, *Struggle for Freedom*, pp. 183–185.

96. *Mercurius Pragmaticus*, 44, Feb. 6–13, 1649.

97. E.g., *ibid.*, 47, Mar. 20–27, 1649; 51, Apr. 17–24, 1649.

98. E.g., *ibid.*, 43, Feb. 20–27, 1649; 47, Mar. 20–27, 1649; 48, Mar. 27–Apr. 4, 1649; 50, Apr. 10–17, 1649.

99. *Ibid.*, 44, Feb. 27–Mar. 5, 1649; 43, Feb. 20–27, 1649.

100. For the price of two pence see *Mercurius Pragmaticus, For King Charls II*, 18, Aug. 14–21, 1649, where the editor claimed that he would "show more sport for two-pence in one hour than can be had at the Bankside for six-pence in three." The two April "counterfeits" were nos. 51 and 52. Various issues in the different series of *Pragmaticus* acknowledged that Londoners were greedy for news, though the editors tended to deprecate this curiosity as another product of revolutionary turmoil.

101. Besides internal evidence, Nedham's return was signaled by the statements in *Mercurius Pragmaticus, (For King Charles II)*, 1, Apr. 17–24, 1649, that "here comes old Prag. himself, new mounted," and that the reader should "Take notice, the last Prag. of the first part ended Num. 41." The new paper also bore the motto "Nemo me impune lacessit," which could be identified with Nedham among others. Finally, one of the counterfeits of this series of *Pragmaticus* included the announcement that its editor had refrained from writing for a long time, but that he was now returning because the former author of *Britanicus* had usurped the name "Pragmaticus" (*Mercurius Pragmaticus, For King Charls II*, 1, Sept. 10–17, 1649, p. 2; the internal punctuation of the title and the spelling of "Charles" was variable in all these series). Nedham, during the four months he was not editing a Royalist weekly, had not entirely withdrawn from propagandizing for the cause. In all likelihood it was he who wrote *A Most Pithy Exhortation*, published early in 1649. Signed by "Mercurius Pragmaticus," this six-page tract was a clever parody of Hugh Peters' speech to the Parliamentary sailors about to go out to battle

Rupert's fleet. Though overdone, it was particularly effective when it poked fun at the sailors for being Independents, leaving their wives at home to be the willing prey of soldiers, and being content with bad food — even if they could be reconciled by the fact that *The Moderate Intelligencer* would "canonize . . . [them] for brave fellows; and Harry Walker shall every Friday write you Admirals names in Hebrew, that their fames may read backwards." Also almost certainly by Nedham was a longer pamphlet, *Digitus Dei*, a pro-Royalist review of the life and death of the Duke of Hamilton published in April. Nedham not only had an inside knowledge of current history, but he could write political poetry not much inferior to Dryden's, as is evident in "An Epitaph upon James Duke of Hamilton" with which his pamphlet concluded. It is, in fact, worth quoting in full:

> "He that three Kingdomes made one flame,
> Blasted their beauty, burn't the frame,
> Himself now here in ashes lies
> A part of this great Sacrifice.
> Here all of HAMILTON remains,
> Save what the other world contains.
> But (Reader) it is hard to tell
> Whether that world be Heav'n or Hell.
> A Scotch man enters Hell at's birth,
> And 'scapes it when he goes to earth,
> Assur'd no worse a Hell can come
> Than that which he enjoy'd at home.
>   How did the Royal Workman botch
> This Duke, halfe-English, and halfe-Scotch:
> A Scot an English Earldom fits,
> As Purple doth your Marmuzets;
> Suits like Nol Cromwell with the Crown,
> Or Bradshaw in his Scarlet-gown.
> Yet might he thus disguis'd (no lesse)
> Have slip't to Heav'n in's English dresse,
> But that he in hope of life became
> [a line is here missing]. . . .
> This mystick Proteus too as well
> Might cheat the Devill, 'scape his Hell,
> Since to those pranks he pleas'd to play,
> Religion ever pav'd the way;
> Which he did to a Faction tie,
> Not to reforme, but crucifie.
> 'Twas he that first alarm'd the Kirke
> To this prepost'rous bloody worke,
> Upon the Kings to place Christs Throne,
> A step, and foot-stoole to his owne;
> Taught Zeale a hundred tumbling tricks,
> And Scriptures twin'd with Politicks;
> The Pulpit made a Juglers-Box,
> Set Law and Gospell in the Stocks,
> As did old Buchanan and Knox,
> In those daies when (at once) the Pox
> And Presbyters a way did find
> Into the world, to plague mankind.
> 'Twas he patch'd up the new Divine,
> Part Calvin, and part Cataline,
> Could too trans-forme (without a Spell)
> Satan into a Gabriel;
> Just like those pictures which we paint

On this side Fiend, on that side Saint.
Both this, and that, and ev'ry thing
He was; for, and against the King;
Rather than he his ends would misse,
Betray'd his Master with a kisse,
And buri'd in one common Fate
The glory of our Church and State:
The Crown too levell'd on the ground;
And having rock't all parties round,
'Faith, it was time then to be gone,
Since he had all his businesse done.
    Next, on the fatall Block expir'd,
He to this Marble-Cell retir'd;
Where all of HAMILTON remains,
But what Eternity contains."

102. See, for example, *Perfect Occurrences*, 129, June 15–22, 1649, p. 121; *Modest Narrative*, 12, June 16–23, 1649, p. 96.

103. *Mercurius Pragmaticus, (For King Charles II.)*, 2, Apr. 24–May 1, 1649, pp. 14f; 3, May 1–8, 1649.

104. *Ibid.*, 7, May 29–June 5, 1649; 8, June 5–12, 1649.

105. *Ibid.*, 9, June 12–19, 1649. New England as a refuge for the regicides was a repeated theme in the Royalist mercuries of 1649.

106. Nedham in all likelihood edited *Mercurius Pragmaticus (For King Charles II.)*, nos. 1 to 9, Apr. 17–June 19, 1649. The rival series, without the "e" in "Charles," extended from nos. 4 to 10, May 8–June 26, 1649, though one or two earlier numbers may not be extant. Each accused the other of being a counterfeit.

107. *Mercurius Pragmaticus, (For King Charls II.)*, 7, May 29–June 5, 1649; 8, June 5–12, 1649, pp. 59f; 9, June 12–19, 1649, pp. 68f.

108. *Ibid.*, 13, July 10–17, 1649; 21, Sept. 4–11, 1649; 15, July 24–31, 1649; 24, Sept. 25–Oct. 2, 1649; 13, July 10–17, 1649; 15, July 24–31, 1649.

109. This recantation, *Certain Considerations Tendered in all humilty*, August 1649, was a functional Hobbesian plea for partial, but not complete, control by the government of the organs of public expression, especially the pulpit.

110. For Wharton's editorship, in addition to internal evidence, see *Elencticus*, 8, June 11–18, 1649, p. 63. Wharton had, apparently, recently escaped from Newgate, to which he had been committed in March.

111. The "Elencticus" whose capture was reported in, for instance, *Impartiall Intelligencer* (no. 8, Apr. 18–25, 1649, p. 64) and *Continued Heads of Perfect Passages* (no. 2, Apr. 20–27, 1649, p. 14) was almost certainly Sheppard. The author of *Mercurius Elencticus, (For King Charls II)*, a typical Royalist weekly that appeared for two weeks in May, is not known, though in all likelihood he was not Wharton or Sheppard.

112. E.g., *Elencticus*, 7, June 4–11, 1649, p. 50; 21, Sept. 10–17, 1649, p. 163.

113. E.g., *ibid.*, 5, May 21–28, 1649, p. 35; 7, June 4–11, 1649, pp. 50ff.

114. *Ibid.*, 9, June 18–25, 1649, p. 66; 19, Aug. 27–Sept. 3, 1649, pp. 147f.

115. Early in 1649 Wharton vigorously expressed himself against censorship (*Elencticus*, 56, Feb. 6–13), as he did intermittently thereafter. In no. 23, Sept. 24–Oct. 1, 1649, pp. 177ff, he gave a full description of the new act, followed by his defiance of it. The next week no *Elencticus* appeared; then in the final four issues (Oct. 8–Nov. 5) Wharton reiterated his defiance and persistently attacked the new official weekly of the Commonwealth, *A Briefe Relation*.

116. *Man in the Moon*, 1, Apr. 16, 1649, p. 3. For Crouch's editorship see Sheppard's *The Weepers*, Sept. 1652; and *Faithfull Scout*, 65, Apr. 9–16, 1652.

117. *Man in the Moon*, 2, Apr. 16–23, 1649, p. 10; Clyde, *Struggle for Freedom*, p. 183.

118. *Man in the Moon,* 21, Sept. 5–12, 1649, pp. 172f.

119. *Ibid.,* 12, June 27–July 4, 1649, p. 102; e.g., 23, Sept. 19–26, 1649, pp. 187f; 24, Sept. 26–Oct. 10, 1649, p. 195 (a double number because of the hotness of pursuit); 31, Nov. 21–28, 1649, pp. 243f (the final 1649 issue of the paper).

120. E.g., *ibid.,* 15, July 25–Aug. 2, 1649, pp. 124f; 24, Sept. 26–Oct. 10, 1649, pp. 200f; 26, Oct. 17–24, 1649, pp. 217f. That Crouch was successful may have been hinted at in his claim (no. 17, Aug. 8–15, 1649, p. 146) that *The Man in the Moon* was being counterfeited.

121. E.g., *ibid.,* 22, Sept. 12–19, 1649, p. 186.

122. *Ibid.,* 18, Aug. 15–23, 1649, p. 152; 20, Aug. 30–Sept. 5, 1649, p. 167.

123. *Ibid.,* 8, May 28–June 5, 1649, pp. 72f; 12, June 27–July 4, 1649, pp. 99f.

124. The act is given in Firth and Rait, *Acts and Ordinances,* II, 245–254, and summarized in Siebert, *Freedom of the Press,* pp. 222f, and Clyde, *Struggle for Freedom,* pp. 187f. It included provisions against hawkers, which drew forth a particularly anguished comment from *Mercurius Pragmaticus (For King Charls II),* 25, Oct. 9–16, 1649.

125. J. G. Muddiman (the real name of "J. B. Williams") has a short article summarizing the situation in late 1649: "The Licensed Newsbooks, 1649 and 1650."

XI

THE COMMONWEALTH NEWSPAPER I
October 1649 to September 1651

Bibliographical Note: Samuel Rawson Gardiner's *History of the Commonwealth and Protectorate, 1649-1656,* is the work on which I have leaned most heavily for the historical background of the years its four volumes cover.

1. For more on Frost see Frank, *Levellers,* pp. 148, 155; Williams, *English Journalism,* p. 122; *Mercurius Elencticus,* 27, Oct. 29–Nov. 5, 1649, pp. 209f.

2. The twelve pages of *A Briefe Relation,* 16, Jan. 1–8, 1650, were entirely given over to foreign news. On a few occasions, however, Frost apparently edited supplements to this paper. Two from late 1649 were *A Very Full and Particular Relation* and *A Perfect and more particular relation,* both of them, as their titles imply, relations rather than newspapers.

3. *Briefe Relation,* 9, Nov. 13–20, 1649, p. 96; 20, Jan. 22–29, 1650, p. 264.

4. *Ibid.,* 39, May 14–21, 1650, p. 570.

5. E.g., *ibid.,* 54, Sept. 10–17, 1650, p. 821.

6. *Briefe Relation,* 17, Jan. 8–15, 1650; see also Clyde, *Struggle for Freedom,* p. 201. Toward the end of its career *A Briefe Relation* shifted printers from Matthew Simmons to William Dugard.

7. In 1651 *Severall Proceedings* sometimes accumulated a page of advertisements.

8. *Ibid.,* 1, Sept. 25–Oct. 9, 1649, p. 3; 5, Oct. 26–Nov. 2, 1649; 7, Nov. 9–16, 1649.

9. Williams, *English Journalism,* p. 129; *Man in the Moon,* 38, Jan. 9–16, 1650, p. 298. Four weeks before this change of editors *Severall Proceedings* boosted Walker's Hebrew lectures (no. 15, Jan. 4–11, 1650, p. 195). From the start the paper was printed by Ibbitson, Walker's regular associate.

10. *Severall Proceedings,* 85, May 8–15, 1651, p. 1295.

11. *Ibid.,* 51, Sept. 12–19, 1650, p. 760; 105, Sept. 25–Oct. 2, 1651.

12. This assumption is based on internal evidence and a remark in *Man in the Moon,* 57, May 29–June 5, 1650, p. 426.

13. E.g., *Perfect Diurnall,* 91 and 92, Sept. 1–15, 1650 — the account of the Battle of Worcester. Also, Pecke received reports from The Hague via a member of the English ambassador's entourage.

14. E.g., *ibid.,* 21, Apr. 29–May 6, 1650, p. 218 (an account of four Royalists who toasted the king and then ate the flesh from their rumps); 34, July 29–Aug. 5, 1650, p. 406 (a story of a nine-week-old child who said "A King, a king," but who, it turned out, was merely an invention of its parents, who wished to publicize their tavern); 49, Nov. 11–18, 1650 (the tale of a cook on a Bremen ship who poisoned the captain and crew); 74, May 5–12, 1651, pp. 1012ff (the account, from Cheshire, of the seventeenth-century equivalent of a flying saucer).

15. *Mercurius Pragmaticus, (For King Charls II),* 30, Nov. 20–27, 1649.

16. *Man in the Moon,* 38, Jan. 9–16, 1650, p. 301.

17. *Ibid.,* 43, Feb. 13–20, 1650, p. 342. For more on Joan see Williams, *English Journalism,* pp. 132f; Clyde, *Struggle for Freedom,* pp. 178, 200f; and Abbott, "First Newspapermen," p. 50. References to her were frequent in the newspapers, both licensed and Royalist, of 1649–50.

18. *Man in the Moon,* 48, Mar. 13–20, 1650, pp. 374f; 49, Mar. 20–29, 1650, p. 384.

19. *Ibid.,* 52, Apr. 24–May 2, 1650, p. 395.

20. Rollins, *Cavalier and Puritan,* p. 58. The final number of *Man in the Moon,* May 29–June 5, 1650, contained no hint that the end was near, except the bitter call for help: where are the Levellers now?

21. E.g., *Man in the Moon,* 38, Jan. 9–16, 1650, p. 203; 43, Feb. 13–20, 1650, pp. 338ff.

22. E.g., *Pragmaticus,* 35, Dec. 25, 1649–Jan. 1, 1650; 37, Jan. 8–15, 1650; 39, Jan. 22–29, 1650; 44, Feb. 26–Mar. 3, 1650; 45, Mar. 5–12, 1650; 51, Apr. 23–30, 1650; 52, Apr. 30–May 7, 1650.

23. E.g., *ibid.,* 42, Feb. 12–19, 1650.

24. E.g., *ibid.,* 36, Jan. 1–8, 1650; 45, Mar. 5–12, 1650; 46, Mar. 12–19, 1650.

25. *Ibid.,* 48, Apr. 2–9, 1650.

26. Williams, *English Journalism,* p. 133. Prior to its demise, *Pragmaticus* skipped three weeks, two in February, one at the end of March.

27. The eighth and last issue (misnumbered 7) of *The Royall Diurnall* came out on April 30, 1650, the first number of *Mercurius Elenticus* on April, 22.

28. In the opening number the editor explained his period of silence by the traps "the viperous brood" had set for him.

29. *Elenticus,* 3, Apr. 29–May 6, 1650; 1, Apr. 22. 1650.

30. One of the editor's sources of optimism was his ostensible conviction, at least twice repeated, that Turkish aid for the Royalists was on the way.

31. *DNB*; J. Milton French, "Milton, Needham, and 'Mercurius Politicus,'" p. 236; Gardiner, *Commonwealth and Protectorate,* I, 252–255.

32. For a summary of this evidence see French, "Milton, Needham, and 'Politicus,'" pp. 236ff; Elmer A. Beller, "Milton and 'Mercurius Politicus,'" pp. 479–487; J. Milton French, *Life Records of John Milton,* II, 311f.

33. E.g., *The Character of Mercurius Politicus,* Aug. 1650, and *The Second Character of Mercurius Politicus,* Oct. 1650, both possibly by John Cleveland; John Webster, *The Picture of Mercurius Politicus,* Oct. 1653; *The Downfall of Mercurius Britannicus-Pragmaticus-Politicus,* Apr. 1660; *A Rope for Pol,* Sept. 1660; James Heath, *A Brief Chronicle of the Late Intestin Warr,* 1663.

34. The prospectus is given in full in French, *Life Records,* II, 310f. From early 1651 to its demise in 1660 *Politicus* was printed by Thomas Newcomb, one of the more successful printers of pro-Commonwealth books, pamphlets, and official papers.

35. *Politicus*, 2, June 13–20, 1650, p. 17; 5, July 4–11, 1650, p. 69; 10, Aug. 8–15, 1650, p. 146.

36. *Ibid.*, 5, July 4–11, 1650, p. 70. Number 29, Dec. 19–26, 1650, p. 486, announced the publication of *Gondibert*, accompanying it with praise for a new book by Hobbes.

37. E.g., *Politicus*, 43, Mar. 27–Apr. 3, 1651, p. 702; 48, May 1–8, 1651, p. 777.

38. E.g., *ibid.*, 54, June 12–19, 1651, *passim*; 60, July 24–31, 1651, pp. 959ff.; 67, Sept. 11–18, 1651, pp. 1061ff.

39. *Politicus*, 13, Aug. 29–Sept. 5, 1650, p. 185, however, alluded to the fact that some people had found the editor's "Satyres . . . offensive."

40. E.g., David Masson, *Life of John Milton*, IV, 324–335; Gardiner, *Commonwealth and Protectorate*, II, 17–20; Williams, *English Journalism*, pp. 134f.

41. French, "Milton, Needham, and 'Politicus,'" p. 244.

42. *Politicus*, 17, Sept. 26–Oct. 3, 1650, p. 278.

43. *Ibid.*, 21, Oct. 24–31, 1650, pp. 341f.

44. *Ibid.*, 39, Feb. 27–Mar. 6, 1651, pp. 623f.

45. *Ibid.*, 53, June 5–12, 1651, pp. 848f.

46. *Ibid.*, 69, Sept. 25–Oct. 2, 1651, p. 1095.

47. For further details see French, *Life Records*, III, 9. Edward Phillips in his *Life of Milton* does mention, however, that Milton and Nedham were friends.

48. *Politicus*, 33, 37, 39, 43, 45, 48, 56, 57, 58, 66; see also French, "Milton, Needham, and 'Politicus,'" pp. 246–249.

49. *Nouvelles Ordinaires* was the only long-run newspaper not collected by Thomason. It was, as far as I know, first resurrected by J. G. Alger in a short note entitled "A French Newspaper in London, 1650–58." The paper has been more fully described by Charles Bastide in *The Anglo-French Entente in the Seventeenth Century*.

50. For the facts of Dugard's life see Bastide, *Entente*, pp. 149–153.

51. Twice early in 1651 *Nouvelles* contained brief announcements about Milton: that his answer to Salmasius was finished, and that it had been published (no. 30, Feb. 2/Jan. 23–Feb. 9/January 30, p. 120, and no. 34, Mar. 2/Feb. 20–Mar. 9/Feb. 27, p. 136).

52. *Ibid.*, 44, May 11/1–18/8, 1651, p. 176; e.g., 33, Feb. 23/13–30/20 [*sic*], 1651, p. 132.

53. *Ibid.*, 6, Aug. 25/15–Sept. 1/Aug. 22, 1650, p. 23; 11, Sept. 22/12–29/19, 1650, p. 41; 20, Nov. 24/14–Dec. 1/Nov. 21, 1650, p. 78; 46, May 25/15–June 1/May 22, 1651, p. 184.

54. *Ibid.*, 14 and 15, Oct. 13/3–27/17, 1650.

55. Bastide, *Entente*, p. 155.

56. Siebert, *Freedom of the Press*, pp. 224f.

57. *The Impartial Scout* was numbered 53 to 61, probably to suggest that it was a continuation of *The Kingdomes Faithfull and Impartiall Scout*. The first seven issues appeared between June 21 and August 9, 1650, the last two on September 20 and 27.

58. *Perfect Passages*, 1, June 28–July 5, 1650, p. 1. Walker's editorship is made clear by internal evidence, of which this quotation is a sample.

59. These two issues, numbered 324 and 325, covered the period July 15–29, 1650.

60. *Perfect Weekly Account*, 1, July 10–17, 1650, p. 527. By this sort of pagination and by labeling the fourth number in this 1650 series no. 70, Border attempted to underline the paper's purported antiquity and continuity.

61. *Weekly Intelligencer*, 1, July 16–23, 1650, p. 1. The paper carried on its title page the notice that it was "Collected by the same hand which formerly drew up" *The Kingdomes Weekly Intelligencer*.

62. E.g., *Weekly Intelligencer*, 1 (the third "number 1," the first being that

of July 16–23, 1650, the second that of Sept. 24–Oct. 1, 1650), Dec. 24–31, 1650, p. 1; 16, Apr. 8–15, 1651, p. 128; 18, Apr. 22–29, 1651, p. 137; 19, Apr. 29–May 6, 1651, p. 151; 8, Feb. 11–18, 1651, p. 57. He also implied that he now had a national rather than a metropolitan audience, though he was seldom patronizing to his rural readers (e.g., nos. 16, Apr. 8–15, 1651, pp. 121f; 33, Aug. 12–19, 1651, p. 256).

63. *Ibid.*, 11, Mar. 4–11, 1651, p. 81; 35, Aug. 26–Sept. 2, 1651, p. 265.

64. *Ibid.*, 21, May 13–20, 1651, p. 168; 15, Apr. 1–8, 1651, p. 113. For Collings' anecdotal skill see, for example, no. 26, June 17–24, 1651, pp. 205–208.

65. *Ibid.*, 9, Feb. 18–25, 1651, p. 72; 13, Mar. 18–25, 1651, pp. 102f; 25, June 10–17, 1651, pp. 193ff.

66. *Faithfull Scout*, 1, Dec. 27, 1650–Jan. 3, 1651, pp. 1f.

67. *Ibid.*, 7, Jan. 31–Feb. 7, 1651, p. 44.

68. E.g., *Perfect Account*, 21, May 28–June 4, 1651, pp. 166f.

69. Earlier, during Cromwell's campaign in Ireland, some sort of official news sheet, referred to in *Severall Proceedings* (no. 18, Jan. 25–31, 1650, pp. 243f) as the "Irish Mercury," was published in Cork; and Williams, *English Journalism*, p. 247, mentions *The Irish Mercury Monethly* and *The Irish Monthly Mercury*, both published at Cork and reprinted in London in February 1650.

70. Elizabeth Alkin, the publisher, was the real name of Parliament Joan.

71. Williams, *English Journalism*, p. 141, gives Sheppard as the editor.

72. These two papers, both printed by F. Neile, were probably an attempt to profit from the public thirst for military news from the north, a supposition corroborated by the opening statement in *The true Informer*. *The Cambridge Bibliography of English Literature*, I, 761, lists one number of a newspaper or relation, *Several Letters from Scotland*, which came out in July.

73. *Diary*, 3, Oct. 6–13, 1651, was distinguished by a doctor's advertisement on the title page.

XII

THE COMMONWEALTH NEWSPAPER II
October 1651 to April 1653

1. For further details see Clyde, *Struggle for Freedom*, pp. 205, 213.

2. Firth and Rait, *Acts and Ordinances*, II, 696–699. For the controversy on censorship see Siebert, *Freedom of the Press*, pp. 226f, and Clyde, *Struggle for Freedom*, pp. 224–233.

3. One of the more interesting advertisements appeared in *A Perfect Diurnall*, 145, Sept. 13–20, 1652: a retraction of an attack on Hugh Peters by Robert Eeles; it was also inserted in *Severall Proceedings*, 156, Sept. 16–23, 1652.

4. *The Perfect Diurnall*, 166, Feb. 7–14, 1653, p. 2505. The following number announced the execution of the man; possibly the horse was reprieved. Many of Pecke's human-interest stories had a slightly anti-Scot bias.

5. *A Perfect Diurnall*, 138–141, July 26–Aug. 23, 1652, *passim*. For the rival printer, John Field, see Plomer, *Dictionary*, p. 74. No counterfeit "Perfect Diurnall" has survived from this period.

6. *The Perfect Diurnall*, 176, Apr. 18–25, 1653, pp. 2661, 2664ff. As another example of Pecke's caution, his paper, until June 1652 and after January 1653, was more regularly entered in the Stationers' Register than were other weeklies.

7. E.g., *Weekly Intelligencer*, 48, Dec. 2–9, 1651, p. 273; 64, Mar. 9–16, 1652, p. 386; 84 (the second week so numbered), Aug. 3–10, 1652, p. 549; 85, Aug. 10–17, 1652, p. 557; 87, Aug. 24–31, 1652, p. 573; 99, Nov. 16–23, 1652, p. 702.

8. *Ibid.,* 66, Mar. 23–30, 1652, p. 405; Samuel Sheppard, *The Weepers,* Sept. 1652, quoted in Williams, *English Journalism,* p. 43.

9. E.g., *Weekly Intelligencer,* 90, Sept. 14–21, 1652, p. 600.

10. *Ibid.,* 64, Mar. 9–16, 1652, p. 382.

11. E.g., *ibid.,* 42, Oct. 21–28, 1651, p. 326. Collings also claimed to have called the attention of the Council of State to errors in Dillingham's *Moderate Messenger* (*Weekly Intelligencer,* 107, Feb. 22–Mar. 1, 1653, p. 758).

12. *Weekly Intelligencer,* 81, July 6–13, 1652, p. 526.

13. E.g., *ibid.,* 66, Mar. 23–30, 1652, p. 405; 85, Aug. 10–17, 1652, p. 564; 94, Oct. 12–19, 1652, p. 636; 97, Nov. 2–9, 1652, pp. 654f; 105, Feb. 8–15, 1653, pp. 741f.

14. *Ibid.,* 105, Feb. 8–15, 1653, p. 735.

15. *Ibid.,* 65, Mar. 16–23, 1652, pp. 394f.

16. *Ibid.,* 66, Mar. 23–30, 1652, p. 399. Collings went on to comment on the wrongness of ministers' meddling in civil affairs. In a later issue he included an attack on Socinian doctrines (no. 79, June 22–29, 1652, p. 504).

17. *Ibid.,* 67, Mar. 30–Apr. 6, 1652, p. 407; 89, Sept. 7–14, 1652, p. 589.

18. *Ibid.,* 92, Sept. 28–Oct. 5, 1652, pp. 617f; 113, Apr. 12–19, 1653, p. 807. Number 106, Feb. 15–22, 1653, p. 750, told the sad story of an accident during a play in Oxfordshire in which sixty were injured — another indication that, both in and out of London, English drama was by no means dead during the Interregnum. (*A Perfect Account,* 11, Feb. 16–23, 1653, p. 887, gave the more likely figure of six for the number injured.)

19. Crouch, not a very reliable informant, implied in *Democritus,* 3, Apr. 13–21, 1652, p. 19, that Border was the editor of *The French Intelligencer.*

20. *French Intelligencer,* 4, Dec. 9–16, 1651, p. 32; 5, Dec. 16–23, 1651, p. 39; 6, Dec. 23–31, 1651, p. 42. Numbers 1 and 2 either never existed or are not extant.

21. *Ibid.,* 8, Jan. 6–13, 1652, p. 56. See also nos. 11, Jan. 27–Feb. 4, 1652, pp. 73f, and 18, Mar. 16–23, 1652, p. 130.

22. *Ibid.,* 10, Jan. 20–27, 1652, p. 65f.

23. *Ibid.,* 16, Mar. 2–9, 1652, pp. 119f.

24. *Ibid.,* 19, Mar. 23–30, 1652, pp. 138ff.

25. *Ibid.,* 18, Mar. 16–23, 1652, pp. 133ff.

26. *Ibid.,* 11, Jan. 27–Feb. 4, 1652, p. 75; 12, Feb. 4–11, 1652, p. 88; 17, Mar. 9–16, 1652, p. 124.

27. The final number of *The French Intelligencer* came out on May 18, 1652, the first number of *The French Occurrences* on May 17. Until September it was printed for, and probably by, George Horton, thereafter by Robert Wood, the man who had printed the *Intelligencer.* The *Occurrences* also occasionally delayed its day of publication to await the foreign posts. For its anti-Commonwealth prophecies see, e.g., nos. 8, June 28–July 5, 1652, p. 64; 13, Aug. 2–9, 1652, pp. 74ff; 17, Aug. 31–Sept. 7, 1652, p. 112.

28. *French Occurrences,* 6, June 14–21, 1652, p. 41. That other editors used this French "Abstract" is indicated by the close similarity of many of their stories from France.

29. *Ibid.,* 11, July 19–26, 1652, p. 68 (the editor's coy refusal to confirm the revolt of some English ships); 19, Sept. 7–14, 1652, p. 128 (his ostensible secretiveness about some English officers in the Venetian service coming to the aid of the Dutch).

30. *Ibid.,* 21, Sept. 20–27, 1652, pp. 137f; 22, Sept. 27–Oct. 4, 1652, p. 147; 31, Nov. 22–29, 1652, p. 202; 28, Nov. 1–8, 1652, p. 189.

31. E.g., *ibid.,* 20, Sept. 13–20, 1652, p. 134; 21, Sept. 20–27, 1652, p. 144; 26, Oct. 18–25, 1652, p. 176.

32. *Perfect Account,* 65, Mar. 24–31, 1652, p. 519.

33. *Ibid.*, 45, Nov. 5-12, 1651, p. 360, and 87, Aug. 25–Sept. 1, 1652, pp. 689, 696; 68, Apr. 14-21, 1652, p. 543; 111, Feb. 16-23, 1653, pp. 883f.

34. *Ibid.*, 84, Aug. 4-11, 1652, p. 671.

35. E.g., *Severall Proceedings*, 186, Apr. 14-21, 1653, p. 2944—the dissolution of the Rump. Starting the following week the paper changed its name from *Severall Proceedings of Parliament* to *Severall Proceedings of State Affairs*. Number 187 also contained a reference to a notice on the door of Parliament announcing a House for rent, followed by: ". . . those that shall abuse the godly of the late Members of Parliament, without a cause, will not be approved of . . . some being such for piety and worth as probably may be our Governours again." Earlier (no. 130, Mar. 18-25, 1652, p. 2017) Walker had included a justification of the weekly press on the basis that it was at least useful for stopping the spread of wild rumors; he also supported a petition asking the government to do more to subsidize postmasters (no. 185, Apr. 7-14, 1653, pp. 2927f).

36. E.g., *ibid.*, 162, Oct. 28–Nov. 4, 1652; 170, Dec. 23-30, 1652.

37. *Nouvelles Extraordinaires*, 140, Mar. 9/Feb. 27, 1653.

38. E.g., *Nouvelles Ordinaires*, 72, Nov. 23/13–30/20, 1651, p. 285; 98, May 23/13–30/20, 1652, p. 392. Number 125, Nov. 28/18–Dec. 5/Nov. 25, 1652, p. 500, contained a notice of Dugard's translation of Milton's *Eikonoklastes*.

39. *Ibid.*, 70, Nov. 9/Oct. 30–Nov. 16/6, 1651, p. 278; 83, Feb. 8/Jan. 29–Feb. 15/5, 1652, p. 329; 147, Apr. 24/14–May 1/Apr. 21, 1653, p. 588. An example of Dugard's caution that probably baffled his French readers was his account of Parliament's investigation of Lilly (no. 123, Nov. 14/4–21/11, 1652, pp. 489f).

40. E.g., *Politicus*, 115, Aug. 12-19, 1652, pp. 1811, 1815; 141, Feb. 17-24, 1653, p. 2260.

41. E.g., *ibid.*, 107, June 17-24, 1652, pp. 1682ff; 147, Mar. 31–Apr. 7, 1653, p. 2345.

42. Among such items were four that dealt with the discomfiture of Salmasius (*ibid.*, 82, Dec. 25, 1651–Jan. 1, 1652, p. 1319; 84, Jan. 8-15, 1652, p. 1344; 111, July 15-22, 1652, p. 1755; 121, Sept. 23-30, 1652, pp. 1907ff).

43. E.g., *ibid.*, 111, July 15-22, 1652, p. 1750; 114, Aug. 5-12, 1652, pp. 1787ff; 117, Aug. 26–Sept. 2, 1652, pp. 1837f (a Johnsonesque description of savagery in the Western Highlands); 124, Oct. 14-21, 1652, pp. 1945f; 143, Mar. 3-10, 1653, pp. 2277f; 126 and 127, Oct. 28–Nov. 11, 1652, pp. 1983, 1994 (Nedham's denunciation of Scottish witchcraft trials).

44. *Ibid.*, 97, Apr. 8-15, 1652, p. 1536; 73, Oct. 23-30, 1651, p. 1166; 113, July 29–Aug. 5, 1652, p. 1782.

45. For a table showing these self-plagiarisms see French, "Milton, Needham, and 'Politicus,'" pp. 242f.

46. The opening of *Politicus*, 113, July 29–Aug. 5, 1652, included four pages from *The Prince*, and Nedham frequently alluded to and paraphrased Machiavelli.

47. *Politicus*, 93, Mar. 11-18, 1652, pp. 1457f; 71, Oct. 9-16, 1651, p. 1127.

48. *Ibid.*, 101, May 6-13, 1652, p. 1586.

49. Nedham received £200 for translating and bringing up to date *Mare Clausum* (*DNB*).

50. In October 1651 either the printer of *Perfect Passages* was confused and published three issues numbered 39, one for the week of Oct. 17-24, the second entitled *Perfect Particulars of Every Daies Intelligence*, for Oct. 24-31, and the third for Oct. 30 [*sic*]–Nov. 7; or, what is more likely, *Perfect Particulars* was a counterfeit, as Walker claimed in nos. 40 and 41 of *Perfect Passages*.

51. *Perfect Passages*, 56, Mar. 5-12, 1652, p. 403; 69, Oct. 8-15, 1652, p. 541. In no. 130 (the paper's numbering was inaccurate) of *Perfect Passages'* continuation, Apr. 22-29, 1653, pp. 1034f, Walker seemed to disapprove of the death penalty for robbery.

52. E.g., *Perfect Passages*, 61, Aug. 13–20, 1652, p. 478; 55, July 2–9, 1652, p. 429.

53. E.g., *ibid.*, 53, June 11–18, 1652, p. 407; 75, Nov. 19–26, 1652, p. 586.

54. *Ibid.*, 72, Oct. 29–Nov. 5, 1652, p. 565. See also Clyde, *Struggle for Freedom*, pp. 234f.

55. *Perfect Passages*, 39 (the first week so numbered), Oct. 17–24, 1651, p. 309.

56. *The Moderate Publisher* (*Perfect Passages'* continuation), 91, Mar. 25–Apr. 1, 1653, p. 778.

57. *Moderate Publisher*, 94, Apr. 15–22, 1653, pp. 813, 809.

58. Siebert, *Freedom of the Press*, p. 226; Clyde, *Struggle for Freedom*, pp. 217, 242.

59. E.g., *Faithfull Scout*, 94, Oct. 29–Nov. 5, 1652, p. 737.

60. *Ibid.*, 72, June 4–11, 1652, pp. 569f. (Border probably got the story from Crouch: see *Democritus*, 7, May 11–19, 1652, p. 56.) See also *Faithfull Scout*, 85, Aug. 29–Sept. 3, 1652, pp. 668f — a proclamation from two drunks.

61. *Faithfull Scout*, 77, July 2–9, 1652, p. 601.

62. *Ibid.*, 44, Nov. 14–21, 1651, p. 338; e.g., 52, Jan. 9–16, 1652, pp. 404f; 53, Jan. 16–23, 1652, pp. 414f; 56, Feb. 6–13, 1652, p. 438. See also, e.g., nos. 90, Oct. 1–8, 1652, p. 707; 107, Mar. 4–11, 1653, pp. 839ff, 844f.

63. It ran four times in *The Faithfull Scout*, first appearing in no. 64, Apr. 2–9, 1652, p. 499.

64. This was the lead story in *ibid.*, 76, June 25–July 2, 1652.

65. E.g., *ibid.*, 45, Nov. 21–28, 1651, pp. 345f; 59, Feb. 27–Mar. 5, 1652, pp. 458f; 60, Mar. 5–12, 1652, p. 466; 62, Mar. 19–26, 1652, p. 488 — where Border approved of four lawyers who hanged themselves.

66. *Ibid.*, 94, Oct. 29–Nov. 5, 1652, p. 739.

67. E.g., *ibid.*, 51, Jan. 2–9, 1652, pp. 393ff; 54, Jan. 23–30, 1652, pp. 419f, 422f; 55, Jan. 30–Feb. 6, 1652, pp. 431f; 62, Mar. 19–26, 1652, pp. 486f; 77, July 2–9, 1652, p. 605; 93, Oct. 22–29, 1652, pp. 728f; 108, Mar. 11–18, 1653, pp. 850f.

68. *Ibid.*, 65, Apr. 19–26, 1652, pp. 510f; 74, June 11–18, 1652, pp. 580f, and 81, July 30–Aug. 6, 1652, pp. 631f.

69. *Ibid.*, 71, May 14–21, 1652, was a counterfeit. Border went after Collings in no. 67, Apr. 23–30, 1652, pp. 522f, and he attacked Crouch's *Democritus* in the *Scout*, for example, in nos. 65 and 66, Apr. 9–23, 1652, pp. 507f, 517, and 92, Oct. 15–22, 1652, p. 726. For some examples of Border's fight with *Britannicus*, see *Faithfull Scout*, 93, Oct. 22–29, 1652, pp. 732ff; 97, Nov. 19–26, 1652, pp. 759ff; 98–102, Nov. 26–Dec. 31, 1652, *passim*.

70. *Democritus*, 3, Apr. 13–21, 1652, p. 19.

71. *Moderate Intelligencer*, 166 [*sic*], Dec. 1–8, 1652, pp. 2599f.

72. *Faithfull Scout*, 103, Feb. 4–11, 1653, p. 807.

73. For Dillingham's editorship see *Weekly Intelligencer*, 107, Feb. 22–Mar. 1, 1653, p. 758, and Manwaring, "Journalism in the . . . Commonwealth," p. 118. Dillingham died in the early 1670's, apparently a prosperous man. (For further details see Manwaring, pp. 118–120.)

74. Clyde, *Struggle for Freedom*, p. 241; Williams, *English Journalism*, pp. 150f. For Mabbott's possible friendship with Milton at this time, see French, *Life Records*, III, 319.

75. *Democritus*, 1, Apr. 8, 1652 ("Tuesday Night"), p. 1.

76. *Ibid.*, 19, Aug. 4–11, 1652, p. 147.

77. *Ibid.*, 17, July 21–28, 1652, p. 136.

78. *Ibid.*, 11, June 8–16, 1652, p. 86.

79. E.g., *ibid.*, 15, July 7–14, 1652, p. 120; 10, June 1–9, 1652, p. 73.

80. For Crouch as a plagiarizer see Rollins, *Cavalier and Puritan*, pp. 60f.

81. *Democritus*, 41, Jan. 19–26, 1653, p. 328. (The numbering and pagination of *Democritus* and *The Laughing Mercury* were continuous, and their only major hiatus occurred during the first three weeks of 1653.)

82. *Democritus*, 43, Feb. 2–9, 1653, p. 341.

83. *Ibid.*, 45, Feb. 16–23, 1653, p. 357.

84. *Ibid.*, 37, Dec. 15–22, 1652, p. 281; also quoted in Rollins, *Cavalier and Puritan*, p. 59. For some other samples of Crouch's poetic skill see nos. 50, Mar. 30–Apr. 6, 1653, p. 393, and 54, Apr. 27–May 4, 1653, p. 425. Crouch was also outspoken against anti-stage laws and the persecution of actors.

85. This paper, which I have not seen, is described in Couper, *Edinburgh Press*, II 166–169. Also reprinted in Leith during this period were a few 1652 numbers of *A Diurnall of Some Passages and Affairs*, probably a version of *A Perfect Diurnall*, and some early 1653 issues of *Politicus* (Couper, II, 43, 169–174). *Mercurius Scoticus* also gets the credit for the first Scottish advertisement, a notice of a book that appeared in no. 19, Dec. 2–9, 1651 (Couper II, 150). Williams, *English Journalism*, pp. 142f, describes a *Mercurius Scoticus* published by Parliament Joan in September 1651 and used by her to trap unwary Royalist customers. Probably it appeared only once.

86. *Bellonius* was printed by "J. C.," and conceivably John Crouch both wrote and printed it.

87. *Democritus*, 3, Apr. 13–21, 1652, p. 19. Sheppard was equally unflattering in *Mercurius Mastix*, 1, Aug. 20–27, 1652, p. 6. *The Cambridge Bibliography of English Literature*, I, 761, lists one number of *The Dutch Intelligencer*, for September 1652.

88. Williams, *English Journalism*, p. 251, lists one number of *Mercurius Zeteticus*, which, if it was a newspaper, would make *Phreneticus* the fourth new weekly of 1652.

89. Rollins, "Sheppard and His Praise of Poets," p. 529.

90. *Pragmaticus*, 1, May 18–25, 1652, pp. 1f. Since late 1651 hawkers had again been noisily busy on the streets of London. See also no. 5, June 15–22, 1652, pp. 34f.

91. *Ibid.*, 2, May 25–June 1, 1652, p. 11.

92. *Ibid.*, 4 and 5, June 8–22, 1652, especially pp. 31f, 39f.

93. The pun appeared in *Britannicus*, 2, July 26–Aug. 2, 1652, p. 18.

94. Williams, *English Journalism*, p. 149, cites Border to the effect that the editor of *Britannicus* had been a cooper, then a tax-collector in Hertfordshire.

95. *Britannicus*, 22, Dec. 14–21, 1652, p. 289. (The first issue in this revived series had been labeled 14.)

96. Clyde, *Struggle for Freedom*, pp. 217, 241; Williams, *English Journalism*, pp. 149f; *Severall Proceedings*, 170, Dec. 23–30, 1652.

97. *Democritus*, 3, Apr. 13–21, 1652, p. 20; *Laughing Mercury*, 28, Oct. 12–20, 1652, p. 218.

98. Such attacks were still frequent in the pamphlets of the day, the most readable of the early 1650's probably being Cleveland's *A Character of a Diurnal-Maker* (November 1653).

99. A month later Sheppard repeated many of these charges in his satiric tract *The Weepers*. For Cottrell, see Plomer, *Dictionary*, p. 54.

100. *Flying Eagle*, 5, Dec. 25, 1652–Jan. 1, 1653, p. 40.

101. Eeles became the printer of *The Faithful Post* with no. 135, May 27–June 3, 1654. For further details about him see Plomer, *Dictionary*, p. 69, Clyde, *Struggle for Freedom*, pp. 114–116, and Frank, *Levellers*, p. 87.

102. *Faithful Post*, 131, Apr. 29–May 6, 1653, p. 698. See also no. 133, May 13–20, 1653, p. 1064. The first five issues had been numbered from 89 through 93; the numeration then jumped at the end of April to no. 131, and went on from there. Internal evidence strongly suggests that Border now had no hand in the paper.

103. *Ibid.*, 89 and 90, Mar. 25–Apr. 8, 1653, pp. 690, 696, 697. The other two illustrations were of a comet and of some Royalist banners.

104. The sixth number of *The Faithful Post* had two headlines, and *Moderate Occurrences* four times used large type in the manner of the *Post*.

XIII

THE NEWSPAPER UNDER
THE PROTECTORATE
May 1653 to September 1655

1. Clyde, *Struggle for Freedom*, p. 246; *Politicus*, 224, Sept. 21–28, 1654, p. 3800.

2. For further details see Siebert, *Freedom of the Press*, pp. 229f; Clyde, *Struggle for Freedom*, pp. 240–250. The government, however, could be rough on offending pamphleteers and printers, many of whom were jailed in 1653.

3. E.g., *Perfect Diurnall*, 241, July 17–24, 1654, pp. 3695f.

4. What happened to Pecke thereafter is shrouded in the mists of time.

5. *Weekly Intelligencer*, 147 (the second issue so numbered), Dec. 6–13, 1653, p. 88. After this issue the numbering and pagination become hopelessly confused.

6. *Ibid.*, Jan. 23–30, 1655, p. 159.

7. E.g., *ibid.*, Oct. 2–9, 1654, p. 137; Aug. 28–Sept. 4, 1655, p. 17.

8. *Ibid.*, 215, July 18–25, 1654, p. 332; 131, Aug. 2–9, 1653, p. 952; 132, Aug. 9–16, 1653, p. 960.

9. *Ibid.*, Feb. 27–Mar. 6, 1655, p. 232; 135, June 21–28, 1653, p. 894. Collings was also tender to the former Royalist editor, George Wharton: e.g., Aug. 14–21, 1655, p. 4.

10. *Ibid.*, May 22–29, 1655, p. 11.

11. *Ibid.*, 214, July 11–18, 1654, pp. 317f; Jan. 16–23, 1655, p. 158.

12. Ibid., Aug. 21–28, 1655, p. 14 (the London ladies); Jan. 9–16, 1655, p. 152 (this beer vat story appeared in most other papers and was promptly made into a ballad, for which see Rollins, *Cavalier and Puritan*, pp. 366–371); June 5–12, 1655, p. 19 (for a fuller description of the Hackney synagogue see *Severall Proceedings*, 297, May 31–June 7, 1655, p. 4714); 120, May 24–31, 1653, p. 861 (the lost child).

13. *Weekly Intelligencer*, 119, May 17–24, 1653, p. 847; 147, Nov. 29–Dec. 6, 1653, pp. 73f. Collings' two descriptions of raids on the players at the Red Bull are also interesting: Dec. 26, 1654–Jan. 2, 1655, p. 158; Sept. 11–18, 1655, pp. 38f.

14. *Ibid.*, Apr. 4–11, 1654, p. 216 (the advertisement was subsequently repeated in other papers: e.g., *Politicus*, May 4–11, 1654, p. 3476); June 26–July 3, 1655, p. 22. (See also Collings' three-page description of Jamaica: Sept. 4–11, 1655, pp. 25ff.) Suggestive of the nineteenth rather than the twentieth century were occasional signs of imperialism, as in Collings' praise of England's potentially world-conquering energy: e.g., Jan. 10–17, 1654, p. 130.

15. *Weekly Intelligencer*, 206, Feb. 21–28, 1654, p. 178; Sept. 11–18, 1655, p. 34.

16. *Faithful Post*, 126, Aug. 26–Sept. 2, 1653, p. 1098.

17. *Great Brittain's Post*, 126, Nov. 2–9, 1653, p. 1076. This number was printed by Wood, the next two by Horton. The Wood-Horton relationship is further complicated by the fact that both men spent some time in jail in late 1653 and/or early 1654 (Williams, *English Journalism*, p. 152; Clyde, *Struggle for Freedom*, pp. 248f). At the end of January, Wood published one number of *The Politique Informer*, the opening of which noted that Horton was in jail and commented: "But give me leave to tell him, the Revolutions and Changes which this Commonwealth hath sustained ought not to be questioned by every Subject. . . ."

18. *The Grand Politique Post* skipped one number and encountered one counterfeit, which was printed by Wood. By the spring of 1654 Horton was out of jail.

19. *Grand Politique Post*, Mar. 7–14, 1654, pp. 133f.

20. *Ibid.*, 167, Feb. 28–Mar. 7, 1654, p. 1332.

21. Since Thomason may have been negligent in collecting it, *The Weekly Post* may have missed fewer weeks. A few times it appeared on Wednesday instead of Tuesday.

22. *Ibid.*, 187, July 11–18, 1654, p. 1479; 201, Oct. 17–24, 1654, p. 1614; 223, Apr. 17–24, 1655, p. 1778.

23. E.g., *ibid.*, 174, Apr. 11–18, 1654, p. 1380; 179, May 16–24, 1654, p. 1413; 184, June 13–20, 1654, p. 1449; 188, July 18–25, 1654, p. 1500; 196, Sept. 12–19, 1654, p. 1566; 199, Oct. 3–10, 1654, p. 1588; 209, Jan. 9–16, 1655, p. 1667; 124 [*sic*], Apr. 24–May 1, 1655, p. 1792. But no. 205, Nov. 21–28, 1654, p. 1648, brought the story of John Harris, the former left-wing editor, up to date: he was apprehended for having forged Cromwell's signature. (A few months later, however, Harris offered to serve as a spy for Cromwell, and in 1660 he was hanged for burglary: Clyde, *Struggle for Freedom*, p. 267; Williams, *English Journalism*, p. 107.)

24. *Weekly Post*, 203, Oct. 31–Nov. 7, 1654, p. 1631 (it also appeared in *Faithfull Scout*, 204, Nov. 3–10, 1654, p. 1639); 231, June 12–19, 1655, p. 1848.

25. The pictures appeared in *Weekly Post*, 193, Aug. 22–29, 1654, p. 1548, and 197, Sept. 19–26, 1654, p. 1572.

26. *Ibid.*, 217, Mar. 6–13, 1655, p. 1736, told the story of a female Faustus from Wapping who sold her soul to the devil.

27. *Ibid.*, 242, Sept. 4–11, 1655, p. 1944; 243, Sept. 11–18, 1655, p. 1948.

28. Note, too, the editor's statement in *Perfect Account*, 134, July 27–Aug. 3, 1653, p. 1063.

29. *Ibid.*, 242, Aug. 22–29, 1655, p. 1931.

30. Clyde, *Struggle for Freedom*, p. 249. When caught she was also peddling *The Moderate Intelligencer*.

31. See the title page of *Democritus*, 89, Nov. 9, 1653–Jan. 25, 1654 [*sic*], and pp. 642, 646ff. This one number was published by Horton.

32. E.g., *Fumigosus*, 55, June 6–13, 1655, p. 428; 70, Sept. 19–Oct. 3, 1655, p. 550 (the final issue).

33. *Ibid.*, 60, July 11–18, 1655, p. 474; 56, June 13–30, 1655, p. 437.

34. *Democritus*, 54, Apr. 27–May 4, 1653, pp. 425f; *Fumigosus*, 27, Nov. 29–Dec. 6, 1654, p. 229. Crouch's inflated stories from places like Turkey and China were invariably part parody.

35. E.g., *Democritus*, 70, Aug. 24–31, 1653, p. 554.

36. *Ibid.*, 84, Feb. 1–8, 1654, p. 463; 85, Feb. 8–15, 1654, p. 467; *Fumigosus*, 21, Oct. 18–25, 1654, p. 185. (Crouch also mentioned a club of women pipe-smokers: *Fumigosus*, 43, Mar. 21–28, 1655, p. 341.)

37. Crouch's knowledge of Jonson, though he never directly alluded to the playwright, is implied in much that he wrote. As for Shakespeare, *Fumigosus*, 14, Aug. 30–Sept. 6, 1654, p. 124, introduced a drinking song by means of a reference to Falstaff. Crouch's sympathy for harassed actors may also be relevant (e.g., no. 23, Nov. 1–8, 1654, p. 197).

38. Two were of eight pages, one giving the Instrument of Government, the other the terms of the Anglo-Dutch peace treaty; the third, in four pages, proclaimed a national day of thanksgiving.

39. *Nouvelles*, 167, Sept. 11/1–18/8, 1653, p. 668; 182, Dec. 25/15, 1653–Jan. 1, 1654/Dec. 22, 1653, p. 706; 240, Jan. 14/4–21/11, 1655, p. 955. (For a fuller account of the fanatical Thoreau John, who not only tried to break into Parliament but wanted to lead the dispersed Jews to Palestine, see *Perfect Diurnall*, 265, Jan. 1–8, 1655, pp. 4061f, and *Weekly Intelligencer*, Jan. 2–9, 1655, pp. 151f.) *Nouvelles*, 260–

265, June 3/May 24–July 15/5, 1655, *passim*, gave relatively full coverage to the massacre of the Piedmontese Protestants and its immediate repercussions.

40. On April 28, 1653, its name was changed from *Severall Proceedings in Parliament* to *Severall Proceedings of State Affairs*, a title which it retained until Sept. 7, 1654. From then until January 2, 1655, it returned to *Severall Proceedings in Parliament*, then for a month went back to *Severall Proceedings of State Affairs*. Finally, from February 22, 1655, to its demise on September 27 it was called *Perfect Proceedings of State Affairs*. Throughout, its numbering and pagination were continuous, and it skipped no weeks.

41. *Severall Proceedings*, 260, Sept. 14–21, 1654, p. 4117.

42. E.g., *ibid.*, 240, Apr. 27–May 4, 1654; 283, Feb. 22–Mar. 1, 1655; 289, Apr. 5–12, 1655; 290, Apr. 12–19, 1655, pp. 4604f; 296, May 24–31, 1655, p. 4698.

43. *Ibid.*, 226, Jan. 19–26, 1654, p. 3576.

44. *Ibid.*, 279, Jan. 25–Feb. 1, 1655, pp. 4416ff. Probably by this time most of Walker's income was coming from his suburban pulpit.

45. *Politicus*, 157, June 9–16, 1653, p. 2506; Clyde, *Struggle for Freedom*, p. 247. Nedham was also taken to task for an alleged error in the story of a debate among four London ministers (John Webster, *The Picture of Mercurius Politicus*, Oct. 1653). From October 1653 to November 1654 *Politicus* was reprinted at Leith, then, until January 1660, at Edinburgh (Couper, *Edinburgh Press*, I, 171f).

46. E.g., *Politicus*, 222, Sept. 7–14, 1654, p. 3760; 246, Feb. 22–Mar. 1, 1655, p. 5162. One strange item reported the arrival in Holland of a group of Brazilian Jews (no. 219, Aug. 17–24, 1654, p. 3715).

47. *Ibid.*, 188, Jan. 12–19, 1654, p. 3198.

48. *Ibid.*, 222, Oct. 19–26, 1654, p. 3864; 276, Sept. 20–27, 1655, p. 5642.

49. E.g., *ibid.*, 155 (misnumbered 153), May 26–June 2, 1653, p. 2472; 224, Sept. 21–28, 1654, p. 3800.

50. *Ibid.*, 208, June 1–8, 1654, p. 3532.

51. *Ibid.*, 220, Aug. 24–31, 1654, pp. 3722f.

52. *Ibid.*, 257, May 10–17, 1655, p. 5340; e.g., 180, Nov. 17–24, 1653, pp. 2888f, and 215, July 20–27, 1654, pp. 3646f; e.g., 236, Dec. 14–21, 1654, pp. 4092f, and 247, Mar. 1–8, 1655, pp. 5171f (an advertisement of the speculative possibilities in Ireland). The Rotterdam ship was discussed in most other papers, but not so fully as in *Politicus*.

53. E.g., *Perfect Diurnall*, 298, Aug. 20–27, 1655, p. 4585; *Politicus*, 271, Aug. 16–23, 1655, p. 5564; J. G. Muddiman, *The King's Journalist 1659–1689*, p. 7.

54. Williams, *English Journalism*, p. 167. Nedham had other sources of income: for instance, in the late summer of 1654 he was paid £20 by the Council of State for "presenting a matter" to it (Fredrick S. Siebert, "Regulation of the Press in the Seventeenth Century — Excerpts from the Records of the Court of the Stationers' Company," p. 387).

55. E.g., *Certain Passages*, Feb. 2–9, 1655, p. 159, made a strong case for Cromwell as a fighter for civil liberties.

56. A fine mixture of piety and credulity occurred in a story about two French virgins who, donning men's clothes, became soldiers, one of them rising to the rank of colonel and then entering a nunnery (*Certain Passages*, 11, Mar. 24–31, 1654, pp. 88f).

57. *Moderate Publisher*, 7, Dec. 2–9, 1653, p. 64; *Certain Passages*, 11, Mar. 24–31, 1654, p. 83.

58. *Certain Passages* also missed a dozen weeks.

59. *Moderate Publisher*, 8, Dec. 9–16, 1653, p. 65; *Certain Passages*, 188 [*sic*], Apr. 27–May 4, 1655.

60. In all likelihood Walker never returned to journalism. In the summer of 1660 he wrote a tract praising Charles II, *Serious Observations lately made touching his Majesty*, on which Crouch appropriately commented in *Fumigosus*. In

1664 Walker may have been appointed to a small benefice; then he disappears. (For further details see Williams, "Henry Walker," pp. 463f.)

61. *Armies Scout*, 119, May 27–June 3, 1653, p. 1023. Earlier Wood had attacked Horton and *The Faithful Post* (*Armies Scout*, 116, May 6–13, 1653, p. 1006). This *Scout*'s numbering and pagination were an approximate continuation of those in *The Faithfull Scout*.

62. One instance of Border's credulity was his apparent acceptance of the tale of an Irish woman with thirty-nine husbands (*Faithfull Scout*, 121, July 15–22, 1653, p. 1087).

63. The most conspicuous of these borrowings consisted of semi-personal obiter dicta. *The Faithfull Scout* also reprinted *The Weekly Post*'s "characters" of a pickpocket and stool pigeon.

64. One of the more interesting of these advertisements was a purported cure for cancer of the breast (*Faithfull Scout*, June 29–July 6, 1655, p. 1871, repeated in subsequent issues).

65. In one number printed by Wood appeared four pictures of devices allegedly being made in Holland to block the Thames (*Faithfull Scout*, 140, Nov. 25–Dec. 2, 1653, pp. 2003f).

66. *Ibid.*, 167, Feb. 24–Mar. 3, 1654, p. 1328. Border may also have had intermittent trouble with the authorities: see, for example, *Democritus*, 77, Oct. 5–12, 1653, p. 605; Clyde, *Struggle for Freedom*, p. 242.

67. *Faithfull Scout*, 204, Dec. 1–8, 1654, p. 1668; July 6–13, 1655, p. 1880.

68. E.g., *ibid.*, 206, Dec. 15–22, 1654, p. 1683; 125, Aug. 12–19, 1653, p. 2024.

69. E.g., *ibid.*, 164, Feb. 3–10, 1654, p. 1302; 184, June 16–23, 1654, p. 1459; 197, Sept. 15–22, 1654, p. 1574.

70. *Ibid.*, 157, Dec. 16–23, 1653, pp. 1254ff.

71. This counterfeit *Scout*, written by a member of the Parliament that had just been dissolved, was published by Horton. Numbered 127, it came out on January 13, 1654.

72. E.g., *Faithfull Scout*, July 13–20, 1655, p. 1886, where Border went so far as to be sympathetic to a man who had denied the divinity of Christ.

73. *Ibid.*, 202, Oct. 20–27, 1654, p. 1621; 229, May 25–June 1, 1655, pp. 1825f.

74. *Ibid.*, 202 [*sic*], Nov. 17–24, 1654, pp. 1649ff; 246, Sept. 21–28, 1655, pp. 1961f. See also no. 243, Sept. 1–8, 1655, pp. 1937f.

75. Internal evidence strongly suggests Border's hand, not Dillingham's.

76. Border borrowed extensively from his own efforts in Tuesday's *Grand Politique Post* and its successor *The Weekly Post*.

77. *Moderate Intelligencer*, 165 and 166, Feb. 16–29 [*sic*], 1654, pp. 1309ff, 1312f.

78. *Ibid.*, 165, Feb. 16–23, 1654, p. 1316, and 174, Apr. 12–19, 1654, p. 1378; 176, Apr. 26–May 3, 1654, p. 1396, and 177, May 3–10, 1654, p. 1404.

79. *Ibid.*, 166, Feb. 23–29, 1654, p. 1332; 169, Mar. 15–23, 1654, p. 1344; 167, Feb. 28–Mar. 8, 1654, p. 1332, and 170, Mar. 22–29, 1654, p. 1353.

80. The counterfeit, numbered 171, appeared on April 5, 1654. Wood apparently published nos. 174 and 175.

81. Williams, *English Journalism*, p. 51.

82. Its first number, May 1–8, 1654, was entitled *Perfect Diurnall Occurrences*; the following week this became *A Perfect Diurnall*.

83. *Fumigosus*, 48, Apr. 25–May 2, 1655, p. 380.

84. *Perfect Diurnall Occurrences*, 1, May 1–8, 1654, p. 8; *A Perfect Diurnall*, 2, May 8–15, 1654, p. 16.

85. E.g., *A Perfect Diurnall*, 12, July 17–24, 1654, p. 95.

86. *Mercurius Pragmaticus*, 8 [*sic*], July 6–13, 1653, pp. 61f.

87. *Ibid.*, p. 57.

88. *Impartial Intelligencer*, 1, June 29–July 6, 1653, p. 1.

89. The extant issue of the revised *Loyal Messenger* is numbered 4 and dated April 3–10, 1654.

90. *Perfect Occurrences*, 2, Feb. 20–27, 1654, p. 16.

91. The one extant issue (no. 2, Mar. 1–8, 1654) slightly suggests Nedham's touch.

92. *Mercurius Aulicus*, 1, Mar. 13–20, 1654, p. 1.

93. The author, John Streater, also wrote eleven numbers of a quasi-newspaper with anti-government implications: *Observations Historical, Political and Philosophical upon Aristotle's First Book of Political Government, together with a narrative of State-Affairs in England, Scotland, and Ireland.* It came out from April to July 1654. Williams, *English Journalism*, p. 256, lists a paper called *The Weekly Abstract*, the first number of which appeared on June 3, 1654, and which may have managed two or three more issues.

94. *Observator*, 1, Oct. 24–31, 1654, pp. 1f.

XIV

THE END

October 1655 to June 1660

Bibliographical Note: For the historical background to this chapter I have relied on Firth's *The Last Years of the Protectorate* and on Godfrey Davies' *The Restoration of Charles II, 1658–1660*.

1. Siebert, *Freedom of the Press*, pp. 230f; Clyde, *Struggle for Freedom*, pp. 323–327.

2. Maurice Ashley, *The Greatness of Oliver Cromwell*, p. 12.

3. Firth, *Last Years*, I, 28.

4. Plomer, *Dictionary*, p. 136; Clyde, *Struggle for Freedom*, p. 251. Numbers 2–22 of *The Publick Intelligencer* were printed by Henry Hills. The one apparent gap in this paper, March 22–29, 1658, was probably the result of Thomason's failure to collect it that single week.

5. On a few occasions the home news in the *Intelligencer* differed from that in *Politicus*, but the differences were trivial: e.g., *Intelligencer*, 99, Sept. 7–14, 1657; 115 [*sic*], Mar. 8–15, 1658.

6. Muddiman, *King's Journalist*, p. 125. Nedham may also have received money from the Edinburgh reprints of *Politicus*. *A Letter of Addresse To the Protector*, Aug. 1657, accused him of being, among other things, "a State Porter, a venalis anima, a mercenary soul . . ." (quoted in Clyde, *Struggle for Freedom*, p. 290).

7. *Politicus*, 432, Sept. 2–9, 1658, p. 802. See also *Intelligencer*, 141, Aug. 30–Sept. 6, 1658.

8. *Politicus*, 399, Jan. 14–21, 1658, pp. 251ff. (This item and most of those that follow, including advertisements, can be found, usually in identical form, in the appropriate number of the *Intelligencer*.) Nedham's treatment of the suicide of another anti-government plotter, Miles Sindercombe, was equally devastating (*Politicus*, 349, Feb. 12–19, 1657, p. 7064).

9. *Politicus*, 354, Mar. 19–26, 1657, p. 7675 — not repeated in the *Intelligencer*.

10. E.g., *Politicus*, 326, Sept. 4–11, 1656, p. 7238; 402, Feb. 4–11, 1658, pp. 293f; 566 (the paper had recently skipped from 445 to 545 in its numbering), May 5–12, 1659, pp. 423f.

11. E.g., *ibid.*, 397, Dec. 31, 1657–Jan. 7, 1658, pp. 223f — the story of a strange man rescued from the sea.

12. E.g., *ibid.*, 286–289, Nov. 29–Dec. 27, 1655, pp. 5804, 5815f, 5836, 5842f, and

293, Jan. 17–24, 1656, pp. 5911f; 340, Dec. 11–18, 1656, pp. 74511ff; 408, Mar. 18–25, 1658, p. 414; 547, Dec. 23–30, 1658, p. 118.

13. *Ibid.*, 300, Mar. 6–13, 1656, pp. 6013f; 424, June 24–July 1, 1658, p. 645.

14. *Ibid.*, 379, Aug. 27–Sept. 3, 1657, pp. 1597f; 443, Nov. 18–25, 1658, pp. 30–32.

15. *Ibid.*, 291, Jan. 3–10, 1656, p. 5881; 305, Apr. 10–17, 1656, p. 6904; 355, Mar. 26–Apr. 2, 1657, p. 7701; 358, Apr. 16–23, 1657, p. 7749.

16. *Ibid.*, 381, Sept. 10–17, 1657, p. 1629; 335, Nov. 6–13, 1656, p. 7378.

17. *Ibid.*, 329, Sept. 25–Oct. 2, 1656, p. 7283.

18. *Ibid.*, 346, Jan. 22–29, 1657, p. 7557; 435, Sept. 23–30, 1658, and 547, Dec. 23–30, 1658, p. 125; 439, Oct. 21–28, 1658, p. 929, and 550, Jan. 13–20, 1659, p. 173; 442, Nov. 11–18, 1658, p. 13.

19. E.g., *ibid.*, 382, Sept. 17–24, 1658, p. 1644; 387, Oct. 22–29, 1658, pp. 56ff.

20. *Ibid.*, 555, Feb. 17–24, 1659, p. 251.

21. *Ibid.*, 416, May 13–20, 1658, pp. 538f.

22. E.g., *ibid.*, 407, Mar. 11–18, 1658, p. 395. A few other editors seem to have known some system of shorthand.

23. E.g., *ibid.*, 416, May 13–20, 1658, p. 532 — the quelling of a Royalist uprising in London.

24. *Ibid.*, 352, Mar. 5–12, 1657, pp. 7641f.

25. *Ibid.*, 353–356, Mar. 12–Apr. 9, 1657, pp. 7657ff, 7673ff, 7690f, 7705f. In the summer of 1657 Nedham's *The Great Accuser cast down* refuted John Goodwin and supported the Protectorate. Long, detailed, sometimes scurrilous, it approved of legislation granting only limited religious toleration, and it attacked Roger Williams, along with Goodwin, for preaching too extreme a concept of freedom of religion (e.g., pp. 64f).

26. *Politicus*, 567, May 12–19, 1659, p. 437; Frank, *Levellers*, pp. 211f, 215, 240f.

27. *The Publick Adviser* was printed by Thomas Newcomb, and Nedham ran notices about the scheme in both his papers: *Politicus*, 361, May 7–14, 1657; *Intelligencer*, 82, May 11–18, 1657. For further details see Williams, *English Journalism*, pp. 167–170, and *Publick Adviser*, 1, May 19–26, 1657, pp. 1f.

28. *Weekly Information*, 1, July 13–20, 1657 (the "Preface"); Williams, *English Journalism*, pp. 170f.

29. *Nouvelles*, 301 and 302, Mar. 9/Feb. 28–Mar. 23/13, 1656, represent one of the few instances of a continued story, the terms of a treaty between England and Sweden; the extras came out in December 1655 (the Anglo-French treaty) and July 1657 (the "Humble Petition and Advice").

30. E.g., *ibid.*, 305, Apr. 6/Mar. 27–Apr. 13/3, 1656, p. 1222; 373, July 19/9–26/16, 1657, p. 1496; 377, Aug. 16/6–23/13, 1657, p. 1514.

31. This 400th number, covering the week of January 24/14–31/21, 1658, contained no hint that it was the last issue; it did contain a comparatively interesting account of George Fox's recent activities.

32. Bastide, *Entente*, p. 163. Williams, *English Journalism*, p. 184, mentions a brief revival of *Nouvelles Ordinaires* in 1663.

33. *Faithful Scout*, 4, May 13–20, 1659, p. 31.

34. *Ibid.*, 1, Apr. 22–29, 1659, pp. 1f.

35. *Loyall Scout*, 25, Oct. 14–21, 1659, pp. 199f; 27, Oct. 28–Nov. 4, 1659, p. 215.

36. *Weekly Post*, 14, Aug. 2–9, 1659, p. 115.

37. *Ibid.*, 20, Sept. 13–20, 1659, pp. 161f.

38. *Ibid.*, e.g., 28, Nov. 8–15, 1659, pp. 217f; 35, Dec. 27, 1659–Jan. 3, 1660, pp. 273f.

39. *Democritus*, 3, May 17–24, 1659, p. 20.

40. E.g., *ibid.*, 8 [*sic*], June 7–14, 1659, pp. 50f.

41. *The Weekly Intelligencer*, with the possible exception of its last two numbers, was published by Coles; and Pecke, not Collings, may have been the editor. Internal evidence, though inconclusive, points to Collings.

42. *Ibid.*, 11, July 12–19, 1659, p. 88, and 20, Sept. 13–20, 1659, pp. 157f; 26, Oct. 25–Nov. 1, 1659, p. 208.

43. E.g., *ibid.*, 25, Oct. 18–25, 1659, p. 199.

44. Wood, *Athenae Oxonienses*, III, 1186; Williams, *English Journalism*, p. 172.

45. E.g., *Politicus*, 575, July 7–14, 1659, pp. 583f. It is possible but not probable that Canne's role was nominal, and that Nedham, without fanfare, kept on editing *Politicus* and the *Intelligencer*.

46. *Politicus*, 592 (the second issue so numbered), Oct. 27–Nov. 3, 1659, pp. 824f.

47. E.g., *ibid.*, 595, Nov. 17–24, 1659, p. 908; 598, Dec. 8–15, 1659, p. 945.

48. *Intelligencer*, 207, Dec. 12–19, 1659; *Politicus*, 599, Dec. 15–22, 1659, pp. 967f.

49. Williams, *English Journalism*, p. 177.

50. For one or two weeks thereafter *Politicus* and the *Intelligencer*, published by Williams and edited by Canne, continued to come out. (For further details see Muddiman, *King's Journalist*, pp. 112f.)

51. E.g., *A Rope for Pol*, May 1660. Other contemporary attacks on Nedham included *A New-Years-Gift for Mercurius Politicus*, Dec. 1659; and *The Downe-fall of Mercurius Britannicus-Pragmaticus-Politicus* and *A Dialogue between Thomas Scot and Marchamont Nedham*, both from the spring of 1660. See also Muddiman, *King's Journalist*, pp. 111f, for an unflattering poem about Nedham in Holland.

52. For Nedham's later career see Firth's article in the *DNB*, though Nedham's post-Restoration pamphlets are themselves instructive. *The Citties Feast To The Lord Protector*, 1661, was a short anti-Cromwell poem. *The True Character Of a Rigid Presbyter*, 1661, at great length and with much repetition lived up to its title. Also in 1661 appeared *A Short History of the English Rebellion*, consisting of 256 four-line stanzas, all but the last four taken from the title-page poems of *Mercurius Pragmaticus*. In 1663 Nedham's *Discourse Concerning Schools and School-Masters* pleaded for higher salaries for teachers and attacked noncon-formist education. In 1665 his *Medela Medicinae* preached modern medicine by advocating a more intelligent use of chemistry and criticizing the traditional shibboleths blocking medical progress. In 1676 and 1677 *A Pacquet of Advice*, *A Second Pacquet of Advices*, and *Honesty's best Policy* went after Shaftesbury and the Whigs, with Nedham playing the part of a loyal and conservative Tory. Then in his final year *The Pacquet-Boat Advice* mildly supported peace with France, a position which Nedham reversed in his last pamphlet, *Christianissimus Christianandus*. Though he never was consistent — and he could be particularly vitriolic when describing the horrors of the Interregnum — he was usually effective.

53. E.g., *Occurrences From Forraigne Parts*, 2, July 5–12, 1659, pp. 9f; 11, Aug. 2–5, 1659, pp. 121f.

54. *Ibid.*, 14, Aug. 12–16, 1659, p. 170. See also no. 3, July 12–19, 1659, pp. 17ff.

55. *Particular Advice*, 47, Dec. 9–16, 1659; *Occurrences From Forraigne Parts*, 42, Nov. 22–29, 1659.

56. *Particular Advice*, 39, Nov. 11–18, 1659, p. 464; *Occurrences From Forraigne Parts*, 38, Nov. 8–15, 1659, p. 456. Possibly, however, Williams hired Canne to edit the news in these two papers.

57. E.g., *Exact Accompt*, 55, Jan. 6–13, 1660, p. 592, and 103, June 22–29, 1660, pp. 1006f; Williams, *English Journalism*, p. 184.

58. Twice it may have been counterfeited: see *A Perfect Diurnal*, 4, Feb. 24, 1660, and 21, Mar. 16, 1660.

59. The first number, Feb. 21, 1660, did briefly mention the bonfires and bells which celebrated the return of the excluded M.P.'s.

60. From May to October 1659 the policy of the Rump was generally liberal and tolerant; in December it changed.

61. *The Faithfull Intelligencer* was attacked by Nedham in *Politicus*, 598, Dec. 8–15, 1659, pp. 951f. The *Intelligencer's* next five numbers, also printed in Edinburgh and edited probably by the same officer, were entitled *Mercurius Britanicus* and came out between December 15, 1659, and January 6, 1660 (Couper, *Edinburgh Press*, I, 176ff). Primarily this paper was intended for Monck's army, and as such it was an effective instrument of propaganda (Davies, *Restoration*, p. 170). Its printer, Christopher Higgins, was active in reprinting London weeklies at least until October 1660 (Couper, *Edinburgh Press*, I, 65); but the first truly Scottish newspaper, *Mercurius Caledonius*, did not appear until early 1661, and then only for a dozen numbers.

62. For further details see Williams, *English Journalism*, pp. 174ff, and Muddiman, *King's Journalist*, pp. 85ff. Pepys, when he met Muddiman early in 1660, was not impressed. At least until May, Muddiman was assisted in his journalistic efforts by a Scot named Giles Dury.

63. Siebert, *Freedom of the Press*, p. 291. For Muddiman's subsequent success with this monopoly see Muddiman, *King's Journalist*, pp. 130f.

64. Siebert, *Freedom of the Press*, p. 291.

65. *Man in the Moon*, Aug. 13–20, 1660.

66. A few other papers may have appeared during the second quarter of 1660, for after March the Thomason Collection is not complete. I have omitted *The Monethly Intelligencer*, the one number of which came out on January 1, 1660. Its prospectus (quoted in Richmond P. Bond, *Studies in the Early English Periodical*, pp. 24f) underlined the fact that it was intended to be a magazine rather than a newspaper.

67. But Parliament's resolution had the effect of promoting newsletters, and for two decades they rather than newspapers supplied news to those who wished to be relatively well informed.

68. *Mercurius Publicus*, 32, May 24–31, 1660, p. 346.

XV

CONCLUSION

1. C. H. Firth's "London During the Civil War" depicts the city's large part in first deposing and then restoring a king.

2. *Faithfull Scout*, 188, July 14–21, 1654, p. 1492. (The letter was reprinted in no. 192, Aug. 11–18, 1654, pp. 1518f.)

3. Richard Baxter, *A Holy Commonwealth*, 1659, as quoted in Richard Schlatter, *Richard Baxter & Puritan Politics*, pp. 87, 97.

INDEX OF
SEVENTEENTH-CENTURY NEWSPAPERS

The notes to the text begin on page 297.
Newspapers appearing in the illustration section are identified "ill."

Perfect Particulars of Every Daies Intelligence, 352
Perfect Passages of Each Dayes Proceedings in Parliament, 94–95, 112–113, 322
Perfect Passages of Every Daies Intelligence, 212, 215, 226–227, 324, 349, 352
Perfect Proceedings of State Affairs, 357
Perfect Relation, or Summarie, A, 306
Perfect Summary of An Exact Dyarie of Some Passages in Parliament, 341
Perfect Summary Of Chief Passages in Parliament, A, 130, 331
Perfect Summary of Exact Passages of Parliament, A, 175–176, 198, 341
Perfect Weekly Account, The, 128, 150, 152, 171–172, 184, 198, 212–213, 330, 340, 349
Phanatick Intelligencer, The, 266
Phoenix of Europe, The, 115
Politique Informer, The, 355
Politique Post, The, 240
Principall Passages of Germany, Italy, France, The . . . Numb. 1, 302
Publick Adviser, The, 258, 263, 360
Publick Intelligencer, The, 255, 256–258, 261–273, 265, 359, 360, 361

relation of Count Mansfeilds last proceedings, A. May 26, 1623. Numb. 33, 300
relation of many memorable passages, A, 299
relation of our last newes, The. July 4 [1623]. Numb. 38, 303
relation of the Duke of Brunswicks march, A. May 7, 1623. Numb. 30, 302
Remarkable Passages, 54
Remarkable Passages in Parliament (1642), 306
Remarkable Passages, Or a perfect Diurnall Of The weekly proceedings, 306
Royall Diurnall, The, 164–165, 205, 338, 348

safe arrivall of Christian Duke of Brunswick, The, 299
Scotch Intelligencer, 313
Scotish Dove, The: discussed, 55–56, 62–64, 92–93, 109–111, 125–126, 315–317; mentioned, 57, 68, 104, 132, 156, 323, 329, 330

Scottish Mercury, The, 313
Several Letters from Scotland, 350
Several Proceedings of Parliament, 239, 352
Severall Proceedings in Parliament, 201–202, 212, 215, 223, 226, 244–245, 246, 247, 347, 350, 357
Severall Proceedings of State Affairs, 352, 357
Some Speciall and considerable Passages, 306
Some Speciall Passages From Hull, Anlaby, and Yorke, 306
Some Speciall Passages From London, Westminster, Yorke, 306
Speciall and Late Passages From The Most Eminent Places, 306, 307
Speciall Passages, 33, 35, 38, 39, 40–41, 45, 306, 310
Speciall Passages and Certain Informations, 306
Speciall Passages and certain Informations from severall places, 307
Speciall Passages from divers parts, 306, 307
Spie, The, 61–62, 315
strangling and death of the Great Turke, The, 299
suprisall of two Imperial townes [July 19, 1622], The, 303
Swedish Intelligencer, The, First, Second, Third, Fourth Parts, 301–302

Treaty traverst, The, 284
true and perfect Diurnall Of all the chiefe passages in Lancashire, A, 306
True and Perfect Diurnall Of the passages in Parliament, A, 306
True and Perfect Dutch Diurnall, The, 251
true and Perfect Informer, The, 251
True and Perfect Journal, A, 318
True Diurnal Occurrances Or, The heads of the Proceedings of Both Houses in Parliament, The, 279, 304
True Diurnall Occurrences, A, 279
True Diurnall Of The Last Weeks Passages In Parliament, A, 279
True Diurnall of the Passages in Parliament (Tucker), 23, 279, 280, 305
True Diurnall of the Passages in Parliament, A, 280
true Diurnall: Or A continued Relation of Irish Occurrences, A, 280

GENERAL INDEX